The Princeton Review®

Cracking the SAT®

2012 Edition

Adam Robinson, John Katzman, and
the Staff of The Princeton Review

PrincetonReview.com

Random House, Inc. New York

The Princeton Review®

The Princeton Review, Inc.
111 Speen Street, Suite 550
Framingham, MA 01701
E-mail: editorialsupport@review.com

ISBN 978-0-375-42829-6
ISSN 1934-239X

Editor: Laura Braswell
Production Editor: Kathy G. Carter
Production Coordinator: Deborah A. Silvestrini

Printed in the United States of America on partially recycled paper.

10 9 8 7 6 5 4 3 2 1

2012 Edition

Acknowledgments

An SAT course is much more than clever techniques and powerful computer score reports. The reason our results are great is that our teachers care so much about their students. Many teachers have gone out of their way to improve the course, often going so far as to write their own materials, some of which we have incorporated into our course manual as well as into this book. The list of these teachers could fill this page.

The Princeton Review would never have been founded without the advice and support of Bob Scheller. Bob's program, Pre-test Review, provides the best sort of competition; his fine results make us work all the harder.

Thanks to Ed Carroll and Eric Ginsberg for reviewing and updating this year's edition.

Finally, we would like to thank the people who truly have taught us everything we know about the SAT: our students.

Special thanks to Adam Robinson, who conceived of and perfected the Joe Bloggs approach to standardized tests and many of the other successful techniques used by The Princeton Review.

Contents

Foreword

Welcome to the 2012 edition of *Cracking the SAT.* The SAT is not a test of aptitude, how good of a person you are, or how successful you will be in life. The SAT simply tests how well you take the SAT. And performing well on the SAT is a skill, one that can be learned like any other. The Princeton Review was founded more than 20 years ago on this very simple idea, and—as our students' test scores show—our approach is the one that works.

Sure, you want to do well on the SAT, but you don't need to let the test intimidate you. As you prepare, remember these two important things about the SAT:

- **It doesn't measure the stuff that matters.** It measures neither intelligence nor the depth and breadth of what you're learning in high school. It doesn't predict college grades as well as your high school grades do, and many schools are still hesitant to use the score from your 25-minute essay in their application decisions at all. Colleges know there is more to you as a student—and as a person—than what you do at a single 4-hour test administration on a random Saturday morning.
- **It underpredicts the college performance of women, minorities, and disadvantaged students.** Historically, women have done better than men in college but worse on the SAT. For a test that is used to help predict performance in college, that's a pretty poor record.

Your preparation for the SAT starts here. We at The Princeton Review spend millions of dollars every year improving our methods and materials. Our teachers take each and every SAT to make sure nothing slips by us, and our books contain the most accurate, up-to-date information available. We're always ready for the SAT, and we'll get you ready too.

However, there is no magic pill: Just buying this book isn't going to improve your scores. Solid score improvement takes commitment and effort from you. If you read this book carefully and work through the problems and practice tests included in the book, not only will you be thoroughly versed in the format of the SAT and the concepts it tests, you will also have a sound overall strategy and a powerful arsenal of test-taking skills that you can apply to whatever you encounter on test day.

In addition to the thorough review in *Cracking the SAT,* we've tied the book to drills and tests on our website—**PrincetonReview.com**—to make it even more efficient at helping you to improve your scores. Before doing anything else, be sure to register at **PrincetonReview.com/cracking.** When you do, you'll gain access to the most up-to-date information on the SAT, detailed score reports for the tests in this book, exercises that will reinforce our techniques, and the opportunity to have your essays scored by our LiveGrader™ service. You'll also find great information on college admissions, online applications, and financial aid.

The more you take advantage of the resources we've included in this book and the online companion tools that go with it, the better you'll do on the test. Read the book carefully and learn our strategies. Take full-length practice tests under actual timed conditions. Analyze your performance and focus your efforts where you need improvement. Perhaps even study with a friend to stay motivated.

This test is challenging, but you're on the right track. We'll be with you all the way.

Good luck!

The Staff of The Princeton Review

...So Much More Online!

More Lessons...

- Step-by-step guide to solving difficult math and verbal problems
- Tutorials that put our strategies into action

More Practice...

- Math drills on Ballparking, Geometry, and Plugging In
- Verbal drills on Sentence Completion and Diction
- Full-length practice test

More Scores...

- Automatic scoring for online test
- Instant scoring for your book tests
- Optional essay scoring with our LiveGrader[SM] service
- Performance analysis to tell you which topics you need to review

More Good Stuff...

- Plan your review sessions with study plans based on your schedule—4 weeks, 8 weeks, 12 weeks

...then College!

- Detailed profiles for hundreds of colleges help you find the school that is right for you
- Information about financial aid and scholarships
- Dozens of Top 10 ranking lists including Quality of Professors, Worst Campus Food, Most Beautiful Campus, Party Schools, Diverse Student Population, and tons more

Register your book now!

- Go to **PrincetonReview.com**
- Look for the link to register your book and follow the on-screen directions!
- Next you will see a Sign Up/Sign In page where you will type in your e-mail address (username) and choose a password.
- Now you're good to go!

princetonreview.com

Look For These Icons Throughout The Book

Go Online   More Great Books

Part I
Orientation

LET'S GET THIS PARTY STARTED!

You are about to unlock a vast repertoire of powerful strategies that have one and only one purpose: to help you get a better score on the SAT. This book contains the collected wisdom of The Princeton Review, which has spent more than 20 years helping students achieve higher scores on standardized tests. We've devoted millions of dollars and years of our lives to cracking the SAT. It's what we do (twisted as it may be), and we want you to benefit from our expertise.

WHAT IS THE PRINCETON REVIEW?

The Princeton Review is the leader in test prep. Our goal is to help students everywhere crack the SAT. Ideally, we'd like the SAT to be eliminated altogether; we think the test is that bad. But until that happens, we'll content ourselves with aiding as many students as possible.

Starting from humble beginnings in 1981, The Princeton Review is now the nation's largest SAT preparation company. We offer courses in more than 500 locations in 12 different countries, as well as online; we also publish best-selling books, like the one you're holding, and software to get students ready for this test.

Our techniques work. We developed them after spending countless hours scrutinizing real SATs, analyzing them with computers, and proving our theories in the classroom. Our methods have been widely imitated, but no one achieves our score improvement.

The Princeton Review Way

This book will show you how to crack the SAT by teaching you to:

- think like the test writers,
- take full advantage of the limited time allowed,
- find the answers to questions you don't understand by guessing intelligently, and
- avoid the traps that the SAT has laid for you (and use those traps to your advantage).

The test is made by the Education Testing Service and they know that our techniques work. For years, ETS claimed that the SAT couldn't be coached. But we've proven that view wrong, and ETS has struggled to find ways of changing the SAT so that The Princeton Review won't be able to crack it—in effect, acknowledging what our students have known all along: that our techniques really do work. The SAT has remained highly vulnerable to our techniques. And the current version of the SAT is even more susceptible to our methods. Read this book, work through the drills, take the practice tests, and you'll see what we mean.

Study

If you were getting ready to take a biology test, you'd study biology. If you were preparing for a basketball game, you'd practice basketball. So, if you're preparing for the SAT, study the SAT. ETS can't test everything (in fact, they test very little), so concentrate on learning what they *do* test.

Chapter 1
The SAT, The Princeton Review, and You

Welcome! Our job is to help you get the best possible score on the SAT. This chapter tells you what to expect from the SAT, and some specifics about the test. It will also explain how to make the most of all your Princeton Review materials, including a bunch of cool stuff online.

GENERAL INFORMATION ABOUT THE SAT

You may have bought this book because you know nothing about the SAT, or perhaps you took the test once and want to raise your score. Either way, it's important to know about the test and the people who write it. Let's take a second to discuss some SAT facts. Some of these may surprise you.

What Does the SAT Test?

Just because the SAT features math, reading, and writing questions doesn't mean that it reflects what you learned in school. You can ace calculus or write like Faulkner and still struggle with the SAT. The test writers say that the test measures "reasoning ability," but actually, all the SAT really measures is how well you take the SAT. It does *not* reveal how smart or how good a person you are.

Who Writes the SAT?

Wait, Who Writes This Test?

You may be surprised to learn that the people who write SAT test questions are NOT teachers or college professors. The people who write the SAT are professional test writers, not superhuman geniuses. So you can beat them at their own game.

Even though colleges and universities make wide use of the SAT, they're not the ones who write the test. That's the job of Educational Testing Service (ETS), a nonprofit company that is in the business of writing tests for college and graduate school admissions. ETS also writes tests for groups as diverse as butchers and professional golfers (who knew?).

ETS is often criticized for the SAT. Many educators have argued that the test does not measure the skills you need for college. In fact, several years ago the University of California, one of the nation's largest university systems, decided that the SAT didn't provide enough information for admissions. ETS scrambled to change the test and introduced the current version of the SAT. It's almost an hour longer than the old SAT and—unlike the old version—tests grammar and includes an essay.

What's on the SAT?

The SAT runs 3 hours and 45 minutes and is divided into 10 sections. These include

- one 25-minute Essay section, requiring you to present your viewpoint on a topic
- two 25-minute Math sections, containing multiple-choice questions and response questions (we call these "grid-ins")
- two 25-minute Critical Reading sections, made up of sentence completions and reading comprehension questions
- one 25-minute Writing section, containing error identification questions, improving sentences questions, and improving paragraphs questions
- one 20-minute Math section, including only multiple-choice questions

- one 20-minute Critical Reading section, again featuring sentence completions and reading comprehension questions
- one 10-minute Writing section containing only improving sentences questions
- one 25-minute Experimental section, which may be Writing, Math, or Critical Reading. There's no way to tell which section is the Experimental, so treat every section as if it will be scored.

The Essay section on the SAT always comes first, while the 10-minute Writing section always comes last. The other six 25-minute sections can be in any order, as can the two 20-minute sections.

Scoring on the SAT

Each subject area on the SAT—Math, Writing, and Critical Reading—is scored on a scale of 200 to 800. The three scores are then totaled, for a combined score between 600 and 2,400. The average SAT score is about 500 per section, or 1,500 total.

You'll receive your score report about two to four weeks after you take the test. It will include your scaled score as well as your percentile rank, which tells you how you performed relative to other people who took the same test. If your score is in the 60th percentile, it means that you scored better than 60 percent of test takers.

One way of thinking of your SAT score is to imagine yourself in a line with 100 other students, all waiting to be seen by an admissions officer. However, the officer can't see every student—some students won't make it through the door. If your SAT score is in the 50th percentile, you'd have fifty other kids in front of you in line. Maybe you'll be seen, maybe not. Wouldn't it be nice to jump the line? If you can boost your SAT score, even by a couple of points, you move up the line and increase your odds of getting through the door. We can help you do that...

More great titles from The Princeton Review
The Best 373 Colleges
College Navigator

Score Choice™

The College Board recently started a program called Score Choice. Normally, colleges get to see every single time you take the SAT. With Score Choice, however, you can tell the College Board which test date or dates (as many or as few as you want) to send to colleges. At first glance, this seems great. "Hey, colleges don't have to see that one bad score from the first time I took the SAT without preparing? Great!" But there are some major problems with it, which you may want to consider before using Score Choice.

First and foremost is that some colleges require that you send them all scores from all times you took the SAT. Score Choice is still new (it first took effect in March 2009), and some colleges aren't very happy about it. They want to know about every single time you take the SAT, and they don't want the College Board telling them which of your SAT scores they're allowed to see. For these colleges, you must submit all scores, and Score Choice is not an option.

Second, many colleges actually just look at your highest scores either for one sitting of a test or, in many cases, per subject across several sittings. If the college just looks at your highest sitting, Score Choice doesn't make any difference, and it's probably not worth bothering with it. The college admissions officer will just look at your highest-scored test date and ignore the other scores. But for the colleges that cherry pick your scores by subject, Score Choice can actually hurt you. For instance, let's say you take the SAT in March and get a 510 in Math, a 400 in Reading, and a 450 in Writing. You retake the SAT in May and get a 410 in Math (ouch), a 500 in Reading (much better), and a 470 in Writing (OK). Many schools look at your best scores per subject and would consider your SAT score to be 510 Math, 500 Reading, and 470 Writing. But if you submitted only one score, the colleges wouldn't have the high points to choose from.

Whether or not you decide to use Score Choice, plan on taking the SAT two or three times. Many colleges frown on taking the SAT four or more times.

A searchable list of colleges and their requested SAT score submission requirements, as well as more information on Score Choice, can be found at the College Board website at www.collegeboard.com.

WHEN IS THE SAT GIVEN?

Stay on Schedule

Plan to take the SAT in either the spring of your junior year or the fall of your senior year. Because you might be expected to take as many as three SAT Subject Tests, don't save everything for the last minute. Sit down with your SAT and SAT Subject Test registration booklets and work out a schedule.

The SAT schedule for the school year is posted at **www.collegeboard.com/student/testing/sat/calenfees.html.** If the test date you're looking for is not posted yet, check this site for updates.

There are two different ways to sign up for the test. You can sign up online by going to **www.collegeboard.com** and clicking on "register for the SAT," or sign up through the mail with an SAT Registration Booklet, which should be available at your school guidance counselor's office.

When you go to the College Board website, take a moment to look at the services they offer and feel free to contact to request any of these services that you want.

Chapter 2
Cracking the SAT: Basic Principles

The first step to cracking the SAT is to know how best to approach the test. The SAT is not like the tests you've taken in school, so you need to learn to look at it in a different way. This chapter will show test-taking strategies that immediately improve your score. Make sure you fully understand these concepts before moving on to Chapter 3. Good luck!

What ETS Is Good At

The folks at ETS have been writing standardized tests for more than 80 years, and they write tests for all sorts of programs. They have administered the test so many times that they know exactly how you will approach it. They know how you'll attack certain questions, what sort of mistakes you'll probably make, and even what answer you'll be most likely to pick. Kinda freaky, isn't it?

However, ETS's strength is also a weakness. Because the test is standardized, the SAT has to ask the same type of questions over and over again. Sure, the numbers or the words might change, but the basics don't. With enough practice, you can learn to think like ETS. But try to use your powers for good, okay?

The SAT Isn't School

Our job isn't to teach you math or English—leave that to your supersmart school teachers. Instead, we're going to teach you the SAT. You'll soon see that the SAT involves a very different skill set.

Be warned that some of the approaches we're going to show you will seem weird or unnatural. In fact, if you tried to pull off some of this stuff in school, your teacher would probably freak. But you must trust us. Try tackling the problems using our techniques, and keep practicing until they become easier. You'll see a real improvement in your score.

Let's take a look at the questions.

How the Test Is Scored

The SAT is scored in an unusual way. For every question you answer correctly you receive 1 raw point. For every question you answer incorrectly you lose $\frac{1}{4}$ of a point. For every question you leave blank you get 0 points.

Your raw score is the combination of these raw points for each section category: Math, Critical Reading, and Writing. Each of your three raw scores is then scaled to a 200–800 score for each subject.

Cracking Multiple-Choice Questions

What's the capital of Azerbaijan?

Give up?

Unless you spend your spare time studying an atlas, you may not even know that Azerbaijan is a real country, much less what its capital is. If this question came up on a test, you'd have to skip it, wouldn't you? Well, maybe not. Let's turn this question into a multiple-choice question—just like all the questions on the SAT Critical Reading and Grammar sections, and the majority of questions you'll find on the SAT Math section—and see if you can figure out the answer anyway.

1. The capital of Azerbaijan is

(A) Washington, D.C.
(B) Paris
(C) Tokyo
(D) London
(E) Baku

The question doesn't seem that hard anymore, does it? Of course, we made our example extremely easy. (By the way, there won't actually be any questions about geography on the SAT.) But you'd be surprised by how many people give up on SAT questions that aren't much more difficult than this one just because they don't know the correct answer right off the top of their heads. "Capital of Azerbaijan? Oh, no! I've never heard of Azerbaijan!"

These students don't stop to think that they might be able to find the correct answer simply by eliminating all of the answer choices they know are wrong.

You Already Know Almost All of the Answers

All but a handful of the questions on the SAT are multiple-choice questions, and every multiple-choice question has five answer choices. One of those choices, and only one, will be the correct answer to the question. You don't have to come up with the answer from scratch. You only have to identify it.

How will you do that?

Look for the Wrong Answers Instead of the Right Ones

Why? Because wrong answers are usually easier to find. After all, there are more of them! Remember the question about Azerbaijan? Even though you didn't know the answer off the top of your head, you easily figured it out by eliminating the four obviously incorrect choices. You looked for wrong answers first.

In other words, you used the Process of Elimination, which we'll call POE for short. This is an extremely important concept, one we'll come back to again and again. It's one of the keys to improving your SAT score. When you finish reading this book, you will be able to use POE to answer many questions that you don't understand.

The great artist Michelangelo once said that when he looked at a block of marble, he could see a statue inside. All he had to do to make a sculpture

It's Not About Circling the Right Answer

Physically marking in your test booklet what you think of certain answers can help you narrow down choices, take the best possible guess, and save time! Try using the following notations:

✔	Put a check mark next to an answer you like.
~	Put a squiggle next to an answer you kinda like.
?	Put a question mark next to an answer you don't understand.
~~A~~	Cross out the letter of any answer choice you KNOW is wrong.

You can always come up with your own system. The key is consistency.

was to chip away everything that wasn't part of it. You should approach difficult SAT multiple-choice questions in the same way, by chipping away everything that's not correct. By first eliminating the most obviously incorrect choices on difficult questions, you will be able to focus your attention on the few choices that remain.

PROCESS OF ELIMINATION (POE)

There won't be many questions on the SAT in which incorrect choices will be as easy to eliminate as they were on the Azerbaijan question. But if you read this book carefully, you'll learn how to eliminate at least one choice on almost any SAT multiple-choice question, if not two, three, or even four choices.

What good is it to eliminate just one or two choices on a five-choice SAT question?

Plenty. In fact, for most students, it's an important key to earning higher scores. Here's another example:

2. The capital of Qatar is

(A) Paris
(B) Dukhan
(C) Tokyo
(D) Doha
(E) London

On this question you'll almost certainly be able to eliminate three of the five choices by using POE. That means you're still not sure of the answer. You know that the capital of Qatar has to be either Doha or Dukhan, but you don't know which.

Should you skip the question and go on? Or should you guess?

Close Your Eyes and Point

You've probably heard a lot of different advice about guessing on multiple-choice questions on the SAT. Some teachers and guidance counselors tell their students never to guess and to mark an answer only if they're absolutely certain that it's correct. Others tell their students not to guess unless they are able to eliminate two or three of the choices.

Both of these pieces of advice are incorrect.

Even ETS is misleading about guessing. Although it tells you that you *can* guess, it doesn't tell you that you *should*. In fact, if you can eliminate even one incorrect choice on an SAT multiple-choice question, guessing from among the remaining choices will usually improve your score. And if you can eliminate two or three choices, you'll be even more likely to improve your score by guessing.

The Big Bad Guessing Penalty

Your raw score on the SAT is the number of questions you got right, minus a fraction of the number you got wrong (except on the grid-ins, which are scored a little differently). Every time you answer an SAT question correctly, you get 1 raw point. Every time you leave an SAT question blank, you get 0 raw points. Every time you answer an SAT question incorrectly, ETS subtracts $\frac{1}{4}$ of a raw point if the question has five answer choices, or nothing if it is a grid-in.

ETS refers to the subtracted fraction as the "guessing penalty." The penalty is supposed to discourage students from guessing on multiple-choice questions (and getting the right answer out of luck). However, let's take a closer look at how the penalty works.

Raw scores can be a little confusing, so let's think in terms of money instead. For every question you answer correctly on the SAT, ETS will give you a dollar. For every multiple-choice question you leave blank, ETS will give you nothing. For every multiple-choice question you get wrong, you will have to give 25 cents back to ETS. That's exactly the way raw scores work.

What happens to your score if you select the correct answer on one question and incorrect choices on four questions? Remember what we said about money: ETS gives you a dollar for the one answer you got right; you give ETS a quarter for each of the four questions you missed. Four quarters equal a dollar, so you end up exactly where you started, with nothing—which is the same thing that would have happened if you had left all five questions blank. Now, what happens if you guess on four questions, but—for each of those questions—you can eliminate one incorrect answer choice? Random odds say you will get one question right—get a dollar—and miss the other three questions—give back 75 cents. You've just gained a quarter! So, guessing can work in your favor.

TO GUESS OR NOT TO GUESS: THAT IS THE QUESTION

If you are confident that you know the answer to a question or that you know how to solve it, just go ahead and select an answer. If you are uncertain about either the answer to a question or how to solve it, see if you can eliminate any wrong answers. We're going to give you lots of tools to eliminate wrong answers, so you'll probably be able to eliminate answers *even* on the hardest questions.

But, should you guess on every question? Well, that depends. In the next chapter, we're going to show you how to set a pacing goal for each section. The pacing goal will tell you how many questions you need to answer for each section. Your goal is to answer that number of questions. If you can get to your pacing goal without guessing, that's great. But most students will need to guess on at least a few questions to reach their pacing goals. When you get to a question you're not sure of, ask yourself, "Can I reach my pacing goal without this question?"

Finally, guess only if you can eliminate *at least one* answer choice. If you can't eliminate one, leave that question blank.

Credit for Partial Information

Want more practice? Check out *11 Practice Tests for the SAT and PSAT*

Earning points for a guess probably seems a little bit like cheating or stealing: You get something you want, but you didn't do anything to earn it.

This is not a useful way to think about the SAT. It's also not true. Look at the following example:

3. The Sun is a

(A) main-sequence star
(B) meteor
(C) asteroid
(D) white dwarf star
(E) planet

If you've paid any attention at all in school for the past ten years or so, you probably know that the Sun is a star. You can easily tell, therefore, that the answer to this question must be either A or D. You can tell this not only because it seems clear from the context that "white dwarf" and "main-sequence" are kinds of stars—as they are—but also because you know for a fact that the Sun is not a planet, a meteor, or an asteroid. Still, you aren't sure which of the two possible choices is correct.

Heads, You Win a Dollar; Tails, You Lose a Quarter

By using POE you've narrowed down your choice to two possibilities. If you guess randomly you'll have a fifty-fifty chance of being correct, like flipping a coin—heads you win a dollar, tails you lose a quarter. Those are extremely good odds on the SAT. So go ahead and guess!

(The answer, by the way, is A. And don't worry, there won't be any questions about astronomy on the SAT.)

ALWAYS PUT PENCIL TO PAPER

At school you probably aren't allowed to write in your textbooks, unless your school requires you to buy them. You probably even feel a little peculiar about writing in the books you own. Books are supposed to be read, you've been told, and you're not supposed to scrawl all over them.

Because you've been told this so many times, you may be reluctant to write in your test booklet when you take the SAT. Your proctor will tell you that you are supposed to write in it—the booklet is the only scratch paper you'll be allowed to use; it says so right in the instructions from ETS—but you may still feel bad about marking it up.

Write Now
Feel free to write all over this book too. You need to get in the habit of making the SAT booklet your own. Do NOT do things in your head. Start now by writing the names of the colleges you really want to attend in the margin below.

Don't Be Ridiculous!

Your test booklet is just going to be thrown away when you're finished with it. No one is going to read what you wrote in it and decide that you're stupid because you couldn't remember what 2 + 2 is without writing it down. Your SAT score won't be any higher if you don't make any marks in your booklet. In fact, if you don't, your score will probably be lower than it should be.

Own Your Test Booklet

You paid for your test booklet; act as though you own it. Scratch work is extremely important on the SAT. Don't be embarrassed about it. After all, writing in your test booklet will help you keep your mind on what you're doing.

- When you work on a geometry problem that provides a diagram, don't hesitate to write all over it. What if there's no diagram? Draw one yourself—don't simply try to imagine it. Keep track of your work directly on the diagram to avoid making careless mistakes.
- On sentence completion questions, you will often need to come up with your own word or two to help you answer a question. Write it down! Trying to retain information in your head leads to confusion and errors. Your test booklet is your scratch paper—use it.
- When you use POE to eliminate a wrong answer choice, physically cross off the answer choice in your test booklet. Don't leave it there to confuse you. You may often need to carefully consider two remaining answer choices. You want to be clear about which answer choices are left in the running.
- When you answer a question but don't feel entirely certain of your answer, circle the question or put a big question mark in the margin beside it. That way, if you have time later on, you can get back to it without having to search through the entire section.

You probably think of scratch paper as something that is useful only for math questions. But you'll need scratch paper on the SAT Critical Reading and Writing sections too. The Critical Reading sections of your booklet should be just as marked up as the Math ones.

Mark Your Answer
When you take the SAT, you should mark all your answers in your test booklet, with a big letter in the margin beside each problem, and then transfer them later onto your answer sheet.

Transfer Your Answers at the End of Each Group

Scratch work isn't the only thing we want you to do in your test booklet. We also want you to mark your answers there. For each group of sentence completions, you should transfer your answers to the answer sheet when you come to the end of the group of questions. For all other questions (except grid-ins), you should transfer your answers one page at a time.

Doing this will save you a great deal of time, because you won't have to look back and forth between your test booklet and your answer sheet every few seconds. You will also be less likely to make mistakes in marking your answers on the answer sheet. However, be sure to give yourself enough time to transfer your answers. Don't wait until the last five minutes.

The only exception to this are the grid-ins, the ten non–multiple-choice math questions. You will need to grid each answer as you find it. We'll tell you all about grid-ins later in the book.

Summary

- When you don't know the right answer to a multiple-choice question, look for wrong answers instead. They're usually easier to find.
- When you find a wrong answer choice, eliminate it. In other words, use POE, the Process of Elimination.
- Intelligent guessing on multiple-choice questions enables you to earn credit for partial information.
- Use your test booklet for scratch paper. Don't be afraid to write all over it; it's yours.
- Transfer your answers to your answer sheet all at once when you reach the end of each group of sentence completions, or one page at a time for all other questions (except for the grid-ins). Give yourself enough time to transfer your answers; don't wait until the last five minutes.

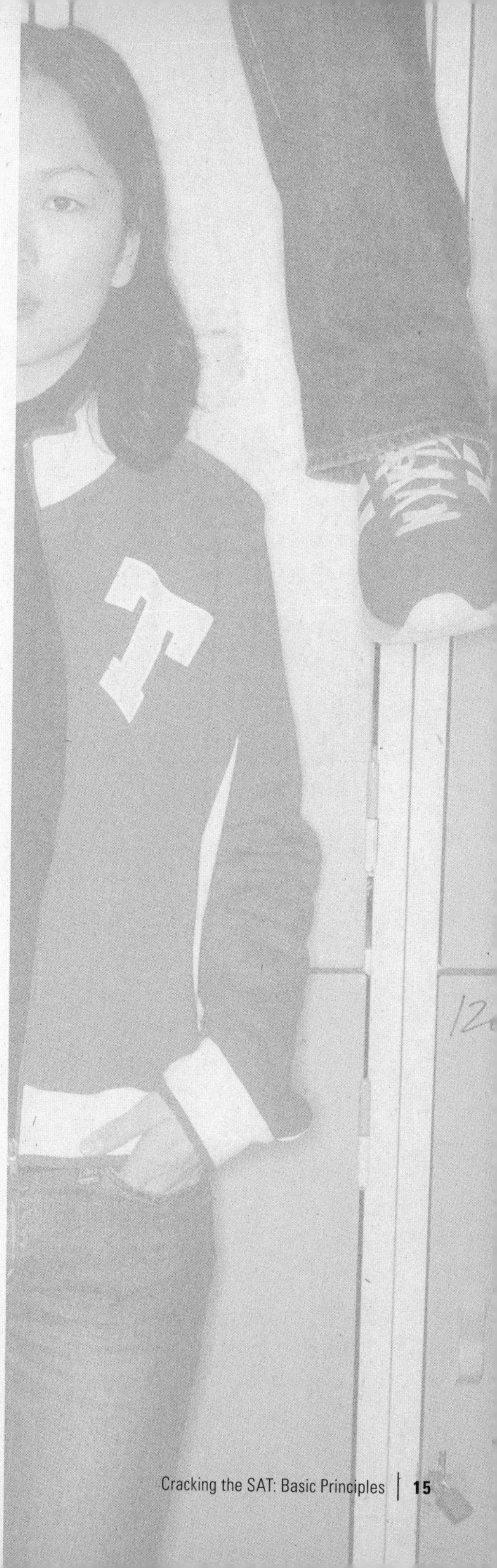

Chapter 3
Cracking the SAT: Advanced Principles

Once you've mastered Process of Elimination (POE) and guessing techniques, you are ready to start applying them to the SAT. In this chapter, you will learn how ETS writes and arranges SAT questions and how knowing this can help you answer more questions correctly.

PUTTING THE BASIC PRINCIPLES TO WORK

In the previous chapter, we reviewed some basic principles of the SAT. We showed you that it is possible to find correct answers by using POE, the Process of Elimination, to get rid of incorrect choices.

But how will you know which answers to eliminate? And how will you know when to guess? In this chapter, we'll begin to show you. We will teach you how to

- take advantage of the order in which questions are asked
- make better use of your time by scoring the easy points first
- use the Joe Bloggs principle to eliminate obviously incorrect choices on difficult questions
- find the traps that ETS has laid for you
- turn those traps into points

To show you how this is possible, we first have to tell you something about the way the SAT is arranged.

ORDER OF DIFFICULTY

Some Do, Some Don't
Not all question types have an order of difficulty. Here's how it breaks down:

Question types with some order of difficulty: Sentence Completions, Math questions, Error IDs, and Improving Sentences.

Question types with no order of difficulty: Long and Short Reading, Improving Paragraphs, and the Essay.

If you have already taken a practice SAT, you may have noticed that the questions seem to get harder as each section progresses. This is not an accident; ETS purposely arranges the questions this way. Why? There are a couple of reasons.

First, starting students with easy questions can lead to a false sense of security. Chances are, after nailing the first three or four questions you start to think that you've got the test beat. That's exactly when ETS starts throwing some traps into the questions for the unwary or the overconfident.

Second, the hard questions are at the end of the section, when you have less time left. Knowing this, you may rush through the beginning of the section, making careless mistakes, just to get to the difficult and frustrating questions at the end.

Easy, Medium, Difficult

Think of each section as being divided into thirds. A third of the questions should be easy. Most test takers get these questions right. Another third of the questions are of medium difficulty. Nearly half of the people taking the test get these questions right. The final third of the questions are difficult. Very few test takers answer these questions correctly.

The Math sections always follow this order of difficulty; thus, in a 20-question Math section, the first seven questions are easy, the next six are medium, and the final seven are difficult. Sentence completions follow a similar pattern. However, most of the other question types are all jumbled up—they follow no particular order of difficulty.

You Have to Pace Yourself

There are some very difficult questions on the SAT that most test takers shouldn't even bother to work on. On the difficult third of every group of questions, there are some questions that almost no one taking the test will get right. Rather than spending too much time on these questions, you should focus your attention on questions that you have a better chance of figuring out.

Rule #1
Any test taker scoring below 700 on either the Math or the Critical Reading section will hurt his or her score by attempting to answer every question.

Because most test takers try to finish every section ("I had two seconds left over!"), almost every test taker hurts his or her score. After all, when you rush, you make mistakes. The solution, for almost anyone scoring less than 700 on a section, is to slow down.

Most test takers could improve their scores significantly by attempting fewer questions and devoting more time to questions they have a better chance of answering correctly. Slow down, score more.

How Will This Help My Score?

Knowing the difficulty level of a question can help you in several ways. Most importantly, it helps you make the best use of your time. Although in terms of difficulty the questions are definitely *not* created equally, each and every single question earns you exactly *one* point. ETS wants you to waste your time on the difficult questions, while missing easy points. Don't play their game.

Make sure you SLOW DOWN and focus your energy on the easy and medium questions before trying the difficult ones. Your job is to get the greatest number of points in the least amount of time. Don't rush through the questions that you're more likely to answer correctly. Get those points. Then with the time you have left, try the difficult questions (those will be loaded with ETS traps!).

Easy to Be Hard
The SAT isn't a huge intellectual challenge; it's just tricky. When we talk about difficult questions on the SAT, we mean ones that people most often get wrong. Flip to one of the practice SATs at the back of this book and look at the more difficult math questions. Do any of them test anything you didn't learn in high school? Probably not. But do they all resemble the kind of straightforward questions you're used to seeing on a regular test? Probably not. ETS specializes in confusing and misleading test takers.

Furthermore, understanding the difficulty level of a question can help you to figure out ETS's trap answers. To do this, we first have to delve into the mind of a typical SAT test taker.

The Importance of Feeling Good

The SAT is a timed test, and ETS doesn't give you a lot of time to work through every question. Plus, there's a tremendous amount of anxiety associated with taking the test. In a situation such as this, many students rely on a sense of what "feels" right when answering questions. The problem is, in many of these cases, ETS is hoping you'll fall for a trap.

Rule #2
Answer easy questions first; save hard questions for last.

Should You Ever Pick an Answer That Feels Right?

Well, that depends on the difficulty level of the question. (See, this whole discussion was leading somewhere.) Consider this:

- On easy multiple-choice questions, ETS's answers seem right to virtually everyone: high scorers, low scorers, and average scorers.
- On medium multiple-choice questions, ETS's answers seem right to high scorers, wrong to low scorers, and sometimes right and sometimes wrong to average scorers.
- On hard multiple-choice questions, ETS's answers seem right to high scorers and wrong to everyone else.

Rule #3
Easy questions have easy answers; hard questions have hard answers.

When doing an easy question, you can trust your gut. But once you hit the medium and difficult questions, the answer that "feels right" may no longer be the best answer.

Why Would ETS Design the Test Like That?

Simply put, they want you to get an average score. If ETS put too many easy questions on the test, then lots of students would get great SAT scores. Sounds pretty good, right?

Well, if you worked in a college admissions office, you might not think so. If almost every student had scores in the 700s for math, reading, and writing, you wouldn't be able to use those scores to make decisions. The colleges would lose faith in the SAT and ETS just wouldn't allow that.

By the way, if ETS put too many hard questions on the test and everybody got really low SAT scores, the colleges would have the same problem. ETS always wants to make sure that there are just enough easy questions to get most students into the average range and just enough hard questions to keep most students from exceeding the average. Pretty twisted, isn't it? So, how do you avoid being average?

Meet Joe Bloggs

The average test taker always goes with his or her gut when taking the SAT. We've seen this average test taker so often that we've decided to give him a name: Joe Bloggs. Joe is the quintessential (good vocabulary word) American high school student. He has average grades and average SAT scores. There's a little bit of him in everyone, and there's a little bit of everyone in him. He isn't brilliant. He isn't dumb. He's just average.

And he's ETS's dream student. He always does what ETS expects and gets an average score as a result.

How Does Joe Bloggs Approach the SAT?

Joe Bloggs *always* trusts his gut. Regardless of the difficulty level of the question, he picks the answer that feels right. And of course, he ends up getting most of the easy questions right, about half of the medium questions right, and almost none of the difficult questions right. That makes ETS very happy because they can give Joe an average score.

Here's an example of a hard question. Let's see how Joe tackles it:

20. Graham walked to school at an average speed of 3 miles an hour and jogged back along the same route at 5 miles an hour. If his total traveling time was 1 hour, what was the total number of miles in the round trip?

(A) 3

(B) $3\frac{1}{8}$

(C) $3\frac{3}{4}$

(D) 4

(E) 5

Which Answer Did Joe Pick?

Question 20 is one of the hardest questions in the math section. Most students get it wrong and, of course, that includes Joe. Can you guess which answer Joe picked? Joe picked answer choice D because it just felt right. Joe read the problem so fast that all that registered was that Graham went to school at 3 miles per hour, returned at 5 miles per hour and that Joe is supposed to find the number of miles in the round trip. Joe figured all he really had to do was to average the two speeds and ETS was waiting with answer choice D. Poor Joe. Does he really think that ETS is going to let him go to a really good college for doing something that easy?

So, what was wrong with Joe's approach? Well, since Graham took the same route to school and then back home, the distance had to be the same. Joe's method, however, assumed that Graham spent half his time going to school and half of it returning home. That can't happen if the distance is the same, right? Graham would have spent less time jogging home. Joe went too fast, made a bad assumption and fell for the ETS trap answer.

ETS's Favorite Wrong Answers

Take another look at question 20. Answer choice D was included to lure Joe Bloggs into a trap. But it isn't the only trap answer choice. Other tempting choices are A and E. Why? Because they are numbers included in the question itself, and Joe Bloggs is most comfortable with familiar numbers. When ETS selects wrong answers to hard questions, it looks for three things.

1. The answer you'd get doing the simplest possible math. In this case, that's D.
2. The answer you'd get after doing some, but not all, of the necessary math.
3. Numbers that are already in the question itself (choices A and E).

ETS doesn't use all of these every time, but there's at least one in every set of difficult answer choices.

THE JOE BLOGGS PRINCIPLE

When you take the SAT a few weeks or months from now, you'll have to take it on your own, of course. But suppose for a moment that ETS allowed you to take it with Joe Bloggs as your partner. Would Joe be of any help to you on the SAT?

You Probably Don't Think So

After all, Joe is wrong as often as he is right. He knows the answers to the easy questions, but so do you. You'd like to do better than average on the SAT, and Joe earns only an average score (he's the average test taker, remember). All things considered, you'd probably prefer to have someone else for your partner.

But Joe might turn out to be a pretty helpful partner, after all. Since his hunches are always wrong on difficult multiple-choice questions, couldn't you improve your chances on those questions simply by finding out what Joe wanted to pick, and then picking something else?

If you could use the Joe Bloggs principle to eliminate one, two, or even three obviously incorrect choices on a hard problem, you could improve your score by guessing among the remaining choices.

We're going to teach you how to make Joe Bloggs your partner on the SAT. When you come to difficult questions on the test, you're going to stop and ask yourself, "How would Joe Bloggs answer this question?" And when you see what he would do, you are going to do something else. Why? Because you know that on hard questions, Joe Bloggs is always wrong.

What If Joe Bloggs Is Right?

Remember what we said about Joe Bloggs at the beginning: He is the average test taker. He thinks the way most people do. If the right answer to a hard question seemed right to most people, the question wouldn't be hard.

Joe Bloggs is right on some questions: the easy ones. But he's always wrong on the hard questions.

Joe's Hunches

Should you always just eliminate any answer that seems to be correct? No! Remember what we said about Joe Bloggs:

1. His hunches are correct on easy questions.
2. His hunches are sometimes correct and sometimes incorrect on medium questions.
3. His hunches are always wrong on difficult questions.

On easy multiple-choice questions, pick the choice that Joe Bloggs would pick. On hard questions, be sure to eliminate the choices that Joe Bloggs would pick.

Putting Joe Bloggs to Work for You

In the chapters that follow, we're going to teach you many specific problem-solving techniques based on the Joe Bloggs principle. The Joe Bloggs principle will help you

- use POE to eliminate incorrect answer choices
- make up your mind when you have to guess
- avoid careless mistakes

The more you learn about Joe Bloggs, the more he'll help you on the test. If you make him your partner on the SAT, he'll help you find ETS's answers on problems you never dreamed you'd be able to solve.

Because This Is So Important, We're Going to Say It Again

Here's a summary of how Joe Bloggs thinks:

Question Type	Joe Bloggs Looks For	Joe Bloggs Selects	Time Joe Spends	How Joe Does
Easy	the answer	the one that seems right	very little	mostly right
Medium	the answer	the one that seems right	not much	so-so
Difficult	the answer	the one that seems right	too much	all wrong!

Here is a summary of how *you* should think:

Question Type	You Should Look For	You Should Select	Time You Should Spend	How You'll Do
Easy	the answer	the one that seems right	enough to not make careless errors	mostly right
Medium	the wrong answers	pick from what's left	most of your time	better than Joe!
Difficult	the wrong answers	pick from what's left	whatever time is left	better than Joe!

SET THE RIGHT GOAL BEFOREHAND

It's very important to set realistic goals. If you're aiming for a 500 on the Critical Reading section, your approach to the SAT is going to be different from that of someone who is aiming for an 800. The following charts will give you some idea of what you realistically need to do to score at various levels on the SAT. Use the chart to gauge your progress as you work through practice tests like those in this book or in The Princeton Review's *11 Practice Tests for the SAT & PSAT.*

Now before you decide you must get a 700 in Critical Reading no matter what, do a reality check: To date, what have you scored on the Critical Reading SAT? The Writing section? The Math? Whatever those numbers are, add 50–90 points to each to determine your goal score. Then get cracking! Work through this book, practice the techniques, and, after a time, take a timed practice test. If you achieve your goal score on the practice test, great! Could you have worked a little more quickly yet maintained your level of accuracy? If so, increase your goal by another 50 points.

In other words, you must set an attainable goal to see any improvement. If you scored a 400 on the last Math SAT you took, and you immediately shoot for a 700, you will be working too quickly to be accurate and won't see any increase in your score. However, if you use the "460–500" pacing guide instead, you may jump from a 400 to a 480! After that, you can work to score over a 500, and so on.

Come back to these pages after each practice test you take to reassess your pacing strategy. Accuracy is more important than speed. Finishing is not the goal; getting more questions right is! Besides, all the hard problems are at the end. If you are missing easy questions due to your haste to get to the difficult questions, you are throwing points away.

By the way, you may notice that the following three charts present slightly different pacing strategies for the Math, Reading and Grammar sections. (Throughout this book, we'll refer to all the Writing sections except the essay as "Grammar" sections.) The Reading pacing chart shows that you should answer a greater percentage of the questions in the section to get a certain score than does the Math pacing chart. Why? Well, on the Math section, it's even more important to slow down. Use the extra time to read problems carefully and to make sure that your calculations are correct. Don't race through every problem just to get to the end. That's what Joe does, and you know what sort of score Joe gets.

Also, the numbers of questions on the charts represent how many questions you should answer. We've already factored in some wrong answers. That's why each line on each chart shows that you should answer a greater number of questions than the points that you need to get that score. So don't blow past your pacing goal because you're worried that you might have made a few mistakes.

And don't be afraid to guess on a few questions in each section to reach your pacing goals.

Go Online
Take the Practice Test to see your current score and the score you should shoot for at PrincetonReview.com/cracking

Rule #4
Accuracy is more important than speed.

Speaking of Goal Setting, Check out

Portable Guidance Counselor

Essential SAT Flashcards

The Best 373 Colleges

Math Pacing Chart

		Answer this many questions				
To get (scaled score)	You need to earn (raw points)	20-question section	18-Question section		16-question section	Total # of questions to attempt
			8 Multiple choice	10 Grid-ins		
350	7	6	2	2	2	12
400	12	7	3	3	4	17
450	19	9	4	4	6	23
500	25	11	5	5	8	29
550	32	14	6	6	10	36
600	38	16	6	7	13	42
650	44	18	7	8	15	48
700	47	all	all	9	all	53
750	52	all	all	all	all	54
800	54	all	all	all	all	54

Critical Reading Pacing Chart

		Answer this many questions			
To get (scaled score)	You need to earn (raw points)	23- to 25-question section	23- to 25-question section	19-question section	Total # of questions to attempt
300	5	6	6	3	15
350	9	8	8	4	20
400	14	11	11	8	30
450	21	15	15	12	42
500	29	20	20	14	54
550	38	23	23	18	64
600	46	all	all	all	65–69
650	53	all	all	all	65–69
700	59	all	all	all	65–69
750	63	all	all	all	65–69
800	67	all	all	all	65–69

Grammar Pacing Chart

		Answer this many questions		
To get (scaled score)	You need to earn (raw points)	35-question section	14-question section	Total # of questions to attempt
35	5	10	5	15
40	11	13	7	20
45	17	18	8	26
50	22	22	9	31
55	27	26	10	36
60	31	27	11	38
65	36	31	all	45
70	40	all	all	49
75	44	all	all	49
80	49	all	all	49

Estimated Writing Scores

Grammar Score (Raw Points)	Essay Score						
	12	10	8	6	4	2	0
80 (49)	800	800	790	750	720	690	680
75 (47)	800	770	730	690	670	640	620
70 (44)	750	710	670	640	610	580	570
65 (41)	710	680	640	600	580	550	530
60 (37)	670	640	600	560	540	510	490
55 (32)	630	590	550	520	490	460	450
50 (27)	590	560	520	480	460	430	410
45 (20)	540	510	470	430	410	380	360
40 (15)	500	470	430	400	370	340	330
35 (9)	460	430	390	350	330	300	280
30 (5)	420	390	350	320	290	260	250
25 (1)	370	340	300	270	240	210	200
20 (-2)	320	290	250	210	200	200	200

More great titles from The Princeton Review

Grammar Smart

Word Smart II

Vocab Help

Learn new vocab with The Vocab Minute, a Princeton Review podcast. Visit www.princetonreview.com for more information.

EMBRACE YOUR POOD

Eww! Embrace your what? POOD is an acronym for Personal Order of Difficulty. The pacing charts show you how many questions you should answer but they don't show you which questions you should answer. So, for example, the pacing chart says that you should answer 14 questions in the 20 question section. Now, you know that the questions get harder as you go. But, what if question 10 is a geometry question and you've forgotten everything you ever knew about geometry? Would it make sense to answer that question? Of course not!

You'd skip the geometry question and hope that you'd know how to answer one of the later questions. That's POOD in action.

In general, you'll want to concentrate your efforts on answering easy and medium questions. So, if you are supposed to answer 14 questions in that 20 question math section, you need to find the best 14 questions for you to answer. Most of them will probably come from the easy and medium questions but it's okay to skip a few questions along the way. That's better than making a blind guess.

Summary

- The problems in many groups of questions on the SAT (except Short and Long Reading) start out easy and gradually get harder. The first question in a group is often so easy that virtually everyone can find ETS's answer. The last question is so hard that almost no one can.
- You should never waste time trying to figure out the answer to a hard question if there are still easy questions that you haven't tried. All questions are worth the same number of points. Why not do the easy ones first?
- Joe Bloggs is the average student. He earns an average score on the SAT. On an easy SAT question, the answer that seems correct to Joe is almost always correct. On medium questions, it is sometimes correct and sometimes not. On hard questions, the answer Joe likes is almost always wrong.
- Most test takers could improve their scores significantly by attempting fewer questions and devoting more time to questions they have a chance of answering correctly.
- It's very important to set realistic goals. If you're aiming for a 500 on Critical Reading, your approach to the SAT is going to be very different from that of someone who is aiming for an 800.
- After each practice exam, go back to the pacing chart. You may need to answer more questions on the next exam to earn the score you want.
- Use POOD, your Personal Order of Difficulty, to decide which questions in a section to answer when trying to reach your pacing goal.

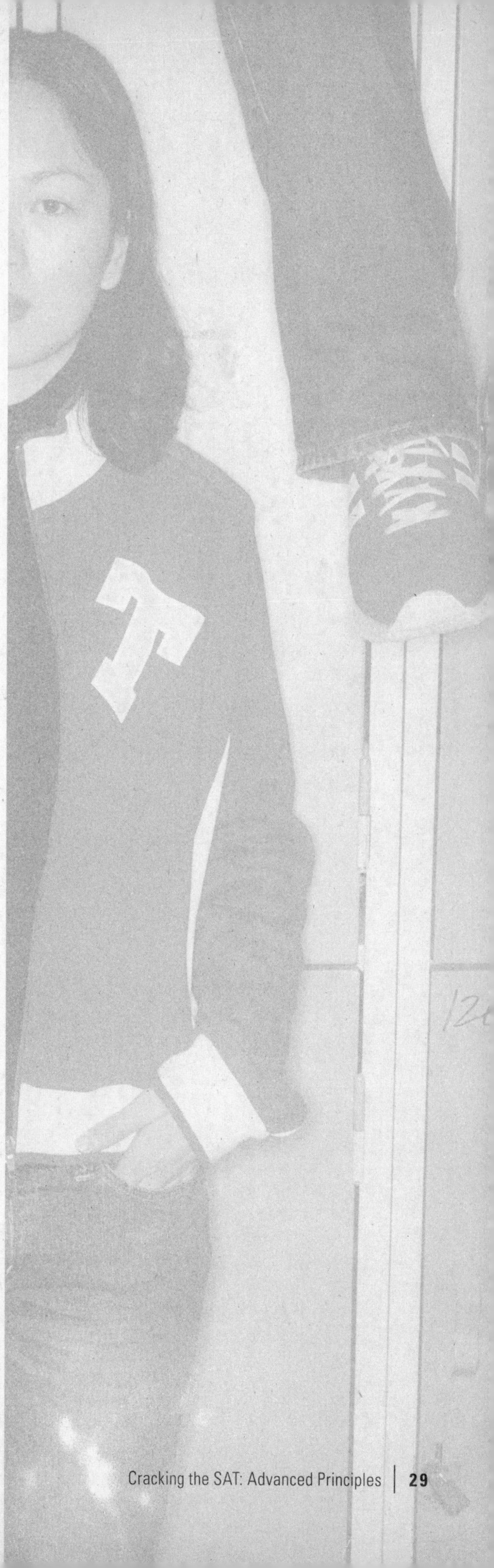

Part II
How to Crack the Critical Reading Section

A FEW WORDS ABOUT WORDS

The SAT contains ten sections. Three of these will be scored Critical Reading sections.

Each of the three scored Critical Reading sections on the SAT contains two types of questions: sentence completions and reading comprehension. In sentence completion questions, you'll be given an incomplete sentence, along with several possible ways to complete it. In reading comprehension questions, you will be given a passage (either long or short) to read, followed by a series of questions asking you about the passage.

WHAT DOES THE CRITICAL READING SECTION TEST?

ETS says that the Critical Reading section tests "verbal reasoning abilities" or "higher order reasoning abilities." You may be wondering exactly what these statements mean, but don't sweat it—they're not true anyway. Critical reading questions test your ability to read and your familiarity with certain words. A strong vocabulary will help you understand what you are reading and allow you to write stronger essays. If you have a big vocabulary, you'll probably do well on the exam. If you have a small vocabulary, you'll have more trouble no matter how many techniques we teach you.

Read What You Like

Some folks think it's necessary to read nothing but books on boring or hard subjects to build a better vocabulary. Not true. Identify something that interests you and find some books on that subject. You'll be spending time on something you enjoy, and hey, you just might learn something.

The best way to improve your reading is by practicing reading. Even certain periodicals—newspapers and some magazines—can improve your verbal performance if you read them regularly. Keep a notebook and a dictionary by your side as you read. When you encounter words you don't know, write them down, look them up, and try to incorporate them into your life. The dinner table is a good place to throw around new words.

Most of us have to encounter new words many times before we develop a firm sense of what they mean. You can speed up this process a great deal by taking advantage of Chapter 8, "Vocabulary." It contains a list of words that are very likely to turn up on the SAT, and some general guidelines about learning new words. If you work through it carefully between now and the time you take the test, you'll have a much easier time on the Critical Reading section. The more SAT words you know, the more our techniques will help you.

Read through Chapter 8 and sketch out a vocabulary-building program for yourself. You should follow this program every day, at the same time that you work through the other chapters of this book.

The techniques described in the Critical Reading chapters that follow are intended to help you take full advantage of your growing vocabulary by using partial information to attack hard questions. In a sense, we are going to teach you how to get the maximum possible mileage out of the words you know. Almost all students miss SAT questions that they could have answered correctly if only they had used our techniques.

Chapter 4
Joe Bloggs and the Critical Reading Section

The Critical Reading section primarily tests vocabulary and reading comprehension skills. However, knowing how ETS expects you to answer the questions and learning to avoid trap answers will help you improve your score. In this chapter we will show you how our average student, Joe Bloggs, can help you answer the questions found on the Critical Reading section of the SAT.

JOE BLOGGS AND THE CRITICAL READING SECTION

Joe Bloggs will be a big help to you on the Critical Reading section. Keep Joe Bloggs in mind as you take the SAT, and you will assuredly increase your score. Let's look at how you can use Joe on the Critical Reading section.

Joe Bloggs and Order of Difficulty

A Reminder
On easy questions, the answers that seem right to Joe really are right; on hard questions, the answers that seem right to Joe are wrong.

The Critical Reading sections of the SAT contain two question types: sentence completions and reading comprehension. As we mentioned before, only the sentence completions follow a definitive order of difficulty. In general, the harder sentence completions test harder vocabulary words. Of course, there's no such thing as a "hard" word or an "easy" word—just words you know and words you don't know. Your best defense against Joe Bloggs answer choices is to increase your vocabulary.

No matter how many words you learn, though, you'll still run across words you don't know on the sentence completions. Not to worry: Joe Bloggs can once again guide you to the right answer. Here's an example of a difficult sentence completion:

Order Of Difficulty (OOD)
Question #8 is the last question in the long sentence completion set. So it is a difficult one. Difficult questions have more trap answers.

8. The researchers believe their experimental and observational data furnish the ------- evidence that proves their hypothesis.

(A) trifling
(B) experiential
(C) intuitive
(D) empirical
(E) microscopic

Analysis

This is a hard question. Only about 8 percent of test takers answer it correctly. More than twice as many of them would have answered it correctly if they had simply closed their eyes and picked one of the choices at random. Why did most test takers—including, of course, our friend Joe Bloggs—do so poorly on this question? They all fell into a cleverly laid trap.

How Does Joe Do It?
On difficult reading questions, Joe Bloggs picks answers that are associated with the topic he's reading about.

Joe reads the sentence and sees that it is about scientists and hypotheses. Instantly, certain words and images spring into his mind. Joe starts looking through the answers for a word commonly associated with science, and he is immediately drawn to choices B and E. Hey, it's called a science *experiment,* right? And scientists need *microscopes* to do their experiments, right? Yeah, that's the ticket…

Don't think like Joe! On hard questions, eliminate any choice or choices that you know will be attractive to Joe. We'll tell you more about how to do this as we go along. (Incidentally, the correct answer to this question is D. *Empirical* means "based on observation.")

Can Joe Help Me on Reading Comprehension Questions?

Even though the reading comprehension questions don't have a strict order of difficulty, knowing how Joe Bloggs approaches this type of question will help you avoid traps and careless mistakes.

When Joe answers a reading comprehension question, he tends to answer from memory. He doesn't go back to the passage to verify his answer. In the Reading Comprehension chapters (Chapters 6 and 7), you'll learn the best way of approaching these problems. Keep in mind that The Princeton Review approach for finding the right answers is practically the opposite of the Joe Bloggs approach. Make sure you use our approach, not Joe's.

Bloggs Magnets

Joe is irresistibly drawn to easy answer choices containing words that remind him of the question. Therefore, on hard sentence completions, you can eliminate such choices.

Putting Joe to Work on the Critical Reading SAT

Generally speaking, the Joe Bloggs principle teaches you to

- trust your hunches on easy questions
- double-check your hunches on medium questions
- eliminate Joe Bloggs answers on difficult questions
- go back to the passage on reading comprehension questions

The next few chapters will teach you how to use your knowledge of Joe Bloggs to add points to your SAT score.

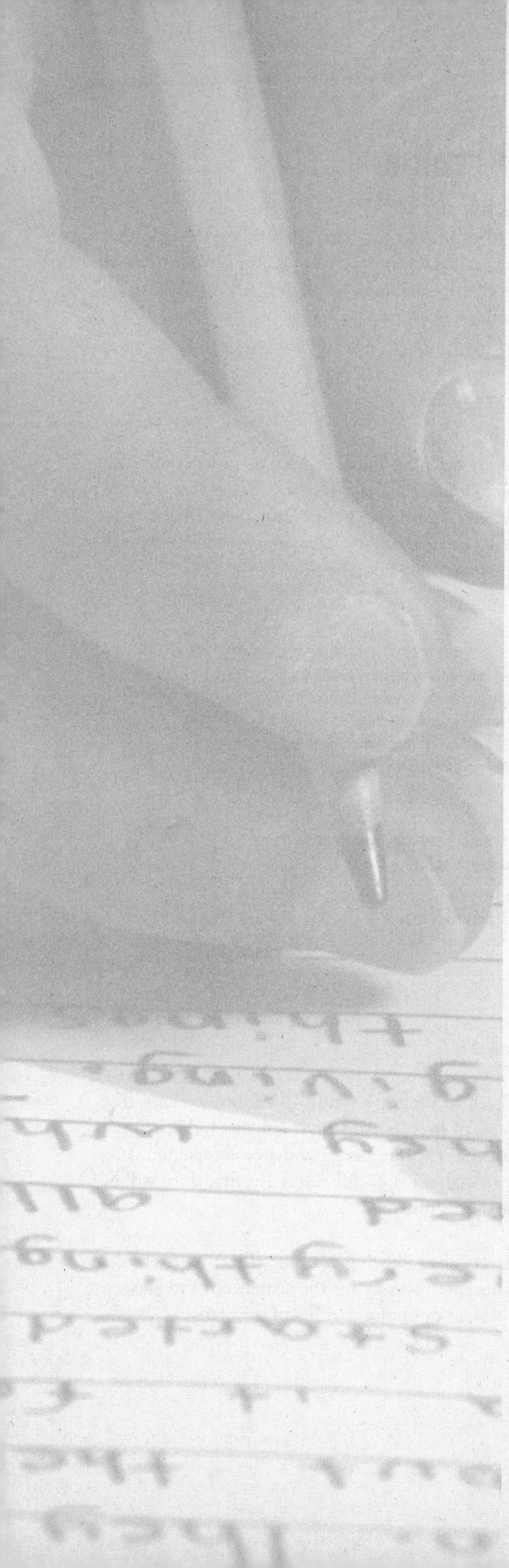

Chapter 5 Sentence Completions

SAT Sentence Completions are sentences from which one or more words have been removed. Your job is to find the missing word or words based on context. This chapter will lead you through a series of steps that will help you accomplish this task with the most accuracy and the least stress. You'll learn how the test writers try to trap you and what techniques you can use to avoid those traps.

SAT SENTENCE COMPLETIONS: CRACKING THE SYSTEM

How will you find the magic word to fill in the blank? By finding the clue that ETS has left for you in the sentence. Each sentence completion contains one or more clues that will tell you what goes in the blank or blanks. All you have to do is find the clues, and you've cracked the question.

The Instructions

Before we begin, take a moment to read the following set of instructions and answer the sample question that follows. Both appear here exactly as they do on the real SAT. Be certain that you know and understand these instructions before you take the SAT. If you learn them ahead of time, you won't have to waste valuable seconds reading them on the day you take the test.

> Each sentence below has one or two blanks, each blank indicating that something has been omitted. Beneath the sentence are five words or sets of words labeled A through E. Choose the word or set of words that, when inserted in the sentence, best fits the meaning of the sentence as a whole.
>
> **Example:**
>
> Desiring to ------- his taunting friends, Mitch gave them taffy in hopes it would keep their mouths shut.
>
> (A) eliminate (B) satisfy (C) overcome
> (D) ridicule (E) silence
>
> Ⓐ Ⓑ Ⓒ Ⓓ ●

ETS's answer to this sample question is E.

Sentence completions appear in each of the test's Critical Reading sections. The questions will be arranged in groups of five, six, and eight sentences (thought not necessarily in that order). Regardless of the number of sentence completions in a section, the questions will follow a rough order of difficulty: The first third will be easy, and the last third will be the most difficult.

Let's begin with an easy question. Try the following example. The answer choices have been removed so you can concentrate solely on the sentence. Read the sentence, look for the clue, and pick a word or phrase that fits in the blank.

1. Even though it is a dead language, rather than fading away, Latin is now being -------.

Here's How to Crack It

What word did you come up with? Probably something like *rediscovered* or *restored*. How did you decide that was the word that you needed? Because of the clue. The clue in the sentence is *rather than fading away*. It tells us that Latin is doing the opposite of *fading away*; it's making a comeback.

Now that you have decided on the kind of word or phrase that goes in the blank, look at the following answer choices. Cross off the answers that are not close to yours (ones that don't mean *rediscovered* or *restored*), and pick the best answer.

(A) forgotten
(B) excavated
(C) mortified
(D) revitalized
(E) revealed

Answer choices A and C are out right away (unless you aren't sure what *mortified* means, in which case you should leave C in). You may find it hard to choose among B, D, and E, but think about which is closest to your word. Can a language be dug up? Not really, so get rid of B. Has Latin been hidden? No, so get rid of E.

The credited response is D. *Revitalized* means "given life."

Mark It!

Make sure you mark each answer, so you can narrow down your choices and guess if you need to! Remember the easy markings:

- ✔ Put a check mark next to an answer you like.
- ~ Put a squiggle next to an answer you kinda like.
- ? Put a question mark next to an answer you don't understand.
- ~~A~~ Cross out the letter of any answer choice you KNOW is wrong.

But Why?

You may be wondering why we didn't just plug each answer into the sentence to see which one sounded right. That's because *all* the answers are designed to *sound* right. Look back to the question we just did. The sentence would sound just fine if you plugged in any one of those answer choices. But only one of them is ETS's answer.

More importantly, plugging each word into the sentence is how Joe Bloggs would solve the question. Does Joe get all sentence completion questions correct? No way. Joe doesn't know that ETS has given him a clue in the sentence that tells him exactly what the answer is. He just plugs in choices and takes a guess.

You, on the other hand, know the inside scoop. In each sentence, ETS must include a clue that reveals the answer. If it didn't, no one would agree on the right answer (there wouldn't *be* a right answer), and lots of people would sue.

ETS will put a clue in every sentence to indicate what goes in the blank. Find it! Once you do, use it to determine the missing word or words. Don't rely on the answer choices—ETS makes them as attractive as possible, so that the Joe Bloggses of the world get caught by trying to find an answer that sounds right. How can you avoid getting caught in the "sounds right" trap?

Cover Up

Cover the answer choices before you begin each sentence completion. (Really do it!) Place your hand or your answer sheet over the five answer choices so that you are not tempted to look at them too soon. Then, read the sentence and underline ETS's clue. Decide what you think the word in the blank should be, and then use POE to get to ETS's answer.

Try another example:

4. Lavender has a ------- effect; its aroma alleviates tension and anxiety.

Here's How to Crack It

Recycle!

ETS often uses a clue that can be used in the blank. Don't spend brain cells coming up with your own word. Recycle the clue! Remember to use anything at your disposal to get to the correct answer quickly and efficiently.

The clue in any sentence completion is always a short, descriptive phrase that tells you what word goes in the blank. What is the clue in this sentence? The last part of the sentence gives you the full picture: *alleviates tension and anxiety.* The clue tells us that lavender relieves stress (tension and anxiety)—so the word we're looking for is something like *calming* or *relaxing.*

Now that you have a target word, use POE to find ETS's answer:

(A) fragrant
(B) joyous
(C) iridescent
(D) soothing
(E) painful

The only word that comes close to meaning calming or relaxing is D, *soothing.* This is ETS's answer.

Step by Step

Before moving on to another example, make sure you know the steps for answering sentence completion questions. Here's a handy list for you to review:

1. Cover up the answer choices.
2. Read the sentence.
3. Underline the clue.
4. Come up with your own word or phrase to go in the blank.
5. Use POE.

Got it? Now take a look at the following question:

Don't Peek!
Cover the answer choices until you come up with your own word.

4. Some developing nations have become remarkably -------, using aid from other countries to build successful industries.

(A) populous
(B) dry
(C) warlike
(D) prosperous
(E) isolated

Here's How to Crack It

The clue in this sentence is *build successful industries.* It indicates that some nations "have become remarkably *successful.*"

Let's look at each answer choice for a word that's close to *successful*:

(A) Does *populous* mean *successful*? No. Cross off this answer.
(B) Does *dry* mean *successful*? Not at all. Cross it off.
(C) Does *warlike* mean *successful*? Nope. Ditch it.
(D) Does *prosperous* mean *successful*? Sure does.
(E) Does *isolated* mean *successful*? Nope. Ditch it.

ETS's answer must be D.

Searching for Clues

Mark It!
Underline the clue!

If you are having trouble finding the clue, ask yourself two simple questions:

1. What is the blank talking about?
2. What *else* does the sentence say about its subject?

For example, look back to the question we just did. What is the blank talking about? Some nations. What else does the sentence say about the nations? They were able to *build successful industries.* This must be the clue of the sentence because it refers to the same thing the blank refers to.

Find and underline the clue in the following sentence. Then fill in the blank with your own word. If you have any trouble, ask:

1. What is the blank talking about?
2. What *else* does the sentence say about its subject?

1. Shaquille O'Neal is such a physically intimidating basketball player that his opponents focus on his ------- and thus underestimate his surprising quickness.

Analysis

What is the blank talking about? Shaquille O'Neal. What else does the sentence say about Shaquille O'Neal? He is a *physically intimidating basketball player.* Therefore, his opponents focus on his *large size.*

Pick a Word, Any Word

The word you come up with to fill the blank doesn't have to be an elegant word, or a hard word, or the perfect word. It doesn't even have to be a word; instead, it can be a phrase—even a clunky phrase—as long as it captures the correct meaning.

In an episode of *The Simpsons,* a lawyer couldn't think of the word *mistrial,* so he asked the judge to declare a "bad court thingie." *Bad court thingie* is an accurate enough substitute for *mistrial* on the SAT. With *bad court thingie* as your "word," POE will get you to *mistrial.*

Recycle the Clue

As we mentioned earlier, you can often just recycle the clue instead of coming up with an entirely new word for the blank. If you can put the clue itself in the blank, you can be sure that you've put your finger on ETS's answer.

Is the blank always the same as the clue? Sometimes the blank is exactly the same, while other times it is exactly the opposite. You must use the rest of the sentence to determine if the blank and the clue are the same or opposite. In other words, you must be on the lookout for "trigger words."

Please Recycle

If the SAT gives you a perfect word or phrase as a clue, then steal it! The SAT just told you exactly what word they want.

Trigger Words

Very often on sentence completions, the most important clue to ETS's answer is a trigger word: a single revealing word or expression that lets you know exactly where ETS is heading. About half of all SAT sentence completions contain trigger words. Combining trigger words with your clue makes filling in the blank a breeze.

Trigger words can either change the direction the sentence is going in or keep it the same. The most common change-direction trigger words are *but, though,* and *although.* These words change the direction or focus of a sentence. The most common same-direction trigger words are *and* and *because.* These are words that maintain the direction of a sentence.

Common Triggers

Same Direction	Change Direction
because	*however*
and	*although/though*
since	*but*
in fact	*in contrast to*
colon (:)	*rather*
semicolon (;)	*despite*
	yet

Both types of trigger words provide terrific clues that you can use to find ETS's answer. To see what we mean, take a look at the following incomplete sentences. For each one, fill in a few words that complete the thought in a plausible way. There's no single correct answer. Just fill in something that makes sense in the context of the entire sentence:

I really like you, *but* ______________________________.
I really like you, *and* ______________________________.

Here's how one of our students filled in the blanks:

I really like you, *but I'm going to leave you.*
I really like you, *and I'm going to hug you.*

Analysis

In the first sentence, the word *but* indicates that the second half of the sentence will contradict the first half. Because the first half of the sentence is positive, the second half must be negative. I like you, *but* I'm going to leave you. The sentence changes direction after the trigger word *but.*

In the second sentence, the word *and* indicates that the second half of the sentence will confirm or support the first half. Because the first half of the sentence is positive, the second half must be positive as well. I like you, *and* I'm going to hug you. In this case, the sentence continues in the same direction after the trigger word *and.*

Other Triggers

Two other types of triggers to look for are punctuation, particularly colons and semicolons, and time triggers. Punctuation triggers are important because they divide the sentence into two pieces: one part with the blank and one without. Most of the time, the part that doesn't include the blank is the clue to the blank. Often you can recycle that part of the sentence into the blank and use it for your word. Time triggers indicate a change in the sentence with the passage of time and help you fill in the blank with the proper word.

DRILL 1

Mark It
Make sure you actually underline the clue and circle the trigger. Put pencil to paper!

Circle the trigger word (if there is one) and underline the clue in each of the following sentences. Then, write your own word in the blank. If you have trouble finding the clue, ask yourself, "What is the blank talking about?" and "What else does the sentence say about this?" Don't worry if you can't think of a single, perfect word for the blank; use a phrase that catches the meaning. Once you've finished these questions, go on to Drill 2 and use POE to find ETS's answer. Answers can be found on page 372.

1. Because theaters refused to show it when it was first released, *Citizen Kane* was ------- failure, though now it is considered one of the greatest American films ever made.

6. Ironically, many of the family-owned small businesses located in the newly revitalized neighborhood downtown are so threatened by increasing rents that they may be ------- by the very economic redevelopment that the city has pursued for so long.

7. When will Hollywood directors stop producing technically slick but emotionally ------- movies and begin creating films filled with authenticity and poignancy?

DRILL 2

Here are the same questions, this time with the answer choices. Refer to your notes from Drill 1 and make a choice for each question. Remember to use POE. Answers can be found on page 372.

1. Because theaters refused to show it when it was first released, *Citizen Kane* was ------- failure, though now it is considered one of the greatest American films ever made.

(A) a revolutionary
(B) a personal
(C) a commercial
(D) an aesthetic
(E) a perennial

6. Ironically, many of the small businesses located downtown are so threatened by increasing rents that they may be ------- by the very economic redevelopment that the city has pursued for so long.

(A) buttressed
(B) bankrupted
(C) hindered
(D) ameliorated
(E) relieved

7. I hope that some day Hollywood directors will stop producing technically slick but emotionally ------- movies and begin creating films filled with authenticity and poignancy.

(A) savvy
(B) vacuous
(C) opulent
(D) urbane
(E) boorish

AND THEN THERE WERE TWO

Roughly half of all sentence completions contain two blanks. Many students fear these questions because they look long and intimidating. But two-blank sentence completions are no more difficult than single-blank sentence completions. In fact, they can be easier because you get two chances to use POE. The key is to take them one blank at a time.

To crack two-blank sentence completions, read the sentence, circling the trigger word(s) and underlining the clue(s), keeping in mind that there may be a clue for *each* blank. Then fill in whichever blank seems easier to you. Once you have filled in one of the blanks, go to the answer choices and check just the words for that blank, using POE to get rid of answers that are not close to yours. Then go back to the other blank, fill it in, and check the remaining choices. You do not need to check both words at one time. If one of the words doesn't work in a blank, then it doesn't matter what the other word is. One strike and the answer is out.

When eliminating answers, draw a line through the entire answer choice. That way you won't get confused and check it again when you are checking the other blank. Even if you do fill in both blanks the first time you read the sentence, check only one blank at a time. It is much easier to concentrate on one word than on a pair of words. Sometimes you'll be able to get rid of four choices by checking only one blank, and you won't even need to check the other blank.

Here's an example of a two-blank sentence completion:

5. While the ------- student openly questioned the teacher's explanation, she was not so ------- as to suggest that the teacher was wrong.

(A) complacent . . suspicious
(B) inquisitive . . imprudent
(C) curious . . dispassionate
(D) provocative . . respectful
(E) ineffectual . . brazen

Shoe Store

If you were shopping for shoes and found a pair you liked, you'd ask the clerk to bring you a pair in your size to try on. Say you tried the right shoe first. If it felt horrible, would you even bother to try on the left shoe? No, because even if the left shoe was comfy, you'd have to wear it with the right shoe, which you already know causes you unspeakable pain. You would look for another pair of shoes. Two-blank sentence completions are like shoes. If one doesn't fit, there's no point trying the other one. Half bad is all bad.

Here's How to Crack It

Let's start with the first blank. The clue is *openly questioned*, and we can simply recycle the clue and put *questioning* in the blank. Now let's take a look at the first-blank words in the answer choices and eliminate any words that are definitely not a good match for *questioning*. Eliminate choices A and E because *complacent* and *ineffectual* have nothing to do with *questioning*. All we want to do at this point is eliminate any words that are way off base. Then we can move on to the second blank.

The clue for the second blank is *suggest that the teacher was wrong*. How would you describe a student who accuses the teacher of being wrong? *Bold* or *rude*, maybe? Look at the remaining choices and get rid of any second words that don't mean something like *bold* or *rude*. C is out—*dispassionate* does not mean *bold* or *rude*. Also, D is out, since this student is anything but *respectful*. ETS's answer must be B.

Notice that we had to eliminate only one of the words in each answer choice to get rid of the entire choice. Attacking this question using POE also made it easier because we could eliminate four answers without much trouble. If four answers are wrong, the one that's left must be ETS's answer.

The Tricky Ones

Every now and then, the clue for one of the blanks in a two-blank sentence completion turns out to be the other blank. What? How can ETS get away with making the clue a *blank*?

Don't worry—if ETS has decided to use one blank as the clue for the other blank, you know it has inserted another way for you to find the answer. Let's look at an example:

6. Most of Rick's friends think his life is unbelievably -------, but in fact he spends most of his time on ------- activities.

(A) fruitful . . productive
(B) wasteful . . useless
(C) scintillating . . mundane
(D) varied . . sportive
(E) callow . . simple

Here's How to Crack It

The trigger word in this sentence is *but*. We gather from the sentence that most of Rick's friends think his life is one way, but in fact it is another. We cannot tell if his friends think his life is great and busy while it's really lousy and slow, or vice versa. However, we do know that our blanks are opposites: The first is positive while the second is negative *or* the first is negative while the second is positive.

Knowing this is enough to get us to ETS's answer. Let's look at each answer choice, keeping in mind that we need a pair of words that are opposites:

(A) *Fruitful* is positive; *productive* is positive. Eliminate this choice.
(B) *Wasteful* is negative; *useless* is negative. Cross it off.
(C) *Scintillating* is positive; *mundane* is negative. Keep it.
(D) *Varied* is positive; *sportive* is positive. Cross it off.
(E) *Callow* is negative; *simple* is neutral. A possibility, but not great.

ETS's answer is C: Rick's life may look *scintillating*, but he spends most of his time on *mundane* activities.

If the clue to one of the blanks is the other blank, look for the trigger word and determine the relationship between the blanks. Then use POE to find ETS's answer.

Are You a Good Word or a Bad Word?

Notice in the last example that we didn't use *words* to fill in the blanks; instead, we looked for positive and negative. On difficult sentence completions, you may find it hard to determine what the word in the blank is supposed to be. However, you will usually have an idea if that word should be a good word (something positive) or a bad word (something negative). Knowing whether a blank is positive or negative can help you eliminate answer choices. If you are unable to come up with your own word, use + or – to get rid of answers and make smart guesses.

Vocab
Don't eliminate words you've never seen before or cannot readily define. Or, in the words of Bob Dylan, "Don't criticize what you can't understand."

Here's an example:

8. Ruskin's vitriolic attack was the climax of the ------- heaped on paintings that today seem amazingly -------.

(A) criticism . . unpopular
(B) ridicule . . inoffensive
(C) praise . . amateurish
(D) indifference . . scandalous
(E) acclaim . . creditable

Here's How to Crack It

A *vitriolic* attack is something bad (and so is simply an *attack,* if you don't know what *vitriolic* means). The climax of a vitriolic attack must also be bad, and therefore the first blank must be a bad word. Already we can eliminate choices C and E (and possibly choice D). We don't have to worry about the second word in these answer choices because we already know that the first word is wrong.

A Gentle Reminder
Your aim is to eliminate wrong answers. Get rid of as many incorrect choices as you can, guess from among the remaining choices, and then move on.

Now look at the second blank. The first part of the sentence says that Ruskin thought the paintings were very bad; today, *amazingly,* they seem—what? Bad?

No! The word in the second blank has to be a *good* word. Choices C and E are already crossed out. We can now also eliminate choices A and D (without bothering to look at the first words again) because the second blank words are bad words. The only choice left is B—ETS's answer. You've correctly answered a very hard question simply by figuring out whether the words in ETS's answer were good or bad. Not bad!

The good-word/bad-word method is also helpful when you have anticipated ETS's answer but haven't found a similar word among the choices. Simply decide whether your anticipated answer is positive or negative, then determine whether each of the answer choices is positive or negative. Eliminate the choices that are different, and you'll find ETS's answer.

WHAT ABOUT JOE?

As you know, the last few questions in each group of sentence completions will be quite difficult. On these hard questions, you will find it useful to remember the Joe Bloggs principle and eliminate choices that you know would attract Joe. Here's an example:

5. The policy of benign ------- was based upon the assumption that citizens were better off when the government kept out of their daily affairs.

(A) regulation
(B) engagement
(C) neglect
(D) democracy
(E) coercion

Here's How to Crack It

Joe Bloggs is attracted to choices containing words that remind him of the subject matter of the sentence. The words in the sentence that Joe notices are *citizens* and *government*—words relating to politics. Which answers attract his attention? Choices A and D. You can therefore eliminate both.

What's the clue in this sentence? It's the phrase *kept out of their daily affairs.* By recycling the clue, you can anticipate the correct answer: "The policy of benign *keeping out of citizens' daily affairs* was based on...." Which answer choice could mean something similar to that? Only C, *neglect.*

Important!
Eliminating Joe Bloggs attractors should always be the first thing you do when considering answer choices on a hard sentence completion. If you don't eliminate them immediately, you run the risk of falling for them as you consider the various choices.

DRILL 3

Putting It All Together

Take all the techniques you've learned and put them into practice. Don't forget to underline your clues and circle your triggers! The numbers reflect where in the section each question would appear. Remember that higher numbers go with harder questions. Answers can be found on page 372.

2. Instead of being ------- by piles of papers, some college admissions officers are trying to ------- the application process by utilizing computers to simplify the procedure.

(A) hindered . . facilitate
(B) bolstered . . retard
(C) disappointed . . arrest
(D) quickened . . accelerate
(E) offended . . innovate

5. In National Park Ranger Nevada Barr's novel *Blind Descent*, the ------- must rescue the endangered victim of a ------- caving accident.

(A) adventurer . . secondary
(B) philanderer . . fictional
(C) protagonist . . perilous
(D) globetrotter . . coincidental
(E) adversary . . hazardous

6. Weather conditions can cause leaves to appear so ------- that they resemble ------- human skin.

(A) lustrous . . opaque
(B) verdant . . scarred
(C) ashen . . sanguine
(D) wizened . . withered
(E) obsolete . . nascent

7. The nonprofit organization was searching for a ------- new employee, one who would courageously support the goals of the organization and become devoted to helping other people.

(A) querulous
(B) novice
(C) proficient
(D) magnanimous
(E) lavish

Summary

- Cover the answer choices. Learn to anticipate ETS's answer by filling in each blank before you look at the answer choices. If you look at the answer choices first, you might be misled.
- Always look for the clue—the key word or words that you need to fill in the blank(s)—and underline it.
- If you have trouble finding the clue, ask yourself:
  - What is the blank talking about?
  - What else does the sentence say about this subject?
- Look for trigger words—revealing words or expressions that give you important clues about the meanings of sentences—and circle them.
- Fill in the blank with any word or phrase that will help you get to ETS's answer. Don't worry if you need to use a clunky or an awkward phrase. If you can, recycle the clue. If you can't come up with any words for the blank, use + or –.
- Use POE to get to the answer.
- Attack two-blank sentence completions by focusing on one blank at a time. Use the same techniques you would use on one-blank questions. If you can eliminate either word in an answer choice, you can cross out the entire choice. If the clue for one of the blanks is the other blank, use the trigger word to determine the relationship between the blanks.
- Never eliminate a choice unless you are sure of its meaning.
- If you can't eliminate any answer choices on a question, skip it.

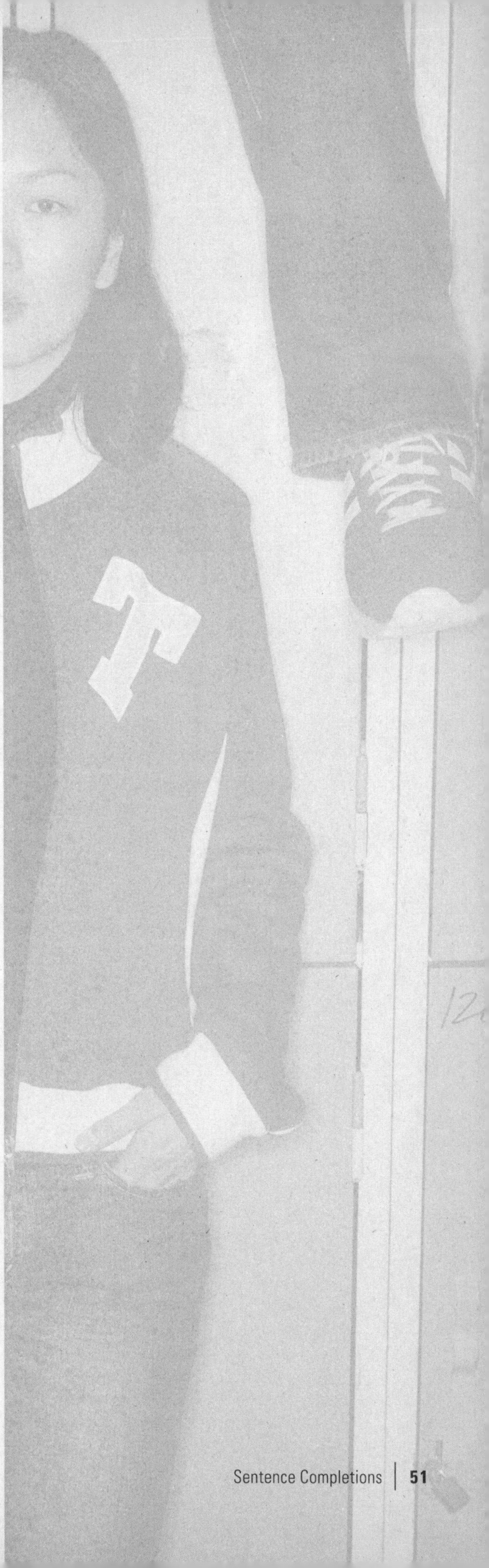

Chapter 6
Reading Comprehension: An Open-Book Test

Questions based on reading passages make up about 70 percent of the Critical Reading sections of the test. These questions may ask you to restate a piece of information from the passage, draw an inference, determine a definition, or to recognize the purpose of a piece of writing. This chapter will introduce you to these different types of questions and provide you with a strategy to handle the long reading passages.

SAT READING COMPREHENSION: CRACKING THE SYSTEM

Passive Reading: Whatever!

Active Reading: Keep your eye on the prize

You read every day. So what's the difference between plain old reading and reading on the Critical Reading section of the SAT? Often, when you read, you read *passively.* When you read a street sign or a magazine (or even sometimes your school books), you are reading just to figure out what the words stand for and to see what might strike you as interesting or important.

On the SAT, you should read *actively.* You will read with an eye toward finding specific information that you need in order to answer a question. Once you've found the necessary information, you need to know not only what the words stand for, but also what they are *really saying.* Sometimes SAT passages are clear and logical, but other times facts, ideas, and opinions are stated indirectly.

Your Task, as Given by ETS

The majority of questions on the Critical Reading sections of the SAT are what we call reading comprehension questions, which refer to a passage or passages. The passage appears first, followed by a series of questions that relate to it. The first two passages you will see in two of the Critical Reading sections will be short; the rest of the passages will be longer.

Let's look at the instructions that ETS gives you for reading comprehension questions:

> Each passage below is followed by questions based on its content. Answer the questions on the basis of what is stated or implied in each passage and in any introductory material that may be provided.

Once you've read the instructions, memorize them, so you don't waste your valuable time reading them when you take the test!

An Open-Book Test

Great news—the SAT is an open-book test! How can you take advantage of this fact? It's easy: don't waste time carefully reading the passage. Instead, follow the strategies we're going to teach you here. You can find the information to answer the questions without spending lots of time getting bogged down in the details of that long, boring passage.

Don't Be Like Joe

ETS writes the reading comprehension section hoping you will act just like Joe Bloggs. Here's what he does—and what you should avoid doing.

- Joe wastes time reading stuff he doesn't need.
- Joe doesn't make sure he knows what the questions are really asking.
- Joe reads carelessly when looking for the answer to a question.
- Joe looks at the answer choices before he has any idea what the answer should look like.
- Joe falls for trap answers designed just for him.

READING COMPREHENSION: YOUR BASIC STRATEGY

To avoid being like Joe, here's how you should approach the reading comprehension questions. Don't worry! We'll come back to this list often!

1. **Read the Italicized Blurb.** It's short, and it helps with the main idea.
2. **Work the passage.** For some passages, you can go right to the questions. (We'll go over how to decide whether or not to do that in a minute.) If you do read the passage, try not to spend more than two minutes on it. Don't get bogged down in the details. Just get a sense of the passage as a whole.
3. **Select a Question.** You should look at the questions in the order they appear and—mostly—you will answer them in order. Reading Comprehension questions don't go in order of difficulty, though, you may want to skip hard ones, at least at first. *Make sure you know what a question is asking* before you answer it. Then *always* go back to the passage before looking at the answer choices.
4. **Read only what you need.** Most of the answers will be located in a small portion of the passage. Sometimes the answer is a couple sentences away from the line reference in the question. A good rule of thumb is to read 5 lines on either side.
5. **Answer the Question.** If possible, use your own words before you go to the answer choices.
6. **POE.** Eliminate the four worst answers.

Now, let's put these steps into practice. A sample passage and questions appear on the next two pages. Don't start working the passage right away. In fact, you can't—the answer choices are missing (they'll be revealed later). Just go ahead to page 58, where we will begin to go through each of these six steps using following the passage on the next two pages as an illustration.

The Fact Bank

Somebody once asked notorious thief Willie Sutton why he robbed banks. "Because that's where the money is," he replied. While reading comprehension is safer and slightly more productive than larceny, the same principle applies: Concentrate on the questions and answer choices because that's where the points are. The passage is just a place for ETS to stash facts and details. You'll find them when you need to. What's the point of memorizing all 67 pesky details about plankton if ETS asks you about only 12?

Sample Passage and Questions

Here is an example of what a reading comprehension passage and questions look like. We will use this passage to illustrate reading comprehension techniques, so you don't need to do the questions right now, but you may want to stick a paper clip on this page to make it easier to flip back to it.

Questions 17–24 are based on the following passage.

The following is an excerpt from an essay published in a weekly San Francisco newspaper column. The author discusses his visit to a beached whale.

I went out, several days ago, to see the whale—I speak in the singular number, because there was only one whale on the beach at that time. My comrade was not well; consequently we travelled slowly, and conversed about distressing diseases and such other matters as I thought would be likely to interest a sick man and make him feel cheerful. Instead of commenting on the mild scenery, we spoke of the ravages of the cholera in the happy days of our boyhood; instead of boasting of the swiftness of our horse, as most persons similarly situated would have done, we chatted gaily of consumption; and when we caught a glimpse of long white lines of waves rolling in silently upon the distant shore, our hearts were gladdened by fond memories of sea-sickness. It was a nice comfortable journey, and I could not have enjoyed it more if I had been sick myself.

When we got to the Cliff House we were disappointed. I had always heard there was such a grand view to be seen there of the majestic ocean, with its white billows stretching far away until it met and mingled with the bending sky; with here and there a stately ship upon its surface, ploughing through plains of sunshine and deserts of shadow cast from the clouds above; and, near at hand, piles of picturesque rocks, splashed with angry surf and garrisoned by drunken, sprawling sea-lions and elegant, long-legged pelicans.

It was a bitter disappointment. There was nothing in sight but an ordinary counter, and behind it a long row of bottles with Old Bourbon, and Old Rye, and Old Tom, and the old, old story of man's falter and woman's fall, in them. Nothing in the world to be seen but these things. We stayed there an hour and a half, and took observations from different points of view, but the general result was the same—nothing but bottles and a bar. They keep a field-glass there, for the accommodation of those who wish to see the sights, and we looked at the bottles through that, but it did not help the matter any to speak of; we turned it end for end, but instead of increasing the view it diminished it.

We left the hotel, then, and drove along the level beach, drowsily admiring the terraced surf, and listening to the tidings it was bringing from other lands in the mysterious language of its ceaseless roar, until we hove in sight of the stranded whale. We thought it was a cliff, an isolated hill, an island—anything but a fish, capable of being cut up and stowed away in a ship. Its proportions were magnified a thousand-fold beyond any conception we had previously formed of them. We felt that we could not complain of a disappointment in regard to the whale, at any rate.

Then the light of inspiration dawned upon me, and I knew what I would do if I kept the hotel, and the whale belonged to me. I would not permit any one to approach nearer than six or eight hundred yards to the show, because at that distance the light mists, or the peculiar atmosphere, or something, exaggerates it into a monster of colossal size. It grows smaller as you go towards it. When we got pretty close to it, the island shrunk into a fish—a very large one for a sardine, it is true, but a very small one for a whale. Distance had been lending immensity to the view. We were disappointed again somewhat; but see how things are regulated! The very source of our disappointment was a blessing to us: As it was, there was just as much smell as two of us could stand; and if the fish had been larger there would have been more, wouldn't there?

The whale was not a long one, physically speaking—say thirty-five feet—but he smelt much longer; he smelt as much as a mile and a half longer, I should say, for we traveled about that distance beyond him before we ceased to detect his fragrance in the atmosphere. My comrade said he did not admire to smell a whale; and I adopt his sentiments while I scorn his language. A whale does not smell like magnolia, nor yet like heliotrope or "Balm of a Thousand Flowers"; I do not know, but I should judge that it smells more like a thousand pole-cats.

These are the questions for the passage. We've removed the answers because, for now, we just want you to see the different question types the SAT will ask. Don't worry about answering these yet.

17. The author and his traveling companion discussed illnesses because

18. The cause of the "bitter disappointment" (line 25) was that

19. The author mentions "a cliff, an isolated hill, an island" (lines 41–42) in order to

20. In lines 47–52, the author suggests that

21. The author would most likely agree with which one of the following about the "blessing" (line 58):

22. As used in line 67, "admire" most nearly means:

23. The final sentence of the passage serves to

24. The author's tone can best be described as

The Blurb

The Strategy
1. **Read the blurb.**

You should always begin by reading the blurb (the italicized stuff above the passage). The blurb tells you whether the passage is fiction or nonfiction and gives you a sense of what the passage will be about. Based on the blurb, you can decide what you will do to Work the Passage (as you'll see in the next step). Also, sometimes knowing what's in the blurb can help you to come up with an answer to a question.

Read the blurb at the beginning of the passage on page 56. Based on the blurb, what do you think the passage will be about? Write your answer in the space below.

____

____

Work the Passage

The Strategy
1. Read the blurb.
2. **Work the passage.**

For nonfiction passages, some people are comfortable going right to the questions. Let's give it a try with this one! For fiction passages, and for all passages if you feel that you need to read the passage first, get through the passage, but read it quickly. Remember: There is no way you can be asked about every single detail in the passage, and you have to go back to the passage for each question anyway. So, don't get stuck in the details. Skim the passage to get a general sense of what it is about.

Select a Question and Read Only What You Need

The Strategy
1. Read the blurb.
2. Work the passage.
3. **Select a question.**

It may seem as though there are lots of different types of questions with very similar and subjective answer choices, but as you will see, almost all questions can be treated in the same way. Let's first take a look at the order in which the questions appear and where in the passage you will find the answers you need.

Difficulty and Chronology

In most sections of the SAT, questions appear in an increasing order of difficulty—but not in reading comprehension. Instead, the questions follow the chronology of the passage. For this reason, you will want to work the questions in the order they appear; as you answer questions, you will be going through the passage from beginning to end. However, don't get stuck on a hard question. If you're having trouble, move on—other questions are likely to be easier. You can always come back to the questions you skipped.

Once you have selected a question, be sure you understand exactly what it is asking.

Line References and Lead Words

Most questions have line references, which makes it easier to find the relevant information. If there is no line reference in a question, you can get an idea of where in the passage to find the answer based on the line references used in the questions before and after—you'll be looking somewhere in between. Also, use names, dates, quotes, italicized words and easily spotted phrases to help you find the correct part of the passage within the chronological range. We call these Lead Words.

The Strategy

1. Read the blurb.
2. Work the passage.
3. Choose and translate a question.
4. **Read only what you need.**

Take a look at the first question:

> **17.** The author and his traveling companion discussed illnesses because

Where do you expect to find the answer to this question? Notice that the next question refers to line 25, so our question should refer to information before line 25. Because it is the first question, it would make sense to start by looking in the first paragraph. Use Lead Words to narrow down the search. From the blurb, you know that the passage is about a visit to a beached whale. The question, however, focuses on illnesses, a topic unlikely to appear much in the passage. So, you can scan the first paragraph looking for something about sickness. It turns out the entire first paragraph is about illnesses. Now you know what to read!

Once you know where to look in the passage, don't make one of Joe's biggest mistakes: reading only the line or sentence mentioned in the question. Usually, the answer to the question will appear a couple of lines above or below the line to which you are sent. In fact, that specific line from the question may very well contain trap answers. Generally, you should read 10 to 15 lines of text, although sometimes a bit more is needed.

Answer the Question

Before you look at the answer choices, you should try to answer the question in your own words. We'll use the passage on page 56 to learn about the different types of reading comprehension questions, and how to determine and articulate the answers. Later, we will look at the answer choices and consider POE.

The Strategy

1. Read the blurb.
2. Work the passage.
3. Choose and translate a question.
4. Read only what you need.
5. **Answer the question.**

Remember this; it's important! *Almost all the questions are going to refer to specific text in the passage.* Don't be creative and don't read too much into the passage. Just find what the author actually wrote.

Detail Questions

Many questions just ask for details about the passage. Let's take a look at Question 17 again.

17. The author and his traveling companion discussed illnesses because

Here's How to Crack It.

This question asks what the author says about why he and his friend talked illnesses. Go to the first paragraph of the passage with that question in mind. When you have an answer, write it down in the empty space provided under the question.

You should have noticed that in lines 3 to 7 the author explains that his friend was not well and the author thought it would make the friend feel better to discuss illnesses. The correct answer to question 17 will contain that information.

Let's try another detail question.

18. The cause of the "bitter disappointment" (line 25) was that

Here's How to Crack It

This question asks what the author says about what caused a "bitter disappointment." Go to the passage, find what you need, and write down the answer to the question. Remember that the answer is unlikely to appear in line 25, but should be in the lines either before or after it.

In this case, the pronoun "it" in line 25 tells you that you should look in the prior paragraph That paragraph talks about the author's expectation for beautiful views, but there's nothing in there about a disappointment, is there?. In that case, you should look at the paragraph containing line 25. Here, the author tells us that all he could see was an old bar, no beautiful views at all. (The blurb told us that the passage is fanciful!)

Purpose Questions

Many questions on the SAT ask why the author wrote something. These questions typically have the words "in order to" or "serves to". At first you might think that these questions require more effort than going to the passage and finding the relevant part—you might think you have to do a lot of generalization or re-read the whole passage. But you don't! An author's purpose will appear in the passage—you just have to find that part.

Let's take a look at a purpose question.

---

19. The author mentions "a cliff, an isolated hill, an island" (lines 41–42) in order to

Here's How to Crack It

This question asks you why the author mentioned the cliff, hill and island. Go the passage and find out what the author actually said about why he mentioned those things. Write down your answer in the space provided.

> **What's the Big Picture?**
> Be careful! ETS will try to trip you up in purpose questions by including answer choices that are about specific details in the relevant line. But you are looking for *the reason* the author used those details, not the details themselves.

The paragraph as a whole explains that the whale was much larger than anything the author expected. The author mentioned the cliff, hill and island in order to explain how surprisingly large the whale was: "Its proportions were magnified a thousand-fold beyond any conception we had previously formed of them."

We will see another purpose question later (number 23), but for now let's continue working in order and looking at other question types.

Suggest/Infer/Imply/Agree Questions

Many questions on the SAT ask what the passage "suggests," what is "implied" by the passage, what "inference" can be drawn from the passage, or with which answer the author "would most likely agree." This all seems to invite creativity and reading between the lines, doesn't it? Don't fall for that trap! Just as with Detail and Purpose questions, the answer must be supported by the *actual text* of the passage.

There *is* one important difference between these question types and Detail questions. With Detail questions, the question is usually narrow enough that you can find the precise answer right away. With Support/Infer/Imply/Agree questions, the answer is often about a fairly minor point that you might not have focused on if you skimmed the passage first. In that case, you might have to do a little more work during the POE step, as we'll see.

Let's take a look at one of these questions.

20. In lines 47–52, the author suggests that

Read the fifth paragraph of the passage and jot down your impressions about what the author is saying. When we evaluate the answer choices, you will see whether the correct answer actually relates to detail on which you thought to focus.

Question 21 is another Suggest/Imply/Infer/Agree question, asking which statement about the blessing the author would most likely agree with. Read around line 58 and jot down what you think the author is saying. We'll discuss the question further in the POE section.

Vocab-in-Context Questions

We call questions that ask what a particular word "most nearly means" (or a similar variation on the phrase) Vocab-in-Context questions. These questions are very similar to Sentence Completion questions. In fact, it's a good idea to use a technique like the ones in the Sentence Completion chapter here: Cross out the word in the passage and come up with your own word based on the clues and triggers.

If you take the time to figure out how the author is using the word, these questions tend not to be very difficult; but Joe Bloggs has trouble with them. He picks the answer choice that contains the most common definition of the word, rather than the answer that accurately reflects how the author is using the word.

Let's take a look at a Vocab-in-Context question.

22. As used in line 67, "admire" most nearly means

Here's How to Crack it

Read a few lines around line 67, and go all the way to the end. Cross out the word *admire*, and write a word that could go into the blank, based upon the clues and triggers.

The paragraph is generally about the terrible stench of the whale. The author's friend said that he "did not _____ to smell a whale," and the author agreed given the bad odor. A good word for the blank might be "want" or something similar.

Question 23 is another Purpose question. It asks why the author wrote the final sentence. Although you've already read that sentence for Question 22, read it (and several additional lines) again with Question 23 in mind, and write down your answer. We will discuss this question in the POE section.

Tone/Attitude Questions

In most nonfiction passages, attitude and tone questions usually relate to the author's feeling or opinion about the subject matter. But in some nonfiction passages, such as the one on page 56, attitude or tone questions can relate to the author's overall "voice." (In fiction passages, such questions often relate to a character's feeling about someone or something.)

Arriving at your own answer to a Tone or Attitude question is often pretty straightforward, but as we'll see in the POE section (which is coming up next, we promise!), the answer choices can contain trap answers and new or difficult vocabulary words.

Let's take a look at Question 24.

24. The author's tone can best be described as

Here's How to Crack It

Hopefully, the work you did while answering the previous questions gave you enough information to come up with an answer to this question. (If not, this is the time to read the passage again.) Write down some words that come to mind about the author's tone.

Remember the blurb at the very beginning? It told us that the passage was "fanciful," and you probably found the passage amusing or at least silly, right? You also might have written down something such as "light-hearted" or anything along those lines.

The Strategy

1. Read the blurb.
2. Work the passage.
3. Choose and translate a question.
4. Read only what you need.
5. Answer the question.
6. **POE**

Process of Elimination

All right. Now we're ready to finally get into the mechanics of POE and the Reading Comprehension section. You should remember the basics of POE from Chapter 2: Once you have an idea of how a question should be answered, you can eliminate the answer choices that don't fit. As we'll see, there are several ways an answer can be incorrect, but they all boil down one key fact: the answer choice is not supported by the text of the passage.

Let's look at the questions for the passage on page 56, this time with the answer choices. As we evaluate the answer choices, we'll go over how to recognize and avoid the types of trap answers that appeal to Joe Bloggs.

POE: The Answer Choice Is Not Supported

Let's take another look at question 17, this time with the answers

17. The author and his traveling companion discussed illnesses because

(A) the cholera epidemic of the era was a grim concern to the travelers
(B) the author hoped to avoid discussing the reason for the journey
(C) the author supposed that the topic would be welcomed by his friend
(D) the travelers were mocking the pretensions enjoyed in elite society
(E) the traveling companion worried about the author's deteriorating health

Here's How to Crack It

From our earlier practice, we know that the answer to this Detail question is that the author believed that his sick friend would feel better if they discussed illnesses.

Did you notice that answer choice (A) refers to a detail—cholera—mentioned in the relevant part of the passage? Watch out for words that are recycled from the passage. The more closely the words of an answer choice track the passage, the more careful you must be, because this is probably ETS trying to trip you up. Answer choices (B) and (D) have nothing to do with anything in the passage.

Avoid Trap Answers!
Recycled Words
Half Right = All Wrong

Let's look at answer choice (E) a little more closely. This choice contains a reference to health, which is related to what we want in the correct answer. But this answer choice gets the details wrong. It was the friend, not the author, who was sick. Answer choices that are only half right (or any amount right other than all right) are all wrong.

Only answer choice (C) is anywhere close to the answer we're looking for. While it may not have a lot of detail, remember that that's not a problem here—it is correct, and that's all that matters. Knowing the answer in advance makes POE much easier.

Let's try the next question.

18. The cause of the "bitter disappointment" (line 25) was that

(A) the whale, which the author and his friend had traveled to see, was no longer on the beach
(B) the previously warm weather had turned rainy and cold, forcing the companions to return home
(C) the hotel in which the author intended to lodge was much older than he had expected
(D) the traveling companions were looking for natural beauty where it would not likely be found
(E) the author's personality precluded enjoyment of a scene that all others would appreciate

Here's How to Crack It

This Detail question was a bit more difficult to answer, but, again, having the answer in mind already makes evaluating the answer choices easier. The author was disappointed because the panoramic views at the beach he expected to see were not visible while he was inside the hotel, remember? Answer choice (D) provides this answer.

Did you see that answer choice (C) uses recycled words? Joe might have picked it, because the lines immediately following line 25 talk about the aging bar. But a careful reading of those lines showed us that the bar itself was not the nature of the disappointment.

Avoid Trap Answers!
Extreme
Goes too Far

Answer choice (E) might also appeal to Joe, because he's likely to read more into a question than he needs to. Leaving aside that the passage provides no support for this answer, the answer is also too extreme. To say that the author cannot enjoy beauty or that all others would enjoy a certain scene goes way too far.

Now let's look at question 19, our Purpose question.

19. The author mentions "a cliff, an isolated hill, an island" (lines 41–42) in order to

(A) describe the nearby scenery as they traveled to the whale
(B) indicate the size of the whale relative to the scenery
(C) show his bravery in traveling over dangerous terrain
(D) express a desire to visit lands brought to mind by the waves
(E) emphasize that the actual size of the whale was unexpected

Here's How to Crack It

Our expected answer to this Purpose question was that the author wanted to emphasize the surprisingly large size of the whale. This is exactly what we find in answer choice (E). Did you notice the Recycled Words in answer choice (D)?

Also, notice that answer choice (B) starts off well but goes too far. The author initially may have thought the whale *was* a cliff or hill from far away, but he never *compared* it to the actual scenery or stated that the whale was in fact as large as an island. ETS loves to use answer choices that go a bit too far, because JOE usually falls for the trap!

On to the Suggest question.

20. In lines 47–52, the author suggests that

(A) when he saw the whale up close, he found it to be even larger than he had expected
(B) he did not have a management role in the hotel that he had visited earlier
(C) if it were up to him, he would not let other travelers come to see the whale
(D) he recognized the ability to make money by charging people to see the whale
(E) he determined to study the effect of atmospheric conditions on perception

Here's How to Crack It

As we discussed, it's sometimes hard to predict how an open-ended Suggest question like this will be answered. You should read the relevant part of the passage to keep the details fresh, but the real work will take place when you do POE. You need to ask yourself whether each answer choice is actually supported by the text. Watch out for all the usual traps.

Sometimes, an answer choice is wrong because of a single word. Answer choice (A), for example, states that the whale was larger up close than the author had expected; in fact, he said it was smaller. There are other trap answers here, too. Answer choice (E) contains recycled words. Answer choice (C) goes too far because the author said only that he would limit how close people could come to the whale. Answer choice (D) is simply not supported.

This leaves answer choice (B). You might have found this choice weird and wanted to eliminate it right away, but it *is* supported by the passage. In lines 48–49 the author states what he would do "if [he] kept the hotel, and the whale belonged to [me]." You can see from this that he doesn't actually "keep" the hotel, which is to say he does not manage it. As we see here, the answer to a Suggest/Infer/Imply/Agree question can relate to a very minor part of the passage, but it will always be supported by the text.

Let's move on to the next question.

21. The author would most likely agree with which one of the following about the "blessing" (line 58):

(A) An even larger whale, while interesting, would smell worse than the whale on the beach
(B) Existing regulations would not prevent the author from seeing a larger whale up close
(C) After the earlier disappointment in the hotel, the author was pleased to have found the whale
(D) The author was amused that his reaction to the whale was consistent with his personality
(E) The author's companion would not have reacted well had the whale been much larger

Here's How to Crack It

Finding the answer to this question might have taken a bit of detective work, because you needed first to figure out what the "source of the disappointment" was before finding out why it was a blessing. The source of the disappointment, as revealed in the lines just before line 58, was the whale's size—the whale was smaller than they had thought when they saw it from a distance. So, why was the smaller size a blessing? The author tells us after line 58 that the whale had a terrible stench, and a larger whale would have smelled even worse!

If you thought about the question in this way, you already know that answer choice (A) is correct. The remaining answer choices are simply not supported by the text of the passage. Which one do you think Joe might choose? (Hint: Read the sentence just before line 58.)

Next up, we'll look at the Vocab-in-Context question.

22. As used in line 67, "admire" most nearly means:

(A) respect
(B) marvel
(C) desire
(D) prize
(E) regard

Here's How to Crack It

When we worked on this question earlier, we understood that the author used admire to mean something like want. Answer choice (C)—desire—is correct. Vocab-in-Context questions are usually not difficult, plus they provide a very quick way to gain a point. So don't skip them! Just don't pick an answer without going back to the passage.

Next up, our other Purpose question:

23. The final sentence of the passage serves to

(A) display the author's knowledge
(B) draw a meaningful contrast
(C) express a burning concern
(D) disagree with a position
(E) articulate an intention

Here's How to Crack It

You probably said the author's purpose was to explain how bad the whale smelled. Notice, however, that the answer choices are more abstract than what we anticipated. When you encounter abstract answer choices, you can still use your initial understanding of the purpose, but you also have to consider how the sentence accomplishes the author's purpose. How does the sentence convey how badly the whale smelled?

In the sentence, the author stated that the whale does not smell like various flowers, but rather smells like pole-cats. The author is contrasting things that smell good (flowers) to things that smell terrible (pole-cats) to make his point. Answer choice (B), therefore, is correct.

Answer choice (A) is incorrect because, although the author may be showing off his knowledge, that is not the purpose of the sentence. Likewise, notice that the author disagreed with his friend's choice of words, but he did not disagree with his friend's sentiments about the smell ("I adopt his sentiments while I scorn his language")—so answer choice (D) is wrong.

Just about done! We'll finish the passage with the Tone question.

24. The author's tone can best be described as

(A) indignant
(B) grave
(C) ambivalent
(D) sardonic
(E) serene

Here's How to Crack It

Earlier, our answer to this question was *sarcastic* or *light-hearted*, remember? Choice (D) is correct.

What if you didn't know the meaning of sardonic? On Tone and Attitude questions, after you eliminate answers that are obviously wrong, go through and get rid of trap answers. Remember: Extreme words are rarely correct, so avoid choices like "wild ecstasy" or "intense hatred." Likewise, words that express lack of caring, interest, or knowledge are rarely correct; avoid choices like *indifferent, puzzled, uninterested,* and *confused.* On the other hand, authors often express moderately stated approval or disagreement, and are often neutral or unbiased, so keep an eye out for choices that mean something similar to those sentiments.

Here, even though the author spoke of disappointments, it's way too extreme to say that his tone was indignant or even grave. Likewise, the author is not ambivalent; he had a great time writing his essay!

Finally, know your Tone/Attitude vocabulary—the words mentioned above and these words:

apathetic	contemptuous	didactic	disdainful	earnest
equivocal	ironic	nonchalant	nostalgic	qualified
resigned	solemn	unabashed	whimsical	wistful

POE: Last Words

Sometimes, you might find it hard to decide between two or even three answers. In that case, it's more important than ever to stick with POE; your task is to look for wrong answers, not the right one—and there are always going to be more wrong answers than right ones! Remember what trap answers look like and try to eliminate those types of answer choices. Sometimes a single word or small phrase is enough to make an answer choice wrong.

We've gone over the four major types of trap answers in this chapter already, but here they are again:

- Recycled Words
- Half Right (= All Wrong)
- Extreme Language
- Goes Too Far

Remember that the typical trap answers for Tone/Attitude questions are:

- Extreme
- Uncaring
- Unknowledgeable

There is one more trap answer that's specific to fiction passages. Be careful not to pick an answer choice that is *too literal.* Watching out for excessively literal answer choices can be especially helpful when you are down to two.

Finally, remember that some questions are just harder than others. It is okay to guess after you have gone as far as you can with POE, or to skip a particularly tricky question and come back later if there is time.

Drill

The paragraphs on the following pages are excerpts from different passages. For each question, read what you need, write down or say the answer to yourself, and use POE to find the answer. You can check your work on pages 373–374.

. . . Even casual fans of the sport of baseball are likely to recognize the impact Babe Ruth had on the sport. Of course, Ruth's feats on the baseball diamond are well-documented: Ruth is among the all-time leaders in home runs, runs batted in, and walks. In addition, he helped the New York Yankees win seven pennants. But what few people realize is the significant impact Babe Ruth had off the field. His larger than life persona and his distinctive physical appearance captured the imaginations of fans of all ages and helped to revitalize the sport of baseball.

14. In lines 33–37, the author suggests that

(A) Babe Ruth succeeded in baseball in part due to his physical size
(B) Babe Ruth hit more home runs than any other player of his time
(C) children of Babe Ruth's era enjoyed watching him play baseball
(D) because of Babe Ruth, the rules of baseball were changed
(E) Babe Ruth had more influence off the field than on the field

. . . In 1770, it is said that an English engineer, Edward Naime, writing at home, accidentally picked up a chunk of this rubber instead of the breadcrumbs commonly used then to remove pencil marks, and discovered its possibilities as an erasing tool. He eventually sold his "rubber squares" throughout the continent. The only inadequacy of those early erasers was that, like food, they spoiled quickly—a problem that remained until 1839, when Charles Goodyear learned to "cure" the rubber to prevent spoilage, and the new and improved eraser became even more popular. . .

12. According to the passage, a problem with early erasers was that they

(A) were costly to ship outside of the continent
(B) tended to rot before they were fully used
(C) lacked the popularity of breadcrumbs
(D) were less effective than rounded erasers
(E) required nearly 70 years to cure

. . . The annals of scientific history are filled with names of great import. August names such as Mendelev, Darwin, and Einstein dominate their respective fields, and the majority of science textbooks sing their praises as well. But what of the names J.L. Meyer, A.R. Wallace, and Hermann Minkowski? These names are not revered, but instead have been relegated to the dustbin of science, known only to the most diligent of scientific scholars. Yet these men developed their own important theories, often at the same time as their better known contemporaries. . .

10. The author mentions "Mendelev, Darwin, and Einstein" (lines 14–15) in order to

(A) examine an important discovery
(B) praise a developing trend
(C) revise a questionable theory
(D) illustrate a repeating pattern
(E) explore an anomalous oversight

. . . Since 1980, hyaluronan has been used to treat humans in a variety of ways: to protect the cornea during eye surgery, to reduce arthritic inflammation, and to prevent formation of scar tissue after surgery. Hyaluronan occurs naturally in humans, but it was originally discovered in the eyes of cows in the 1930s. At the time, there was no commercially viable way to extract hyaluronan to test its therapeutic potential. Years later, scientists not only discovered the compound was contained in rooster combs but also developed a method to extract it from them. Veterinarians used hyaluronan for years before the extraction method patent was sold to a major pharmaceutical company in 1980.

17. It can be inferred from lines 43–49 that

(A) after 1980, veterinarians were prohibited from using hyaluronan
(B) scientists did not initially anticipate that hyaluronan would be useful
(C) hyaluronan has been extracted from humans, cows and rooster combs
(D) a financial impediment relating to hyaluronan has been resolved
(E) hyaluronan's most important use is to prevent scar tissue after surgery

. . . When he sat at that desk he would be taking up, he though of not his own career, but the career of the entity who had occupied the office through generations, and would occupy it in perpetual succession. Vaguely he began to miss something. The sensation was like that of one who has long worn a ring on his finger, but omits to put it on one morning. For that person there is a vague sense of something missing throughout the day. Bonbright did not know what he felt the lack of—it was his identity.

24. The word "omits" (line 64) most nearly means:

(A) removes
(B) deletes
(C) neglects
(D) desists
(E) forbears

. . . Yet, the original *Star Wars* trilogy offers much more than fantasy and adventure. The movies remind us of our noblest instincts—and our basest. Darth Vader's iron rule recalls many totalitarian regimes throughout history, and Yoda's wisdom and innate goodness reflects heroes such as Mahatma Gandhi and Nelson Mandela. The ramshackle freedom fighters mirror seemingly doomed but ultimately successful revolutionaries, from George Washington to Lech Walesa. We relate to the innocence of Luke, the raffish attitude of Han Solo, and the strength of Leia. Yes, *Star Wars* may take place "a long time ago in a galaxy far, far away," but it continues soundly to resonate in the here and now. . .

19. The author's attitude toward *Star Wars* can best be described as

(A) complete adoration
(B) sincere admiration
(C) certain indifference
(D) qualified aversion
(E) blatant distaste

. . . The word *telescope* literally means "far-seeing," but all telescopes do not "see" in the same way. While the most common types of telescope use a system of mirrors and lenses to gather light from distant objects, other telescopes employ very different ways of seeing. Radio telescopes, for example, do not "see" at all; rather, they use antennae to pick up radio waves emitted by celestial objects. Other telescopes, such as X-ray telescopes, infrared telescopes, and ultraviolet telescopes, can see wavelengths imperceptible to the human eye. NASA's next major telescope project—heralded as a breakthrough—will rely on a combination of these types of methods . . .

21. The author's mention of "X-ray telescopes, infrared telescopes, and ultraviolet telescopes" (lines 51–52) serves to

(A) demonstrate that the mechanisms by which telescopes receive information differ
(B) provide evidence that the design of NASA's upcoming telescope will be innovative
(C) underscore the importance of revising the accepted definition of how telescopes "see"
(D) establish that telescope technologies using imperceptible wavelengths are essential
(E) support the thesis that the use of mirrors and lenses in telescopes has become outdated

. . . Originally used for architecture, terra-cotta was transformed into an artistic material during the Renaissance. Sculptors in particular began to use the fired clay to make "bozzetti," rough drafts of sculptures that would later be created out of stone, bronze, or other more traditional materials. These rough drafts, however, often created more interest than the finished works. During the eighteenth century, art aficionados began collecting terra-cotta models for exhibitions in their homes and at salons. Collectors maintained that the models presented a more accurate representation of an artist's talent, and created a sustainable market for larger sculptures. . . .

15. It can be inferred from the passage that in the eighteenth century

(A) collectors were finally able to recognize a sculptor's talent
(B) terra-cotta's use for architecture remained fashionable
(C) some finished sculptures continued to interest collectors
(D) there was no sustainable market for smaller sculptures
(E) artists sometimes used terra-cotta for a finished work

Line

. . . Because Western classical music encompasses such a variety of styles and spans more than a thousand years, it is difficult to identify the genre's primary characteristics. A monastic chant that relies solely on the human voice and an orchestral symphony utilizing multiple instruments are both classical, yet neither sounds remotely like the other. Even the title "classical" is misleading, given that music historians uniformly recognize the years from A.D. 1750 to 1827 as the Classical era of classical music. Despite this inability to definitely pinpoint the nature of classical music, people of all musical backgrounds continue to find the label useful. . .

11. The author would most likely agree with which one of the following statements?

(A) People will never reach agreement about the proper use of the term classical music.
(B) A useful label must definitively pinpoint the nature of the object the label describes.
(C) The year in which a piece of music was created is a useful indicator of the music's genre.
(D) It is necessary that classical music utilize instruments.
(E) Not all music labeled as classical must share similar characteristics and rhythms.

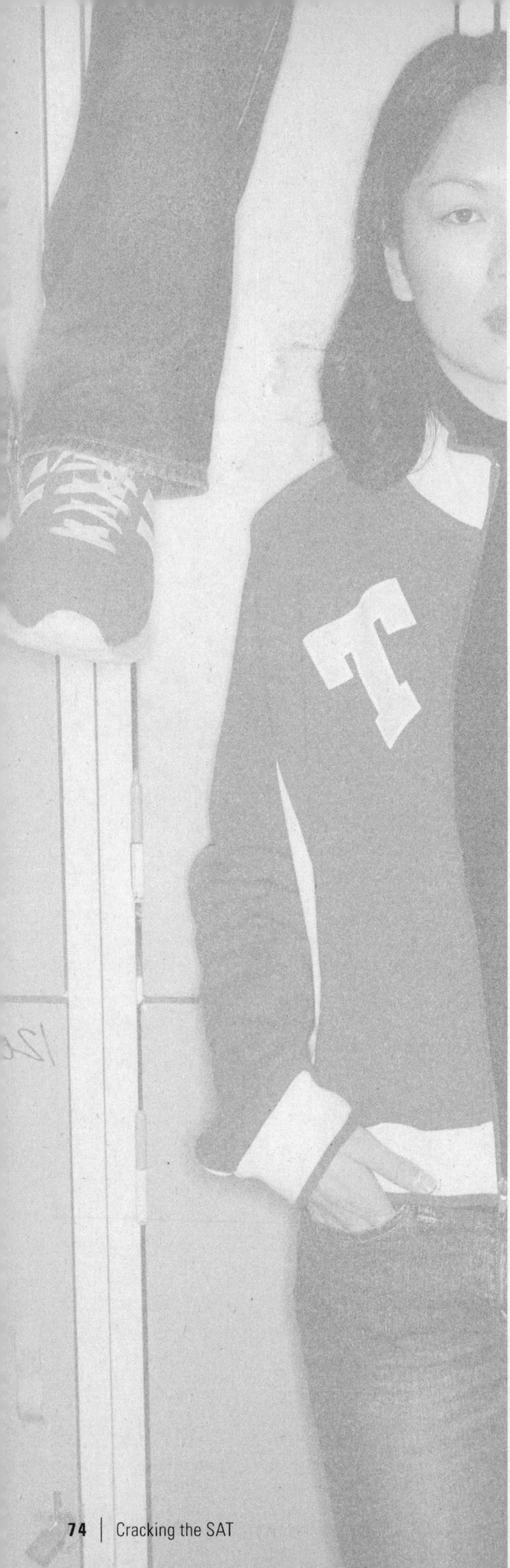

Summary

- Reading comprehension questions account for more than two-thirds of all the points on the Critical Reading sections.
- Reading comprehension questions are *not* presented in order of difficulty, but they are in rough chronological order. Don't be afraid to skip a hard question, and don't worry if you can't answer every question. Most people can't.
- Reading comprehension is like an open-book test. Instead of reading through the whole passage carefully, seek out the information you need based on the questions.
- Approach reading comprehension passages by reading the blurb first. Then, decide whether you will go right to the questions or skim the passage.
- Translate the questions into your own words. You can't answer a question if you don't understand what it's asking.
- Use line references, lead words, and chronology to help you find ETS's answer in the passage. Always start reading a few lines above the line reference or the lead words and read until you have the answer.
- Answer the questions in your own words before you read ETS's answers. You will avoid Joe Bloggs answer choices by knowing what the answer is before you read any of the choices.
- Use POE to get rid of choices that don't match yours. Cross out incorrect choices as you go. You should have a definite sense of zeroing in on ETS's answer. If you don't cross out incorrect choices, you'll waste time and energy rereading wrong answer choices.
- When using POE, look for answers with the following characteristics:
    - not mentioned at all in the passage
    - recycled words
    - half-right, half-wrong
    - extreme language
    - the opposite of what is said in the passage
    - too literal (fiction)

Chapter 7
Reading Comprehension: Wait, There's More!

In this chapter, we'll take a look at short and dual passages with an eye toward pointing out minor differences in approach. Also, every now and then, ETS likes to add a question type other than the typical ones discussed in the last chapter. We'll take a look at those question types here.

SHORT PASSAGES AND MINOR QUESTION TYPES

Short passages don't have an intro blurb, so your strategy when attacking these passages involves one less step. Because the passages are so short, you might decide to Work the Passage first, by skimming it to get a sense of what's there. You might even decide to just go ahead and read the whole thing But even though it's short, you still don't want to get bogged down in the details, and remember: You've got a lot of test still to go. You might want to just go to the first question, and then read the passage looking for the answer to that question.

Short Passages Strategy

1. ~~Read the Blurb~~
2. Work the Passage
3. Select a Question
4. Read only what you need
5. Answer the Question
6. POE

When you're looking for the answer, you should still read several lines of text around the relevant line. Be sure you know what the answer should look like before you go to the answer choices, and then engage in your usual POE, watching out for those same trap answers.

Sometimes the short passages in a section are harder than the long passages. ETS is hoping that you'll spend so much time on those four measly questions that you don't have enough time to do the easier questions about the long passage! Remember that reading comprehension questions are never in order of difficulty, and knowing when to guess or skip a question is important to improving your overall score.

Let's take a look some short passages. We'll work through the passages on the next page together, using them to examine the minor question types that may also appear as questions to the longer passages discussed in Chapter 6. However, keep in mind that you should still expect to see a lot of the more common question types discussed in Chapter 6 in short passages on your test.

Questions 6–7 are based on the following passage.

After more than thirty years of study, Japanese researchers claim to have identified a new species of baleen whale. In 1970, nine adult whales were killed in the Indian Ocean for research purposes. Through recent DNA analysis of samples from these whales, the Japanese scientists obtained what they believe is sufficient data to identify a new species. Aside from differences in both internal and external physical features, there were significant differences between the genetic material of these whales and that of the most similar species of whale used for comparison, the fin whale. Other researchers in this field have cautiously pointed out that DNA comparisons with seven other similar species were not conducted.

6. The author's primary purpose in writing the passage was to

(A) describe two species of whale
(B) criticize an incomplete analysis
(C) survey uses of DNA analysis
(D) explain a recent discovery
(E) justify the killing of whales

7. Which of the following would most undermine the researchers' conclusion that they discovered a new species of whale?

(A) The nine adult whales were born in the Artic Sea and came to the Indian Ocean as adults.
(B) The fin whale and the baleen whale are known to feed upon the same species of fish.
(C) The DNA profile of the nine adult whales is similar to that of a whale species not studied.
(D) There have been major advances in the technology of DNA profiling since 1970.
(E) The seven similar species of whale not in the study are found only in the Pacific Ocean.

Questions 8–9 are based on the following passage.

Adopting a completely computerized voting system is unfeasible. If ballots are recorded only in a machine's memory with no physical proof, a recount becomes impossible. Vigilant election officials may ensure integrity and security at the polls, yet accidental or malicious errors could be introduced into software long before election day. If a voter chooses "X," but the machine records "Y," there is no way to recover the intended vote. If computers are used in voting, there should also be a paper ballot that permits voters to verify their choices. This ballot would allow the voter's intent to be confirmed at any later date. Advances in technology are beneficial and should be integrated into the voting process to improve accessibility and ease of ballot casting, but we should not reject paper ballots entirely.

8. The situation described in lines 4–10 ("Vigilant election . . . verify their choices") is most analogous to

(A) A couple expecting their first baby reads several books about the different stages of child development, from infancy to adulthood.
(B) An observer of a family of gorillas takes photographs of the gorillas in addition to writing down observations about their behavior.
(C) An established computer manufacturer provides free word processing and anti-virus software as part of every new computer sold.
(D) A car dealership that sells only select models decides to expand its inventory to include additional models with a broader variety of options.
(E) A politician running for re-election releases an advertisement attacking the challenger for malicious lies without verifying the content of the ad.

9. All of the following reasons not to adopt an entirely computerized voting system are given in the passage EXCEPT

(A) both paper ballot and electronic voting systems are by nature insecure
(B) a machine may make a mistake in recording a person's intended vote
(C) even the best election officials may be unable to judge the integrity of software
(D) physical evidence could aid in discerning a voter's objective
(E) tampering or mistakes in the computer program could remain undiscovered until it is too late

Primary Purpose Questions

What's the Point?
Sometimes ETS asks for the Main Point instead of the Primary Purpose. Try to figure out the main idea the author wants you to know, avoiding answers that ar too broad or too narrow.

Primary purpose questions are similar to the Purpose questions we discussed in the previous chapter, except these are asking about the author's purpose in writing the passage overall. If you encounter a primary purpose question in a long passage, you should save it for the end, after you've read most or all of the passage while answering the other questions. Try question 6, below, following the usual steps.

6. The author's primary purpose in writing the passage was to

(A) describe two species of whale
(B) criticize an incomplete analysis
(C) survey uses of DNA analysis
(D) explain a recent discovery
(E) justify the killing of whales

Here's How to Crack It

Start by coming up with an answer in your own words. The author states that a new species of whale was discovered and describes the evidence supporting the discovery. So it's a safe bet to say the author's purpose was to talk about this discovery and the process leading up to it. Answer choice (D) correctly states this purpose.

Answer choices (A) and (B) are too narrow. While (A) refers to the fact that two whale species were discussed, it lacks any reference to the discovery of a new species. Answer choice (B) uses recycled words from the last sentence of the passage (remember that those indicate a trap answer!), but the author's purpose in writing the passage was not to make that criticism.

Answer choice (C) is too broad. While the author does explain how DNA analysis was used to support the discovery of a new species, this answer claims that the entire purpose of the passage is to discuss DNA.

Answer choice (E) is just wrong; the author neither supports nor criticizes that whales were killed for research.

Weaken/Strengthen Questions

Questions asking you to weaken or strengthen a statement by the author are rare, but they do show up from time to time, so you should know how to tackle them. Be careful and figure out exactly what the author believes, then find the answer choice that most clearly makes that belief either false (for weaken) or true (for strengthen). Try question 7.

---

7. Which of the following would most undermine the researchers' conclusion that they discovered a new species of whale?

   (A) The nine adult whales were born in the Artic Sea and came to the Indian Ocean as adults.

   (B) The fin whale and the baleen whale are known to feed upon the same species of fish.

   (C) The DNA profile of the nine adult whales is similar to that of a whale species not studied.

   (D) There have been major advances in the technology of DNA profiling since 1970.

   (E) The seven similar species of whale not in the study are found only in the Pacific Ocean.

Here's How to Crack It

This question is asking you to find the answer that undermines the author's conclusion that the researchers discovered a new species of whale. So, let's begin by finding the basis for the author's conclusion—why does the author believe that researchers have discovered a new species? The author relies principally on DNA analysis: compared to the similar fin whales, the whales under study have different genetic material. Thus, in order to undermine the conclusion, our answer choice will need to state that the whales under study do have different genetic material as compared to some other whale.

Answer choice (A) relates to the original location of the whales. The author didn't use location to support the conclusion, so this answer choice provides irrelevant information—it doesn't strengthen OR weaken the conclusion.

Answer choice (B) is about the fish the fin whale and potentially new species of whale use for food. Given that these whales have different genetic material, the fact that they happen to have similar diets does not undermine the DNA analysis. Cross it out.

Answer choice (C) is probably correct. Although it's not a terribly strong answer choice, it at least calls into question whether the study correctly compared the whales under study to only a single other species of whale. But let's go through the other two choices to make sure.

Answer choice (D) relates to advances in DNA technology. This isn't relevant because the DNA technology was sophisticated enough when the study was conducted to determine that the fin whale and other whale species were different, which is what's important here. Additionally, neither the author nor the author's critics address DNA technology advances.

Answer choice (E) may seem appealing at first because it mentions other similar species of whales. However, rather than focusing on the DNA of these species, the answer choice provides information about the species' location, which neither supports nor undermines the author's conclusion. The information is irrelevant, just like in choice (A).

Analogy Questions

Analogy questions can be a bit tricky, so we can be thankful that they don't show up very often! Unlike just about every other Reading Comprehension question type, the answer choices in analogy questions contain information that is not directly related to the passage. Rather, the information shares some characteristics with something in the passage. Your job is to find the answer that is the tightest fit. Let's flesh this out with question 8.

8. The situation described in lines 4–10 ("Vigilant election . . . verify their choices") is most analogous to

(A) A couple expecting their first baby reads several books about the different stages of child development, from infancy to adulthood.

(B) An observer of a family of gorillas takes photographs of the gorillas in addition to writing down observations about their behavior.

(C) An established computer manufacturer provides free word processing and anti-virus software as part of every new computer sold.

(D) A car dealership that sells only select models decides to expand its inventory to include additional models with a broader variety of options.

(E) A politician running for re-election releases an advertisement attacking the challenger for malicious lies without verifying the content of the ad.

Here's How to Crack It

Your first task is to read the relevant section of the passage. We're told that no matter how careful election officials are, computer errors are still possible and that, therefore, it is important to have a paper ballot as a back-up. In considering the answer choices, don't look specific for information about voting or computers! That's a trap (and something Joe Bloggs would do). Rather, try to find an answer choice that relates to establishing a back-up in case there are errors—which is the general gist of the passage.

Answer choice (B) works. By taking photographs of the gorillas *in addition* to written observations, the observer has created a back-up for later review. Any errors in the observer's notes can be detected by looking at the photos, just as errors relating to peoples' votes can be detected by looking at the back-up paper ballot.

None of the other answer choices deals with creating a back-up. Did you notice, though, that both computers and elections are the subject of incorrect answer choices?

Except/Least/Not Questions

In Except/Least/Not questions, you are usually asked to find the one answer choice that is *not* supported by the passage. Because four of the answer choices *are* supported, these questions can be tricky and a bit more time-consuming than other questions. Nevertheless, POE still applies. You are looking for four answers that are supported by the actual text of the passage and one that is not.

Also, be careful not to lose track of the question. Sometimes people forget midway through the answer choices that they are looking for the *unsupported* answer choice and then pick one of the choices that is supported! For this reason, instead of crossing out answer choices as you find support for them, try using a check mark next to each answer choice that is supported by the passage. Whatever you don't check is the correct answer.

Take a look at question 9.

9. All of the following reasons not to adopt an entirely computerized voting system are given in the passage EXCEPT

(A) both paper ballot and electronic voting systems are by nature insecure
(B) a machine may make a mistake in recording a person's intended vote
(C) even the best election officials may be unable to judge the integrity of software
(D) physical evidence could aid in discerning a voter's objective
(E) tampering or mistakes in the computer program could remain undiscovered until it is too late

Here's How to Crack It

Because you can't predict what answer will not be supported, just go through each answer choice and ask yourself whether it is supported by the text of the passage.

Answer choices (B) through (E) all find support in the passage. A paraphrase of each answer choice actually appears in the passage as a reason against adopting an entirely computerized voting system. Answer choice (A), however, is not entirely supported because nothing in the passage says that paper voting systems are by their nature insecure.

DUAL PASSAGES

You should expect to see two sets of Dual Passages, one short set and one long set.

Strategy for Dual Passages

The six steps you learned in the last chapter are the same, but Step 3—Select a Question—requires special focus.

> When doing dual passages, first do questions about the first passage, then do questions about the second passage, and finally do questions about both passages.

For single passages, chronology counts. The same goes for dual passages and their questions, but there's a slight twist. The questions for Passage 1 will come before the questions for Passage 2, and the questions for each passage follow the order of the passage, just like single-passage questions. But dual questions—questions about *both* passages—can pop up anywhere. Skip those questions until you've gone through all of the single-passage questions. You might want to write down the question numbers as you skip them and/or mark the question numbers themselves so they catch your eye before you move on.

For short dual passages, it's not unusual for all four questions to relate to both passages. In that case, you will want to skim both passages during the Work the Passage step before going to the questions.

Two-Passage Questions

For questions asking about both passages, it's helpful to use the same strategy you use for two-blank Sentence Completions. First, find the answer for the first passage (or the second passage if that one is easier) and use POE to narrow down the answer choices. Then find the answer in the other passage and use POE to arrive at the correct answer. This will save time and keep you from confusing the two passages when you're evaluating the answer choices.

Always keep in mind that the same POE criteria apply, no matter how two-passage questions are presented.

- If a question is about what is supported by *both* passages, make sure that you find specific support in both passages, and be wary of all the usual trap answers.
- If a questions is about an issue on which the authors of the two passages disagree, make sure you find support in each passage for the author's particular opinion.
- If the question asks how one author would respond to the other passage, find out what was said in that other passage, and then find out exactly what the author you are asked about said on that exact topic.

The bottom line is that if you are organized and remember your basic reading comprehension strategy, you'll see that two-passage questions are no harder than single-passage questions!

In the drill at the end of this chapter, you'll have a chance to work on dual passages. But first, let's talk a little bit about vocabulary that's important for the Reading Comprehension section.

READING COMPREHENSION VOCABULARY

In addition to knowing the regular vocabulary listed in the next chapter, you should also know the reading comprehension words below. You probably know most of them from school, but be sure to look up any that are unfamiliar.

aesthetic	discern	indifferent	refute
allusion	discredit	interpret	relevant
ambivalent	disengaged	ironic	repudiate
anecdote	disinterested	justify	resigned
assert	dismissive	metaphor	reverent
assess	disparage	nostalgia	rhetoric
belied	disparity	objective	satire
characterize	dispassionate	partisan	scornful
compare	dubious	personification	scrutinize
concur	elicit	phenomenon	simile
contempt	endorse	plausible	speculate
contrast	equivocate	pragmatic	subjective
conventional	exemplify	prove	substantiate
convey	hyperbole	provoke	undermine
debunk	hypothesis	qualified	underscore
digression	illustrate	reconcile	yield

Drill

Now you're ready to try a complete set of passages from a reading comprehension section! Use your new skills to crack the passages and questions on the following pages. You can check your answers on page 374–376.

Each passage below is followed by questions based on its content. Answer the questions on the basis of what is stated or implied in each passage and in any introductory material that may be provided.

Questions 9–12 are based on the following passages.

Passage 1

Every work of art is the child of its age and, in many cases, the mother of our emotions. It follows that each period of culture produces an art of its own that can never be repeated. Efforts to revive the art principles of the past will at best produce an art that is stillborn. It is impossible for us to live and feel as did the ancient Greeks. In the same way those who strive to follow the Greek methods in sculpture achieve only a similarity of form, the work remains soulless for all time. Such imitation is mere aping. Externally the monkey completely resembles a human being; he will sit holding a book in front of his nose, and turn over the pages with a thoughtful aspect, but his actions have for him no real meaning.

Passage 2

The style of architecture has been guessed at as everything from Romanesque and Gothic to Flamboyant Renaissance and Moorish. The truth is that the court is a thoroughly original conception; the architect has clothed his preconceived design in forms that he has borrowed from all these styles as they happened to suit his artistic purpose. The spirit of the court is clearly Gothic, due to the accentuation of the vertical lines. The rounded arches, modified in feeling by the decorative pendent lanterns, hint of the awakening of the Renaissance period in Spain, during the fourteenth and fifteenth centuries, when the vertical lines, and decorative leaf and other symbolic ornaments of the severer Gothic, were so charmingly combined with classic motives.

9. Unlike the author of Passage 2, the author of Passage 1 makes significant use of

(A) historical references
(B) specific dates
(C) metaphorical comparisons
(D) visual description
(E) artistic analysis

10. Both passages agree that an artist who borrows the artistic styles of earlier eras

(A) can produce a work of art that is satisfying in its own right
(B) may borrow from Moorish styles but not Greek styles
(C) will achieve better results for architecture than sculpture
(D) might be successful in accurately imitating earlier forms
(E) should do so only after receiving appropriate training

11. Which of the following aspect of artistic creation is addressed in Passage 2 but not in Passage 1?

(A) The way in which choices of form can reveal the artist's vision
(B) The difficulty artists have in borrowing methods from earlier eras
(C) The interest of some artists in looking to the past for inspiration
(D) The creative use by an artist of forms copied from contemporaries
(E) The principles underlying the artistic conventions of ancient artists

12. The author of Passage 2 would most likely respond to lines 2–5 ("It follows that . . . stillborn") in Passage 1 by arguing that

(A) artistic endeavors are always successful
(B) old art forms can be used to innovative effects
(C) Gothic art is more easily borrowed than is Greek art
(D) sculpture is a particularly difficult art form to master
(E) the fourteenth century provides a vital exception

Questions 13–24 are based on the following passages.

These passages discuss how people have affected chimpanzees. The first passage is a selection from a book on primátes and their habitats. The second passage is a selection from materials distributed by an animal welfare organization.

Passage 1

While the countenance of a young chimpanzee may not reveal it, chimpanzees are our closest genetic relatives. When one examines the behavior of chimpanzees, the similarities to humans abound. Studies reveal that the developmental cycle of a chimpanzee parallels that of a human. In the wild, chimpanzees nurse for five years and are considered young adults at age 13. Mothers typically share life-long bonds with their adult sons and daughters. Chimpanzees communicate nonverbally, using human-like interactions such as hugs, kisses, pats on the back, and tickling. Many chimpanzee emotions, such as joy, sadness, fear, boredom, and depression, are comparable to human emotions.

Chimpanzees are currently found living freely in 21 African countries, from the west coast of the continent to the eastern African nations of Uganda, Rwanda, Burundi, and Tanzania. However, chimpanzees are disappearing from their natural habitats in Africa. Several factors are responsible. Africa currently has one of the highest growth rates in the world, and the exploding human population is creating a snowballing demand for the limited natural resources. Forests, the preferred habitat of the chimpanzee, are razed for living space, crop growing, and grazing for domestic livestock. Consequently, the habitat of the chimpanzee is shrinking and becoming fragmented. Since logging is the primary economic activity in the forests of central Africa, providing many jobs and improving the livelihoods of poor, rural populations, the fate of chimpanzees living in the wild does not look promising. Their outcome is further impacted by poachers who abduct baby chimpanzees (usually killing protective adults in the process) and sell them to dealers for resale as pets or performers. Increased legislative restrictions and penalties have reduced the export of young chimpanzees, but the threat has by no means vanished: approximately 10,000 wild-caught chimpanzees were exported from Africa in the past decade.

Passage 2

Chimpanzees suffer greatly as a consequence of their genetic similitude with humans.

Chimpanzees are suited to living freely in forests, not as family pets. However, the appealing demeanor of infant chimps erroneously suggests that they can fit into a household. By age five, chimps are stronger than most human adults and soon become destructive and resentful of discipline. When efforts to discipline are unsuccessful, the pet chimpanzee typically spends much of its day in a cage. These attempts rarely preclude the pet's ultimate expulsion from the home.

Chimpanzees are fancied by the entertainment industry for their perspicacity and agility. While chimps possess the ability to perform, they lack the inherent motivation to conform to expectations so unlike those of their native milieu. Although it is possible to train animals using only positive reinforcement, this requires time and patience often lacking in the circus, television, and film industries. Many exotic animal trainers admit that they beat their performers during training. Once chimpanzees have reached puberty, however, even the threat of pain cannot check the recalcitrance of those disinclined to perform. When chimps become impossible to subjugate, they must be discarded.

There is almost no good fate for captive chimpanzees, who, given the opportunity, can live well into their sixties. When chimpanzees are expelled from a home or circus, they are typically sent to a medical research laboratory or euthanized. Zoos rarely accept these chimpanzees, who have forgotten, or perhaps never learned, how to comport themselves according to the strict social conventions of chimpanzee groups; these retired chimps would probably never safely integrate into an existing group of chimpanzees. A scarce slot in sanctuary looks to be the best hope for mankind's closest living relative.

13. It is likely that the authors of Passages 1 and 2 would agree that

(A) chimps should be valued because of their genetic closeness to humans
(B) enacting new legislation would effectively protect the chimpanzees
(C) humans are a substantial contributor to the problems faced by chimpanzees
(D) chimps can be dangerous and unpredictable and should be treated with caution
(E) only through heroic and unprecedented measures can the chimp be saved

14. Lines 4–12 ("Studies reveal . . . human emotions") suggest that

(A) chimpanzees and humans share all the same emotions
(B) chimpanzees are capable of learning sign language
(C) infant chimpanzees in the wild require their mother's milk
(D) male chimpanzees do not help in raising their offspring
(E) chimpanzees pat each other on the back for moral support

15. The author of Passage 1 mentions the "exploding human population" (line 19) in order to

(A) explain a consequence
(B) present a solution
(C) praise a development
(D) criticize a policy
(E) demand a response

16. According to Passage 1, forests in Africa are cleared to allow for all of the following EXCEPT

(A) agrarian cultivation
(B) essential employment
(C) added human domiciles
(D) increased fuel production
(E) feeding farm animals

17. The author of Passage 1 would most likely agree with which one of the following?

(A) New restrictions on logging in African should be imposed.
(B) Poachers pose a greater harm to chimpanzees than do loggers.
(C) The impact of logging extends well beyond chimpanzees .
(D) Poachers of chimpanzees have little interest in adult animals.
(E) Chimpanzees in Africa have no prospect of surviving.

18. The author of Passage 2 would most likely respond to the assertion in Passage 1 that chimpanzees use "human-like interactions such as hugs, kisses, pats on the back, and tickling" (lines 9–10) by pointing out that

(A) these interactions paradoxically are a reason for chimpanzees' problems
(B) without these interactions, chimpanzees would not succeed in the wild
(C) humans and chimpanzees are able to communicate with each other
(D) chimpanzees have difficulty communicating after being held captive
(E) additional resources are required to care for retired chimpanzees

19. The author of Passage 2 mentions the "appealing demeanor" of infant chimpanzees (line 39) in order to

(A) provide a contrast to their strength at age five
(B) explain why people might keep them as pets
(C) clarify the reluctance to impose needed discipline
(D) underscore their similarity to human infants
(E) describe their success living freely in forests

20. In Passage 2, the word "check" (line 55) most nearly means

(A) investigate
(B) transmit
(C) impede
(D) divide
(E) approve

21. Which of the following, if true, would most undermine the statement in Passage 2 that "there is almost no good fate for captive chimpanzees" (line 58)?

(A) People are angered by the treatment of the chimpanzees.
(B) Many well-trained chimpanzees enjoy living in zoos.
(C) The number of sanctuaries has increased in recent years.
(D) Only a few chimpanzees live to be older than 70 years.
(E) Successful chimpanzees in the film industry are well paid.

22. The phrase "given the opportunity" (line 59) suggests that captive chimpanzees

(A) are prone to free from captive settings
(B) might see a reduced lifespan in captivity
(C) are underestimated by their human captors
(D) should be used for medical research
(E) can integrate with wild chimpanzees

23. A major difference between the two passages is that Passage 1 is more concerned with

(A) legal restrictions and penalties, while Passage 2 is concerned with root causes
(B) actions of humans, while Passage 2 is concerned with actions of chimpanzees
(C) the lifespan of chimpanzees, while Passage 2 is concerned only with adults
(D) rebuilding a species, while Passage 2 is concerned with protecting the species
(E) chimpanzees in the wild, while Passage 2 is concerned with captive chimpanzees

24. As compared to the attitude of the author of Passage 2 toward human treatment of chimpanzees, the attitude of the author of Passage 1 can be described as more

(A) condescending
(B) understanding
(C) indifferent
(D) complimentary
(E) exasperated

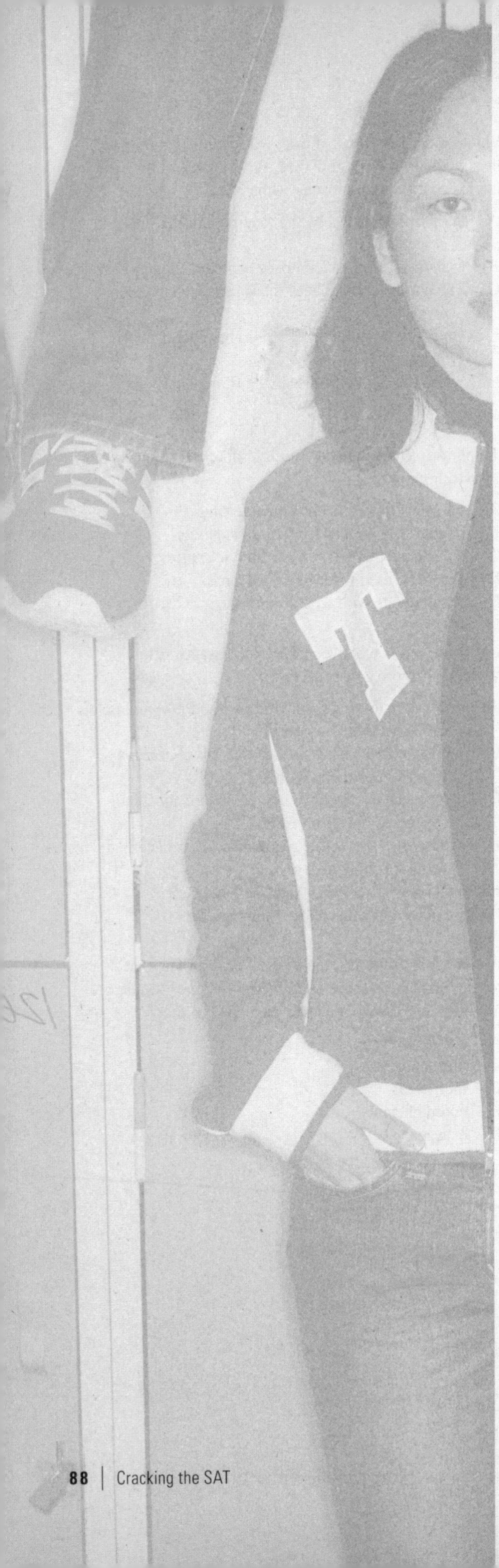

Summary

- Approach short reading passages the same way you approach long passages.
- For dual passages, do questions about the first passage first, questions about the second passage second, and dual questions last. Remember that even with dual questions, you must find support in the passages.
- If the short passages are hard, don't spend too much time on them. They contain only four out of 24 questions!
- Some of the minor question types can be harder than the more common questions types. Use POE and guess, or even skip harder questions. Do the best you can, but don't get bogged down in them!
- Know your reading comprehension vocabulary.

Chapter 8
Vocabulary

Learning new vocabulary is an important step in maximizing your Critical Reading score. It is also a habit that will benefit you no matter what career you choose to pursue later in life. In this chapter you will find a number of ways to improve your vocabulary and maximize your SAT score.

WORDS, WORDS, WORDS

A great way to improve your reading and essay-writing skills is to improve your vocabulary. The more words you know on the test, the easier it will be. It's as simple as that. For this reason, it's important that you get to work on your vocabulary *immediately*.

The Hit Parade

The SAT is very, very repetitive. Over and over again, the SAT tests words such as *pragmatic*, *ambivalent*, *reticent*, and *benign*. So instead of memorizing every single word in the English language, you can just focus your time memorizing those words that show up repeatedly on the SAT.

That's where the Hit Parade comes in. The Hit Parade are the words that we at the Princeton Review have noticed show up frequently on the SAT. Why does ETS think you really need to know the definition of *bombastic* or *capricious*? Who knows? But since they've asked about these words so often, go ahead and learn the Hit Parade, so you can be prepared next time you see the word *magnanimous*. In fact, start right now: *pragmatic*, *ambivalent*, *reticent*, *benign*, *bombastic*, *capricious*, and *magnanimous* are some of the most common words tested on the SAT, so try to memorize these seven words today.

Each word on the Hit Parade is accompanied by its definition, a pronunciation guide, and a sentence that uses the word.

Learn the Words in Groups

The Hit Parade has been arranged by groups of related words. Learning groups of related words can better help you remember each word's meaning. Even when you don't remember the exact meaning of a word, you may remember what group it is from. This will give you an idea of the word's meaning, which can help you use POE to get to an answer.

Make each group of words a part of your life. Rip out one of the group lists, carry it around with you, and use the words throughout your day. For example, on Monday you may feel like using *derogatory* words (see the "If You Can't Say Anything Nice" list), but on Friday you may wish to be more *laudatory* (see the "One Person Can Change the World" list).

Don't Memorize the Dictionary

Only a tiny percentage of all the words in the English language are ever used on the SAT. Generally speaking, the SAT tests the kinds of words that an educated adult—your English teacher, for example—would know without having to look them up. It tests the sorts of words that you encounter in your daily reading, from a novel in English class to the newspaper.

How to Memorize New Words

Here are three effective methods for learning new words.

1. **Flash Cards:** You can make your own flash cards out of 3 × 5 index cards. Write a word on one side and the definition on the other. Then quiz yourself on the words, or practice with a friend. You can carry a few cards around with you every day and work on them in spare moments, like when you're riding on the bus.
2. **The Image Approach:** The image approach involves letting each new word suggest a wild image to you, then using that image to help you remember the word. For example, the word *enfranchise* means "to give the right to vote." *Franchise* might suggest to you a McDonald's franchise. You could remember the new word by imagining people lined up to vote at a McDonald's. The weirder the image, the more likely you'll be to remember the word.
3. **Mnemonics:** Speaking of "the weirder, the better," another way to learn words is to use mnemonics. A mnemonic (the first "m" is silent) is a device or trick, such as a rhyme or a song, that helps you remember something. *In fourteen hundred ninety-two, Columbus sailed the ocean blue* is a mnemonic that helps you remember a date in history. The funnier or the stranger you make your mnemonic, the more likely you are to remember it. Write down your mnemonics (your flash cards are a great place for these).

Even if you are not able to think of a mnemonic for *every* Hit Parade word, sometimes you'll end up learning the word just by thinking about the definition long enough.

Look It Up

Well-written general publications—like the *New York Times* and *Sports Illustrated*—are good sources of SAT words. You should regularly read them or similar publications that are dedicated to topics that interest you. When you come across a new word, write it down, look it up, and remember it. You can make flash cards for these words as well.

Before you can memorize the definition of a word you come across in your reading, you have to find out what it means. You'll need a real dictionary for that. ETS uses two dictionaries in writing the SAT: the *American Heritage Dictionary* and *Merriam-Webster's New Collegiate Dictionary*. You should own a copy of one or the other. (You'll use it in college too—it's a good investment.)

Keep in mind that most words have more than one definition. The dictionary will list these in order of frequency, from the most common to the most obscure. ETS will trip you up by testing the second, third, or even the fourth definition of a familiar-sounding word. For example, the word *pedestrian* shows up repeatedly on the SAT. When ETS uses it, though, it never means a person on foot—the definition of *pedestrian* with which you're probably most familiar. ETS uses it to mean common, ordinary, banal—a *secondary* definition.

Very often, when you see easy words on hard SAT questions, ETS is testing a second, third, or fourth definition with which you may not be familiar. The Hit Parade will help prepare you for these tricks. So grab those index cards and get ready to improve your vocabulary!

The Hit Parade

ARE YOU TALKIN' TO ME?

candid **KAN did**

completely honest, straightforward

Candace's candidness overwhelmed her business colleagues, who were not used to such honesty.

conjecture **kun JEK chur**

inference; guesswork

At this point, Kimaya's hypothesis about single-cell biorhythms is still conjecture: She doesn't have conclusive evidence.

didactic **die DAK tik**

instructive

The tapes were entertaining and didactic; they both amused and instructed children.

effusive **ef YOO siv**

showing excessive emotion; overflowing

Accepting his Oscar for Best Supporting Sound Editor, Ben delivered the most effusive speech in Academy Awards history: he cried, he hugged people, he blew kisses to the audience, and then he cried some more.

euphemism **YOO fuh miz um**

a mild, indirect, or vague term substituting for a harsh, blunt, or offensive term

"To pass away" is a common euphemism for dying.

extrapolate **ek STRAP uh layt**

to infer or estimate by extending or projecting known information

Seeing the wrecked bike and his daughter's skinned knees, Heath extrapolated that she had had a biking accident.

incoherent **in ko HEAR unt**

lacking cohesion or connection

Maury's sentences were so incoherent that nobody understood a word.

insinuate **in SIN yoo ayt**

to imply or communicate stealthily

Sean insinuated that Grace stole the arsenic, but he never came out and said it.

loquacius **low KWAY shus**

very talkative

I'm not eloquent, so I'll just come out and say it: Bobby is loquacious and will talk, and talk, and talk.

lucid **LOO sid**

easily understood; clear

Our teacher provides lucid explanations of even the most difficult concepts so that we can all understand them.

rhetoric **RET uh rik**

the art of using language effectively and persuasively

Since they are expected to make speeches, most politicians and lawyers are well-versed in the art of rhetoric.

WHAT'S UP, TEACH?

acumen **AK yoo men**

quickness, accuracy, and keenness of judgment or insight

Judge Ackerman's legal acumen was so well regarded that he was nicknamed the "Solomon of the South."

adroit **uh DROYT**

dexterous; deft

An adroit balloon-animal maker, Adrianna became popular at children's parties.

ascertain **as er TAYN**

to find out, as through investigation or experimentation

The private investigator had long suspected my dog; before long, he ascertained that Toto was indeed the murderer.

astute **uh STOOT**

shrewd; clever

Stewart is financially astute; he invests wisely and never falls for scams.

circumspect **SER kum spekt**

careful; prudent; discreet

Ned's circumspect manner makes him a wise appointment to the diplomatic corps.

disseminate **dis SEM uh nayt**

to scatter widely, as in sowing seed

The news about Dave's embarrassing moment at the party disseminated quickly through the school; by the end of the day, everyone knew what had happened.

erudition **er yuh DISH un**

deep, extensive learning

Professor Rudy's erudition was such that she could answer any question her students put to her.

pedantic **puh DAN tik**

excessively concerned with book learning and formal rules

Pedro's pedantic tendencies prompted him to remind us constantly of all the grammatical rules we were breaking.

perspicacious **per spih KAY shus**

shrewd; clear-sighted

Persephone's perspicacious mind had solved so many cases that the popular private investagator was able to retire.

pragmatic **prag MAT ik**

practical

Never one for wild and unrealistic schemes, Matt took a pragmatic approach to research.

precocious **pre KO shus**

exhibiting unusually early intellectual aptitude or maturity

Bobby Fisher's precocious intellect made him one of the world's best chess players before he could even drive.

prolific **pro LIFF ick**

very productive; producing great qualities

Charles Harold St. John Hamilton was the world's most prolific author; it is estimated he wrote the equivalent of one thousand novels.

prospectus **pro SPEK tus**

formal proposal

Before writing my thesis, I had to submit a detailed prospectus to the department for approval.

rudimentary **roo duh MEN tuh ree**

basic; elementary; in the earliest stages of development

Josh's rudimentary golf skills were easily overpowered by Tiger Woods's amazing performance on the green.

WHEN THE GOING GETS TOUGH

abstruse **ab STROOS**

difficult to understand

Abby found her professor's lecture on non-Euclidian geometry abstruse; she doubted anyone else in class understood it either.

callous **KAL us**

emotionally hardened; unfeeling

Callie's callous remark about her friend's cluttered room really hurt his feelings.

convoluted **kon vo LOO tid**

intricate; complex

The directions were so convoluted that we became hopelessly lost.

disaffected **DIS a fek ted**

having lost faith or loyalty; discontent

The disaffected cat trainer had finally quit his job when he realized you just can't train cats, no matter how much you yell at them.

enigma **en IG ma**

a puzzle, mystery, or riddle

The emu was an enigma; you could never tell what she was thinking.

inscrutable **in SKROOT uh bul**

difficult to fathom or understand; impenetrable

The ancient poet's handwriting was so inscrutable, that even the most prominent Latin scholars could not read the manuscript.

reticent **RET uh sint**

inclined to keep silent; reserved

Rosanna's reticent behavior caused the interviewer to think her incapable of conversing with other students.

staid **STAYD**

unemotional; serious

Mr. Estado was well known for his staid demeanor; he stayed calm even when everyone else celebrated the team's amazing victory.

CULTURAL ARTIFACTS

arcane **ar KAYN**

known or understood by only a few

The dusty archive includes an arcane treasure trove of nautical charts from the Age of Discovery.

assimilate **uh SIM uh layt**

to absorb or become absorbed; to make or become similar

Keisha assimilated so quickly at her new school that she was named head of the social committee a month after enrolling.

autonomy **aw TAHN uh mee**

independence; self-determination

Candice gained autonomy upon moving out of her parents' house into her own apartment.

cosmopolitan **koz mo PAHL i tun**

worldly; widely sophisticated

Inga was surprisingly cosmopolitan considering that she had never left her tiny hometown in Norway.

derivative (n) **duh RIV uh tiv**

something that comes from another source

Special Victims Unit and *Criminal Intent* are derivatives of the original *Law and Order* drama series.

esoteric **es oh TAIR ik**

intended for or understood by only a small group

Esme's play is extremely esoteric; someone not raised in Estonia would find it difficult to follow.

gaffe **GAF**

a clumsy social error; a faux pas

Geoff committed the gaffe of telling his date that he'd gone out with her sister the night before.

idiosyncrasy **ID ee oh SINK ruh see**

characteristic peculiar to an individual or group

She had many idiosyncrasies, one of which was washing her socks in the dishwasher.

insular **IN suh ler**

isolated; narrow or provincial

The family was so insular that no one else could get near them.

orthodox **OR thuh doks**

adhering to the traditional and established, especially in religion

My father held an orthodox view of baseball; he believed that the field should be outside and made of real grass.

potentate **PO tun tayt**

one who has the power and position to rule over others; monarch

An omnipotent potentate is a person to be reckoned with; great power in the hands of a great leader is a powerful combination.

CAST OUT

castigate **KAS tih gayt**

to scold, rebuke, or harshly criticize

Mr. Castile preferred not to castigate student misbehavior publicly; instead, he would quietly send the troublemaker to the principal's office.

censure **SEN shur**

to issue official blame

In recent years the FCC has censured networks for the provocative antics of Super Bowl halftime acts; what goes on during the game, however, usually escapes the organization's notice.

denounce **duh NOWNTS**

to condemn openly

In many powerful speeches throughout his lifetime, Martin Luther King, Jr. denounced racism as immoral.

reclusive **ree KLOO siv**

seeking or preferring seclusion or isolation

Our neighbors were quite reclusive, hardly ever emerging from behind the closed doors of their home.

relinquish **ree LING kwish**

to retire from; give up or abandon

Ricky relinquished his career in order to search for the source of the world's best relish.

renounce **ree NOWNTS**

to give up (a title, for example), especially by formal announcement

Nancy renounced her given name and began selling records under the moniker "Boedicia."

vituperative **vie TOOP ur uh tiv**

marked by harshly abusive condemnation

The vituperative speech was so cruel that the members left feeling completely abused.

THERE'S NO WAY AROUND IT

circumscribe **SER kum skryb**

to draw a circle around; to restrict

The archeologist circumscribed the excavation area on the map.

contiguous **kun TIG yoo us**

sharing an edge or boundary; touching

The continental United States consists of 48 contiguous states.

I'LL BE THE JUDGE OF THAT!

conciliatory **kon SIL ee uh tor ee**

appeasing; soothing; showing willingness to reconcile

After arguing endlessly with them for weeks, Connie switched to a more conciliatory tone with her parents once prom season arrived.

credible **KRED uh bul**

capable of being believed; plausible

The shocking but credible report of mice in the kitchen kept Eddie up all night.

exonerate **eg ZON er ayt**

to free from blame

Xena was exonerated of all charges.

incontrovertible **in kahn truh VERT uh bul**

indisputable; not open to question

The videotape of the robbery provided incontrovertible evidence against the suspect—he was obviously guilty.

indict **in DITE**

to officially charge with wrongdoing or a crime

President Nixon's aides were indicted during the Watergate scandal.

litigious **luh TIJ us**

prone to engage in lawsuits

Letitia was a litigious little girl; at one point, she tried to sue her dog.

partisan (adj.) **PAR tiz un**

devoted to or biased in support of a party, group, or cause

Today's partisan politics are so antagonistic that it's difficult to reach a successful compromise on any issue.

parity **PA ruh tee**

equality, as in amount, status, or value (antonym: disparity)

The judges at the Olympics must score each athlete's performance with parity; such impartial treatment is hard since one always wants to root for one's own country.

rectitude **REK ti tood**

moral uprightness; righteousness

Thanks to his unerring sense of fairness and justice, Viktor was a model of moral rectitude; his hometown even erected a statue in his honor.

remiss **ree MISS**

lax in attending to duty; negligent

Cassie was remiss in fulfilling her Miss America duties; she didn't even come close to ending world hunger.

repudiate **ree PYOO dee ayt**

to reject the validity or authority of

I repudiated the teacher's arguments about Empress Wu Zetian's reputation by showing him that the reports of her cruelty were from unreliable sources.

sanctimonious **sank ti MO nee us**

feigning piety or righteousness

The sanctimonious scholar had actually been plagiarizing other people's work for years.

scrupulous **SKROO pyoo lus**

principled, having a strong sense of right and wrong; conscientious and exacting

Evan's scrupulous behavior began to annoy his friends when he called the cops on them for toilet papering their teacher's house.

solicitous **so LIS it us**

concerned

The parents asked solicitous questions about the college admissions officer's family.

substantiate **sub STAN shee ayt**

to support with proof or evidence; verify

The argument was substantiated by clear facts and hard evidence.

veracity **vuh RA si tee**

adherence to the truth; truthfulness

Since Vera was known for her veracity, it came as a complete shock when her family found out she'd lied on her application.

vindicate **VIN dih kayt**

to free from blame

Mrs. Layton was finally vindicated after her husband admitted to the crime.

FLATTERY WILL GET YOU NOWHERE

cajole **kuh JOL**

to urge with repeated appeals, teasing, or flattery

The sweet-talking senior cajoled an impressionable junior into seeing *The Lord of the Rings* for the tenth time.

chicanery **chik AY ner ee**

trickery

The candidate accused his debate opponent of resorting to cheap chicanery to sway the electorate.

obsequious **ob SEEK wee us**

fawning and servile

Kevin was so obsequious that even his teachers were embarrassed; as a result, his sucking up rarely led to better grades.

sycophant **SIK uh fent**

insincere, obsequious flatterer

Siggie is such a sycophant; he slyly sucks up to his teachers, and reaps the rewards of his behavior.

ONE PERSON CAN CHANGE THE WORLD

altruism **AL troo iz im**

unselfish concern for the welfare of others; selflessness

Alta, a model of altruism, gave her movie ticket to someone who needed it more.

eminent **EM uh nent**

distinguished; prominent

Emeril Lagasse is one of the most eminent chefs working today; every TV watcher knows how well-known and highly regarded he is.

empathy **em puh THEE**

identification with and understanding of another's situation, feelings, and motives

Emily is one of my most empathetic friends; she can always relate to my emotions.

extol **ek STOL**

to praise highly

Tollivan extolled the virtues of the troll while his teacher looked on amazed.

laudatory **LAW duh tor ee**

full of praise

The principal's speech was laudatory, congratulating the students on their SAT scores.

magnanimous **mag NAN im us**

courageously or generously noble in mind and heart

The magnanimous prince cared deeply for his country and its people.

philanthropic **fil un THROP ik**

humanitarian; benevolent; relating to monetary generosity

Phil was a philanthropic soul, always catering to the needy and the underprivileged.

reciprocate **ree SIP ro kayt**

to mutually take or give; to respond in kind

The chef reciprocated his rival's respect; they admired each other so much that they even traded recipes.

GET RID OF IT

defunct **duh FUNKT**

no longer existing or functioning

The theory that the world was flat became defunct when Magellan sailed to the West and didn't fall off the earth.

eradicate **er RAD i kayt**

to get rid of as if by tearing it up by the roots; abolish

Radcliffe did her best to eradicate the radishes from her farm.

quell **KWEL**

to put down forcibly; suppress

Nell quelled the fight over the quiche by throwing it out the window—she had long given up on reasoning with her sisters.

raze **RAYZ**

to level to the ground; demolish

It is difficult to raze a city building without demolishing other structures around it.

squelch **SKWELCH**

to crush as if by trampling; squash

Sam wanted to keep squash as pets, but Quentin squelched the idea.

supplant **suh PLANT**

to usurp the place of, especially through intrigue or underhanded tactics

The ants prepared to supplant the roaches as the dominant insect in the kitchen; their plan was to take the roaches by surprise and drive them out.

stymie **STY mee**

to thwart or stump

Stan was stymied by the Sudoku puzzle; he just couldn't solve it.

IF YOU CAN'T SAY ANYTHING NICE

abase **uh BAYS**

to lower in rank, prestige, or esteem

Bayard's withering restaurant review was an attempt to abase his former friend, the owner.

deride **duh RIDE**

to mock contemptuously

Derrick was derided for wearing two different colored socks, but he couldn't help it—it was laundry day.

derogatory **duh RAH guh tor ee**

insulting or intended to insult

The unethical politician didn't just attack his opponent's views; he also made derogatory remarks about the other candidate's family and personal hygiene.

disparage **dis PAR uj**

to speak of negatively; to belittle

Wanda disparaged Glen by calling him a cheat and a liar.

effrontery **eh FRON ter ee**

brazen boldness; presumptuousness

The attorney's effrontery in asking such personal questions so shocked Esther that she immediately ran from the office.

ignominy **IG nuh mi nee**

great personal dishonor or humiliation; disgraceful conduct

Ignacio felt great ignominy after the scandal broke.

impugn **im PYOON**

to attack as false or questionable

Instead of taking the high road, the candidate impugned his opponent's character.

mar **MAR**

to damage, especially in a disfiguring way

The perfect day was marred by the arrival of storm clouds.

pejorative (adj) **puh JOR uh tiv**

disparaging, belittling, insulting

Teachers should refrain from using pejorative terms as *numbskull* and *idiot* to refer to other teachers.

vex **VEKS**

to annoy or bother; to perplex

Bex's mom was vexed when Bex was very vague about her whereabouts for the evening.

vindictive **vin DIK tiv**

disposed to seek revenge; revengeful; spiteful

Vincenzo was very vindictive; when someone hurt him, he responded by vigorously plotting revenge.

OVERKILL

bombastic **bom BAS tik**

given to pompous speech or writing

The principal's bombastic speech bombed in the eyes of the students; it only furthered their impression of him as a pompous jerk.

ebullience **eh BOO li ents**

intense enthusiasm

A sense of ebullience swept over the lacrosse fans crowd when their team won the game.

exorbitant **eg ZOR bit int**

exceeding all bounds, as of custom or fairness

I wanted to buy a Porsche, but the price was exorbitant, so instead I purchased a used mail truck.

exuberant **eg ZOO bur ent**

full of unrestrained enthusiasm or joy

William was exuberant when he found out that he'd gotten into the college of his choice.

embellish **em BELL ish**

to ornament or decorate; to exaggerate

One can never trust that Anwar's stories are realistic; his details are almost always embellished so that his experiences sound more interesting than they really are.

flagrant **FLAY grent**

extremely or deliberately shocking or noticeable

Too many flagrant fouls can get you kicked out of a basketball game.

gratuitous **gruh TOO uh tus**

given freely; unearned; unnecessary

The film was full of gratuitous sex and violence inessential to the story.

lavish (adj) **LAV ish**

extravagant

Lavanya's wedding was a lavish affair.

lugubrious **luh GOO bree yus**

mournful, dismal, or gloomy, especially to an exaggerated or ludicrous degree

Lucas's lugubrious eulogy for his pet lobster quickly became ridiculous.

opulent **OP yoo lent**

displaying great wealth

The ophthalmologist's opulent home was the envy of his friends; the crystal chandeliers, marble floors, and teak furniture must have cost a fortune.

ornate **or NAYT**

elaborately decorated

The wood carvings were so ornate that you could examine them many times and still notice things you had not seen before.

penchant **PEN chent**

a strong inclination or liking

Penny's penchant for chocolate-covered ants led her to munch on them all day.

redundant **ree DUN dint**

needlessly repetitive

The author's speech was terribly redundant, repeating the same phrases, saying the same thing over and over, and constantly reiterating the same point.

ubiquitous **yoo BIK wit us**

being or seeming to be everywhere at the same time; omnipresent

Kenny had a ubiquitous little sister; wherever he turned, there she was.

THROUGH SOMEONE ELSE'S EYES

vicarious **vie KA ree us**

felt or undergone as if one were taking part in the experience or feelings of another

Stan, who was never athletic but loved sports, lived vicariously through his brother, a professional basketball player.

vignette **vin YET**

a short scene or story

The poodle vignette in my new film expresses the true meaning of Valentine's Day.

LOTS 'N' LOTS

amalgam **uh MAL gum**

a combination of diverse elements; a mixture

The song was an amalgam of many different styles, from blues to hip hop to folk.

inundate **IN un dayt**

to overwhelm as if with a flood; to swamp

The day after the ad ran, Martha was inundated with phone calls.

multifarious **mul ti FAYR ee us**

diverse; various

The multifarious achievements of Leonardo da Vinci, ranging from architecture and painting to philosophy and science, are unparalleled in our century.

multiplicity **mul tuh PLI sit ee**

state of being various or manifold; a great number

A multiplicity of views is essential to a healthy multicultural democracy.

IT'S GETTING BETTER ALL THE TIME

alleviate **uh LEE vee ayt**

to ease a pain or burden

Alvin meditated to alleviate the pain from the headache he got after taking the SAT.

beneficial **ben uh FISH ul**

producing or promoting a favorable result; helpful

According to my doctor, tea's beneficial effects may include reducing anxiety.

cathartic **kuh THAR tik**

relaxing after an emotional outburst

Cathy found that yelling at her idiotic coworkers for a while had a cathartic effect, and she was able to calmly go back to work.

curative **KYUR uh tiv**

able to heal or cure

The aloe had a curative effect on my sunburn; within hours, the flaking had stopped.

palliative **PAL lee uh tiv**

relieving or soothing the symptoms of a disease or disorder without effecting a cure

Watching professional polo on TV became a palliative for the screaming child; it was the only thing that would quiet him.

therapeutic **thair uh PYOO tik**

having or exhibiting healing powers

The therapeutic air of the Mediterranean cured Thomas of his asthma.

MODEL BEHAVIOR

complement (n) **KOM plem ent**

something that completes, goes with, or brings to perfection

The lovely computer is the perfect complement to the modern furnishings in Abby's apartment.

epitome **ep IT o mee**

a representative or example of a type

She is the epitome of selflessness; no matter how much or little she has, she always gives to others.

felicitous **fuh LIH sih tus**

admirably suited; apt

Jamie Foxx made a felicitous speech when he won his Oscar.

LIAR, LIAR, PANTS ON FIRE

belie **bee LIE**

to misrepresent or disguise

He smiled in order to belie his hostility.

debunk **duh BUNK**

to expose untruths, shams, or exaggerated claims

The university administration debunked the myth that bunk beds are only for children by installing them in every dorm on campus.

dubious **DOO bee us**

doubtful; of unlikely authenticity

Jerry's dubious claim that he could fly like Superman didn't win him any summer job offers.

duplicitous **doo PLIS uh tus**

deliberately deceptive

The duplicitous man duplicated dollars and gave the counterfeits to unsuspecting vendors.

fabricate **FAB ruh kayt**

to make up in order to deceive

Fabio fabricated the story that he used to play drums for Metallica; he has never actually held a drumstick in his life.

fallacy **FAL uh see**

a false notion

The idea that there is only one college for you is a fallacy.

mendacious **men DAY shus**

lying; untruthful

John's mendacious statements on the stand sealed his fate; he was found guilty of lying to the court about his role in the crime.

specious **SPEE shus**

having the ring of truth or plausibility but actually false

Susie's specious argument seemed to make sense, but when I looked more closely, it was clearly illogical.

SITTIN' ON THE FENCE

ambiguous **am BIG yoo us**

open to more than one interpretation

Big's eyes were an ambiguous color: in some lights, brown, and in others, green.

ambivalent **am BIV uh lint**

simultaneously feeling opposing feelings; uncertain

Amy felt ambivalent about her dance class: on one hand, she enjoyed the exercise, but on the other, the choice of dances bored her.

apathetic **ap uh THET ik**

feeling or showing little emotion

The apathetic students didn't even bother to vote for class president.

capricious **kuh PREE shus**

impulsive and unpredictable

The referee's capricious behavior angered the players; he would call a foul for minor contact, but ignore elbowing and kicking.

equivocal **e KWIV uh kul**

open to two or more interpretations and often intended to mislead; ambiguous (antonym: unequivocal)

The politician made so many equivocal statements during the scandal that no one could be sure what, if anything, he had admitted to.

erratic **e RAT ik**

markedly inconsistent

Erroll's erratic behavior made it difficult for his friends to predict what he would do in a given moment.

impetuous **im PET choo us**

suddenly and forcefully energetic or emotional; impulsive and passionate

Mr. Limpet was so impetuous that we never knew what he would do next.

impetus **IM pit us**

an impelling force or stimulus

A looming deadline provided Imelda with the impetus she needed to finish her research paper.

sporadic **spo RAD ik**

occurring at irregular intervals; having no pattern or order in time

Storms in Florida are sporadic; it's hard to predict when they're going to occur.

vacillate **VA sil ayt**

to sway from one side to the other; oscillate

The cook vacillated between favoring chicken and preferring fish; he just couldn't decide which to prepare.

whimsical **WIM zi kul**

characterized by whim; unpredictable

Egbert rarely behaved as expected; indeed, he was a whimsical soul whose every decision was anybody's guess.

I JUST CAN'T TAKE IT ANYMORE

flag (v.) **FLAG**

to decline in vigor or strength; to tire; to droop

After several few days climbing mountains in pouring rain, our enthusiasm for the hiking trip began to flag.

jaded **JAY did**

worn out; wearied

Jade's experiences had jaded her; she no longer believed that the junk stacked in her garage was going to make her rich.

SHE'S CRAFTY

clandestine **klan DEST in**

done secretively, especially to deceive; surreptitious

I met the secret agent in an alleyway, where she handed me the plans for the clandestine operation.

subterfuge **SUB ter fyoozh**

a deceptive stratagem or device

The submarine pilots were trained in the art of subterfuge; they were excellent at faking out their enemies.

surreptitious **sir up TISH us**

secretive; sneaky

Sara drank the cough syrup surreptitiously because she didn't want anyone to know that she was sick.

JUST A LITTLE BIT

dearth **DERTH**

scarce supply; lack

There was a dearth of money in my piggybank; it collected dust, not bills.

modicum **MAHD ik um**

a small, moderate, or token amount

A modicum of effort may result in a small score improvement; to improve significantly, however, you must study as often as possible.

paucity **PAW sit ee**

smallness in number; scarcity

The struggling city had a paucity of jobs and therefore a high level of poverty.

squander **SKWAN der**

to spend wastefully

Carrie squandered her savings on shoes and wasn't able to buy her apartment.

temperate **TEM per ut**

moderate; restrained (antonym: intemperate)

Temperate climates rarely experience extremes in temperature.

tenuous **TEN yoo us**

having little substance or strength; shaky

Her grasp on reality is tenuous at best; she's not even sure what year it is.

I WILL SURVIVE

diligent **DIL uh jint**

marked by painstaking effort; hardworking

With diligent effort, they were able to finish the model airplane in record time.

maverick **MAV rik**

one who is independent and resists adherence to a group

In the movie *Top Gun,* Tom Cruise played a maverick who often broke rules and did things his own way.

mercenary **MUR sin air ee**

motivated solely by a desire for money or material gain

Mercer is a mercenary lawyer; he'll argue for whichever side pays him the most for his services.

obstinate **OB stin it**

stubbornly attached to an opinion or a course of action

Despite Jeremy's broken leg, his parents were obstinate; they steadfastly refused to buy him an XBox.

proliferate **pro LIF er ayt**

to grow or increase rapidly

Because fax machines, pagers, and cell phones have proliferated in recent years, many new area codes have been created to handle the demand for phone numbers.

tenacity **te NAS uh tee**

persistence

With his overwhelming tenacity, Clark was finally able to interview Brad Pitt for the school newspaper.

vigilant **VIJ uh lent**

on the alert; watchful

The participants of the candlelight vigil were vigilant, as they had heard that the fraternity across the street was planning to egg them.

CONNECT THE DOTS

extraneous **ek STRAY nee us**

irrelevant; inessential

The book, though interesting, had so much extraneous information that it was hard to keep track of the important points.

juxtapose **JUK stuh pohz**

to place side by side, especially for comparison or contrast

Separately the pictures look identical, but if you juxtapose them, you can see the differences.

novel (adj) **NOV il**

fresh; original; new

It was a novel idea, the sort of thing no one had tried before.

superfluous **soo PUR floo us**

extra; unnecessary

If there is sugar in your tea, honey would be superfluous.

synergy **SIN er jee**

combined action or operation

The synergy of hydrogen and oxygen creates water.

tangential **tan JEN chul**

merely touching or slightly connected; only superficially relevant

Though Abby's paper was well written, its thesis was so tangential to its proof that her teacher couldn't give her a good grade.

I WRITE THE SONGS

aesthetic **es THET ik**

having to do with the appreciation of beauty

Aesthetic considerations determined the arrangement of paintings at the museum; as long as art looked good together, it didn't matter who had painted it.

aural **AW rul**

of or related to the ear or the sense of hearing

It should come as no surprise that musicians prefer aural to visual learning.

cacophony **kuh KAH fuh nee**

discordant, unpleasant noise

Brian had to shield his ears from the awful cacophony produced by the punk band onstage.

dirge **DERJ**

a funeral hymn or lament

The dirge was so beautiful that everyone cried, even those who hadn't known the deceased.

eclectic **e KLEK tik**

made up of a variety of sources or styles

Lou's taste in music is quite eclectic; he listens to everything from rap to polka.

incongruous **in KAHN groo us**

lacking in harmony; incompatible

My chicken and jello soup experiment failed; the tastes were just too incongruous.

sonorous **SAHN ur us**

producing a deep or full sound

My father's sonorous snoring keeps me up all night unless I close my door and wear earplugs.

strident **STRY dent**

loud, harsh, grating, or shrill

The strident shouting kept the neighbors awake all night.

DUDE, THIS SUCKS!

debacle **duh BAHK ul**

disastrous or ludicrous defeat or failure; fiasco

Jim's interview was a complete debacle; he accidentally locked himself in the bathroom, sneezed on the interviewer multiple times, and knocked over the president of the company.

debilitate **duh BIL i tayt**

impair the strength of; weaken

Deb ran the New York City marathon without proper training; the experience left her debilitated for weeks.

tumultuous **tum UL choo us**

noisy and disorderly

The tumultuous applause was so deafening that the pianist couldn't hear the singer.

IT'S ALL IN THE TIMING

anachronistic **ah nak ruh NIS tik**

the representation of something as existing or happening in the wrong time period

I noticed an anachronism in the museum's ancient Rome display: a digital clock ticking behind a statue of Venus.

archaic **ar KAY ik**

characteristic of an earlier time; antiquated; old

"How dost thou?" is an archaic way of saying "How are you?"

dilatory **DIL uh tor ee**

habitually late

Always waiting until the last moment to leave home in the morning, Dylan was a dilatory student.

ephemeral **e FEM er ul**

lasting for only a brief time

The importance of SAT scores is truly ephemeral; when you are applying, they are crucial, but once you get into college, no one cares how well you did.

redolent **RED uh lint**

fragrant; aromatic; suggestive

The aroma of apple pie wafted into my room, redolent of weekends spent baking with my grandmother.

temporal **TEM per ul**

of, relating to, or limited by time

One's enjoyment of a Starbuck's mocha latte is bound by temporal limitations; all too soon, the latte is gone.

WHO CAN IT BE NOW?

onerous **O ner us**

troublesome or oppressive; burdensome

The onerous task was so difficult that Ona thought she'd never get through it.

portent **POR tent**

indication of something important or calamitous about to occur; omen

A red morning sky is a terrible portent for all sailors — it means that stormy seas are ahead.

prescience **PRE shens**

knowledge of actions or events before they occur; foreknowledge; foresight

Preetha's prescience was such that people wondered if she was psychic; how else could she know so much about the future?

BOOORING

austere **aw STEER**

without decoration; strict

The gray walls and bare floors of his monastery cell provided an even more austere setting than Brother Austen had hoped for.

banal **buh NAL**

drearily commonplace; predictable; trite

The poet's imagery is so banal that I think she cribbed her work from *Poetry for Dummies.*

hackneyed **HAK need**

worn out through overuse; trite

All Hal could offer in the way of advice were hackneyed old phrases that I'd heard a hundred times before.

insipid **in SIP id**

uninteresting; unchallenging; lacking taste or savor

That insipid movie was so predictable that I walked out.

prosaic **pro ZAY ik**

unimaginative; dull (antonym: poetic)

Rebecca made a prosaic mosaic consisting of identical, undecorated tiles.

soporific **sah puh RIF ik**

inducing or tending to induce sleep

The congressman's speech was so soporific that even his cat was yawning.

vapid **VAP id**

lacking liveliness, animation, or interest; dull

Valerie's date was so vapid that she thought he was sleeping with his eyes open.

IT ALL CHANGES SO FAST

brevity **BRE vi tee**

the quality or state of being brief in duration

Brevity = briefness. (You can't get any shorter than that!)

expedient **ek SPEE dee ent**

appropriate to a purpose; convenient; speedy

It was more expedient to use Federal Express than to use the post office.

transient **TRAN zhent**

passing quickly in time or space

Jack Dawson enjoyed his transient lifestyle; with nothing but the clothes on his back and the air in his lungs, he was free to travel wherever he wanted.

FULL ON

augment **awg MENT**

to make greater, as in size, extent, or quantity; to supplement

The model Angele Franju is rumored to have augmented her studies in chemistry with a minor in German literature.

bolster **BOWL ster**

to hearten, support or prop up

The class bolstered Amelia's confidence; she had no idea she already knew so much.

burgeon **BER jun**

to grow and flourish

The burgeoning Burgess family required a new house because its old one had only one bedroom.

copious **KO pee us**

plentiful; having a large quantity

She took copious notes during class, using up five large notebooks.

distend **dis TEND**

to swell out or expand from internal pressure, as when overly full

The balloon distended as it was filled with helium, much like Mike's stomach after he ate an entire turkey on Thanksgiving.

grandiose **gran dee OHS**

great in scope or intent; grand

The party was a grandiose affair; hundreds of richly dressed guests danced the night away.

prodigious **pruh DIJ us**

enormous

Steven Spielberg's prodigious talent has made him the most successful film producer and director of our time.

profundity **pro FUN di tee**

great depth of intellect, feeling, or meaning

The actor's profundity surprised the director, who had heard that he was a bit of an airhead.

redouble **ree DUB ul**

to make twice as great; to double

Rita redoubled her efforts to become president of her class by campaigning twice as hard as before.

scintillating **SIN til ay ting**

brilliant

The writer's scintillating narrative diverted Izabel's attention away from her other guests.

DON'T MAKE WAVES

averse **uh VERS**

strongly disinclined

Ava proved so averse to homework that she would break out in hives at the mere mention of it.

conspicuous **kun SPIK yoo us**

easy to notice; obvious (antonym: inconspicuous)

The red tuxedo was conspicuous among all the classic black ones. What was he thinking?

demure **duh MYUR**

modest and reserved

Muriel was the most demure girl in the class, always sitting quietly in the back of the room and downplaying any compliments she received.

diffidence **DIF uh dins**

timidity or shyness

Lea's diffident nature often prevented her from speaking out in class.

docile **DAHS ul**

submissive to instruction; willing to be taught

The SAT class was so docile that the teacher wondered if she was in the right room.

innocuous **in NAHK yoo us**

having no adverse effect; harmless

The plants were as innocuous as they looked; we suffered no ill effects from eating their leaves.

placid **PLAS id**

calm or quiet; undisturbed

Lake Placid was the place to go for those in need of a quiet vacation.

quiescent **kwee ES sint**

quiet, still, or at rest; inactive

Quinn's quiescent behavior made him an ideal roommate.

DO YOU AGREE?

concord **KON kord**

agreement (antonym: discord)

The class was in concord about the necessity to perform *Hamlet,* rather than *King Lear,* in the spring show.

concur **kun KUR**

to agree

The board concurred that the con artist who had stolen their money had to be convicted.

dogmatic **dog MAT ik**

stubbornly attached to insufficiently proven beliefs

Avik was dogmatic in his belief that the power lines were giving his dog headaches.

fastidious **fas TID ee us**

carefully attentive to detail; difficult to please

Kelly, always so fastidious, dramatically edited our group's report.

intransigence **in TRAN zi jents**

refusal to moderate a position or to compromise

Jeff was so intransigent in his views that it was impossible to have a rational debate with him.

jocular **JOK yoo ler**

characterized by or given to joking

Yung-Ji's jocular disposition helped him gain popularity.

meticulous **muh TIK yoo lus**

extremely careful and precise

Since Kelly was so meticulous, we asked her to proofread our group's report.

OFFICER FRIENDLY

affable **AF uh bul**

easy-going; friendly

My mom always said that the key to being affable is the ability to make others laugh.

alacrity **uh LAK ruh tee**

promptness in response; cheerful readiness; eagerness

I was so happy when I got the acceptance letter from the University of Alaska that I sprinted home with great alacrity to share the good news.

amiable **AY mee uh bul**

friendly; agreeable; good-natured

Mr. Amis was so amiable that he let us call him "Big A."

benign **be NINE**

kind and gentle

Uncle Ben is a benign and friendly man who is always willing to help.

sanguine **SAN gwin**

cheerfully confident; optimistic

Harold's sanguine temperament kept him cheerful, even through somber times.

NASTY BOYS

belligerent **buh LIH jer int**

eager to fight; hostile or aggressive

The prosecutor was reprimanded for his belligerent cross-examination of the witness, who had dissolved into tears.

cantankerous **kan TANK er us**

ill-tempered and quarrelsome; disagreeable

The dog hid under the tank as a result of the cat's cantankerous disposition.

contentious **kun TEN shus**

quarrelsome

The contentious debate over science class content is increasingly making the news.

deleterious **del uh TER ee us**

having a harmful effect

It was only once he started his test that Murray realized the deleterious effects of one too many Red Bulls; he couldn't concentrate, and his hands were shaking so much he could barely write.

exacerbate **eg ZA ser bayt**

to increase the severity, violence, or bitterness of; aggravate

Alan's procrastination problems were exacerbated by the monkeys who kept throwing bananas at him while he tried to concentrate.

flippant **FLIP ent**

disrespectfully humorous or casual

Flap's flippant remarks to the teacher got him sent to the principal's office.

insolent **IN suh lint**

insulting in manner or speech

The insolent prime minister stuck her tongue out at the queen.

nefarious **nuh FAYR ee us**

flagrantly wicked; vicious

Dorothy's kindness and bravery triumphed over the nefarious antics of the Wicked Witch of the West.

pernicious **per NISH us**

extremely or irrevocably harmful; deadly

The fertilizer's pernicious effects were not immediately obvious, but researchers became suspicious when all their petunias died.

rancorous **RANK er us**

marked by bitter, deep-seated ill-will

They had such a rancorous relationship that no one could believe that they had ever gotten along.

repugnant **ree PUG nent**

arousing disgust or aversion; offensive or repulsive

The pug's behavior at the dog park was repugnant, causing other dogs to avoid him altogether.

supercilious **SUPE er sil lee us**

disdainful; haughty; arrogant

The nobleman traveled through the town with a supercilious expression, sneering at the peasants as he was carried past them.

EARTH, WIND, AND FIRE

arboreal **ar BOR ee ul**

relating to or resembling a tree or trees

The Rocky Mountain National Forest will celebrate its arboreal splendor with an Arbor Day concert.

invocation (n) **in vo KAY shun**

a call (usually upon a higher power) for assistance, support, or inspiration

The group invoked the god of war as their protector on the field of battle.

stratify **STRAT i fy**

to layer or separate into layers

Jonas studied the stratified bedrock and was able to see which time periods went with which layers.

variegated **VAR ee ih gay tid**

having streaks, marks, or patches of a different color or colors; varicolored

The wood's markings were so variegated that Mr. Vargas assumed they had been painted on.

verdant **VUR dent**

green with vegetation

The garden was verdant after the rain.

OTHER WORDS

As important as Hit Parade words are, they aren't the only words on the SAT. As you go about learning the Hit Parade, you should also try to incorporate other new words into your vocabulary. The Hit Parade will help you determine what kinds of words you should be learning—good solid words that are fairly difficult but not impossible.

One very good source for SAT words is whatever you're already reading. Magazines that interest you and books you read for school, or just for fun, are treasure troves of good vocabulary; just take the time to look up words you don't already know. Reading can only help your chances of earning a higher score on the SAT.

Part III
How to Crack the Math Section

A FEW WORDS ABOUT SAT MATH

As we've mentioned before, the SAT isn't your normal school test. The same is true of the Math portion of the SAT. There are two types of questions that you'll run into: multiple-choice and student-produced response questions. We've talked before about multiple-choice, so let's talk about these strange questions known as student-produced response questions. These questions are the only non-multiple-choice questions on the SAT, other than the essay; instead of selecting ETS's answer from among several choices, you will have to find the answer on your own and mark it in a grid, which is why we call them Grid-Ins. The Grid-In questions on your test will be drawn from arithmetic, algebra, and geometry, just like regular SAT math questions. However, the format has special characteristics, so we will treat them a bit differently. You'll learn more about them later in this book.

What Does the Math SAT Measure?

ETS says that the Math SAT measures "mathematical reasoning abilities" or "higher-order reasoning abilities." Unfortunately, or fortunately for you, this is not true. The Math section is merely a brief test of arithmetic, algebra, and a bit of geometry—when we say a "bit," we mean it. The principles you'll need to know are few and simple. We'll show you which ones are important. Most of them are listed for you at the beginning of each section.

Order of Difficulty

As was true of the sentence completion questions, questions on the Math section are arranged in order of difficulty. The first question in each section will be the easiest in that section, and the last will be the hardest; in this case, harder doesn't mean tougher—it means trickier. In addition, the questions within the grid-in question groups will also be arranged in order of difficulty. The difficulty of a problem will help you determine how to attack it.

You Don't Have to Finish

We've all been taught in school that when you take a test, you have to finish it. If you answered only two-thirds of the questions on a high school math test, you probably wouldn't get a very good grade. But as we've already seen, the SAT is not at all like the tests you take in school. Most students don't know about the difference, so they make the mistake of doing all the problems on each Math section of the SAT.

Because they have only a limited amount of time to answer all the questions, most students are always in a rush to get to the end of the section. At first, this seems reasonable, but think about the order of difficulty for a minute. All the easy questions are at the beginning of a Math section, and the hard questions are at the end. So when students rush through a Math section, they're actually spending less time on the easier questions (which they have a good chance of getting right), just so they can spend more time on the harder questions (which they have very little chance of getting right). Does this make sense? Of course not.

Here's the secret: On the Math section, you don't have to answer every question in each section. In fact, unless you're trying to score 600 or more, you shouldn't even look at the difficult last third of the Math questions. Most students can raise their math scores by concentrating on getting all the easy and medium questions correct. In other words…

Slow Down!

Most students do considerably better on the Math section when they slow down and spend less time worrying about the hard questions (and more time working carefully on the easier ones). Haste causes careless errors, and careless errors can ruin your score. In most cases, you can actually *raise* your score by answering *fewer* questions. That doesn't sound like a bad idea, does it? If you're shooting for an 800, you'll have to answer every question correctly. But if your target is 550, you should ignore the hardest questions in each section and use your limited time wisely.

If you got 70 percent on a math test in school, you'd feel pretty lousy—that's a C minus, below average. But the SAT is not like school. Getting 42 out of 60 questions correct (70%) would give you a math score of about 600—that's 100 points *above* the national average.

To make sure you're working at the right pace in each Math section, refer to the Math Pacing Chart on page 26. The chart will tell you how many questions you need to answer in each section to achieve your next score goal.

Calculators

Students are permitted (but not required) to use calculators on the SAT. You should definitely take a calculator to the test. It will be extremely helpful to you, as long as you know how and when to use it and don't get carried away. We'll tell you more about calculators as we go along.

The Princeton Review Approach

We're going to give you the tools you need to handle the easier questions on the Math section, along with several great techniques to help you crack some of the more difficult ones. But you must concentrate first on getting the easier questions correct. Don't worry about the difficult third of the Math section until you've learned to work carefully and accurately on the easier questions.

When it does come time to look at some of the harder questions, the Joe Bloggs principle will help you once again; this time to zero in on ETS's answer. You'll learn what kinds of answers appeal to Joe in math, and how to avoid those answers. Just as you did in the Critical Reading section, you'll learn to use POE to find ETS's answer by getting rid of obviously incorrect answers.

Generally speaking, each chapter in the Math section of this book begins with the basics and then gradually moves into more advanced principles and techniques. If you find yourself getting lost toward the end of the chapter, don't worry. Concentrate your efforts on principles you can understand but still need to master.

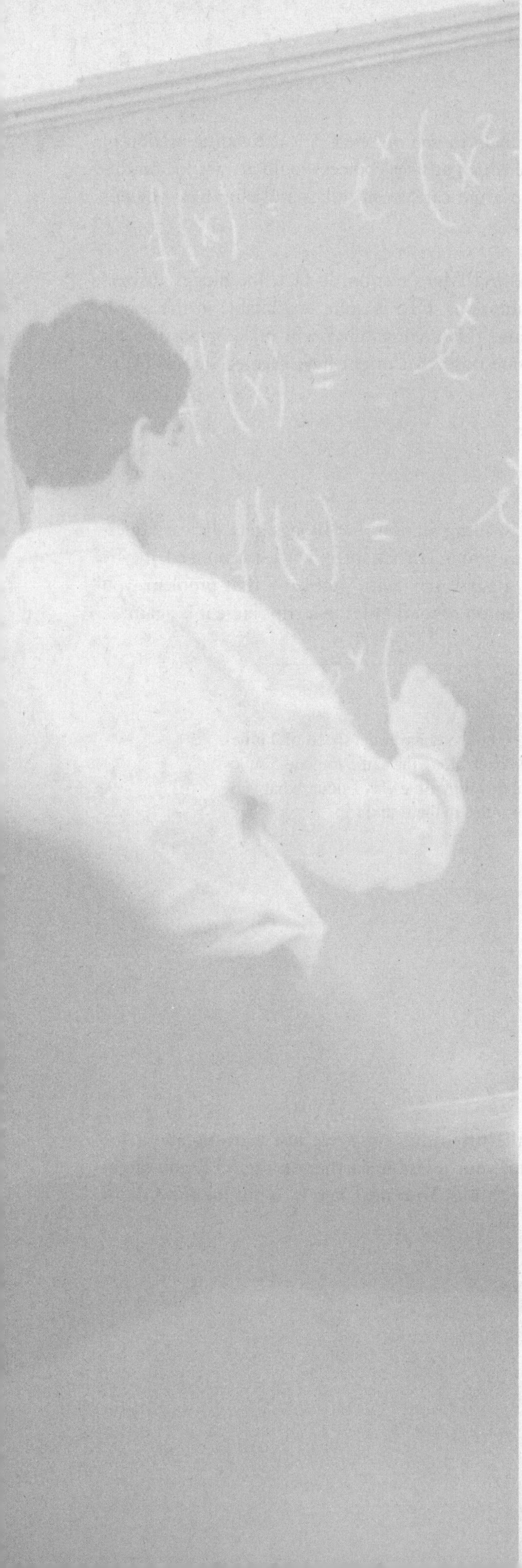

Chapter 9
Joe Bloggs and the Math Section

In Chapter 4 you learned how Joe Bloggs, our model average student, can help you avoid trap answers on the Critical Reading sections of the SAT. Well, that's not all he can do. In this chapter you will see that we can learn from Joe on the Math sections of the test too. By keeping in mind what Joe is likely to do on difficult math questions, you can avoid those same mistakes and maximize your math score.

HEY, JOE!

Joe Bloggs has already been a big help to you on the Critical Reading section of the SAT. By learning to anticipate which answer choices would attract Joe on difficult questions, you know how to avoid careless mistakes and eliminate obvious incorrect answers.

You can do the same thing on the SAT Math section. In fact, Joe Bloggs answers are even easier to spot on math questions. ETS is quite predictable in the way it writes incorrect answer choices, and this predictability will make it possible for you to zero in on its answers to questions that might have seemed impossible to you before.

How Joe Thinks

No Problem

Joe Bloggs is attracted to easy solutions arrived at through methods that he understands.

As was true on the SAT Critical Reading section, Joe Bloggs gets the easy questions right and the hard questions wrong. In Chapter 3, we introduced Joe by showing you how he approached a particular math problem. That problem, you may remember, involved the calculation of total miles in a trip. Here it is again:

20. Graham walked to school at an average speed of 3 miles an hour and jogged back along the same route at 5 miles an hour. If his total traveling time was 1 hour, what was the total number of miles in the round trip?

(A) 3

(B) $3\frac{1}{8}$

(C) $3\frac{3}{4}$

(D) 4

(E) 5

When we showed this problem the first time, you were just learning about Joe Bloggs. Now that you've made him your invisible partner on the SAT, you ought to know a great deal about how he thinks. Your next step is to put Joe to work for you on the Math sections.

Here's How to Crack It

This problem was the last in a 20-question Math section. Therefore, it was the hardest problem in that section. Naturally, Joe got it wrong.

The answer choice most attractive to Joe on this problem is D. The question obviously involves an average of some kind, and 4 is the average of 3 and 5, so Joe picked it. Choice D just seemed like the right answer to Joe. (Of course, it wasn't the right answer; Joe gets the hard ones wrong.)

Because this is true, we know which answers we should avoid on hard questions: answers that seem obvious or that can be arrived at simply and quickly. If the answer really were obvious and if finding it really were simple, the question would be easy, not hard.

Joe Bloggs is also attracted to answer choices that simply repeat numbers from the problem. This means, of course, that you should avoid such choices. In the problem about Graham's going to school, you can also eliminate choices A and E, because 3 and 5 are numbers repeated directly from the problem. Therefore, they are extremely unlikely to be ETS's answer.

Avoid Repeats
Joe Bloggs is attracted to answer choices that simply repeat numbers from the problem.

We've now eliminated three of the five answer choices. Even if you couldn't figure out anything else about this question, you'd have a fifty-fifty chance of guessing correctly. Those are excellent odds, considering that we really didn't do any math. By eliminating answer choices that we knew were wrong, we were able to beat ETS at its own game. (ETS's answer to this question is C, by the way.)

Putting Joe to Work on the Math SAT

Generally speaking, the Joe Bloggs principle teaches you to

- trust your hunches on easy questions.
- double-check your hunches on medium questions.
- eliminate Joe Bloggs answers on difficult questions.

The rest of this chapter is devoted to using Joe Bloggs to zero in on ETS's answers to difficult questions. Of course, your main concern is still to answer all easy and medium questions correctly. But if you have some time left at the end of a Math section, the Joe Bloggs principle can help you eliminate answers on a few difficult questions, so that you can venture some good guesses. And as we've already seen, smart guessing means more points. (In Chapter 15, you'll learn how he can help you with grid-ins.)

DON'T GET TRAPPED

Let's take a look at some common situations you will come across on the SAT and find out how best to handle them.

Hard Questions = Hard Answers

As we've just explained, hard questions on the SAT simply don't have correct answers that are obvious to the average person. Avoiding the "obvious" choices will take some discipline on your part, but you'll lose points if you don't. Even if you're a math whiz, the Joe Bloggs principle will keep you from making careless mistakes.

Here's an example:

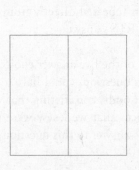

20. The figure above is a square divided into two nonoverlapping regions. What is the greatest number of nonoverlapping regions that can be obtained by drawing any two additional straight lines?

(A) 4
(B) 5
(C) 6
(D) 7
(E) 8

Joe Likes to Share

When it comes to the goofy "nonoverlapping region" questions, Joe's own good nature gets the best of him and he assumes that he must divide the figure evenly. That's why he likes to pick C on this problem. But, *nowhere does the question say the regions must be equal in size.* Read carefully.

Here's How to Crack It

This is the last question from a Math section. Therefore, it's extremely difficult. One reason it's so difficult is that it is badly written. (ETS's strengths are mathematical, not verbal.) Here's a clearer way to think of it: The drawing is a pizza cut in half; what's the greatest number of pieces you could end up with if you make just two more cuts with a knife?

The most obvious way to cut the pizza would be to make cuts perpendicular to the center cut, dividing the pizza into six pieces, like this:

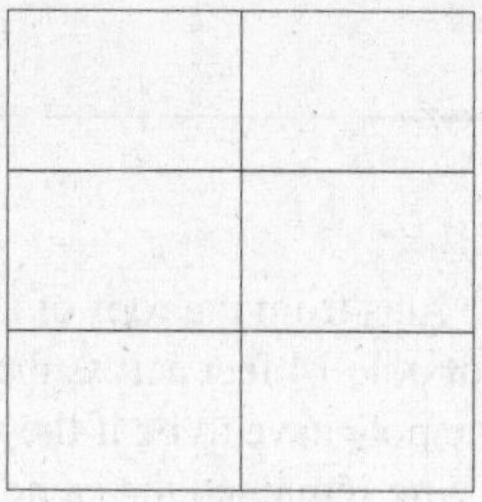

There, that was fast and easy. So that means 6 is ETS's answer, right? Wrong. That was too easy, which means that 6 can't possibly be ETS's answer, and choice C can be eliminated. If finding ETS's answer were that simple, Joe Bloggs would have gotten this question right and it would have been an easy question, not a difficult one.

Will this fact help you eliminate any other choices? Yes, because you know that if you can divide the pizza into at least six pieces, neither five nor four could be the greatest number of pieces into which it can be divided. Six is a greater number than either five or four; if you can get six pieces you can also get five or four. You can thus eliminate choices A and B as well.

Now you've narrowed it down to two choices. Which will you pick? You shouldn't waste time trying to find the exact answer to a question like this. It isn't testing any mathematical principle, and you won't figure out the trick unless you get lucky. If you can't use another of our techniques to eliminate the remaining wrong answer, you should just guess and go on. Heads you win a dollar, tails you lose a quarter. (ETS's answer is D. Our third technique, incidentally, will enable you to zero in on it exactly. Keep reading.)

In case you're wondering, here's how ETS divides the figure:

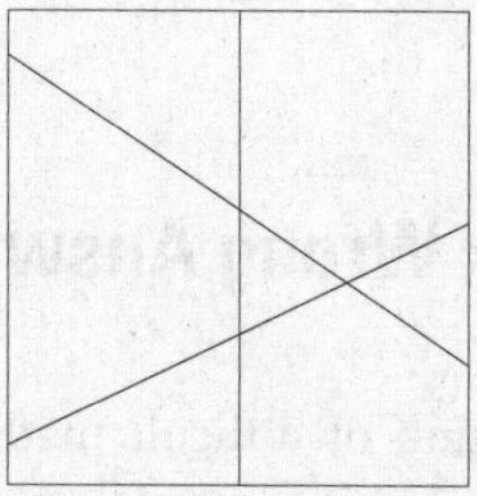

Discipline
When you actually take the SAT, you may find that you are irresistibly attracted to an "obvious" choice on a hard SAT math question. You'll look at the problem and see no other possible solution. If this happens, you may say to yourself, "Aha! I've found an exception to the Joe Bloggs rule!" Don't be tempted. Eliminate obvious answers.

Here's another example:

18. A 50-foot wire runs from the roof of a building to the top of a 10-foot pole 14 feet across the street. How much taller would the pole have to be if the street were 16 feet wider and the wire remained the same length?

(A) 2 feet
(B) 8 feet
(C) 14 feet
(D) 16 feet
(E) 18 feet

Here's How to Crack It

Which answer seems simple and obvious? Well, if the wire stays the same length, and the street is 16 feet wider, then it seems obvious that the pole would have to be 16 feet higher.

What does that mean? It means that we can eliminate choice D. If 16 feet were the correct answer, then Joe Bloggs would get this problem right and it would be an easy question, not one of the hardest in the section.

Choice C repeats a number from the problem, which means we can be certain that it's wrong too.

If you don't know how to do this problem, working on it further probably won't get you anywhere. You've eliminated two choices; guess if you need the question to reach your pacing goal and then move on. (ETS's answer is B. Use the Pythagorean theorem—see Chapter 14.)

Simple Operations = Wrong Answers on Hard Questions

Joe Bloggs doesn't usually think of difficult mathematical operations, so he is attracted to solutions that use very simple arithmetic. Therefore, any answer choice that is the result of simple arithmetic should be eliminated on hard SAT math questions.

Here's an example:

17. A dress is selling for $100 after a 20 percent discount. What was the original selling price?

(A) $200
(B) $125
(C) $120
(D) $80
(E) $75

Here's How to Crack It

When Joe Bloggs looks at this problem, he sees "20 percent less than $100" and is attracted to choice D. Therefore, you must eliminate it. If finding the answer were that easy, Joe Bloggs would have gotten it right. Joe is also attracted to choice C, which is 20 percent more than $100. Again, eliminate.

Temptation
Joe Bloggs attractors often obscure more sensible answer choices.

With two Joe Bloggs answers out of the way, you ought to be able to solve this problem quickly. The dress is on sale, which means that its original price must have been more than its current price. That means that ETS's answer has to be greater than $100. Two of the remaining choices, A and B, fulfill this requirement. Now you can ask yourself:

(A) Is $100 20 percent less than $200? No. Eliminate.
(B) Is $100 20 percent less than $125? Could be. This must be ETS's answer. (It is.)

Here's another example:

16. If 3 parallel lines are cut by 3 nonparallel lines, what is the maximum number of intersections possible?

(A) 9
(B) 10
(C) 11
(D) 12
(E) 13

Here's How to Crack It

The problem asks you for the *maximum,* or greatest number, so Joe will want to pick the biggest number. What is the maximum number among the choices? It is 13; therefore, you can eliminate choice E. By the *simple = wrong* rule that we just discussed, you can also eliminate choice A. Joe's preference for simple arithmetic makes him think that the answer to this problem can be found by multiplying 3 by 3. The simple operation leads quickly to an answer of 9, which must therefore be wrong.

ETS's answer is D. Here's how it's found:

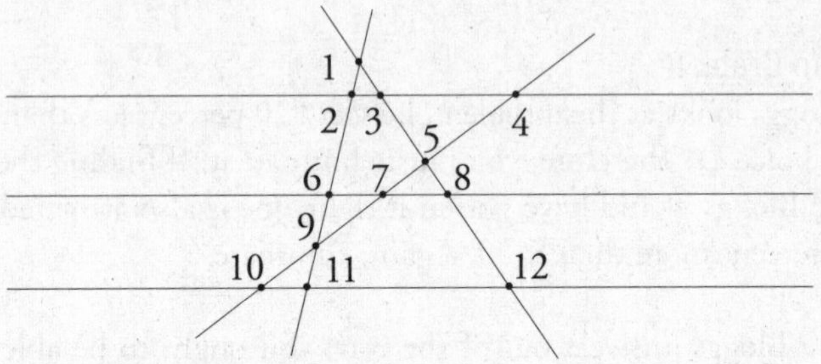

"It Cannot Be Determined"

Occasionally on the Math section, the fifth answer choice on a problem will be:

(E) It cannot be determined from the information given.

The Joe Bloggs principle makes these questions easy to crack. Why? Joe Bloggs can never determine the correct answer on difficult SAT problems. Therefore, when Joe sees this answer choice on a difficult problem, he is greatly attracted to it.

What Does This Mean?

It means that if "it cannot be determined" is offered as an answer choice on a difficult problem, it is usually wrong.

Here's an example:

19. If the average of x, y, and 80 is 6 more than the average of y, z, and 80, what is the value of $x - z$?

(A) 2
(B) 3
(C) 6
(D) 18
(E) It cannot be determined from the information given.

Here's How to Crack It

This problem is the next-to-last question in a section. It looks absolutely impossible to Joe. Therefore, he assumes that the problem must be impossible to solve. Of course, he's wrong. Eliminate choice E. If E were ETS's answer, Joe would be correct and this would be an easy problem.

Choice C simply repeats a number from the problem, so you can eliminate that choice also. Because you already eliminated two answer choices, the odds are in your favor if you need to guess.

ETS's answer is D. Don't worry about how to solve this problem right now. It's only important that you understand how to eliminate Joe Bloggs answers to get closer to ETS's answer. If you have to guess, that's okay. Besides, that was a hard question; you should be concentrating on answering all the easy and medium questions correctly.

Why Is This Choice Here?

The test writers include the "It cannot be determined from the information given" choice because they understand how the average test taker's mind works. When Joe Bloggs picks this choice on a hard question, he's thinking, "If I can't get it, no one can."

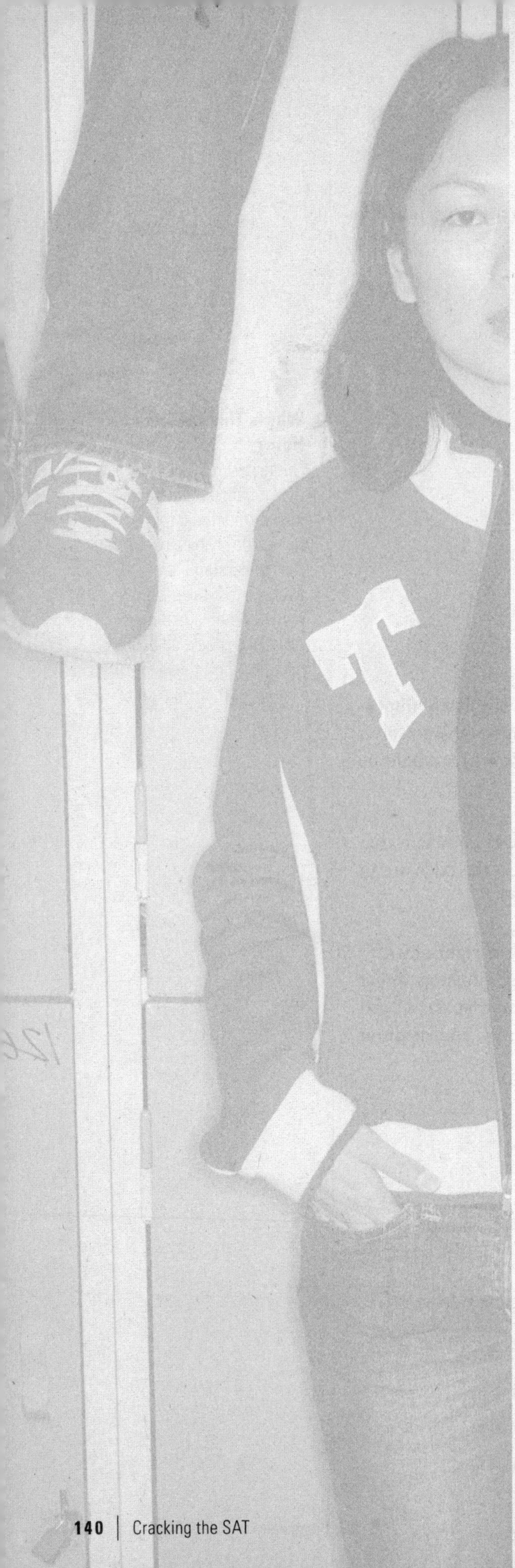

Summary

- Joe Bloggs gets the easy math questions right and the hard ones wrong.
- On difficult problems, Joe Bloggs is attracted to easy solutions arrived at with methods he understands. Therefore, you should eliminate obvious, simple answers on difficult questions.
- On difficult problems, Joe Bloggs is also attracted to answer choices that simply repeat numbers from the problem. Therefore, you should eliminate any such choices.
- On difficult problems that ask you to find the least or greatest number that fulfills certain conditions, you can eliminate the answer choice containing the least or greatest number.
- On difficult problems, you can almost always eliminate any answer choice that says, "It cannot be determined from the information given."
- The point of Joe Bloggs is not to get to ONE answer choice; it's to improve your odds when you must guess, and eliminate answer choices that could distract you or seem right if you made a careless error.

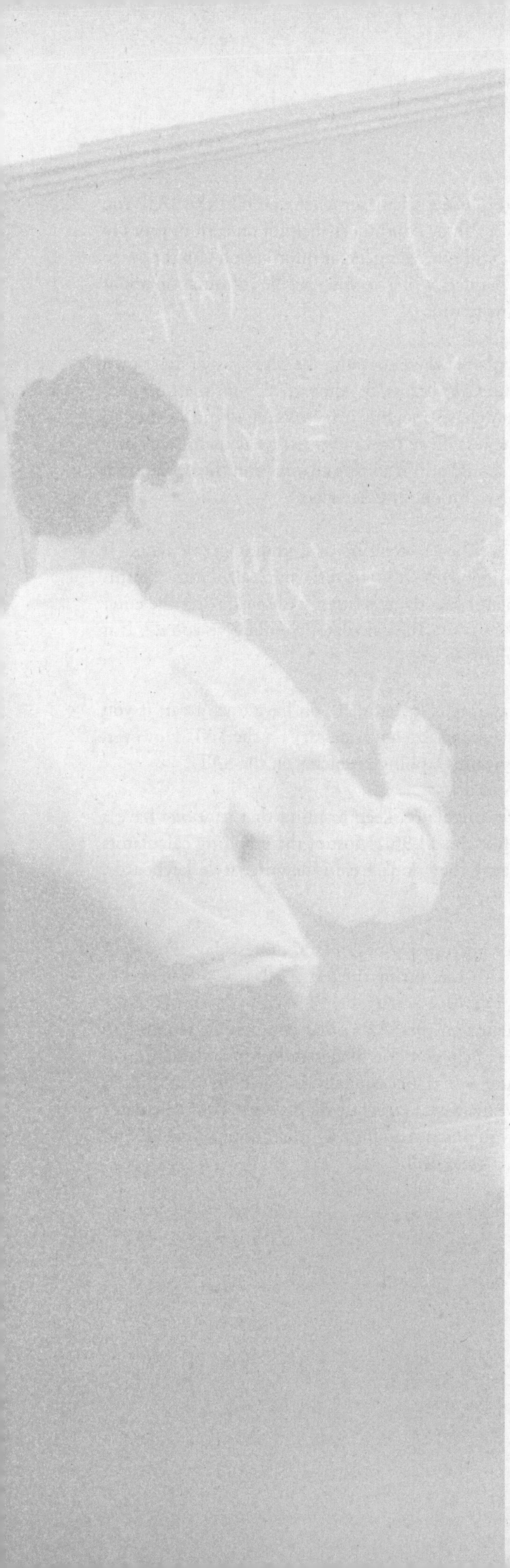

Chapter 10
The Calculator

A calculator is an important tool on the SAT. ETS states that the SAT contains no questions requiring you to use a calculator, but it also says that students are strongly encouraged to take a calculator. We agree; a calculator is a reliable tool to use and it is a good idea to have one for the Math sections of the SAT. This chapter will introduce some basic information about how and when to use your calculator most effectively on this test.

THE CALCULATOR

You are allowed (but not required) to use a calculator when you take the SAT. You should definitely do so. A calculator can be enormously helpful on certain types of SAT math problems. This chapter will give you general information about how to use your calculator. Other math chapters will give you specific information about using your calculator in particular situations.

Gee, ETS Must Really Like Me

Why else would it let you use a calculator? Well, friend, a calculator can be a crutch and an obstacle at times. ETS hopes that many test takers will waste time using their machines to add 3 + 4. When it comes to simple calculations, your brain and pencil are faster than the fastest calculator.

You'll need to take your own calculator when you take the SAT. If you don't own one now, you can buy one for around $15 or less, or you can ask your math teacher about borrowing one. If you do purchase one, buy it far enough ahead of time to practice with it before you take the test. Even if you now use a calculator regularly in your math class at school, you should still read this chapter and the other math chapters carefully and practice the techniques we describe.

Make sure that your calculator is either a scientific or a graphing calculator. It must perform the order of operations correctly. To test your calculator, try this problem. Type it in to your calculator exactly as written without hitting the enter or equals key until the end: $3 + 4 \times 6 =$. The calculator should give you 27. If it gives you 42, it's not a good calculator to use.

Many students already own a graphing calculator. If you have one, great; if you don't, don't sweat it. Graphing calculators are not necessary on the SAT. However, if you have one, it may simplify certain graphing problems on the SAT.

If you do decide to use a graphing calculator, keep in mind that it *cannot* have a QWERTY-style keyboard on it (like the TI-95). Most of the graphing calculators have typing capabilities, but because they don't have typewriter-style keyboards, they are perfectly legal.

Also, you *cannot* use the calculator on your phone. In fact, on test day, leave your phone at home; you can't have it with you during the test at all.

The only danger in using a calculator on the SAT is that you may be tempted to use it in situations in which it won't help you. Joe Bloggs thinks his calculator will solve all his difficulties with math. It won't. Occasionally, it may even cause him to miss a problem that he might have answered correctly on his own. Your calculator is only as smart as you are. But if you practice and use a little caution, you will find that your calculator will help you a great deal.

What a Calculator Is Good at Doing

Here is a complete list of what a calculator is good at on the SAT.

- Arithmetic
- Decimals
- Fractions
- Square roots
- Percentages
- Graphs (if it is a graphing calculator)

We'll discuss the calculator's role in most of these areas in the next few chapters.

Calculator Arithmetic

Adding, subtracting, multiplying, and dividing integers and decimals is easy on a calculator. You need to be careful only when you key in the numbers. A calculator will give you an incorrect answer to an arithmetic calculation only if you press the wrong keys. Here are two tips for avoiding mistakes on your calculator.

1. Check every number on the display as you key it in.
2. Press the *on/off* or *clear all* key after you finish each problem or after each separate step.

The main thing to remember about a calculator is that it can't help you find the answer to a question you don't understand. If you wouldn't know how to solve a particular problem using pencil and paper, you won't know how to solve it using a calculator either. Your calculator will help you, but it won't take the place of a solid understanding of basic SAT mathematics.

Calculators Don't Think
A calculator crunches numbers and often saves you a great deal of time and effort, but it is not a substitute for your problem-solving skills.

Use Your Paper First

Before you use your calculator, be sure to set up the problem or equation on paper; this will keep you from getting lost or confused. This is especially important when solving the problem involves a number of separate steps. The basic idea is to use the extra space in your test booklet to make a plan, and then use your calculator to execute it.

Working on scratch paper first will also give you a record of what you have done if you change your mind, run into trouble, or lose your place. If you suddenly find that you need to try a different approach to a problem, you may not have to go all the way back to the beginning. This will also make it easier for you to check your work, if you have time to do so.

Write Things Down
You paid for the test booklet; make the most of it. Keep track of your progress through each problem by writing down each step.

Don't use the memory function on your calculator (if it has one). Because you can use your test booklet as scratch paper, you don't need to juggle numbers within the calculator itself. Instead of storing the result of a calculation in the calculator, write it on your scratch paper, clear your calculator, and move to the next step of the problem. A calculator's memory is fleeting; scratch paper is forever.

Order of Operations

In Chapter 11, we will discuss the proper order of operations when solving equations in which several operations must be performed. Be sure you understand this information, because it applies to calculators as much as it does to pencil-and-paper computations. (We will teach you a mnemonic device that will enable you to remember this easily.) You must always perform calculations in the proper order.

Summary

- You should definitely use a calculator on the SAT.
- Take your own calculator when you take the test. You don't need a fancy one. Make sure your calculator doesn't beep or have a typewriter-style keyboard.
- Even if you already use a calculator regularly, you should still practice with it before the test.
- Be careful when you key in numbers on your calculator. Check each number on the display as you key it in. Clear your work after you finish each problem or after each separate step.
- A calculator can't help you find the answer to a question you don't understand. (It's only as smart as you are!) Be sure to use your calculator as a tool, not a crutch.
- Set up the problem or equation on paper first. By doing so, you will eliminate the possibility of getting lost or confused.
- Don't use the memory function on your calculator (if it has one). Scratch paper works better.
- Whether you are using your calculator or paper and a pencil, you must always perform calculations in the proper order.
- If your calculator runs on batteries, make sure it has fresh ones at test time! Change them a day or two before.

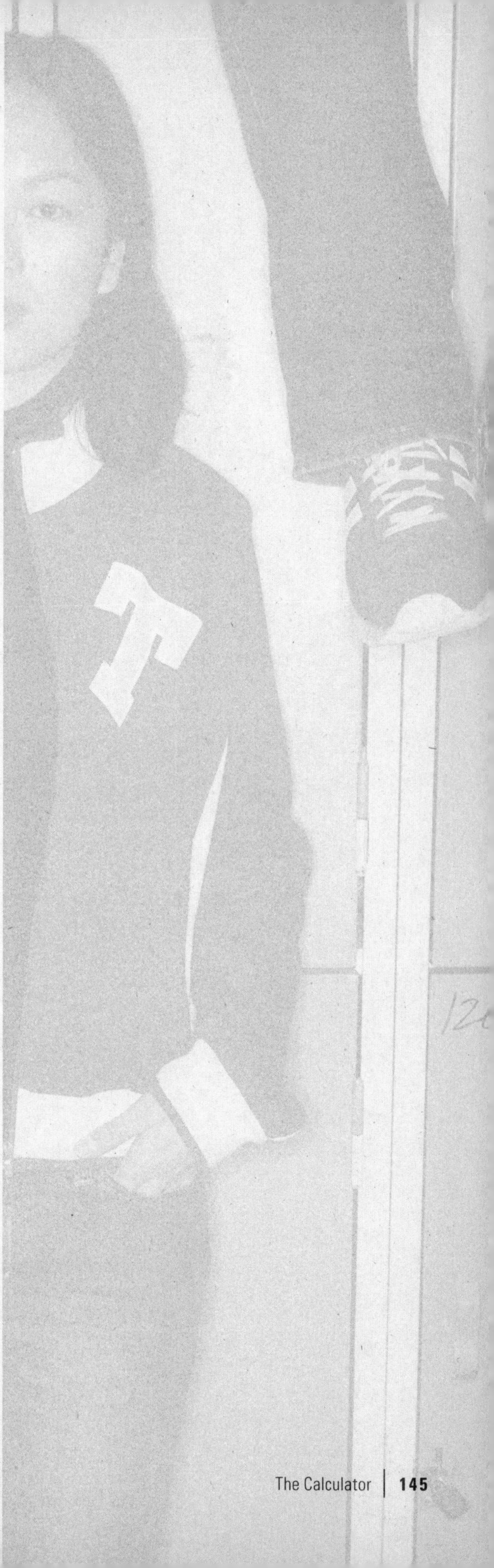

Chapter 11
Fun with Fundamentals

Although we'll show you which mathematical concepts are most important to know for the SAT, this book relies on your knowledge of basic math concepts. If you're a little rusty, this chapter is for you. Read on for a quick review of the math fundamentals you'll need to know before you continue.

THE BUILDING BLOCKS

As you go through this book you might discover that you're having trouble with stuff you thought you already knew—like fractions, or square roots. If this happens, it's probably a good idea to review the fundamentals. That's where this chapter comes in. Our drills and examples will refresh your memory if you've gotten rusty, but if you have serious difficulty with the following chapters, even after reviewing the material in this chapter, then you should consider getting extra help. For this purpose, we recommend our own *Math Workout for the SAT,* which is designed to give you a thorough review of all the fundamental math concepts that you'll need to know on the SAT. Always keep in mind that the math tested on the SAT is different from the math taught in school. If you want to raise your score, don't waste time studying math that ETS never tests.

Let's talk first about what you should expect to see on the test.

THE MATH BREAKDOWN

No Need to Know
Here are a few things that you *won't* need to know to answer SAT math questions: calculus, trigonometry, and the quadratic formula. Essentially, the SAT tests the math you learned in junior high and your first two years of high school.

Three of the nine scored sections on the SAT are Math sections. Two of the scored Math sections will last 25 minutes each; the third will last 20 minutes.

The math questions on your SAT will be drawn from the following four categories:

1. Arithmetic
2. Basic Algebra I and II
3. Geometry
4. Basic probability/statistics

The math questions on your SAT will appear in two different formats:

1. Regular multiple-choice questions
2. Grid-Ins

THE INSTRUCTIONS

Each of the three scored Math sections on your SAT will begin with the same set of instructions. We've reprinted these instructions, just as they appear on the SAT, in the Math sections of the practice tests in this book. These instructions include a few formulas and other information that you may need to know in order to answer some of the questions. You should learn these instructions ahead of time so you don't have to waste valuable time referring to them during the test.

Still, if you do suddenly blank out on one of the formulas while taking the test, you can always refresh your memory by glancing back at the instructions. Be sure to familiarize yourself with them thoroughly ahead of time, so you'll know which formulas are there.

BASIC PRINCIPLES OF SAT NUMBERS

Before moving on, you should be certain that you are familiar with some basic terms and concepts that you'll need to know for the math sections of the SAT. This material isn't at all difficult, but you must know it cold. If you don't, you'll waste valuable time on the test and lose points that you easily could have earned.

Positive and Negative

There are three rules regarding the multiplication of positive and negative numbers.

1. positive × positive = positive
2. negative × negative = positive
3. positive × negative = negative

Integers

Integers are the numbers that most of us are accustomed to thinking of simply as "numbers." Integers are numbers that have no fractional or decimal part. They can be either positive or negative. The positive integers are:

1, 2, 3, 4, 5, 6, 7, and so on

The negative integers are:

–1, –2, –3, –4, –5, –6, –7, and so on

Zero (0) is also an integer, but it is neither positive nor negative.

Note that positive integers get bigger as they move away from 0, while negative integers get smaller. In other words, 2 is bigger than 1, but –2 is smaller than –1. This number line should give you a clear idea of how negative numbers work.

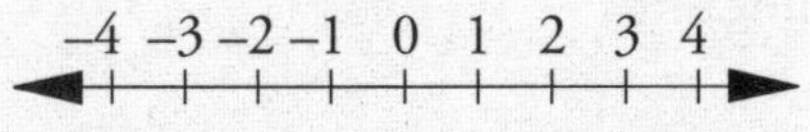

You should also remember the types of numbers that are *not* integers. Here are some examples:

$$-2.7, .625, 15.898, -9.8, \frac{2}{13}, -\frac{3}{4}$$

Basically, integers are numbers that have *no* fractions or decimals. So if you see a number with a fraction or non-zero decimal, it's *not* an integer.

Negative Land

Think of integers as steps on a staircase leading up from the cellar (the negatives), through a doorway (zero), and above the ground (the positives). Five steps down (–5) is farther below ground than four steps down (–4) because you're one step farther away from the cellar door (0). Integers are like stairs, because when climbing stairs, you can't use a fraction of a step.

Odd and Even

Even numbers are integers that can be divided by 2 leaving no remainder. Here are some examples of even numbers:

–4, –2, 0, 2, 4, 6, 8, 10, and so on

You can always tell at a glance whether a number is even: It is even if its final digit is even (divisible by 2). Thus 999,999,999,994 is an even number because 4, the final digit, is an even number.

Odd numbers are integers that have a remainder when divided by 2. Here are some examples of odd numbers:

–5, –3, –1, 1, 3, 5, 7, 9, and so on

You can always tell at a glance whether a number is odd: It is odd if its final digit is odd. Thus, 444,444,444,449 is an odd number because 9, the final digit, is an odd number.

Several rules always hold true with odd and even numbers:

even + even = even   even × even = even

odd + odd = even   odd × odd = odd

even + odd = odd   even × odd = even

Pick a Number, Any Number...

If you aren't sure about one of these rules, it's safer to try an example than guess. Say you need to know what kind of number you get when you add an odd number and an even number to solve a problem but you can't remember the rule. Just try an example like 2 + 5 = 7 and you'll know that even + odd = odd.

Distinct Numbers

You might see problems on the SAT that mention "distinct numbers." Don't let this throw you. All ETS means by distinct numbers is different numbers. For example, the set of numbers 2, 3, 4, and 5 is a set of distinct numbers, whereas 2, 2, 3, and 4 would not be a set of distinct numbers because 2 appears twice. Easy concept, tricky wording.

Digits

There are ten digits:

0, 1, 2, 3, 4, 5, 6, 7, 8, 9

All integers are made up of digits. In the integer 3,476, the digits are 3, 4, 7, and 6. Digits are to numbers as letters are to words.

The integer 645 is called a "three-digit number" for obvious reasons. Each of its digits has a different name depending on its place in the number:

5 is called the *units* digit.
4 is called the *tens* digit.
6 is called the *hundreds* digit.

But what if we didn't use an integer? If we had a number such as 645.32, which contains decimal places, we would know that it's a little bit bigger than 645. Each decimal place tells us how much bigger.

3 is called the *tenths* digit.
2 is called the *hundredths* digit.

Thus the value of any number depends on which digits are in which places. The number 645.32 could be rewritten as follows:

6	×	100	=	600
+ 4	×	10	= +	40
+ 5	×	1	= +	5
+ 3	×	0.1	= +	.3
+ 2	×	0.01	= +	.02
				645. 32

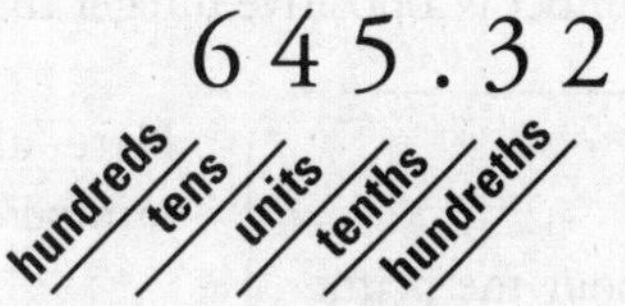

Factors

The factors of an integer are all of the integers that divide into it evenly. For example, the factors of 30 are 1, 2, 3, 5, 6, 10, 15, and 30.

Which Is Which?
The largest *factor* of a number is *that number*.

The smallest *multiple* of a number is *that number*.

Multiples

A multiple of a number is any product of an integer and the given number. For example, 10, 20, 50, 180, and 370 are all multiples of 10. Make sure you know the difference between a factor and a multiple.

Remainders

If an integer cannot be divided evenly by another number, the integer left over at the end of the division is called the remainder. Decimals cannot be remainders.

The best way to figure out a remainder is to actually do the long division. For example, if you want to find the remainder when 25 is divided by 3, set up and start solving a long division problem. Here's what it would look like:

Leftovers
Be careful when figuring remainders on your calculator. On your calculator, 25 divided by 3 is 8.3333333, but .3333333 is not the remainder. The remainder is 1, or .33333333 of 3. So do the long division instead!

$$\begin{array}{r} 8 \\ 3\overline{)\ 25} \\ -\underline{24} \\ 1 \end{array}$$

The 1 that is left over after you subtract the 24 is the remainder.

Consecutive Integers

Consecutive integers are integers listed in increasing order of size without any integers missing in between. For example, –1, 0, 1, 2, 3, 4, and 5 are consecutive integers; 2, 4, 5, 7, and 8 are not. Nor are –1, –2, –3, and –4 consecutive integers, because they are decreasing in size.

Prime Numbers

A prime number is a positive integer that is divisible only by itself and by 1.

Here are a few important facts about prime numbers:

- 0 and 1 are not prime numbers.
- 2 is the smallest prime number.
- 2 is the only even prime number.
- Not all odd numbers are prime: 1, 9, 15, 21, and many others are *not* prime.

> The Prime Directive
>
> The SAT frequently asks questions about the prime numbers smaller than 30, so make sure you have these memorized: **2, 3, 5, 7, 11, 13, 17, 19, 23,** and **29.**
>
> Also, notice that 1 is not prime? There will often be a trap answer choice on SAT questions that assumes that you think that 1 is a prime number. So remember: 1 is NOT prime.

Standard Symbols

The following standard symbols are used frequently on the SAT:

SYMBOL	MEANING
$=$	is equal to
$\neq$	is not equal to
$<$	is less than
$>$	is greater than
$\leq$	is less than or equal to
$\geq$	is greater than or equal to

THERE ARE ONLY SIX OPERATIONS

There are only six arithmetic operations that you will ever need to perform on the SAT:

1. Addition ($3 + 3$)
2. Subtraction ($3 - 3$)
3. Multiplication (3×3 or $3 \cdot 3$)
4. Division ($3 \div 3$)
5. Raising to a power (3^3)
6. Finding a square root ($\sqrt{3}$)

If you're like most students, you probably haven't paid much serious attention to these topics since junior high school. You'll need to learn about them again if you want to do well on the SAT. By the time you take the test, using them should be automatic. All the arithmetic concepts are fairly basic, but you'll have to know them cold. You'll also have to know when and how to use your calculator, which will be quite helpful.

In this chapter, we'll deal with each of these six topics.

What Do You Get?

You should know the following arithmetic terms:

- The result of addition is a *sum* or *total.*
- The result of subtraction is a *difference.*
- The result of multiplication is a *product.*
- The result of division is a *quotient.*
- In the expression 5^2, the 2 is called an *exponent.*

The Six Operations Must Be Performed in the Proper Order

Do It Yourself
Some calculators automatically take order of operations into account, and some don't. Either way, you can very easily go wrong if you are in the habit of punching in long lines of arithmetic operations. The safe, smart way is to clear the calculator after every individual operation, performing PEMDAS yourself.

Whichever Comes First
Addition and subtraction are interchangeable in the order of operations. Solve whichever operation comes first, reading left to right. The same is true of multiplication and division. And remember: If you don't solve in order from left to right, you could end up with the wrong answer!
Example:
$24 \div 4 \times 6 = 24 \div 24 = 1$
wrong
$24 \div 4 \times 6 = 6 \times 6 = 36$
right

Very often, solving an equation on the SAT will require you to perform several different operations, one after another. These operations must be performed in the proper order. In general, the problems are written in such a way that you won't have trouble deciding what comes first. In cases in which you are uncertain, you need to remember only the following sentence:

Please Excuse My Dear Aunt Sally;
she limps from *left* to *right.*

That's PEMDAS, for short. It stands for Parentheses, Exponents, Multiplication, Division, Addition, and Subtraction. First, you clear the parentheses; then you take care of the exponents; then you perform all multiplication and division at the same time, from *left* to *right,* followed by addition and subtraction, from *left* to *right.*

The following drill will help you learn the order in which to perform the six operations. First, set up the equations on paper. Then, use your calculator for the arithmetic. Make sure you perform the operations in the correct order.

DRILL 1

Solve each of the following problems by performing the indicated operations in the proper order. Answers can be found on page 376.

1. $107 + (109 - 107) =$ ____________

2. $(7 \times 5) + 3 =$ ____________

3. $6 - 3\,(6 - 3) =$ ____________

4. $2 \times [7 - (6 \div 3)] =$ ____________

5. $10 - (9 - 8 - 6) =$ ____________

Parentheses Can Help You Solve Equations

Using parentheses to regroup information in SAT arithmetic problems can be very helpful. In order to do this, you need to understand a basic law that you have probably forgotten since the days when you last took arithmetic—*the distributive law*. You don't need to remember the name of the law, but you do need to know how it works.

The Distributive Law

If you're multiplying the sum of two numbers by a third number, you can multiply each number in your sum individually. This comes in handy when you have to multiply the sum of two variables.

If a problem gives you information in "factored form"—$a\,(b + c)$—then you should distribute the first variable before you do anything else. If you are given information that has already been distributed—$(ab + ac)$—then you should factor out the common term, putting the information back in factored form. Very often on the SAT, simply doing this will enable you to spot ETS's answer.

For example:

Distributive: $6(53) + 6(47) = 6(53 + 47) = 6(100) = 600$

Multiplication first: $6(53) + 6(47) = 318 + 282 = 600$

You get the same answer each way, so why get involved with ugly arithmetic? If you use the distributive law for this problem, you don't even need to use your calculator.

The drill on the following page illustrates the distributive law.

DRILL 2

Rewrite each problem by either distributing or factoring, whichever is called for, then solve. Questions 3, 4, and 5 have no numbers in them; therefore, they can't be solved with a calculator. Answers can be found on page 376.

1. $(6 \times 57) + (6 \times 13) =$ ____________
2. $51(48) + 51(50) + 51(52) =$ ________
3. $a(b + c - d) =$ ____________
4. $xy - xz =$ ____________
5. $abc + xyc =$ ____________

Fractions and Your Calculator

You can also use your calculator to solve fraction problems. When you do, ALWAYS put each of your fractions in a set of parentheses. This will insure that your calculator knows that they are fractions. Otherwise, the order of operations will get confused. On a scientific calculator, you can write the fraction in two different ways:

> You will have a fraction key, which looks similar to "$a\,{}^{b}\!/_{c}$." If you wanted to write $\frac{5}{6}$, you'd type "5 $a\,{}^{b}\!/_{c}$ 6"
>
> You can also use the division key, because a fraction bar is the same as "divided by." Be aware that your answer will be a decimal for this second way, so we recommend the first.

On a graphing calculator, you'll use the division bar to create fractions. Keep in mind that, whatever calculator you are using, you can always turn your fractions into decimals before you perform calculations with them. Just be aware that the answer won't always be exact.

FRACTIONS

A Fraction Is Just Another Way of Expressing Division

The expression $\frac{x}{y}$ is exactly the same thing as $x \div y$. The expression $\frac{1}{2}$ means nothing more than $1 \div 2$. In the fraction $\frac{x}{y}$, x is known as the numerator (hereafter referred to as "the top") and y is known as the denominator (hereafter referred to as "the bottom").

Adding and Subtracting Fractions with the Same Bottom

To add two or more fractions that all have the same bottom, simply add up the tops and put the sum over the common bottom. For example:

$$\frac{1}{100}+\frac{4}{100}=\frac{1+4}{100}=\frac{5}{100}$$

Subtraction works exactly the same way:

$$\frac{4}{100} - \frac{1}{100} = \frac{4-1}{100} = \frac{3}{100}$$

Adding and Subtracting Fractions with Different Bottoms

In school you were taught to add and subtract fractions with different bottoms, or denominators, by finding a common bottom. To do this, you have to multiply each fraction by a number that makes all the bottoms the same. Most students find this process annoying.

Fortunately, we have an approach to adding and subtracting fractions with different bottoms that simplifies the entire process. Use the example below as a model. Just multiply in the direction of each arrow, and then either add or subtract across the top. Lastly, multiply across the bottom.

$$\frac{1}{3} + \frac{1}{2} =$$

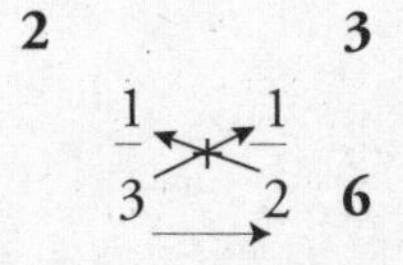

$$\frac{2+3}{6} = \frac{5}{6}$$

We call this procedure the *Bowtie* because the arrows make it look like a bowtie. Use the Bowtie to add or subtract any pair of fractions without thinking about the common bottom, just by following the steps above.

> **Calculating Fractions**
>
> Let's say you wanted to find $\frac{1}{3} + \frac{1}{2} =$ using your calculator. For a scientific calculator, you'd type in "(1 $a^b\!/_c$ 3) + (1 $a^b\!/_c$ 2) =" The answer will come up looking like something similar to 5⌋6, which means 5/6. On a graphing calculator, you'd type in (1/3) + (1/2) [ENTER]. This gives you the repeating decimal .833333. Now hit the [MATH] button and hit the [>FRAC] button and press [ENTER]. The calculator will now show "5/6." The shortcut to turn a decimal into a fraction on a TI-80 series graphic calculator is [MATH][ENTER][ENTER]. Remember those parentheses for all fraction calculations!

Multiplying All Fractions

Multiplying fractions is easy. Just multiply across the top, then multiply across the bottom.

Here's an example:

$$\frac{4}{5} \times \frac{5}{6} = \frac{20}{30}$$

When you multiply fractions, all you are really doing is performing one multiplication problem on top of another.

You should never multiply two fractions before looking to see if you can reduce either or both. If you reduce first, your final answer will be in the form for which ETS is looking. Here's another way to express this rule: Simplify before you multiply.

$$\frac{63}{6} \times \frac{48}{7} = \frac{\overset{9}{\cancel{63}}}{6} \times \frac{48}{\underset{1}{\cancel{7}}} = \frac{\overset{9}{\cancel{63}}}{\underset{1}{\cancel{6}}} \times \frac{\overset{8}{\cancel{48}}}{\underset{1}{\cancel{7}}} =$$

$$\frac{9}{1} \times \frac{8}{1}$$

$$\frac{72}{1} = 72$$

Dividing All Fractions

Just Do It
When dividing (don't ask why) just flip the last one and multiply.

To divide one fraction by another, flip over (or invert) the second fraction and multiply. Doing this is extremely easy, as long as you remember how it works.

Here's an example:

$$\frac{2}{3} \div \frac{4}{3} =$$

$$\frac{2}{3} \times \frac{3}{4} = \frac{6}{12} = \frac{1}{2}$$

Be careful not to cancel or reduce until after you flip the second fraction. You can even do the same thing with fractions whose tops and/or bottoms are fractions. These problems look quite frightening but they're actually easy if you keep your cool.

Here's an example:

$$\frac{4}{\frac{4}{3}} =$$

$$\frac{4}{1} \div \frac{4}{3} =$$

$$\frac{4}{1} \times \frac{3}{4} =$$

$$\frac{\cancel{4}}{1} \times \frac{3}{\cancel{4}} =$$

$$\frac{3}{1} = 3$$

Reducing Fractions

When you add or multiply fractions, you will very often end up with a big fraction that is hard to work with. You can almost always reduce such a fraction into one that is easier to handle.

To reduce a fraction, divide both the top and the bottom by the largest number that is a factor of both. For example, to reduce $\frac{12}{60}$, divide both the top and the bottom by 12, which is the largest number that is a factor of both. Dividing 12 by 12 yields 1; dividing 60 by 12 yields 5. The reduced fraction is $\frac{1}{5}$.

If you can't immediately find the largest number that is a factor of both, find any number that is a factor of both and divide both the top and bottom by that. Your calculations will take a little longer, but you'll end up in the same place. In the previous example, even if you don't see that 12 is a factor of both 12 and 60, you can no doubt see that 6 is a factor of both. Dividing top and bottom by 6 yields $\frac{2}{10}$. Now divide by 2. Doing so yields $\frac{1}{5}$. Once again, you have arrived at ETS's answer.

Start Small
It is not easy to see that 26 and 286 have a common factor of 13, but it's pretty clear that they're both divisible by 2. So start from there.

Fast Reduction
If you are calculator savvy, reducing fractions will be a breeze. To reduce fractions in your scientific calculator, just type in the fraction and hit the equals key. If you are using a graphing calculator, type in the fraction, find the [>FRAC] function, and hit enter.

Converting Mixed Numbers to Fractions

A mixed number is a number such as $2\frac{3}{4}$. It is the sum of an integer and a fraction. When you see mixed numbers on the SAT, you should usually convert them to ordinary fractions.

Here's a quick and easy way to convert mixed numbers.

- Multiply the integer by the bottom of the fraction.
- Add this product to the top of the fraction.
- Place this sum over the bottom of the fraction.

For example, let's convert $2\frac{3}{4}$ to a fraction. Multiply 2 (the integer part of the mixed number) by 4 (the bottom of the fraction). That gives you 8. Add that to the 3 (the top of the fraction) to get 11. Place 11 over 4 to get $\frac{11}{4}$.

The mixed number $2\frac{3}{4}$ is exactly the same as the fraction $\frac{11}{4}$. We converted the mixed number to a fraction because fractions are easier to work with than mixed numbers.

DRILL 3

Try converting the following mixed numbers. Answers can be found on page 376.

1. $8\frac{1}{3}$

2. $2\frac{3}{7}$

3. $5\frac{4}{9}$

4. $2\frac{1}{2}$

5. $6\frac{2}{3}$

Just Don't Mix

For some reason, ETS thinks it's okay to give you mixed numbers as answer choices. On grid-ins, however, if you use a mixed number, ETS won't give you credit. You can see why. In your grid-in box $3\frac{1}{4}$ will be gridded in as 3 1 / 4, which looks like $\frac{31}{4}$; not the answer you thought you were using, was it?

Fractions Behave in Peculiar Ways

Joe Bloggs has trouble with fractions because they don't always behave the way he thinks they ought to. For example, because 4 is obviously greater than 2, Joe Bloggs sometimes forgets that $\frac{1}{4}$ is less than $\frac{1}{2}$. He becomes especially confused when the top is some number other than 1. For example, $\frac{2}{6}$ is less than $\frac{2}{5}$.

Joe also has a hard time understanding that when you multiply one fraction by another, you will get a fraction that is smaller than either of the first two. For example:

$$\frac{1}{2} \times \frac{1}{4} = \frac{1}{8}$$

$$\frac{1}{8} < \frac{1}{2}$$

$$\frac{1}{8} < \frac{1}{4}$$

A Final Word About Fractions and Calculators

Throughout this section we've given you some hints about your calculator and fractions. While you should understand how to work with fractions the old-fashioned way, your calculator can be a tremendous help if you know how to use it properly. Make sure that you practice with your calculator so that working with fractions on it becomes second nature before the test.

DRILL 4

Work these problems with the techniques you've read about in this chapter so far. Then check your answers by solving them with your calculator. If you have any problems, go back and review the information just outlined. Answers can be found on page 377.

1. Reduce $\frac{18}{6}$. ____________________

2. Convert $6\frac{1}{5}$ to a fraction. ____________________

3. $2\frac{1}{3} - 3\frac{3}{5} =$ ____________________

4. $\frac{5}{18} \times \frac{6}{25} =$ ____________________

5. $\frac{3}{4} \div \frac{7}{8} =$ ____________________

6. $\dfrac{\frac{2}{5}}{5} =$ ____________________

7. $\dfrac{\frac{1}{3}}{\frac{3}{4}} =$ ____________________

DECIMALS

A Decimal Is Just Another Way of Expressing a Fraction

Fractions can be expressed as decimals. To find a fraction's decimal equivalent, simply divide the top by the bottom. (You can do this easily with your calculator.) For example:

$$\frac{3}{5} =$$

$$3 \div 5 = 0.6$$

Adding, Subtracting, Multiplying, and Dividing Decimals

Manipulating decimals is easy with a calculator. Simply punch in the numbers—being especially careful to get the decimal point in the right place every single time—and read the result from the display. A calculator makes these operations easy. In fact, working with decimals is one area on the SAT where your calculator will prevent you from making careless errors. You won't have to line up decimal points or remember what happens when you divide. The calculator will keep track of everything for you, as long as you punch in the correct numbers to begin with. Just be sure to practice carefully before you go to the test center.

DRILL 5

Answers can be found on page 377.

1. $0.43 \times 0.87 =$ ____________________

2. $\frac{43 + 0.731}{0.03} =$ ____________________

3. $3.72 \div 0.02 =$ ____________________

4. $0.71 - 3.6 =$ ____________________

Place Value
Compare decimals place by place, going from left to right.

Comparing Decimals

Some SAT problems will ask you to determine whether one decimal is larger or smaller than another. Many students have trouble doing this. It isn't difficult, though, and you will do fine as long as you remember to line up the decimal points and fill in missing zeros.

Here's an example:

> **Problem:** Which is larger, 0.0099 or 0.01?
> **Solution:** Simply place one decimal over the other with the decimal points lined up, like this:
>
> 0.0099
> 0.01

To make the solution seem clearer, you can add two zeros to the right of 0.01. (You can always add zeros to the right of a decimal without changing its value.) Now you have this:

> 0.0099
> 0.0100

Which decimal is larger? Clearly, 0.0100 is, just as 100 is larger than 99. (Remember that $0.0099 = \frac{99}{10{,}000}$, while $0.0100 = \frac{100}{10{,}000}$. Now the answer seems obvious, doesn't it?)

Analysis

Joe Bloggs has a terrible time on this problem. Because 99 is obviously larger than 1, he tends to think that 0.0099 must be larger than 0.01. But it isn't. Don't get sloppy on problems like this! ETS loves to trip up Joe Bloggs with decimals. In fact, any time you encounter a problem involving the comparison of decimals, you should stop and ask yourself whether you are about to make a Joe Bloggs mistake.

EXPONENTS AND SQUARE ROOTS

Exponents Are a Kind of Shorthand

Many numbers are the product of the same factor multiplied over and over again. For example, $32 = 2 \times 2 \times 2 \times 2 \times 2$. Another way to write this would be $32 = 2^5$, or "thirty-two equals two to the fifth power." The little number, or *exponent,* denotes the number of times that 2 is to be used as a factor. In the same way, $10^3 = 10 \times 10 \times 10$, or 1,000, or "ten to the third power," or "ten cubed." In this example, the 10 is called the *base* and the 3 is called the *exponent.* (You won't need to know these terms on the SAT, but you will need to know them to follow our explanations.)

Exponents and Your Calculator

Raising a number to a power is shown in two different ways on your calculator, depending on the type of calculator you have. A scientific calculator will use the y^x button. You'll have to type in your base number first, then hit the y^x key, then type the exponent. So 4^3 will be typed in as "4 y^x 3 =" and you'll get 64. If you have a calculator from the TI-80 series, your button will be a ^ sign. You'll enter the same problem as "4^3 [ENTER]." Think of these two keys as the "to the" button, because you say "4 to the 3rd power."

Multiplying Numbers with Exponents

When you multiply two numbers with the same base, you simply add the exponents. For example, $2^3 \times 2^5 = 2^{3+5} = 2^8$.

Warning

The rules for multiplying and dividing exponents do not apply to addition or subtraction:

$2^2 + 2^3 = 12$

$(2 \times 2) + (2 \times 2 \times 2) = 12$

It does not equal 2^5 or 32.

Dividing Numbers with Exponents

When you divide two numbers with the same base, you simply subtract the exponents. For example, $\frac{2^5}{2^3} = 2^{5-3} = 2^2$.

Raising a Power to a Power

When you raise a power to a power, you multiply the exponents. For example, $(2^3)^4 = 2^{3 \times 4} = 2^{12}$

Warning

Parentheses are very important with exponents, because you must remember to distribute powers to everything within them. For example: $(3x)^2 = 9x^2$, not $3x^2$. Similarly, $\left(\frac{3}{2}\right)^2 = \frac{3^2}{2^2}$, not $\frac{9}{2}$. But the distribution rule applies only when you multiply or divide. $(x + y)^2 = x^2 + 2xy + y^2$, not $x^2 + y^2$.

MADSPM

To remember the exponent rules, all you need to do is remember the acronym MADSPM. Here's what it stands for:

- Multiply → Add
- Divide → Subtract
- Power → Multiply

Whenever you see an exponent problem, you should think MADSPM. The three MADSPM rules are the only rules that apply to exponents.

Here's a typical ETS exponent problem:

14. For the equations $\frac{a^x}{a^y} = a^{10}$ and $(a^y)^3 = a^x$, if $a > 1$, what is the value of x ?

(A) 5
(B) 10
(C) 15
(D) 20
(E) 25

Here's How to Crack It

This problem looks pretty intimidating with all those variables. In fact, you might be about to cry "POOD" and go on to the next problem. That might not be a bad idea but before you skip the question, pull out those MADSPM rules.

For the first equation, you can use the Divide-Subtract rule: $\frac{a^x}{a^y} = a^{x-y} = a^{10}$. In other words, the first equation tells you that $x - y = 10$.

For the second equation, you can use the Power-Multiply rule: $\left(a^y\right)^3 = a^{3y} = a^x$. So, that means that $3y = x$.

Now, it's time to substitute: $x - y = 3y - y = 10$. So, $2y = 10$ and $y = 5$. Be careful, though! Don't choose answer A. That's the value of y but the question wants to know the value of x. Since $x = 3y$, $x = 3(5) = 15$, which is answer C.

Don't forget that you could also do this question by plugging in the answer choices. Of course, you still need to know the MADSPM rules to do the question that way.

Calculator Exponents

You can compute simple exponents on your calculator. Make sure you have a scientific calculator with a y^x key. To find 2^{10}, for example, simply use your y^x key, punching 2 in for the y value and 10 in for the x value. This may be especially useful if you are asked to compare exponents.

The Peculiar Behavior of Exponents

Raising a number to a power can have quite peculiar and unexpected results, depending on what sort of number you start out with. Here are some examples.

- If you square or cube a number greater than 1, it becomes larger. For example, $2^3 = 8$.
- If you square or cube a positive fraction smaller than one, it becomes smaller.

  For example, $\left(\frac{1}{2}\right)^3 = \frac{1}{8}$.
- A negative number raised to an even power becomes positive. For example, $(-2)^2 = 4$.
- A negative number raised to an odd power remains negative. For example, $(-2)^3 = -8$.

You should also have a feel for relative sizes of exponential numbers without calculating them. For example, 2^{10} is much larger than 10^2. ($2^{10} = 1{,}024$; $10^2 = 100$.) To take another example, 2^5 is twice as large as 2^4, even though 5 seems only a bit larger than 4.

See the Trap

ETS is hoping that you won't know these strange facts about exponents, so the test writers will throw them in as trap answers. Knowing the peculiar behavior of exponents will help you avoid these tricky pitfalls in a question.

Square Roots

The radical sign ($\sqrt{\ }$) indicates the square root of a number. For example, $\sqrt{25} = 5$. Note that square roots cannot be negative. If ETS wants you to think about a negative solution they'll say $x^2 = 25$ because then $x = 5$ or $x = -5$.

The Only Rules You Need to Know

Here are the only rules regarding square roots that you need to know for the SAT:

1. $\sqrt{x}\sqrt{y} = \sqrt{xy}$. For example, $\sqrt{3}\sqrt{12} = \sqrt{36} = 6$.
2. $\sqrt{\frac{x}{y}} = \frac{\sqrt{x}}{\sqrt{y}}$. For example, $\sqrt{\frac{5}{4}} = \frac{\sqrt{5}}{\sqrt{4}} = \frac{\sqrt{5}}{2}$.
3. $\sqrt{x}$ = positive root only. For example, $\sqrt{16} = 4$.

Note that rule 1 works in reverse: $\sqrt{50} = \sqrt{25} \times \sqrt{2} = 5\sqrt{2}$. This is really a kind of factoring. You are using rule 1 to factor a large, clumsy radical into numbers that are easier to work with. And remember that radicals are just fractional exponents, so the same rules of distribution apply.

Roots and Your Calculator

The other important key is the root key. On a scientific calculator it is often the same button as y^x but you'll have to hit shift first. The symbol is $\sqrt[x]{y}$. So "the 4th root of 81" would be "81 $\sqrt[x]{y}$ 4 = ." Sometimes the calculator will have y^x or $\sqrt[x]{y}$ as x^y or $\sqrt[y]{x}$. They mean the same thing. Just know which number you're supposed to type in first.

The root key in the TI-80 graphing calculator series varies, but the most common symbol is the square root sign, which you can get to by pressing "[SHIFT] x^2." In case you want to find the 3rd, 4th, or other root of a number, there is a button in the [MATH] directory for $\sqrt[3]{\ }$ or $\sqrt[x]{\ }$. In the case of the $\sqrt[x]{\ }$, you have to type in the root you want, then hit [MATH] and $\sqrt[x]{\ }$, and finally hit your base number. For example, if you wanted to find the 4th root of 81, you'd type "4 [MATH]," then select $\sqrt[x]{\ }$, then type 81 and press [ENTER]. If you look at it on the screen, it will appear as "4 $\sqrt[x]{\ }$ 81," which is similar to how you'd write it. You can also use the ^ symbol if you remember that a root is the same as the bottom part of a fractional exponent. We'll go over this in more detail in the fractions section.

Careless Errors

Don't make careless mistakes. Remember that the square root of a number between 0 and 1 is *larger* than the original number. For example, $\sqrt{\frac{1}{4}} = \frac{1}{2}$, and $\frac{1}{2} > \frac{1}{4}$.

Negative and Fractional Exponents

So far we've dealt with only positive integers for exponents, but they can be negative integers as well as fractions. The same concepts and rules apply, but the numbers just look a little weirder. Keep these concepts in mind:

- Negative exponents are a fancy way of writing reciprocals:

$$x^{-n} = \frac{1}{x^n}$$

- Fractional exponents are a fancy way of taking roots and powers:

$$x^{\frac{y}{z}} = \sqrt[z]{x^y}$$

Here's an example:

18. If $x > 0$, which of the following is equivalent to $\sqrt{x^3}$?

I. $x + x^{\frac{1}{2}}$

II. $\left(x^{\frac{1}{2}}\right)^3$

III. $\left(x^2\right)\left(x^{-\frac{1}{2}}\right)$

(A) None
(B) I and II only
(C) I and III only
(D) II and III only
(E) I, II and III

Here's How to Crack It

This problem really tests your knowledge of exponents. First, convert $\sqrt{x^3}$ into an exponent since all the roman numerals contain expressions with exponents. (Plus, exponents are easier to work with because they have those nice MADSPM rules.) So, using the definition of a fractional exponent, $\sqrt{x^3} = x^{\frac{3}{2}}$. You want the items in the roman numerals to equal $x^{\frac{3}{2}}$.

Now, it's time to start working with the roman numerals. For roman numeral I, ETS is trying to be tricky. (There's a surprise.) There's no exponent rule for adding exponent expressions with like bases. So, $x + x^{\frac{1}{2}} \neq x^{\frac{3}{2}}$. (If you were uncertain, you could try a number for x. If $x = 4$, then $\sqrt{4^3} = 8$ but $4 + 4^{\frac{1}{2}} = 4 + 2 = 6$.) Cross off any answer with roman numeral I. So, B, C and E are all gone.

Now, all you really need to do is try either II or III. If either works, the answer is D. For roman numeral II, use the power-multiply rule: $\left(x^{\frac{1}{2}}\right)^3 = x^{\left(\frac{1}{2}\right)(3)} = x^{\frac{3}{2}}$. So, since roman numeral II works, D is the correct answer.

If you simply must know what's going on with roman numeral III, use the multiply-add rule: $(x^2)\left(x^{-\frac{1}{2}}\right) = x^{2+\left(-\frac{1}{2}\right)} = x^{\frac{3}{2}}$. But, remember that you had already chosen an answer. Using good POE on a roman numeral question often means that you don't need to check all the roman numerals.

Summary

- There are only six arithmetic operations tested on the SAT: addition, subtraction, multiplication, division, exponents, and square roots.
- These operations must be performed in the proper order (PEMDAS), beginning with operations inside parentheses.
- Apply the distributive law whenever possible. Very often, this is enough to find ETS's answer.
- A fraction is just another way of expressing division.
- You must know how to add, subtract, multiply, and divide fractions. And don't forget that you can also use your calculator.
- In any problems involving large or confusing fractions appear, try to reduce the fractions first. Before you multiply two fractions, for example, see if it's possible to reduce either or both of the fractions.
- If you know how to work out fractions on your calculator, use it to help you with questions that involve fractions. If you intend to use your calculator for fractions, make sure you practice. You should also know how to work with fractions the old-fashioned way.
- A decimal is just another way of expressing a fraction.
- Use a calculator to add, subtract, multiply, and divide decimals.
- Exponents are a kind of shorthand for expressing numbers that are the product of the same factor multiplied over and over again.
- To multiply two exponential expressions with the same base, add the exponents.
- To divide two exponential expressions with the same base, subtract the exponents.

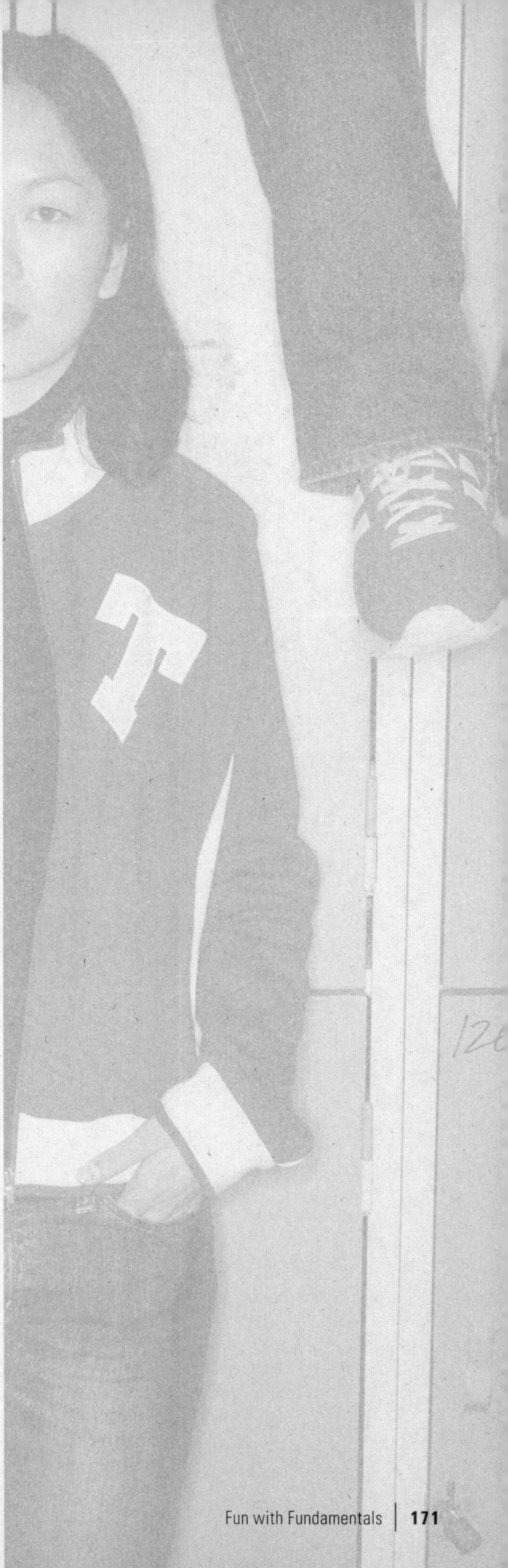

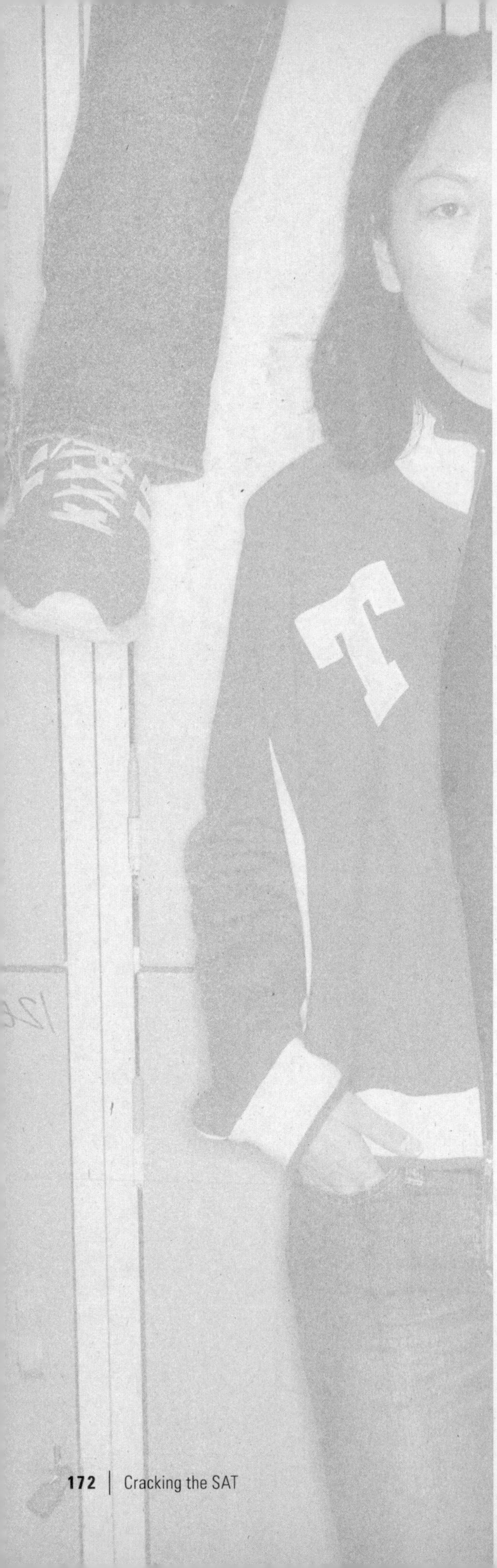

- To raise one exponential expression to another power, multiply the exponents.
- To remember the exponent rules, think MADSPM.
- When you raise a positive number greater than 1 to a power greater than 1, the result is larger. When you raise a positive fraction less than 1 to an exponent greater than 1, the result is smaller. A negative number raised to an even power becomes positive. A negative number raised to an odd power remains negative.
- When you're asked for the square root of any number $\sqrt{x}$, you're being asked for the positive root only.
- Here are the only rules regarding square roots that you need to know for the SAT:

$$\sqrt{x} \times \sqrt{y} = \sqrt{xy}$$

$$\sqrt{\frac{x}{y}} = \frac{\sqrt{x}}{\sqrt{y}}$$

$$x^{-n} = \frac{1}{x^n}$$

$$x^{\frac{y}{z}} = \sqrt[z]{x^y}$$

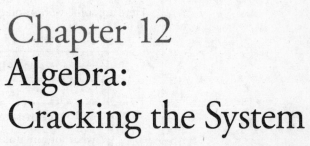

Chapter 12
Algebra: Cracking the System

In the last chapter we reviewed some fundamental math concepts featured on the SAT. Many questions on the SAT combine simple arithmetic concepts with more abstract algebraic concepts. This is one way the test writers raise the difficulty level of a question—they replace numbers with variables, or letters that stand for unknown quantities. In this chapter you will learn multiple ways to answer these algebraic questions, including avoiding algebra altogether.

SAT ALGEBRA: CRACKING THE SYSTEM

The SAT generally tests algebra concepts that you probably learned in the eighth or ninth grade. So unless you suffer from arithmophobia (fear of numbers), you are probably pretty familiar with the level of math on the test. In fact, many people who take the SAT are currently taking math classes, such as calculus or trigonometry, that cover topics far more advanced than those on the SAT.

Mark It!
Always write out the question as you translate.

The SAT Math section tests not only your math skills, but also your reading skills. It is important that you read the questions carefully and translate the words in the problem into mathematical symbols.

Here are some words and their equivalent symbols:

WORD	SYMBOL
is	=
of, times, product	× (multiply)
what (or any unknown value)	any letter (*x*, *k*, *b*)
more, sum	+
less, difference	−
ratio, quotient	÷

Here are two examples:

Words: 14 is 5 more than some number.

Equation: $14 = 5 + x$

Words: If one-eighth of a number is 3, what is one-half of the same number?

Equation: $\frac{1}{8}n = 3,\ \frac{1}{2}n = ?$

Later in the chapter we're going to show you some extremely important techniques for bypassing a great majority of the algebra on the test, but first we need to go over some of the basics. If you feel comfortable with your algebra skills, feel free to skip ahead.

BASIC PRINCIPLES: FUNDAMENTALS OF SAT ALGEBRA

Many problems on the SAT require you to work with variables and equations. In algebra class you learned to solve equations by "solving for x" or "solving for y." To do this, you isolate x or y on one side of the equal sign and put everything else on the other side. The good thing about equations is that, to isolate the variable, you can do anything you want to them—add, subtract, multiply, divide, square—provided you perform the same operation to all the numbers in the equation.

Hence, the golden rule of equations:

> Whatever you do to the items on one side of the equal sign, you must do to the items on the other side of it as well.

Let's look at a simple example of this rule:

1. If $2x - 15 = 35$, what is the value of x?

Here's How to Crack It

You want to isolate the variable. First, add 15 to each side of the equation. Now you have the following:

$$2x = 50$$

Divide each side of the equation by 2. Thus, x equals 25.

A Little Terminology

Here are some words that you will need to know to follow this chapter. The words themselves won't show up on the SAT, so after you finish the chapter you can forget about them.

Term: An equation is like a sentence, and a term is the equivalent of a word. For example, 9×2 is a term in the equation $9 \times 2 + 0x = 5y$.

Expression: If an equation is like a sentence, then an expression is like a phrase or a clause. An expression is a combination of terms and mathematical operations with no equal or inequality sign. For example, $9 \times 2 + 3x$ is an expression.

Polynomial: A polynomial is any expression containing two or more terms. Binomials and trinomials are both polynomials.

Solving For Expressions

Some SAT algebra problems ask you to find the value of an expression rather than the value of a variable. In most cases, you can find the value of the expression without finding the value of the variable.

Math Class Solution:
In math class, you would find the value of x and then plug that value into the provided expression. So, subtract 2 from both sides to find that $4x = 2$. Then divide both sides by 4 to find that $x = \frac{1}{2}$. Then, $4x - 6 = 4\left(\frac{1}{2}\right) - 6 = -4$. So, the answer is B.

5. If $4x + 2 = 4$, what is the value $4x - 6$?

(A) –6
(B) –4
(C) 0
(D) 4
(E) 8

The Princeton Review Solution:

Since ETS is asking for the value of an expression ($4x - 6$) rather than the value of x, you correctly suspect that there might be a shortcut. So, you look for a way to turn $4x + 2$ into $4x - 6$ and realize that subtracting 8 from both sides of the equation will do just that.

So, you just do $(4x + 2) - 8 = 4 - 8 = -4$ and you've got answer B.

The Princeton Review solution will save you time—provided that you see it quickly. So, while you practice, you should train yourself to look for these sorts of direct solutions whenever you are asked to solve for the value of an expression.

Learn Them, Love Them
Don't get bogged down looking for a direct solution. Always ask yourself if there is a simple way to find the answer. If you train yourself to think in terms of shortcuts, you won't waste a lot of time. However, if you don't see a quick solution, get to work. Something may come to you as you labor away.

However, don't worry too much if you don't always see the faster way to solve a problem like this one. The math class way will certainly get you the right answer.

Here's another example:

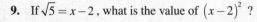

9. If $\sqrt{5} = x - 2$, what is the value of $(x-2)^2$?

(A) $\sqrt{5}$
(B) $\sqrt{7}$
(C) 5
(D) 9
(E) 25

Here's How to Crack It

If you were to attempt the math class way, you'd find that $x = \sqrt{5} + 2$ and then you'd have to substitute that into the provided expression. There's got to be an easier way!

The problem is much easier if you look for some sort of direct solution. Then, you notice that all the problem wants you to do is to square the expression on the right of the equal sign. Well, if you square the expression on the right, then you'd better square the expression on the left, too. So, $\left(\sqrt{5}\right)^2 = 5 = (x-2)^2$ and the answer is C. That was pretty painless by comparison.

Solving Simultaneous Equations

Some SAT problems will give you two equations involving two variables and ask for the value of an expression. These problems are very similar to the problems on the previous page. ETS would like you to solve for the value of each variable. But, all you really need to do is add or subtract the equations.

Here's an example:

If $4x + y = 14$ and $3x + 2y = 13$, then $x - y = ?$

Here's How to Crack It

You've been given two equations here. But instead of being asked to solve for a variable (x or y), you've been asked to solve for an expression ($x - y$). Why? Because there must be a direct solution.

In math class, you're taught to multiply one equation by one number and then subtract equations to find the second variable. You're also taught to solve one equation for one variable in terms of a second variable and to substitute that value into the second equation to solve for the first variable.

Forget it. These methods are far too time consuming to use on the SAT, and they put you at risk of making mistakes. There's a better way. Just stack them on top of each other, then add or subtract the two equations; either addition or subtraction will produce an easy answer. Let's try it.

Adding the two equations gives you this:

$$\begin{array}{r} 4x + \ \ y = 14 \\ +\ 3x + 2y = 13 \\ \hline 7x + 3y = 27 \end{array}$$

Unfortunately, that doesn't get us anywhere. So try subtracting:

$$\begin{array}{c} 4x + \ \ y = 14 \\ (3x + 2y = 13) \end{array}$$

When you subtract equations, just change the signs of the second equation and add. So the equation above becomes:

$$\begin{array}{r} 4x + \ \ y = \ \ 14 \\ +(-3x - 2y = -13) \\ \hline x - \ \ y = \ \ \ 1 \end{array}$$

The value of $(x - y)$ is precisely what you are looking for, so this must be ETS's answer.

Solving Inequalities

In an equation, one side equals the other. In an inequality, one side does not equal the other. The following symbols are used in inequalities:

$\neq$	is not equal to
$>$	is greater than
$<$	is less than
$\geq$	is greater than or equal to
$\leq$	is less than or equal to

Solving inequalities is pretty much like solving equations. You can collect similar terms, and you can simplify by doing the same thing to both sides. All you have to remember is that if you multiply or divide both sides of an inequality by a negative number, the direction of the inequality symbol changes. For example, here's a simple inequality:

$$x > y$$

Now, just as you can with an equation, you can multiply both sides of this inequality by the same number. But if the number you multiply by is negative, you have to change the direction of the symbol in the result. For example, if we multiply both sides of the inequality above by –2, we end up with the following:

$$-2x < -2y$$

Remember: When you multiply or divide an inequality by a negative number, you must reverse the inequality sign.

Hungry Gator
Think of the inequality sign as the mouth of a hungry alligator. The alligator eats the bigger number.

Simplifying Expressions

If a problem contains an expression that can be factored, it is very likely that you will need to factor it to solve the problem. So, you should always be on the lookout for opportunities to factor. For example, if a problem contains the expression $2x + 2y$, you should see if factoring it to produce the expression $2(x + y)$ will help you to solve the problem.

If a problem contains an expression that is already factored, you should consider using the distributive law to expand it. For example, if a problem contains the expression $2(x + y)$, you should see if expanding it to $2x + 2y$ will help.

Here are five examples that we've worked out:

1. $4x + 24 = 4(x) + 4(6) = 4(x + 6)$
2. $\frac{10x-60}{2} = \frac{10(x)-10(6)}{2} = \frac{10(x-6)}{2} = 5(x-6) = 5x-30$
3. $\frac{x+y}{y} = \frac{x}{y} + \frac{y}{y} = \frac{x}{y} + 1$
4. $2(x + y) + 3(x + y) = (2 + 3)(x + y) = 5(x + y)$
5. $p(r + s) + q(r + s) = (p + q)(r + s)$

Something to Hide
Because factoring or expanding is usually the key to finding ETS's answer on such problems, learn to recognize expressions that could be either factored or expanded. This will earn you more points. ETS will try to hide the answer by factoring or expanding the result.

Multiplying Binomials

Multiplying binomials is easy. Just be sure to use FOIL (first, outer, inner, last):

$$
\begin{aligned}
(x + 2)(x + 4) &= (x + 2)(x + 4) \\
&= (x \times x) + (x \times 4) + (2 \times x) + (2 \times 4) \\
&\quad \text{FIRST OUTER INNER LAST} \\
&= x^2 + 4x + 2x + 8 \\
&= x^2 + 6x + 8
\end{aligned}
$$

TERMinology

Remember: A *term* is a number, variable, or a number *and* variable that are combined by multiplication or division. So in the expression $6x + 10 = y$, $6x$, 10 and y are all terms. $6x + 10$, however, is not a term because a term includes only variables and their coefficients. .

Combine Similar Terms First

In manipulating long, complicated algebraic expressions, combine all similar terms before doing anything else. In other words, if one of the terms is $5x$ and another is $-3x$, simply combine them into $2x$. Then you won't have as many terms to work with. Here's an example:

$$
\begin{aligned}
&(3x^2 + 3x + 4) + (2 - x) - (6 + 2x) = \\
&3x^2 + 3x + 4 + 2 - x - 6 - 2x = \\
&3x^2 + (3x - x - 2x) + (4 + 2 - 6) = \\
&3x^2
\end{aligned}
$$

Evaluating Expressions

Sometimes ETS will give you the value of one of the variables in an algebraic expression and ask you to find the value of the entire expression. All you have to do is plug in the given value and see what you come up with.

Here is an example:

Problem:

If $2x = -1$, then $(2x - 3)^2 = ?$

Solution:

Don't solve for x; simply plug in -1 for $2x$, like this:

$$
\begin{aligned}
(2x - 3)^2 &= (-1 - 3)^2 \\
&= (-4)^2 \\
&= 16
\end{aligned}
$$

Solving Quadratic Equations

To solve quadratic equations, remember everything you've learned so far: Look for direct solutions and either factor or expand when possible.

Here's an example:

If $(x + 3)^2 = (x - 2)^2$, then $x =$

Here's How to Crack It

Expand both sides of the equation using FOIL:

$$(x + 3)(x + 3) = x^2 + 6x + 9$$

$$(x - 2)(x - 2) = x^2 - 4x + 4$$

$$x^2 + 6x + 9 = x^2 - 4x + 4$$

Now you can simplify. Eliminate the x^2's, because they are on both sides of the equal sign. Now you have $6x + 9 = -4x + 4$, which simplifies to:

$$10x = -5$$

$$x = -\frac{1}{2}$$

Factoring Quadratics

To solve a quadratic, you might also have to factor the equation. Factoring a quadratic basically involves doing a reverse form of FOIL.

For example, suppose you needed to know the factors of $x^2 + 7x + 12$. Here's what you would do:

1. Write down 2 sets of parentheses and put an x in each one because the product of the first terms is x^2.

   $x^2 + 7x + 12 = (x \quad)(x \quad)$

Factoring
When factroring an equation like $x^2 + bx + c$, think "**A.M.**" Find two numbers that **A**dd up to the middle term (b) and **M**ultiply to give the last term (c).

2. Look at the number at the end of the expression you are trying to factor. Write down its factors. In this case, the factors of 12 are 1 and 12, 2 and 6 and 3 and 4.
3. To determine which set of factors to put in the parentheses, look at the coefficient of the middle term of the quadratic expression. In this case, the coefficient is 7. So, the correct factors will also either add or subtract to get 7. Write the correct factors in the parentheses.
$$x^2 + 7x + 12 = (x \_\_ 3)(x \_\_ 4)$$
4. Finally, determine the signs for the factors. To get a positive 12, both the 3 and the 4 are both positive or both negative. But, since 7 is also positive, the signs must both be positive.
$$x^2 + 7x + 12 = (x + 3)(x + 4)$$

You can always check that you have factored correctly by FOILing the factors to see if you get the original quadratic expression.

Now, try this one:

---

16. In the expression $x^2 + kx + 12$, k is an integer and $k < 0$. Which of the following is a possible value of k?

(A) –13
(B) –12
(C) –6
(D) 7
(E) It cannot be determined from the information given.

Here's How to Crack It

Of course, you're going to eliminate E because that's the Joe Bloggs answer. While you are eliminating answers, you can also get rid of D because the question says that $k < 0$.

To solve the question, you need to factor. This question is just a twist on the example used above. Don't worry that we don't know the value of k. The question said that k was an integer and that means that you probably need to consider only the integer factors of 12. The possible factors of 12 are 1 and 12, 2 and 6, and 3 and 4. Since 12 is positive and k is negative, the you'll need subtraction signs in both factors.

The possibilities are:

$$x^2 + kx + 12 = (x - 1)(x - 12)$$

$$x^2 + kx + 12 = (x - 2)(x - 6)$$

$$x^2 + kx + 12 = (x - 3)(x - 4)$$

If you FOIL each of these sets of factors, you'll get:

$(x-1)(x-12) = x^2 - 13x + 12$

$(x-2)(x-6) = x^2 - 8x + 12$

$(x-3)(x-4) = x^2 - 7x + 12$

The correct answer is A, as –13 is the only value from above included in the answers. Of course, you didn't need to write them all out if you started with 1 and 12 as your factors.

ETS FAVORITES

ETS plays favorites when it comes to quadratic equations. There are three equations that they use all the time. You should memorize these and be on the lookout for them. Whenever you see a quadratic that contains two variables, it is almost certain to be one of these three.

$$(x + y)(x - y) = x^2 - y^2$$

$$(x + y)^2 = x^2 + 2xy + y^2$$

$$(x - y)^2 = x^2 - 2xy + y^2$$

Here's an example of how ETS is likely to test these equations. Try it:

11. If $2x - 3y = 5$, what is the value of $4x^2 - 12xy + 9y^2$?

(A) $\sqrt{5}$
(B) 5
(C) 12
(D) 25
(E) 100

Here's How to Crack It

Look! A quadratic equation with two variables! What do you think ETS is up to? Yes, that's right, it's one of their favorites.

In this case, work with $2x - 3y = 5$. If you square the left side of the equations, you get

$$(2x - 3y)^2 = 4x^2 - 12xy + 9y^2$$

That's precisely the expression for which you need to value. It's also the third of the equations from the box. Now, since you squared the left side, all you need to do is square the 5 on the right side of the equation to discover that the expression equals 25, answer D.

Did you notice that this question was just another version of ETS asking you to solve for the value of an expression rather than for a variable? Quadratics are one of their favorite ways to do that.

SOLVING QUADRATICS SET TO ZERO

Before factoring most quadratics, you need to set the equation equal to zero. Why? Well, if $ab = 0$, what do you know about a and b? At least one of them must equal 0, right? That's the key fact you need to solve most quadratics.

Here's an example:

9. If $3 - \frac{3}{x} = x + 7$, and $x \neq 0$, which of the following is a possible value for x ?

(A) −7
(B) −1
(C) 1
(D) 3
(E) 7

Here's How to Crack It

ETS has tried to hide that the equation is actually a quadratic. Start by multiplying both sides of the equation by x to get rid of the fraction.

$$x\left(3-\frac{3}{x}\right)=x(x+7)$$

$$3x - 3 = x^2 + 7x$$

Now, just rearrange the terms to set the quadratic equal to 0. You'll get $x^2 + 4x + 3 = 0$. Now, it's time to factor:

$$x^2 + 4x + 3 = (x + 1)(x + 3) = 0$$

So, at least one of the factors must equal 0. If $x + 1 = 0$, then $x = -1$. If $x + 3 = 0$, then $x = -3$. Since -1 is answer B, that's the one you want.

WHEN VALUES ARE ABSOLUTE

Absolute value is just a measure of the distance between a number and 0. Since distances are always positive, the absolute value of a number is also always positive. The absolute value of a number is written as $|x|$.

When solving for the value of a variable inside the absolute value bars, it is important to remember that variable could be either positive or negative. For example, if $|x| = 2$, then $x = 2$ or $x = -2$ since both 2 and -2 are a distance of 2 from 0.

Joe Bloggs Is Always Positive

When ETS asks you to solve an equation involving an absolute value, it is very likely that the correct answer will be the negative result. Why? Because Joe doesn't think about the negative result!

Here's an example:

$$|x + 3| = 6$$

$$|y - 2| = 7$$

9. For the equations shown above, which of the following is a possible value of $x - y$?

(A) –14
(B) –4
(C) –2
(D) 1
(E) 14

Here's How to Crack It

To solve the first equation, set $x + 3 = 6$ and set $x + 3 = -6$. If $x + 3 = -6$, then the absolute value would still be 6. So, x can be either 3 or –9. Now, do the same thing to solve for y. Either $y = 9$ or $y = -5$.

To get the credited answer, you need to try the different combinations. One combination is $x = -9$ and $y = -5$. So, $x - y = -9 - (-5) = -4$, which is answer B.

PRINCETON REVIEW ALGEBRA, OR HOW TO AVOID ALGEBRA ON THE SAT

Now that you've reviewed some basic algebra, it's time for some Princeton Review algebra. At The Princeton Review, we like to avoid algebra whenever possible. You read that correctly: We're going to show you how to avoid doing algebra on the SAT. Now, before you start crying and complaining that you love algebra and couldn't possibly give it up, just take a second to hear us out. We have nothing against algebra—it's very helpful when solving problems, it works all the time, it impresses your friends—but on the SAT, using algebra can actually hurt your score. And we don't want that.

But Algebra Would Never Hurt Me!

We know it's difficult to come to terms with this. But if you use algebra on the SAT, you're doing exactly what ETS wants you to do. You see, when the test writers design the problems on the SAT, they expect the students to use algebra to solve them. ETS builds little traps into the problems to take advantage of that fact. But if you don't use algebra, there's no way you can fall into those traps.

My Best Friend
Plugging In allows you to use your calculator on most algebra problems!

Plus, when you avoid algebra, you have one other powerful tool at your disposal: your calculator! Even if you have a super-fancy calculator that plays games and doubles as a global positioning system, chances are it doesn't do algebra. Arithmetic, on the other hand, is easy for your calculator. It's what calculators were invented for.

Our goal, then, is to turn all the algebra on the SAT into arithmetic. We do that using something we call *Plugging In.*

PLUGGING IN THE ANSWER (PITA)

Algebra uses letters to stand for numbers, but very few other things do. You don't go to the grocery store to buy *x* eggs or *y* gallons of milk. Most people think in terms of numbers, not letters that stand for numbers.

You should think in terms of numbers on the SAT as much as possible. On many SAT algebra problems, even very difficult ones, you will be able to find ETS's answer without using any algebra at all. You will do this by working backward from the answer choices instead of trying to solve the problem using math-class algebra.

Plugging In the Answer is a technique for solving word problems in which the answer choices are all numbers. Many algebra problems on the SAT can be solved simply and quickly by using this powerful technique.

In algebra class at school, you solve word problems by using equations. Then, if you're careful, you check your solution by Plugging In your answer to see if it works. Why not skip the equations entirely by simply checking the five solutions ETS offers on the multiple-choice questions? One of these has to be correct. You don't have to do any algebra, you will seldom have to try more than two choices, and you will never have to try all five. Note that you can use this technique only for questions that ask for a specific amount.

Here's an example:

9. Zoë won the raffle at a fair. She will receive the prize money in 5 monthly payments. If each payment is half as much as the previous month's payment and the total of the payments is $496, what is the amount of the first payment?

(A) $256
(B) $96
(C) $84
(D) $16
(E) $4

Here's How to Crack It

ETS would like you to go through all the effort of setting up this equation:

$$p+\frac{1}{2}p+\frac{1}{4}p+\frac{1}{8}p+\frac{1}{16}p=496$$

Then, of course, they want you to solve the equation. But, look at all those fractions! There are lots of opportunities to make a mistake and you can bet that ETS has figured most of them out so they can have a trap answer waiting. So, let's work with the answers instead.

To work with the answer choices, first you need to know what they represent so that you can label them. In this case, the question asks for the first payment, so write something like first payment over the answers.

Now, it's time to start working the steps of the problem. But first, notice that the answer choices are in numerically descending order. ETS likes to keep their problems organized so they will always put the answers in order. You can use that to your advantage by starting with answer choice C.

Grab answer choice C and ask yourself something like, "If the first payment is $84, what's the next thing I can figure out?" In this case, you could figure out the second payment. So, make a chart and write down 42 (half of 84) next to the 84. Keep doing that to find the values of the third, fourth, and fifth payments.

Representation
Make sure you know what the numbers in the answer choices represent. Be sure to label them!

When you have worked all the steps, your problem should look like this:

9. Zoë won the raffle at a fair. She will receive the prize money in 5 monthly payments. If each payment is half as much as the previous month's payment and the total of the payments is $496, what is the amount of the first payment?

	1st PMT	2nd PMT	3rd PMT	4th PMT	5th PMT
(A)	$256				
(B)	$96				
(C)	$84	42	21	10.50	5.25
(D)	$16				
(E)	$4				

You need to determine if that was the correct answer. The problem says that the total is supposed to be $496, so add up the payments: 84 + 42 + 21 + 10.50 + 5.25 = 162.75, which is much smaller than 496. So, cross off choices C, D and E.

Now, all you need to do is try answer B. If B works, then you're done. And, if B doesn't work, you're still done because the answer must be A. That's putting your POE to good use! If the first payment is $96, then the payments are 96 + 48 + 24 + 12 + 6 = 186, which is still too small. That means the answer must be A and you don't really need to check it.

Here are the steps for solving a problem using the PITA approach:

To solve a problem by Plugging In the Answers

1. Label the answer choices.
2. Starting with answer C, work the steps of the problem. Be sure to write down a label for each new step.
3. Look for something in the problem that tells you what must happen for the answer to be correct.
4. When you find the correct answer, STOP.

Here's another problem that PITA makes easy:

14. The units digit of a two digit number is 3 times the tens digit. If the digits are reversed, the resulting number is 36 more than the original number. What is the original number?

(A) 26
(B) 36
(C) 39
(D) 54
(E) 93

Here's How to Crack It

It's pretty hard to come up with the algebraic equation to solve this one, so try Plugging In the Answers. First, label the answers as the original number.

Start at choice C. If the original number is 39, what must be true? The units digit is supposed to be 3 times the tens digit and 9 is three times 3, so don't rule this answer choice out yet. Next, the problem says to reverse the digits, so the new number would be 93. Finally, the difference is supposed to be 36 but 93 – 39 = 54, so this answer gets eliminated.

Which Way?
Sometimes, it's hard to tell if you need a bigger number or a smaller number if C didn't work. Don't fret. Just pick a direction and go! Spend your time trying answers, rather than worrying about going in the wrong direction.

It's hard to tell if you need a bigger number or smaller number, so just pick a direction and try it. Let's try A. If the original number is 26, then the units digit is three times the tens digit. So far, so good. Next, if the digits are reversed, the new number is 62. Finally, 62 – 26 = 36. Bingo! A is the answer.

Always make sure that you follow *all* of the steps of a problem. If you had just checked to be sure that the units digit was three times the tens digit, you might have chosen answer C and been wrong!

One last thing about PITA. Here's how you spot that you can use this approach to solve the problem.

Three ways to know that it's time for PITA:

1. There are numbers in the answer choices.
2. The question asks for a specific amount such as "what was the first payment."
3. You have the urge to write an algebra equation to solve the problem.

Plugging In: Advanced Principles

Plugging In is the same on difficult problems as it is on easy and medium ones. You just have to watch your step and make certain you don't make any careless mistakes or fall for Joe Bloggs answers.

Here's one of our examples:

15. A baseball team won 54 more games than it lost. If the team played a total of 154 games and there were no ties, how many games did the team win?

(A) 50
(B) 98
(C) 100
(D) 102
(E) 104

Here's How to Crack It

Doesn't seem so bad, right? Well, that's what Joe thinks, too. What would Joe choose? If you thought that Joe might choose C, you've tapped into your inner Joe and you can use that knowledge to eliminate wrong answers. Joe likes answer C because he thinks all he needs to do is 154 – 54 = 100. But, that's just too easy to be the answer to a hard question like number 15. Cross off C!

If you're itching to write an equation, that's a sure sign that it's time for PITA. So, start by labeling the answer choices as *games won*. Since C has been eliminated, start at choice D. If the team won 102 games, what else can you figure out? The team lost 102 – 54 = 48 games. How will you know if that's the right answer? The team is supposed to have played 154 games but with choice D the team has played only 102 + 48 = 150 games. That's not enough, so cross off D. The team needs to have won more games, so the answer must be E. (It is. Really. You can check it if you'd like.)

Here's another example:

17. Committee *A* has 18 members and Committee *B* has 3 members. How many members from Committee *A* must switch to Committee *B* so that Committee *A* will have twice as many members as Committee *B* ?

(A) 4
(B) 6
(C) 7
(D) 11
(E) 15

Here's How to Crack It

Because it's fairly hard to write the correct equation to solve this problem, only a very small percentage of students get it right. But, if you plug in the answers, you won't have any trouble.

This problem is about two committees, so the first thing you should do is quickly draw a picture in your test booklet to keep from getting confused:

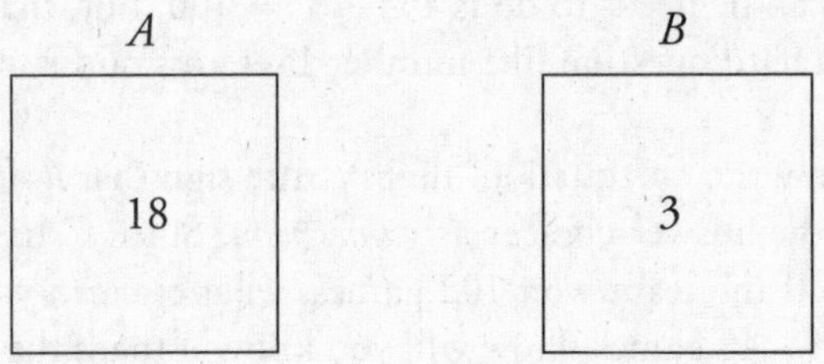

Now plug in the answer choices, starting with answer choice C. If you move 7 members out of Committee *A,* there will be 11 members left in *A* and 10 members in *B.* Is 11 twice as many as 10? No, eliminate.

As you work through the choices, keep track of them, like this:

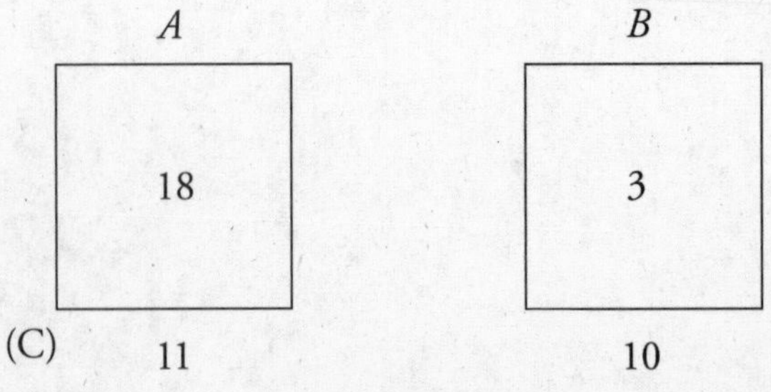

Choice C didn't work. To make the question work out right, you need more members in Committee *A* and fewer in Committee *B*. In other words, you need to try a smaller number. Try the smallest one, choice A. Moving 4 members from Committee *A* will leave 14 in *A* and 7 in *B*. Is 14 twice as many as 7? Yes, of course. This is the answer.

PLUGGING IN YOUR OWN NUMBERS

Plugging In the Answers enables you to find the answer on problems when the answer choices are all numbers. What about problems that have answer choices containing variables? On these problems, you will usually be able to find the answer by Plugging In your own numbers.

Plugging In is easy. It has three steps:

1. Pick numbers for the variables in the problem.
2. Use *your* numbers to find an answer to the problem.
3. Plug your numbers from step 1 into the answer choices to see which choice equals the answer you found in step 2.

Hey, Smarty!
If you think you can improve your SAT Math score without learning to plug in, you're in for an unpleasant surprise. Seriously, this technique applies strictly to the SAT, and it works. Just bear in mind: This is a multiple-choice test; the correct answers are already right there on the page.

The Basics of Plugging In Your Own Numbers

This sort of Plugging In is simple to understand. Here's an example:

3. If Jayme will be j years old in 3 years, then in terms of j, how old was Jayme 5 years ago?

(A) $j-8$
(B) $j-5$
(C) $j-3$
(D) $j+5$
(E) $j+8$

Get Real
There is nothing abstract about the SAT (except maybe its relevance). So, if the problem says that Tina is *x* years old, why not plug in your own age? That's real enough. You don't have to change your name to Tina. (Anyway, only ancient Roman children can be *x* years old.)

When to Plug In

- Phrases like "in terms of *k*" in the question
- Variables in the answers
- Unspecified values and fractions

Here's How to Crack It

First, pick a number for *j*. Pick something easy to work with, like 10. In your test booklet, write 10 directly above the letter *j* in the problem, so you won't forget.

If $j = 10$, then Jayme will be 10 years old in 3 years. That means that she is 7 right now. Because the problem asked you how old she was 5 years ago, just calculate $7 - 5 = 2$. She was 2! Write a nice big 2 in you test booklet and circle it. That's your target. The correct answer will be the choice that, when you plug in 10 for *j*, equals 2.

Now plug in!

Plug in 10 for *j* in A and you get $10 - 8$, or 2. This is the number that you are looking for, so this must be the right answer! Go ahead and try the other choices just to make sure that you're right and to practice Plugging In.

Here's another example:

Plugging In Works

Don't try to solve problems like this by writing equations and "solving for *x*" or "solving for *y*." Plugging In is faster, easier, and less likely to produce errors.

12. The sum of four consecutive positive even integers is *x*. In terms of *x*, what is the sum of the second and third integers?

(A) $\frac{x-12}{4}$

(B) $\frac{x-6}{2}$

(C) $2x+6$

(D) $\frac{x}{2}$

(E) $\frac{x^2-3x}{4}$

Here's How to Crack It

Let's pick four numbers: 2, 4, 6, and 8. The sum of these four is 20, so $x = 20$; write that in your test booklet. The second and third numbers, 4 and 6, add up to 10; this is your target number, circle it. You are looking for the choice that will equal 10 when you plug in 20. Try each choice:

(A) $\frac{20-12}{4}=2$ Nope!

(B) $\frac{20-6}{2}=7$ Nope!

(C) $2(20)+6=46$ Too big!

(D) $\frac{20}{2}=10$ Looks good. This is the correct answer.

(E) $\frac{20^2-3(20)}{4}=?$ Waaaay too big!

Which Numbers?

Although you can plug in any number, you can make your life much easier by Plugging In "good" numbers—numbers that are simple to work with or that make the problem easier to manipulate. Picking a small number, such as 2, will usually make finding the answer easier. If the problem asks for a percentage, plug in 10 or 100. If the problem has to do with minutes, try 30 or 120.

Be Good

"Good" numbers make a problem less confusing by simplifying the arithmetic. This is your chance to make the SAT easier.

Except in special cases, you should avoid Plugging In 0 and 1; these numbers have weird properties. Using them may allow you to eliminate only one or two choices at a time. You should also avoid Plugging In any number that appears in the question or in any of the answer choices. These could make more than one answer match your target.

Many times you'll find that there is an advantage to picking a particular number, even a very large one, because it makes solving the problem easier.

Here's an example:

---

14. If 60 equally priced downloads cost x dollars, then how much do 9 downloads cost?

(A) $\frac{20}{3x}$

(B) $9x - 60$

(C) $\frac{20x}{3}$

(D) $60x + 9$

(E) $\frac{3x}{20}$

Here's How to Crack It

Should you plug in 2 for x? You could, but Plugging In 120 would make the problem easier. After all, if 60 downloads cost a total of $120, then each download costs $2. Write $x = 120$ in your test booklet.

If each download costs $2, then 9 downloads cost $18. Write an 18 in your test booklet and circle it. You are looking for the answer choice that works out to 18 when you plug in $120 for x. Let's try each choice:

(A) $\frac{20}{3(120)} \neq 18$

(B) $9(120) - 60 \neq 18$

(C) $\frac{20(120)}{3} \neq 18$

(D) $60(120) + 9 \neq 18$

(E) $\frac{3(120)}{20} = 18$ Here's your answer.

Let's try another example:

20. A watch loses x minutes every y hours. At this rate, how many hours will the watch lose in one week?

(A) $7xy$

(B) $\frac{2x}{5y}$

(C) $\frac{5y}{2x}$

(D) $\frac{14y}{5x}$

(E) $\frac{14x}{5y}$

That's OOD

Check where you are in the Order Of Difficulty (OOD). ETS expects you to do algebra here and mess it up. Plug in!

Here's How to Crack It

This is an extremely difficult problem for students who try to solve it the math-class way. You'll be able to find the answer easily, though, if you plug in carefully.

What numbers should you plug in? As always, you can plug in anything. However, if you think just a little bit before choosing the numbers, you can make the problem easier to understand. There are three units of time—minutes, hours and weeks—and that's a big part of the reason this problem is hard to understand. If you choose units of time that are easy to think about, you'll make the problem easier to handle.

Start by choosing a value for x, which represents the number of minutes that the watch loses. You might be tempted to choose $x = 60$ and that would make the math pretty easy. However, it's usually not a good idea to choose a conversion factor such as 60, the conversion factor between minutes and hours, when plugging in. It would actually turn out okay on this problem but when dealing with time, 30 is usually a safer choice. So, write down $x = 30$.

Next, you need a number for y, which represents the number of hours. Again, you might be tempted to use $y = 24$ but that's the conversion factor between hours and days. So, how about $y = 12$ as a safer choice? Write down $y = 12$.

Now, it's time to solve the problem to come up with a target. If the watch loses 30 minutes every 12 hours, then it loses 60 minutes every 24 hours. Put another way, the watch loses an hour each day. In one week, the watch will lose 7 hours. That's your target so be sure to circle it.

Now, you just need to check the answer choices to see which one gives you 7 when $x = 30$ and $y = 12$.

(A) $7xy = 7(30)(12)$ = Something too big! Cross it off.

(B) $\frac{2x}{5y} = \frac{2(30)}{5(12)} = \frac{60}{60} = 1$. Eliminate it.

(C) $\frac{5y}{2x} = \frac{5(12)}{2(30)} = \frac{60}{60} = 1$. Also wrong.

(D) $\frac{14y}{5x} = \frac{14(12)}{5(30)} = \frac{168}{150} = \frac{28}{25}$ Cross it off.

(E) $\frac{14x}{5y} = \frac{14(30)}{5(12)} = \frac{420}{60} = 7$. Choose it!

Inequalities

Plugging In works on problems containing inequalities, but you will have to follow some different rules. Plugging In one number is often not enough; to find ETS's answer, you may have to plug in several numbers, including weird numbers like –1, 0, 1, $\frac{1}{2}$, and $-\frac{1}{2}$.

The five numbers just mentioned all have special properties. Negatives, fractions, 0, and 1 all behave in peculiar ways when, for example, they are squared. Don't forget about them!

Sometimes it can actually be easier or faster to simplify. Here's an example:

Weird Numbers
As you may have noticed, some numbers have uncommon properties. Because of this, we plug them in only under certain circumstances, usually when solving.

- Inequalities
- MUST BE problems

8. If $-3x + 6 \geq 18$, which of the following must be true?

(A) $x \leq -4$
(B) $x \leq 6$
(C) $x \geq -4$
(D) $x \geq -6$
(E) $x = 2$

What Are the Weird Numbers?

- Fractions
- Negatives
- Big numbers
- 1 and 0

Here's How to Crack It

The inequality in the problem can be simplified quite a bit:

$$-3x + 6 \geq 18$$

$$-3x \geq 12$$

$$-x \geq 4$$

We're close to one of the answer choices, but not quite there yet. Multiply both sides by –1 to make x positive. *Remember to change the direction of the inequality sign!*

$$x \leq -4$$

So choice A is the answer.

Other Special Cases

Sometimes SAT algebra problems will require you to determine certain characteristics of a number or numbers. Is x odd or even? Is it small or large? Is it positive or negative?

On questions like this, you will probably have to plug in more than one number and/or plug in weird numbers, just as you do on problems containing inequalities. Sometimes ETS's wording will tip you off. If the problem states only that $x > 0$, you know for certain that x is positive but you don't know that x is an integer. See what happens when you plug in a fraction.

Here are some other tip-offs you should be aware of when you're trying to eliminate answers.

If the problem asked for this	and you plugged in this	also try this, just to be sure
an integer	3	1, 0, or –1
a fraction	$\frac{1}{4}$	$-\frac{1}{4}$
two even numbers	2, 4	2, –2
a number	an integer	a fraction
a number	an even number	an odd number
a number	a small number	a huge number
a multiple of 7	7	7,000 or –7
consecutive numbers	1, 2, 3	–1, 0, 1
$x^2 = 4$	2	–2
$xy > 0$	(2, 4)	(–2, –4)
$x = 2y$	(4, 2)	(–4, –2) or (0, 0)

Must Be True

Must is a very strong word in a math problem. It means that whatever condition you are given needs to work for every number that you are allowed to try. When you plug in on a question that uses *must,* it is very likely that you will need to plug in at least twice to find the answer. If you choose the first answer that meets the condition, you could wind up choosing something that ***could be true*** rather than something that *must be true.*

Try the following problem:

14. If $a - b$ is a multiple of 7, which of the following must also be a multiple of 7 ?

(A) ab

(B) $a + b$

(C) $\frac{a+b}{2}$

(D) $\frac{b-a}{2}$

(E) $b - a$

Here's How to Crack It

Because there are variables in the answer choices, you can plug in. First, plug in easy numbers that make the given statement ($a - b$ is a multiple of 7) true. Make $a = 14$ and $b = 7$. So the whole thing would be 7, which is indeed a multiple of 7. The question asks which of the following must also be a multiple of 7. Plug in the number and cross off any answer choices that are not true.

(A) 14(7) = 98 is a multiple of 7, so keep it.

(B) 14 + 7 = 21 is a multiple of 7, so keep it.

(C) $\frac{14+7}{2}$ is not a multiple of 7. Cross it off.

(D) $\frac{7-14}{2}$ is not a multiple of 7. Cross it off.

(E) 7 – 14 = –7 is a multiple of 7, so keep it.

Since the question asks for something that *must* be true and you are left with three answer choices, you must plug in again. The first time you plugged in, you used two other multiples of 7 ($a = 14$ and $b = 7$) to satisfy the condition. But it doesn't say that a and b must be multiples of 7, just that the *expression* must be. So now, plug in two numbers that are *not* multiples of 7, but still make the statement true. Plug in 10 for a and 3 for b. The statement becomes 10 – 3 = 7, which works. Now check the answers that you didn't eliminate the first time:

(A) (10)(3) = –30. Cross it off.
(B) 10 + 3 = 13. Cross it off.
(E) 3 – 10 = –7. It still works
(and is the only one left), so keep it.

The answer is (E).

Plugging In: Advanced Principles

As you have just learned, you should plug in whenever you don't know what a number is. But you can also plug in when you have numbers that are too big, too ugly, or too inconvenient to work with. On such problems you can often find the answer simply by using numbers that aren't as ugly as the ones you've been given.

Here's an example:

16. In a marathon, runners who finish 1st through 75th receive gift certificates; those who finish 76th and higher do not. If 312 runners participated in the race, how many did NOT receive gift certificates?

(A) 75
(B) 76
(C) 236
(D) 237
(E) 238

Here's How to Crack It

This is a number 16—a difficult question. Finding the answer has to be harder than simply subtracting 76 from 312 to get 236, which means that C has to be wrong. Cross it out. (You can also immediately eliminate A and B as they are way too small.)

One way to find the answer would be to count this out by hand. But to count from 76 to 312 would take forever. You can achieve the same result by using simpler numbers instead.

It doesn't matter which numbers you use. How about 7 and 11? The difference between 7 and 11 is 4. But if you count out the numbers on your hand—7, 8, 9, 10, 11—you see that there are five numbers. In other words, if we were looking at runners 7 through 11, the number of runners would have been 1 greater than the difference between 7 and 11. The answer therefore will be 1 greater than the difference between 76 and 312, in other words, D.

ADVANCED PRINCIPLES OF SAT ALGEBRA

Solving Rational Equations

A rational equation is basically a fraction with a polynomial in the numerator and a polynomial in the denominator. Rational equations look scary, but there are very simple ways of solving them. One way is to factor out like terms and then cancel. All in all, ETS can't get too messy here, so they will keep the math nice and tidy.

Try one:

Quick and Painless
Use your calculator!

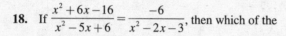

18. If $\dfrac{x^2+6x-16}{x^2-5x+6}=\dfrac{-6}{x^2-2x-3}$, then which of the following could be a value of x ?

(A) –7
(B) –5
(C) 0
(D) 6
(E) 16

Here's How to Crack It

Hate factoring? PITA! Start with answer choice C and plug in 0 for x. Does everything work out? In this case, it doesn't. Keep trying other answer choices until you find one that works. Choice A does, so that's the correct answer choice. See? These are all bark and no bite.

Solving Radical Equations

Radical equations are just what the name suggests: an equation with a radical ($\sqrt{\ }$) in it. Not to worry, just remember to get rid of the radical first by raising both sides to that power.

Here's an example:

7. If, $7\sqrt{x} - 24 = 11$, what is the value of x ?

(A) $\sqrt{5}$
(B) $\sqrt{7}$
(C) 5
(D) 25
(E) 35

Here's How to Crack It

Start by adding 24 to both sides to get $7\sqrt{x} = 35$. Now, divide both sides by 7 to find that $\sqrt{x} = 5$. Finally, square both sides to find that $x = 25$, which is answer D.

Don't forget that you can also get the answer by using PITA. If you are ever unsure about how to solve an equation, PITA is a great approach.

Note It Well!
Though $f(x)$ is the most common way to show that an equation is a mathematic function, any letter can be used. So you may see $g(x)$ or $h(d)$. Know that you're still dealing with a function.

Functions

A function is just a machine for producing ordered pairs. You put in one number and the machine spits out another. The most common function is an $f(x)$ function. You've probably dealt with it in your algebra class.

Let's look at a problem:

9. If $f(x) = x^3 - 4x + 8$, then $f(5) =$

(A) 67
(B) 97
(C) 113
(D) 147
(E) 153

Here's How to Crack It

Any time you see a number inside the parentheses, such as $f(5)$, plug in that number for x. The question is actually telling you to plug in! Let's do it:

$$f(5) = 5^3 - 4(5) + 8$$
$$f(5) = 125 - 20 + 8$$
$$f(5) = 113$$

That's choice C.

What the *f*?
Anytime you see the notation $f(x)$, know that f isn't a variable. It's the name of the function. When you say it out loud it's "f of x."

Sometimes you'll get more complicated questions. As long as you know that when you put in x your function will spit out another number, you'll be fine. Try this next one:

20. Let the function g be defined by $g(x) = 5x + 2$. If

$\sqrt{g\left(\frac{a}{2}\right)} = 6$, what is the value of a ?

(A) $\frac{1}{\sqrt{6}}$

(B) $\frac{1}{\sqrt{2}}$

(C) $\frac{5}{2}$

(D) $\frac{34}{5}$

(E) $\frac{68}{5}$

PITA!

Don't forget that you can often plug in the answer choices on function questions! Noticing a pattern yet? Just a few cheap tricks can unlock a lot of easy points.

Here's How to Crack It

This may look complicated, but just following the directions. You know that $g(x) = 5x + 2$. You also know that $\sqrt{g\left(\frac{a}{2}\right)} = 6$. First, get rid of the square root by squaring both sides. Now you have $g\left(\frac{a}{2}\right) = 36$. Usually there's an x inside the parentheses. Treat this the same. This statement says that g of some number equals 6. We know that g of some number is the same as $5x + 2$. So $5x + 2 = 6$. Simplify and you get $\frac{34}{5}$. Careful, you're not done. You now know that $\frac{a}{2} = \frac{34}{5}$, so $a = \frac{68}{5}$, or D.

Even though these questions may have looked like one you might get on an algebra test, remember you're still dealing with ETS. Sometimes they'll throw you a curveball by inserting a function question that has crazy symbols instead of $f(x)$. Just follow the directions of the function and you'll do fine.

Here's an example:

---

14. If $x \# y = \frac{1}{x - y}$, what is the value of $\frac{1}{2} \# \frac{1}{3}$?

(A) 6

(B) $\frac{6}{5}$

(C) $\frac{1}{6}$

(D) –1

(E) –6

Here's How to Crack It

Finding ETS's answers is just a matter of simple substitution. Just substitute $\frac{1}{2}$ and $\frac{1}{3}$ for x and y in the function.

$$\frac{1}{2} \# \frac{1}{3} = \frac{1}{\frac{1}{2} - \frac{1}{3}}$$

$$= \frac{1}{\frac{1}{6}}$$

$$= 6$$

ETS's answer, therefore, is choice A.

WHAT'S THE POINT?

Why did math folks come up with functions? To graph them of course! When you put in a value for x, and your machine (or function) spits out another number, that's your y. You now have an ordered pair. Functions are just another way to express graphs. Knowing the connection between functions and graphs is useful, because ETS will show you a graph and ask you questions about it.

DRILL

Work these problems using the Plugging In techniques and algebra tips we've covered in this chapter. Answers can be found on pages 377–378.

4. If 4 more than twice a number is 6 less than that number, what is the number?

(A) −10
(B) 2
(C) 10
(D) 16
(E) 24

6. If n is a negative integer, which of the following must be a positive integer?

(A) $n + 2$
(B) $2n$
(C) $2n + 4$
(D) $n^2 - 5$
(E) $n^2 + 1$

7. Ashley is 7 years younger than Sarah and three times as old as Cindy. If Cindy is c years old, how old is Sarah in terms of c?

(A) $c - 7$

(B) $\frac{c}{3}$

(C) $\frac{c}{3} + 7$

(D) $3c$

(E) $3c + 7$

8. If r and s are both odd integers, which of the following must be an even integer?

(A) $\frac{r+s}{2}$

(B) $\frac{rs}{2}$

(C) rs

(D) $2rs$

(E) $3rs$

9. John buys 40 sacks of flour for y dollars. At the same rate, how much would it cost to buy 12 sacks of flour?

(A) $\frac{y}{10}$

(B) $\frac{y}{3}$

(C) $3y$

(D) $\frac{3y}{10}$

(E) $\frac{10y}{3}$

11. If x percent of 50 is 20 percent of y, what is the value of x in terms of y?

(A) $\frac{2y}{5}$

(B) $\frac{5y}{2}$

(C) $2y$

(D) $5y$

(E) $10y$

12. If Alex can fold 12 napkins in x minutes, how many napkins can he fold in y hours?

(A) $\frac{720}{xy}$

(B) $\frac{xy}{720}$

(C) $\frac{720y}{x}$

(D) $\frac{720x}{y}$

(E) $720xy$

13. Alice had to read 350 pages of a book over the weekend. If on Sunday, she read 50 pages more than half the amount she read on Saturday, how many pages did she read on Saturday?

(A) 150
(B) 175
(C) 200
(D) 225
(E) 250

14. If $xy < 0$, which of the following must be true?

I. $x + y = 0$
II. $2y - 2x < 0$
III. $x^2 + y^2 > 0$

(A) I only
(B) III only
(C) I and III
(D) II and III
(E) I, II, and III

15. Alan, Fred, and Mark are going to buy a computer that costs $540. If Alan pays $40 more than Fred and Fred pays twice as much as Mark, then how much does Mark pay?

(A) $100
(B) $140
(C) $160
(D) $200
(E) $240

16. Allie has three fewer than twice the number of coins that Jonathan has. If Jonathan gave 2 coins to Allie, she would have three times as many coins as he would. How many coins does Allie have?

(A) 2
(B) 3
(C) 5
(D) 7
(E) 9

18. If $2t + \frac{(s-r)}{3} = r$, what is s in terms of r and t?

(A) $2r - 3t$
(B) $2(r - 3t)$
(C) $2(2r - 3t)$
(D) $2(2r + 3t)$
(E) $3(2r - t)$

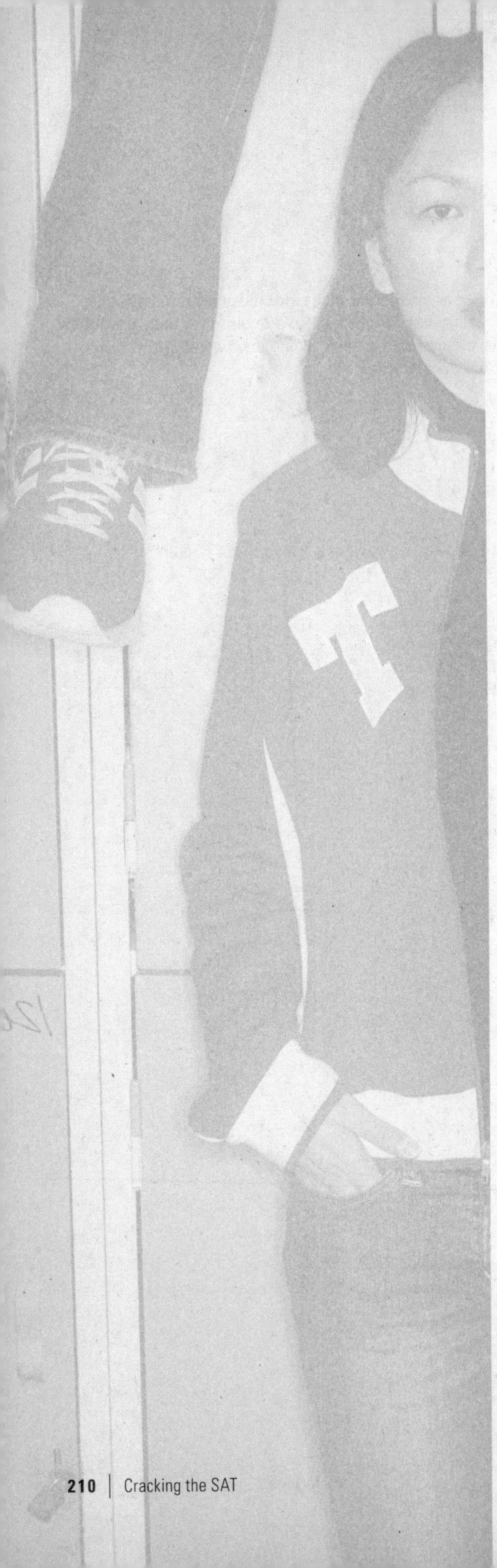

Summary

- Don't "solve for x" or "solve for y" unless you absolutely have to. (Don't worry; your math teacher won't find out.) Instead, look for direct solutions to SAT problems. ETS never uses problems that *necessarily* require time consuming computations or endless fiddling with big numbers. There's almost always a trick—if you can spot it.
- If a problem contains an expression that can be factored, factor it. If it contains an expression that already has been factored, unfactor it.
- To solve simultaneous equations, simply add or subtract the equations.
- When an algebra question has numbers in the answer choices, plug each of the numbers in the answer choices into the problem until you find one that works.
- Plugging In your own numbers is the technique for multiple-choice problems whose answer choices contain variables. It has three steps:
  1) Pick numbers for the variables in the problem.
  2) Use your numbers to find an answer to the problem.
  3) Plug your numbers from step 1 into the answer choices to see which choice equals the answer you found in step 2.
- When you plug in, use "good" numbers—ones that are simple to work with and that make the problem easier to manipulate.
- Plugging In works on problems containing inequalities, but you will have to be careful and follow some different rules. Plugging in one number is often not enough; to find ETS's answer, you may have to plug in several numbers.
- You can also plug in when you have numbers that are too big, too ugly, or too inconvenient to work with.
- Learn to recognize SAT function problems. Sometimes they have funny symbols. Solve them like playing "Simon Says"—do what you are told.

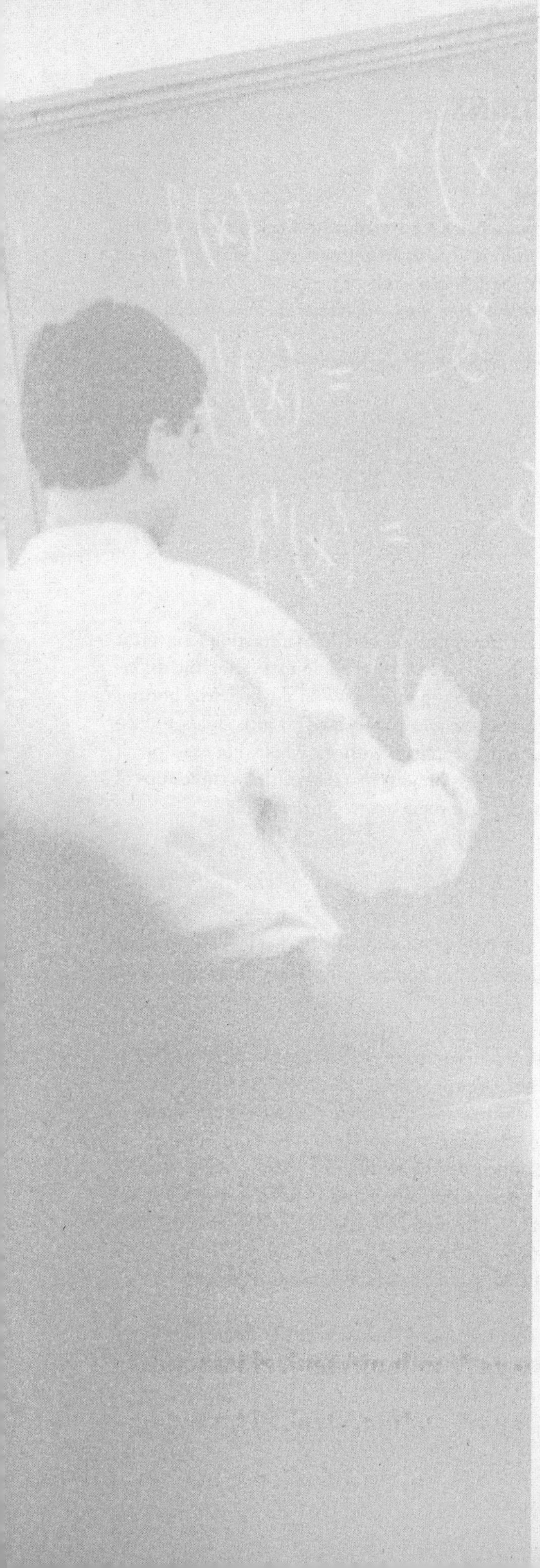

Chapter 13
Advanced Arithmetic

Now that we have reviewed some mathematical fundamentals and some algebra, it is time to jump into our review of the more advanced arithmetic concepts you will find on the SAT. Many math questions test concepts you learned in junior high school, such as averages and proportions. Some difficult questions build on these basic concepts and require you to combine multiple techniques. In this chapter we will brush off the cobwebs and review the advanced arithmetic you'll need to know for the SAT.

RATIOS AND PROPORTIONS

A Ratio Is a Comparison

Many students get extremely nervous when they are asked to work with ratios. But there's no need to be nervous. A ratio is a comparison between the quantities of ingredients you have in a mixture, be it a class full of people or a bowl of cake batter. Ratios can be written to look like fractions—don't get them confused.

The ratio of x to y can be expressed in the following three ways:

1. $\frac{x}{y}$
2. the ratio of x to y
3. $x{:}y$

Part, Part, Whole

Ratios vs. Fractions

Keep in mind that a ratio compares part of something to another part. A fraction compares part of something to the whole thing.

Ratio: $\frac{\text{part}}{\text{part}}$

Fraction: $\frac{\text{part}}{\text{whole}}$

Ratios are a lot like fractions. In fact, anything you can do to a fraction (convert it to a decimal or percentage, reduce it, and so on), you can do to a ratio. The difference is that a fraction gives you a part (the top number) over a whole (the bottom number), while a ratio typically gives you two parts (boys to girls, CDs to cassettes, sugar to flour), and it is your job to come up with the whole. For example, if there is one cup of sugar for every two cups of flour in a recipe, that's three cups of stuff. The ratio of sugar to flour is 1:2. Add the parts to get the whole.

Ratio to Real

If a class contains 3 students and the ratio of boys to girls in that class is 2:1, how many boys and how many girls are there in the class? Of course: There are 2 boys and 1 girl.

Now, suppose a class contains 24 students and the ratio of boys to girls is still 2:1. How many boys and how many girls are there in the class? This is a little harder, but the answer is easy to find if you think about it. There are 16 boys and 8 girls.

How did we get the answer? We added up the number of "parts" in the ratio (2 parts boys plus 1 part girls, or 3 parts all together) and divided it into the total number of students. In other words, we divided 24 by 3. This told us that the class contained 3 equal parts of 8 students each. From the given ratio (2:1), we knew that two of these parts consisted of boys and one of them consisted of girls.

An easy way to keep track of all this is to use a tool we call the *Ratio Box*. Every time you have a ratio problem, set up a Ratio Box with the information provided in the problem and use it to find ETS's answer.

Here's how it works:

Let's go back to our class containing 24 students, in which the ratio of boys to girls is 2:1. Quickly sketch a table that has columns and rows, like this:

	Boys	Girls	Whole
Ratio (parts)	2	1	3
Multiply By			
Actual Number			24

This is the information you have been given. The ratio is 2:1, so you have 2 parts boys and 1 part girls, for a total of 3 parts. You also know that the actual number of students in the whole class is 24. You start by writing these numbers in the proper spaces in your box.

Your goal is to fill in the two empty spaces in the bottom row. To do that, you will multiply each number in the *parts* row by the same number. To find that number, look in the last column. What number would you multiply by 3 to get 24? You should see easily that you would multiply by 8. Therefore, write an 8 in all three blanks in the *Multiply By* row. (The spaces in this row will always contain the same number, although of course it won't always be an 8.) Here's what your Ratio Box should look like now:

	Boys	Girls	Whole
Ratio (parts)	2	1	3
Multiply By	8	8	8
Actual Number			24

The next step is to fill in the empty spaces in the bottom row. You do that the same way you did in the last column, by multiplying. First, multiply the numbers in the boys column ($2 \times 8 = 16$). Then multiply the numbers in the girls column ($1 \times 8 = 8$).

Here's what your box should look like now:

	Boys	Girls	Whole
Ratio (parts)	2	1	3
Multiply By	8	8	8
Actual Number	16	8	24

Now you have enough information to answer any question that ETS might ask you. For example:

- What is the ratio of boys to girls? You can see easily from the ratio (parts) row of the box that the ratio is 2:1.
- What is the ratio of girls to boys? You can see easily from the ratio (parts) row of the box that the ratio is 1:2.
- What is the total number of boys in the class? You can see easily from the bottom row of the box that it is 16.
- What is the total number of girls in the class? You can see easily from the bottom row of the box that it is 8.
- What fractional part of the class is boys? There are 16 boys in a class of 24, so the fraction representing the boys is $\frac{16}{24}$, which can be reduced to $\frac{2}{3}$.

As you can see, the Ratio Box is an easy way to find, organize, and keep track of information on ratio problems. And it works the same no matter what information you are given. Just remember that all the boxes in the *Multiply By* row will always contain the same number.

Here's another example:

Mark It!
Always draw the Ratio Box when working with ratio questions!

10. In a jar of red and green jelly beans, the ratio of green jelly beans to red jelly beans is 5:3. If the jar contains a total of 160 jelly beans, how many of them are red?

(A) 30
(B) 53
(C) 60
(D) 100
(E) 160

Here's How to Crack It

First, sketch out a Ratio Box.

	Green	Red	Whole
Ratio (parts)	5	3	8
Multiply By			
Actual Number			160

Now find the multiplier. What do you multiply by 8 to get 160? You multiply 8 by 20. Now write 20 in each box on the *Multiply By* row.

	Green	**Red**	**Whole**
Ratio (parts)	5	3	8
Multiply By	20	20	20
Actual Number			160

The problem asks you to find how many red jelly beans there are. Go to the red column and multiply 3 by 20. The answer is 60. ETS's answer is C. Notice that you would have set up the box in exactly the same way if the question had asked you to determine how many jelly beans were green. (How many are green? The answer is 5×20, which is 100.)

Don't forget that you can use more than one technique to solve a problem. There's no reason why you can't combine the ratio box with some form of plugging in. In fact, if one technique makes the problem easy, two techniques might make it downright simple!

Here's a problem where combining techniques is just the ticket:

17. In Miss Hoover's class, the ratio of boys to girls is x to y. If the total number of children in the class is five times the number of boys in the class, which of the following is an expression for the number of girls in the class, in terms of x and y ?

(A) $\frac{5x}{x+y}$

(B) $\frac{5x^2}{x+y}$

(C) $\frac{5xy}{x+y}$

(D) $5x$

(E) $5xy$

What You Need

Always keep an eye on what you are being asked. You don't want to do more work than necessary. Question 10 never asks about green jelly beans, so leave that box empty.

Here's How to Crack It

Since the problem uses the word *ratio,* you definitely want to use the ratio box. However, the ratio box works best with numbers rather than variables. What to do? Plug in, of course! Make $x = 3$ and $y = 2$. So the total of the ratio is 5. Since the question says that the total number of students is 5 times the number of boys, we know that the total number of students is 5(3) or 15. Now, it's time to draw the ratio box and fill in what you know:

	Boys	Girls	Total
Ratio (parts)	3	2	5
Multiply By			
Actual Number			15

Now, it's time to use the box to find the target. Since the question wants to know about the number of girls in the class, don't bother with the number of boys. Here's what your filled-in box should look like:

	Boys	Girls	Total
Ratio (parts)	3	2	5
Multiply By		3	3
Actual Number		6	15

In this example, there are 6 girls in the class. Don't forget to circle your target. Now, all you need to do is find which answer equals 6 when $x = 3$ and $y = 2$. Only answer choice C works.

Proportions Are Equal Ratios

Some SAT math problems will contain two proportional, or equal, ratios from which one piece of information is missing.

Here's an example:

5. If 2 packages contain a total of 12 doughnuts, how many doughnuts are there in 5 packages?

(A) 12
(B) 24
(C) 30
(D) 36
(E) 60

Here's How to Crack It

This problem simply describes two equal ratios, one of which is missing a single piece of information. Here's the given information represented as two equal ratios:

$$\frac{2 \text{ (packages)}}{12 \text{ (doughnuts)}} = \frac{5 \text{ (packages)}}{x \text{ (doughnuts)}}$$

Because ratios can be written so they look like fractions, we can treat them exactly like fractions. To find the answer, all you have to do is figure out what you could plug in for x that would make $\frac{2}{12} = \frac{5}{x}$. Now cross-multiply:

$$\frac{2}{12} \times \frac{5}{x}$$

$$\text{so, } 2x = 60$$

$$x = 30$$

The answer is C.

Fraction Magic
Which way can I simplify? Here's the easy trick to remember: Always simplify in the direction of the symbol; that is, a multiplication sign (×) shows you can simplify diagonally and an equal sign (=) says simplify straight across.

Direct and Indirect Variation

What's in a Name?
When you see *variation*, think *proportion*.

Problems dealing with direct variation (a fancy term for proportion) are exactly what you've just seen: If one quantity grows or decreases by a certain amount (a factor), the other quantity grows or decreases by the same amount. Indirect variations (also known as *indirect proportions*) are just the opposite of that. As one quantity grows or decreases, the other quantity decreases or grows by the same factor.

The main formula you want to remember for indirect proportions is:

$$x_1y_1 = x_2y_2$$

Try one:

Translate!
Direct means divide. Since *indirect* is the opposite, indirect means multiply..

15. The amount of time it takes to consume a buffalo carcass is inversely proportional to the number of vultures. If it takes 12 vultures 3 days to consume a buffalo, how many fewer hours will it take if there are 4 more vultures?

(A) $\frac{1}{4}$

(B) $\frac{3}{4}$

(C) 18

(D) 24

(E) 54

Here's How to Crack It

For inverse proportions, follow the formula. First, convert the days: 3 days is equal to 72 hours. Now set up the equation: (12 vultures)(72 hours) = (16 vultures)(x). We solve to get $x = 54$, which is 18 fewer hours. The answer is C.

Since ratios and proportions are related concepts, you might be wondering how you can tell when you should set the problem up as a proportion and when you should use a ratio box. Here are some guidelines to help you decide.

- If the question gives you a *ratio* and an *actual number*, use a ratio box.
- If the question compares items that have *different units* (like feet and seconds), set up a proportion.
- If you don't need the total column in the ratio box, then you can also do the question by setting up a proportion.

PERCENTAGES

Percentages Are Fractions

There should be nothing frightening about a percentage. It's just a convenient way of expressing a fraction whose bottom is 100.

Percent means "per 100," or "out of 100." If there are 100 questions on your math test and you answer 50 of them, you will have answered 50 out of 100, or $\frac{50}{100}$, or 50 percent. To think of it another way:

$$\frac{\text{part}}{\text{whole}} = \frac{x}{100} = x \text{ percent}$$

Memorize These Percentage-Decimal-Fraction Equivalents

These show up all the time, so go ahead and memorize them.

$0.01 = \frac{1}{100} = 1$ percent $\quad 0.25 = \frac{1}{4} = 25$ percent

$0.1 = \frac{1}{10} = 10$ percent $\quad 0.5 = \frac{1}{2} = 50$ percent

$0.2 = \frac{1}{5} = 20$ percent $\quad 0.75 = \frac{3}{4} = 75$ percent

Another Way
You can also convert fractions to percentages by cross-multiplying:

$$\frac{3}{4} = \frac{x}{100}$$
$$4x = 3(100)$$
$$x = \frac{3(100)}{4}$$
$$x = 75$$

Converting Percentages to Fractions

To convert a percentage to a fraction, simply put the percentage over 100 and reduce. For example:

$$80 \text{ percent} = \frac{80}{100} = \frac{8}{10} = \frac{4}{5}$$

Converting Fractions to Percentages

Because a percentage is just another way to express a fraction, you shouldn't be surprised to see how easy it is to convert a fraction to a percentage. To do so, simply use your calculator to divide the top of the fraction by the bottom of the fraction, and then multiply the result by 100. Here's an example:

Problem: Express $\frac{3}{4}$ as a percentage.

Solution: $\frac{3}{4} = 0.75 \times 100 = 75$ percent.

Converting fractions to percentages is easy with your calculator.

Converting Percentages to Decimals

To convert a percentage to a decimal, simply move the decimal point *two places to the left.* For example: 25 percent can be expressed as the decimal 0.25; 50 percent is the same as 0.50 or 0.5; 100 percent is the same as 1.00 or 1.

Converting Decimals to Percentages

To convert a decimal to a percentage, just do the opposite of what you did in the preceding section. All you have to do is move the decimal point *two places to the right.* Thus, 0.5 = 50 percent; 0.375 = 37.5 percent; 2 = 200 percent.

The following drill will give you practice working with fractions, decimals, and percentages.

DRILL 1

Fill in the missing information in the following table. Answers can be found on page 379.

	Fraction	Decimal	Percent
	$\frac{1}{5}$	.2	20%
1.	$\frac{1}{2}$		
2.		3.0	
3.			0.5%
4.	$\frac{1}{3}$		

Word	Symbol
is	=
greater than	+
of	× (multiply)
percent	/100
what	*n* (variable)

Translation, Please!

On a math test like the SAT, we can convert (or translate) words into arithmetic symbols. Here are some of the most common:

Joe Bloggs Doesn't Speak Math

Problem: What number is 10 percent greater than 20?

Joe Bloggs makes careless errors on questions like this because he doesn't think about what the words he's reading translate to in math. You won't if you take them slowly and remember what those words look like when you use mathematical symbols. Let's use the chart above to write this question in math. *What number* means "variable" so we can write that as n (or x or whatever number works for you!). *Is* means "equals," so now we have $n = 10\%$. *Greater than* translates to +. So now we've got our equation:

$$n = 10\% + 20$$

10 percent of 20 is 2, so

$$n = 2 + 20$$
$$n = 22.$$

You will see the words *of, is, product, sum,* and *what* pop up a lot in the Math sections of the SAT. Don't let these words fool you because they all translate into simple math functions. Memorize all of these terms and their math equivalents. It will save you time on the test and make your life with the SAT much nicer.

What Percent of What Percent of What?

On harder SAT questions, you may be asked to determine the effect of a series of percentage increases or decreases. The key point to remember on such problems is that each successive increase or decrease is performed on the result of the previous one.

Here's an example:

Bite-Size Pieces
Always handle percentage problems in bite-size pieces: one piece at a time.

15. A business paid $300 to rent a piece of office equipment for one year. The rent was then increased by 10% each year thereafter. How much will the company pay for the first three years it rents the equipment?

(A) $920
(B) $960
(C) $990
(D) $993
(E) $999

Here's How to Crack It

This problem is a great place to use bite-sized pieces. You know that the business paid $300 to rent the piece of office equipment for the first year. Then, you were told that the rent increases by 10 percent for each year thereafter. That's a sure sign that you're going to need the rent for the second year, so go ahead and calculate it. For the second year, the rent is $300+\left(\frac{10}{100}\times 300\right)=330$

Now, the problem tells you that the business rents the equipment for three years. So, you need to do the calculation one more time. At this point, you might want to set up a chart to help keep track of the information.

Year 1: $300

Year 2: $330

Year 3: $\$363=330\left(\frac{10}{100}\times 330\right)$

To find the answer, all you need to do is add up the costs for each of the three years:

Year 1:	$300
Year 2:	$330
Year 3:	$363
	$993

The correct answer is D, $993.

What Percent of What Percent of . . . Yikes!

Sometimes you may find successive percentage problems in which you aren't given actual numbers to work with. In such cases, you need to plug in some numbers.

Here's an example:

17. A number is increased by 25 percent and then decreased by 20 percent. The result is what percent of the original number?

(A) 80
(B) 100
(C) 105
(D) 120
(E) 125

Here's How to Crack It

You aren't given a particular number to work with in this problem—just "a number." Rather than trying to deal with the problem in the abstract, you should immediately plug in a number to work with. What number would be easiest to work with in a percentage problem? Why, 100, of course.

1. 25 percent of 100 is 25, so 100 increased by 25 percent is 125.
2. Now you have to decrease 125 by 20 percent; 20 percent of 125 is 25, so 125 decreased by 20 percent is 100.
3. 100 (our result) is 100 percent of 100 (the number you plugged in), so ETS's answer, once again, is B.

Remember: Never try to solve a percentage problem by writing an equation if you can plug in numbers instead. Plugging in on percentage problems is faster, easier, and more accurate. Why work through long, arduous equations if you don't have to?

Careful

Number 17 is a difficult question. Beware of percentage change problems in the hard questions. The answers to these problems almost always defy common sense. Unless you are careful, you may fall for a Joe Bloggs attractor.

More Plugging In with Percents

Sometimes ETS will give you a percent problem that uses variables rather than numbers. They'd like you to get confused because you're not used to seeing percent questions like these. However, if you remember to plug in and to translate the words in the problem, these problems are no big deal.

Here's an example:

18. Which of the following is equivalent to $\frac{1}{x}$ of 37% of y ?

(A) $\frac{37y}{x}$

(B) $\frac{37}{x}$% of xy

(C) $\frac{37}{100x}$% of y

(D) $\frac{37}{x}$% of $\frac{y}{x}$

(E) 37% of $\frac{y}{x}$

Here's How to Crack It

If there were numbers in the problem, you could pull out your trusty calculator and get to the answer pretty easily. So, fill in some numbers for the variables! If you make $x = 2$ and $y = 100$, you'll have some pretty nice number to work with. With the numbers inserted, the problem now reads:

18. Which of the following is equivalent to $\frac{1}{2}$ of 37% of 100 ?

Now, it's time to translate. Don't forget that *of* means *multiply* and *percent* means *over 100*. So, the words in the problem translate to $\frac{1}{2}\times\frac{37}{100}\times 100=\frac{37}{2}$. So, $\frac{37}{2}$ (or 18.5, if you prefer decimals) is the target. It's time to go find that in the answer choices. Remember to translate them, as well. Here are the results:

(A) $\frac{37\times 100}{2}=185$ Wrong!

(B) $\left(\frac{37}{2}\%\right)\times 2\times 100=\frac{185}{100}\times 200=37$ Wrong!

(C) $\left(\frac{37}{100\times 2}\%\right)\times 100=\frac{\frac{37}{200}}{100}\times 100=\frac{37}{200}$ Wrong!

(D) $\left(\frac{37}{2}\%\right)\times\frac{100}{2}=\left(\frac{185}{100}\right)\times 50=9.25$ Wrong!

(E) $\frac{37}{100}\times\frac{100}{2}=\frac{37}{2}$ Right!

So, the answer is E.

Percent Change

There's one more thing that you should know about percents. Some problems will ask for a percent increase or decrease. For these problems, use the following formula.

$$\%\ change=\frac{Difference}{Original}\times 100$$

Most of the time that you use the formula, it will be pretty clear which number you should use for the original. However, if you're not sure, remember that you should use the *smaller* number for the original if you are finding a percent *increase.* You should use the *larger* number for the original if you are finding a percent *decrease.*

Here's an example of how to use the formula:

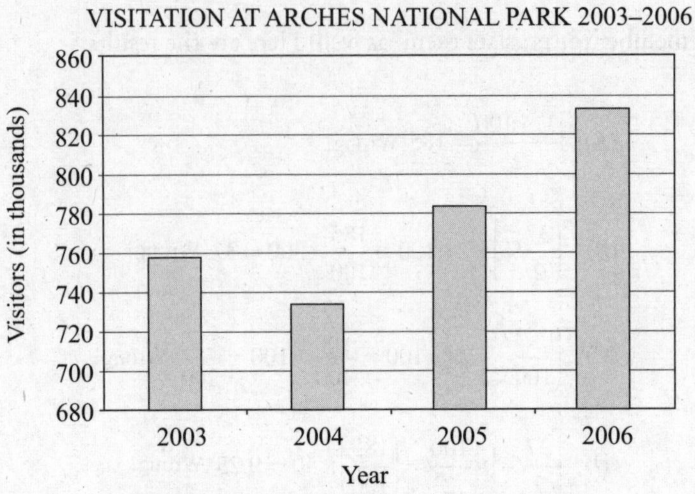

8. The chart shown above shows the number of visits, in thousands, at Arches National Park for the years 2003 to 2006. Which of the following is the closest approximation of the percent increase in the number of visits from 2004 to 2006?

(A) 1.5%
(B) 5%
(C) 15%
(D) 20%
(E) 115%

Here's How to Crack It

First, you need to get the data from the chart. In 2004, the chart shows that there were approximately 730,000 visitors to Arches. In 2006, the chart shows that there were about 830,000 visitors to the park. Now, it's time to use the percent change formula. The difference is about 100,000 and the original is the 730,000 visitors in 2004:

$$\%\ increase = \frac{100{,}000}{730{,}000} \times 100 \approx 15\%$$

You could punch the number into the calculator, or you could approximate since the numbers in the answers are pretty far apart. The fraction in the formula is about $\frac{1}{7}$ and that's greater than $\frac{1}{10}$, which is 10%, but less than $\frac{1}{5}$, which is 20%. The correct answer is C.

AVERAGES

What Is an Average?

The average (also called the *arithmetic mean*) of a set of n numbers is simply the sum of all the numbers divided by n. In other words, if you want to find the average of three numbers, add them up and divide by 3. For example, the average of 3, 7, and 8 is $\frac{(3+7+8)}{3}$, which equals $\frac{18}{3}$, or 6.

That was an easy example, but ETS does not always write average questions with clear solutions. That is, ETS doesn't always give you the information for averages in a way that is easy to work with. For that reason, we have a visual aid, like the Ratio Box for ratios, that helps you organize the information on average questions and find ETS's answer.

We call it the *Average Pie*. Here's what it looks like:

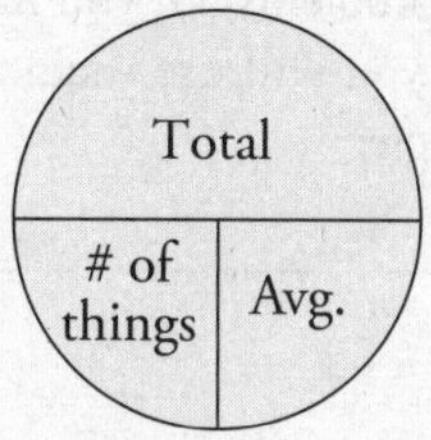

The *total* is the sum of all the numbers you're averaging, and the *number of things* is the number of elements you're averaging. Here's what the Average Pie looks like using the simple average example we just gave you.

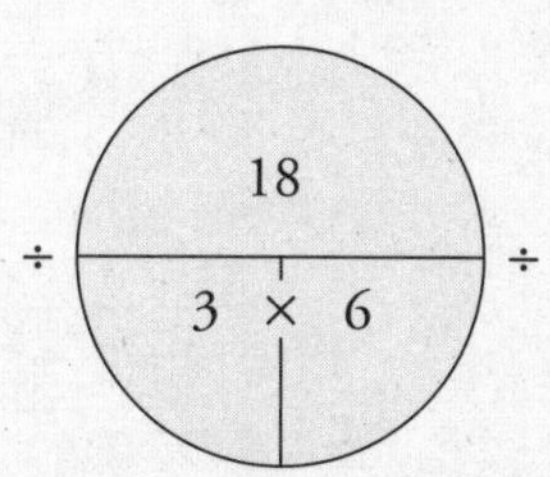

Here's how the Average Pie works mathematically. The line in the middle means *divide*. If you know the total and the number of things, just divide to get the average (18 ÷ 3 = 6). If you know the total and the average, just divide to get the number of things (18 ÷ 6 = 3). If you know the average and the number of things, simply multiply to get the total (6 × 3 = 18). The key to most average questions is finding the total.

Total
When calculating averages and means, always find the total. It's the one piece of information that ETS loves to withhold.

Here's another simple example:

Problem: If the average of three test scores is 70, what is the total of all three test scores?

Solution: Just put the number of things (3 tests) and the average (70) in the pie. Then multiply to find the total, which is 210.

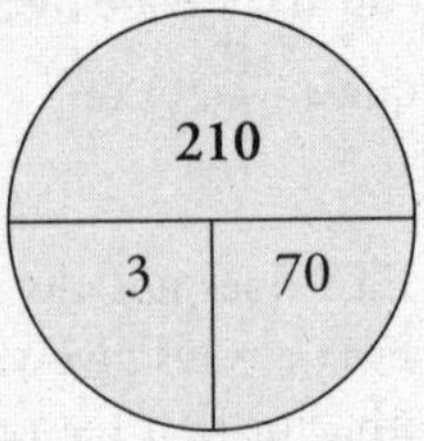

Mark It!
Make sure you're drawing a new average pie each time you see the word *average* in a question.

Averages: Advanced Principles

To solve most difficult average problems, all you have to do is fill out one or more Average Pies. Most of the time you will use them to find the total of the number being averaged. Here's an example:

10. Maria has taken four chemistry tests and has an average (arithmetic mean) score of 80. If she scores a 90 on her fifth chemistry test, what is her average for these five tests?

(A) 80
(B) 81
(C) 82
(D) 84
(E) 85

Here's How to Crack It

Start by drawing an average pie and filling in what you know. You can put 4 in for the number of things and 80 for the average. You can calculate that Maria has gotten 320 total points on her first four tests. Your pie should look like this:

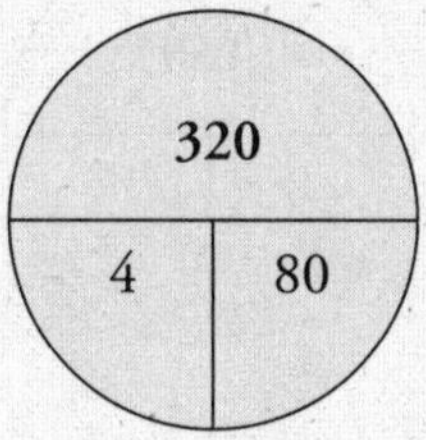

Now, draw another average pie and fill in what you know. This time, there are five tests. The question wants to know the average, so you also need to fill the total. The total for all five tests is the total from the first four tests plus the score from the fifth test: 320 + 90 = 410. Put that on the pie and divide to find the average:

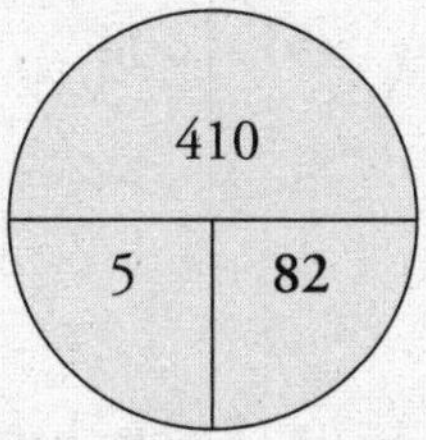

The answer is C, 82.

Now let's try a difficult test question:

20. If the average (arithmetic mean) of eight numbers is 20, and the average of five of these numbers is 14, what is the average of the other three numbers?

(A) 14
(B) 17
(C) 20
(D) 30
(E) 34

Here's How to Crack It

Start by drawing an Average Pie for all eight numbers; then multiply to find the total.

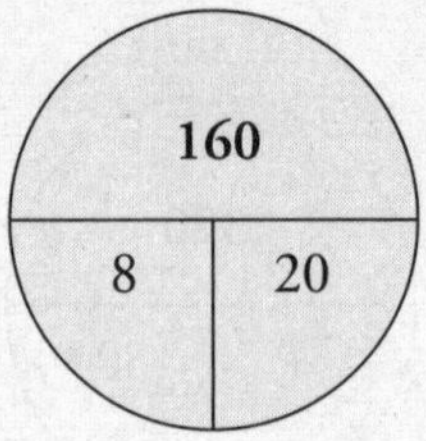

The total of the eight numbers is 160. Now draw another Average Pie for five of the numbers.

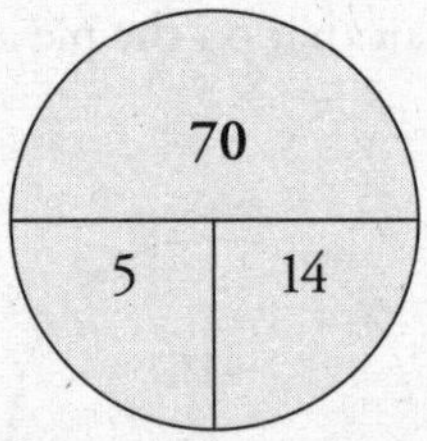

The total of those five numbers is 70. (Remember: Those are five out of the original eight numbers.) To find the average of the other three numbers, you need the total of those three numbers. You have the total of all eight numbers, 160, and the total of five of those numbers, 70, so you can find the total of the other three by subtracting 70 from 160. That means the total of the three remaining numbers is 90. It's time to create one more Average Pie to find the average of those three numbers.

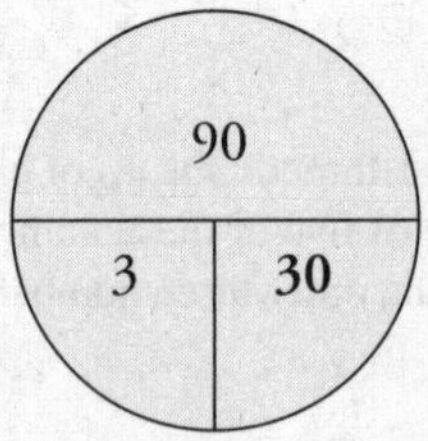

The average is 30, so the answer is D.

Don't forget that you can also plug in when using the average pie.

16. The average (arithmetic mean) of a list of 5 numbers is n. When an additional number is added to the list, the average of all 6 numbers is $n + 3$. Which of the following is the value, in terms of n, of the number added to the list?

(A) n
(B) $5n$
(C) $n + 6$
(D) $n + 18$
(E) $6n + 18$

Here's How to Crack It

Plug in for the value of n. If $n = 20$, then you can use the average pie to find the total of the five numbers on the list.

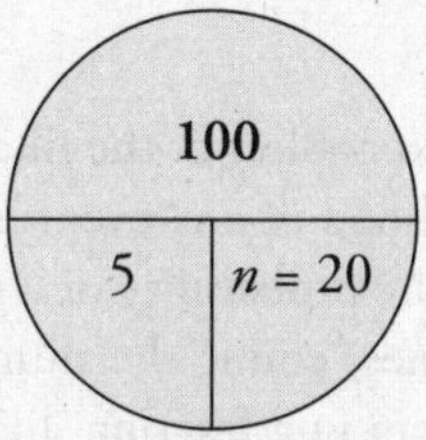

As shown on the average pie above, the total of the 5 numbers is 100. Now, it's time for another average pie. For this pie, you know that there are 6 numbers and that their average is $20 + 3 = 23$.

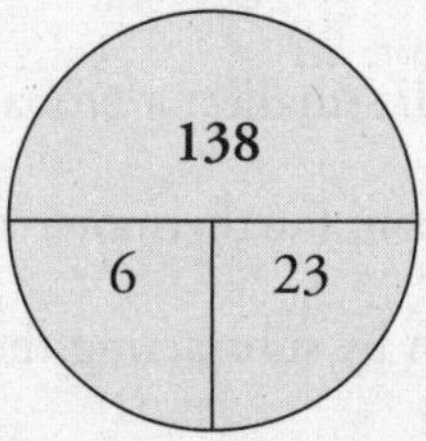

Using the average pie as shown above, the total of the six numbers is 138. Since the difference in the two totals was caused by the addition of the sixth number, the sixth number must be $138 - 100 = 38$. That's the target, so be sure to circle it. Only answer D is 38 when $n = 20$.

On the SAT, you'll also need to know two other topics related to averages: *median* and *mode.*

What Is a *Median*?

Missing the Middle?
To find the median of a set containing an even number of items, take the average of the two middle numbers.

The median of a list of numbers is the number that is exactly in the middle of the list when the list is arranged from smallest to largest, as on a number line. For example, in the group 3, 6, 6, 6, 6, 7, 8, 9, 10, 10, 11, the median is 7. Five numbers come before 7 in the list, and 5 come after. Remember it this way: *Median* sounds like *middle.*

What Is a *Mode*?

A la Mode
If two numbers appear in a sequence the same amount of times, like 1, 2, 2, 3, 3, 4, then they're both the mode. Likewise, if every number appears the same amount of times, like 1, 1, 8, 8, 9, 9, then they're *all* modes.

The mode of a group of numbers is the number in the list that appears most often. In the list 3, 4, 4, 5, 7, 7, 8, 8, 8, 9, 10, the mode is 8, because it appears three times while no other number in the group appears more than twice. Remember it this way: *Mode* sounds like *most.*

PROBABILITY

Probability is a mathematical expression of the likelihood of an event. The basis of probability is simple. The likelihood of any event is discussed in terms of all of the possible outcomes. To express the probability of a given event, *x,* you would count the number of possible outcomes, count the number of outcomes that give you what you want, and arrange them in a fraction, like this:

$$\text{Probability of } x = \frac{\text{number of outcomes that are } x}{\text{total number of possible outcomes}}$$

Every probability is a fraction. The largest a probability can be is 1; a probability of 1 indicates total certainty. The smallest a probability can be is 0, meaning that it's something that cannot happen. Furthermore, you can find the probability that something WILL NOT happen by subtracting the probability that it WILL happen from 1. For example, if the weatherman tells you that there is a 0.3 probability of rain today, then there must be a 0.7 probability that it won't rain, because 1 – 0.3 = 0.7. Figuring out the probability of any single event is usually simple.

When you flip a coin, there are only two possible outcomes, heads and tails; the probability of getting heads is therefore 1 out of 2, or $\frac{1}{2}$. When you roll a die, there are six possible outcomes, 1 through 6; the odds of getting a 6 is therefore $\frac{1}{6}$. The odds of getting an even result when rolling a die are $\frac{1}{2}$ because there are 3 even results in 6 possible outcomes.

Here's an example of a probability question:

12. A bag contains 7 blue marbles and 14 marbles that are not blue. If one marble is drawn at random from the bag, what is the probability that the marble is blue?

(A) $\frac{1}{7}$

(B) $\frac{1}{3}$

(C) $\frac{1}{2}$

(D) $\frac{2}{3}$

(E) $\frac{3}{7}$

Here's How to Crack It

Here, there are 21 marbles in the bag, 7 of which are blue. The probability that a marble chosen at random would be blue is therefore $\frac{7}{21}$, or $\frac{1}{3}$. The correct answer is B.

Some probability questions might include variables. Not to worry. Plugging in will save the day!

Here's an example:

---

17. A jar contains only red marbles and white marbles. If the probability of selecting a red marble is $\frac{r}{y}$, which of the following expressions gives the probability of selecting a white marble in terms of r and y ?

(A) $\frac{r-y}{y}$

(B) $\frac{y-r}{y}$

(C) $\frac{y}{y-r}$

(D) $\frac{r}{y}$

(E) $\frac{y}{r}$

Here's How to Crack It

Plug in! You could make the probability of choosing a red marble be $\frac{2}{3}$. Then $\frac{r}{y} = \frac{2}{3}$ which means that $r = 2$ and $y = 3$.

Now, to get the numerical answer, you need to remember that the probabilities of all the things that can happen always add up to 1. Since there are only red marbles and white marbles in the jar, choosing a red marble or choosing a white marble are the only things that can happen. So, the probability of selecting a white marble can be found by subtracting the probability of getting a red marble from 1: Probability of white $= 1 - \frac{2}{3} = \frac{1}{3}$. That's your target, so circle it.

Now, go find the answer that gives you $\frac{1}{3}$ when $r = 2$ and $y = 3$. Answer B is $\frac{y-r}{y} = \frac{3-2}{3} = \frac{1}{3}$. Since no other answer evaluates to $\frac{1}{3}$, B is the answer.

PERMUTATIONS

A permutation is an arrangement of objects of a definite order. The simplest sort of permutations question might ask you how many different arrangements are possible for six different chairs in a row, or how many different four-letter arrangements of the letters in the word FUEL are possible. Both of these simple questions can be answered with the same technique.

Just draw a row of boxes corresponding to the positions you have to fill. In the case of the chairs, there are six positions, one for each chair. You would make a sketch like this:

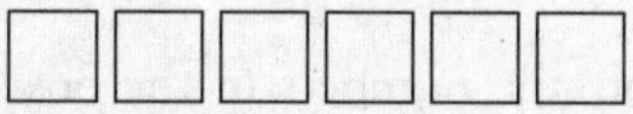

Then, in each box, write the number of objects available to be put into that box. Keep in mind that objects put into previous boxes are no longer available. For the chair-arranging example, there would be six chairs available for the first box; only five left for the second box; four for the third, and so on until only one chair remained to be put into the last position. Finally, just multiply the numbers in the boxes together, and the product will be the number of possible arrangements, or permutations.

6	5	4	3	2	1	= 720

There are 720 possible permutations of a group of six chairs. This number can also be written as 6!. That's not a display of enthusiasm—the exclamation point means *factorial*. The number is read "six factorial," and it means $6 \times 5 \times 4 \times 3 \times 2 \times 1$, which equals 720. A factorial is simply the product of a series of integers counting down to 1 from the specified number. For example, the number 70! means $70 \times 69 \times 68 \ldots 3 \times 2 \times 1$.

The number of possible arrangements of any group with n members is simply $n!$. In this way, the number of possible arrangements of the letters in FUEL is 4!, because there are four letters in the group. That means $4 \times 3 \times 2 \times 1$ arrangements, or 24. If you sketched four boxes for the four letter positions and filled in the appropriate numbers, that's exactly what you'd get.

Don't Forget Your Calculator!

Look at your calculator for the factorial sign. It can simplify your life. On a scientific calculator, it is often a shift key and the symbol is $x!$. On a graphing calculator, it can usually be found in [MATH] in [Probability]. Knowing where the key is and how to use it can speed things along. Don't forget about your parentheses!

Advanced Permutations

Permutations get a little trickier when you work with smaller arrangements. For example, what if you were asked how many two-letter arrangements could be made from the letters in FUEL? It's just a modification of the original counting procedure. Sketch two boxes for the two positions. Then fill in the number of letters available for each position. As before, there are four letters available for the first space, and three for the second; the only difference is that you're done after two spaces:

$$\boxed{4}\,\boxed{3} = 12$$

As you did before, multiply the numbers in the boxes together to get the total number of arrangements. You should find there are twelve possible two-letter arrangements from the letters in FUEL.

That's all there is to permutations. The box-counting procedure is the safest way to approach them. Just sketch the number of positions available, and fill in the number of objects available for each position, from first to last—then multiply those numbers together.

Try one:

17. Hal wrote 7 essays in his English class. He wants to put all 7 essays in his portfolio and is deciding in what order to place the essays. In how many different orders can Hal arrange his essays?

(A) 49
(B) 420
(C) 5,040
(D) 5,670
(E) 10,549

Here's How to Crack It

There are seven essays that could be first. Once an essay is selected for first place, there are six left that could be second, then five that could be third, four that could be fourth, three that could be fifth, two that could be sixth, and one that will be last. Multiply all of those choices together: $7 \times 6 \times 5 \times 4 \times 3 \times 2 \times 1 = 5{,}040$. The correct answer is C.

There's one final thing to know about counting problems. Sometimes, some of the positions might have some restrictions on what you can put there. Be sure that you remember those restrictions when you write down how many things could go in each of those positions.

Here's an example:

---

19. In the three digit integer 735, the digits are all different and the hundreds digit and the units digit are both prime. How many three digit integers have digits that are all different and have both prime hundreds and units digits?

(A) 24
(B) 96
(C) 120
(D) 160
(E) 250

Here's How to Crack It

Since there are three digits in the number, start by drawing out three boxes. The hundreds digit needs to be prime, so it could be any of the digits 2, 3, 5, or 7. (Don't forget that 1 is not prime!) So, there are 4 choices for the hundreds digit. Write 4 in your first box. The problem will be easier to think about if you fill in the choices for the more restricted of the remaining two boxes next. So, jump over to the last box. The units digit also needs to be prime but it also needs to be different from the hundreds digit. That means there are only 3 choices left for the units digit. Finally, it's time to fill in the box for the tens digit. It doesn't need to be prime but it does need to be different from the hundreds and the units digits. So, rather than there being 10 choices (the digits 0 through 9), there are really only 8 choices left. To finish the problem, all you need to do is multiply the choices together: $4 \times 8 \times 3 = 96$. The correct answer is B.

DRILL 2

Work these problems using the advanced algebra techniques and algebra tips we've covered in this chapter. Answers can be found on pages 379–380.

$20-2x$

$20-x$

20

$20+x$

$20+2x$

5. What is the average (arithmetic mean) of the list of numbers above?

(A) 20

(B) 100

(C) $20+\frac{x}{5}$

(D) $4+x$

(E) $\frac{100}{x}$

8. Henry needs to choose 2 statues to arrange on his lawn. If he has 9 statues, how many total arrangements of statues are possible?

(A) 18
(B) 36
(C) 72
(D) 81
(E) 108

9. The amount of time that Amy walks is directly proportional to the distance that she walks. If she walks a distance of 2.5 miles in 50 minutes, how many miles will she walk in 2 hours?

(A) 3
(B) 4.5
(C) 5
(D) 6
(E) 6.5

10. A total of 140,000 votes were cast for two candidates, Skinner and Whitehouse. If Skinner won by a ration of 4 to 3, how many votes were cast for Whitehouse?

(A) 30,000
(B) 40,000
(C) 60,000
(D) 80,000
(E) 105,000

14. Which of the following is equivalent to 1/4 of 18% of 616?

(A) 18% of 2464
(B) 4.5% of 154
(C) 72% of 616
(D) 18% of 154
(E) 18.25% of 616

16. Of all the houses in a certain neighborhood, 80% have garages. Of those houses with garages, 60% have two-car garages. If there are 56 houses with garages that are not two-car garages, how many houses are there in the neighborhood?

(A) 26
(B) 93
(C) 117
(D) 125
(E) 156

18. On Tuesday, a watchmaker made 4 more watches than he had made during the previous day. If he made 16% more watches on Tuesday than on Monday, how many watches did he make on Tuesday?

(A) 16
(B) 20
(C) 21
(D) 25
(E) 29

Summary

- A ratio can be expressed as a fraction, but ratios are not fractions. A ratio compares parts to parts; a fraction compares a part to the whole.
- Use a Ratio Box to solve ratio questions.
- Direct proportion is $\frac{x_1}{y_1} = \frac{x_2}{y_2}$. Indirect proportion is $x_1y_1 = x_2y_2$.
- A percentage is just a convenient way of expressing a fraction whose bottom is 100.
- To convert a percentage to a fraction, put the percentage over 100 and reduce.
- To convert a fraction to a percentage, use your calculator to divide the top of the fraction by the bottom of the fraction. Then multiply the result by 100.
- To convert a percentage to a decimal, move the decimal point two places to the left. To convert a decimal to a percentage, move the decimal point two places to the right.
- In problems that require you to find a series of percentage increases or decreases, remember that each successive increase or decrease is performed on the result of the previous one.
- If you need to find the percent increase or decrease use % change = $\frac{\textit{difference}}{\textit{original}} \times 100$
- To find the average (arithmetic mean) of several values, add up the values and divide the total by the number of values.
- Use the Average Pie to solve problems involving averages. The key to most average problems is finding the total.

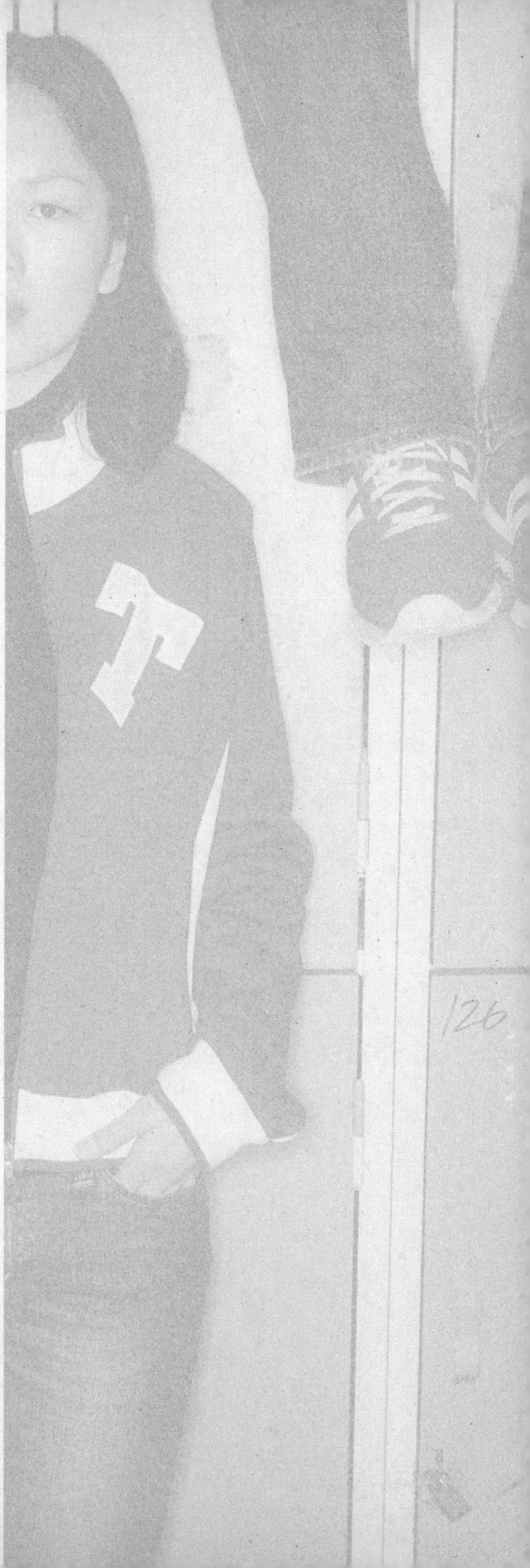

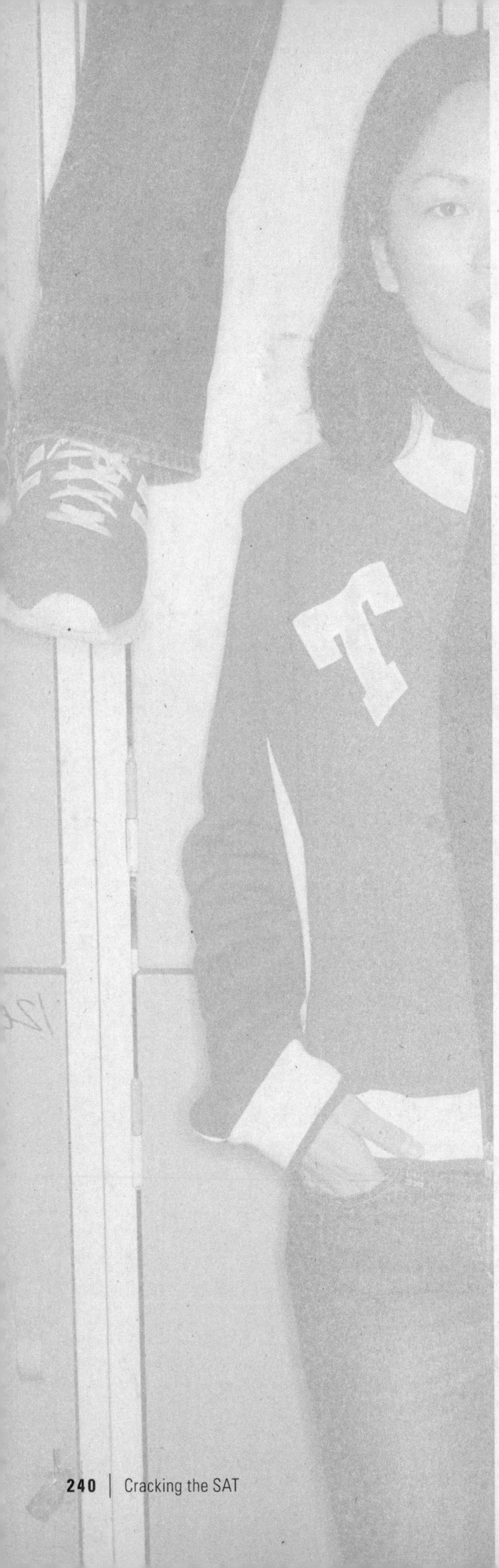

- The median of a group of numbers is the number that is exactly in the middle of the group when the group is arranged from smallest to largest, as on a number line. If there are an even number of numbers, the median is the average of the two middle numbers.
- The mode of a group of numbers is the number in the group that appears most often.
- Probability is expressed as a fraction:

  $$\text{Probability of } x = \frac{\text{number of outcomes that are } x}{\text{total number of possible outcomes}}$$

- To find permutations, or possible orders of objects, use factorials. A factorial is the whole series of integers counting down from the given number, all multiplied together.

Chapter 14
Geometry

While high school geometry can be amazingly complex and involve numerous proofs and theorems, SAT geometry is limited to testing a few basic rules. In fact, many of the rules the SAT tests are ones you learned in middle school. The SAT even provides you with most of the formulas you need at the beginning of each Math section. In this chapter you will learn how to apply these rules and formulas to the questions in the test. You will also learn that harder questions don't test harder geometry; rather these questions simply are tricker or involve more steps.

Reference Information

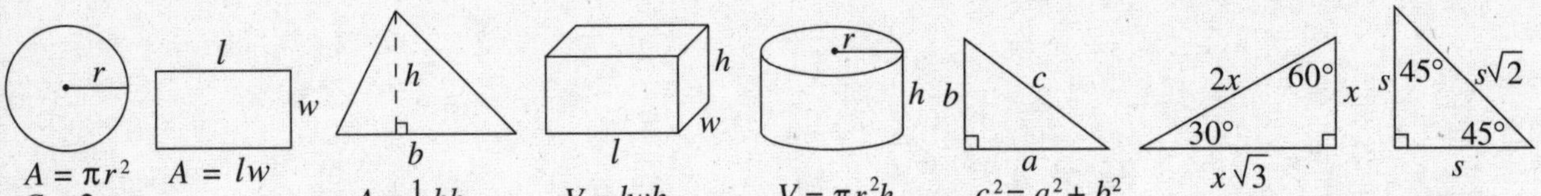

$A = \pi r^2$
$C = 2\pi r$

$A = lw$

$A = \frac{1}{2}bh$

$V = lwh$

$V = \pi r^2 h$

$c^2 = a^2 + b^2$

Special Right Triangles

The number of degrees of arc in a circle is 360.

The sum of the measures in degrees of the angles of a triangle is 180.

SAT GEOMETRY: CRACKING THE SYSTEM

About a third of the math problems on the SAT will involve geometry. Fortunately, you won't have to prove theorems or memorize tons of terms and formulas. That's right, most of the geometric formulas you'll need are on the first page of each Math section on the test, in the box entitled, "Reference Information."

ETS Tries to Be Helpful

Not only do you not need any advanced geometric knowledge, but ETS helps you by giving you some basic geometric formulas in the front of each Math section.

Why would ETS give you all these geometric formulas? Because the SAT is not a geometry test like the ones you might see in school. ETS doesn't care about proofs because it doesn't want to spend the time and money to grade proofs. You need to know some rules of geometry, but not the way you do in a real geometry class.

Don't be afraid to look back to grab a formula that you need!

The Princeton Review Way

The key to cracking SAT geometry is to gather all the available information in the problem. The best way to do that is to follow these simple steps:

1. **Know the rules!** The SAT doesn't require any advanced geometric knowledge, but you will have to know the basics backward and forward.
2. **Fill in the missing info.** SAT geometry problems almost always leave out important information. Fill it in! Don't forget to draw any missing pictures.
3. **Write down any formulas required.** All the area and volume formulas that you need will be provided. Write 'em down and fill in the values that you know.
4. **Solve for any missing info.** After you fill in the formula, solve.

Some problems won't require you to work through all the steps. For easier geometry problems, you might need only steps 1 and 2. For harder problems, you may need all four steps. Either way, get in the habit of looking for missing information and filling it into the diagram.

Let's get started with step 1: learning the basic rules.

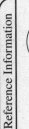

BASIC PRINCIPLES: FUNDAMENTALS OF SAT GEOMETRY

The SAT doesn't test any really difficult geometry, but you will need a thorough knowledge of several fundamental rules. You will use these fundamentals in applying the techniques that we will teach you later in the chapter. You don't need to linger over these rules if you have already mastered them. But be sure you understand them completely before you move on. Some of these rules will be provided in the instructions on your SAT, but you should know them before you go to the test center. Consulting the instructions as you work is a waste of time. (On the other hand, if the Pythagorean theorem suddenly vaporizes from your brain while you are taking the test, don't hesitate to peek back at the instructions.)

We divide SAT geometry into five basic topics:

- Degrees and angles
- Triangles
- Circles
- Rectangles and squares
- Odds and ends

Degrees and Angles

1. **A circle contains 360 degrees.**

   Every circle contains 360 degrees. Each degree is $\frac{1}{360}$ of the total distance around the outside of the circle. It doesn't matter whether the circle is large or small; it still has exactly 360 degrees.

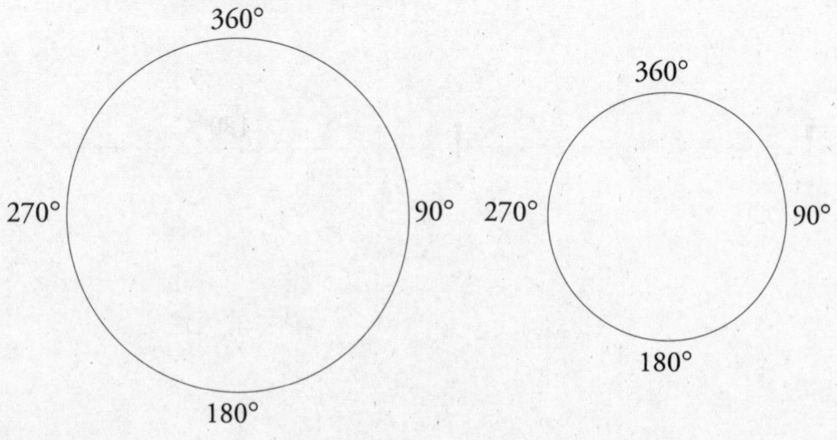

2. **When you think about angles, remember circles.**
An angle is formed when two line segments extend from a common point. If you think of the point as the center of a circle, the measure of the angle is the number of degrees enclosed by the lines when they pass through the edge of the circle. Once again, the size of the circle doesn't matter; neither does the length of the lines.

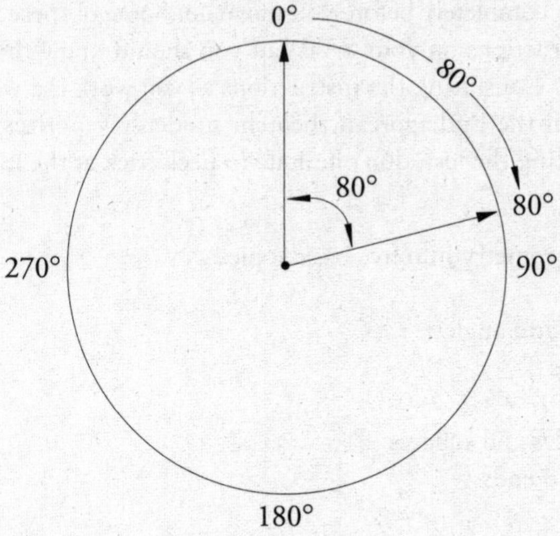

3. **A line is a 180-degree angle.**
You probably don't think of a line as an angle, but it is one. Think of it as a flat angle. The following drawings should help:

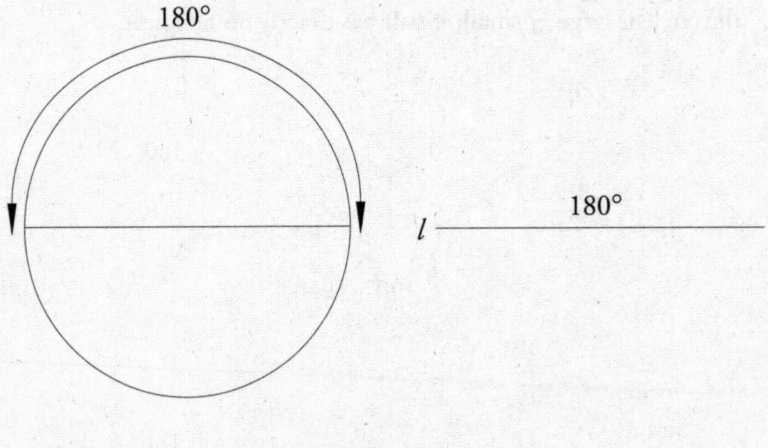

4. **When two lines intersect, four angles are formed.**
The following diagram should make this clear. The four angles are indicated by letters.

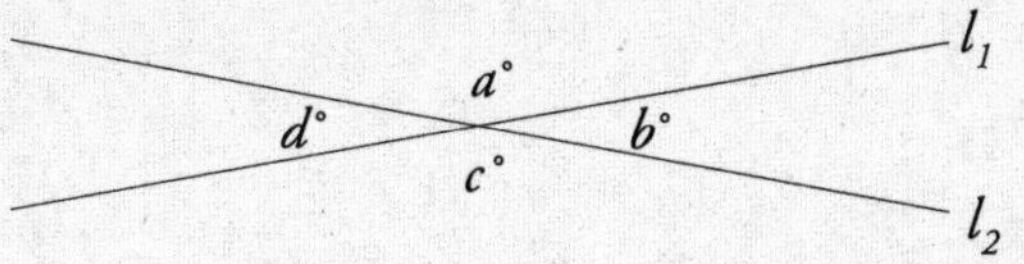

5. **When two lines intersect, the angles opposite each other will have the same measures.**
Such angles are called *vertical angles*. In the following diagram, angles a and c are equal; so are angles b and d.

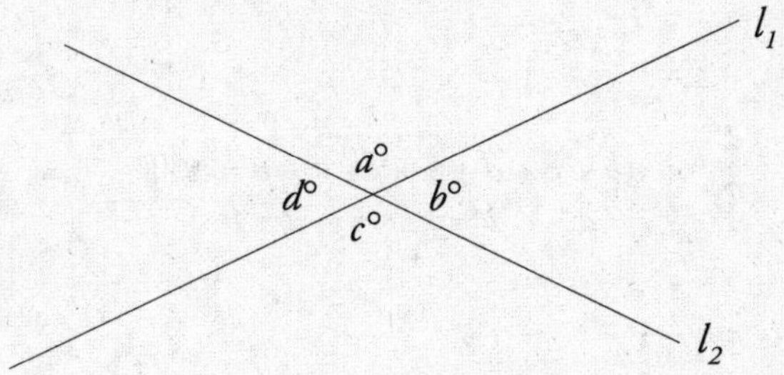

$$a + b + c + d = 360°$$
$$a = c,\ b = d$$

The measures of these four angles add up to 360 degrees. (Remember the circle.)

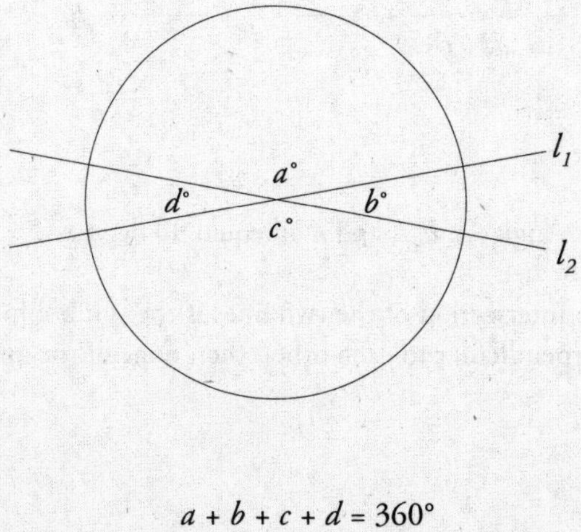

$$a + b + c + d = 360°$$

It doesn't matter how many lines you intersect through a single point. The total measure of all the angles formed will still be 360 degrees.

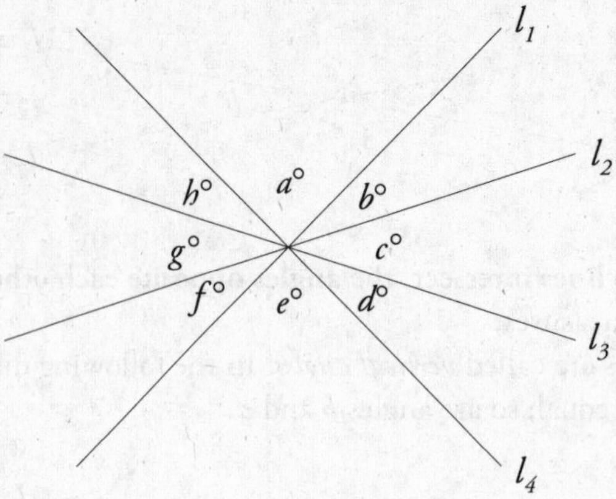

$$a + b + c + d + e + f + g + h = 360°$$
$$a = e, b = f, c = g, d = h$$

Perpendicular
(adj) meeting at right (90°) angles

6. **If two lines are perpendicular to each other, each of the four angles formed is 90 degrees.** A 90-degree angle is called a *right angle.*

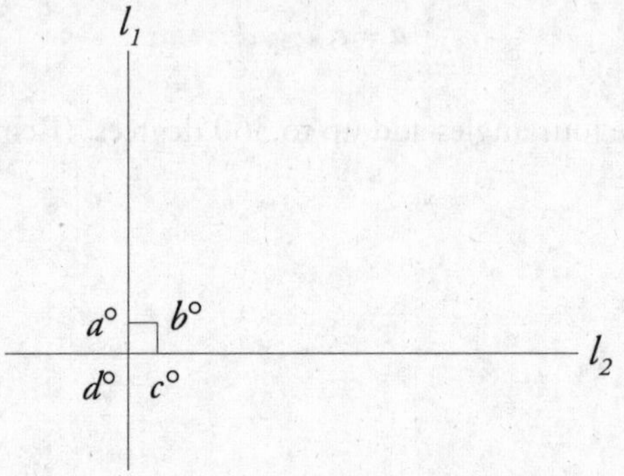

Angles *a, b, c,* and *d* all equal 90 degrees.

Flip and Negate
If two lines are perpendicular, then their slopes are negative reciprocals; i.e., if l_1 has a slope of 2 and l_2 is perpendicular to l_1, then l_2 must have a slope of $-\frac{1}{2}$.

The little box at the intersection of the two lines is the symbol for a right angle. If the lines are not perpendicular to each other, then none of the angles will be right angles.

7. **When two parallel lines are cut by a third line, all of the small angles are equal, all of the big angles are equal, and the sum of any big angle and any small angle is 180 degrees.**

Parallel lines are two lines that never intersect, and the rules about parallel lines are usually taught in school with lots of big words. But we like to avoid big words whenever possible. Simply put, when a line cuts through two parallel lines, two kinds of angles are created: big angles and small angles. You can tell which angles are big and which are small just by looking at them. All the big angles look equal, and they are. The same is true of the small angles. Lastly, any big angle plus any small angle always equals 180 degrees. (ETS likes rules about angles that add up to 180 or 360 degrees.)

Parallel lines have the same slope.

In any geometry problem, never assume that two lines are parallel unless the question or diagram specifically tells you so. In the following diagram, angle *a* is a big angle, and it has the same measure as angles *c, e,* and *g,* which are also big angles. Angle *b* is a small angle, and it has the same measure as angles *d, f,* and *h,* which are also small angles.

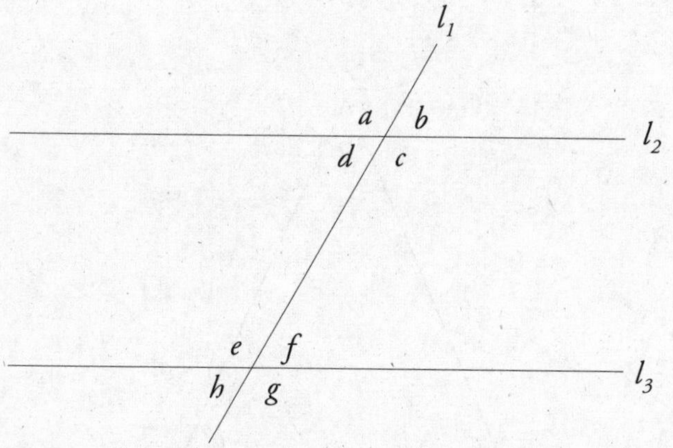

$$a = c = e = g$$
$$b = d = f = h$$

You should be able to see that the degree measures of angles *a, b, c,* and *d* add up to 360 degrees. So do those of angles *e, f, g,* and *h.* If you have trouble seeing it, draw a circle around the angles. What is the degree measure of a circle? Also, the sum of any small angle (such as *d*) and any big angle (such as *g*) is 180°.

Triangles

1. **Every triangle contains 180 degrees.**
   The word *triangle* means "three angles," and every triangle contains three interior angles. The measure of these three angles always adds up to exactly 180 degrees. You don't need to know why this is true or how to prove it. You just need to know it. And we mean *know* it.

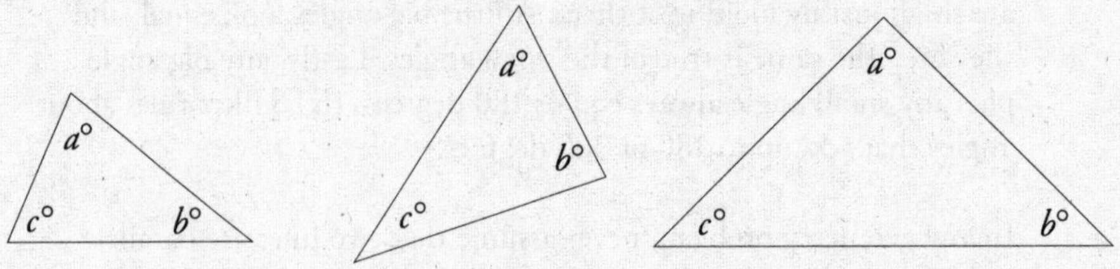

$a + b + c = 180°$ $a + b + c = 180°$ $a + b + c = 180°$

Your Friend the Triangle
If ever you are stumped by a geometry problem that deals with a quadrilateral, hexagon, or circle, look for the triangles that you can form by drawing lines through the figure.

2. **An isosceles triangle is one in which two of the sides are equal in length.**
   The angles opposite those equal sides are also equal because, as we just mentioned, angles opposite equal sides are also equal.

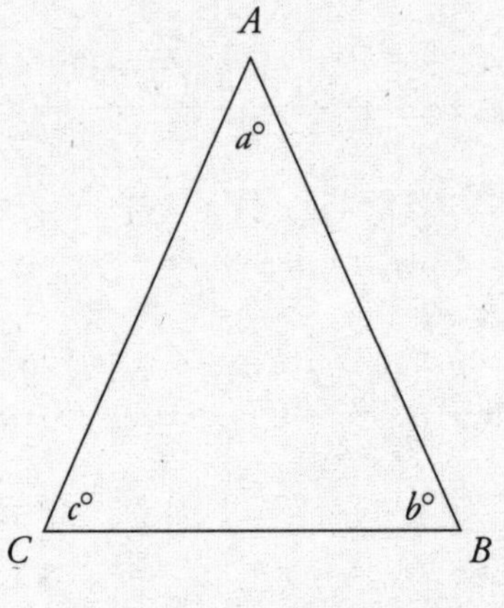

$AB = AC \quad AB \neq BC$
$c = b \quad c \neq a$

3. **An equilateral triangle is one in which all three sides are equal in length.**
Because the angles opposite equal sides are also equal, all three angles in an equilateral triangle are equal too. (Their measures are always 60 degrees each.)

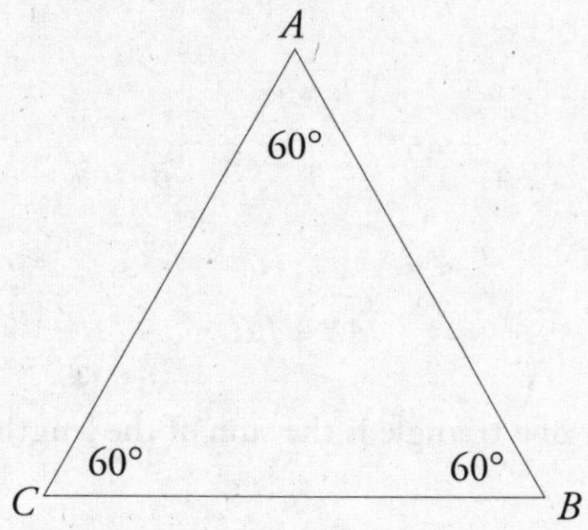

$AB = BC = AC$

An equilateral triangle is also isoceles.

4. **A right triangle is a triangle in which one of the angles is a right angle (90 degrees).**
The longest side of a right triangle, which is always opposite the 90-degree angle, is called the *hypotenuse*.

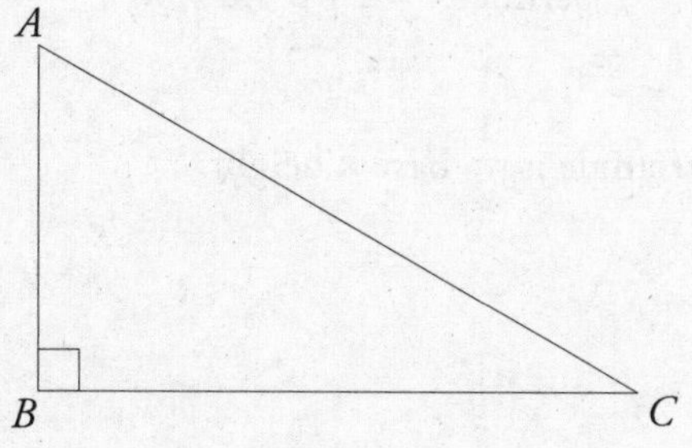

AC is the hypotenuse.

Some right triangles are also *isosceles*. The angles in an isosceles right triangle always measure 45°, 45°, and 90°.

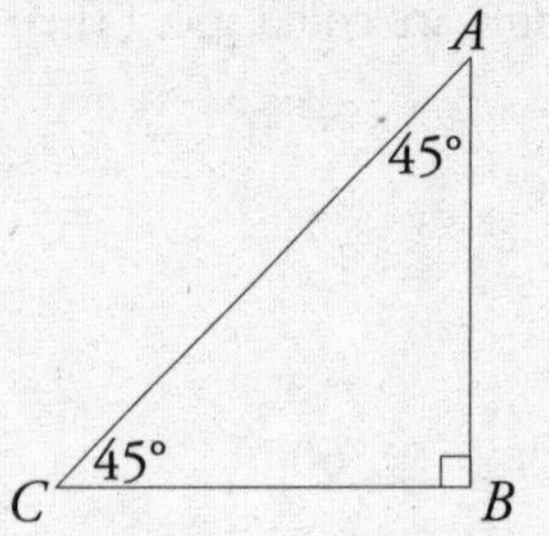

$AB = BC$

5. **The perimeter of a triangle is the sum of the lengths of its sides.**

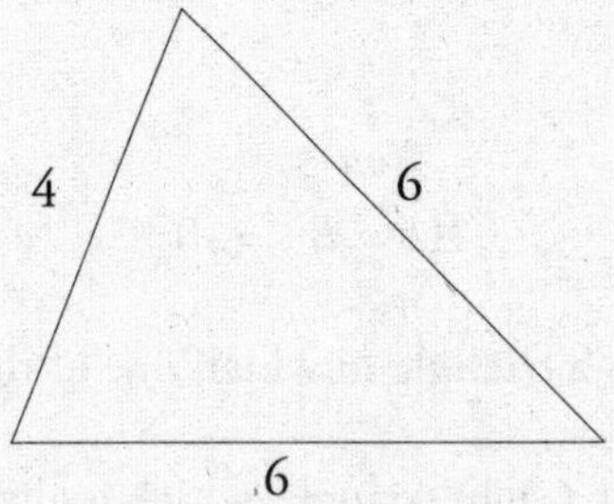

perimeter = 4 + 6 + 6 = 16

In or Out
The height can be found with a line dropped inside or outside the triangle—just as long as it's perpendicular to the base.

6. **The area of a triangle is $\frac{1}{2}$ base × height.**

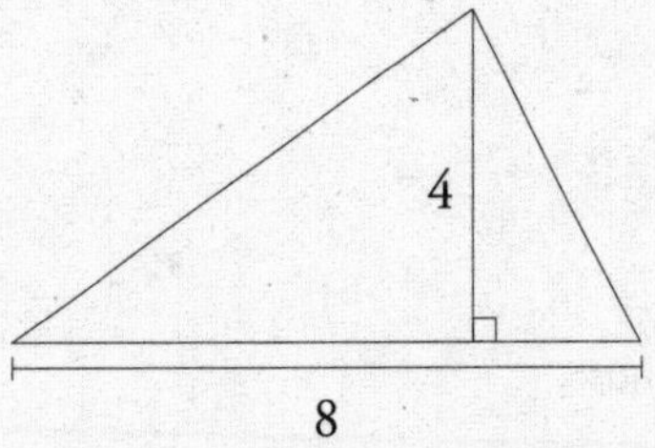

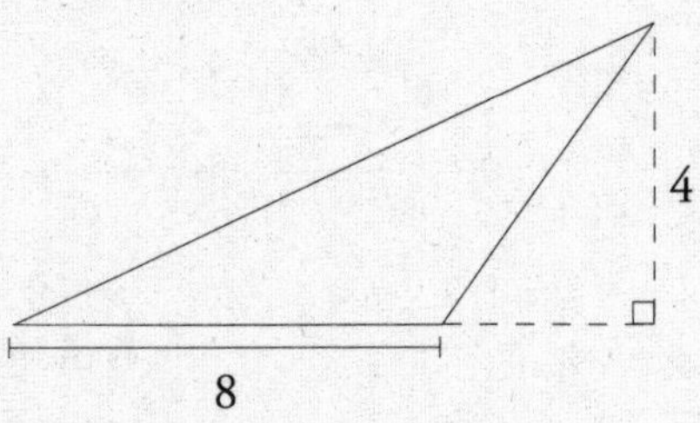

area = $\frac{1}{2}(8 \times 4) = 16$

area = $\frac{1}{2}(8 \times 4) = 16$

The Pythagorean Theorem

The Pythagorean theorem states that in a right triangle, the square of the hypotenuse equals the sum of the squares of the other two sides. As we told you earlier, the hypotenuse is the longest side of a right triangle; it's the side opposite the right angle. The square of the hypotenuse is its length squared. Applying the Pythagorean theorem to the following drawing, we find that $c^2 = a^2 + b^2$.

Pythagorean Theorem:
$a^2 + b^2 = c^2$, where c is the hypotenuse of a right triangle. Learn it, love it.

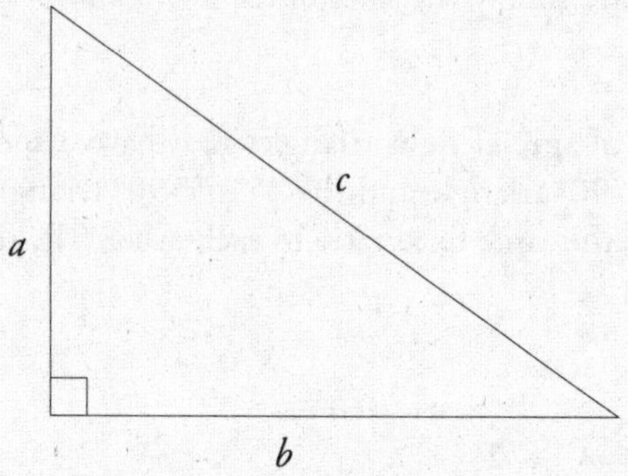

If you forget the Pythagorean theorem, you can always look it up in the box at the beginning of the Math section.

Your Friend the Rectangle
Be on the lookout for problems in which the application of the Pythagorean theorem is not obvious. For example, every rectangle contains two right triangles. That means that if you know the length and width of the rectangle, you also know the length of the diagonal, which is the hypotenuse of both triangles.

Special Right Triangles

There are many questions for which you won't need the Pythagorean theorem. ETS writes very predictable geometry questions involving right triangles, and reuses certain relationships. In these questions the triangles being used have particular ratios. There are two different types of special right triangles. The first involves the ratio of sides and the second involves the ratio of angles.

The most common special right triangles with side ratios are known as Pythagorean triplets. ETS's two favorites are:

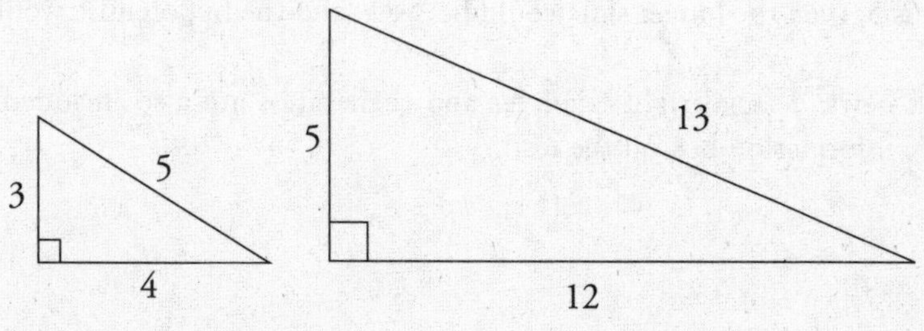

Relax; it's just a ratio. A 3:4:5 triangle may be hiding, disguised as 6:8:10, or 18:24:30. It's all the same ratio though, so be on the lookout.

Remember Ratios?
The great thing about 45°-45°-90° and 30°-60°-90° triangles is that, because they have particular ratios, you can use your Ratio Box!

If you memorize these two sets of Pythagorean triplets (3-4-5 and 5-12-13), you'll often be able to find ETS's answer without using the Pythagorean theorem. If ETS gives you a triangle with a side of 3 and a hypotenuse of 5, you know right away that the other side has to be 4. Likewise, if you see a right triangle with sides of 5 and 12, you know the hypotenuse must be 13.

ETS also likes to use right triangles with sides that are simply multiples of the common Pythagorean triplets. For example, you might see a 6-8-10 or a 10-24-26 triangle. These sides are simply the sides of the 3-4-5 and 5-12-13 triangles multiplied by 2.

There are two types of special right triangles that have a specific ratio of angles. They are the 30°-60°-90° triangle and the 45°-45°-90° triangle. The sides of these triangles always have the same fixed ratio to each other. The ratios are as follows:

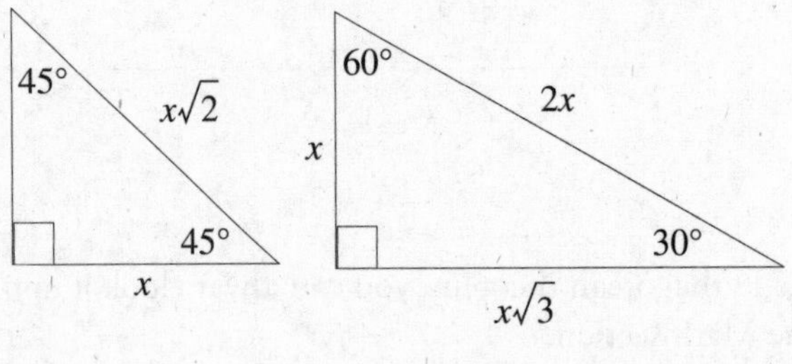

Let's talk about a 45°-45°-90° triangle first. Did you notice that this is also an isosceles right triangle? The sides will always be the same. And the hypotenuse will always be the side times $\sqrt{2}$. Its ratio of side to side to hypotenuse is always $1 : 1 : \sqrt{2}$. For example, if you have a 45°-45°-90° triangle with a side of 3, then the second side will also be 3 and the hypotenuse will be $3\sqrt{2}$.

Now let's talk about a 30°-60°-90° triangle. The ratio of shorter side to longer side to hypotenuse is always $1 : \sqrt{3} : 2$. For example, if the shorter side of a 30°-60°-90° triangle is 5, then the longer side would be $5\sqrt{3}$ and the hypotenuse would be 10.

The best news? Special right triangles and their ratios are also included in your reference information box on the test!

Angle-Side Relationships in Triangles

The longest side of any triangle is opposite the largest interior angle; the shortest side is opposite the smallest angle. In the following triangle, side *a* is longer than side *b*, which is longer than side *c*, because 80 > 60 > 40.

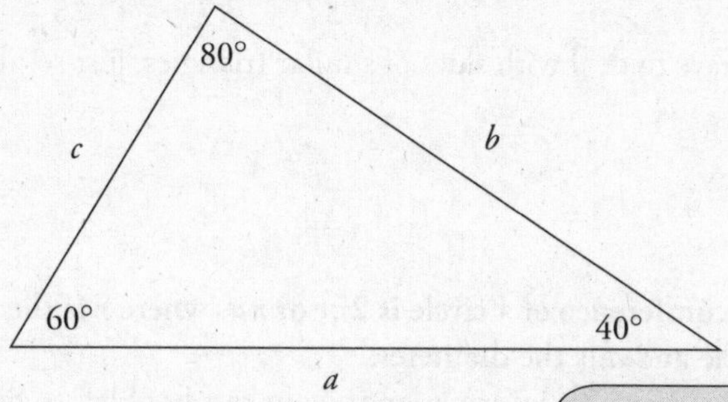

The same rule applies to isosceles and equilateral triangles. An isosceles triangle, remember, is one in which two of the sides are equal in length; therefore, the angles opposite those sides are also equal. In an equilateral triangle, all three sides are equal; so are all three angles.

Similar Triangles

Similar triangles have the same shape, but they are not necessarily the same size. Having the same shape means that the angles of the triangles are identical. Look at the following two similar triangles:

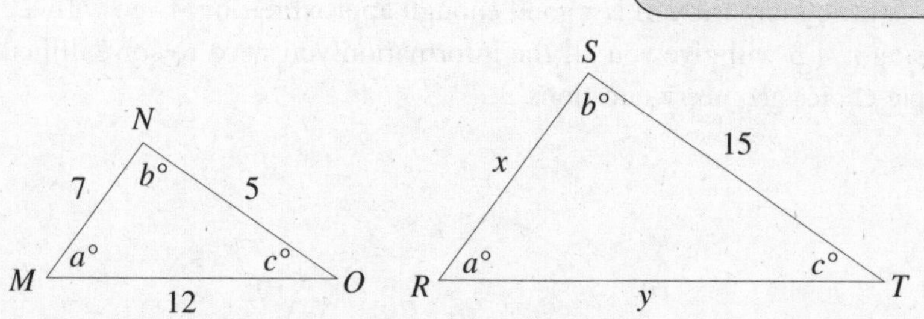

These two triangles both have the same set of angles, but they aren't the same size. Whenever this is true, the sides of one triangle are proportional to those of the other. Notice that sides *NO* and *ST* are both opposite the angle that is *a*°. These are called corresponding sides, because they correspond to the same angle. So the lengths of $\overline{NO}$ and $\overline{ST}$ are proportional to each other. In order to figure

The Third Side Rule

It is simply impossible for the third side of a triangle to be longer than the total of the other two sides. Nor can the third side of a triangle be shorter than the difference between the other two sides. Imagine a triangle with sides *a*, *b*, and *c*: $a - b < c < a + b$.

Symbols

ETS doesn't always write things out. Here's a list of symbols ETS might use, along with a translation of each one into English:

Symbol	**Meaning**
ΔABC	triangle *ABC*
$\overline{AB}$	line segment *AB*
AB	the length of line segment *AB*

Learn these symbols and keep an eye out for them!

out the lengths of the other sides we set up a proportion: $\frac{MN}{RS} = \frac{NO}{ST}$. Now fill in the information that you know: $\frac{7}{x} = \frac{5}{15}$. Cross-multiply and you find that $x = 21$. You could also figure out the length of y: $\frac{NO}{ST} = \frac{MO}{RT}$. So, $\frac{5}{15} = \frac{12}{y}$, and $y = 36$. Whenever you have to deal with sides of similar triangles, just set up a proportion.

Circles

Some Formulas
Area = πr^2
Circumference = $2\pi r$ or πd
Diameter = $2r$

1. **The circumference of a circle is $2\pi r$ or πd, where r is the radius of the circle and d is the diameter.**
   You'll be given this information in your test booklet, so don't stress over memorizing these formulas. You will always be able to refer to your test booklet if you forget them. Just keep in mind that the diameter is always twice the length of the radius (and that the radius is half the diameter).

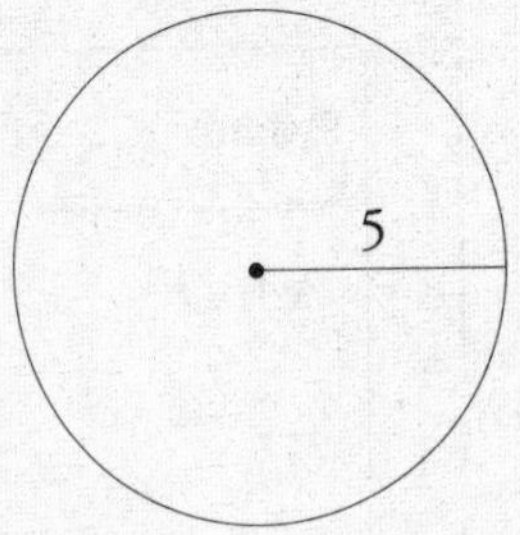

circumference = $2 \times \pi \times 5 = 10\pi$

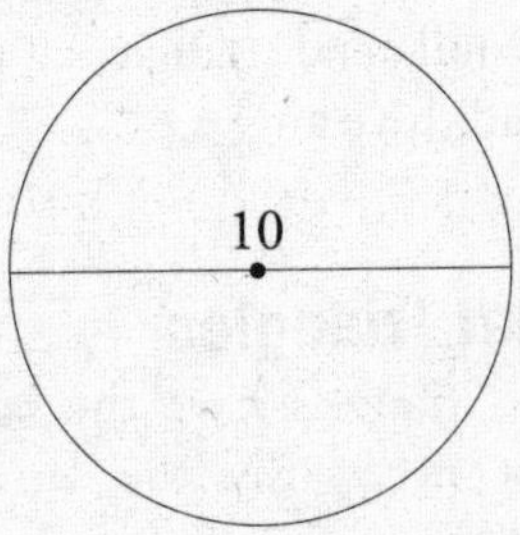

circumference = 10π

Leave That π Alone!
Most of the time, you won't multiply π out in circle problems: Because the SAT answers will be in terms of π (6π instead of 18.849...), you an save yourself some trouble by leaving your work in terms of π.

In math class you probably learned that $\pi = 3.14$ (or even 3.14159). On the SAT, $\pi = 3^+$ (a little more than 3) is a good enough approximation. Even with a calculator, using $\pi = 3$ will give you all the information you need to solve difficult SAT multiple-choice geometry questions.

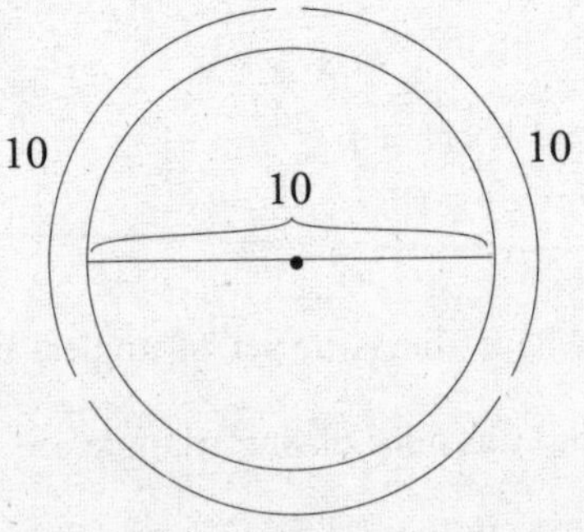

circumference = about 30

2. **The area of a circle is πr^2, where r is the radius of the circle.**

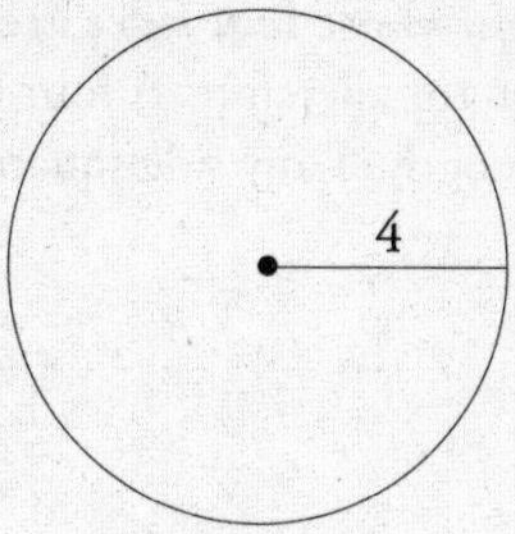

area = $\pi 4^2 = 16\pi$

3. **A tangent is a line that touches a circle at exactly one point. Any radius drawn from that tangent point forms a 90-degree angle.**

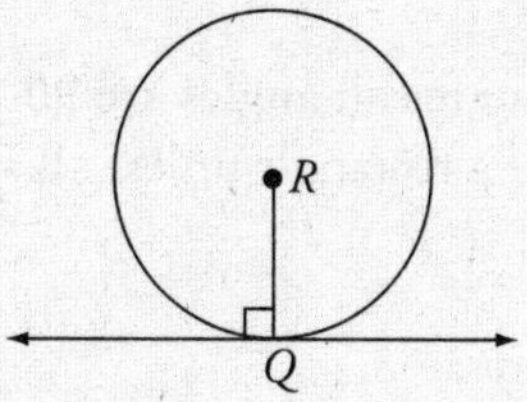

Circles Have Names?
If the SAT refers to Circle R, it means that the center of the circle if point R.

Rectangles and Squares

1. **The perimeter of a rectangle is the sum of the lengths of its sides.** Just add them up.

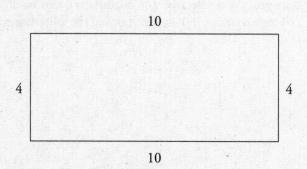

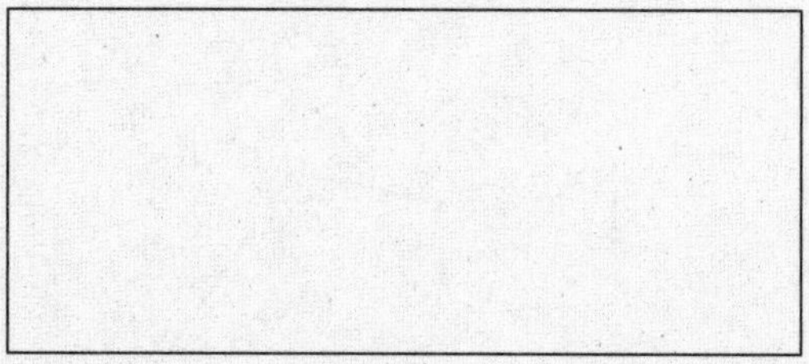

perimeter = 10 + 4 + 10 + 4 = 28

Little Boxes
Here's a progression of quadrilaterals from least specific to most specific:
quadrilateral is any 4-sided figure
↓
parallelogram is a quadrilateral in which opposite sides are parallel
↓
rectangle is a parallelogram in which all angles = 90 degrees
↓
square is a rectangle in which all sides are equal

2. **The area of a rectangle is length × width.**
The area of the preceding rectangle, therefore, is 10 × 4, or 40.

3. **A square is a rectangle whose four sides are all equal in length.**
The perimeter of a square, therefore, is four times the length of any side. The area is the length of any side squared.

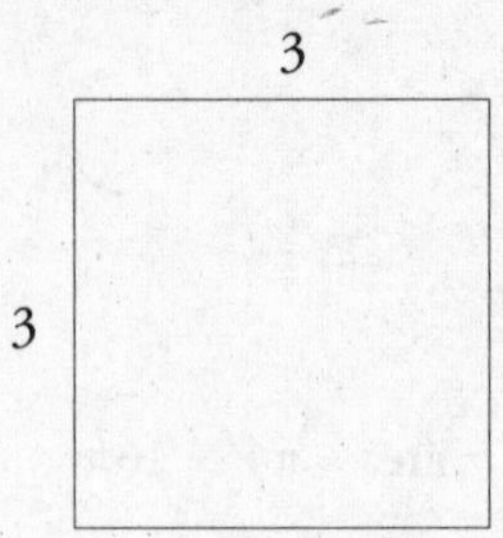

$$\text{perimeter} = 4\ (3) = 12$$
$$\text{area} = 3^2 = 9$$

4. **In rectangles and squares all angles are 90-degree angles.**
It can't be a square or a rectangle unless all angles are 90 degrees.

Polygons

Polygons are two-dimensional figures with three or more straight sides. Triangles and rectangles are both polygons. So are figures with five, six, seven, eight, or any greater number of sides. The most important fact to know about polygons is that any one of them can be divided into triangles. This means that you can always determine the sum of the measures of the interior angles of any polygon.

For example, the sum of the interior angles of any four-sided polygon (called a *quadrilateral*) is 360 degrees. Why? Because any quadrilateral can be divided into two triangles, and a triangle contains 180 degrees. Look at the following example:

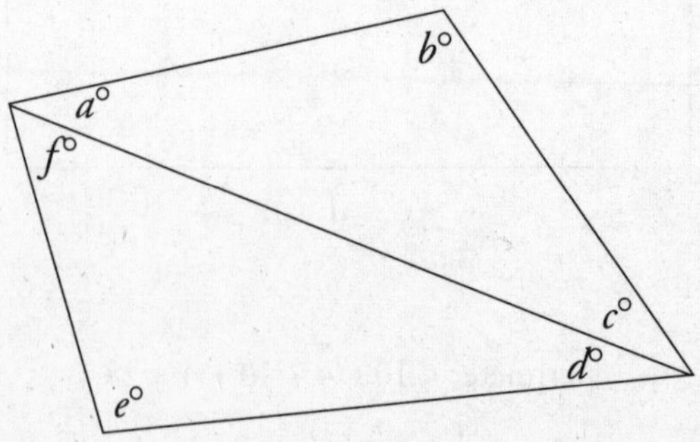

In this polygon, $a + b + c = 180$ degrees; so does $d + e + f$. That means that the sum of the interior angles of the quadrilateral must be 360 degrees $(a + b + c + d + e + f)$.

A *parallelogram* is a quadrilateral whose opposite sides are parallel. In the following parallelogram, side AB is parallel to side DC, and AD is parallel to BC. Because a parallelogram is made of two sets of parallel lines that intersect each other, Fred's theorem applies to it as well: The two big angles are equal, the two small angles are equal, and a big angle plus a small angle equals 180 degrees. In the figure below, big angles A and C are equal, and small angles B and D are equal. Also, because A is a big angle and D is a small angle, $A + D = 180$ degrees.

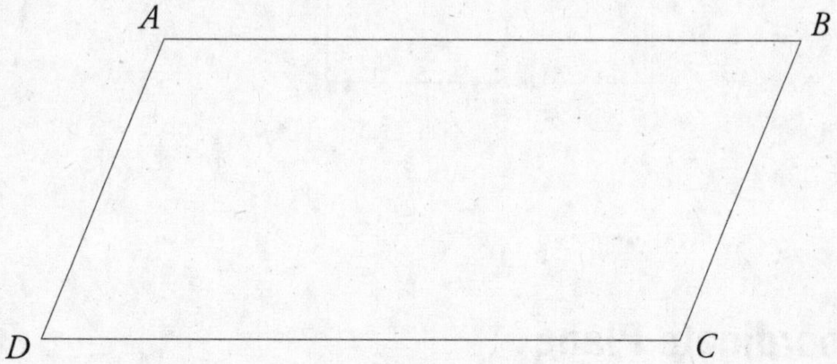

Volume

ETS will occasionally ask a question that will require you to calculate the volume of a rectangular solid (a box or a cube). The formula for the volume of a rectangular solid is length × width × height. Because length, width, and height are equal in a cube, the volume of a cube can be calculated simply by cubing (where do you think they get the name?) the length of any edge of the cube.

No Sweat
In the rare case when ETS asks you to find the volume of a figure other than a rectangular solid, the formula will either be provided with the question or will appear in the instructions.

Volume = $8 \times 4 \times 3 = 96$

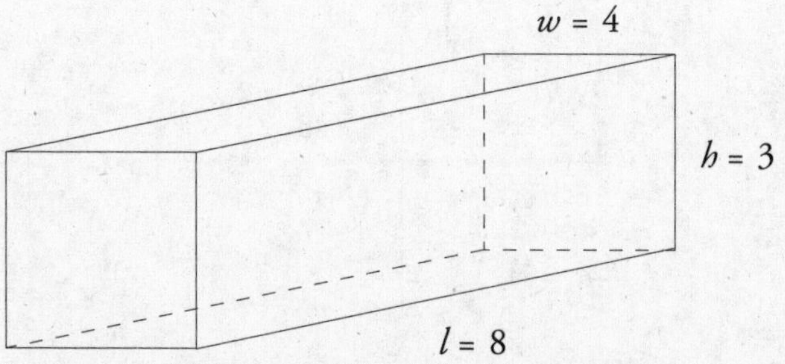

Volume = 3^3 = 27

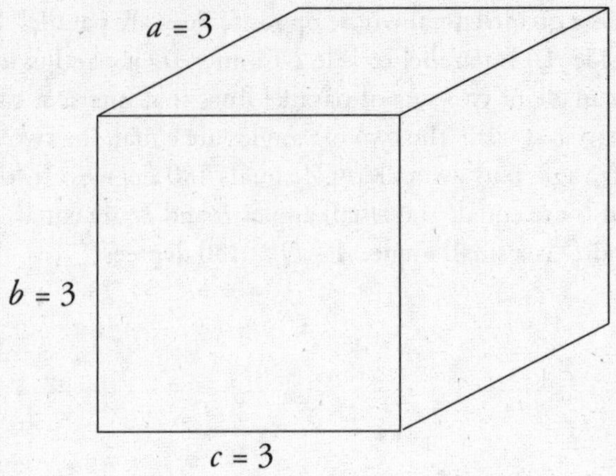

The Coordinate Plane

A coordinate plane is made up of two number lines that intersect at a right angle. The horizontal number line is called the *x*-axis, and the vertical number line is the *y*-axis.

Quadrants

A coordinate plane has four distinct areas known as quadrants. The quadrants are numbered counterclockwise. They help determine generally whether *x* and *y* are positive or negative. Quadrant I is the upper right-hand corner, where *x* and *y* are both positive. Quadrant II is the upper left-hand corner, where *x* is negative and *y* is positive. Quadrant III is the lower left-hand corner where both *x* and *y* are negative. Quadrant IV is the lower right-hand corner where *x* is positive and *y* is negative. Sometimes knowing what quadrant a point is in and what that means is all you need to find ETS's answer.

The four areas formed by the intersection of the axes are called *quadrants*. The location of any point can be described with a pair of numbers (*x*, *y*), just the way you would point on a map: (0, 0) are the coordinates of the intersection of the two axes (also called the *origin*); (1, 2) are the coordinates of the point one space to the right and two spaces up; (–1, 5) are the coordinates of the point one space to the left and five spaces up; (–4, –2) are the coordinates of the point four spaces to the left and two spaces down. All these points are located on the diagram below.

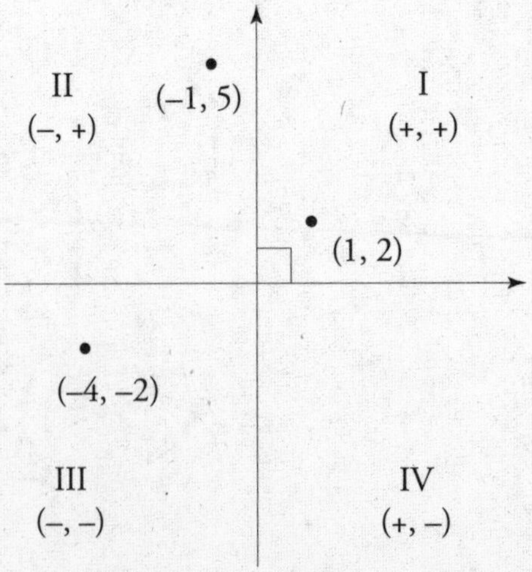

Some of the questions on the SAT may require you to know certain properties of lines on the coordinate plane. Let's talk about them.

Slope

You always read a graph from left to right. As you read the graph how much the line goes up or down is known as the slope. Slope is the rate of change of a line and is commonly known as "rise over run." It's denoted by the letter *m*. Essentially, it's the change in the *y*-coordinates over the change in *x*-coordinates and can be found with the following formula:

$$m = \frac{(y_2 - y_1)}{(x_2 - x_1)}$$

This formula uses the coordinates (x_1, y_1) and (x_2, y_2).

Let's do an example. If you have the points (2, 3) and (7, 4), the slope of the line created by these points would be:

$$m = \frac{(4-3)}{(7-2)}$$

So the slope of a line with points (2, 3) and (7, 4) would be $\frac{1}{5}$, which means that every time you go up 1 unit, you travel to the right 5 units.

Equation of a Line

The equation of a line can take multiple forms. The most common of these is known as the slope-intercept form. If you know the slope and the *y*-intercept, you can create the equation of a given line. A slope-intercept equation takes the form $y = mx + b$, where *m* is the slope and *b* is the *y*-intercept.

Ways to Remember
Having trouble remembering that the *x*-coordinate comes before the *y*-coordinate in an ordered pair? Just remember the phrase "*x* before *y*, walk before you fly." The letter *x* comes before *y* in the dictionary.

Let's say that we know that a certain line has a slope of 5 (which is the same as $\frac{5}{1}$) and a y-intercept of 3. The equation of the line would be $y = 5x + 3$. You could graph this line simply by looking at this form of the equation. First, draw the y-intercept, (0, 3). Next, plug in a number for x and solve for y to get a coordinate pair of a point on the line. Now connect the point you just found with the y-intercept you already drew, and voilà, you have a line. If you want more points, you can create a table such as this one:

x	y
–2	–7
–1	–2
0	3
1	8

Take a look at the finished product:

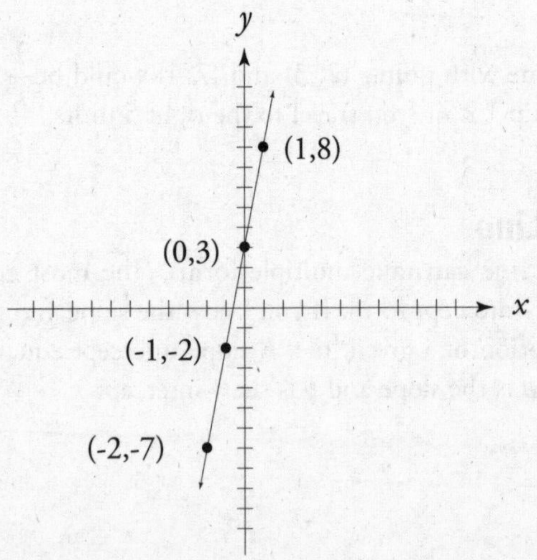

Things You Can Do to a Line

The **midpoint** formula gives the midpoint of ST, with points $S\ (x_1, y_1)$ and $T\ (x_2, y_2)$. It's simply the average of the x-coordinates and the y-coordinates. In our example, the midpoint would be $\frac{(x_1 + x_2)}{2}, \frac{(y_1 + y_2)}{2}$.

The **distance** formula looks quite complicated. The easiest way to solve the distance between two points is to connect them and form a triangle. Then use the Pythagorean theorem. Many times, the triangle formed is one of the common Pythagorean triplets (3-4-5 or 5-12-13).

Remember Functions?

Sometimes, instead of seeing the typical $y = mx + b$ equation, or something similar, you'll see $f(x) = mx + b$. Look familiar? Graphs are just another way to show information from a function. Functions show information algebraically and graphs show functions geometrically (as pictures).

Here's an example. The function $f(x) = 3x - 2$ is shown graphically as the following:

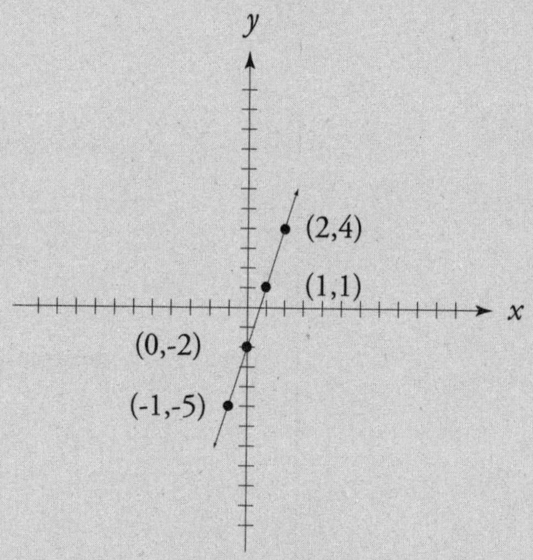

If you're not comfortable with graphs, feel free to skip the oddball graphing question, but for most of you, these aren't half as frustrating as some other topics (fractions, for example). The reason ETS asks function questions is to test whether you can figure out the relationship between a function and its graph. To tackle these questions, you need to know that the independent variable, the x, is on the x-axis, and the dependent variable, the $f(x)$, is on the y-axis. For example, if you see a function of $f(x) = 7$, then you need to understand that this is a graph of a horizontal line where $y = 7$.

Graphing Functions

One type of function question you might be asked is how the graph of a function would shift if you added a value to it. Again, there are not going to be a lot of these questions, so feel free to skip the few that appear if you don't feel comfortable answering them.

Here is a quick guide (c is a constant) for the graph of $f(x) = x^2$:

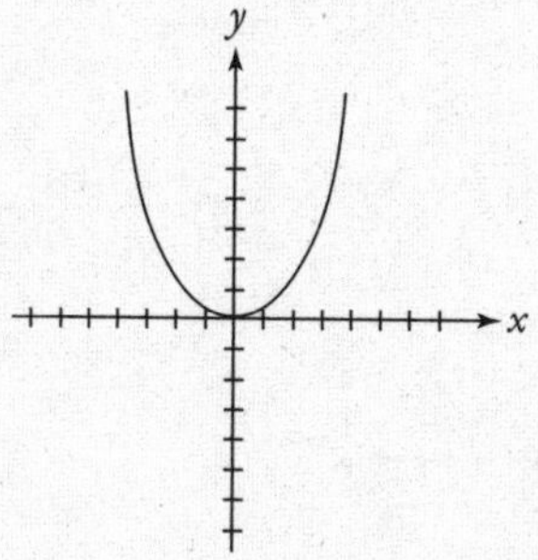

For $f(x) + c$, the graph will shift up c units. Like this:

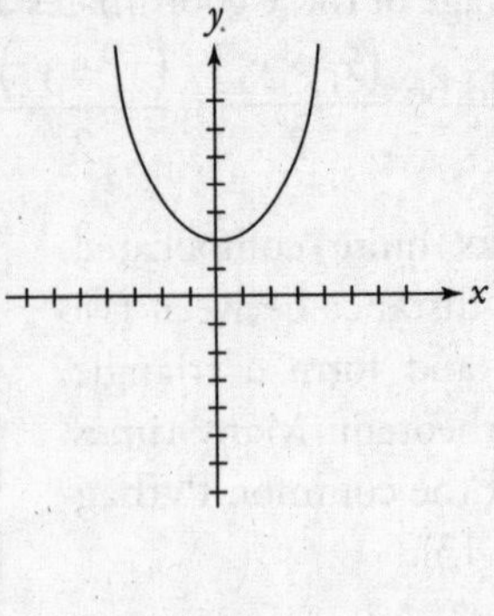

Conversely, $f(x) - c$ will shift the graph down by c units:

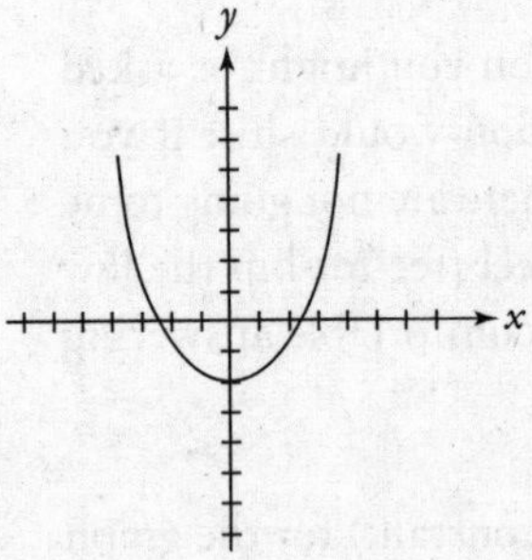

For $f(x + c)$, the graph will shift c units to the left:

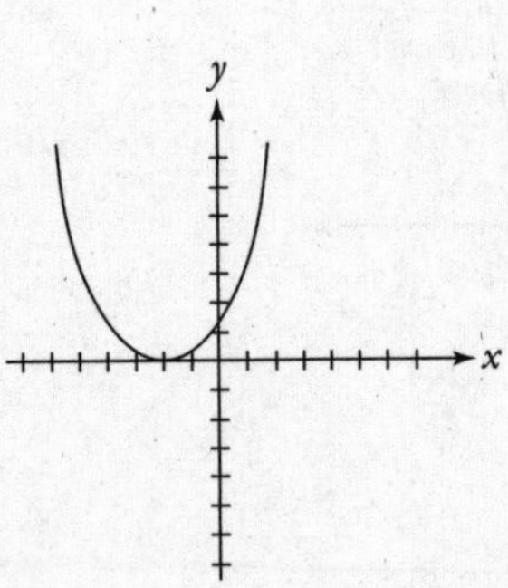

For $f(x - c)$, the graph will shift to the right by c units:

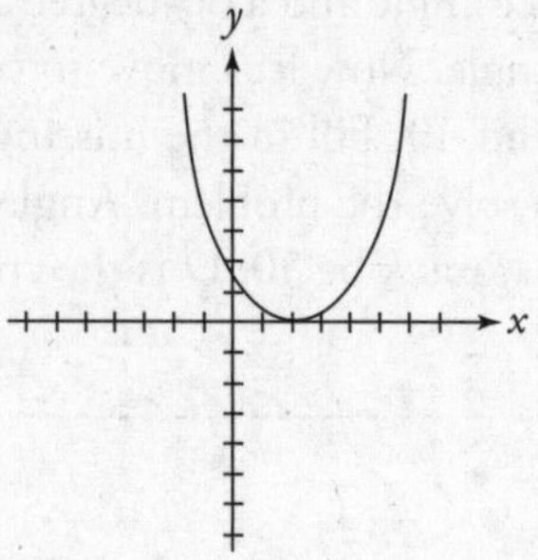

You may have realized how easy these problems would become if you simply put them into your graphing calculator. If you've got one, type in the function; if not, remember the four simple rules for transforming graphs (see the chapter summary for these).

BASIC PRINCIPLES: PRACTICE

Okay, now that you've mastered the rules, you're ready to knock out some problems.

Warm up with this one:

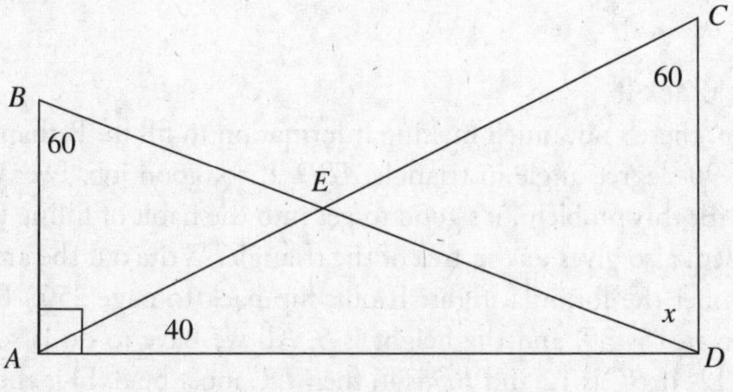

6. What is the value of x in the figure above?

(A) 20
(B) 30
(C) 40
(D) 50
(E) 60

Here's How to Crack It

Look at the way ETS presents the problem. We have two triangles, but only two angles are given in each figure. Let's start filling in the missing information. Triangle *ABD* has a 90-degree angle and a 60-degree angle. What's missing? Write 30 degrees in for the third angle. Now let's move to triangle *ACD*. This figure has angle measurements of 60 and 40. Fill in the missing third angle of 80. Now we have enough information to solve the problem. Angle *D* is 80 degrees and part of it is 30, so the leftover part, *x*, must be 50. D is the correct answer.

Here's another one:

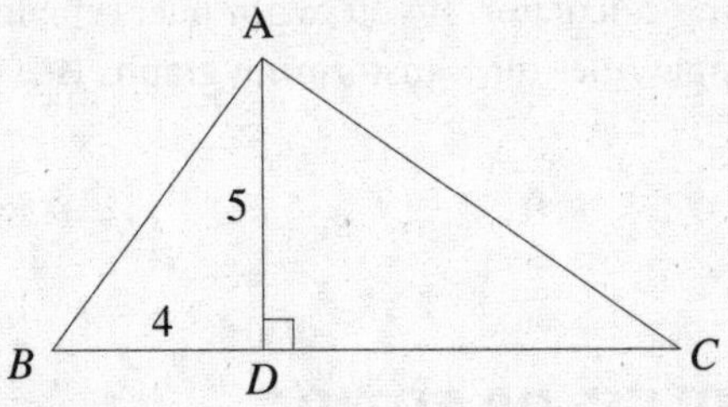

Write It Down!
Always write down the appropriate formula and fill in what you know.

8. If the area of ΔABC in the figure above is 30, what is the length of DC ?

(A) 2
(B) 4
(C) 6
(D) 8
(E) 12

Here's How to Crack It

In this problem, there's not much missing information to fill in. Perhaps you filled in the missing 90-degree angle in triangle *ABD*. If so, good job. Even though it's not important for this problem, it's good to get into the habit of filling in information. The problem also gives us the area of the triangle. Write out the area formula. (You do remember the formula, right? If not, flip back to page 250.) Fill in what you know. The area is 30, and the height is 5. All we have to do is solve for the base, which is 12. If *BC* is 12 and *BD* is 4, then *DC* must be 8. D is the answer.

Now you're warmed up. Let's try a more challenging problem:

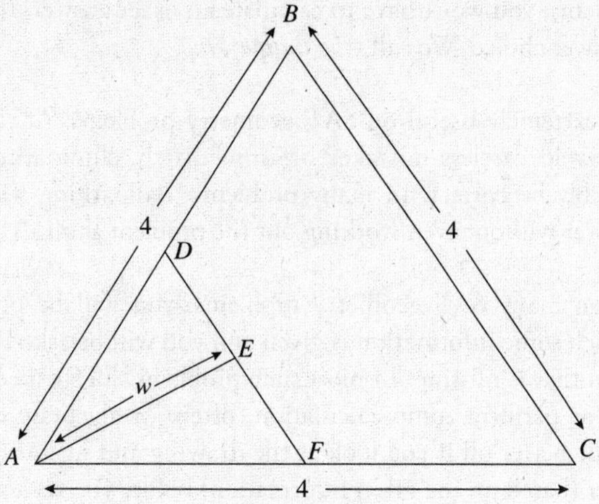

10. Triangle ABC is equilateral and angle AEF is a right angle. D is the midpoint of AB, F is the midpoint of AC, and E is the midpoint of DF. What is the value of w ?

(A) 1

(B) $\sqrt{3}$

(C) 2

(D) $2\sqrt{2}$

(E) $2\sqrt{3}$

Here's How to Crack It

This problem has a lot more going on in it. But if we take it piece by piece, we'll crack it. Let's start filling in some information. The first thing the problem tells us is that triangle ABC is equilateral. Mark 60 degree angles on the figure. Next, we see that angle AEF is a right angle. Write that in as well. The problem also conveniently tells us that D and F are the midpoints of AB and AC, respectively. Therefore, AD and AF are 2. Finally, the last piece of information reveals that E is the midpoint of DF; mark DE and EF as equal.

Now, what do we have? Triangle AEF is a right triangle, with a hypotenuse of 2 and a leg of 1. Hmm, perhaps the good ol' Pythagorean theorem can help us. Plug the numbers into the theorem, and you'll see that the answer is B.

BALLPARKING

You may be thinking, "Wait a second, isn't there an easier way?" By now, you should know that of course there is, and we're going to show you. On many SAT geometry problems, you won't have to calculate an exact answer. Instead, you can estimate an answer choice. We call this *Ballparking*.

Ballparking is extremely useful on SAT geometry problems. At the very least, it will help you avoid careless mistakes by immediately eliminating answers that could not possibly be correct. In many problems, Ballparking will allow you to find ETS's answer without even working out the problem at all.

Pictures
Unless otherwise stated, the diagram ETS supplies you with is drawn to scale.

For example, on many SAT geometry problems, you will be presented with a drawing in which some information is given and you will be asked to find some of the information that is missing. In most such problems, ETS expects you to apply some formula or perform some calculation, often an algebraic one. But you'll almost always be better off if you look at the drawing and make a rough estimate of ETS's answer (based on the given information) before you try to work it out.

The basic principles you just learned (such as the number of degrees in a triangle and the fact that $\pi \approx 3$) will be enormously helpful to you in Ballparking on the SAT. You should also know the approximate values of several common square roots. Be sure to memorize them before moving on. Knowing them cold will help you solve problems and save time, even if your calculator has a square root function.

Rocket Science?
The SAT is a goofy college admissions test, not an exercise in precision. Because 50 of its 60 math questions are multiple-choice, you can afford to approximate numbers like π, $\sqrt{2}$, and $\sqrt{3}$ (3+, 1.4, and 1.7+, respectively).

Square Roots

$$\sqrt{1} = 1$$
$$\sqrt{2} \approx 1.4$$
$$\sqrt{3} \approx 1.7+$$
$$\sqrt{4} = 2$$

Happy Holidays!
February 14 (2/14) is Valentine's Day, so $\sqrt{2} = 1.4$.
March 17 (3/17) is St. Patrick's Day, so $\sqrt{3} = 1.7$.

You will also find it very helpful if you have a good sense of how large certain common angles are. Study the following examples.

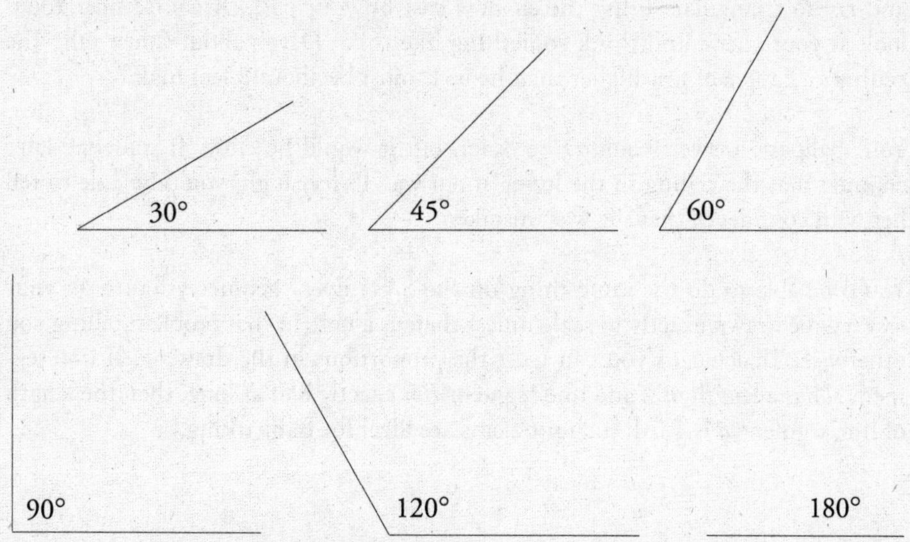

To get a little practice using the material you've memorized to help you Ballpark, do the drill on the following page.

How High Is the Ceiling?

If your friend stood next to a wall in your living room and asked you how high the ceiling was, what would you do? Would you get out your trigonometry textbook and try to triangulate using the shadow cast by your pal? Of course not. You'd look at your friend and think something like this: "Dave's about 6 feet tall. The ceiling's a couple of feet higher than he is. It must be about 8 feet high."

The Correct Choice

Remember that the SAT is a multiple-choice test. This means that you don't always have to come up with an answer; you just have to identify the correct one from among the five choices provided.

Your ballpark answer wouldn't be exact, but it would be close. If someone later claimed that the ceiling in the living room was 15 feet high, you'd be able to tell her with confidence that she was mistaken.

You'll be able to do the same thing on the SAT. Every geometry figure on your test will be drawn exactly to scale unless there is a note in that problem telling you otherwise. That means you can trust the proportions in the drawing. If line segment *A* has a length of 2 and line segment *B* is exactly half as long, then the length of line segment *B* is 1. All such problems are ideal for Ballparking.

When You Can't Measure, Sketch, or Ballpark

You will sometimes encounter geometry problems that have no diagrams, diagrams not drawn to scale, or diagrams containing only partial information. In these cases, you should use the given information to sketch your own complete diagram and then use your drawing as a basis for Ballparking. Don't hesitate to fill your test booklet with sketches and scratch work: This is precisely what you are supposed to do. Finding ETS's answer will be much harder, if not impossible, if you don't take full advantage of the information ETS gives you.

Here's an example:

16. All faces of a cube with a 4-meter edge are covered with striped paper. If the cube is then cut into cubes with 1-meter edges, how many of the 1-meter cubes have striped paper on exactly one face?

(A) 24
(B) 36
(C) 48
(D) 60
(E) 72

Here's How to Crack It

This problem doesn't have a diagram. It would be much easier to solve if it did. What should you do? Draw a diagram, of course! Just sketch the cube quickly in your test booklet and mark it off into 1-meter cubes as described. Your sketch might look like this:

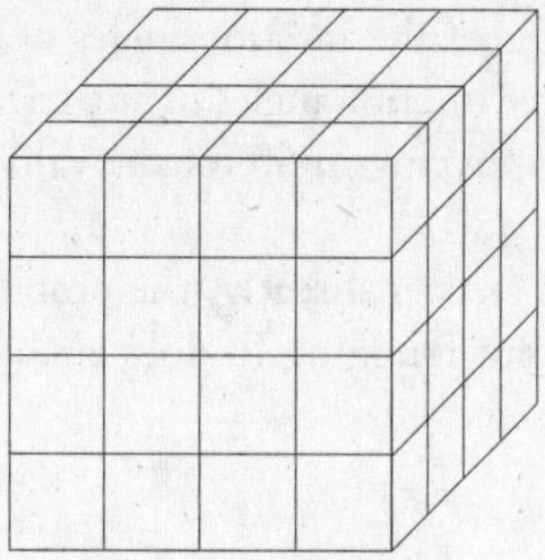

You should be able to see that there are four cubes on each side of the big cube that will have striped paper on only one face (the four center cubes—all the other cubes have at least two exterior sides). Because a cube has six sides, this means that ETS's answer is choice A.

PLUGGING IN

As you learned in Chapter 13, Plugging In is one of the most powerful techniques for solving SAT algebra problems. It is also very useful on geometry problems. On some problems, you will be able to plug in ballpark values for missing information and then use the results either to find ETS's answer directly or to eliminate answers that could not possibly be correct.

Here's an example:

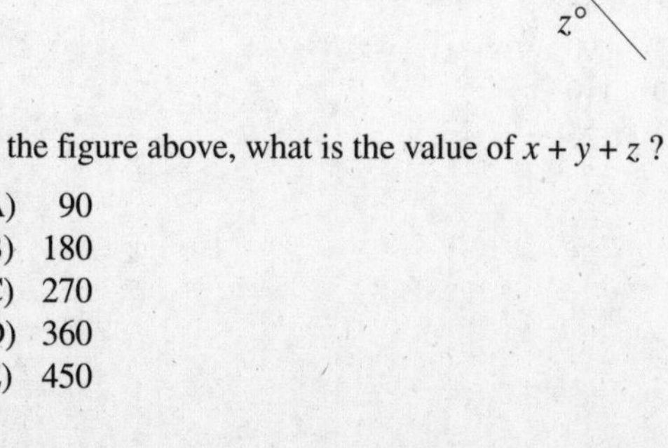

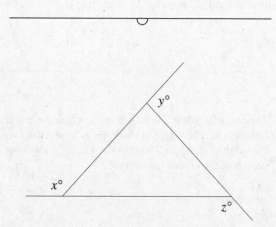

16. In the figure above, what is the value of $x + y + z$?

(A) 90
(B) 180
(C) 270
(D) 360
(E) 450

Here's How to Crack It

We don't know the measures of the interior angles of the triangle in the drawing, but we do know that the three interior angles of any triangle add up to 180, and 180 divided by 3 is 60. Now, simply plug in 60 for the value of each interior angle.

This doesn't give you ETS's answer directly; the problem does not ask you for the sum of the interior angles. But Plugging In does enable you to find ETS's answer. Look at the redrawn figure:

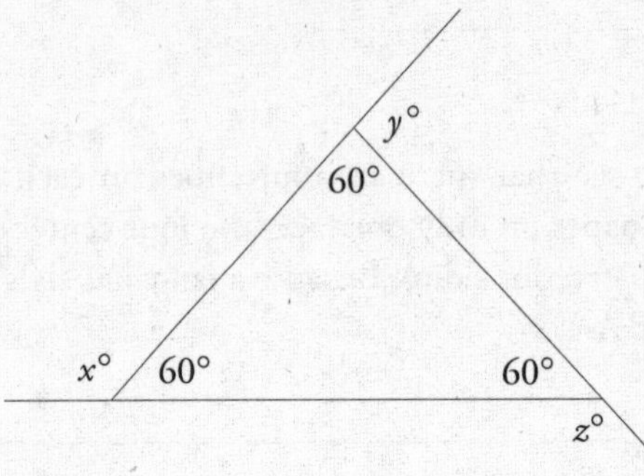

If the marked interior angle is 60, what must x be? Remember that every line is a 180-degree angle. That means that the measure of x must be 180 – 60, or 120. You can now do the same thing for the other two angles. Using this method you find that x, y, and z each equal 120. That means that $x + y + z = 360$. ETS's answer, therefore, is choice D.

Ballparking like this won't always give you ETS's exact answer, but it will usually enable you to eliminate at least three of the four incorrect choices. Other kinds of geometry problems also lend themselves to Plugging In.

Here's another example:

20. The base of triangle *T* is 40 percent less than the length of rectangle *R*. The height of triangle *T* is 50% greater than the width of rectangle *R*. The area of triangle *T* is what percent of the area of rectangle *R* ?

(A) 10
(B) 45
(C) 90
(D) 110
(E) 125

Here's How to Crack It

This is a really hard problem. You should recognize that A, C, and D are Joe Bloggs answers and should be eliminated. Even if you don't see this, you'll still be able to find the right answer by sketching and Plugging In.

When Plugging In, always use numbers that are easy to work with. Let's say the length of the rectangle is 10; that means that the base of the triangle, which is 40 percent smaller, is 6. Now if we plug 4 in for the width of rectangle *R*, then the height of triangle *T* is 6. You should come up with two sketches that look like this:

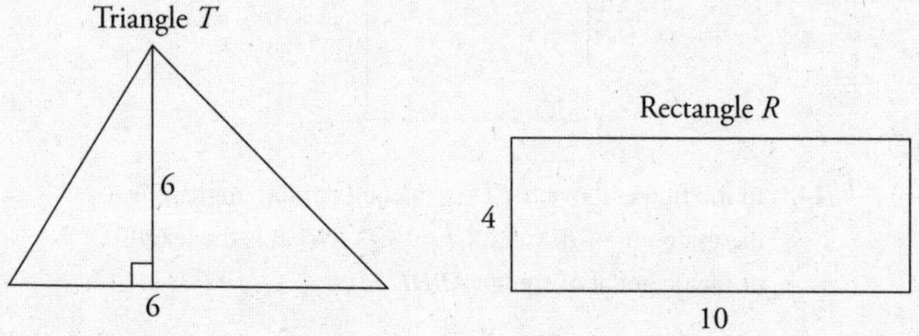

T has an area of $\frac{1}{2}bh$, or 18. *R* has an area of 40. Now set up the translation:

$18 = \frac{x}{100}(40)$ where *x* represents what percent the triangle is of the rectangle. Solve for *x* and you get 45. The correct answer is B.

As you can see, advanced geometry problems actually don't involve any advanced principles. Rather, these problems are harder simply because they combine multiple concepts (and therefore require a lot more work). However, if you follow The Princeton Review's strategy—and know your basic rules—you should have a pretty good handle on these.

Let's give another difficult one a shot:

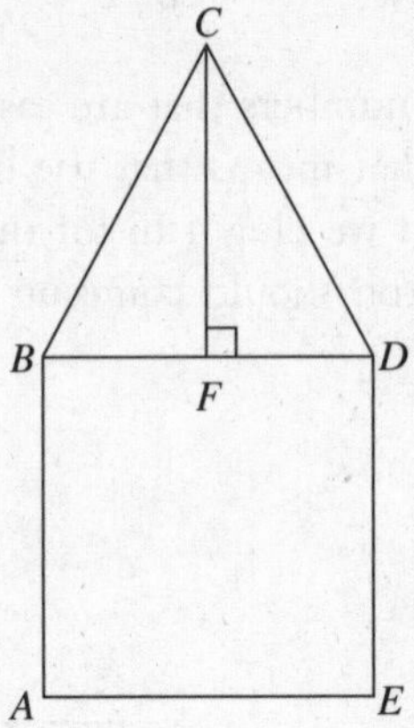

14. In the figure above, BCD is an equilateral triangle, F is the midpoint of BD, and $CF = 3\sqrt{3}$. What is the length of the diagonal of square $ABDE$?

(A) $3\sqrt{2}$
(B) $3\sqrt{3}$
(C) 6
(D) $6\sqrt{2}$
(E) $6\sqrt{3}$

Here's How to Crack It

First, you should fill in the missing angles on triangle BCD. It looks like we have a 30°-60°-90° right triangle for FCD. This is one of ETS's favorite triangles. In fact, the test writers love it so much that they provide all the information you need to know about it in the beginning of each Math section. Even so, it might be helpful to memorize the relationship of sides in the 30°-60°-90° triangle. If the smallest side, which is opposite the 30-degree angle, is x, then the hypotenuse will be $2x$. The medium-length side opposite the 60-degree angle will be $x\sqrt{3}$.

Conveniently, the side opposite the 60-degree angle is $3\sqrt{3}$. Therefore, x must be 3. And if side DF is 3, then so too must be side BF. You've now discovered that the side of the square is 6; you're in the home stretch. Because you need the diagonal of the square, you can use the Pythagorean theorem. $6^2 + 6^2 = c^2$. Solving for the diagonal, you should get $6\sqrt{2}$, which is D.

Had enough? Maybe we should try one more.

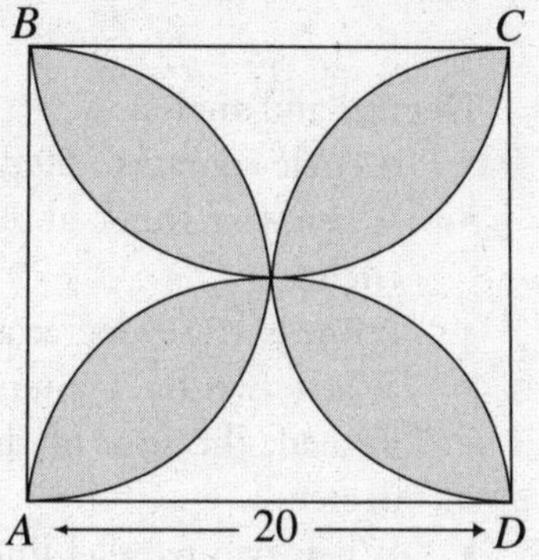

19. The shaded region in square *ABCD* above is composed of the intersections of circular regions. What is the area of the shaded region?

(A) 20π
(B) $40(\pi - 2)$
(C) $200(\pi - 2)$
(D) 100π
(E) 400π

Here's How to Crack It

This problem is a nightmare. Notice the difficulty level—it's right up there at the top. But even the most difficult problems can be cracked if you know how to approach them. Instead of doing all of the math, which would take ages, let's engage in a little Ballparking. Start with what you know: You have a square with a side length of 20. The question asks for the area of the leaf-shaped portions. The entire area of the square is 400. Ballpark the amount of the picture taken up by the shaded region; it looks to be around half. So we need an answer around 200. Let's go to the choices:

(A) $20\pi \approx 60$ Too small
(B) $40(\pi - 2) \approx 40$ Too small
(C) $200(\pi - 2) \approx 200$ Looks good!
(D) $100\pi \approx 314$ Too big
(E) $400\pi \approx 1{,}200$ Way too big!

The answer is C.

You may think that this isn't the "right" way to do the problem, but that's not the issue. The goal is to get as many points as possible, by any means possible. In most areas of your life, we wouldn't recommend that sort of mindset, but for the SAT it's okay.

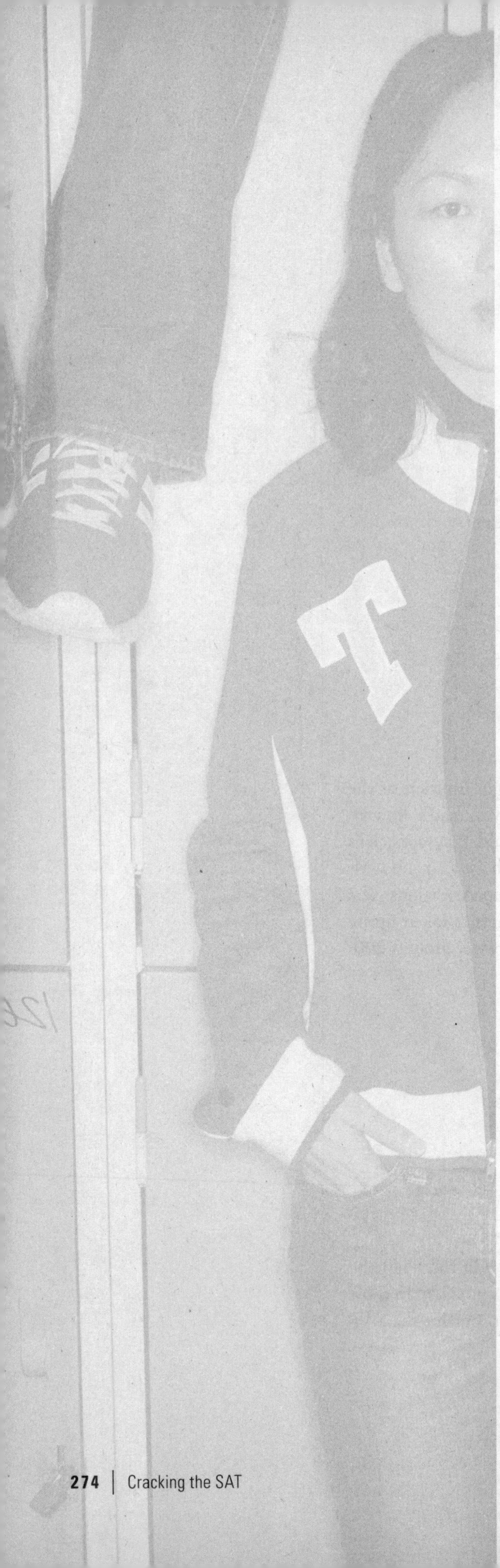

Summary

- Degrees and angles:
  - A circle contains 360 degrees.
  - When you think about angles, remember circles.
  - A line is a 180-degree angle.
  - When two lines intersect, four angles are formed; the sum of their measures is 360 degrees.
  - When two parallel lines are cut by a third line, the small angles are equal, the big angles are equal, and the sum of a big angle and a small angle is 180 degrees.

- Triangles:
  - Every triangle contains 180 degrees.
  - An isosceles triangle is one in which two of the sides are equal in length, and the two angles opposite the equal sides are equal in measure.
  - An equilateral triangle is one in which all three sides are equal in length, and all three angles are equal in measure (60 degrees).
  - A right triangle is one in which one of the angles is a right angle (90 degrees).
  - The perimeter of a triangle is the sum of the lengths of its sides.
  - The area of a triangle is $\frac{1}{2}bh$.
  - The height *must* form a right angle with the base.
  - The Pythagorean theorem states that in a right triangle, the square of the hypotenuse equals the sum of the squares of the other two sides. Remember ETS's favorite Pythagorean triplets (3-4-5 and 5-12-13).
  - Remember the other special right triangles 45°-45°-90° and 30°-60°-90°.
  - Similar triangles have the same angles and their lengths are in proportion.

- Circles:
  - The circumference of a circle is $2\pi r$ or πd, where r is the radius of the circle and d is the diameter.
  - The area of a circle is πr^2, where r is the radius of the circle.
  - A tangent touches a circle at one point; any radius that touches that tangent forms a 90-degree angle.

- Rectangles and squares:
  - The perimeter of a rectangle is the sum of the lengths of its sides.
  - The area of a rectangle is *length* × *width*.
  - A square is a rectangle whose four sides are all equal in length.
  - Any polygon can be divided into triangles.
  - The volume of a rectangular solid is *length* × *width* × *height*. The formulas to compute the volume of other three-dimensional figures are supplied in the instructions at the front of every Math section.
  - You must know how to locate points on a grid.

- When you encounter a geometry problem on the SAT, Ballpark the answer before trying to work it out.

- You must be familiar with the size of certain common angles.

- Most SAT geometry diagrams are drawn to scale. Use your eyes before you use your pencil. Try to eliminate impossible answers.

- When a diagram is not drawn to scale, redraw it.

- When no diagram is provided, make your own; when a provided diagram is incomplete, complete it.

- When information is missing from a diagram, ballpark and plug in.

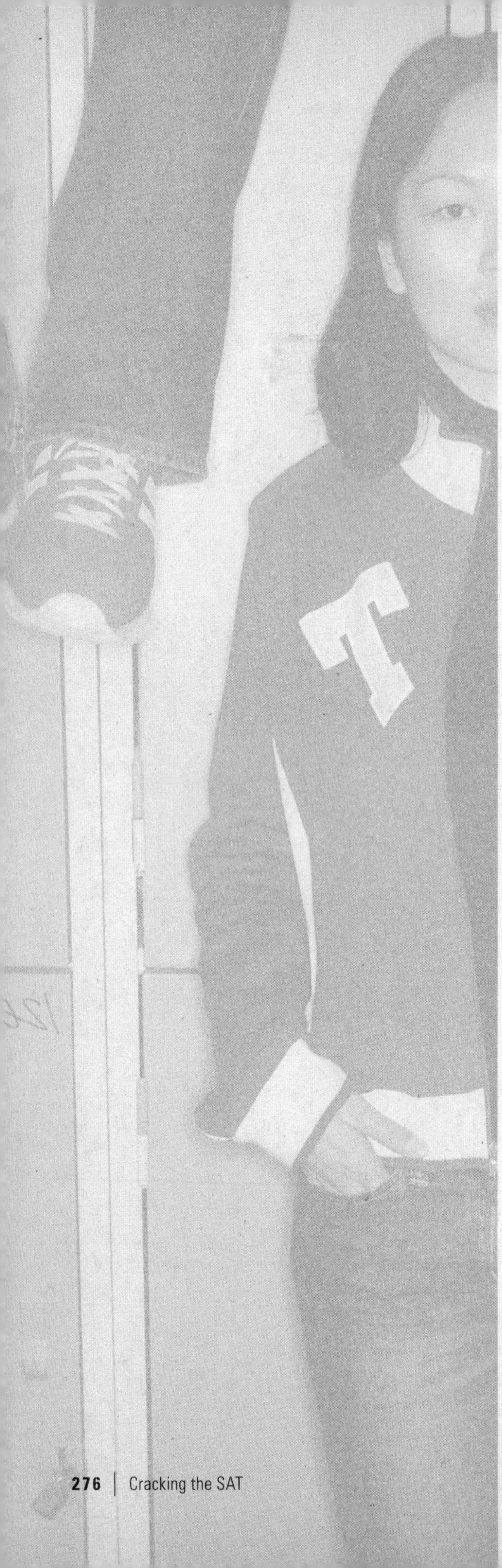

- Some extremely difficult SAT geometry problems can be solved quickly and easily through sketching and Ballparking, but you will have to stay on your toes. The way to do this is always to ask yourself three questions:
  - What information have I been given?
  - What information have I been asked to find?
  - What is the relationship between these two pieces of information?

Chapter 15
Grid-Ins: Cracking the System

Ten of the fifty-four math questions found on the SAT will require you to produce your own answer. Although the format of these questions is different from that of the multiple-choice questions, the mathematical concepts tested are no different. In this chapter we will show you how to apply what you have learned in the previous chapters to these new questions.

WHAT IS A GRID-IN?

One of the Math sections on your SAT will contain a group of ten problems without multiple-choice answers. ETS calls these problems "Student-Produced Responses." We call them *Grid-Ins,* because you have to mark your answers on a grid printed on your answer sheet. The grid looks like this:

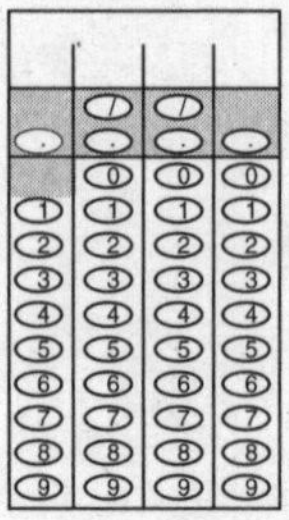

Despite their format, Grid-Ins are just like other math questions on the SAT, and many of the techniques that you've learned so far still apply. You can still use Plugging In and other great techniques, such as the Ratio Box and the Average Pie. You can still use the order of difficulty and your knowledge of Joe Bloggs to avoid making obvious mistakes on hard questions. Your calculator will still help you out on many problems as well. So Grid-Ins are nothing to be scared of. In fact, many Grid-In questions are simply regular SAT multiple-choice math problems with the answer choices lopped off. The only difference is that you have to arrive at your answer from scratch, rather than choose from among five possibilities.

You will need to be extra careful when answering Grid-In questions, however, because the grid format increases the likelihood of careless errors. It is vitally important that you understand how the Grid-In format works before you take the test. In particular, you'll need to memorize ETS's rules about which kinds of answers count and which don't. The instructions may look complicated, but we've boiled them down to a few rules for you to memorize and practice.

Order of Difficulty: Grid-Ins

Questions 9–11 Easy
Questions 12–15 Medium
Questions 16–18 Difficult

Take a look at the grid again. Because of the way it's arranged, ETS can use only certain types of problems for Grid-Ins. For example, you'll never see variables (letters) in your answer (although there can be variables in the question), because the grid can only accommodate numbers. This is good for you because no matter how good you are at algebra, you're probably better at arithmetic.

Keep Your Quarter

You don't lose points for wrong answers in the Grid-In section.

Also, this means that your calculator will be useful on several questions. As always, be careful to set up the problem on paper before you carefully punch the numbers into your calculator. Because you have to write in the answer on the grid yourself, you have to be more careful than ever to avoid careless mistakes.

Grid-Ins are scored somewhat differently than multiple-choice questions on the SAT. On multiple-choice questions, you lose a fraction of a raw score point for every incorrect answer. However, *nothing* is deducted for an incorrect answer on a Grid-In. An incorrect answer on one of these questions is no worse for your score than a question left blank. And, by the same token, a blank is just as costly as an error. Therefore, you *should be very aggressive in answering these questions.* Don't leave a question blank just because you're worried that the answer you've found may not be correct. ETS's scoring computers treat incorrect answers and blanks exactly the same. If you have arrived at an answer, you have a shot at earning points, and if you have a shot at earning points, you should take it.

We're not saying guess blindly. But if you work a problem and are unsure of your answer, enter it anyway. There is no penalty for getting it wrong.

THE INSTRUCTIONS

Here are the instructions for the Grid-In sections as they will appear on your SAT:

Directions: For Student-Produced Response questions 29-38, use the grids at the bottom of the answer sheet page on which you have answered questions 21-28.

Each of the remaining 10 questions requires you to solve the problem and enter your answer by marking the circles in the special grid, as shown in the examples below. You may use any available space for scratch work.

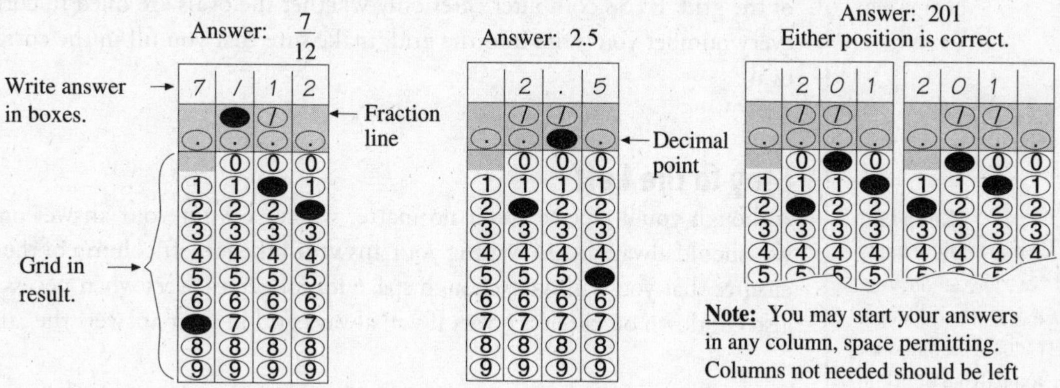

Note: You may start your answers in any column, space permitting. Columns not needed should be left blank.

- Mark no more than one circle in any column.
- Because the answer document will be machine-scored, **you will receive credit only if the circles are filled in correctly.**
- Although not required, it is suggested that you write your answer in the boxes at the top of the columns to help you fill in the circles accurately.
- Some problems may have more than one correct answer. In such cases, grid only one answer.
- No question has a negative answer.
- **Mixed numbers** such as $3\frac{1}{2}$ must be gridded as 3.5 or 7/2. (If

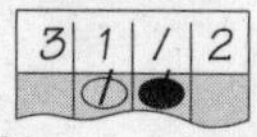

is gridded, it will be interpreted as $\frac{31}{2}$, not $3\frac{1}{2}$.)

- **Decimal Answers:** If you obtain a decimal answer with more digits than the grid can accommodate, it may be either rounded or truncated, but it must fill the entire grid. For example, if you obtain an answer such as 0.6666..., you should record your result as .666 or .667. **A less accurate value such as .66 or .67 will be scored as incorrect.**

Acceptable ways to grid $\frac{2}{3}$ are:

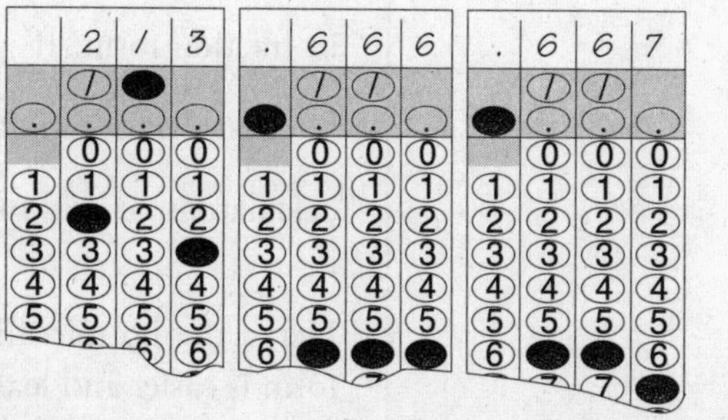

What the Instructions Mean

Of all the instructions on the SAT, these are the most important to understand thoroughly before you take the test. Pity the unprepared student who takes the SAT cold and spends ten minutes of potential point-scoring time reading and puzzling over ETS's confusing instructions. We've translated these unnecessarily complicated instructions into a few important rules. Make sure you know them all well.

Fill In the Boxes

Watch Out

Negatives, π, and % cannot be gridded in! For a Grid-In question involving % or $, the SAT will tell you to ignore the % or $ symbol. But negative numbers, non-integer square roots, and π can't be gridded in, so they'll never be an answer for this type of problem.

Always write your answer in the boxes at the top of the grid before you darken the ovals below. Your written answers won't affect the scoring of your test; if you write the correct answer in the boxes and grid in the wrong ovals, you won't get credit for your answer (and you won't be able to appeal to ETS). However, writing in the answers first makes you less likely to make an error when you grid in, and it also makes it easier to check your work.

Fill In the Ovals Correctly

As we just pointed out, you receive no credit for writing in the answer at the top of the grid. ETS's computer cares only whether the ovals are filled in correctly. For every number you write into the grid, make sure that you fill in the corresponding oval.

Stay to the Left

Keep Left

No matter how many digits are in your answer, always start gridding in the left-most column. That way, you'll avoid omitting digits and losing points.

Although you'll receive credit no matter where you put your answer on the grid, you should always begin writing your answer in the far left column of the grid. This ensures that you will have enough space for longer answers when necessary. You'll also cut down on careless errors if you always grid in your answers the same way.

FRACTIONS OR DECIMALS: YOUR CHOICE

You can grid in an answer in either fraction or decimal form. For example, if your answer to a question is $\frac{1}{2}$, you can either grid in $\frac{1}{2}$ *or* .5. It doesn't matter to ETS because $\frac{1}{2}$ equals .5; the computer will credit either form of the answer. That means you actually have a choice. If you like fractions, grid in your answers in fraction form. If you like decimals, you can grid in the decimal. If you have a fraction that doesn't fit in the grid, you can simply convert it to a decimal on your calculator and grid in the decimal.

Here's the bottom line: When gridding in fractions or decimals, use whichever form is easier and least likely to cause careless mistakes.

Decimal Places and Rounding

When you have a decimal answer of a value less than 1, such as .45 or .678, many teachers ask you to write a zero before the decimal point (for example, 0.45 or 0.678). On Grid-In questions, however, ETS doesn't want you to worry about the zero. In fact, there is no 0 in the first column of the grid. If your answer is a decimal less than 1, just write the decimal point in the first column of the grid and then continue from there.

Lop

Why do extra work for ETS? After all, they won't give you extra points. If your decimal doesn't fit in the grid, lop off the extra digits and grid in what does fit.

You should also notice that if you put the decimal point in the first column of the grid, you have only three places left to write in numbers. But what if your decimal is longer than three places, such as .87689? In these cases, ETS will give you credit if you round off the decimal so that it fits in the grid. But you'll *also* get credit, however, if you just enter as much of the decimal as will fit.

For example, if you had to grid in .87689, you could just write .876 (which is all that will fit) and then stop. You need to grid in only whatever is necessary to receive credit for your answer. Don't bother with extra unnecessary steps. You don't have to round off decimals, so don't bother.

If you have a long or repeating decimal, however, be sure to fill up all the spaces in the grid. If your decimal is .666666, you *must* grid in .666. Just gridding in .6 or .66 is not good enough.

Reducing Fractions

If you decide to grid in a fraction, ETS doesn't care if you reduce the fraction or not. For example, if your answer to a problem is $\frac{4}{6}$, ETS will give you credit if you grid in $\frac{4}{6}$ or reduce it to $\frac{2}{3}$. So if you have to grid in a fraction, and the fraction fits in the grid, don't bother reducing it. Why give yourself more work (and another chance to make a careless error)?

Relax

If your answer is a fraction and it fits in the grid (fraction bar included), don't reduce it. Why bother? ETS won't give you an extra point. However, if your fraction doesn't fit, reduce it or turn it into a decimal on your calculator.

The only time you might have to reduce a fraction is if it doesn't fit in the grid. If your answer to a question is $\frac{15}{25}$, it won't fit in the grid. You have two options: Either reduce the fraction to $\frac{3}{5}$ and grid that in, or use your calculator to convert the fraction to .6. Choose whichever process makes you the most comfortable.

Don't Mix

Never grid in a mixed number. Change it into a top-heavy fraction or its decimal equivalent.

Mixed Numbers

ETS's scoring machine does not recognize mixed numbers. If you try to grid in $2\frac{1}{2}$ by writing "2 1/2," the computer will read this number as $\frac{21}{2}$. You have to convert mixed numbers to fractions or decimals before you grid them in. To grid in $2\frac{1}{2}$, either convert it to $\frac{5}{2}$ or its decimal equivalent, which is 2.5. If you have to convert a mixed number to grid it in, be very careful not to change its value accidentally.

Don't Worry

The vast majority of Grid-In answers will not be difficult to enter in the grid. ETS won't try to trick you by purposely writing questions that are confusing to grid in. Just pay attention to these guidelines and watch out for careless errors.

GRIDDING IN: A TEST DRIVE

To get a feel for this format, let's work through two examples. As you will see, Grid-In problems are just regular SAT math problems.

10. If $a + 2 = 6$ and $b + 3 = 21$, what is the value of $\frac{b}{a}$?

Here's How to Crack It

You need to solve the first equation for *a* and the second equation for *b*. Start with the first equation, and solve for *a*. By subtracting 2 from both sides of the equation, you should see that $a = 4$.

Now move to the second equation, and solve for *b*. By subtracting 3 from both sides of the second equation, you should see that $b = 18$.

The question asked you to find the value of $\frac{b}{a}$. That's easy. The value of *b* is 18, and the value of *a* is 4. Therefore, the value of $\frac{b}{a}$ is $\frac{18}{4}$.

That's an ugly-looking fraction. How in the world do you grid it in? Ask yourself: "Does $\frac{18}{4}$ fit?" Yes! Grid in $\frac{18}{4}$.

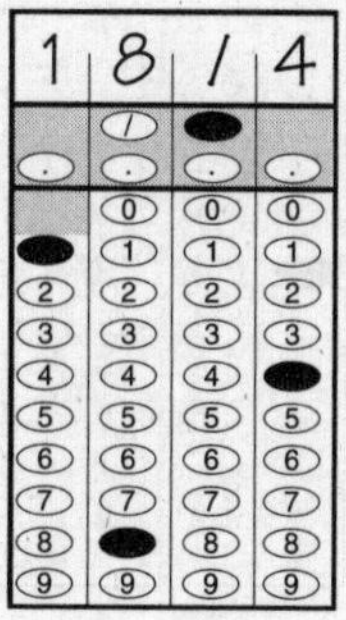

Your math teacher wouldn't like it, but ETS's computer will. You shouldn't waste time reducing $\frac{18}{4}$ to a prettier fraction or converting it to a decimal. Spend that time on another problem instead. The fewer steps you take, the less likely you will be to make a careless mistake.

Here's another example. This one is quite a bit harder.

15. Forty percent of the members of the sixth-grade class wore white socks. Twenty percent wore black socks. If twenty-five percent of the remaining students wore gray socks, what percent of the sixth-grade class wore socks that were not white, black, or gray? (Disregard the % when gridding your answer.)

Here's How to Crack It

The problem doesn't tell you how many students are in the class, so you can plug in any number you like. This is a percentage problem, so the easiest number to plug in is 100. Forty percent of 100 is 40; that means 40 students wore white socks. Twenty percent of 100 is 20. That means that 20 students wore black socks.

Your next piece of information says that 25 percent of the remaining students wore gray socks. How many students remain? Forty, because 60 students wore either white or black socks, and 100 – 60 = 40. Therefore, 25 percent of these 40—10 students—wore gray socks.

How many students are left? 30. Therefore, the percentage of students not wearing white, black, or gray socks is 30 out of 100, or 30 percent. Grid it in, and remember to forget about the percent sign.

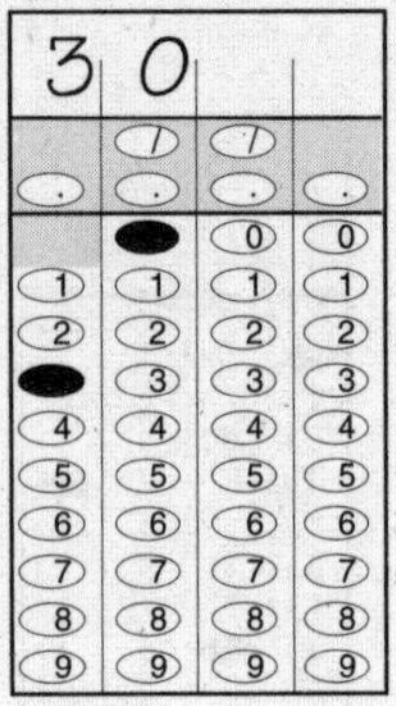

ORDER OF DIFFICULTY

Like all other questions on the Math SAT, Grid-In problems are arranged in order of increasing difficulty. In each group of ten, the first third is easy, the second third is medium, and the final third is difficult. As always, the order of difficulty will be your guide to how much faith you can place in your hunches.

Remember to focus on the questions you know how to answer first. Don't spend time on questions that you have no idea how to work, but if you're able to plug in or take an educated guess, go ahead and grid in that answer. Again, there's no penalty for getting it wrong.

Keep in mind, of course, that many of the math techniques that you've learned are still very effective on Grid-In questions. Plugging In worked very well on question number 15 on the previous page.

Here's another difficult Grid-In question that you can answer effectively by using a technique you've learned before:

18. Grow-Up potting soil is made from only peat moss and compost in a ratio of 3 pounds of peat moss to 5 pounds of compost. If a bag of Grow-Up potting soil contains 12 pounds of potting soil, how many pounds of peat moss does it contain?

Here's How to Crack It

To solve this problem, set up a Ratio Box (the Ratio Box is explained in detail in Chapter 13).

	Peat Moss	Compost	Whole
Ratio (parts)	3	5	8
Multiply By			
Actual Number			12 (lbs)

What do you multiply by 8 to get 12? If you don't know, divide 12 by 8 on your calculator. The answer is 1.5. Write 1.5 in each of the boxes on the *multiply by* row of your Ratio Box.

	Peat Moss	Compost	Whole
Ratio (parts)	3	5	8
Multiply By	1.5	1.5	1.5
Actual Number			12 (lbs)

The problem asks you how many pounds of peat moss are in a bag. To find out, multiply the numbers in the Peat Moss column. That is, multiply 3 × 1.5, and you get 4.5. ETS's answer is 4.5.

	Peat Moss	Compost	Whole
Ratio (parts)	3	5	8
Multiply By	1.5	1.5	1.5
Actual Number	4.5 (lbs)		12 (lbs)

Grid it in like this:

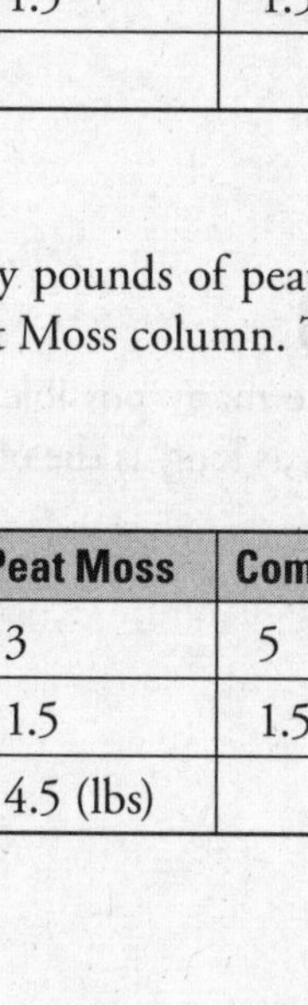

Joe Bloggs and Grid-In Questions

Say No to Joe
If it takes you only four seconds to answer any Grid-In question from numbers 16 through 18, you've probably goofed. Check your work. Difficult questions have difficult answers.

On Grid-In questions, you obviously can't use the Joe Bloggs principle to eliminate tempting but incorrect answer choices, because there aren't any choices from which to choose. But you can—and must—use your knowledge of Joe Bloggs to double-check your work and keep yourself from making careless mistakes or falling into traps.

The basic idea still holds true: Easy questions have easy answers, and hard questions have hard answers. On hard questions, you must be extremely suspicious of answers that come to you easily or through simple calculations.

Unfortunately, your knowledge of Joe Bloggs alone will never lead you all the way to ETS's answers, the way it sometimes does on multiple-choice questions. In order to earn points on Grid-In questions, you're going to have to find the real answers, and you're going to have to be extremely careful when you enter your answers on your answer sheet. But Joe Bloggs may help you find the correct path to ETS's answer. On a hard problem, you may be torn between two different approaches, one easy and one hard. Which should you pursue? The harder one. Joe will take the easy path and, as always on hard questions, it will lead him to the wrong answer.

More Than One
Some Grid-In questions have several possible correct answers. None is more correct than any other, so grid in the first one you find and move on.

RANGE OF ANSWERS

Some Grid-In problems will have many possible correct answers. It won't matter which correct answer you choose, as long as the one you choose really is correct.

Here's an example:

12. What is one possible value of x such that $\frac{1}{4} < x < \frac{1}{3}$?

Here's How to Crack It

Joe Bloggs has trouble imagining how anything could squeeze between $\frac{1}{4}$ and $\frac{1}{3}$, but you know there are lots and lots of numbers in there. Any one of them will satisfy ETS.

The numbers in this problem are both fractions, but your answer doesn't have to be. The easiest approach is to forget about math-class solutions and head straight for your calculator (or your mental calculator). Convert $\frac{1}{4}$ to a decimal by dividing 1 by 4, which gives you .25. Now convert $\frac{1}{3}$ to a decimal by dividing 1 by 3, which gives you .333. All you need to answer the question is any number that falls between those two decimals. How about .26? Or .3? Or .331? Your answer merely has to be bigger than .25 and smaller than .333. Pick one, grid it in, and move on.

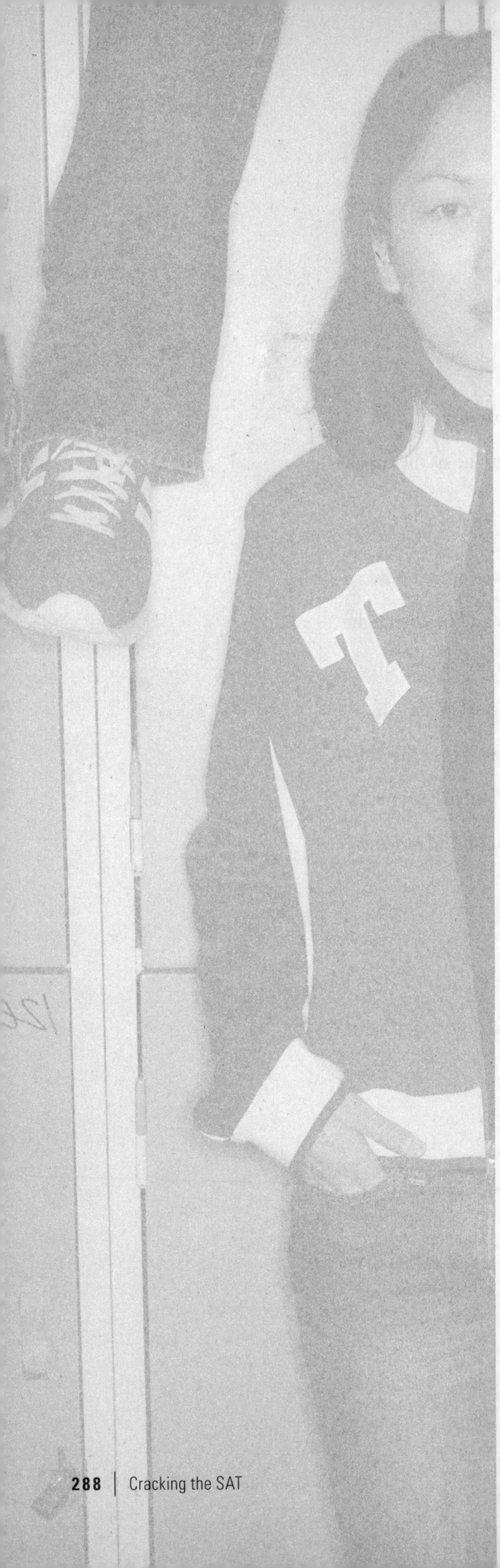

Summary

- One of the Math sections on your SAT will contain a group of ten problems without multiple-choice answers. ETS calls these problems "Student-Produced Responses." We call them *Grid-Ins,* because you have to mark your answers on a grid printed on your answer sheet.
- Despite their format, Grid-Ins are really just like other math questions on the SAT, and many of the same techniques that you have learned still apply.
- The grid format increases the likelihood of careless errors. Know the instructions and check your work carefully.
- There is no guessing penalty for Grid-Ins, so you should always grid in your answer, even if you're not sure that it's correct.
- Always write the numbers in the boxes at the top of the grid before you (carefully) fill in the corresponding ovals.
- Grid in your answer as far to the left as possible.
- If the answer to a Grid-In question contains a fraction or a decimal, you can grid in the answer in either form. When gridding in fractions or decimals, use whichever form is easier and least likely to cause careless mistakes.
- There's no need to round decimals, even though it is permitted.
- If you have a long or repeating decimal, be sure to fill up all the spaces in the grid.
- If a fraction fits in the grid, you don't have to reduce the fraction before gridding it in.
- ETS's scoring machine does not recognize mixed numbers. Convert mixed numbers to fractions or decimals before gridding them in.
- Some Grid-In questions will have more than one correct answer. It doesn't matter which answer you grid in, as long as it's one of the possible answers.

- Like all other questions on the Math SAT, Grid-In problems are arranged in order of increasing difficulty. In each group of ten, the first third is easy, the second third is medium, and the final third is difficult.
- On Grid-Ins, as on all other SAT sections, easy questions have easy answers, and hard questions have hard answers. On hard Grid-Ins, you must be extremely suspicious of answers that come to you easily or through simple calculations.
- Negatives, π, square roots, and % cannot be gridded in.

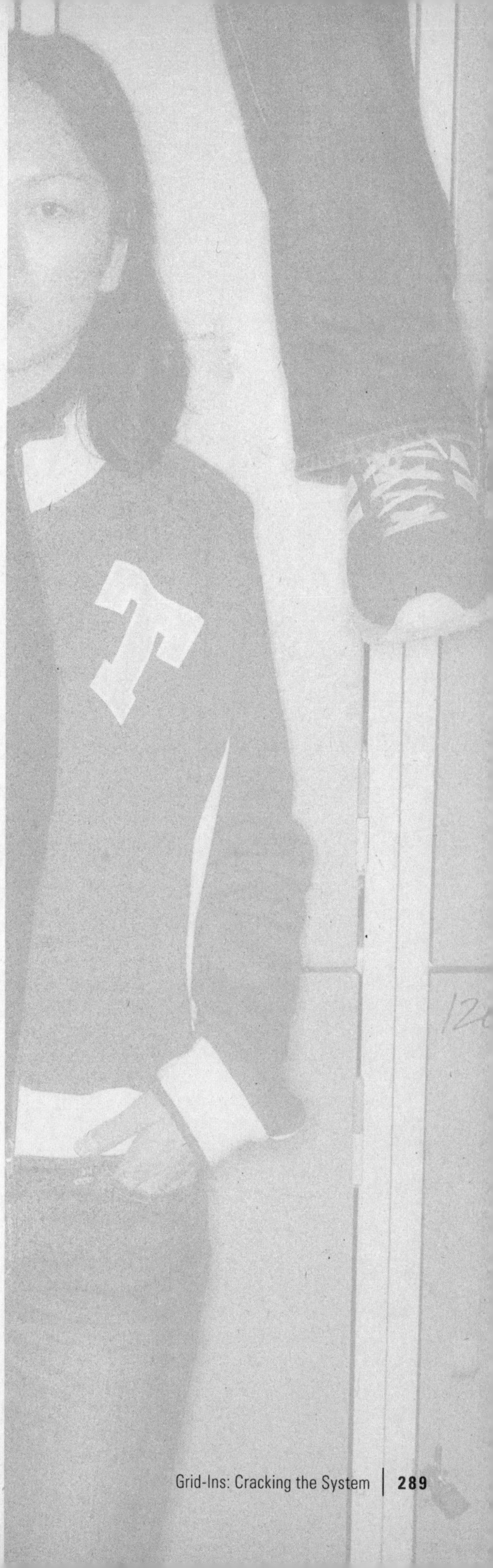

Chapter 16 Putting It All Together

Now that you have reviewed the mathematical concepts you need to know for the SAT, it is time to start practicing what you've learned. This chapter contains a comprehensive practice drill on which you can practice your skills and techniques. Good luck!

PUTTING IT ALL TOGETHER...

Here's your chance to combine everything you learned in the math chapters and give yourself some extra drills before the practice tests. Remember to practice the techniques we've taught you, even if you could arrive at the answer in a different way. This is the only way to improve your problem recognition skills (knowing what technique to use on what type of problem).

The problem numbers represent where you would see them on the actual SAT. All numbers of multiple-choice questions are based on a 25-minute section, so you can use that as a gauge for recognizing question difficulty. The answers and explanations are located in Part VI.

Good luck!

13. If $a > b$ and $a^2 - 2ab + b^2 = 169$, what is the value of $a - b$?

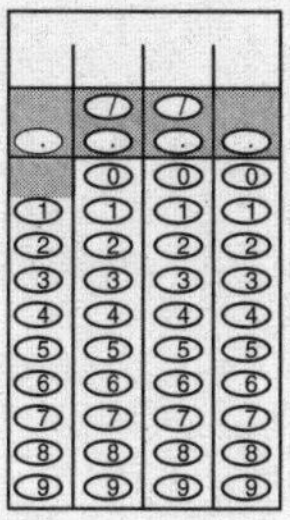

15. If a is 63% and c is $\frac{3}{8}$, which of the following is the closest equivalent of the ratio of a to c ?

(A) 0.006
(B) 0.236
(C) 0.381
(D) 0.595
(E) 1.680

11. In right triangle ABC, the longest side, AB, is 4 feet long, and angles BAC and ABC are equal. What is the perimeter of the triangle in feet?

(A) 8

(B) $4\sqrt{2}$

(C) $4+4\sqrt{2}$

(D) 12

(E) $8+4\sqrt{2}$

18. There are 5 cyclists in a race. If the first-place finisher receives a gold medal, the second-place finisher receives a silver medal, and the third-place finisher receives a bronze medal, how many different permutations are possible for the medal winners?

(A) 5
(B) 12
(C) 20
(D) 50
(E) 60

12. If $a + 2b = 10$, and $b - a = 2$, what is the value of b ?

(A) 10
(B) 8
(C) 6
(D) 4
(E) 2

---

8. If the perimeter of a square is 28, what is the length of the diagonal of the square?

(A) $2\sqrt{14}$
(B) $7\sqrt{2}$
(C) $7\sqrt{3}$
(D) 14
(E) $28\sqrt{2}$

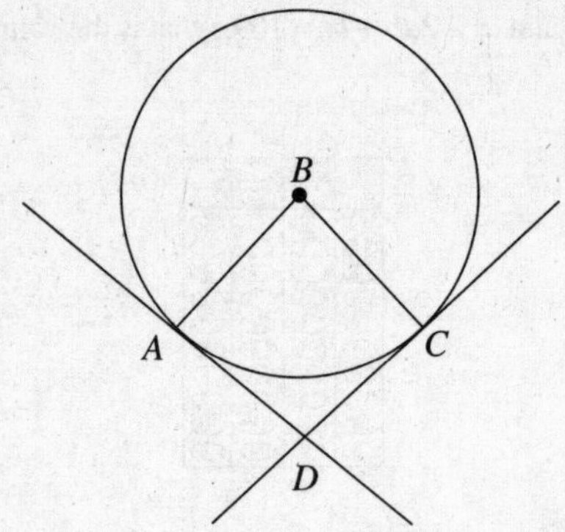

Note: Figure not drawn to scale.

17. In the figure above, DA and DC are tangent to the circle with center B at points A and C, respectively. If $\angle ABC = \frac{2}{7}\angle ADC$, what is the degree measure of $\angle ADC$?

(A) 40
(B) 51
(C) 129
(D) 140
(E) 154

---

10. A photographer is arranging 5 photographs in a row from left to right for a display. If all 5 photographs will be used, how many different arrangements can the photographer make?

(A) 5
(B) 24
(C) 25
(D) 120
(E) 390,625

13. At Ernie's Fruit Stand, 3 apples and 5 cherries cost $1.25. 15 apples and 100 cherries cost $9.25. What is the cost of 6 apples and 35 cherries?

(A) $3.25
(B) $3.50
(C) $3.62
(D) $4.00
(E) $5.25

15. According to local safety regulations, no transit bus may carry more than 66 people in it at one time. Right now, there are 42 people on a particular transit bus. At the next stop, *n* people enter the bus, but no one exits. If the total number of people on that transit bus is not over the limit, in terms of *n*, how many people are on the bus?

(A) $n + 42 \leq 66$
(B) $n + 42 \geq 66$
(C) $n - 42 \leq 66$
(D) $n - 42 \geq 66$
(E) $n \geq 66 - 42$

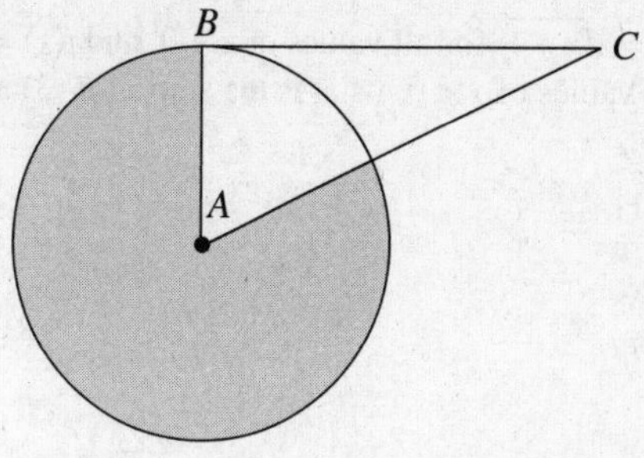

Note: Figure not drawn to scale.

18. The circle above with center *A* has an area of 21. *BC* is tangent to the circle with center *A* at point *B*. If $AC = 2AB$, what is the area of the shaded region?

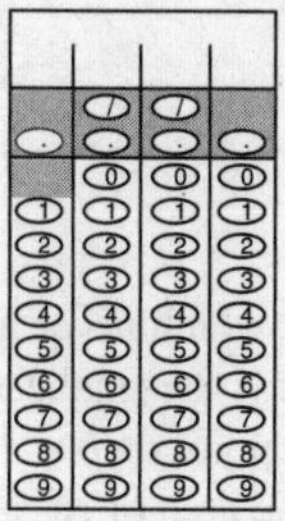

14. If $f(x) = |x| + 1$ and $g(x) = x - 3$, what is the value of $f(g(1))$?

(A) –2
(B) – 1
(C) 1
(D) 2
(E) 3

15. If $f(x) = \sqrt{x+1}$ for all values of $x \geq 0$, and $f(x) = x^2 + 2$ for all values of $x < 0$, what is the sum of $f(-3)$ and $f(8)$?

(A) 5
(B) 11
(C) 14
(D) 68
(E) 77

12. Two lines, a and b, which never intersect, are both tangent to circle C. If the smallest distance between any point on a and any point on b is 4 less than triple that distance, what is the area of circle C ?

(A) $\frac{\pi}{4}$

(B) π

(C) 2π

(D) 4π

(E) 9π

16. One sheet of metal can be melted down to make a spherical ball with a radius of 2 centimeters. How many such sheets would have to be melted down to make a spherical ball of radius 6 centimeters? (The volume V of a sphere with radius r is given by $V = \frac{4}{3}\pi r^3$.)

(A) 3
(B) 9
(C) 16
(D) 27
(E) 216

17. Let $f(a, b) = a^2 - b^2$. If $f(5, d) = 9$, what is the positive value of d ?

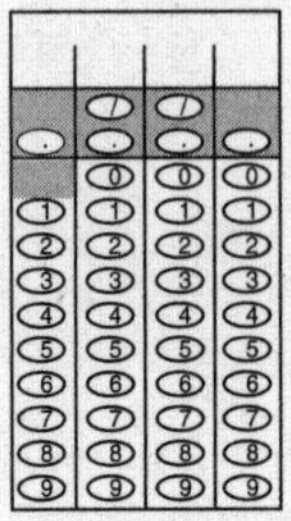

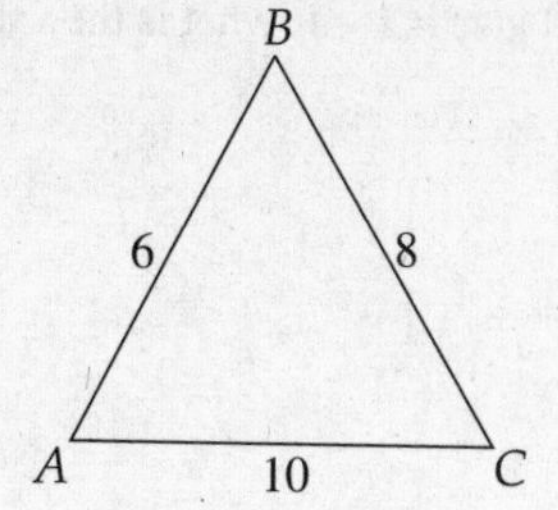

Note: Figure not drawn to scale.

13. What is the measure, in degrees, of the largest angle in the above triangle?

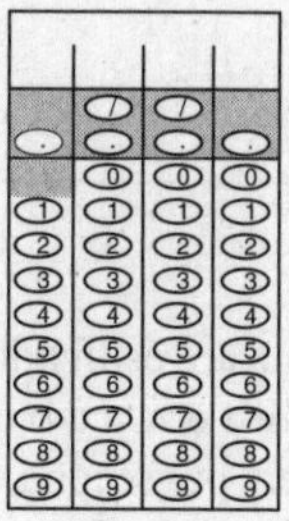

10. If the product of $x^2 - 6x + 5$ and $2x^2 - 7x + 3$ is 0, then x could equal any of the following numbers EXCEPT

(A) $\frac{1}{2}$

(B) 1

(C) 2

(D) 3

(E) 5

13. Jon is making omelets. He has 3 different spices, 4 different vegetables, and 2 different types of eggs. If he will use one spice, one vegetable, and one type of egg, how many combinations of these ingredients can he make?

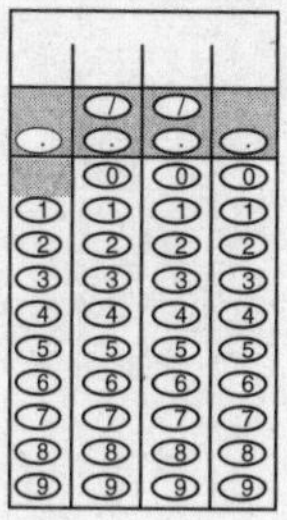

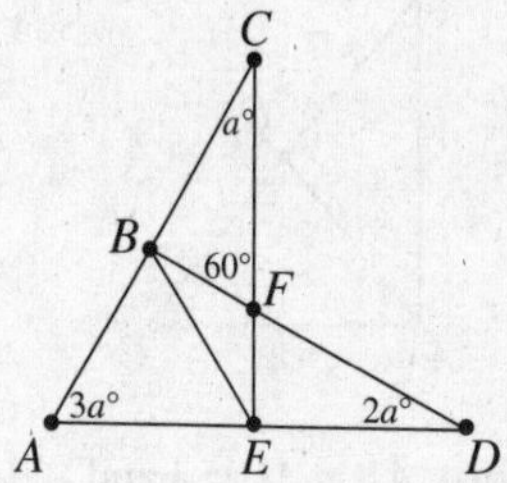

17. In the figure above, *AC*, *CE*, and *BD* intersect at the points shown above. What is the value of *a* ?

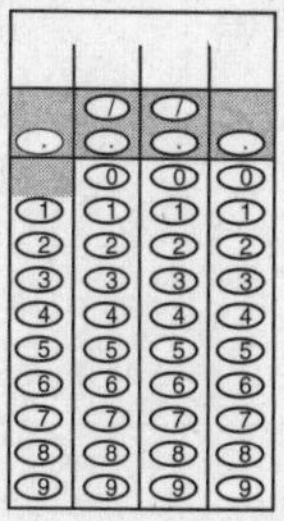

$$5 < \sqrt{n} < 9$$

18. If n is an integer that satisfies the inequality above, what is the sum of the largest possible value of n and the smallest possible value of n?

(A) 2
(B) 4
(C) 100
(D) 106
(E) 117

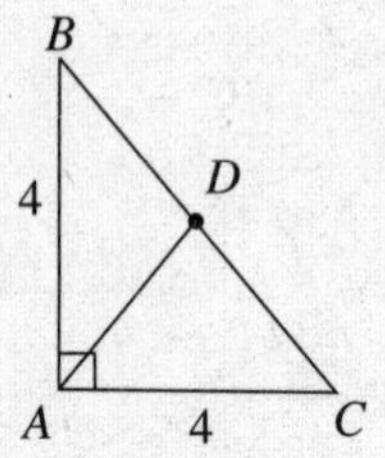

12. In the figure above, $AB = AC = 4$ and $\angle BAC$ and $\angle ADC$ are right angles. What is AD ?

(A) $2\sqrt{2}$
(B) $2\sqrt{3}$
(C) $4\sqrt{2}$
(D) $4\sqrt{3}$
(E) 8

14. If $f(x) = x^2$ and $g(x) = x - 1$, what is the value of $f(g(3))$?

(A) 2
(B) 4
(C) 6
(D) 8
(E) 9

20. Carlos and Katherine are estimating acceleration by rolling a ball from rest down a ramp. At 1 second, the ball is moving at 5 meters per second (m/s); at 2 seconds, the ball is moving at 10 m/s; at 3 seconds, the ball is moving at 15 m/s; and at 4 seconds, it is moving at 20 m/s. When graphed on an xy-plane, which equation best describes the ball's estimated acceleration where y expresses speed and x expresses time?

(A) $y = 5x + 5$
(B) $y = 25x$
(C) $y = -5x + 5$
(D) $y = 5x$
(E) $y = (4x + 1)^2 + 5$

17. The average (arithmetic mean) number of computers fixed by a technician was 15 per day for the first 20 days of the month. After another 10 days, the average number of computers fixed over all 30 days was 18 per day. What was the average number of computers fixed in the last 10 days?

(A) 24
(B) 27
(C) 29
(D) 32
(E) 35

20. If $y = 3^x$ and x and y are both integers, which of the following is equivalent to $9^x + 3^{x+1}$?

(A) y^3

(B) $3y + 3$

(C) $y(y + 3)$

(D) $y^2 + 3$

(E) $3(y + 3)$

Part IV
How to Crack the Writing Section

CAN YOU REALLY TEST WRITING ON A STANDARDIZED TEST?

ETS thinks so, but we would beg to differ. What the SAT calls a writing test is really a test of some grammar rules and your ability to crank out an essay in 25 minutes. But those two skills don't really indicate anything about your writing ability. All this section tests is your ability to conform to what essay graders at ETS consider "good" writing. Based on these standards, William Shakespeare, Ernest Hemingway, and e.e. cummings would all be considered bad writers.

How Can That Be?

Once again, it's all about the "best" answer. In the real world, no one writes an essay in 25 minutes, and many acclaimed writers have a fairly loose conception of grammar. But the SAT is not like the real world, as by now you've surely realized. All we can do is suppress our anger and try to do the best we can on the SAT.

WHAT'S IN THE WRITING SECTION?

In official ETS language, the Essay section and sections with multiple-choice grammar questions are called the "Writing section." However, we'll often just use the terms "Essay section" and "Grammar section" so you'll know exactly what we're talking about.

You will see three types of multiple-choice questions in the Grammar sections: error identifications (a.k.a. error ID, where you're asked to find which part of the sentence is wrong), improving sentences (where you're asked to make a sentence sound better), and improving paragraphs (where you fix errors in a poorly written passage).

Now, before you get worried about all of the grammar rules you've forgotten (or never managed to learn), relax; you have seen this section before. It's simply the PSAT's Writing Skills section, with a new name, but the same old attitude. As on the PSAT, ETS is checking only a few, select rules of grammar. Regardless of whether you remember these rules from the PSAT, we will be going over each of the ones you'll need.

The essay is not as bad as it sounds either. The College Board will present either a statement of opinion (roughly a paragraph long) made by a notable person, or two statements from different people. Then you'll write a two-page essay (approximately) arguing how you feel about the statement(s), and why. Heck, ETS is even kind enough to give you a few options to start approaching the topic.

How to Ace the Writing Section

- Review and learn the rules of grammar, SAT-style.
- Memorize your plan of attack for each type of question.
- Know which questions to do right away and which to skip until the end.
- Understand what the essay graders want from you.

Chapter 17 Grammar

There will be two sections, one short and one long, dedicated to testing your knowledge of English grammar rules and style preferences. Although there are many grammar rules, ETS tests only a few of them, and you probably already know many of them. In this chapter, you will review the rules being tested and learn how to apply these basic rules to the three types of questions found on the Writing sections.

GRAMMAR STRATEGY

Every question type on the SAT can be cracked, and Grammar section questions are no exception. While reviewing the basic grammar you need, you will also learn how to crack error ID and improving sentences questions. After you solidify your approach to these question types, you'll learn how to crack improving paragraphs questions by employing the grammar and skills you've already mastered. Of course, you need to practice this stuff to really make it work. After working through the drills in this chapter, be sure to take a full-length practice test.

Joe Bloggs and the Grammar Sections

No Order of Difficulty
Remember the types of questions that don't follow a clear order of difficulty?
Critical Reading:
the long and short reading passage questions
Writing:
improving paragraphs and the essay

Just as they do in the Critical Reading sections, some of the questions in the Grammar section don't follow a noticeable order of difficulty. However, knowing how Joe approaches questions in these sections can still help you achieve a better score.

Joe's biggest mistake on the grammar questions is basing his answers on what sounds right. This approach, unfortunately, is just about the worst way to go about answering the questions. Most people do not speak in a grammatically correct way. Consider the following conversation:

Alex (answering the phone): Hello? Who's there?

Briana: It's me.

Alex: Oh hey, where you at?

Briana: Me and my friends are headed to the movie theater. You coming?

Alex: Cool. I'll be there.

Keep Track of Where You Are
Statistically, more students miss the last few questions in each question type. Remember Joe Bloggs when you hit the end of any Grammar section. If it sounds too good to be true, it probably is!

Now note the same conversation, edited for grammatical correctness:

Alex: Hello? Who's there?

Briana: It is I.

Alex: Oh, hey. At what location are you?

Briana: My friends and I are going to the movie theater. Would you like to join us?

Alex: Indeed. I shall be there.

Chances are you don't talk like this, so it sounds strange to your ear. But that doesn't mean it's wrong. Joe thinks that awkward or weird-sounding sentences or phrases must be wrong. ETS uses this tendency to set traps. Look at the following sentence:

The inconsistencies in (A) the witness's testimony notwithstanding (B), the jury had no choice but to conclude that the suspect was not guilty (C) of the charges leveled (D) against him. No error (E)

Analysis

Joe reads this sentence and something just *sounds* wrong to him. He can't exactly put his finger on it, but he knows that he's supposed to find an error. So Joe decides that something must be wrong with choice B because he would never use a word such as *notwithstanding.* Once again, poor Joe has played right into ETS's devious little hands. ETS hopes that you select answers based on how you would speak.

In this case, the sentence is actually fine as written. Now, you may have noticed that or you might have fallen for a Joe Bloggs answer. In any case, the questions in the Grammar sections can be some of the most frustrating on the test. You can't always be sure of the best answer, but make sure you get rid of any answers you know to be wrong.

The Importance of POE

Process of Elimination is extremely important on grammar questions. On many questions, you won't be 100 percent certain of the best answer. Even so, you can still eliminate as many wrong answers as you can and then take a guess. Be aggressive!

To Do or Not to Do

Remember that not all grammar questions are arranged in order of difficulty; therefore, to do well, you need to determine when a problem is hard and should be skipped. What makes a question hard? It either contains grammar that you don't know, or it's long and time-consuming. As a general rule, you will approach the section like this: Plan on going through the section twice. On your first pass, do the questions that are easiest for you. These should include some of each question type. Make sure you hit some or all of the improving paragraphs questions on the first pass, because they are almost always easy or medium. Once you've been through the section once, answering all of the questions you know how to do, go back and try the more difficult questions. Answer them only if you can eliminate at least one answer choice, and stick with your pacing.

Is It Difficult for You?

Remember that you have particular strengths and weaknesses when it comes to grammar. So, even if you're in a section that has an order of difficulty, make sure you're starting with questions that you know you can do.

Before we begin reviewing ETS's grammar, let's take a peek at the first two question types you'll see on the Grammar sections.

Error ID

This is an example of an error ID question that has no error. No error
(underlined: "This" = A, "example" = B, "that" = C, "has" = D, "No error" = E)

To check out which colleges have "Dorms Like Palaces," take a look at the rankings on your online student tools. If you haven't registered yet, go to PrincetonReview.com/cracking

An error ID question gives you a sentence that has four words or phrases underlined, each with a corresponding letter underneath. At the end of each sentence will be "No error"—choice E. There are some important things you need to know about error IDs.

- There is never more than one error per sentence.
- If there is an error, it's always underlined.
- Approximately 20 percent of all error ID questions are correct as written, so don't be afraid to pick choice E.
- Error IDs are short, and you should usually be able to eliminate at least one answer choice, so guess on all error ID questions.
- Do error ID questions first.

Improving Sentences

This is an example of an improving sentences question <u>that does not contain</u> an error.

(A) that does not contain
(B) that has not been containing
(C) which has not been contain
(D) which is not being with
(E) about which there is nothing to indicate it being with

Improving sentences questions give you a sentence, part or all of which is underlined. The underlined part may or may not contain a grammatical error. There are some important things you need to know about improving sentences questions.

- Answer choice A is a reprint of the underlined section. Therefore, if you decide that the sentence contains no error, choose answer choice A.
- Approximately 20 percent of all improving sentences questions are correct as written, so don't be afraid to pick choice A.
- If you decide the underlined portion of the sentence contains an error, eliminate choice A. Also, eliminate any other choice that does not fix the error.
- If you are unsure whether the sentence contains an error, look to your answer choices for a clue (more on this later).
- KISS: Keep It Short and Sweet. Concise answers are preferable.

Grammar? Ugh!

To do well on the Grammar sections, you need to remember some basic grammar rules. Now, don't get worked up about being tested on grammar. SAT grammar is not difficult, nor is it extensive. In fact, the Grammar sections really test only five basic grammatical concepts:

1. Sentence structure
2. Verbs
3. Nouns
4. Pronouns
5. Prepositions
6. Other little things

These are the five areas in which a sentence can "go wrong." They will function as a checklist for you—every time you read a sentence, you will look at these five areas to find the error. If you don't find one after checking these five things, then there probably isn't one.

Everything Is Just Ruined

Remember: Only the underlined portion can have an error. Don't try to fix things that aren't underlined.

No Error?

As we've mentioned, 20 percent of error ID questions and improving sentences questions contain no error. If you've used your checklist and can't find a mistake, chances are there isn't one. Because the questions get tougher, though, we find that "No Error" is more likely to be the answer on the second half of error ID questions than on the first.

We will use error ID questions to illustrate the first four areas of grammar. Before we get going on the grammar stuff, let's learn how to crack an error ID question.

Cracking Error IDs

As we mentioned, an error ID question is a short sentence that has four words or phrases underlined and lettered. Your job is to determine if any one of those four underlined segments contains an error. If it does, you are to blacken the corresponding oval on your answer sheet. If not, you are to choose E, "No error."

Let's look at an example of an error ID to learn how to beat these questions:

Jose told the school counselor his plan (A): he will (B) attend college, major in criminal justice (C), and to become (D) a lawyer. No error (E)

To check out which colleges have the "Most Beautiful Campuses," take a look at the rankings on your online student tools. If you haven't registered yet, go to PrincetonReview.com/cracking

The Approach

To solve an error ID, you need to look at the sentence one piece at a time. As you read through the sentence, pause after each underlined segment and ask, "Is there anything wrong yet?" Run through the first five categories of your grammar checklist:

- Sentence structure problem
- Verb problem
- Noun problem
- Pronoun problem
- Preposition problem

If these five areas check out, cross off each segment as you go (it's not your answer).

Look at the first segment of this sentence: *Jose told the school counselor his plan*.... Is there a problem with the phrase *his plan*? No. Put a slash through answer choice A. Next segment: *he will*.... Any problem with this verb? No, it's in the future tense and it's Jose's plan we're talking about, so everything is fine. Cross it off.

Continuing on: *major in criminal justice*.... No problem here—cross off C. Keep going: *and to become a lawyer.* Wait a minute—something doesn't sound right. *To become* is a verb. Notice in this example, there is a series of activities (verbs): *attend, major, to become.* When in a series, all the verbs need to have the same form. Therefore *to become* should be *become.* The answer is D.

By the way, you have just learned the first verb rule: When a series of activities is described in a sentence, make sure all the verbs are expressed the same way—make sure they are *parallel.*

Trim the Fat

Often an error ID will contain extraneous phrases that distract from the meat of the sentence and cause you to miss an error. How can you avoid getting waylaid by distracting phrases? Trim the fat. As you work through a sentence, cross off anything that is not essential to the sentence: prepositional phrases, phrases offset by commas, and so on. Crossing out the distracting phrases puts the important parts of a sentence, the subject and verb for example, together and prevents you from making careless errors.

Let's look at another example:

Math, <u>developed</u> over 2,000 years ago, <u>have been</u> a favorite <u>of</u> teachers and school children <u>alike for</u> generations. <u>No error</u>

(A: developed; B: have been; C: of; D: alike for; E: No error)

Here's How to Crack It

First, trim the fat. What's the subject of the sentence? *Math.* Once you see that there is no problem with choice A, *developed,* you can cross off the stuff between the commas—it's there to distract you. What's the verb? *Have been.* "*Math have been?*" Don't think so. *Math* is singular, so it needs a singular verb. The answer is B.

Be Aggressive

Error IDs are typically short and uncomplicated. Be aggressive as you go through these sentences. Read the sentence quickly once, keeping your checklist in mind. If you spot a problem, jump to it—you don't need to labor over the whole sentence if your eye is drawn to a problem right away.

As we review the first four areas of grammar, you will work through a bunch of error ID questions. This will give you a feel for how they work and how easy it is to guess and eliminate aggressively on these questions.

> **Do I Have to Read the Whole Thing?**
> Once you've found the error, do you need to read the rest of the sentence? Yes. If you're sure of the error you've found, a quick read will be easy and reassuring. If you are not so sure, you will need to read the rest of the sentence to be sure you haven't missed anything. Because error IDs are short and sweet, take a quick second to read them through.

SENTENCE STRUCTURE

Not only will the SAT test your ability to distinguish nouns, verbs, and such, but it will also test your knowledge of how sentences fit together. The main culprits when it comes to sentence structure errors are **clauses**.

Clauses

There are two types of clauses: independent (or main) and subordinate.

Independent (or Main) Clauses

The independent clause is the easier one to spot; it could stand alone and be a sentence all by itself. When you join two independent clauses, you have a few different options. Let's take a look at the following sentences:

> Susie wanted to go shopping. She wanted to go to the sale.

Here we just have two independent clauses, each of which is its own sentence. If you have too many of these in an essay it can start to sound stilted. One way to make your original sentences flow more smoothly is to connect them with a comma and a conjunction.

> Susie wanted to go shopping, and she wanted to go to the sale.

You could also join them with a semicolon.

> Susie wanted to go shopping; she wanted to go to the sale.

The Errors

SAT Traps
These are very common errors on the SAT. Always make sure that your independent clauses are separated by something: a period, a comma and conjunction, or a semicolon. Don't be fooled!

The previous sentences are grammatically correct and show different ways to combine main clauses. ETS will test your knowledge of these clauses with the following errors:

1. Comma Splice

   Susie wanted to go shopping, she wanted to go to the sale.

   This sentence has two independent clauses separated by only a comma. This is incorrect.

When to Punctuate
Missing or incorrect punctuation won't show up on Error ID, so that's one less thing to worry about on those questions.

2. Run-On Sentence

   Susie wanted to go shopping she wanted to go to the sale.

   You will see two independent clauses stuck together with nothing separating them. This is also wrong.

Subordinate (Dependent) Clauses

Unlike an independent clause, a dependent clause can't stand on its own. It needs an independent clause to latch onto. Let's look at the following sentence:

Since Sam is very dirty, he needs a bath.

This sentence has both an independent clause ("he needs a bath") and a dependent clause ("Since Sam is very dirty"). Often subordinate clauses fall either at the beginning or end of a sentence, separated by a comma or conjunction. However, this isn't always the case. Look at this sentence:

The shirt *that he put on* was too small.

In this case, the subordinate clause came in the middle. Notice that our independent clause is still intact, because if you remove the dependent clause (in italics), the sentence becomes: The shirt was too small. The clause can stand alone. There's your test for independent clauses!

The Errors

The main trap that ETS will throw at you when it comes to dependent clauses is called a **sentence fragment**. Look at the following sentence:

When the students entered the school, much to their dismay, and following the announcement.

Well, this just sounds bad, right? Here's the problem: You have 3 subordinate clauses and no independent clauses. When this happens, you have to fix the problem by finding the answer that keeps the idea of the sentence intact while inserting an independent clause.

VERBS

A verb is an action word. It tells what the subject of the sentence is doing. You've already seen two kinds of errors. There are a total of three things about a verb to check out:

1. Does it **agree** with its subject?
2. Is it **parallel** in structure to the other verbs in the sentence?
3. Is it in the proper **tense**?

Do They Agree?

The rule regarding subject-verb agreement is simple: singular with singular, plural with plural. If you are given a singular subject (*he, she, it*), then your verb must also be singular (*is, has, was*). (In case you don't remember, the subject of the sentence is the noun that the verb modifies—the person or thing that is *doing* the action.)

Easy enough, except, as you have already seen, ETS has a way of putting lots of stuff between the subject and the verb to make you forget whether your subject was singular or plural. Remember *Math* from the example on page 311?

Look at another one:

The answers given by (A) the commission appears (B) to contradict the earlier (C) testimony of its (D) members. No error (E)

To check out which colleges offer the "Most Diverse Student Population," take a look at the rankings on your online student tools. If you haven't registered yet, go to PrincetonReview.com/cracking

Here's How to Crack It

At first glance, this sentence may appear fine. But let's pull it apart. What is the sentence about? The *answers*—a plural subject. If the subject is plural, then the verb must be plural too. *Appears* is the verb modifying *answers,* but it is a singular verb—no can do. The answer is B.

Why did the sentence sound okay at first? Because of the stuff stuck between *answers* and *appears.* The phrase *given by the commission* places a singular noun right before the verb. Get rid of the extraneous stuff (i.e., trim the fat) and the error becomes obvious.

Knowing When It's Singular

Sometimes you may not know if a noun is singular or plural, making it tough to determine whether its verb should be singular or plural. Of course you know nouns like *he* and *cat* are singular, but what about *family* or *everybody*? The following is a list of "tricky" nouns—technically called collective nouns. They are nouns that typically describe a group of people but are considered singular and thus need a singular verb:

The family *is*
The jury *is*
The group *is*
The team *is*
The audience *is*
The congregation *is*
The United States (or any other country) *is*

The following pronouns also take singular verbs:

Either *is*
Neither *is*
None *is*
Each *is*
Anyone *is*
No one *is*
Everyone *is*

And or *Or*

Subjects joined by *and* are plural: Bill and Pat *were* going to the show. However, nouns joined by *or* can be singular or plural—if the last noun given is singular, then it takes a singular verb; if the last noun given is plural, it takes a plural verb.

John Keats and Percy Bysshe Shelley, each (A) of whom (B) is an accomplished Romantic poet, (C) is (D) still well known today. No error (E)

To check out which colleges have the "Most Homogeneous Student Population," take a look at the rankings on your online student tools. If you haven't registered yet, go to PrincetonReview.com/cracking

Here's How to Crack It

Once again ETS is trying to trip you up by separating the subject from the verb. You know what to do—trim the fat! What's the subject? *John Keats and Percy Bysshe Shelley.* We know the subject is plural because of the *and.* Cross off the stuff between commas and you have *John Keats and Percy Bysshe Shelley...is.* Can we use the singular verb *is* with our plural subject? No way—the answer is D.

Are They Parallel?

The next thing you need to check out about a verb is whether it and the other verbs in the sentence are parallel. In the first example used in this chapter, Jose was going to *attend, major,* and *to become.* The last verb, *to become,* is not written in the same form as the other verbs in the series. In other words, it's not parallel. The sentence should read, *Jose will attend college, major in criminal justice, and become a lawyer.*

Try another example:

As a new member (A) of the secret society, George was (B) required (C) to shine the senior members' shoes, to carry their books, and never revealing (D) the identities of the other members. No error (E)

Here's How to Crack It

If an error ID contains an underlined verb that is part of a series of activities, isolate the verbs to see if they are parallel. In this sentence, George is required *to shine, to carry,* and *revealing.* What's the problem? He should be required *to shine, to carry,* and *to reveal.* The answer is D.

Are You Tense?

As you know, verbs come in different tenses—for example, *is* is present tense, while *was* is past tense. You've probably heard of other tenses like "past perfect." Well, first of all, don't worry about identifying the kind of tense used in a sentence—you will never be asked to identify verb tense, only to make sure that the tense is consistent throughout a sentence.

For the most part, verb tense should not change within a sentence. Look at the following example:

In Colonial times, children often do not attend high school, knowing that they were needed to help with the family business. No error

(A: In; B: do not attend; C: knowing that; D: to help with; E: No error)

Here's How to Crack It

Our subject? *Children*. Our verb? *Attend*—which would be fine if the sentence hadn't started out with *In Colonial times*.... Is the sentence talking about children attending (or not attending) school right now? No, it's talking about Colonial times. The verb should be *attended*—the answer is B. If you missed that clue, you could have found another one by examining the other verbs in the sentence. The phrase *were needed* is in the past tense, and because it's not underlined, we know the other verbs in the sentence should match it.

NOUNS

The only thing you really have to check for with nouns is agreement. Agreement is a big thing for most grammarians, ETS included. Verbs must agree with their subjects, nouns must agree with other nouns, and pronouns must agree with the nouns they represent. When you read an error ID, if you come across an underlined noun, check to see if it refers to or is associated with any other nouns in the sentence. If so, make sure they match in number.

For example:

Some animals, <u>such as</u> the hedgehog, appear <u>quite</u> timid
A B

but <u>they can become</u> fierce enemies when they perceive a
C

threat to their <u>baby</u>. <u>No error</u>
D E

Here's How to Crack It

Take it one piece at a time. ...*such as the hedgehog*... sounds good. Cross off A.

Continuing on, *appear quite timid*.... No problem that we can see. Cross it off. Going on, *but they can become fierce enemies*... checks out. The subject is *some animals,* not *the hedgehog.* So cross off C.

The last part of the sentence reads *when they perceive a threat to their baby. Their* is okay; we're referring to a bunch of animals. But what about *baby*? Because we are discussing *some animals,* which is plural, we need to make sure *baby* is plural as well—in other words it should read the *babies* of *some animals.* The answer is D.

PRONOUNS

As with verbs, there are three things you need to check when you have pronouns:

1. Do they **agree**?
2. Are they **ambiguous**?
3. Do they use the right **case**?

I Agree

Pronouns
Subject → Verb
Singular → Singular
Plural → Plural

As you know, a pronoun is a little word that is inserted to represent a noun (*he, she, it, they,* and so on). As with everything else, pronouns must agree with their nouns: The pronoun that replaces a singular noun must also be singular, and the pronoun that replaces a plural noun must be plural. If different pronouns are used to refer to the same subject or one pronoun is used to replace another, the pronouns must also agree.

This may seem obvious, but it is also the most commonly violated rule in ordinary speech. How often have you heard people say, *Everyone must hand in their application before leaving.* Remember from our list of singular pronouns that *everyone* is singular? But *their* is plural. This sentence is incorrect.

To spot a pronoun agreement error, look for pronouns that show up later in a sentence. If you see a pronoun underlined, find the noun or pronoun it is replacing and make sure the two agree. Let's look at an example:

Everyone in the department (A) who worked with (B) Heather personally congratulated her on her promotion (C) and told her how much they (D) enjoyed her company. No error (E)

Here's How to Crack It

Is there an underlined pronoun late in this sentence? There sure is: *they.* Let's trim the fat to check this sentence:

Everyone... who worked... congratulated her... and told her... they enjoyed...

Everyone is singular, but *they* is plural, so it cannot replace *everyone.*

The answer is D.

To Whom Do You Refer?

When a pronoun appears in a sentence, it should be infinitely clear which noun it replaces. For example:

> After looking over the color samples, Mary agreed with Martha that her porch should be painted green.

Whose porch is being painted green? Mary's or Martha's? This sentence would be unacceptable to ETS because it is not perfectly clear to whom the word *her* in the sentence is referring. This is pronoun ambiguity, and it is unacceptable on the SAT.

If you see a pronoun late in a sentence, check to see if it clearly refers to a noun. Be especially wary if the early part of the sentence contains two singular or two plural nouns. Try the example on the next page.

Hey, What's "That"?
A pronoun replaces a noun, but you always have to be clear which noun it replaces. It's not enough for you to guess. In ETS's world, you have to know for sure. If not, that's the error.

The drummer <u>told</u> (A) the guitar player that <u>he</u> (B) was an integral part <u>of the band</u> (C) and could not easily <u>be replaced</u> (D). <u>No error</u> (E)

Here's How to Crack It

Let's take it apart a piece at a time. *The drummer told*.... Do a quick tense scan of the sentence. Is it past tense? Yes. Cross off A and go on.

Let's check the next answer choice:

The drummer told the guitar player that he was an integral part....

Who was an integral part? It is not clear whether the pronoun *he* is referring to the drummer or the guitar player. The answer is B.

Case? What Case?

Pronouns come in two "flavors," known as cases: subjective or objective. The subject, as you know, is the person or thing performing the action in the sentence. The object is the person or thing *receiving* the action. Think of it this way: An object just sits there. It doesn't *do* anything; rather, things are done to it. The subject, by contrast, does something.

When it comes to pronouns, subjects and objects are represented by different pronouns. For example, *I* is a subjective pronoun, as in *I did it,* while *me* is an objective pronoun, as in *it happened to me.* Most of the time, you will know if the wrong pronoun case (as it's called) is used because the sentence will sound funny. However, this is another area that is often butchered in our spoken language. When in doubt, trim the fat to figure out whether the pronoun is the subject (performing the action) or the object (receiving the action).

Subject Pronouns

Singular	Plural
I	We
You	You
He	They
She	They
It	They
Who	Who

Object Pronouns

Singular	Plural
Me	Us
You	You
Him	Them
Her	Them
It	Them
Whom	Whom

Try the following example:

The safety check of the new vehicle, including
A

an inspection of the brakes and wheel alignment,
B

was performed by the mechanic and him. No error
C D E

Here's How to Crack It

Read through the sentence, checking each underlined segment. *The safety check of the new vehicle*.... No problem here—cross off A and move on. Next segment: ...*an inspection of*.... Again, it seems fine. Cross it out and keep going.

To check the next two, do a little cutting: *The safety check... was performed by the mechanic and him. Performed by* is fine. What about *him*? Get rid of *the mechanic* to check: *The safety check... was performed by... him. Him* is an objective pronoun and, in this sentence, is used correctly. *He performed* would need the subjective pronoun; *performed by him* is the correct use of the objective pronoun. The answer is E, no error.

I or *Me*?

Are you frequently being corrected on the *I* versus *me* thing? If so, you're not alone. In the example we just did, if you were to replace *him* with either *I* or *me*, which would it be? You would use *me* because you need an object pronoun. It is often difficult to tell which case to use when the pronoun is coupled with another noun or pronoun. If you are having trouble deciding which case to use, remember to trim the fat: In this case, remove the other person (*the mechanic* in the example we just did).

Which One Is Correct?

The book belongs to Jerry and I.

The book belongs to Jerry and me.

To check out which colleges are "Located in Great College Towns," take a look at the rankings on your online student tools. If you haven't registered yet, go to PrincetonReview.com/cracking

If you're not sure, take Jerry out of the picture:

The book belongs to ______.

Me, of course. It's much easier to tell which is correct if the extraneous stuff is removed. Here's a tricky one:

Clare is more creative than me.

Clare is more creative than I.

Be careful. This may look as though the pronoun is an object, but actually the sentence is written in an incomplete form. What you are really saying in this sentence is *Clare is more creative than I am*. The *am* is understood. When in doubt, say the sentence aloud, adding on the *am* to see whether it is hiding at the end of the sentence.

Don't Be Passive

One final note about subjects and objects: ETS prefers sentences written in the active voice to the passive voice. If a sentence is written in the active voice, the subject of the sentence is doing something. If a sentence is written in the passive voice, the main player becomes an object and things happen to him.

Which of the following is written in the active voice?

She took the SAT.

The SAT was taken by her.

She took the SAT is active because *she* is the subject of the sentence and *she* is doing something. *The SAT was taken by her* is passive because *her* is now the object of *by,* not the subject of the sentence. This will be important to know when attacking improving sentences questions.

PREPOSITIONS

Remember prepositions? *About, above, across, around, along...* You use prepositions all the time to add information to a sentence. Using different prepositions can change the meaning of a sentence. For example:

I am standing *by* you.
I am standing *for* you.
I am standing *near* you.
I am standing *under* you.

Common SAT Prepositions

about	before	for	on	toward
above	behind	from	out	under
across	below	in	over	until
after	between	inside	since	up
against	down	like	through	with
around	during	near	throughout	without
at	except	off	to	

Drill 1

In the English language, certain words must be paired with certain prepositions. These pairs of words are called *idioms*. There are really no rules to idioms, so you need to just use your ear and memorize ones that are tricky. Here is a list of some common idioms you may come across. Fill in the blanks with the missing prepositions (some may have more than one possibility). Answers can be found on page 384.

1. I am *indebted* _____ you.

2. I am *resentful* _____ you.

3. I am *delighted* _____ you.

4. I am *jealous* _____ you.

5. I am *worried* _____ you.

6. I am *astounded* _____ you.

7. The women had a *dispute* ____ politics.

8. You have a *responsibility* ____ take care of your pet.

9. My friends are not so *different* ____ your friends.

Try an error ID example:

After seeing Andy fall into the crocodile pit, his girlfriend admitted that she was worried for him. No error

(A: After; B: fall into; C: admitted that; D: worried for; E: No error)

Here's How to Crack It

Let's pull it apart: *After seeing Andy fall into....* Both of these seem okay so let's move on. Next phrase: *his girlfriend admitted that....* No problem there. How about the next part, *worried for him.* You may have heard people say this, but it's wrong. The preposition that should accompany *worry* is *about.* The answer is D.

ERROR ID AND YOUR GRAMMAR CHECKLIST

Let's do a quick review. On error ID questions, have your grammar checklist ready (keep it in your head, or jot it on your test booklet). It should look like this:

1. Is there an underlined **verb**? If so,
   (a) does it **agree** with its subject?
   (b) is it **parallel** in structure to the other verbs in the sentence?
   (c) is it in the proper **tense**?
2. Is there an underlined **noun**? If so,
   (a) does it **agree** in number with any other noun to which it refers?
3. Is there an underlined **pronoun**? If so,
   (a) does it **agree** with the noun/pronoun it represents?
   (b) can you tell to which noun it refers or is it **ambiguous**?
   (c) does it use the right **case** (subjective or objective)?
4. Is there an underlined **preposition**? If so,
   (a) is it the **right one**?

When you approach error ID questions, remember the following:

- Read them with your checklist in mind.
- Cross off underlined stuff that is right.
- Trim the fat.
- Don't be afraid to pick E, "No error."
- Guess if you don't know the answer.

Drill 2

Use the following drill to solidify your error ID strategy.

Answers can be found on page 384.

1. Although many (A) young children would like to (B) have pets, most find it (C) difficult to be responsible to (D) another living creature at such a tender age. No error (E)

2. I told (A) my English teacher that the best part (B) of the novel is where (C) the antagonist finally realized the error of his (D) ways. No error (E)

3. It (A) was only last month that (B) the hockey playoffs finally ended (C), but the new season has started (D) today. No error (E)

4. The postman assured (A) his customers (B) that neither sleet nor snow were (C) the cause of (D) the delay in their mail delivery. No error (E)

5. Sports journalists have debated (A) whether it is a more strenuous (B) task to box for ten rounds (C) or running a marathon (D). No error (E)

6. Regular exercise and a healthy diet will (A) not only increase (B) a person's energy level but also (C) improving (D) physical fitness. No error (E)

IMPROVING SENTENCES

So far we have been concentrating on error ID questions while reviewing grammar. The good news is that improving sentences questions test a lot of the same grammar. Let's look at a sample question to see how to crack these questions.

> **Cut It Out**
> Improving sentences uses (A) for "no error" instead of (E), as error ID does. Use your ear: Does the sentence sound wrong? Cross (A) out immediately and you're on your way.

Although both Senator Fritz and Senator Pierce have proposed plans to reduce the deficit, only one of the two are viable.

(A) only one of the two are viable
(B) only one of the two is viable
(C) only one of the two plans are viable
(D) only one of the two plans is viable
(E) one only of the two plans has been viable

Here's How to Crack It

There are two ways to go about cracking an improving sentences question. The preferable way is for you to identify the error as you read the underlined part of the sentence. How will you do that, you ask? By using your handy-dandy grammar checklist, of course. Let's try it on this example. The underlined portion of the sentence says *only one of the two are viable.* Let's run through your list. Is there an underlined verb? Yes—*are.* Does it agree with its subject? What is its subject? If we trim the fat (in this case, the prepositional phrase of the two) we can easily see the subject is one. Is it correct to say *one are*? Of course not.

> **A Couple of Good Rules to Live By**
> Here are some very good points that will be very helpful for you when solving improving sentences:
>
> - Eliminate any answer choice that changes the meaning of the original sentence.
> - After you've gotten rid of any grammatical errors and you're down to two answer choices that are error-free, choose the shorter one.

So you've identified the problem. However, improving sentences questions require you to go further than just identifying the error—they also require you to fix the error, thus "improving" the sentence. To do this, you will use your old friend: Process of Elimination. First, we know that answer choice A is simply a repeat of the underlined portion; therefore, once you've identified an error, cross off answer choice A.

Next, scan the rest of the answer choices and cross off any answer choices that don't fix the problem you've identified. In our example, we know the verb *are* is wrong. What answer choice can we get rid of? Answer choice C.

So far, we have eliminated answer choices A and C. Let's look at the remaining choices to see how they fix the error we found. Answer choice B changes *are* to *is,* a singular verb. That works. Answer choice D does the same thing. Both of these choices are possible. Answer choice E changes the verb to *has been.* A quick glance at the sentence tells us that this is in the wrong tense—we need present tense. Cross off answer choice E.

To check out which colleges have the "Most Politically Active Students," take a look at the rankings on your online student tools. If you haven't registered yet, go to PrincetonReview.com/cracking

Okay, down to two. The last thing to check is the difference between the two choices that fixed the original problem. Sometimes the underlined portion of the sentence contains a secondary error that also needs to be fixed. Other times, an answer may fix the original problem but introduce a new error. In this example, the difference between B and D is that B uses the vague language *only one of the two is viable* while D clarifies *only one of the two plans is viable.* We know that ETS hates to be ambiguous, and B does not make it as clear that the sentence is referring to one of the two plans as opposed to one of the two senators. Therefore, our answer is D.

Back-up Plan?

Let's say you couldn't tell if there was an error in the example we just did. You thought it might be okay, but you weren't sure. How could you check? By scanning your answer choices. Your answer choices can tip you off to the error contained in a sentence by revealing what is being fixed in each choice. In the example we just did, a quick scan of the answer choices reveals that the verb is being altered:

(A) ...are...
(B) ...is...
(C) ...are...
(D) ...is...
(E) ...has been...

Once you pick up on the error being tested, you can try to figure out which form is correct. Let's try another example, using our back-up plan to illustrate how it works:

When students are told they will be tested on a subject, you tend to be more anxious and find it harder to retain the information.

(A) you tend to be more anxious and find it harder to retain the information
(B) students being more anxious find it harder to retain the information
(C) they tend to be more anxious and find it harder to retain information that will be tested
(D) they tend to be more anxious and find it harder to retain the information
(E) you tend toward anxiety and a failure to retain information

Here's How to Crack It

When you first read this sentence, you may feel that something is wrong, but you may not be able to pinpoint what it is. No problem—let your answer choices do the work for you. A quick scan of the answer choices reveals a possible pronoun problem:

(A) you…
(B) students…
(C) they…
(D) they…
(E) you…

Now that you know what to check, let's trim the fat:

When students are told they will be tested… you…

Is *you* the right pronoun to represent *students*? No. Cross off A and any other answer that doesn't fix the *you*. That leaves us with B, C, and D. If you have no idea how the rest of the sentence should read, you've still given yourself great odds of "guessing" this question correctly. But let's forge ahead.

Answer choice B doesn't make any sense upon closer inspection. Cross it off. Now you're down to two. Which answer choice is more clear and less awkward? Answer choice D:

> *When students are told they will be tested… they tend to be more anxious and find it harder to retain the information.*

Other Little Things

We mentioned back at the beginning of this chapter that your grammar checklist should include a number 5: "other little things." In addition to testing the four main areas we've already reviewed, other little grammar things will be tested on the improving sentences questions. Let's look at some of these little grammar tidbits so you are ready for them when they turn up.

If everything else checks out, the sentence may be testing other little things, such as

- faulty comparisons
- misplaced modifiers
- adjectives/adverbs
- diction

To check out which colleges have the "Least Politically Active Students," take a look at the rankings on your online student tools. If you haven't registered yet, go to PrincetonReview.com/cracking

Can You Compare?

There are several little things ETS tries to trip you up with when it comes to comparing. These things are not difficult, but they are notoriously misused in spoken English, so you will need to make a note of them. First, when comparing two things, make sure that what you are comparing can be compared. Sound like double-talk? Look at the following sentence:

> Larry goes shopping at Foodtown because the prices are better than Shoprite.

Sound okay? Well, sorry—it's wrong. As written, this sentence says that the prices at Foodtown are better than Shoprite—the entire store. What Larry means is the prices at Foodtown are better than the *prices* at Shoprite. You can compare only like things (prices to prices, not prices to stores).

While we're on the subject of Foodtown, how often have you seen this sign?

> Express Checkout: Ten items or less.

Unfortunately, supermarkets across America are making a blatant grammatical error when they post this sign. When items can be counted, you must use the word *fewer*. If something cannot be counted, you would use the word *less*. For example:

> If you eat fewer french fries, you can use less ketchup.

Other similar words include *many* (can be counted) versus *much* (cannot be counted):

> *Many* hands make *much* less work.

Another pair to watch out for is *number* (can be counted) versus *amount* (cannot be counted):

> The same *number* of CDs played different *amounts* of music.

Two's Company; Three or More Is...?

Finally, the English language uses different comparison words when comparing two things than when comparing more than two things. The following examples will jog your memory:

- **more** (for two things) vs. **most** (for more than two)
  Given Alex and Dave as possible dates, Alex is the *more* appealing one.
  In fact, of all the guys I know, Alex is the *most* attractive.
- **less** (for two things) vs. **least** (for more than two)
  I am *less* likely to be chosen than you are.
  I am the *least* likely person to be chosen from the department.
- **better** (for two things) vs. **best** (for more than two)
  Taking a cab is *better* than hitchhiking.
  My Princeton Review teacher is the *best* teacher I have ever had.
- **between** (for two things) vs. **among** (for more than two)
  Just *between* you and me, I never liked her anyway.
  Among all the people here, no one likes her.

Try this one:

Suzie was excited because her fantasy baseball team <u>was far better than Justin</u>.

(A) was far better than Justin
(B) did far better as Justin
(C) was far better than Justin's team
(D) did seem superior to Justin
(E) was far better than the team of Justin

Here's How to Crack It

What is being compared in this sentence? Susie is comparing her team with Justin. Can she do that? No! She really wants to compare her team with Justin's team.

Because you have identified an error, immediately cross off A. Next, cross off any other answer choice that doesn't fix the error. That gets rid of B and D. Now compare our remaining choices. While E technically fixes our comparison problem, it is awkwardly worded. ETS's answer is C.

Misplaced Modifiers

A modifier is a descriptive word or phrase inserted in a sentence to add dimension to the thing it modifies. For example:

> *Because he could talk,* Mr. Ed was a unique horse.

Because he could talk is the modifying phrase in this sentence. It describes a characteristic of Mr. Ed. Generally speaking, a modifying phrase should be right next to the thing it modifies. If it's not, the meaning of the sentence may change. For example:

> Every time he goes to the bathroom outside, John praises his new puppy for being so good.

Who's going to the bathroom outside? In this sentence, it's John! There are laws against that! The descriptive phrase *every time he goes to the bathroom outside* needs to be near *puppy* for the sentence to say what it means.

When you are attacking improving sentences questions, watch out for sentences that begin with a descriptive phrase followed by a comma. If you see one, make sure the thing that comes after the comma is the person or thing being modified.

Try the following example:

<u>Clearly one of the most distinctive and impressive skylines in the country</u>, New York City is a breathtaking sight to behold.

(A) Clearly one of the most distinctive and impressive skylines in the country
(B) Being one of the most distinctive and impressive skylines in the country
(C) Possessing one of the most distinctive and impressive skylines in the country
(D) Its skyline may be the most distinctive and impressive in the country
(E) More distinctive and impressive in its skyline than any other place in the country

Here's How to Crack It

Is New York City a type of skyline? No, so cross off A. We need an answer that will make the opening phrase modify *New York City.* Answer choice B is still modifying *skyline,* so cross it off. All three other choices fix the problem, but C does it the best. D makes the sentence ungrammatical, and E is correct but awkward. The answer is C.

Adjectives/Adverbs

Misplaced modifiers aren't the only descriptive errors ETS test writers throw at you. Another way they try to trip you up is by using adjectives where they should use adverbs and vice versa. Remember that an *adjective* modifies a noun, while an *adverb* modifies verbs, adverbs, and adjectives. The adverb is the one that usually has *-ly* on the end. In the following sentence, circle the adverbs and underline the adjectives:

> The stealthy thief, desperately hoping to evade the persistent police, ran quickly into the dank, dark alley after brazenly stealing the stunningly exquisite jewels.

First, let's list the adjectives along with the nouns they modify: *stealthy* thief, *persistent* police, *dank* alley, *dark* alley, *exquisite* jewels. Now for the adverbs with the words they modify: *desperately* hoping (verb), ran (verb) *quickly*, *brazenly* stealing (verb), *stunningly* exquisite (adjective).

Now try the following improving sentences example:

A bacterium may not reproduce for months, but a sudden influx of heat, moisture, or food <u>can cause its growth rate to increase tremendous</u>.

(A) can cause its growth rate to increase tremendous
(B) can tremendously increase its growth rate
(C) increase the tremendous growth rate of it
(D) increases its growth rate in a tremendous way
(E) tremendously causes the growth rate to increase

Here's How to Crack It

Hopefully you identified the error as soon as you read the sentence. What should the last word in the sentence be? *Tremendously*. Cross off A, and also D, because it doesn't fix the error and changes the meaning of the sentence. C is way out there, so cross it off too. In E, the placement of the *tremendously* is awkward and slightly changes the meaning of the sentence. ETS's answer is B.

Diction

Finally, ETS may occasionally slip in a diction error just to keep you on your toes. Diction means choice of words. Diction errors are tough to spot because the incorrect word often looks a lot like the word that should have been used. For example:

> None of the neighbors can stand it when the noisome garage band practices next door.

Unless the band is known for their offensive odor, "noisome"—something with an extremely unpleasant smell—is the wrong word. It sounds just enough like "noisy" to trick some students, though. Here's another example:

> The candidate's campaign strategy was to equivocate his opponents' policies to those of their unpopular predecessor.

"Equivocate" sounds a lot like "equate"—or any word meaning "equal" for that matter—but they're false cognates: words that sound similar but mean different things. "Equivocate" means to use ambiguous language to avoid committing: another thing candidates do, but incorrect in this context.

Drill 3

Before we move on to improving paragraphs questions, try putting together what you've learned. Do the following error ID and improving sentences questions using your grammar checklist. Remember to trim the fat and use POE. On improving sentences questions, do not hesitate to check out the answer choices for a clue to help you spot the error. You may wish to jot down your grammar checklist before you begin. Answers can be found on page 385.

1. After the electricity went (A) out, Dora stumbled blind (B) about (C) her apartment searching for (D) a candle. No error (E)

2. Heeding the advice (A) of their (B) wise instructor, Rasheed and Ben each brought (C) a pencil and a calculator to the test. (D) No error (E)

3. None of the fish (A) in the aquarium is (B) native to this part of the world, having instead (C) been imported from (D) overseas. No error (E)

4. Because we are (A) brothers, I don't think we should (B) allow petty disagreements to come between (C) you and I. (D) No error (E)

5. Psychologists have found that (A) it is difficult to think clear (B) when in a pressure situation, especially (C) when under (D) a time limit. No error (E)

6. After (A) all of the day's chores was completed (B) the family sat down (C) to a splendid (D) dinner. No error (E)

7. Critics often debate whether the role of art is one that is simply aesthetic or if it should be instructional.

(A) one that is simply aesthetic or if it should be instructional
(B) simply one that is aesthetic or being instructional
(C) one that is simply aesthetic or if it should have instruction as well
(D) simply an aesthetic one or an instructional one
(E) aesthetic or should it be instructional

8. The civil engineers who designed the city's streets in the 1800s could never have foreseen the sprawling metropolis that the town would have soon become.

(A) never have foreseen the sprawling metropolis that the town would have soon become
(B) never have foreseen that the small town would soon become a sprawling metropolis
(C) have not foreseen the small town turning into a sprawling metropolis
(D) not have foreseen the sprawling metropolis that the small town became
(E) have never foreseen the small town being such a sprawling metropolis

9. The director felt that the actress was perfect for the part, since he wanted her to research the character first.

(A) the part, since he wanted her to
(B) the part, however the director wanted the actress to
(C) the part, but he wanted her to
(D) the part, only after she had to
(E) the part, but wanting her to

10. Cable television, which strikes some television watchers as a modern convenience, actually debuted in the 1940s, it was used only in rural areas at first.

(A) Cable television, which strikes some television watchers as a modern convenience, actually debuted in the 1940s, it was used only in rural areas at first.
(B) Used only in rural areas at first, cable television, which strikes some television watchers as a modern convenience, actually debuted in the 1940s.
(C) To be used only in rural areas, and striking some television watchers as a modern convenience, cable television actually debuted in the 1940s.
(D) Debuting in 1940s, it was used only in rural areas at first and strikes some television watchers as a modern convenience is cable television.
(E) Cable television was used only in rural areas at first, striking some television watchers as a modern convenience and actually debuting in the 1940s.

11. Jade is commonly found in two colors, either green or the color is white, which is the more precious of the two.

(A) either green or the color is white, which is the more precious of the two
(B) either green or white, although white jade is more precious than green jade
(C) the color is either green or the color is white, with white being the more precious
(D) with green or white as the color and white the most precious of the two
(E) those colors are green and white, which is the more precious

12. The term "mach" does not refer to the speed of an aircraft or vehicle; rather they are the ratio of the speed of sound to the speed of the craft.

(A) rather they are the ratio of the speed of sound to the speed of the craft
(B) they are the ratio of the speed of sound to the speed of the craft rather
(C) instead it is the ratio of the speed of sound to the speed of the craft
(D) rather they are referring to the ratio of the speed of sound and the craft
(E) instead, it refers to the ratio of the speed of sound to the speed of the craft

IMPROVING PARAGRAPHS

After you have found and answered all of the error ID and improving sentences questions you can easily do, move on to the improving paragraphs questions. These questions come last in the section, and they are almost always easy or medium in difficulty.

The improving paragraphs questions require you to make corrections to a "first draft" of a student's essay to improve it. The essay is typically three or four paragraphs long, and each paragraph contains numbered sentences.

Here is a sample passage:

> **(1)** I'm not sure exactly how I turned out to be a hockey fan. **(2)** My father was always a big football fan, my mom loves baseball. **(3)** And my brothers and sisters don't like hockey, either. **(4)** In any case, I've loved hockey for as long as I can remember.
>
> **(5)** But despite my love of hockey, I wasn't really that good at playing it. **(6)** Part of the problem is my skating, as in I'm not very good at it. **(7)** I didn't even learn to skate until I was twelve. **(8)** Most hockey players have been skating for their entire lives. **(9)** Still, I wanted to play and I asked my father to have me enrolled in a hockey camp. **(10)** He did and I went to it, not knowing what to expect. **(11)** On the first day of the camp, I barely knew how to put my equipment on. **(12)** Although the other kids were all about my age, they seemed to know so much more and be better players. **(13)** The first day on ice I was intimidated because they were all so good. **(14)** I thought that I didn't belong, but I love hockey so much that I wanted to stay. **(15)** I wanted badly to be able to play the sport that I loved.
>
> **(16)** And it was worth it. **(17)** After I got more comfortable with my skills, I became confident. **(18)** The coaches at the camp really helped me a lot. **(19)** They told me exactly what I needed to do to be better. **(20)** Now, I've been playing hockey for three years and while I'm not the best player on the ice, I'm certainly one of the most passionate.

Go to the Questions

Instead of wasting a lot of time reading the rough draft, skim it only for the main idea and structure. Then go directly to the questions. There are far more errors in the passage than you'll ever be asked about—reading the passage first will waste your time and confuse you.

Also, for many of the questions, the sentences you need to fix are reprinted right under the question, so you won't necessarily need to go back to the paragraph to answer a question.

Red Pencil Fever

There are probably more errors in the passage than you'll be asked to correct. Who cares? Worry only about the ones for which you'll get points—the ones in the questions.

There are three basic types of questions that you will be asked:

1. **Revision questions:** These questions ask you to revise sentences or parts of sentences in much the same way as improving sentences questions do.
2. **Combination questions:** These questions ask you to combine two or more sentences to improve the quality and/or flow of the paragraph.
3. **Content questions:** These questions ask you about passage content, typically by asking you to insert a new sentence or paragraph.

Revision Questions

As we mentioned, these questions are very similar to improving sentences questions. Therefore, you can follow the same basic approach. One warning: *There is normally no such thing as "No error" on improving paragraphs questions. Do not assume that A is merely a repeat of the given sentence.*

Even though the sentence you are revising is provided for you, you may still need to go back to the passage to gain some context when trying to fix a sentence. Before going back, however, use POE. If you have spotted an error in the given sentence, cross off answers that don't fix it. Also, cross off answer choices that contain obvious errors. After doing some POE, go back and read a few sentences before and after the given sentence. This should be enough context for you to determine the best edit.

Try the following revision question—refer back to the sample passage when needed.

In context, which is the best way to revise sentence 6 (reproduced below)?

Part of the problem is my skating, as in I'm not very good at it.

(A) One of the problems was my limited skating ability.
(B) Not skating well was a big problem of mine.
(C) A problem was that my skating needed to be better than it was.
(D) Of my problems, I would say that my bad skating was the biggest.
(E) Skating, I'm not very good at it, was part of my problems.

Here's How to Crack It

The correct revision will be concise and unambiguous. It will also flow well. We can get rid of choices B, D, and E before going back to the passage. Choice B is as clunky as the given sentence; choices D and E are awkwardly written.

After doing some elimination, go back and read, beginning with sentence 5. The author states that he wasn't good at playing. Why not? Apparently the problem is his skating. Answer A is the best choice. When you read this segment, the word *next* should be jumping into your brain. Sentence 6 seems out of place until you realize that it is a new thought, the next step. ETS's answer is A.

Combination Questions

Combination questions are revision questions with a twist: You are working with two sentences instead of one. The sentences are almost always reprinted for you under the question, and you can usually answer these questions without going back to the passage at all. As with revision questions, do what you can first, then go back to the passage if necessary.

To combine sentences you will need to work with conjunctions. If the sentences are flowing in the same direction, look for an answer with words such as *and, since,* and *as well as*. If the sentences seem to be flowing in opposite directions, look for trigger words in the answer choices such as *however, but,* and *on the contrary*.

Try the following without going back to the passage:

Which of the following represents the most effective way to combine sentences 18 and 19 (reproduced below)?

The coaches at the camp really helped me a lot. They told me exactly what I needed to do to be better.

(A) The coaches who helped me a lot told me exactly what I needed to do be better.

(B) Those coaches at the camp who told me exactly what I needed to do to be better were the ones who helped me the most.

(C) Helping me a lot was the coaches, telling me exactly what I needed to do.

(D) By telling me exactly what was needed to be done by me the coaches helped me a lot.

(E) The coaches at the camp really helped me by telling me exactly what I needed to do to get better.

Trigger Happy

When you combine two sentences, make sure that they're combined with the right trigger: *same-direction* or *change-direction*.

Here's How to Crack It

First, the sentences are moving in the same direction. Your job is to find a clear, concise way to combine them. A and B are out because they are poorly worded. Choice C contains an agreement error, and D is passive. The best answer is E. Note that you can answer this question without going back to the passage.

Try another:

Which of the following represents the best revision of sentences 7 and 8 (reproduced below) ?

I didn't even learn to skate until I was twelve. Most hockey players have been skating for their entire lives.

(A) I didn't even learn to skate until I was twelve, even though most hockey players have been skating for their entire lives.

(B) I didn't even learn to skate until was twelve, compared with most hockey players have been skating for their entire lives.

(C) I learned to skate when I was twelve; most hockey players have been skating for their entire lives.

(D) Although most hockey players have been skating for their entire lives, I didn't even learn to skate until I was twelve.

(E) Skating, which most hockey players have been doing their entire lives, I didn't learn how until I was twelve.

Here's How to Crack It

First, check the flow of the sentence. It appears as if the sentences are going in opposite directions. Get rid of A and C, which don't change the direction. Answer choice B compares the two ideas but doesn't establish a contrast. E is horribly awkward, so ditch it. The best answer is D.

Content Questions

ETS will occasionally ask you a question regarding the content of the passage. These questions may ask:

1. Which sentence should immediately follow or precede the passage?
2. Which sentence should be inserted into the passage?
3. What is the best description of the passage as a whole?

If you are asked the third question, you will need to skim the whole passage. However, you will more likely be asked one of the first two questions. To answer these, you will need to read the relevant paragraph.

Try this example using the sample passage from earlier in this section:

Which of the following sentences, if added after sentence 4, would best serve to link the first paragraph to the second paragraph?

(A) I found it quite odd that I ended up loving hockey.
(B) I wanted to be more than just a passionate hockey fan, though.
(C) My brothers loved baseball, while my sisters were bigger fans of football.
(D) Perhaps it was my uncle, a big hockey fan, who helped me to love the game.
(E) Actually, hockey is not a very popular sport in the United States.

Here's How to Crack It

To solve this question, you need to read the first paragraph and the first sentence of the second paragraph quickly. At the end of the first paragraph, he states his love for the game. The next paragraph talks about playing the sport. Find the answer that connects these two ideas.

A, C, and D are out because they focus on the "problems" theme from the first paragraph instead of making a transition to the second paragraph. E is not implied anywhere in the passage. The answer is B.

MORE THAN GRAMMAR

When you look at improving paragraphs questions, you're going to see more than grammar rules. You will need to know the rules we've discussed, but it's not just about that. When you're answering these questions, keep the following things in mind:

- **Think about what the author is trying to convey.** Your job here is to improve the paragraphs that they give you. Think about if you were to edit a friend's essay. The way to make it better is to help him get his point across as clearly and effectively as possible. To do that you have to know what he's trying to do and say with the essay. That's what you're doing here.
- **Pay attention to the logical flow of ideas.** Many of the questions are going to ask, either directly or indirectly, about the order in which ideas are presented. You want to make sure that each part of the essay leads to the next, that there is a logical progression.
- **Avoid ambiguity and wordiness.** The most effective revisions are short and precise. You don't want to ramble on, you know, say what was already said. You want to be able to get your point across in as few words as possible, without going overboard or repeating yourself again. And again. Got it?

Final Words of Wisdom

As with all the sections of the SAT, you are rewarded for answering the question. Don't be afraid to do some POE and guess. You will almost always be able to eliminate some answer choices, so allow your partial knowledge to earn you credit on the test.

Drill 4

Try the following improving paragraphs drill to practice what you have learned. Answers can be found on pages 385–386.

(1) Many people dismiss comic books as just something for kids. **(2)** But comic books, sometimes they are called graphic novels, have held an important place in our culture. **(3)** You may be surprised to find out that comic books, in one form or another, has a beginning in 19th century Europe. **(4)** In the United States, the golden age of comics is generally thought to be in the 1930s. **(5)** Those years saw the birth of two of the most popular characters of all time. **(6)** Superman was introduced in 1938 and Batman then follows in 1939. **(7)** The attraction of these two characters, to both adult and children readers alike, elevates the comic book in the public consciousness.

(8) Today, comic books are a major industry. **(9)** They are able to generate millions and millions of dollars in licensing and movies, as well as toys and other collectibles. **(10)** Even old favorites like Batman and Superman, now seventy years old, keep coming out new comics. **(11)** No longer just for kids, the stories of graphic novels are increasingly complex. **(12)** Now, you can even take a class on the writing of comic books at your local college. **(13)** You can't say that comics are just for kids anymore.

1. In context, what is the best version of sentence 2, reproduced below?

But comic books, sometimes they are called graphic novels, have held an important place in our culture.

(A) (As it is now)
(B) But comic books, also called graphic novels, have long held an important place in our culture.
(C) But comic books, which are also called graphic novels by some people, hold an important place in our culture.
(D) Comic books, sometimes being called graphic novels, hold an important place in our culture.
(E) Comic books, or graphic novels as they are called, are important to our culture.

2. Which of the following would be the best subject for a paragraph immediately preceding this essay?

(A) A discussion of popular children's toys
(B) An overview of 19th century European culture
(C) A critical perspective on the writing style of graphic novels
(D) An examination of the toy and game industry
(E) An analysis of the appeal of comic books to youngsters

3. The author wishes to divide the first paragraph into two shorter paragraphs. The most appropriate place to begin a new paragraph would be

(A) between sentences 1 and 2
(B) between sentences 2 and 3
(C) between sentences 3 and 4
(D) between sentences 4 and 5
(E) between sentences 5 and 6

4. In sentence 3, the word *you* could best be replaced with which of the following?

(A) Young people
(B) They
(C) Europeans
(D) Comic book fans
(E) Comic book detractors

5. Which word could best replace *birth* in sentence 5 ?

(A) resurgence
(B) production
(C) beginning
(D) creation
(E) addition

6. Which would be the best way to revise and combine the underlined portions of sentences 8 and 9 (reproduced below) ?

Today, comic books are <u>a major industry. They are able to generate</u> millions and millions of dollars in licensing and movies, as well as toys and other collectibles.

(A) a major industry, generating
(B) a major industry, which has generated
(C) a major industry, ably generating
(D) a major industry, being responsible for generating
(E) a major industry, one that has been generating

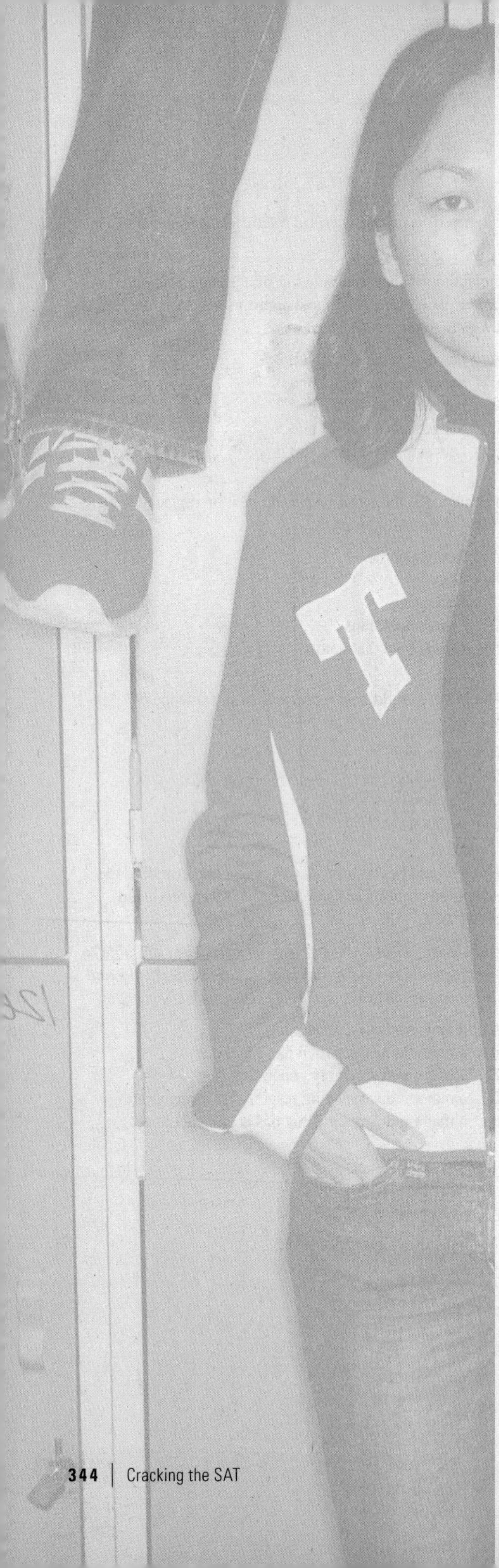

Summary

- Don't forget to use POE on writing questions.
- To solve an error ID, read the sentence and look for an error. If nothing strikes you as incorrect, check each underlined word for the errors that occur for its part of speech.
- To solve an improving sentence, read the original sentence and look for an error. If nothing strikes you as incorrect, go to the answer choices and look for errors in the answers. Remember that if a part of speech changes among the answer choices it is likely to contain an error.
- When it comes to sentence structure, make sure independent and dependent clauses are being used correctly. Avoid
    - comma splices: two independent clauses connected by a comma
    - run-on sentences: two independent clauses not separated by anything
    - sentence fragments: two dependent clauses with no independent clauses
- A verb is a word that shows action or a state of being. Check any underlined verb for agreement, parallelism, and tense.
- A noun is a person, place, thing, or idea. Check any underlined noun for agreement with related or connected nouns in the sentence.
- A pronoun is a word that replaces a noun. Check any underlined noun for agreement with the noun it replaces, ambiguity or unclearness, and case.
- Remember that *everyone, no one, either/neither,* and *each* are singular and take singular verbs and singular pronouns. A group of people—such as the government, the family, or the company—is also singular.

- Prepositions are words that show position or place, such as *in, of, with,* and *by*. Check any underlined preposition for idiom errors.
- Descriptive phrases must always be kept near the noun they are describing. Be especially attentive to long, descriptive phrases at the beginning of the sentences; the nouns that follow must be the things the opening phrases are describing.
- On improving paragraphs questions, don't bother reading or correcting the entire essay.
- Also, on improving paragraphs questions, consider what point the author is making, the logical flow of ideas, and clarity.
- Keep in mind that right answers are usually short, clear, and direct. Wrong answers are usually long, redundant, and unclear.

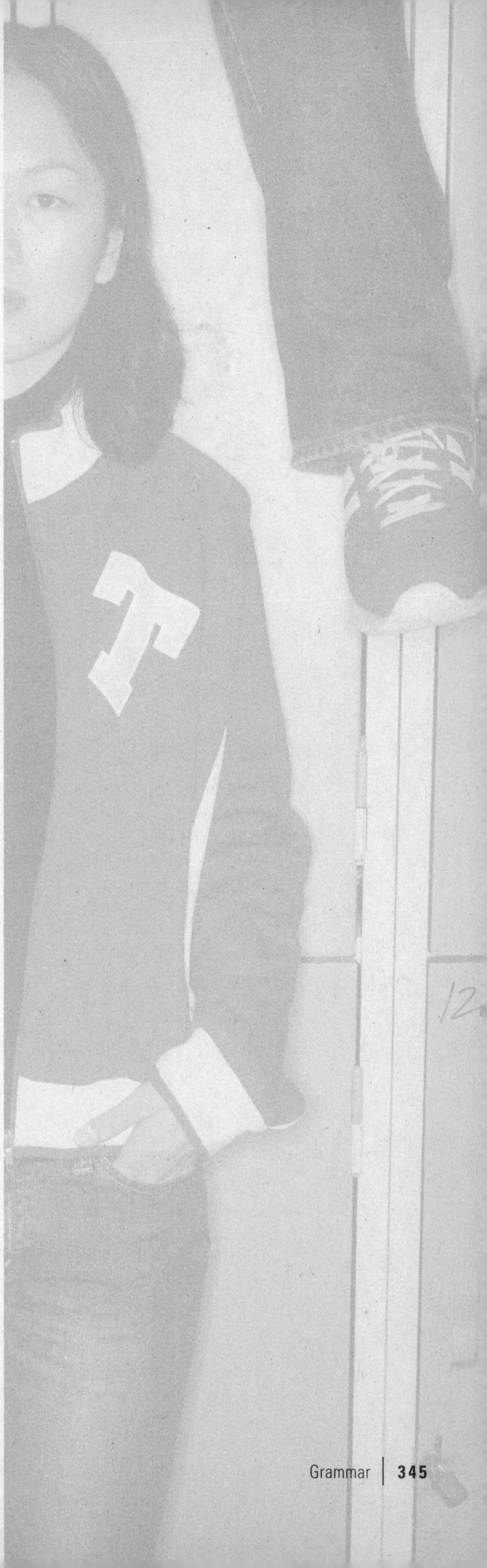

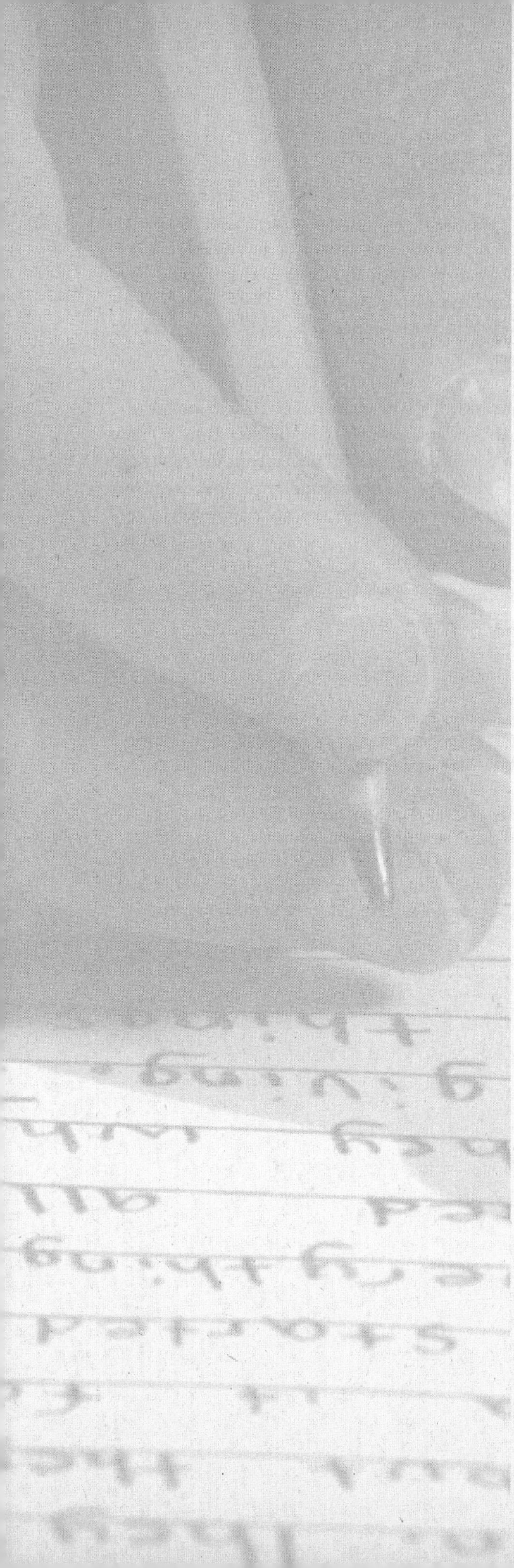

Chapter 18
Essay

The Essay section will always be the first thing you see on the test. You will have 25 minutes to write a coherent response to a given prompt. Although you probably have written essays in the past, you may not have had to write one quite like this before. In this chapter, we will show you how to address the prompt, brainstorm ideas, and write a high-scoring essay in the scant time given.

NOT YOUR TYPICAL ESSAY

We've finally arrived at the last part of your SAT prep, which is the first part of your SAT—the essay. The Writing section is not about writing a great essay that would bring a tear to your Language Arts teacher's eyes or be published in a literary journal. For that kind of writing to be worth the trouble, there would have to be someone carefully reading and evaluating your essay. Don't worry: With readers spending only a few minutes on each essay, that won't really happen on the SAT.

ETS says the essay is graded "holistically." That means essay readers look at the overall impression that the essay makes and give you a score accordingly. However, because there are so many to get through, each grader spends an average of only two to three minutes for each essay. In that short amount of time, what sort of impression can you, as a student, make? Well, with the right approach, a very good one.

In this section we'll give you some tips about what you *should* concentrate on for the SAT essay, and how to pick up the most points possible.

First let's read through the instructions and a sample assignment.

The essay gives you an opportunity to show how effectively you can develop and express ideas. You should, therefore, take care to develop your point of view, present your ideas logically and clearly, and use language precisely.

Your essay must be written on the lines provided on your answer sheet—you will receive no other paper on which to write. You will have enough space if you write on every line, avoid wide margins, and keep your handwriting to a reasonable size. Remember that people who are not familiar with your handwriting will read what you write. Try to write or print so that what you are writing is legible to those readers.

Important Reminders:

- A pencil is required for the essay. An essay written in ink will receive a score of zero.
- Do not write your essay in your test book. You will receive credit only for what you write on your answer sheet.
- An off-topic essay will receive a score of zero.
- If your essay does not reflect your original and individual work, your test scores may be canceled.

Here's a sample essay topic:

You have twenty-five minutes to write an essay on the topic assigned below.
DO NOT WRITE ON ANOTHER TOPIC. AN OFF-TOPIC ESSAY WILL RECEIVE A SCORE OF ZERO.

Think carefully about the issue presented in the following excerpt and the assignment below.

> In his poem "In Memoriam," romantic poet Alfred Lord Tennyson expresses his view that loss is an unavoidable consequence of love. Yet, rather than shunning love because of this, Tennyson resolves to accept both the experience of love and the pain that inevitably comes with it. As he writes in his often quoted passage, "Tis better to have loved and lost than never to have loved at all."
>
> Adapted from James R. Kincaid, *Tennyson's Major Poems*

Assignment: Are people unwise to pursue love even when they know it will cause them pain? Plan and write an essay in which you develop your point of view on this issue. Support your position with reasoning and examples taken from your reading, studies, experience, or observations.

DO NOT WRITE YOUR ESSAY IN YOUR TEST BOOK. You will receive credit only for what you write on your answer sheet.

Although you can't write the essay itself in the test booklet, the test booklet is a great place to jot down notes before you write your actual essay on the answer sheet.

So What Does This Really Mean?

You'll notice the instructions tell you to "think carefully about the issue being presented," and "plan and write an essay in which you develop your point of view on this issue." How much time do you have for all of this planning, developing, AND writing? Twenty-five minutes. That means ETS is not expecting a polished work on par with Hemingway; in fact, your essay will be graded as if it were your rough draft (which it is). So you should really take a couple of minutes to figure out your view and to jot down a few examples before you begin writing.

What Are the Essays About?

You will read a quotation or short passage that states one or more opinions on some generic topic and you will then write an essay discussing your position or viewpoint on that opinion.

How Are the Essays Scored?

The essay, which is graded by two people, is scored on a scale of 1 to 6 (low to high).

Two people will read your essay, and each will give it a score on a scale of 1 to 6 (6 is the highest). These two scores are added together and multiplied by a mysterious conversion factor that translates the raw score so it equals about 30 percent of your overall writing raw score. It's added to the raw score from your multiple-choice Grammar section, and then this total raw score is converted to the familiar 200–800 scale. If, by some chance, the readers differ by more than one point (and this is very rare) a third "master" reader will be called in to score the essay.

What ETS Says Is Graded

ETS publications tell you that readers are encouraged to look at what has been done well, rather than what hasn't been done. According to ETS the highest score of 6 is reserved for an essay that "effectively and insightfully develops a point of view"; "is well organized and clearly focused"; uses "clearly appropriate examples, reasons, and other evidence to support its position"; and "demonstrates meaningful variety in sentence structure" and "a varied, accurate, and apt vocabulary," though it may have "minor errors." Even an essay with a score of 6 does NOT have to be perfect. As long as your essay is well organized with fully developed ideas, you can make a couple of errors and still get a 6. On the other hand, a low score of 1 goes to an essay that "provides little or no evidence to support its position," "is disorganized or unfocused," and "contains pervasive errors in grammar, usage, or mechanics that persistently interfere with meaning." (Visit **www.collegeboard.com** to read the entire set of essay-scoring guidelines.)

How Quickly Your Essay Is Graded

Your essay counts for about 30% of your overall Writing score.

Think about your high school English teacher and how long he or she takes to get writing assignments back to you. Days? Weeks sometimes? Well, imagine that your teacher had to grade ten times as many essays in one-tenth the time. Suddenly the time he or she might have to look at your essay is shortened to a few minutes. The ETS reader (who is most likely a high school or college English teacher in real life) is in exactly that crazy situation—he or she may be reading 100 or 200 essays in one sitting. Careful scrutiny under these circumstances is simply not possible. As a result, there are very few things the reader will really have time to look for, and we're going to tell you all about them.

What Does This Mean for Your Essay?

It means "don't sweat the small stuff," but do sweat the structure and develop your thesis. It means that one or two misspellings probably won't break your score, but not having a good topic and argument for each paragraph will. So a missing apostrophe is not a cause for alarm. On the other hand, you'll want to make sure what you write is relevant and that you start with a strong topic sentence and conclusion. Our techniques will help you write a clear, concise essay that will earn you a solid score. To ace this section, grab the reader's attention right from the start and finish strong.

What Really Matters: The Big Three

ETS graders focus on three major things when looking at your essay. If you pay attention to these issues as you write, your essay will finish strong.

1. **Clear Point of View**
   Every essay should have a clear thesis. In other words: What do you think? The essay directions even tell you to state your point of view. So make sure that the grader knows exactly what your point of view is.
   You have only 25 measly minutes to write your essay. You may be tempted to argue every single issue that you can think of, and show why both sides have valid points. Although in the real world it's certainly good to think reasonably about both sides of an issue, you don't have time or space enough to argue both sides convincingly here. So pick a side and stick to it. Don't straddle the fence.
   You may not feel comfortable arguing forcefully for one side. If so, don't worry about it. Remember: This essay exists solely to get you a decent Writing score. Even if you don't think that "people are unwise to pursue love if it causes them pain," it's an easier essay to write (and grade) than an essay whose thesis is "there are many possibilities, really." The SAT is asking you a "yes" or "no" question. Don't answer "maybe."
2. **Support Your Position**
   Go back and look at the directions for the essay from a couple pages ago. Notice that they tell you to support your position with reasoning and examples taken from your reading, studies, experience, or observations? That's the meat of your essay. It's not enough to just say "yes" or "no"; you have to explain why you think yes or no.
   In addition to having an example, you need to show the grader how that example proves your point. It's not enough to say "Gatsby from *The Great Gatsby* shouldn't have pursued love because it caused him pain"; we want to know what, exactly, happened with Gatsby. The more you support your position, the more convincing your position is.
3. **Have a Logical Structure**
   You may have written five-paragraph essays in school. Those essays start with an introduction, have three body paragraphs, and then end with a conclusion. You won't have the time or space to write a full five-paragraph essay and explain each example, so we're going to limit ourselves to two good examples, rather than rushing through three mediocre ones.

Having a logical structure will help not only the rushed and uncaring grader locate your main points easily, but will also help you as you write. What's your first paragraph? The introduction! What do you have to do? State your thesis, and mention your examples. What are your next two paragraphs? Examples. Explain each example, and connect it to your thesis. And last, of course, is the conclusion paragraph. Restate your thesis, and you're done.

Is it a boring essay if it's always the same like that? Sure, it can be. But do you care about being exciting in any other portion of the SAT? Do you ever change your answer to an SAT math question because your answer is boring? Nope. So why would you do it here? Your goal with the essay is to make it easy for the grader to see how great you are. A logical structure can help do exactly that.

If you love writing, all this may seem like the wrong way to focus your attention. But our purpose is to help you raise your SAT score, and it will help to know what the College Board readers are really looking for. Don't forget, this essay is about getting your point across in the best rough draft possible.

Ready for some practice?

Some Sample Essays

Think Like a Grader
The best way to understand what is required of your essay is to step in the shoes of the graders. They want organization, clear and concise thoughts, and good examples that fit the thesis.

Let's take a look at a couple of sample essays written on the following topic:

> In his poem "In Memoriam," romantic poet Alfred Lord Tennyson expresses his view that loss is an unavoidable consequence of love. Yet, rather than shunning love because of this, Tennyson resolves to accept both the experience of love and the pain that inevitably comes with it. As he writes in his often quoted passage, "Tis better to have loved and lost than never to have loved at all."
>
> Adapted from James R. Kincaid, *Tennyson's Major Poems*

Assignment: Are people unwise to pursue love even when they know it will cause them pain? Plan and write an essay in which you develop your point of view on this issue. Support your position with reasoning and examples taken from your reading, studies, experience, or observations.

Give yourself two minutes to read each essay. Take a second to jot down the good and bad points of each. Think about what you didn't notice and what you noticed right away.

Essay Number One

I agree with the sentiment that it is better to experience love than not to experience it at all. A life filled with love is most certainly better than a life without love. You cannot always worry about whether or not you will lose the love you work hard for.

Romeo from Romeo and Juliet by William Shakespeare, who was a play wright from Victorian England, shows how important love is. He died for his love, Juliet, who was a Capulet. Romeo was a Montague. Their love though, was worth it, even though they both died because of it.

In all aspects of life, whether it is sports, personal relationships, or study, you should work hard to be the best. You should always strive for "love" and not be concerned about losing. As in sports, when it is better to try really hard and get a home run sometimes than to only be mediocre and get a single.

In personal relationships as well, you can't be afraid of losing your love. Just having had a wonderful experience, whether in personal relationships, or outside of them is worth the pain of loss.

Your Score

Essay Number Two

It is better to experience love, even if it brings pain, then to live a dull love less life. Love is one of the things that makes us truly human, and although it often comes hand in hand with unbearable pain, it is still ultimately worth it. Gregor from The Metamorphosis and mathematician John Nash both show how important love is to humanity.

Gregor awoke and found he was a giant bug. He was stuck in his room, cut off from his family and friends. His first worry was about his job, because he was a traveling salesman. His family, when they find out about Gregor's transformation, seal him off in the room, barely feeding him. Gregor lived a life simply devoted to work, and providing for his family. He avoided aiming for true, passionate love, and so when he turned into an insect he didn't have anyone close enough to him to care for him in his monstrous state. This shows that love is worth it, despite the pain, because it connects us to each other.

John Nash was a mathematician who created game theory and worked on many other mathematical subjects. He suffered from schizophrenia, so he knew how painful it was to be alone. But it was his wife who we was really able to connect to, although they had troubles due to his reclusive nature and mental problems. Through her love, he was able to control some of his mental problems, and when he won the Nobel prize for his work, as shown in the movie A Beutiful Mind, he dedicated it to her. His love for his wife was worth the pain, cause it helped him deal with other pains in his life.

Gregor lived a life without love, and found that when bad things happened he had no one he really loved, and no one who loved him enough to help him. John Nash, however, truly loved his wife, and that love helped him work through his pain. Love can be painful, but it can help deal with other pains in the world.

Your Score

How the Graders See These Essays

Essay One would have received a 3 from each grader, for a total score of 6 out of 12. Although it has two examples, both examples are very vague. The first example, about *Romeo and Juliet*, doesn't really connect with the thesis. How do we know that Romeo's love for Juliet was worth it? The second example is incredibly vague, and just rambles about love and sports for a while.

Essay Two would have received a 5 from each grader, for a total score of 10 out of 12. Although there are definitely small problems with this essay, such as spelling mistakes, and saying "cause" rather than "because," overall it is very clear what the author thinks and why she thinks it. All the details from each example directly connect to show why the author thinks that love, even with pain, is worthwhile.

Step 1: Thinking It Through

The prompt is there to help you understand the context for your essay, but you don't need to mention the given quotes. You can if it will help you to launch yourself into the essay, but the real task that you're given is in the assignment and that's what graders are looking to see if you accomplished.

> Modern ethics is suspicious of those who serve only their own self-interest and instead praises the selfless among us for their dedication to the greater good. However, this distinction is less clear in the context of a capitalist society, where each individual citizen is responsible for his own welfare, and cannot rely on society to help him in times of need. Indeed, one must sometimes act in selfish ways to survive.
>
> Adapted from C. S. Parker, "No Big Macs in the Kalahari"

Assignment: Is it better to focus on your own good or that of others? Plan and write an essay in which you develop your point of view on this issue. Support your position with reasoning and examples taken from your reading, studies, experience, or observations.

Follow the Directions!
Make sure you read the assignment. And pay attention to "plan and write" and "support your position." These are what the graders will be looking for!

Point of View

What's your point of view on the previous topic? What would your thesis be? Remember: You're not graded on your thesis alone, but this is the launching pad for your essay. Make sure that it clearly states what position you've decided to take.

Don't Straddle!
Make sure you're not straddling the fence. Pick one side of the argument and show that you've clearly done so in your thesis.

Putting Pen to Paper: Brainstorm!

You've chosen a side and a thesis. Great! Now you need to come up with some good, concrete examples that specifically prove your point.

Choose examples that are

- real (not hypothetical or made up)
- specific
- related to a topic you're familiar with

Your turn. Brainstorm on the above prompt. What examples can you come up with? Don't stick to three. Come up with as many as you can in the next three minutes.

Step 2: Introduction

Now that you know your thesis and your examples, it's time to start writing. The general structure for the essay should be: introduction, two examples, and conclusion. If you have two really solid, detailed, relevant examples, stick to those. Don't throw in a third because you think you have to.

With your introduction, you want to state your point of view clearly. Your entire essay has to connect back to your thesis, so make sure that your thesis is stated directly. Your goal is to state that you agree or disagree with the assignment.

Don't just state that you agree or disagree, of course. Restate "I agree" or "I disagree" as a full sentence, such as "You should focus on your own good, which can help others," or "It is better to focus on the good of others rather than on yourself."

Once you've stated your thesis, you can elaborate a little bit. You'll use specific examples later on, so for now just explain why you believe what you do. Something such as "People know what is best for themselves better than they know what is better for others," or "Civilization is built on the fact that people help others over themselves." Emphasize the point you've made with your thesis; don't confuse it.

You want to finish your introduction by previewing the examples you're going to talk about. This shows your reader that you've organized your thoughts. Otherwise it looks as though you're just rambling on without evidence, and maybe without a point!

Write out your introduction for our original prompt:

Step 3: Examples

You've given the reader a roadmap to the argument you're going to make. Now, let's argue! Remember: Although you're going to write three examples if you can, it's more important to have two really specific, well-developed examples than to include three examples that you rush through and don't examine in enough detail.

The Body of Your Argument

In writing your body paragraphs, you need to supply the readers with everything they need to know, and nothing else. You want your body paragraphs to give enough detail to show that you know the subject you're discussing and demonstrate how it helps to prove your thesis. And that's it. Don't put in random facts to prove you know your subject if it doesn't help your argument!

After writing a concise, detailed, fat-free body paragraph, you must explain why it supports your argument. Don't assume that your readers understand the connection between the two. Explain yourself.

> It's All About Transitions
>
> You're going to have to transition from your introduction into your first body paragraph, from first body paragraph to second body paragraph, and so on. Make sure that your essay flows smoothly from one paragraph to the next. You can accomplish this through the use of **transitions**. Transitional words and phrases show your intentions to your reader. They're like signs on the side of the road of the journey on which you're taking your reader.

That's Why We Read That: Good Examples

You know all those books you had to read in English class? All of those make great examples. First off, you've read them (hopefully), which always helps. Second, your teacher probably explained many of the big ideas and themes of those books in class, which makes it easy to reference those big ideas in your essay.

History examples can also be great. Avoid big, vague examples like "World War II" or "The Crusades." Instead, use specific examples, like "The *Titanic*," "Landing on the Moon," or "The Battle of Gettysburg." Specific examples will give you more details to use, which will give you more to connect to your thesis.

You don't have to be an expert in your examples, you just have to know enough to write three to five sentences about them. Try to focus on the details that connect directly to your thesis. Everything you write should exist only to support your opinion.

Getting Personal

Let's talk for a moment about the personal anecdote example. Make sure you don't get caught up telling your story; instead focus on explaining *why* your experience is relevant to your argument. Here are some ways to use your personal examples most effectively.

- Make sure your example supports your thesis.
- Don't pad your example with irrelevant details. Stay on topic!
- Explain very clearly why this example supports your argument.
- As a guide, remember that it's an appropriate example if you were going to write about it for your college essay.

Let's Try It!

Return to your introductory paragraph to refresh your memory. Now write your first body paragraph. Make sure to transition smoothly from your intro into this paragraph.

In Conclusion

Always leave yourself a couple of minutes to write a fabulous conclusion. You started your essay with a hook. Now you want to leave your reader thinking about your subject. It's more important to write two well-thought-out body paragraphs and a great conclusion than to write three mediocre body paragraphs and then have no time for a conclusion. The second scenario will lead your graders to believe that your essay is poorly organized.

Your conclusion doesn't have to be long, but make sure you wrap up your argument. Refer back to your examples and your original thesis. Sum up what you've said and answer the question, "Why do you see it this way?"

Let's Try It!

Write a conclusion for your essay:

____

____

____

____

____

Timing Is Everything

One of the hardest things about the essay is balancing your time. You have 25 minutes to write, which is not a lot. Here's a rough guideline to help keep you on track:

> **First 3 minutes**: Think. Organize. Take a point of view. Brainstorm, and write down the examples you've picked.
> **Next 17–20 minutes**: Write. Try to balance your time between the intro and body paragraphs.
> **Last 2–5 minutes**: Conclusion. If you haven't done so already, begin writing your conclusion.

Take a breath. You're done!

Sample Essay

Give yourself 25 minutes and see how you do on this essay topic.

> History has shown us that liberty is not a guaranteed, natural possession. The great landmarks of liberty, such as the American Bill of Rights and the Emancipation Proclamation, were all gained only through the sacrifices of many visionaries and patriots. We should be ever mindful that freedom, if we are to preserve it, must be safeguarded with our lives.
>
> Adapted from Bernard L. Berzon

Assignment: Do you believe that one should sacrifice life for liberty? Plan and write an essay in which you develop your point of view on this issue. Support your position with reasoning and examples taken from your reading, studies, experience, or observations.

Some Reminders

You now know all you need to know to write a great essay. Here are a few tips that may help you get that extra point.

- Speak like you speak. Use big words only if you know how to use them.
- Avoid overly casual writing. You're writing for an adult, not for your peers. Your own voice should come through, but it should be your best voice.
- Don't address the parts of your essay with words like "for example," "in conclusion," or "this proves."
- Create a mix of long and short sentences.
- Write legibly.

The Princeton Review Diagnostic Test Form

ESSAY

SECTION 1

Begin your essay on this page. If you need more space, continue on the next page. Do not write outside of the essay box.

Continue on the opposite side if necessary.

PLEASE DO NOT WRITE IN THIS AREA

SERIAL #

The Princeton Review
Diagnostic Test Form

Continued from previous page.

PLEASE PRINT YOUR INITIALS

First	Middle	Last

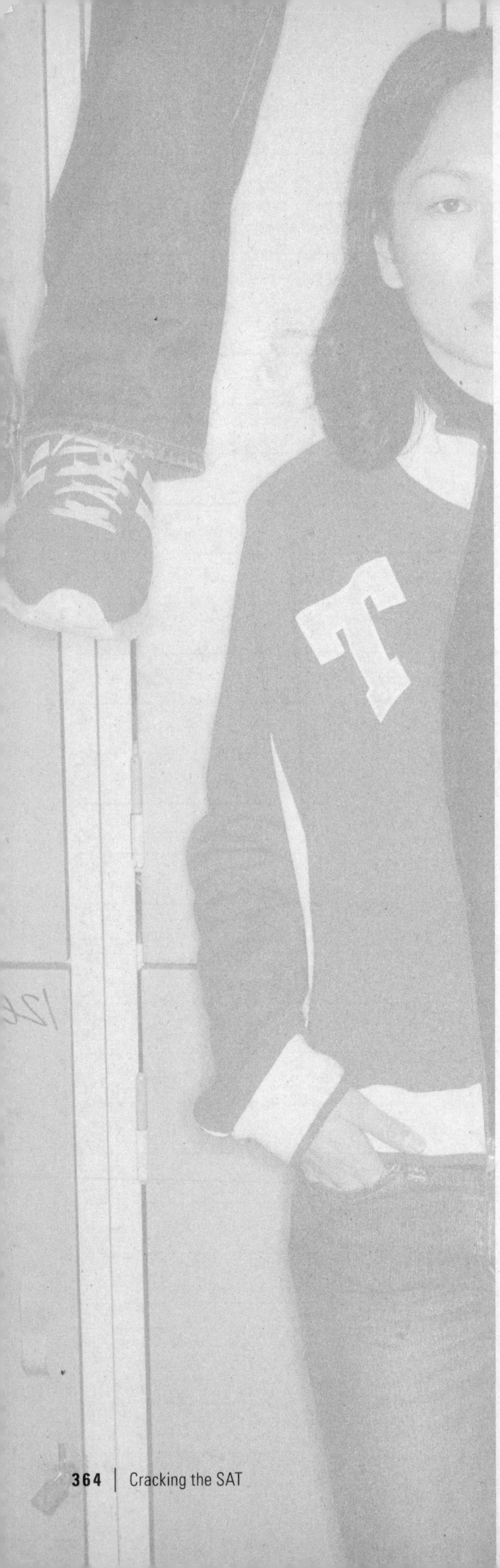

Summary

- There are two graders who grade your essay on a scale of 1 to 6. They have only a few minutes to read each essay. A great way to help with your essay is to learn to think like a reader.
- Focus on the big three.
  - Clear Point of View
  - Support Your Position
  - Have a Logical Structure
- Pick a side. Make sure you have a point of view and stick to it. Remember there are no right answers, so feel free to pick an unpopular side. Just make sure you can support it.
- Brainstorm ideas before picking your best two or three examples.
- Your introduction should foreshadow the examples you're going to use to prove your point.
- Your body paragraphs should contain concrete, detailed information that is appropriate to your argument.
- You need to finish your essay with a solid conclusion, even if it means using only two great examples rather than three mediocre ones.
- Keep in mind some helpful hints:
  - Don't use big words you're not comfortable with just to sound smarter.
  - Avoid overly casual writing.
  - Don't address the essay.
  - Create a mix of long and short sentences.
  - Write legibly.

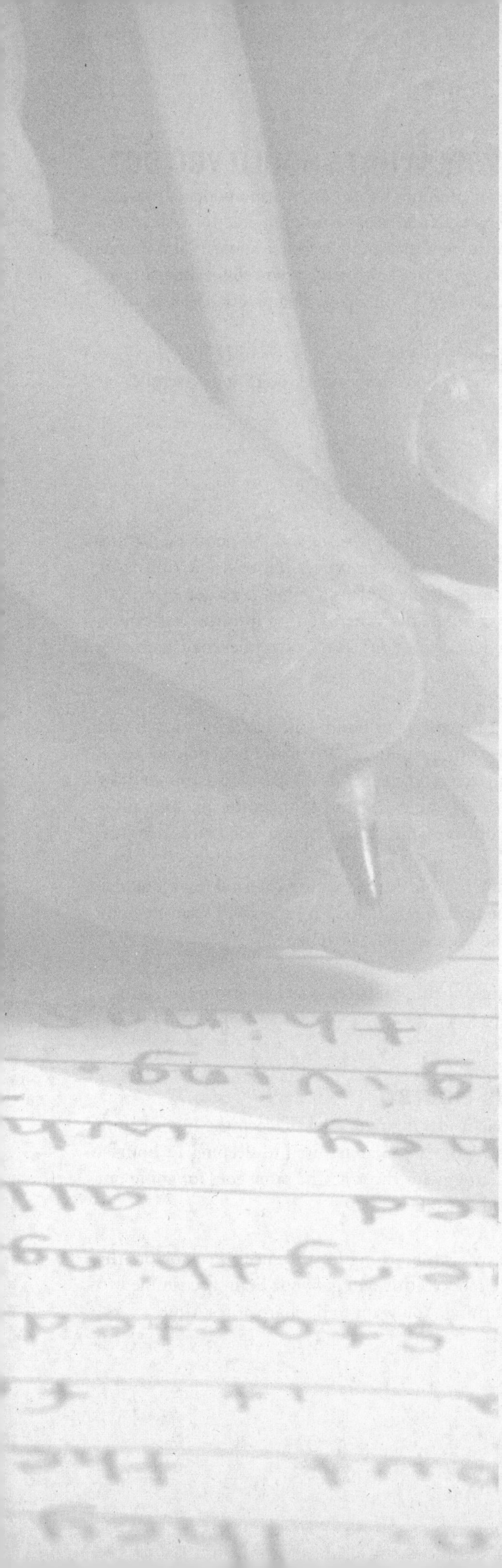

Part V
Taking the SAT

THE SAT IS A WEEK AWAY. WHAT SHOULD YOU DO?

Get a copy of a full-length SAT from your guidance counselor or online at sat.collegeboard.com and PrincetonReview.com.

First of all, you should practice the techniques we've taught you on lots of practice tests. If you haven't done so already, take and score the three practice tests at the back of this book, as well as the practice tests on our website. You can also download a practice test from the College Board's website, **www.collegeboard.com.** Your guidance counselor may be able to give you a copy of a practice SAT as well.

If you want more practice, pick up a copy of our very own *11 Practice Tests for the SAT & PSAT* at your local bookstore or through our website, at **PrincetonReview.com/bookstore**.

Getting Psyched

The SAT is a big deal, but you don't want to let it scare you. Sometimes students get so nervous about doing well that they freeze up on the test and ruin their scores. The best thing to do is to think of the SAT as a game. It's a game you can get good at, and beating the test can be fun. When you go into the test center, just think about all those poor students who don't know how to eyeball geometry diagrams.

The best way to keep from getting nervous is to build confidence in yourself and in your ability to remember and use our techniques. When you take practice tests, time yourself exactly as you will be timed on the real SAT. Develop a sense of how long 25 minutes is and how much time you can afford to spend on cracking difficult problems. If you know ahead of time what to expect, you won't be as nervous.

Of course, taking a real SAT is much more nerve-racking than taking a practice test. Prepare yourself ahead of time for the fact that 25 minutes will seem to go by a lot faster on a real SAT than it did on your practice tests.

It's all right to be nervous; the point of being prepared is to keep from panicking.

Should You Sleep for 36 Hours?

Some guidance counselors tell their students to get a lot of sleep the night before the SAT. This probably isn't a good idea. If you aren't used to sleeping 12 hours a night, doing so will just make you groggy for the test. The same goes for going out all night: Tired people are not good test takers.

A much better idea is to get up early each morning for the entire week before the test and do your homework before school. This will get your brain accustomed to functioning at that hour of the morning. You want to be sharp at test time.

Before dinner the night before the test, spend an hour or so reviewing the Hit Parade. This will make the list fresh in your mind in the morning. You might also practice estimating some angles and looking for direct solutions on a few real SAT math problems. You don't want to exhaust yourself, but it will help to brush up.

Furthermore

Here are a few pointers for test day and beyond:

1. Eat a good breakfast before the test—your brain needs energy.
2. Work out a few SAT problems on the morning of the test to help dust off any cobwebs in your head and get you started thinking analytically.
3. Arrive at the test center early. Everyone is headed to the same place at the same time.
4. You must take acceptable identification to the test center on the day of the test. According to ETS, acceptable identification must include a recognizable photograph and your name. Acceptable forms of ID include your driver's license, a school ID with a photo, or a valid passport. If you don't have an official piece of ID with your signature and your photo, you can have your school make an ID for you using a Student ID form provided by the College Board. Complete instructions for making such an ID are found on the College Board's website and in the *SAT Registration Bulletin*. According to ETS, the following forms of ID are *unacceptable:* a birth certificate, a credit card, or a Social Security card.
   Make sure you read all of the rules in the *Registration Bulletin*, because conflicts with ETS are just not worth the headache. Your only concern on the day of the test should be beating the SAT. To avoid hassles and unnecessary stress, make *absolutely certain* that you take your admissions ticket and your ID with you on the day of the test.
5. The only outside materials you are allowed to use on the test are No. 2 pencils (wooden, NOT mechanical), a wristwatch (an absolute necessity), and a calculator. ETS's latest rule is that mechanical pencils are not allowed. We're not sure why, but you should take lots of sharpened wooden pencils just to be safe. Digital watches are best, but if it has a beeper, make sure you turn it off. Proctors will confiscate pocket dictionaries, word lists, portable computers, and the like. Proctors have occasionally also confiscated stopwatches and travel clocks. Technically, you should be permitted to use these, but you can never tell with some proctors. Take a watch and avoid the hassles.
6. Some proctors allow students to bring food into the test room; others don't. Take some fruit (especially bananas) with you and see what happens. If you don't flaunt them, they probably won't be confiscated. Save them until your break and eat outside the test room, as discreetly as possible.

#1: Eat Breakfast
You'll work better on a satisfied stomach.

#2: Try Some Problems
Get your mind moving.

#3: Show Up Early
Leave time for traffic.

#4: Take ID
A driver's license, a passport, or a school photo ID will do.

#5: Take Equipment
At least 12 sharpened No. 2 pencils, a watch, and a calculator.

#6: Take Fruit or Other Energy Food
Grapes or oranges can give you an energy boost if you need it.

#7: Your Desk...
should be comfortable and suited to your needs.

7. You are going to be sitting in the same place for more than three hours, so make sure your desk isn't broken or unusually uncomfortable. If you are left-handed, ask for a left-handed desk. (The center may not have one, but it won't hurt to ask.) If the sun is in your eyes, ask to move. If the room is too dark, ask someone to turn on the lights. Don't hesitate to speak up. Some proctors just don't know what they're doing.

#8: Your Test...
should be printed legibly in your booklet.

8. Make sure your booklet is complete. Booklets sometimes contain printing errors that make some pages impossible to read. One year more than ten thousand students had to retake the SAT because of a printing error in their booklets. Also, check your answer sheet to make sure it isn't flawed.

#9: Skipping
You can skip around within a section, but not between sections.

9. As you know, you can skip around within a section as much as you want. However, you can't skip around from one section to another. Even if you finish a section early, you can't look back at a previous section or jump ahead. Use the extra time to take a few deep breaths, and then go back to any questions in the section that you weren't sure about.

#10: Breaks
You will probably get several—take advantage of them!

10. You will probably get a short break after each hour of testing. Ask for it if your proctor doesn't give it to you. You should be allowed to go to the bathroom at this time. The breaks are a very good idea. Be sure to get up, move around, and clear your head.

#11: Cancel with Care
Don't cancel your scores just because you feel icky. Think it over carefully, and NEVER cancel on the same day as the test. Make sure you have a really good reason, like you fainted. Remember: You can always retake the test.

11. ETS allows you to cancel your SAT scores. Unfortunately, you can't cancel only your Math, your Writing, or your Critical Reading—it's all or nothing. You will also have to cancel them before you know what your scores are. You can cancel scores at the test center by asking your proctor for a "Request to Cancel Test Scores" form. You must complete this form and hand it in before you leave the test center. If you decide to cancel your scores after you leave, you can do so by contacting ETS by cable, overnight delivery, or e-mail (sat@ets.org). The address is in the *Registration Bulletin,* or you can call ETS at 609-771-7600 to find out where to send your score cancellation request.

We recommend that you not cancel your scores unless you know you made so many errors or left out so many questions that your score will be unacceptably low. Don't cancel your scores on test day just because you have a bad feeling—even the best test takers feel a little shaky after the SAT. You've got five days to think it over.

#12: Bubble with Care
A stray mark can hurt your score.

12. Make sure you darken all your responses before the test is over. At the same time, erase any extraneous marks on the answer sheet. **A stray mark in the margin of your answer sheet can result in correct responses being marked as wrong.**

13. Don't assume that your test was scored correctly. Send away for ETS's Question and Answer Service whenever it is offered. It costs money, but it's worth it. You'll get back copies of your answer sheet, a test booklet, and an answer key. Check your answers against the key and complain if you think your test has been scored incorrectly. (Don't throw away the test booklet you receive from the Question and Answer Service. If you're planning to take the SAT again, save it for practice. If you're not, give it to your guidance counselor or school library.)

#13: Keep Tabs on ETS
Get a copy of your SAT, your answer sheet, and an answer key. Make sure your score is accurate.

14. You deserve to take your SAT under good conditions. If you feel that your test was not administered properly (the high school band was practicing outside the window, or your proctor hovered over your shoulder during the test), call us immediately at 800-2-REVIEW and we'll tell you what you can do about it.

#14: We're Here for You
The Princeton Review is proud to advise students who have been mistreated by ETS.

16. Don't assume that your first [illegible] read over the [illegible] question and answers before you [illegible] difficult questions, but it's common. You'll get [illegible] questions at the [illegible] chapter and an answer key. Check your answers against the key and continue if you [illegible] these [illegible] test book [illegible] in your [illegible] practice [illegible]

17. You deserve to take your ACT under good conditions. [illegible] you [illegible] the [illegible] practice outside the [illegible] your [illegible] should [illegible] and [illegible] what you can do about it.

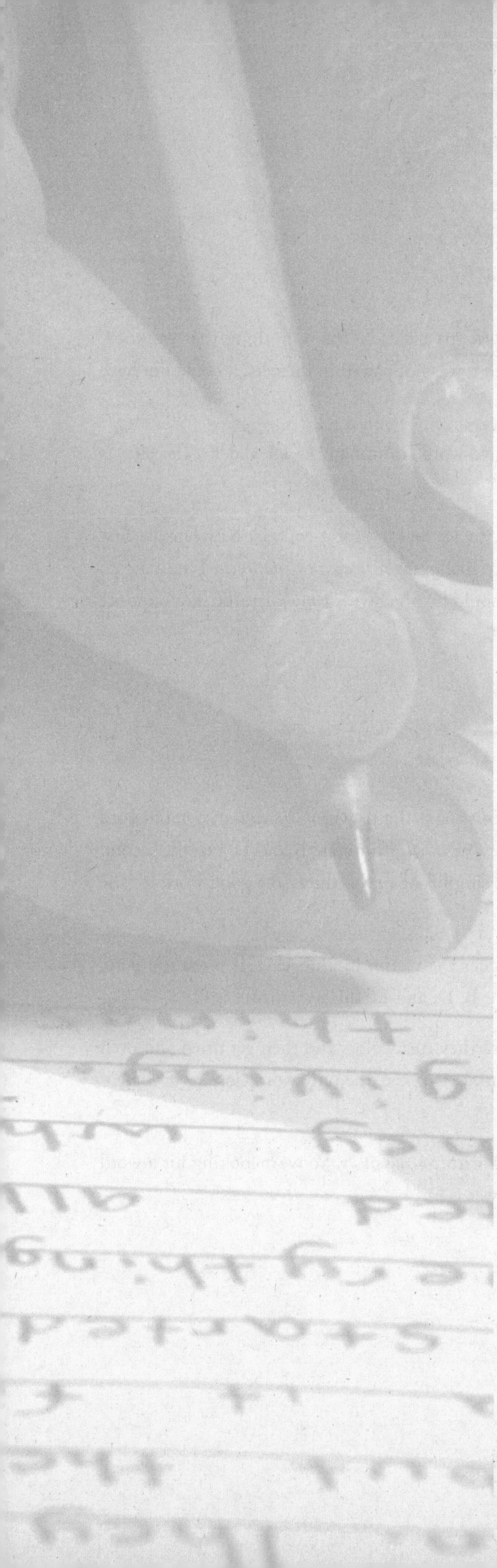

Part VI
Answer Key to Drills

CHAPTER 5

Drills 1 and 2
Pages 44–45

1. **C** The blank is concerned with what *Citizen Kane was* (past tense). The only thing that we know about the past is that *theaters refused to show it.* Since it was not played in theaters, it could not have made any money, therefore C.

6. **B** The buildings are *threatened*, so we need a negative word. Eliminate A, D, and E. The clue is *increasing rents*, so B is the best choice.

7. **B** Lots of triggers in this one. First, *but* tells us that we are looking for a contrast between the first blank and *technically slick*, therefore we want a word like *unsophisticated* or *simplistic*. Eliminate A, C, and D. The sentence also states that the films should be filled with *poignancy*, the best opposite of which is *vacuous*.

Drill 3
Page 50

2. **A** A good clue for the first blank is *simplify the procedure* and the trigger is *instead of*; a good word for the first blank would have to do with being *not simplified.* Eliminate B and D. For the second blank, officers are trying to do something that will simplify the procedure, so a good word for the blank is *help.* The answer is A.

5. **C** For the first blank, think what type of person rescues the victim in a novel. It is often the hero. *Hero* is a good word for the first blank. Eliminate A, B, D, and E. The best answer is C.

6. **D** Think about how leaves can be affected by weather. They turn colors and then get dried and even a little wrinkly. So a good word for the second blank is *wrinkly.* The only word close to *wrinkly* is *withered.* The best answer is D.

7. **D** The clue is the second half of the sentence, starting with *courageously.* So we're looking for a word that means "supportive and devoted." The best answer is D.

CHAPTER 6

Drill
Pages 71–73

14. **C** Babe Ruth's personality and appearance captured the imagination of people of all ages, which includes children. Choice B is too extreme, and choice E goes too far. We are not given specific information to support choice A. The reference in choice D to "rules" makes it wrong; baseball was revitalized, but that doesn't mean rules were changed. The best answer is C.

12. **B** Like food, the early erasers tended to rot quickly. Although we are told that the erasers were popular within the Continent, there's no information about shipping costs to support choice A. Choices C and D find no support in the passage. Choice E refers to the 70-year period between the invention of the eraser and the invention of the curing process. However, the answer choice states that the curing process itself takes 70 years. The best answer is B.

10. **E** The author writes about the fame of Mendelev, Darwin, and Einstein, but the question asks why the author mentions them. The remainder of the excerpt discusses three other scientists who, according to the author, made significant discoveries, and yet are essentially unknown. The author believes that these other scientists should be famous as well. Choices A and C relate to a specific discovery and theory; the author did not mention the famous scientists in order to discuss such particulars. Because there is no trend or pattern discussed in the passage, choices B and D are not supported. The best answer is E.

17. **D** The author explained that for a time "there was no commercially viable way to extract hyaluronan," but that later a method was developed and sold to a pharmaceutical company. Choice A is not supported; just because physicians now use hyaluronan does not mean veterinarians are prohibited from doing so. Choice B is contradicted. Choice C is contradicted; we are told that hyaluronan is extracted from rooster combs. Choice E is extreme and not supported. The best answer is D.

24. **C** In context, *omits* means *forgets*. C is the best answer.

19. **B** The author has a positive attitude towards *Star Wars*. Choices C, D, and E are *not* positive. Choice A is extreme. The best answer is B.

21. **A** The author mentions a variety of telescopes to show that "all telescopes do not 'see' in the same way." While choice B might be a true statement, the author didn't mention other telescopes to make this point. Choices C and E find no support in the text of the passage. Choice D is extreme and does not state the correct purpose. The best answer is A.

15. C The author wrote that the terra-cotta rough drafts "often created more interest than the finished works." We are not told that terra-cotta works *always* created more interest or that finished works stopped being of interest. Choice A goes too far; some collectors believed the terra-cotta revealed talent more accurately, but they did not claim that talent previously had gone unrecognized. Choices B and E, however logical, are not supported by the text of the passage. Choice D is not supported and is extreme. The best answer is C.

11. E The author writes that a "monastic chant that relies solely on the human voice and an orchestral symphony utilizing multiple instruments are both classical, yet neither sounds remotely like the other." Choice A is not supported and is arguably contradicted. Choices B, C, and D are contradicted. The best answer is E.

CHAPTER 7

Drill
Pages 85–87

9. C Passage 1 contains several metaphors, including referring to certain art as "stillborn" and "soulless," and referring to a particular artistic process as "aping." Although Passage 2 does contain a limited use of metaphor, metaphors are featured more substantially in Passage 1. Both passages use historical references and artistic analysis, so choices A and E are wrong. Neither passage mentions specific dates, so choice B is wrong. Passage 2, but not Passage 1, uses visual description; choice D is wrong. The best answer is C.

10. D Although the authors disagree about the artistic merit of using older forms, both authors agree that it is technically possible to do so. Choice A is wrong because the authors are in disagreement about the point in the answer. Choices B and C relate to factual differences between the passages, but not issues on which the authors are in agreement or disagreement. Choice E is not supported by the text of either passage. The best answer is D.

11. A The point of Passage 2 is that an artist can use older forms in a new way so as to create his or her own vision. The author of Passage 1 does not discuss this possibility. Choice B is wrong as it is consistent with Passage 1, not Passage 2. The information in choice C is discussed in both passages, while the information in choice E is discussed in neither passage; both choices are wrong. Choice D erroneously refers to "contemporaries." The best answer is A.

12. B The author of Passage 2 disagrees that borrowing artistic forms from the past must be bad. To the contrary, Passage 2 states that the old forms *can* be used in new ways. Choice A is extreme. Choices C, D, and E are not supported by the text of Passage 2. The best answer is B.

13. **C** Although the authors address the issue from different perspectives, they agree that humans are creating problems for chimpanzees. Choice A goes too far; the authors do not claim that the reason chimps should be valued is their genetic closeness to humans. The remaining answer choices clearly do not reflect the primary purpose. The best answer is C.

14. **C** The author of Passage 1 states that "chimpanzees nurse for five years." Choice A is extreme. Choices B, D, and E are not supported by the text of the passage. The best answer is C.

15. **A** The author mentions population growth as part of a lengthy explanation about how this growth affects chimpanzees. The author does not offer a solution or demand a reaction, so choices B and E are wrong. The author does not criticize the growth, which wouldn't be called a policy anyway, so choice D is wrong. The author does not praise the population growth, of course, so choice C is wrong. The best answer is A.

16. **D** Answer choices A, B, C, and E are all supported by the text of the passage Answer choice D is the only one that is not mentioned. The best answer is D.

17. **D** The author tells us that poachers take baby chimpanzees. The author does not call for logging restrictions and even explains why logging is important to the African poor, so choice A is wrong. The author does not discuss whether logging or poaching is worse, so choice B is not supported. Choice C is not supported because the author discusses only chimpanzees. Choice E is extreme. The best answer is D.

18. **A** The author of Passage 2 tells us that chimpanzees "suffer greatly as a consequence of their genetic similitude with humans" and that their "appealing demeanor" leads people to believe they can fit into a household. Choices B, C, and D are not supported by the text of the passage. Choice E may reflect the author's belief, but it does not represent how the author would respond to the text referenced in the question. The best answer is A.

19. **B** The author of Passage 2 tells us that the "appealing demeanor" of chimpanzees leads people to believe the animals can fit into a household as pets. The remaining answer choices do not provide a reason for the author's comment, even if some of the answer choices are mentioned in the passage. The best answer is B.

20. **C** In context, *check* means *stop*. The best answer is C.

21. **C** The author believes that the fate of chimpanzees is poor for several reasons, including the lack of sanctuary slots. Even assuming choices A, B, D, and E to be true (as required by the question), none of these choices relates directly to the author's stated reasons for the poor fate of the chimpanzees. The best answer is C.

22. **B** The phrase "given the opportunity" is used to describe the lengthy life-span of chimpanzees in the wild. Choices A and C might contain true statements, but they do not relate to the author's use of the quoted phrase. Choices D and E are contradicted. The best answer is B.

23. **E** The principal difference between the two passages is that Passage 1 concerns chimpanzees in the wild, while Passage 2 concerns chimpanzees in captivity. The author of Passage 1 mentions legal restrictions briefly, but that does not amount to a major difference, so choice A is wrong. Both passages are concerned with actions of humans, so choice B is wrong. Both passages discuss chimpanzees of all ages, so choice C is wrong. The author of Passage 1 does not discuss ways to help chimpanzees, so choice D is wrong. The best answer is E.

24. **B** The authors of both passages discuss how the actions of people are negatively affecting chimpanzees. However, the author of Passage 1 does explain that poor people in Africa need deforested land to live and look to the logging industry as a means to survive. Thus, the author of Passage 1 is more understanding. The best answer is B.

CHAPTER 11

Drill 1
Page 154

1. 109
2. 38
3. –3
4. 10
5. 15

Drill 2
Page 156

1. $6(57+13) = 6 \times 70 = 420$
2. $51(48 + 50 + 52) = 51(150) = 7{,}650$
3. $ab + ac - ad$
4. $x(y - z)$
5. $c(ab + xy)$

Drill 3
Page 161

1. $\frac{25}{3}$
2. $\frac{17}{7}$
3. $\frac{49}{9}$
4. $\frac{5}{2}$
5. $\frac{20}{3}$

Drill 4
Page 162

1. 3
2. $\frac{31}{5}$
3. $-1\frac{4}{15}$ or $-\frac{19}{15}$
4. $\frac{1}{15}$
5. $\frac{6}{7}$
6. $\frac{2}{25}$
7. $\frac{4}{9}$

Drill 5
Page 163

1. 0.3741
2. 1,457.7
3. 186
4. –2.89

CHAPTER 12

Drill
Pages 208–209

4. **A** For this question, we should try Plugging In the Answers. Starting with C, we can Plug In 10 for the number. First, we can take 10 and multiply it by 2, then add 4. This gives us 24. To check if this is right, we can take 10 and subtract 6. This gives us 4. So C is not the correct answer. Since the two results came out to be 24 and 4, we can try a smaller number to try and narrow it down. If we Plug In choice B, we get 2 × 2 = 4. Adding 4 to this gives us 8. Does this equal 2 – 6? No. So let's try A. We first get –10 × 2 = –20. Adding 4 gives us –16. Is this equal to –10 – 6? Yes. The answer is choice A.

6. **E** With a "must be" question, we should Plug In. Let's make $n = -2$. We then plug into the answer choices. Choices A, B, and C don't give us a positive integer and can be eliminated. Since we have two choices left, we need to Plug In again. Let's try $n = -3$. Using this number eliminates D, leaving us with E.

7. **E** Plug In a number for c. If we say that $c = 5$, we can calculate that Ashley is 15. That means Sarah is 15 + 7, which equals 22. This is our target. Plugging 5 into the answer choices for c gives us E as our answer.

8. **D** The words "must be" mean this is a good place to Plug In. Let's Plug In values for r and s. We can make $r = 3$ and $s = 5$. Using these numbers in the answer choices, the only choice that gives us an even integer is D.

9. **D** Here, we can Plug In our own number for y dollars. Let's make $y = 80$. That makes each sack of flour cost 2 dollars. Then, 12 sacks of flour would cost 12 × 2 = 24. This is our target answer. When we plug 80 in for y in the answer choices, we get D as our answer.

11. **A** A problem with variables means Plugging In! Let's first plug in for x. If we say that $x = 10$, then 10 percent of 50 gives us 5. Now, we can figure out what y is. To solve, we can use our percent translation terms. If 5 is 20 percent of y, this becomes $5 = \frac{20}{100}y$. Solving for y gives us 25. When we plug in 25 for y in the answer choices, the only choice that works is A.

12. **C** Two variables tells us this is a great place to Plug In. Let's pick numbers that make the math easy. We can try $x = 30$ and $y = 2$. So in 2 hours there are 4 periods of 30 minutes each: $12 \times 4 = 48$. Alex can fold 48 napkins in 2 hours. 48 is our target. Plugging into our answer choices gives us C as the only answer.

13. **C** Since the problem is asking for a specific amount, this is a good place to PITA. Starting with C, if we say that Alice read 200 pages on Saturday, we can figure out how many she read on Sunday. We take 200 and divide it by 2. This gives us 100. Now, we add 50 to it. This gives us 150 pages that Alice read on Sunday. To check to see if we're right, we add 200 for Saturday and 150 for Sunday. Do these add to 350? Yes. The correct answer is C.

14. **B** Here, the words "must be" again indicate a good place to Plug In. We need numbers for x and y that will give us a negative value. Let's try $x = -1$ and $y = -2$. If we plug these into the statements in the roman numerals, we find that I is false, but II and III are true. We can eliminate any answer choice that contains I. This leaves B and D. Let's try different numbers and see if we can eliminate another choice. If we try $x = -3$ and $y = -2$, we find that II is false and III is still true. This leaves us with B as the only correct answer.

15. **A** This problem is asking for a specific amount, so we should probably PITA. Starting with choice C, if we assume that Mark pays $160 dollars, then Fred pays twice that, or $320, and Alan pays $360. To check if this is correct, we add the three values together. This gives us $840, which is too much. We can eliminate C and also D and E. If we try B, the sum of all three becomes $740, which is still too much. Choice A is the only one left, but even when we check it, the sum of the three is $540.

16. **D** The easiest way to do this question is with PITA. Let's start with choice C. If Allie has 5 coins, that means that Jonathan has 4 coins. To check if this is the right answer, we add 2 coins to Allie and subtract 2 from Jonathan. This gives us 7 for Allie and 2 for Jonathan. Since 7 is not three times as much as 2, we can eliminate C and anything less. When we try D, it gives us the correct answer.

18. **C** With multiple variables, we should definitely Plug In. To try and make the math easy, let's Plug In first for r. We can make $r = 3$. To make the fraction easier to work with, let's make $s = 6$. That means that $t = 1$. So our target is 6. We plug in 3 and 1 for r and t, respectively, in the answer choices. We get our target answer in choice C.

CHAPTER 13

Drill 1
Page 221

1.	$\frac{1}{2}$	0.5	50
2.	$\frac{3}{1}$	3.0	300
3.	$\frac{1}{200}$	0.005	0.5
4.	$\frac{1}{3}$	$0.333\overline{3}$	$33\frac{1}{3}$

Drill 2
Page 238

5. **A** Variables in the answers? Plug in! Make up a value for x. Let's say that x is 3. The list of numbers then becomes 20 – 2(3), 20 – 3, 20, 20 + 3, 20 + 2(3), so the list is 14, 17, 20, 23, and 26. To find the average, make an average pie: we know the number of things (5) and the total (14 + 17 + 20 + 23 + 26 = 100), so the average is 100 ÷ 5 = 20, answer choice (A).

8. **C** Henry has two spaces on his lawn for statues, so draw two boxes. For the first box, he has 9 options of statues to choose from. He chooses one statue out of the 9, and now he has only 8 statues to choose from for the other statue. So there are a total of 9 × 8 = 72 total arrangements of the 2 statues.

9. **D** Since we know the time that Amy walked and the distance she walked are directly proportional, we can set up a proportion to show her distance ÷ time. We want to know how many miles she'll walk in two hours, so put in 120 (60 × 2) minutes in the section half of the ratio: $\frac{2.5}{50} = \frac{x}{120}$. To solve, cross multiply, and you'll get $50x = 2.5 \times 120$; $50x = 300$; $x = 6$ miles, answer choice (D).

10. C Since this is a ratio question, let's draw a ratio box. We know the ratio for the votes for Skinner and Whitehouse, and the total number of votes cast. Fill in the total by adding the ratio (4 + 3 = 7), and then find the multiplier by seeing how many times 7 goes into 140,000 (140,000 ÷ 7 = 20,000).

Skinner	Whitehouse	Total
4	3	7
× 20,000	× 20,000	× 20,000
80,000	60,000	140,000

The question wants to know how many votes Whitehouse received, which is 60,000, answer (C).

14. D Start out by finding 1/4 of 18 percent of 616 by translating to math: $\frac{1}{4} \times \frac{18}{100} \times 616$. Plug that into your calculator (remember to use parentheses for your fractions) and you'll get 27.72. That's the number we're looking for. Convert each answer to math and plug in to your calculator to see which one gives you 27.72. (D), 18% of 154, is 27.72.

16. D Start by figuring out what percent of the houses do not have two-car garages. Since 60% of the houses with garages have two-car garages, 40% of the houses with garages do not have two-car garages. In other words, 40% of 80% of the houses do not have two-car garages. Translate that into math to get $\frac{40}{100} \times \frac{80}{100} = 0.32$, or 32% of the houses. The problem tells us that 56 houses do not have two-car garages, which means 32% of the houses equals 56. Translating into math gives us $\frac{32}{100} \times x = 56$. Solve for *x*, and you'll get 125, answer choice (D).

18. E Let's try out the answers, and see which one works. Start with (C). If the watchmaker made 21 watches on Tuesday, then he must have made 17 watches on Monday. We know that he should have made 16% more watches on Tuesday than on Monday, so let's use the Percent Change formula (difference ÷ original) and see if we get 16%: $\frac{4}{17} \approx 23.5\%$, which is too big. Eliminate answer choice (C). We want the 4 watches to be a smaller percent of the total, so we need a bigger total. Try a bigger answer choice, like (E). If he made 29 watches on Tuesday, then he made 25 watches on Monday. Now the percent change is $\frac{4}{25} = 0.16 = 16\%$, which is exactly what we wanted.

CHAPTER 16

Answers and Explanations to Putting It All Together... Pages 293–299

13. **13** Use the common quadratic: $(x - y)^2 = x^2 - 2xy + y^2$. So, $a^2 - 2ab + b^2 = (a - b)^2$. That means $(a - b)^2 = 169$. Take the square root of both sides to find $a - b = 13$ or -13; but don't forget $a > b$ and $a - b > 0$, so $a - b = 13$.

15. **E** First, convert a and c to decimals. 63% is $63 \div 100 = 0.63$, and $\frac{3}{8}$ is $3 \div 8 = 0.375$. The ratio of a to c is $\frac{a}{c}$. So, $\frac{0.63}{0.375} = 1.68$. To save time, you can ballpark the answer, since $a > c$ and E is the only choice greater than 1.

11. **C** Draw out the triangle. If it's a right triangle, and the two other angles are equal, then this is a 45°-45°-90° triangle. That tells us sides BC and AC are both the same, and that AB is the hypotenuse. Using the Pythagorean theorem, we know that $a^2 + b^2 = c^2$. Since a and b are the same, and $c = 4$, $a^2 + a^2 = 4^2$. Solve, for $a = 2\sqrt{2}$. The perimeter is therefore $2\sqrt{2} + 2\sqrt{2} + 4 = 4 + 4\sqrt{2}$, answer (C).

18. **E** There are 5 cyclists that could be first. Then, once you use one for the first spot, there are 4 that could be second, then 3 that could be third and that is all. Remember: Who cares about fourth or fifth place, since they're not getting a medal? So, there are $5 \times 4 \times 3 = 60$ places in which the cyclists finish.

12. **D** Plug in the answers for the value of b to find the values of a and b that work in both equations. Plugging in choice D, if $b = 4$, then $a + 2(4) = 10$; so, $a = 2$. Plug these values into the second equation: Does $4 - 2 = 2$? Yes, so D is correct. Alternatively, rewrite the second equation as $-a + b = 2$. Then, add the two equations together. This yields $3b = 12$. Divide by 3 to get $b = 4$.

8. **B** The perimeter of a square is $4s$. So, $28 = 4s$. Divide by 4 to find $s = 7$. The diagonal of a square divides the square into two 45:45:90 triangles, with sides in the ratio of $x{:}x{:}x\sqrt{2}$. If the side is 7, the diagonal is $7\sqrt{2}$.

17. **D** The angles in quadrilateral $ABCD$ (or any other quadrilateral) must add up to 360°. Since A and C are tangent points, we know that $\angle BAD = \angle BCD = 90°$, so we get $\angle ABC + \angle ADC = 180°$. From the question, $\angle ABC = \frac{2}{7}\angle ADC$. We can substitute and solve: $\frac{2}{7}\angle ADC + \angle ADC = 180°$, so $\frac{9}{7}\angle ADC = 180°$, so $\angle ADC = 140°$.

10. **D** There are 5 pictures that could be first. Then, once you use one for the first spot, there are 4 that could be second, then 3 that could be third, then 2 that could be fourth, then 1 that could be fifth. So, there are $5 \times 4 \times 3 \times 2 \times 1 = 120$ ways to arrange the photographs.

13. **B** Rewrite these statements as equations, where a = the price of an apple and c = the price of a cherry: $3a + 5c = 1.25$ and $15a + 100c = 9.25$. Add the equations together to get $18a + 105c = 10.50$, then divide everything by 3 to get $6a + 35c = 3.50$.

15. **A** If n represents the number of people that are added to the number of people already on the bus (42), you know that the new total on the bus is $n + 42$. Since that number is not *over the limit* of 66, but *could be equal to* the limit, you know that $n + 42 \leq 66$.

18. **17.5 or $\frac{35}{2}$** The trick is to recognize that ABC is a 30-60-90 right triangle. $\angle ABC$ must equal 90° since a tangent line must be perpendicular to the radius of a circle drawn to the point of tangency. Only a 30-60-90 has a hypotenuse (AC) equal to double the length of one of the sides (AB). (You can also use the Pythagorean theorem to show this.) This means that $\angle BAC = 60°$, so the shaded region has a central angle measure of $360° - 60° = 300°$. To get the area, use the proportion $\frac{\text{Central Angle}}{360} = \frac{\text{Sector Area}}{\text{Circle Area}}$, or $\frac{300}{360} = \frac{s}{21}$. Reduce, cross-multiply, and solve to get $s = 17.5$.

14. **E** First, find $g(1)$ by Plugging In 1 for x in $g(x) = x - 3$. So, $g(1) = (1) - 3 = -2$. Next, find $f(-2)$ by Plugging In -2 for x in $f(x) = |x| + 1$. So, $f(-2) = |-2| + 1 = 2 + 1 = 3$. (The bar marks are absolute value, which is the distance from zero on a number line.)

15. **C** Because -3 is less than 0, find $f(-3)$ by Plugging In -3 for x in $f(x) = x^2 + 2$. So, $(-3)^2 + 2 = 9 + 2 = 11$. Because 8 is greater than 0, find $f(8)$ by Plugging In 8 for x in $f(x) = \sqrt{x+1}$. So, $f(8) = \sqrt{8+1} = \sqrt{9} = 3$. *Sum* means to add. So, $11 + 3 = 14$.

12. **B** Since a and b are parallel, and are both tangent to the circle, the distance between a and b is equal to the diameter of circle C. If we let d equal the distance between a and b, we get the equation $d = 3d - 4$, which solves to $d = 2$. Since the diameter of circle C is 2, the radius is 1, and its area $= \pi(1)^2 = \pi$.

16. **D** Start by finding the volume of a sphere with radius 2 cm, to find how much metal is in one sheet. Using the formula supplied by the problem, $V = \frac{4}{3}\pi(2)^3 = \frac{4}{3}\pi \times 8 \approx 33.5$ cubic centimeters. Now find the volume of a sphere with radius 6: $V = \frac{4}{3}\pi(6)^3 = \frac{4}{3}\pi(216) \approx 904.3$ cubic centimeters. Since each metal sheet has a volume of 33.5 cubic centimeters, we need to know how many sheets it would take to make a volume of 904.3 cubic centimeters. $904.3 \div 33.5 \approx 27$, answer choice (D).

17. **4** Plug 5 and d into the equation: $f(5, d) = 9$. So, $(5)^2 - (d)^2 = 9$. So, $25 - d^2 = 9$. Subtract 25 from both sides, then multiply by negative 1 to find $d^2 = 16$. So, $d = \pm 4$. The question asks for the positive value of d. So, $d = 4$.

13. **90** $6^2 + 8^2 = 10^2$. Since this triangle works in the Pythagorean theorem, it is a right triangle, meaning it has a 90-degree angle. (You can also recognize that the sides are in a ratio of 3-4-5.) Since the three angles in any triangle add up to 180 degrees, the right angle must be the largest angle.

10. **C** Factor $x^2 - 6x + 5$ into $(x - 5)(x - 1)$. Factor $2x^2 - 7x + 3$ into $(2x - 1)(x - 3)$. So if their product is equal to zero, that means $(x - 5)(x - 1)(2x - 1)(x - 3) = 0$, or $x = 5, 1, \frac{1}{2}$, or 3. Eliminate A, B, D, and E. Alternatively, you can plug the answer choices into the equations and multiply, but that could take some time.

13. **24** For problems in which you choose one item each from different sources, multiply the number of items in each of the sources together. So, Jon has $3 \times 4 \times 2 = 24$ ways to make omelets.

17. **20** The sum of the angles in triangle *ABD* must be 180. So, $3a + 2a + \angle ABD = 180$. Thus, $\angle ABD = 180 - 5a$. The sum of the angles in triangle *BCF* must be 180. So, $a + 60 + \angle CBF = 180$. Thus, $\angle CBF = 120 - a$. Because $\overline{AC}$ is a line segment $\angle ABD + \angle CBF = 180$. Plug in the angles in terms of a: $(180 - 5a) + (120 - a) = 180$. Combine like terms to find $300 - 6a = 180$. Subtract 300 to find $-6a = -120$. Divide by -6 to find $a = 20$.

18. **D** Find the smallest and largest values for n. Although n has to be an integer, $\sqrt{n}$ doesn't have to be an integer. The smallest value for n is 26, because $5 < \sqrt{26}$. The largest value of n is 80, because $\sqrt{80} < 9$. The sum of 26 and 80 is 106, answer choice (D).

12. **A** Because angles that are opposite sides of equal length are equal, $\angle ABC = \angle BCA = 45$. Because $\angle ADC$ is 90 and $\angle BCA = 45$, triangle *ADC* is a 45:45:90 triangle, with sides in the ratio of $x{:}x{:}x\sqrt{2}$. The side across from the 90-degree side is 4, so $x\sqrt{2} = 4$. Divide by $\sqrt{2}$ to find that $x = \frac{4}{\sqrt{2}} = \frac{4}{\sqrt{2}} \times \frac{\sqrt{2}}{\sqrt{2}} = \frac{4\sqrt{2}}{2} = 2\sqrt{2}$.

14. **B** First, find $g(3)$ by Plugging In 3 for x in $g(x) = x - 1$. So, $g(3) = (3) - 1 = 2$. Next, find $f(2)$ by Plugging In 2 for x in $f(x) = x^2$. So, $(2)^2 = 4$. That means $f(g(3)) = 4$.

20. **D** Draw a line through or close to the points given: (0, 0), (1, 5), (2, 10), (3, 15), (4, 20). Then use POE. The line is linear, not quadratic, so you can eliminate E. It is also clear that the line begins at the origin, so the y-intercept will be 0. This will eliminate A and C. A slope of 25 is far too big—ballpark—so we can eliminate B, leaving D.

17. **A** Since we're dealing with averages, let's draw some Average Pies. First off, we know the total number of days (20) and the average (15), so the total number of computers fixed over the first 20 days is (20×15) 300. After another 10 days, the average goes up to 18, so draw another Average Pie: the average is 18, and the number of days is now 30, so the total number of computers fixed over 30 days is (18×30) 540, meaning that in the last 10 days there were $(540 - 300)$ 240 computers fixed. Draw one last Average Pie, and you'll find there were an average of $(240 \div 10)$ 24 computers fixed over the last 10 days.

20. C We've got variables in the answer choices, which means this is a perfect Plug In problem. Let's make up an easy value for x, such as 2. $9^x + 3^{x+1}$ then becomes $9^2 + 3^{2+1} = 81 + 27 = 108$. We plugged in $x = 2$, so let's use that to find y: $y = 3^x$, so $y = 3^2 = 9$. Now Plug In $y = 9$ to each answer choice, and see which one gives you 108. Answer choice (C) is $y(y + 3)$, which is $9(12) = 108$, which is the answer.

CHAPTER 17

Drill 1
Page 324

1. to
2. of, for
3. by, for
4. of
5. about
6. by
7. over
8. to
9. from

Drill 2
Page 326

1. D The correct idiomatic phrase is "responsible for."

2. C *Where* is an adverb that is being equated with the noun *part.* The blank needs a noun instead. It should say "the best part of the novel was the point at which...."

3. D The phrase *has started* is in the wrong tense. It should be *started.*

4. C In the case of *neither...nor* the verb must agree with the word after *nor.* In this case that is *snow,* which is singular.

5. D When comparing, the phrases should be parallel. So *running a marathon* should be *to run a marathon.* Changing *to box* to *boxing* would also be correct, but this is not an option.

6. D When using the phrase *not only...but also* the phrases following those terms must be parallel. Since *improving* is the wrong form of the verb when it's in the future perfect tense (when combined with the word "will"), you must change *improving* to *improve.*

Drill 3
Pages 335–336

1. **B** The word *blind* modifies *stumbled.* Since adjectives modify only nouns and adverbs modify everything else, *blind* should be *blindly.*

2. **E**

3. **E**

4. **D** The phrase should be "between you and me."

5. **B** The word *clear* modifies *think.* Again, adjectives modify only nouns, so you need an adverb here. *Clear* should be *clearly.*

6. **B** *Was completed* refers to *chores,* which is plural. So *was completed* should contain the plural form of the verb: "were completed."

7. **D** The simplest, most straightforward answer is D.

8. **B** The phrase *would have soon become* is incorrect. The best answer is B.

9. **C** The conjunction *since* doesn't work within the sentence. It should be *but.* Answer B is unnecessarily long. Answer E contains an -ing word, which is incorrect—and one of ETS's favorite kinds of wrong answers. The best answer is C.

10. **B** The sentence as is contains a run-on. *It was used only in rural areas at first* can stand alone as a sentence. Answer C changes the meaning of the sentence. Answer D contains an ambiguous pronoun (*it*). Answer E also changes the meaning of the sentence. The best answer is B.

11. **B** When using the phrase *either...or* the phrases after each word should be parallel. B is short, direct, and has a correct parallelism.

12. **E** *They* is a pronoun that refers to the term *mach,* which is singular. Eliminate A, B, and D. Also, the sentence talks about what *mach* refers to, not what *mach* is. The best answer is E.

Drill 4
Page 343

1. **B** The current sentence is incorrect because *they are called graphic novels* can stand alone as a sentence. C, D, and E are all in the wrong tense; C is also unnecessarily wordy. B is the clearest, best answer.

2. **E** The first paragraph talks about comic books and starts off by mentioning kids. So the best topic for a previous paragraph would be one that includes both of those things. The best answer is E.

3. **C** Sentence 3 talks about comic books in Europe while Sentence 4 talks about comic books in the United States. This is a good break. The best answer is C.

4. **E** The first sentence talks about those who dismiss comic books. So the *you* would best refer to those who dismiss them. The best answer is E.

5. **D** The word *birth* refers to comic book characters. The best word to replace it is *creation*. The best answer is D.

6. **A** Since the comic books are what generates the money, answer A is the shortest and clearest way to combine those two sentences.

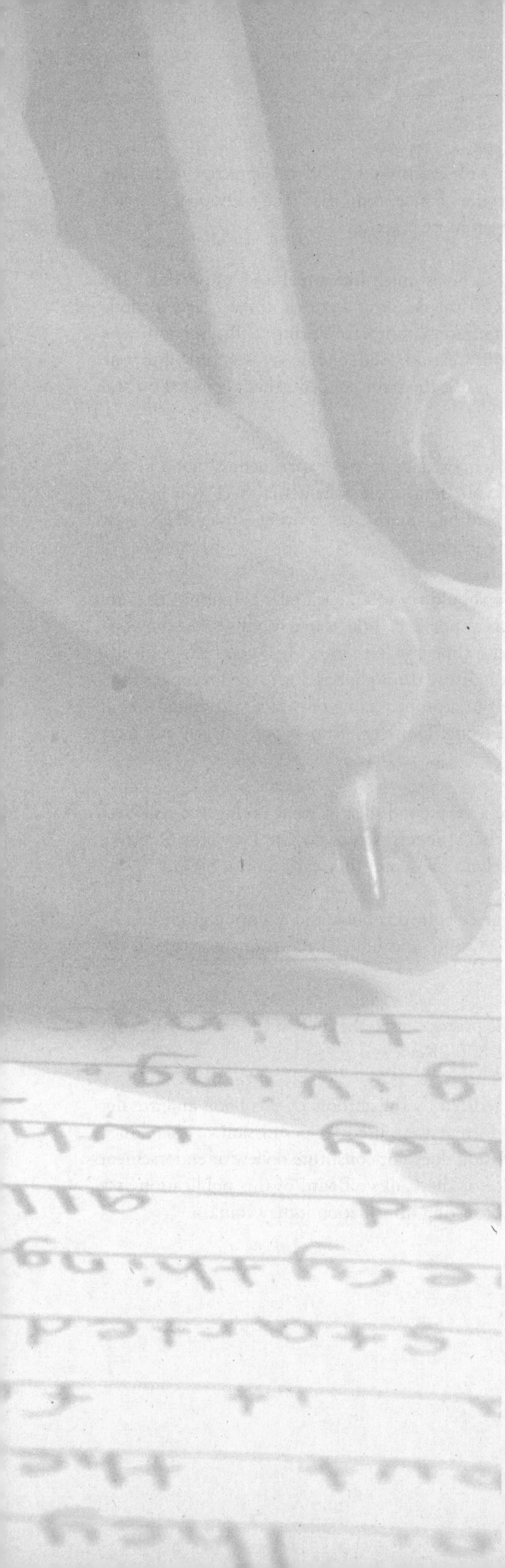

Part VII
The Princeton Review SAT Practice Tests and Explanations

Keep Working
It is difficult to tell if a section is experimental, so you should treat all of the sections as if they count toward your score.

The best way to learn our techniques for cracking the SAT is to practice them. The following practice tests will give you a chance to do that. The additional practice tests on our website will provide even more practice.

These practice tests were designed to be as much like a real SAT as possible. The tests in this book contain three Critical Reading sections, three Math sections, three Writing sections (one 25-minute Grammar/Writing Skills section, one 10-minute Grammar/Writing Skills section, and one Essay section), and one Experimental section. Our questions test the same concepts that are tested on real SATs.

Because one of the sections in each practice test is experimental, none of the questions in it will count toward your final score. The actual SAT will have an Experimental section—critical reading, math, or writing—that ETS now euphemistically terms an "equating section."

When you take a practice test, you should try to take it under conditions that are as much like real testing conditions as possible. Take it in a room where you won't be disturbed, and have someone else time you. (It's too easy if you time yourself.) You can give yourself a brief break halfway through, but don't stop for longer than five minutes or so. To put yourself in a proper frame of mind, you might take it on a weekend morning. One more thing: Don't use scrap paper; you will not have any when you take the real SAT.

After taking our tests, you'll have a very good idea of what taking the real SAT will be like. In fact, we've found that students' scores on The Princeton Review's practice tests correspond very closely to the scores they earn on real SATs.

The answers to the questions on the tests in this book and a scoring guide can be found beginning on pages 444, 524, 606, and 680. The answer sheets are in the back of the book.

If you have any questions about the practice tests, the SAT, ETS, or The Princeton Review, give us a call, toll-free, at 1-800-2Review.

The following practice tests were written by the authors of this book and are not actual SATs. The directions and format were used by permission of the Educational Testing Service. This permission does not constitute review or endorsement by the Educational Testing Service or the College Board of this publication as a whole or of any sample questions or testing information it may contain.

HOW TO SCORE YOUR SAT PRACTICE TESTS

This book includes three practice tests. You can figure out your score on each of these tests with the same formula used by the College Board:

> # of questions you get correct – (# of questions you get incorrect ÷ 4) = raw score

The College Board then takes your raw score, along with the raw score of every other test taker in the country, and figures out a curve. Finally, it assigns each raw score to a number on a scale from 200 to 800. This is your scaled score.

NOTE: Each practice test contains an unidentified, unscored section that simulates the Experimental section on the real SAT. Questions from these sections are NOT included when calculating your raw or scaled scores.

To figure out your scaled score for each subject, use the scoring worksheet that follows each SAT practice test. Let's look at the subjects one at a time:

Writing

Step One Count up the number of your correct answers for the two multiple-choice Writing sections. This is the number that goes in the first box.

Step Two Count up the number of your incorrect answers for the multiple-choice Writing sections. Divide this number by 4, and place this number in the second box.

Step Three Subtract the second number from the first. This is your Grammar raw score. This is the number that goes in the third box.

Step Four Look up the number from the third box in the Writing Multiple-Choice Subscore Conversion Table. This is your Grammar scaled subscore.

Step Five The essay is scored on a scale from 2–12. It is based upon the score that two graders give you, each on a scale from 1–6. Be sure to register at **PrincetonReview.com/cracking** to gain access to our LiveGrader™ Service. Your essay can be scored by our graders there. Take your 2–12 grade and double it so that it is from 4–24. This is the number that goes in the fourth box.

Step Six Add the fourth box to the third. This is your raw score. This number goes in the fifth box.

Step Seven Look up the number from the fifth box in the SAT Score Conversion Table. This is your scaled score.

Critical Reading

Step One Count up the number of your correct answers for the three Critical Reading sections of the test. This is the number that goes in the first box.

Step Two Count up the number of your incorrect answers for the three Critical Reading sections of the test. Divide this number by 4. This is the number that goes in the second box.

Step Three Subtract the second number from the first. This is your raw score. This is the number that goes in the third box.

Step Four Look up the number from the third box in the SAT Score Conversion Table. This is your scaled score.

Math

Step One Count up the number of correct grid-in answers. This is the number that goes in the first box.

Step Two Count up the number of your correct answers for the multiple-choice questions in the three Math sections of the test. This is the number that goes in the second box.

Step Three Count up the number of your incorrect answers for the multiple-choice questions in the three Math sections of the test. **Do NOT include any grid-in questions you may have answered incorrectly.** Divide this number by 4 and place this number in the third box.

Step Four Subtract the third number from the second, then add the first number. This is your raw score. This is the number that goes in the fourth box.

Step Five Look up the number from the fourth box in the SAT Score Conversion Table. This is your scaled score.

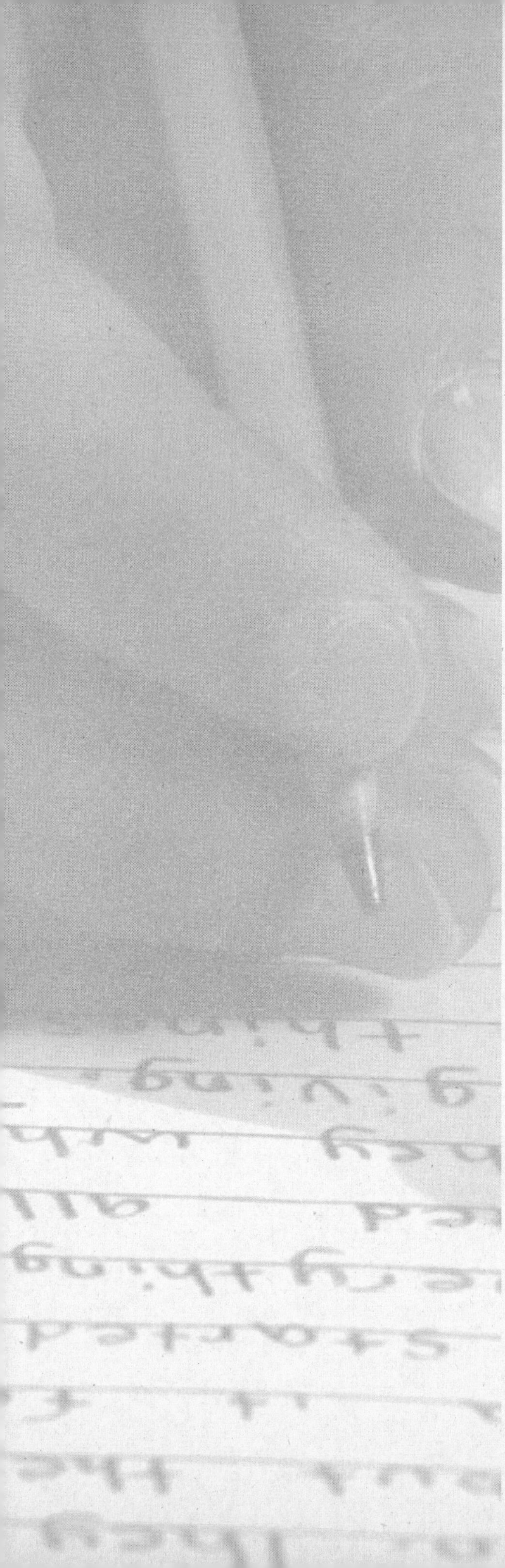

Chapter 19
Practice Test 1

SECTION 1
ESSAY
Time — 25 minutes

Turn to Section 1 of your answer sheet to write your essay.

The essay gives you an opportunity to show how effectively you can develop and express ideas. You should, therefore, take care to develop your point of view, present your ideas logically and clearly, and use language precisely.

Your essay must be written on the lines provided on your answer sheet—you will receive no other paper on which to write. You will have enough space if you write on every line, avoid wide margins, and keep your handwriting to a reasonable size. Remember that people who are not familiar with your handwriting will read what you write. Try to write or print so that what you are writing is legible to those readers.

You have twenty-five minutes to write an essay on the topic assigned below. DO NOT WRITE ON ANOTHER TOPIC. AN OFF-TOPIC ESSAY WILL RECEIVE A SCORE OF ZERO.

Think carefully about the issue presented in the following excerpt and the assignment below.

> No great man lives in vain. The history of the world is but the biography of great men.
> Adapted from Thomas Carlyle, "The Hero as Divinity"
> In historic events, the so-called great men are labels giving names to events, and like labels they have but the smallest connection with the event itself.
> Adapted from Leo Tolstoy, *War and Peace*

Assignment: Can the daily actions of average people have a significant impact on the course of history? Plan and write an essay in which you develop your point of view on this issue. Support your position with reasoning and examples taken from your reading, studies, experience, or observations.

DO NOT WRITE YOUR ESSAY IN YOUR TEST BOOK. You will receive credit only for what you write on your answer sheet.

BEGIN WRITING YOUR ESSAY ON PAGE 3 OF THE ANSWER SHEET (FOUND AT THE BACK OF THE BOOK).

STOP

If you finish before time is called, you may check your work on this section only. Do not turn to any other section in the test.

SECTION 2
Time — 25 minutes
20 Questions

Turn to Section 2 of your answer sheet to answer the questions in this section.

Directions: For this section, solve each problem and decide which is the best of the choices given. Fill in the corresponding circle on the answer sheet. You may use any available space for scratchwork.

Notes

1. The use of a calculator is permitted.
2. All numbers used are real numbers.
3. Figures that accompany problems in this test are intended to provide information useful in solving the problems. They are drawn as accurately as possible EXCEPT when it is stated in a specific problem that the figure is not drawn to scale. All figures lie in a plane unless other wise indicated.
4. Unless otherwise specified, the domain of any function f is assumed to be the set of all real numbers x for which $f(x)$ is a real number.

Reference Information

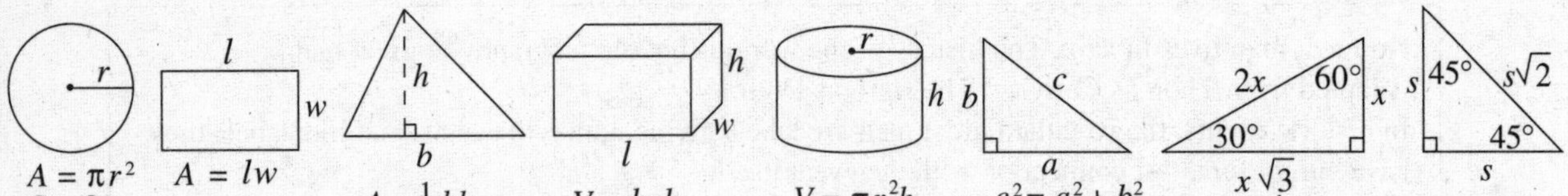

$A = \pi r^2$
$C = 2\pi r$

$A = lw$

$A = \frac{1}{2}bh$

$V = lwh$

$V = \pi r^2 h$

$c^2 = a^2 + b^2$

Special Right Triangles

The number of degrees of arc in a circle is 360.

The sum of the measures in degrees of the angles of a triangle is 180.

1. Andrea subscribed to four publications that cost $12.90, $16.00, $18.00, and $21.90 per year, respectively. If she made an initial payment of one-half of the total yearly subscription cost, and paid the rest in four equal monthly payments, how much was each of the four monthly payments?

(A) $8.60
(B) $9.20
(C) $9.45
(D) $17.20
(E) $34.40

2. If $\frac{2x}{x^2+1} = \frac{2}{x+2}$, what is the value of x ?

(A) $-\frac{1}{4}$

(B) $\frac{1}{4}$

(C) $\frac{1}{2}$

(D) 0

(E) 2

GO ON TO THE NEXT PAGE

3. A survey of Town X found an average (arithmetic mean) of 3.2 persons per household and a mean of 1.2 televisions per household. If 48,000 people live in Town X, how many televisions are in Town X ?

(A) 15,000
(B) 16,000
(C) 18,000
(D) 40,000
(E) 57,600

If I do not have any flour, I am not able to make cookies.

4. If the statement above is true, which of the following statements must be true?

(A) If I did not make cookies, I must not have had flour.
(B) If I made cookies, I must have had flour.
(C) If I have flour, I must be able to make cookies.
(D) If I was able to make cookies, I must not have had any flour.
(E) If I am not able to make cookies, I must not have any flour.

5. Let the function f be defined such that $f(x) = x^2 - c$, where c is a constant. If $f(-2) = 6$, what is the value of c?

(A) −10
(B) −2
(C) 0
(D) 2
(E) 6

6. If $9b = 81$, then $\sqrt{b} \times \sqrt[3]{3b} =$

(A) 9
(B) 27
(C) 81
(D) 243
(E) 729

GO ON TO THE NEXT PAGE

7. What is the diameter of a circle with a circumference of 5 ?

(A) $\frac{5}{\pi}$

(B) $\frac{10}{\pi}$

(C) 5

(D) 5π

(E) 10π

8. If the product of (1 + 2), (2 + 3), and (3 + 4) is equal to one-half the sum of 20 and x, what is the value of x ?

(A) 10
(B) 85
(C) 105
(D) 190
(E) 1,210

9. If $\sqrt{x} = 2^2$, then $x =$

(A) 1
(B) 2
(C) 4
(D) 8
(E) 16

MERCHANDISE SALES

Type	Amount of Sales	Percent of Total Sales
Shoes	$12,000	15%
Coats	$20,000	25%
Shirts	x	40%
Pants	y	20%

10. According to the table above, $x + y =$

(A) $32,000
(B) $48,000
(C) $60,000
(D) $68,000
(E) $80,000

GO ON TO THE NEXT PAGE

Note: Figure not drawn to scale.

11. If $AB > CD$, which of the following must be true?

I. $AB > BC$
II. $AC > BD$
III. $AC > CD$

(A) I only
(B) II only
(C) III only
(D) II and III only
(E) I, II, and III

12. If $f(x) = |(|x| - 3)|$, what is the value of $f(1)$?

(A) −2
(B) −1
(C) 1
(D) 2
(E) 3

13. A researcher found that the number of bacteria in a certain sample doubles every hour. If there were 6 bacteria in the sample at the start of the experiment, how many bacteria were there after 9 hours?

(A) 54
(B) 512
(C) 1,536
(D) 3,072
(E) 6,144

14. If $f(x) = x^2 + 2$, which of the following could be a value of $f(x)$?

(A) −2
(B) −1
(C) 0
(D) 1
(E) 2

GO ON TO THE NEXT PAGE

15. How many numbers from 1 to 200 inclusive are equal to the cube of an integer?

(A) One
(B) Two
(C) Three
(D) Four
(E) Five

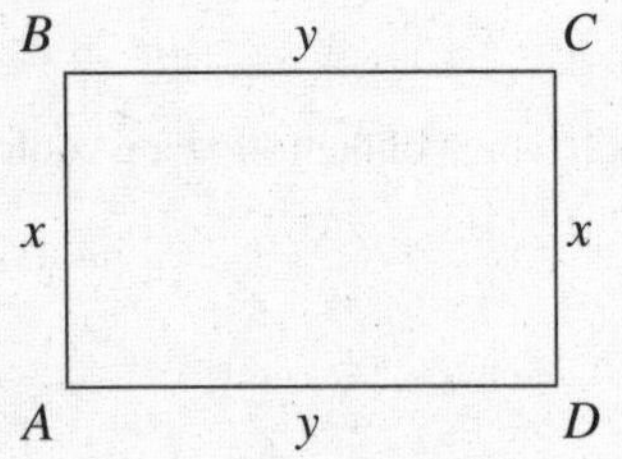

16. If the perimeter of rectangle *ABCD* is equal to *p*, and $x = \frac{2}{3}y$, what is the value of *y* in terms of *p* ?

(A) $\frac{p}{10}$

(B) $\frac{3p}{10}$

(C) $\frac{p}{3}$

(D) $\frac{2p}{5}$

(E) $\frac{3p}{5}$

17. A basketball team had a ratio of wins to losses of 3:1. After the team won six games in a row, its ratio of wins to losses became 5:1. How many games had the team won <u>before</u> winning six games in a row?

(A) 3
(B) 6
(C) 9
(D) 15
(E) 24

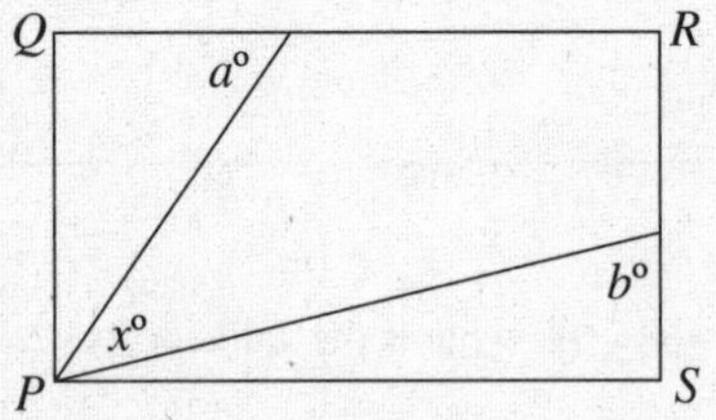

18. In rectangle *PQRS* above, what is $a + b$ in terms of x ?

(A) $90 + x$
(B) $90 - x$
(C) $180 + x$
(D) $270 - x$
(E) $360 - x$

GO ON TO THE NEXT PAGE

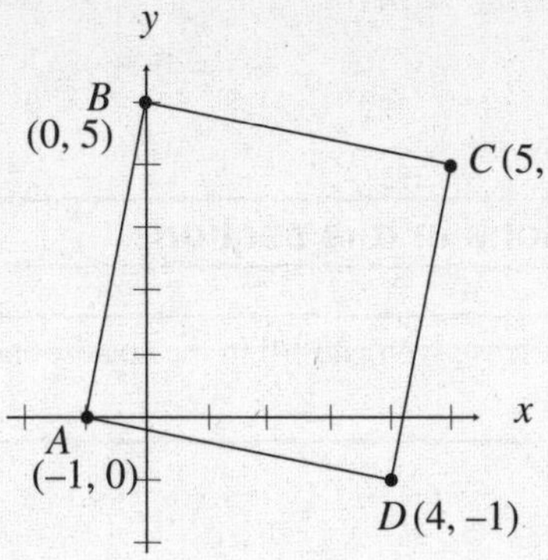

19. What is the area of square *ABCD* ?

(A) 25
(B) $18\sqrt{2}$
(C) 26
(D) $25+\sqrt{2}$
(E) 36

20. A square is inscribed in a circle with radius *r*. What is the probability that a randomly selected point within the circle will NOT be within the square?

(A) $\dfrac{\pi-2}{\pi r^2}$

(B) $\dfrac{\pi-2}{\pi}$

(C) $\dfrac{\pi-\frac{1}{2}}{\pi}$

(D) $\dfrac{1-r}{\pi}$

(E) $\dfrac{r}{\pi}$

STOP

If you finish before time is called, you may check your work on this section only. Do not turn to any other section in the test.

SECTION 3
Time — 25 minutes
24 Questions

Turn to Section 3 of your answer sheet to answer the questions in this section.

Directions: For each question in this section, select the best answer from among the choices given and fill in the corresponding circle on the answer sheet.

Each sentence below has one or two blanks, each blank indicating that something has been omitted. Beneath the sentence are five words or sets of words labeled A through E. Choose the word or set of words that, when inserted in the sentence, best fits the meaning of the sentence as a whole.

Example:

Desiring to ------- his taunting friends, Mitch gave them taffy in hopes it would keep their mouths shut.

(A) eliminate (B) satisfy (C) overcome (D) ridicule (E) silence

Ⓐ Ⓑ Ⓒ Ⓓ ●

1. To prevent household fires, all flammable liquids, oily rags, and other ------- materials should be properly disposed of.

(A) combustible (B) unctuous (C) restricted (D) diluted (E) extinguishable

2. Mark was intent on maintaining his status as first in his class; because even the smallest mistakes infuriated him, he reviewed all his papers ------- before submitting them to his teacher.

(A) explicitly (B) hastily (C) honestly (D) unconsciously (E) meticulously

3. Because Jenkins neither ------- nor defends either side in the labor dispute, both parties admire his journalistic -------.

(A) criticizes . . vitality
(B) attacks . . neutrality
(C) confronts . . aptitude
(D) dismisses . . flair
(E) protects . . integrity

4. It is ironic that the ------- insights of the great thinkers are voiced so often that they have become mere -------.

(A) original . . clichés
(B) banal . . beliefs
(C) dubious . . habits
(D) philosophical . . questions
(E) abstract . . assessments

5. Some anthropologists claim that a few apes have been taught to communicate using rudimentary sign language, but skeptics argue that the apes are only ------- their trainers.

(A) emulating (B) condoning (C) instructing (D) acknowledging (E) belaboring

6. Most people imagine organ fugues to be ------- and -------, due to their technical difficulty and challenging counterpoint.

(A) diminutive . . uplifting
(B) harmonious . . petrifying
(C) daunting . . esoteric
(D) cacophonous . . enchanting
(E) inscrutable . . classical

7. Since many disadvantaged individuals view their situations as ------- as well as intolerable, their attitudes can best be described as -------.

(A) squalid . . obscure
(B) unpleasant . . bellicose
(C) acute . . sanguine
(D) inalterable . . resigned
(E) political . . perplexed

8. Only when one actually visits the ancient ruins of marvelous bygone civilizations does one truly appreciate the sad ------- of human greatness.

(A) perspicacity (B) magnitude (C) artistry (D) transience (E) quiescence

GO ON TO THE NEXT PAGE

Directions: Each passage below is followed by questions based on its content. Answer the questions on the basis of what is stated or implied in each passage and in any introductory material that may be provided.

Questions 9–10 are based on the following passage.

Many of the techniques recommended to relieve writer's block actually involve writing. Exercises such as brainstorming and clustering are meant to loosen up the writer and unstop pent-up creativity. But what if the root of the problem were neurological? Recent research on the antipodal condition of hypergraphia has shown that the overwhelming desire to write is a side effect of temporal lobe epilepsy. Located in the area near the ear on both sides of the brain, the temporal lobes control hearing, speech, and memory—all crucial to the task of communicating. Writer's block is usually accompanied by depression, which is said to mimic frontal lobe impairment.

9. The question posed by the author in lines 4–5 serves to

(A) criticize traditional therapies for writer's block
(B) reflect on the information provided earlier in the passage
(C) transition into a new perspective on understanding writer's block
(D) introduce more information on neurological disorders
(E) highlight the contrast between the two problems

10. The author's primary purpose in the passage is to

(A) compare two problems faced by writers
(B) present a possible cause of writer's block
(C) provide detailed information about the temporal lobe
(D) question current therapeutic techniques for writing problems
(E) describe the side effects of epilepsy

Questions 11–12 are based on the following passage.

Paris is a circular city divided into 20 sectors called *arrondissements*, which spiral out from the center of the city. Romans inhabited the islands that make up the heart of Paris in the first century A.D. and built a wall to protect their territory. New walls were built in concentric circles as the city expanded, the sites of which were transformed into some of today's streets. The first twelve *arrondissements* were laid out by 1795 and the surrounding suburban areas were annexed in 1860 to add eight more.

11. The tone and content of the passage is most appropriate for which of the following?

(A) An urban planning proposal
(B) A traveler's guidebook
(C) A satire magazine
(D) An art history textbook
(E) A book of Roman history

12. According to the passage, which of the following has most influenced the layout of Paris?

(A) The decreasing population of the city
(B) The ritual importance of the spiral symbol
(C) A need for defense
(D) Roman experiments in solid geometry
(E) The desire to improve upon Roman architectural styles

GO ON TO THE NEXT PAGE

Questions 13–24 are based on the following passage.

The following passage is an excerpt from nineteenth-century British explorer David Livingston's memoirs of his journeys to Africa.

The Expedition left England on the 10th of March, 1858, in Her Majesty's Colonial Steamer "Pearl," commanded by Captain Duncan; and, after enjoying the generous hospitality of our friends at Cape Town, with the obliging attentions of Sir George Grey, and receiving on board Mr. Francis Skead, R.N., as surveyor, we reached the East Coast in the following May.

Our first object was to explore the Zambesi, its mouths and tributaries, with a view to their being used as highways for commerce and Christianity to pass into the vast interior of Africa. When we came within five or six miles of the land, the yellowish-green tinge of the sea in soundings was suddenly succeeded by muddy water with wrack, as of a river in flood. The two colours did not intermingle, but the line of contact was as sharply defined as when the ocean meets the land. It was observed that under the wrack—consisting of reeds, sticks, and leaves—and even under floating cuttlefish bones and Portuguese "men-of-war" (Physalia), numbers of small fish screen themselves from the eyes of birds of prey, and from the rays of the torrid sun.

The Zambesi pours its waters into the ocean by four mouths, namely, the Milambe, which is the most westerly, the Kongone, the Luabo, and the Timbwe (or Muselo). After the examination of three branches by the able and energetic surveyor, Francis Skead, R.N., the Kongone was found to be the best entrance. The immense amount of sand brought down by the Zambesi has in the course of ages formed a sort of promontory, against which the long swell of the Indian Ocean, beating during the prevailing winds, has formed bars, which, acting against the waters of the delta, may have led to their exit sideways. The Kongone is one of those lateral branches, and safest, inasmuch as the bar has nearly two fathoms on it at low water, and the rise at spring tides is from twelve to fourteen feet. The bar is narrow, the passage nearly straight, and, were it buoyed and a beacon placed on Pearl Island, would always be safe to a steamer. When the wind is from the east or north, the bar is smooth; if from the south and south-east, it has a heavy break on it, and is not to be attempted in boats. A strong current setting to the east when the tide is flowing, and to the west when ebbing, may drag a boat or ship into the breakers. If one is doubtful of his longitude and runs east, he will soon see the land at Timbwe disappear away to the north; and coming west again, he can easily make out East Luabo from its great size; and Kongone follows several miles west. East Luabo has a good but long bar, and not to be attempted unless the wind be north-east or east. It has sometimes been called "Barra Catrina," and was used in the embarkations of slaves. This may have been the "River of Good Signs," of Vasco de Gama, as the mouth is more easily seen from the seaward than any other; but the absence of the pillar dedicated by that navigator to "St. Raphael," leaves the matter in doubt. No Portuguese live within eighty miles of any mouth of the Zambesi.

The Kongone is five miles east of the Milambe, or western branch, and seven miles west from East Luabo, which again is five miles from the Timbwe. We saw but few natives, and these, by escaping from their canoes into the mangrove thickets the moment they caught sight of us, gave unmistakeable indications that they did not have a very favourable opinion of white men. They were probably fugitives from Portuguese slavery. In the grassy glades buffaloes, wart-hogs, and three kinds of antelope were abundant, and the latter easily obtained. A few hours' hunting usually provided venison enough for a score of men for several days.

13. The passage provides the most information about which aspect of Livingston's journey?

(A) The people he met
(B) The colors of the surrounding environment
(C) The time he spent in Africa
(D) The river system on which he traveled
(E) The type of food available

14. According to the passage, Livingston explored the Zambesi primarily in order to

(A) map the course of the river and its tributaries
(B) attempt to make contact with the Portuguese settlers that live along it
(C) find a safe route along the coast of Africa
(D) determine whether the waterway could be used for trade
(E) be the first to survey a new land

15. As used in the passage, the word "torrid" (line 20) most nearly means

(A) pleasant
(B) frightening
(C) hurried
(D) hidden
(E) scorching

GO ON TO THE NEXT PAGE

16. It may be inferred from the discussion of the bar in the Kongone River that

(A) under certain wind conditions, a ship traveling over the bar would most likely pass safely
(B) a beacon will soon be built on Pearl Island to help guide ships over the bar
(C) if the wind comes from the east or south, the bar in the Kongone River will be smooth
(D) of all the rivers in Africa, the Kongone is the best way of reaching the interior of Africa
(E) ships should not attempt to travel the Kongone unless the wind is from the northeast

17. According to the passage, a strong current on the Kongone

(A) may, depending on the tide, increase the danger to a boat traveling along the river
(B) will make the river impassable to most ships
(C) increases the water level from two fathoms to twelve to fourteen feet
(D) led de Gama to name the river the "Barra Catrina"
(E) caused an immense amount of sand to form a promontory in the river

18. The author most likely mentions Vasco de Gama (line 49) in order to

(A) indicate that other explorers have already charted the course of the river
(B) refer to a previous navigator that Livingston admires
(C) demonstrate a possible connection between Livingston's expedition and that of a another navigator
(D) explain why no Portuguese live within eighty miles of the river
(E) reveal why there is a pillar dedicated to St. Raphael at the mouth of the river

19. The tone of the passage may best be described as

(A) disinterested
(B) enthusiastic
(C) passionate
(D) personally revealing
(E) objective

20. The mention of the natives in the final paragraph suggests that

(A) most of the inhabitants of Africa do not have a favorable view of Livingston
(B) the people Livingston encountered had little interest in making contact with him
(C) there were not many people living along the rivers that Livingston explored
(D) the Portuguese had enslaved a great many of the native inhabitants of Africa
(E) the native inhabitants were upset by the arrival of Livingston

21. The primary function of the first paragraph is to

(A) give the reader a glimpse into Livingston's private life
(B) establish Livingston's personal characteristics and skills as an explorer
(C) provide a brief prelude to the later details in the passage
(D) emphasize the lackadaisical nature of Livingston and his companions
(E) explain why Livingston was in Africa

GO ON TO THE NEXT PAGE

22. The passage lists which of the following as a factor in Livingston's designation as Kongone as the "best" entrance to the Zambesi for boat travel?

(A) The ease with which a boat can travel on the river, regardless of the current or the wind direction
(B) The abundant food, including antelope and buffalo, that can be found along the banks of the river
(C) The lack of native inhabitants living near the river
(D) The presence of prominent land features that make it easy for a navigator to find the Kongone
(E) The beacon placed on Pearl Island

23. Based on the passage, which of the following may be properly inferred about the Kongone?

(A) The waters of the Kongone are home to a large variety of cuttlefish and small fish.
(B) The water levels in the Kongone change significantly with the tides.
(C) The Kongone is the most westerly of the four mouths of the Zambesi.
(D) The Kongone has the smoothest bar of any of the mouths of the Zambesi.
(E) The Kongone was often used by the Portuguese for the disembarkation of slaves.

24. The passage states that East Luabo offers which advantage to navigators?

(A) Of the tributaries of the Zambesi, it is the most prominent to a viewer approaching from the sea.
(B) No Portuguese live within eighty miles of East Luabo.
(C) Its bar is safe to boaters under most conditions.
(D) East Luabo is more familiar to European navigators than the other mouths of the Zambesi.
(E) It is the only tributary of the Zambesi that had previously been charted.

STOP

If you finish before time is called, you may check your work on this section only.
Do not turn to any other section in the test.

NO TEST MATERIAL ON THIS PAGE.

SECTION 4
Time — 25 minutes
20 Questions

Turn to Section 4 of your answer sheet to answer the questions in this section.

Directions: For this section, solve each problem and decide which is the best of the choices given. Fill in the corresponding circle on the answer sheet. You may use any available space for scratchwork.

Notes

1. The use of a calculator is permitted.
2. All numbers used are real numbers.
3. Figures that accompany problems in this test are intended to provide information useful in solving the problems. They are drawn as accurately as possible EXCEPT when it is stated in a specific problem that the figure is not drawn to scale. All figures lie in a plane unless other wise indicated.
4. Unless otherwise specified, the domain of any function f is assumed to be the set of all real numbers x for which $f(x)$ is a real number.

Reference Information

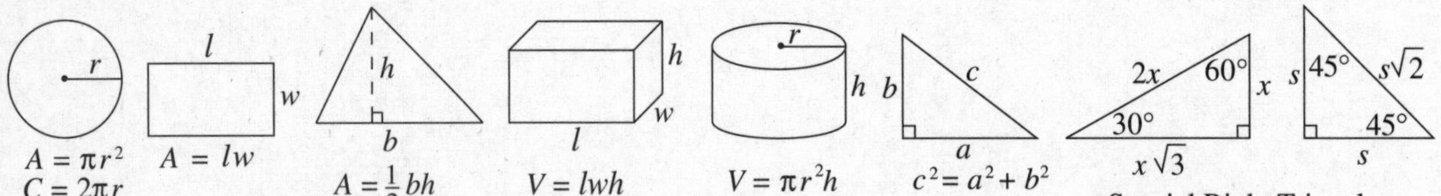

$A = \pi r^2$ $C = 2\pi r$ $A = lw$ $A = \frac{1}{2}bh$ $V = lwh$ $V = \pi r^2 h$ $c^2 = a^2 + b^2$

Special Right Triangles

The number of degrees of arc in a circle is 360.

The sum of the measures in degrees of the angles of a triangle is 180.

1. If $2 + a = 2 - a$, what is the value of a ?

(A) -1
(B) 0
(C) 1
(D) 2
(E) 4

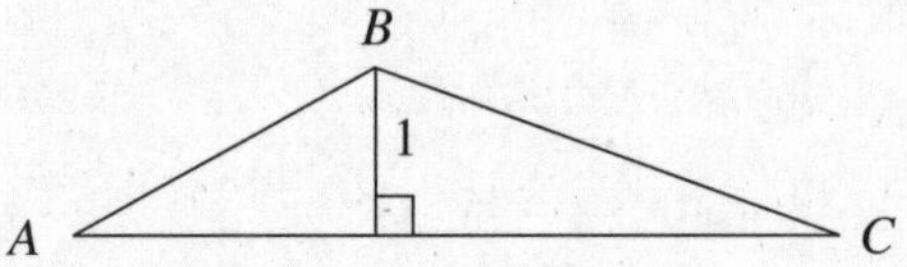

2. If $AC = 4$, what is the area of ABC above?

(A) $\frac{1}{2}$

(B) 2

(C) $\sqrt{7}$

(D) 4

(E) 8

GO ON TO THE NEXT PAGE

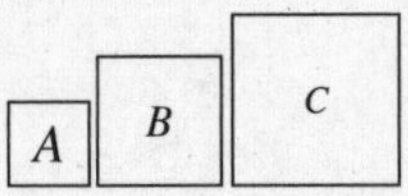

3. In the figure above, the perimeter of square A is $\frac{2}{3}$ the perimeter of square B, and the perimeter of square B is $\frac{2}{3}$ the perimeter of square C. If the area of square A is 16, what is the area of square C ?

(A) 24
(B) 36
(C) 64
(D) 72
(E) 81

4. A bakery uses a special flour mixture that contains corn, wheat, and rye in the ratio of 3:5:2. If a bag of the mixture contains 5 pounds of rye, how many pounds of wheat does it contain?

(A) 2
(B) 5
(C) 7.5
(D) 10
(E) 12.5

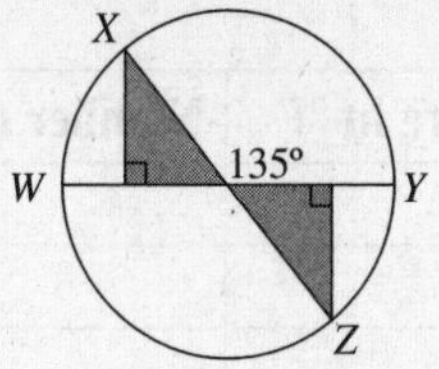

5. If $\overline{WY}$ and $\overline{XZ}$ are diameters with lengths of 12, what is the area of the shaded region?

(A) 36
(B) 30
(C) 18
(D) 12
(E) 9

6. If the product of x and y is 76, and x is twice the square of y, which of the following pairs of equations could be used to determine the values of x and y?

(A) $xy = 76$
$x = 2y^2$
(B) $xy = 76$
$x = (2y)^2$
(C) $x + y = 76$
$x = 4y^2$
(D) $x + y = 76$
$x = 4y$
(E) $xy = 76$
$x = 2y$

GO ON TO THE NEXT PAGE

Temperature in °F	Number of Customers
10	4
20	9
30	37
40	66
50	100

7. A coffee shop noticed that the outside temperature affected the number of customers who came to the shop that day, as shown in the table above. Which of the following graphs best represents the relationship between the outside temperature and the number of customers, as indicated by the table?

(A)

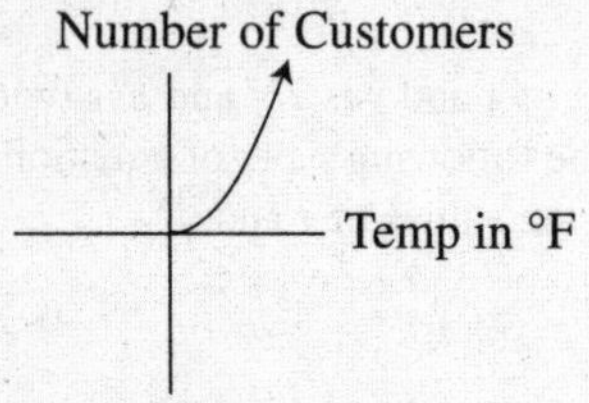

(B)

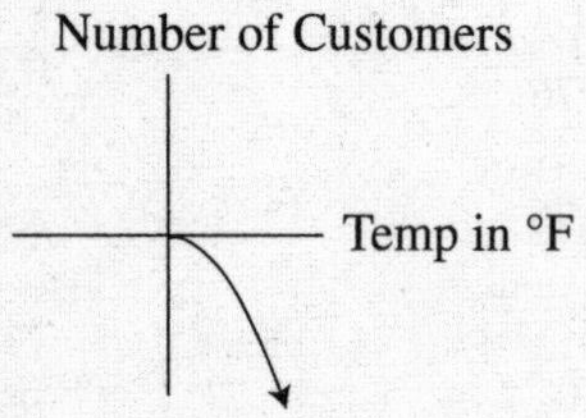

(C)

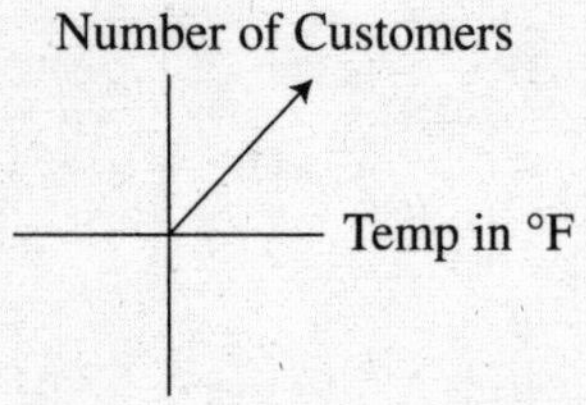

(D)

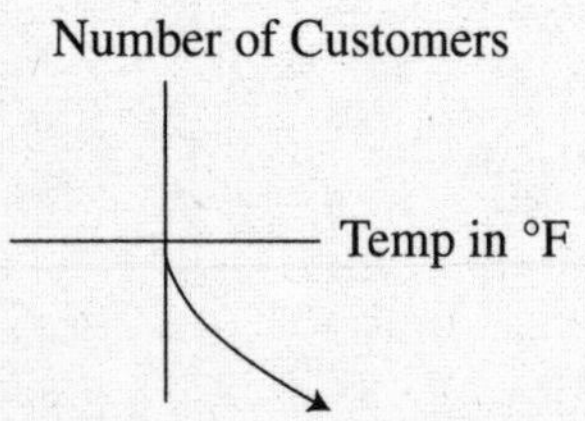

(E)

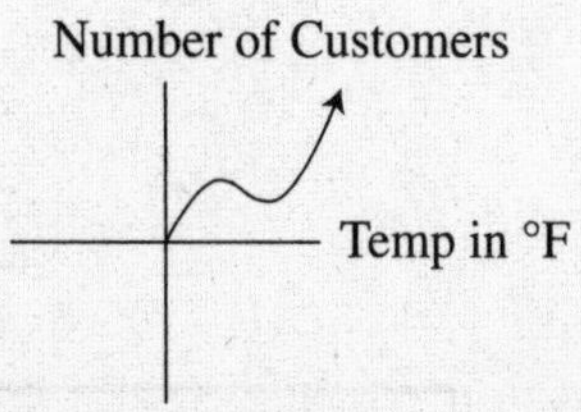

8. If c is positive, what percent of $3c$ is 9 ?

(A) $\frac{c}{100}\%$

(B) $\frac{c}{3}\%$

(C) $\frac{9}{c}\%$

(D) 3%

(E) $\frac{300}{c}\%$

D (–6, 3)

E (–1, –1)

F (–1, 3)

9. The coordinates of points D, E, and F in the xy-plane are given above. What is the perimeter of ΔDEF ?

(A) 12

(B) 20

(C) $9+\sqrt{17}$ (approximately 13.12)

(D) $9+\sqrt{41}$ (approximately 15.40)

(E) $\sqrt{150}$ (approximately 12.25)

GO ON TO THE NEXT PAGE

10. Fifteen percent of the coins in a piggy bank are nickels and five percent are dimes. If there are 220 coins in the bank, how many are <u>not</u> nickels or dimes?

(A) 80
(B) 176
(C) 180
(D) 187
(E) 200

11. At the beginning of 1999, the population of Rockville was 204,000 and the population of Springfield was 216,000. If the population of each city increased by exactly 20% in 1999, how many more people lived in Springfield than in Rockville at the end of 1999 ?

(A) 2,400
(B) 10,000
(C) 12,000
(D) 14,400
(E) 43,200

12. If $x + y = z$ and $x = y$, then all of the following are true EXCEPT

(A) $2x + 2y = 2z$

(B) $x - y = 0$

(C) $x - z = y - z$

(D) $x = \frac{z}{2}$

(E) $z - y = 2x$

13. In a list of seven integers, 13 is the lowest member, 37 is the highest member, the mean is 23, the median is 24, and the mode is 18. If the numbers 8 and 43 are then included in the list, which of the following will change?

I. The mean
II. The median
III. The mode

(A) I only
(B) I and II only
(C) I and III only
(D) II and III only
(E) I, II, and III

GO ON TO THE NEXT PAGE

14. If $|x| \neq 0$, which of the following statements must be true?

(A) x is positive.

(B) $2x$ is positive.

(C) $\frac{1}{x}$ is positive.

(D) x^2 is positive.

(E) x^3 is positive.

15. Rock climbing routes are rated on a numbered scale with the highest number representing the most difficult route. Sally tried a range of shoe sizes on each of several routes of varying difficulty and found that when she wore smaller shoes, she could climb routes of greater difficulty. If D represents the difficulty rating of a route Sally successfully climbed and s represents the size of the shoes she wore on such a route, then which of the following could express D as a function of s ?

(A) $D(s) = s^2$

(B) $D(s) = \sqrt{s}$

(C) $D(s) = 4s$

(D) $D(s) = s - 3.5$

(E) $D(s) = \frac{45}{s}$

16. If $a^2b = 12^2$, and b is an odd integer, then a could be divisible by all of the following EXCEPT

(A) 3
(B) 4
(C) 6
(D) 9
(E) 12

17. An equilateral triangle has sides of length x. If a second equillateral triangle has sides of length $2x$, what is the ratio of the area of the first triangle to the area of the second?

(A) $1 : 16$
(B) $\sqrt{3} : 2$
(C) $1 : 2$
(D) $1 : 4$
(E) $1 : \sqrt{3}$

GO ON TO THE NEXT PAGE

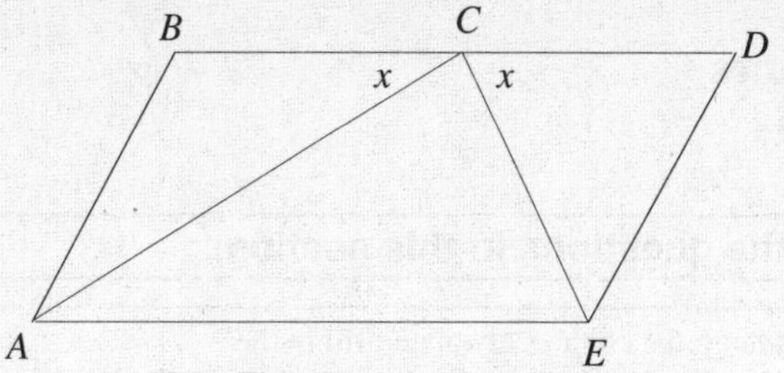

<u>Note:</u> Figure not drawn to scale.

18. In the figure above, $\overline{BD} \parallel \overline{AE}$. If the length of $\overline{CE}$ is 3, what is the length of $\overline{AC}$?

(A) 3
(B) 4
(C) 5
(D) $3\sqrt{3}$
(E) It cannot be determined from the information given.

---

19. If $(a - 5)(b + 5) < 0$, then which of the following must be true?

(A) $a < 5$
(B) $a \neq -5$
(C) $b \neq -5$
(D) $b > -5$
(E) $a > 5$

20. The value of the *n*th term of a sequence is given by the expression $a^{3n} - 3$. If the second term of the sequence is 61, which of the following could be the value of *a* ?

I. −2
II. 2
III. 4

(A) I only
(B) II only
(C) III only
(D) I and II only
(E) II and III only

STOP

If you finish before time is called, you may check your work on this section only. Do not turn to any other section in the test.

SECTION 5
Time — 25 minutes
35 Questions

Turn to Section 5 of your answer sheet to answer the questions in this section.

Directions: For each question in this section, select the best answer from among the choices given and fill in the corresponding circle on the answer sheet.

The following sentences test correctness and effectiveness of expression. Part of each sentence or the entire sentence is underlined; beneath each sentence are five ways of phrasing the underlined material. Choice A repeats the original phrasing; the other four choices are different. If you think the original phrasing produces a better sentence than any of the alternatives, select choice A; if not, select one of the other choices.

In making your selection, follow the requirements of standard written English; that is, pay attention to grammar, choice of words, sentence construction, and punctuation. Your selection should result in the most effective sentence—clear and precise, without awkwardness or ambiguity.

EXAMPLE:

Bobby Flay baked his first cake and he was thirteen years old then.

(A) and he was thirteen years old then
(B) when he was thirteen
(C) at age thirteen years old
(D) upon the reaching of thirteen years
(E) at the time when he was thirteen

Ⓐ●ⒸⒹⒺ

1. Laura Southworth, a children's author who is beginning to attract the notice of critics and librarians alike, wrote and illustrated her first story *Tika* and she was only seven years old then.

   (A) and she was only seven years old then
   (B) at age seven years old only
   (C) when she was only seven years old
   (D) upon the reaching of only seven years
   (E) at the time when she was only seven

2. Many building technologies are changing significantly in the last two thousand years, but today's concrete is still similar to the concrete of Roman times.

   (A) are changing
   (B) have changed
   (C) had changed
   (D) are going to change
   (E) change

3. The video class that meets on Thursdays makes use of the innovative software MAYA, which enables students to design and build a virtual stage set, a home, or even a city in three dimensions.

   (A) makes use of the innovative software MAYA, which enables students to design and build
   (B) using the innovative software MAYA and enabling students to design and build
   (C) besides making use of the innovative software MAYA, enables students to design and build
   (D) because it makes use of the innovative software MAYA, it enables students to design and build
   (E) not only making use of the innovative software MAYA, but also enabling students in the design and building of

4. The ancient belief of all matter being in continuous motion seems borne out by modern discoveries about atomic structure.

   (A) of all matter being in continuous motion
   (B) is that all matter is in continuous motion
   (C) which is that all matter is in continuous motion
   (D) that all matter is in continuous motion
   (E) of all matter that is in continuous motion

5. If Marcel Proust's memory had not been felicitously stirred by the taste of a madeleine, he might never have been moved to write *Remembrance of Things Past.*

   (A) had not been felicitously stirred by the taste of a madeleine
   (B) had not been stirred by means of the felicitous taste of a madeleine
   (C) were not to be felicitously stirred by the taste of a madeleine
   (D) were not to be stirred by the taste of a felicitous madeleine
   (E) should not be stirred by the felicitous taste of a madeleine

GO ON TO THE NEXT PAGE

6. The game hadn't ended yet, but Sarin knows that his chances of winning are slipping away by the second and he needs a miracle.

(A) knows that his chances of winning are slipping away by the second and he needs a miracle
(B) knew that he had no chance of winning and in a second he would need a miracle
(C) knows that winning is a long shot and that he needs a miracle
(D) knew that his chances to win were slipping away by the second and a miracle is what he needed
(E) knew that his chances of winning were slipping away by the second and he needed a miracle

7. When preparing to write a research paper, you should gather information from books, periodicals, and the Internet, and your documenting of sources should be carefully done.

(A) and your documenting of sources should be carefully done
(B) and document your sources carefully
(C) and you should document your careful sources
(D) because your sources need to be documented carefully
(E) yet you need to carefully document your sources

8. Because it has rich limestone similar to the Rhine Valley, Pennsylvania's Lehigh Valley attracted many German settlers who had brought traditional farming methods with them from home.

(A) the Rhine Valley
(B) the Rhine Valley did
(C) it has the Rhine Valley
(D) the Rhine Valleys
(E) that of the Rhine Valley

9. Catherine II of Russia died at 67, and her reputation still surviving as one of the forward-looking, enlightened monarchs of Europe.

(A) 67, and her reputation still surviving as one of the forward-looking, enlightened monarchs of Europe
(B) 67, however her reputation is surviving as one of the forward-looking, enlightened monarchs of Europe
(C) 67, her reputation as one of the forward-looking, enlightened monarchs of Europe still surviving
(D) 67; her reputation as one of the forward-looking, enlightened monarchs of Europe still survives
(E) 67; and her reputation as being one of the more forward-looking, enlightened monarchs of Europe will always survive

10. You may not realize that it is still possible to pick one's own fruit from an orchard; the supermarket is not the only place where fruit is available today.

(A) You may not realize that it is still possible to pick one's own fruit from an orchard
(B) One may not realize that it is still possible to pick your own fruit from an orchard
(C) Picking your own fruit from the orchard
(D) Although many don't realize it, picking fruit from the orchard is still an option
(E) Picking your own fruit from the orchard can be a possibility

11. The Bauhaus school of design, craft, and architecture held many theories in common with the De Stijl movement; however, it instigated a paradigm shift in design.

(A) however, it instigated a paradigm shift in design
(B) however, they instigated a paradigm shift in design
(C) however, the Bauhaus school instigated a paradigm shift in design
(D) and the Bauhaus school instigated a paradigm shift in design
(E) and a paradigm shift was instigated by the Bauhaus school

GO ON TO THE NEXT PAGE

The following sentences test your ability to recognize grammar and usage errors. Each sentence contains either a single error or no error at all. No sentence contains more than one error. The error, if there is one, is underlined and lettered. If the sentence contains an error, select the one underlined part that must be changed to make the sentence correct. If the sentence is correct, select choice E. In choosing answers, follow the requirements of standard written English.

EXAMPLE:

The other players and her significantly improved
A B C

the game plan created by the coaches. No error
D E

Ⓐ●ⒸⒹⒺ

12. Two of Charles Dickens' most famous characters, Oliver
A

Twist and David Copperfield, were an orphan who
B

fell upon hard luck as children, but found happiness later
C D

in life. No error
E

13. A number of horticultural arts, including bonsai and
A B

ikebana, began in Japan. No error
C D E

14. When my sister and me visited the eulogized city of Troy,
A B

we noticed it was much smaller than the epic tales had
C D

suggested. No error
E

15. Complete exhausted from a hard day at work, Evelyn fell
A B

asleep on the bus and, when she finally awoke, found that
C

she had missed her stop. No error
D E

16. There is many benefits to biking; it is both a rigorous
A B

form of exercise and an environmentally sustainable,
C D

conscious mode of transportation. No error
E

17. Despite having had no formal training, Jackie was
A

nonetheless able to master the piano by listening
B

to recordings, reading instructional books, and
C

she practiced on her own. No error
D E

18. Of all the jingoists in the country, that politician,
A B

known for fanatical patriotism, appears to be the more
C D

dangerous. No error
E

19. Many scholars consider *Ulysses* James Joyce's greatest
A B

work; however, many readers find *Dubliners* more
C D

accessible. No error
E

20. Dentists agree that brushing your teeth three times a day
A B

promote good dental health and a more attractive smile.
C D

No error
E

GO ON TO THE NEXT PAGE

21. Two current television trends, the home improvement show craze and the "hot rod" automobile fad, seem (A) to show a dissatisfaction with (B) our domestic spaces and indicating (C) a desire for something riskier (D) and more exciting. No error (E)

22. Before (A) handing in her (B) assignment, Michelle checked (C) all of her sources twice; her greatest fear being (D) receiving any grade lower than a B. No error (E)

23. Species of monkeys living among (A) a variety of creatures in the rainforest come in contact with (B) predators and prey alike as it swings (C) through (D) the trees. No error (E)

24. The pitch of the note that a stringed instrument (A) makes (B) depends on the length, weight, and tension of the string: highest (C) notes are produced by (D) shorter, lighter, or tighter strings. No error (E)

25. When his daughter asked him hundreds of questions (A) about the blue whale model suspended (B) in the American Museum of Natural History, the father had exercised (C) patience (D) and answered every query. No error (E)

26. I choose (A) to carry my necessities in my pockets, and (B) most other women prefer (C) to use (D) purses. No error (E)

27. Saif knew that the other applicants (A) weren't as good as (B) him, (C) so he wasn't surprised when the company offered him (D) the lucrative position. No error (E)

28. Noelle and Natalie argued at great length (A) about the authenticity (B) of the painting; finally (C) Noelle decided that she (D) was right. No error (E)

29. Not (A) everyone would agree (B) that Lawrence Olivier's performance in *Henry V* was (C) superior to Kenneth Branagh. (D) No error (E)

GO ON TO THE NEXT PAGE

Directions: The following passage is an early draft of an essay. Some parts of the passage need to be rewritten.

Read the passage and select the best answers for the questions that follow. Some questions are about particular sentences or parts of sentences and ask you to improve sentence structure or word choice. Other questions ask you to consider organization and development. In choosing answers, follow the requirements of standard written English.

Questions 30–35 are based on the following passage.

(1) Many laws seem to be created for the purpose of protecting people from themselves. **(2)** Some examples are age limits for off-road vehicles, seatbelt requirements for cars, and wearing a helmet when riding a motorcycle. **(3)** Opponents of these laws feel that their rights are being restricted. **(4)** If it doesn't hurt anyone else, why should there be a law? **(5)** But if they become injured, it can raise insurance rates for everyone.

(6) In another context, consider people putting aside money for their retirement. **(7)** Suppose they work for a fast-growing company, the hot new stock pick. **(8)** Many employees invest heavily in the stock. **(9)** The stock price plummets, their savings disappear.

(10) Laws preventing people from having too much company stock in their retirement accounts could protect them from financial disaster. **(11)** It isn't easy to find the proper balance between individual rights and the common good. **(12)** Some people will think that the new law goes too far. **(13)** Others complaining that it doesn't go far enough. **(14)** If it is too much, we can stand up and fight it. **(15)** Although we may not agree with every law, some minor inconveniences are part of living in our society.

30. Which of the following is the best revision of the underlined portion of sentence 1 (reproduced below) ?

Many laws seem to be created for the purpose of protecting people from themselves.

(A) (as it is now)
(B) in order to protect people
(C) as a result of protecting people
(D) so that people will have protection
(E) that let people be protected

31. What is the best way to deal with sentence 6 ?

(A) Replace "another context" with "a similar vein."
(B) Replace the word "context" with "way."
(C) Insert the words "you could" before "consider."
(D) Delete the word "another."
(E) Omit the entire sentence.

32. In which of the following ways could sentences 8 and 9 (reproduced below) best be written?

Many employees invest heavily in the stock. The stock price plummets, their savings disappear.

(A) (As they are now)
(B) Employees can invest heavily in the stock; then the stock price plummets, their savings will disappear.
(C) After the employees invest heavily in the stock, the plummeting stock price causes their savings to disappear.
(D) When employees invest heavily in the stock, it is then that the stock price can plummet and their savings disappear.
(E) If employees invest heavily in the stock and the stock price plummets, their savings will disappear.

33. What should be done with sentence 10 ?

(A) Insert "On the other hand" at the beginning.
(B) Switch it with sentence 7.
(C) Move it to the end of the second paragraph.
(D) Change "their" to "his."
(E) Change "accounts" to "account."

34. Which of the following most effectively revises the underlined portions of sentences 12 and 13 (reproduced below) in order to combine the sentences?

Some people will think that the new law goes too far. Others complaining that it doesn't go far enough.

(A) far: some others complaining
(B) far, others complain
(C) far; others are complaining
(D) far; others have complained
(E) far, while others will complain

35. Which of the following sentences could best be deleted without detracting from the flow of the passage?

(A) Sentence 3
(B) Sentence 7
(C) Sentence 11
(D) Sentence 14
(E) Sentence 15

STOP

If you finish before time is called, you may check your work on this section only.
Do not turn to any other section in the test.

NO TEST MATERIAL ON THIS PAGE.

GO ON TO THE NEXT PAGE

SECTION 6
Time — 25 minutes
18 Questions

Turn to Section 6 of your answer sheet to answer the questions in this section.

Directions: For this section, solve each problem and decide which is the best of the choices given. Fill in the corresponding circle on the answer sheet. You may use any available space for scratchwork.

Notes

1. The use of a calculator is permitted.
2. All numbers used are real numbers.
3. Figures that accompany problems in this test are intended to provide information useful in solving the problems. They are drawn as accurately as possible EXCEPT when it is stated in a specific problem that the figure is not drawn to scale. All figures lie in a plane unless other wise indicated.
4. Unless otherwise specified, the domain of any function *f* is assumed to be the set of all real numbers *x* for which *f*(*x*) is a real number.

Reference Information

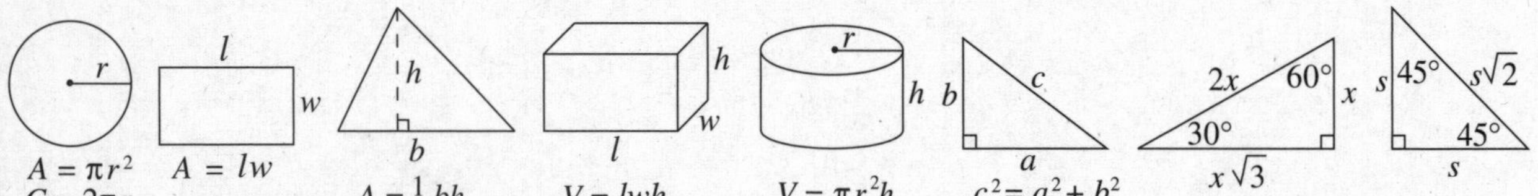

$A = \pi r^2$ $C = 2\pi r$ $A = lw$ $A = \frac{1}{2}bh$ $V = lwh$ $V = \pi r^2 h$ $c^2 = a^2 + b^2$ Special Right Triangles

The number of degrees of arc in a circle is 360.

The sum of the measures in degrees of the angles of a triangle is 180.

1. When k is subtracted from 10, and the difference is divided by 2, the result is 3. What is the value of k ?

(A) 3
(B) 4
(C) 6
(D) 10
(E) 16

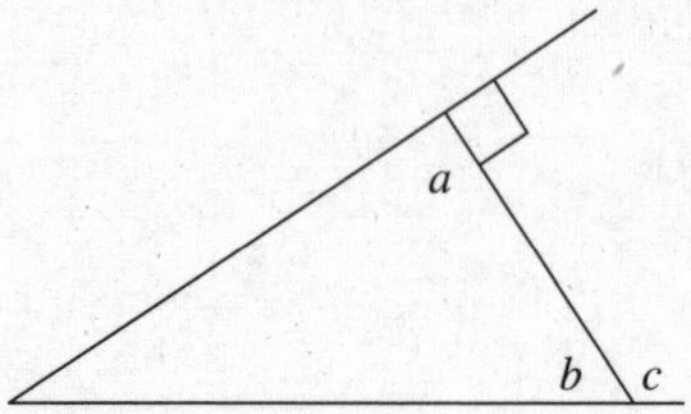

2. In the figure above, what is the value of $a + b + c$?

(A) 180
(B) 240
(C) 270
(D) 360
(E) It cannot be determined from the information given.

GO ON TO THE NEXT PAGE

3. Steve ran a 12-mile race at an average speed of 8 miles per hour. If Adam ran the same race at an average speed of 6 miles per hour, how many minutes longer did Adam take to complete the race than did Steve?

(A) 9
(B) 12
(C) 16
(D) 24
(E) 30

4. Which of the following is equivalent to $\frac{4a}{3} \bullet 6a$?

(A) $\frac{8a^2}{3}$

(B) $\frac{10a^2}{3}$

(C) $\frac{24a}{3}$

(D) $8a^2$

(E) $24a^2$

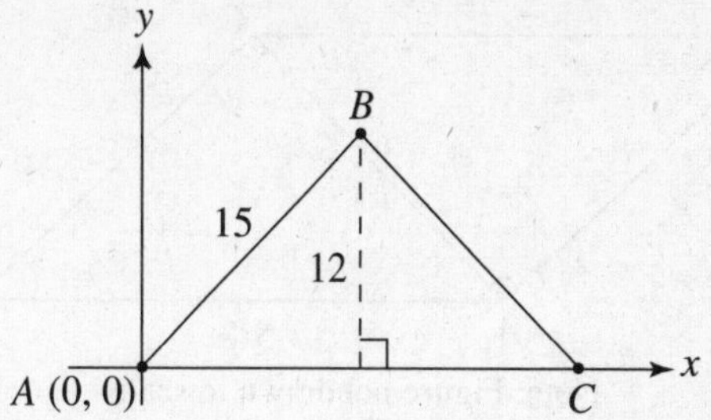

5. In the figure above, side $\overline{AB}$ of $\triangle ABC$ contains which of the following points?

(A) (3, 2)
(B) (3, 5)
(C) (4, 6)
(D) (4, 10)
(E) (6, 8)

6. A college student bought 11 books for fall classes. If the cost of his anatomy textbook was three times the mean cost of the other 10 books, then the cost of the anatomy textbook was what fraction of the total amount he paid for the 11 books?

(A) $\frac{2}{13}$

(B) $\frac{3}{13}$

(C) $\frac{3}{11}$

(D) $\frac{3}{10}$

(E) $\frac{10}{13}$

GO ON TO THE NEXT PAGE

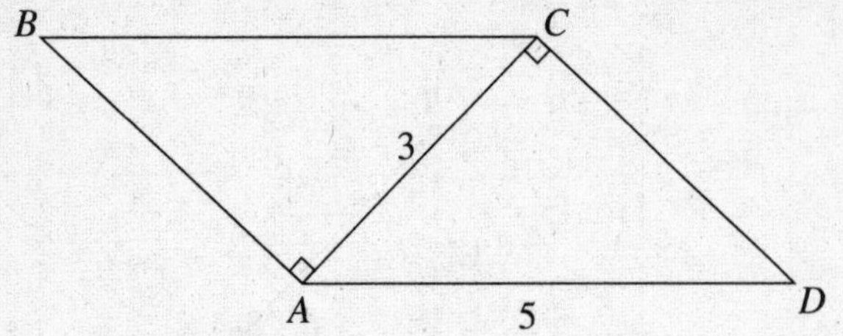

Note: Figure not drawn to scale.

7. In parallelogram *ABCD* above, $AC = 3$ and $AD = 5$. What is the area of *ABCD* ?

(A) 12
(B) 15
(C) 18
(D) 20
(E) It cannot be determined from the information given.

8. The recipe for a pie recommends that the pie be baked for at least 50 minutes, but not more than 60 minutes. If *b* is the number of minutes a pie, baked within the recommended time, is baked, which of the following represents all possible values of *b*?

(A) $|b - 55| = 5$
(B) $|b + 55| < 5$
(C) $|b + 55| > 5$
(D) $|b - 55| < 5$
(E) $|b - 55| > 5$

GO ON TO THE NEXT PAGE

Directions: For Student-Produced Response questions 9–18, use the grids to the right of the answer document page on which you have answered questions 1–8.

Each of the remaining 10 questions requires you to solve the problem and enter your answer by marking the circles in the special grid, as shown in the examples below. You may use any available space for scratch work.

Answer: $\frac{7}{12}$

Write answer in boxes. →

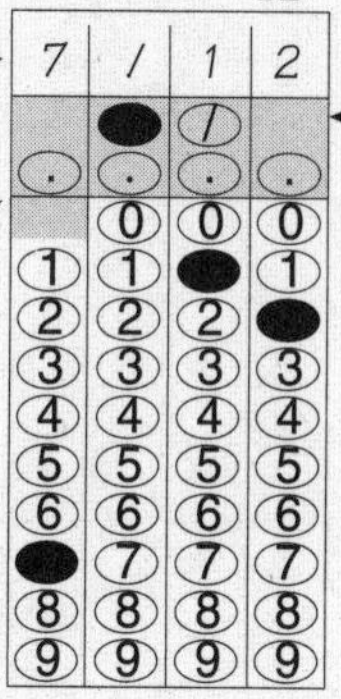

← Fraction line

Grid in result. →

Answer: 2.5

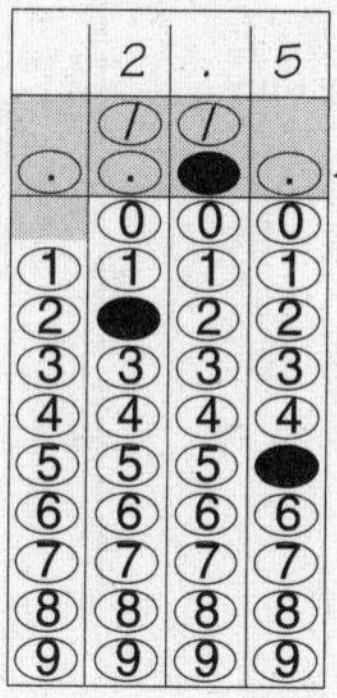

← Decimal point

Answer: 201
Either position is correct.

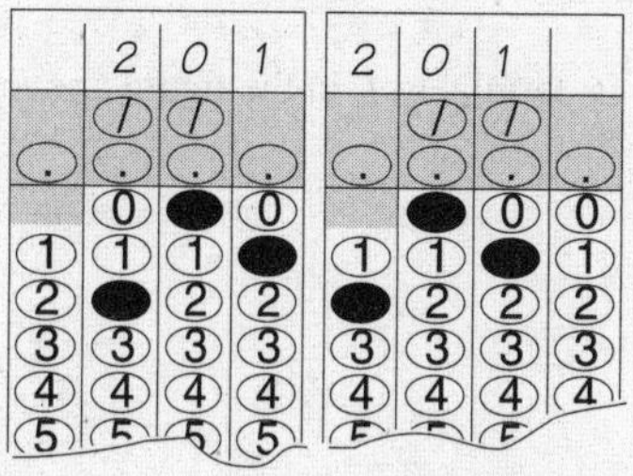

Note: You may start your answers in any column, space permitting. Columns not needed should be left blank.

- Mark no more than one circle in any column.
- Because the answer document will be machine-scored, **you will receive credit only if the circles are filled in correctly.**
- Although not required, it is suggested that you write your answer in the boxes at the top of the columns to help you fill in the circles accurately.
- Some problems may have more than one correct answer. In such cases, grid only one answer.
- No question has a negative answer.
- **Mixed numbers** such as $3\frac{1}{2}$ must be gridded as 3.5 or 7/2. (If 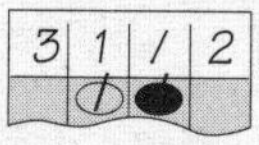 is gridded, it will be interpreted as $\frac{31}{2}$, not $3\frac{1}{2}$.)

- <u>**Decimal Answers:**</u> If you obtain a decimal answer with more digits than the grid can accommodate, it may be either rounded or truncated, but it must fill the entire grid. For example, if you obtain an answer such as 0.6666..., you should record your result as .666 or .667. **A less accurate value such as .66 or .67 will be scored as incorrect.**

Acceptable ways to grid $\frac{2}{3}$ are:

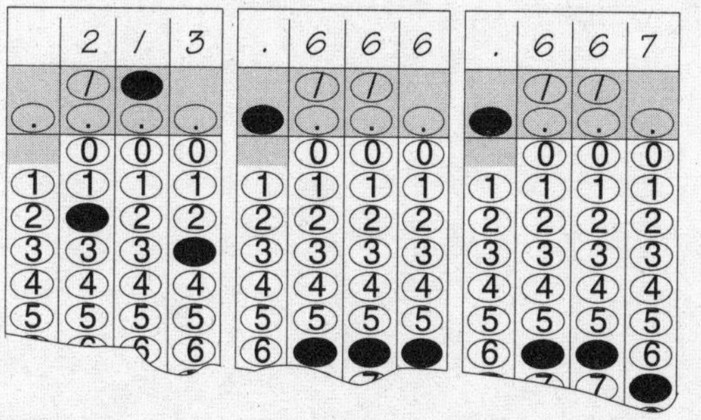

9. If $\frac{x+2x+3x}{2}=6$, what is the value of x ?

10. When n is divided by 5, the remainder is 4. When n is divided by 4, the remainder is 3. If $0 < n < 100$, what is one possible value of n ?

GO ON TO THE NEXT PAGE

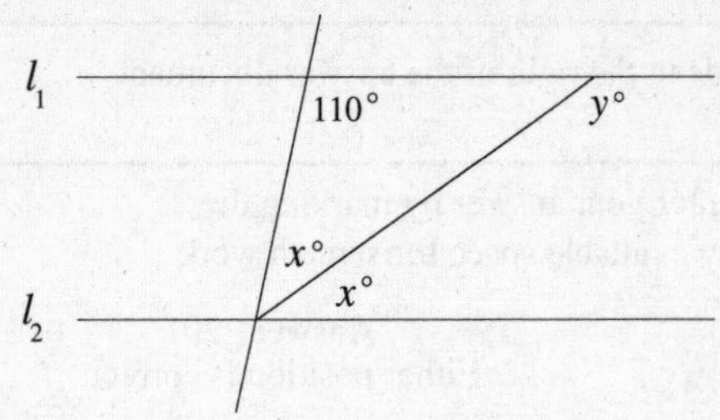

11. If l_1 is parallel to l_2 in the figure above, what is the value of y ?

12. If $x^2 = 16$ and $y^2 = 4$, what is the greatest possible value of $(x - y)^2$?

13. There are 250 students in 10th grade at Northgate High School. All 10th graders must take French or Spanish, but not both. If the ratio of males to females in 10th grade is 2 to 3, and 80 of the 100 French students are male, how many female students take Spanish?

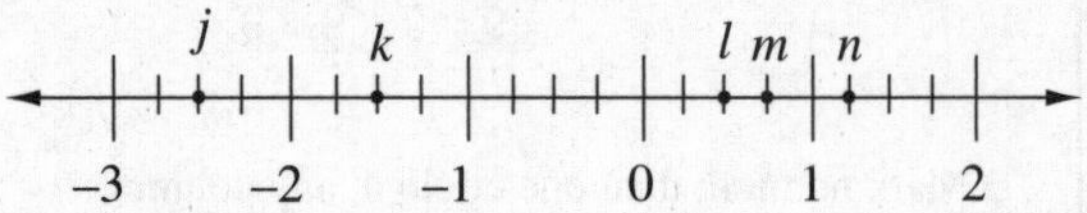

14. On the number line above, j, k, l, m, and n are coordinates of the indicated points. What is the value of $\frac{jk}{lmn}$?

GO ON TO THE NEXT PAGE

15. Hanna is arranging tools in a toolbox. She has one hammer, one wrench, one screwdriver, one tape measure, and one staple gun to place in 5 empty spots in her toolbox. If all of the tools will be placed in a spot, one tool in each spot, and the hammer and screwdriver fit only in the first 2 spots, how many different ways can she arrange the tools in the spots?

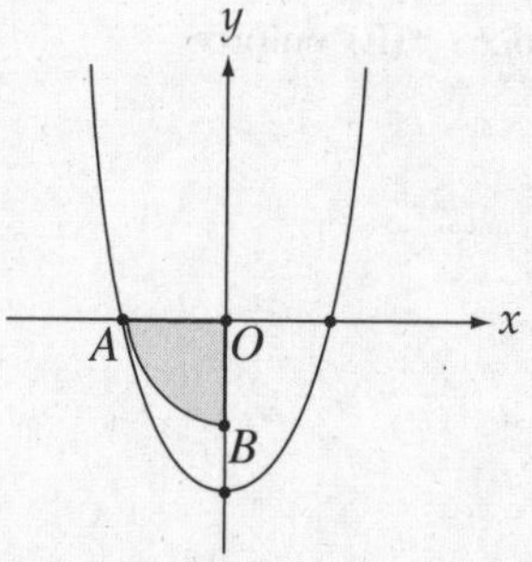

16. In the figure above, AB is the arc of the circle with center O. Point A lies on the graph of $y = x^2 - b$, where b is a constant. If the area of shaded region AOB is π, then what is the value of b ?

17. $\overline{AB}$ is perpendicular to $\overline{BD}$ and $\overline{AB}$ and $\overline{CD}$ bisect each other at point X. If $AB = 8$ and $CD = 10$, what is the length of $\overline{BD}$?

18. A researcher found that the amount of sleep that she allowed her mice to get was inversely proportional to the number of errors the mice made, on average, in a maze test. If mice that got 2 hours of sleep made 3 errors in the maze test, how many errors, on average, do mice with 5 hours of sleep make?

STOP

If you finish before time is called, you may check your work on this section only.
Do not turn to any other section in the test.

SECTION 7
Time — 25 minutes
24 Questions

Turn to Section 7 of your answer sheet to answer the questions in this section.

Directions: For each question in this section, select the best answer from among the choices given and fill in the corresponding circle on the answer sheet.

Each sentence below has one or two blanks, each blank indicating that something has been omitted. Beneath the sentence are five words or sets of words labeled A through E. Choose the word or set of words that, when inserted in the sentence, best fits the meaning of the sentence as a whole.

Example:

Desiring to ------- his taunting friends, Mitch gave them taffy in hopes it would keep their mouths shut.

(A) eliminate (B) satisfy (C) overcome (D) ridicule (E) silence

Ⓐ Ⓑ Ⓒ Ⓓ ●

1. If it is true that morality cannot exist without religion, then does not the erosion of religion herald the ------- of morality?

(A) regulation (B) basis (C) belief (D) collapse (E) value

2. Shaken by two decades of virtual anarchy, the majority of people were ready to buy ------- at any price.

(A) stability (B) emancipation (C) prosperity (D) liberty (E) enfranchisement

3. Certain animal behaviors, such as mating rituals, seem to be -------, and therefore ------- external factors such as climate changes, food supply, or the presence of other animals of the same species.

(A) learned . . immune to
(B) innate . . unaffected by
(C) intricate . . beleaguered by
(D) specific . . confused with
(E) memorized . . controlled by

4. The stoic former general led his civilian life as he had his military life, with simplicity and ------- dignity.

(A) benevolent (B) informal (C) austere (D) aggressive (E) succinct

5. Although bound to uphold the law, a judge is free to use his discretion to ------- the cruel severity of some criminal penalties.

(A) mitigate (B) understand (C) condone (D) provoke (E) enforce

GO ON TO THE NEXT PAGE

Directions: Each passage below is followed by questions based on its content. Answer the questions on the basis of what is stated or implied in each passage and in any introductory material that may be provided.

Questions 6–9 are based on the following passages.

Passage 1

Geological Evolutionary theory, the idea of scientifically dating Earth, is a relatively recent concept. Seventeenth-century scientists began to use geological evidence to bolster the idea that Earth evolved over time. In the eighteenth century, British scientist James Hutton posited his theory of Uniformity. According to this theory, processes that changed the Earth in the past are still at work today. In the nineteenth century, Charles Darwin expanded the idea of geological evolution to include biological evolution. Combining Hutton and Darwin's theories, scientists then used fossil evidence to begin dating the Earth. Compared to other geological sciences, Geological Evolutionary theory is still relatively new, and many of its fundamental assumptions are constantly challenged.

Passage 2

Geological Evolutionary theory is based on a simple assumption: older rock strata came first and hence, should lie underneath younger rock strata. While distinct layers or "strata" of rock of varying ages are a commonly observed phenomenon, the order of the layers does not necessarily correlate to the presumed age of the rocks themselves. The Heart Mountain Thrust in Wyoming is one such thorn in the side of evolutionary geologists. At Heart Mountain, 50 separate blocks of Paleozoic strata are resting horizontally on top of Eocene beds which are supposed to be 250 million years younger. Numerous theories for this seeming anomaly have been put forth; however, none has yet emerged as an intuitive truth.

6. It can be inferred from Passage 1 that

(A) theories of the Earth's age evolved from the work of more than one scientist
(B) there is general agreement on theories of geological evolution
(C) geologists used biological evolution to disprove the theory of Uniformity
(D) geology is a new, and therefore inexact, science
(E) attempts to scientifically date the Earth began with Hutton's work

7. Passage 1 is unlike Passage 2 in that Passage 1

(A) attempts to prove a theory while Passage 2 attempts to disprove it
(B) places a theory in time while Passage 2 offers an example to contradict it
(C) proves a new geological theory while Passage 2 offers a counterexample
(D) contradicts an existing theory while Passage 2 proves one
(E) criticizes a popular theory while Passage 2 defends it

8. Which of the following statements about Geological Evolutional theory is supported by both passages?

(A) Geological Evolutionary theory has not yet been proven to be true.
(B) Geological Evolutionary theory cannot yet explain the placement of Paleozoic strata.
(C) Geological Evolutionary theory is not yet old enough to be true.
(D) Geological Evolutionary theory is a commonly observed phenomenon.
(E) Geological Evolutionary theory is not as old as the theory of Uniformity.

9. Passage 2 is best described as

(A) a confirmation of a firmly established theory
(B) an exception to a generally accepted truth
(C) an itemization of the flaws of newly established theory
(D) a discussion of an intuitively plausible hypothesis
(E) a potential exception to an observable theory

GO ON TO THE NEXT PAGE

Questions 10–15 are based on the following passage.

The following passage is an excerpt from a book by novelist Gregor von Rezzori.

Skushno is a Russian word that is difficult to translate. It means more than dreary boredom; a spiritual void that sucks you in like a vague but intensely urgent longing. When I was thirteen, at a phase that educators used to call "the awkward age," my parents were at their wits' end. We lived in the Bukovina, today an almost astronomically remote province in southeastern Europe. The story I am telling seems as distant—not only in space but also in time—as if I'd merely dreamed it. Yet it begins as a very ordinary story.

I had been expelled by a *consilium abeundi*—an advisory board with authority to expel unworthy students—from the schools of the then kingdom of Rumania, whose subjects we had become upon the collapse of the Austro-Hungarian Empire after the first great war. An attempt to harmonize the imbalances in my character by means of strict discipline at a boarding school in Styria (my people still regarded Austria as our cultural homeland) nearly led to the same ignominious end, and only my pseudo-voluntary departure from the institution in the nick of time prevented my final ostracism from the privileged ranks of those for whom the path to higher education was open. Again in the jargon of those assigned the responsible task of raising children to become "useful members of society," I was a "virtually hopeless case." My parents, blind to how the contradictions within me had grown out of the highly charged difference between their own natures, agreed with the schoolmasters; the mix of neurotic sensitivity and a tendency to violence, alert perception and inability to learn, tender need for support and lack of adjustability, would only develop into something criminal.

One of the trivial aphorisms my generation owes to Wilhelm Busch's *Pious Helene* is the homily "Once your reputation's done / You can live a life of fun." But this optimistic notion results more from wishful thinking than from practical experience. In my case, had anyone asked me about my state of mind, I would have sighed and answered, "*Skushno!*" Even though rebellious thoughts occasionally surged within me, I dragged myself, or rather I let myself be dragged, listlessly through my bleak existence in the snail's pace of days. Nor was I ever free of a sense of guilt, for my feeling guilty was not entirely foisted upon me by others; there were deep reasons I could not explain to myself; had I been able to do so, my life would have been much easier.

10. It can be inferred from the passage that the author's parents were

(A) frustrated by the author's performance in school
(B) oblivious to the author's inability to do well in school
(C) wealthy, making them insensitive to the needs of the poor
(D) schoolmasters who believed in the strict disciplining of youth
(E) living in Russia while their son lived in Bukovina

11. Lines 14–23 are used by the author to demonstrate that

(A) the author posed an imminent danger to others
(B) the schools that the author attended were too difficult
(C) the tactics used to make the author more obedient were failing
(D) the author was often criticized by both his schoolmasters and classmates
(E) the author's academic career was nearing an end

12. In lines 16–17, the author implies that Styria

(A) belongs to his people
(B) is in Austria
(C) does not belong to Austria
(D) is not a lenient boarding school
(E) belongs to Hungary rather than Austria

13. The word "ignominious" in line 17 means

(A) dangerous
(B) harsh
(C) unappreciated
(D) disreputable
(E) discriminating

14. The passage as a whole suggests that the author felt

(A) happy because he was separated from his parents
(B) upset because he was unable to maintain good friendships
(C) melancholy and unsettled in his environment
(D) suicidal and desperate because of his living in Russia
(E) hopeful because he'd soon be out of school

15. The passage indicates that the author regarded the aphorism mentioned in the last paragraph with

(A) relief because it showed him that he would eventually feel better
(B) dissatisfaction because he found it unrealistic
(C) contempt because he saw it working for others
(D) bemusement because of his immunity to it
(E) sorrow because his faith in it nearly killed him

GO ON TO THE NEXT PAGE

Questions 16–24 are based on the following passage.

The following passage, published in 1986, is from a book written by a zoologist.

The domestic cat is a contradiction. No other animal has developed such an intimate relationship with humanity, while at the same time demanding and getting such independent movement and action. The cat manages to remain a tame animal because of the sequence of its upbringing. By living both with other cats (its mother and littermates) and with humans (the family that has adopted it) during its infancy and kittenhood, the cat becomes attached to and considers that it belongs to both species. It is like a child that grows up in a foreign country and, as a consequence, becomes bilingual. The young cat becomes bimental. It may be a cat physically, but mentally it is both feline and human. Once it is fully adult, however, most of its responses are feline ones, and it has only one major reaction to its human owners. It treats them as pseudoparents. The reason is that they took over from the real mother at a sensitive stage of the kitten's development and went on giving it milk, solid food, and comfort as it grew up.

This is rather different from the kind of bond that develops between human and dog. The dog sees its human owners as pseudoparents, as does the cat. On that score the process of attachment is similar. But the dog has an additional link. Canine society is group-organized; feline society is not. Dogs live in packs with tightly controlled status relationships among the individuals. There are top dogs, middle dogs, and bottom dogs, and under natural circumstances they move around together, keeping tabs on one another the whole time. So the adult pet dog sees its human family both as pseudoparents and as the dominant members of the pack, hence the dog's renowned reputation for obedience and its celebrated capacity for loyalty. Cats do have a complex social organization, but they never hunt in packs. In the wild, most of their day is spent in solitary stalking. Going for a walk with a human, therefore, has no appeal for them. And as for "coming to heel" and learning to "sit" and "stay," they are simply not interested. Such maneuvers have no meaning for them.

So the moment a cat manages to persuade a human being to open a door (that most hated of human inventions), it is off and away without a backward glance. As it crosses the threshold, the cat becomes transformed. The kitten-of-human brain is switched off and the wildcat brain is clicked on. The dog, in such a situation, may look back to see if its human packmate is following to join in the fun of exploring, but not the cat. The cat's mind has floated off into another, totally feline world, where strange, bipedal* primates have no place.

Because of this difference between domestic cats and domestic dogs, cat-lovers tend to be rather different from dog-lovers. As a rule, cat-lovers have a stronger personality bias toward working alone, independent of the larger group. Artists like cats; soldiers like dogs. The much-lauded "group loyalty" phenomenon is alien to both cats and cat-lovers. If you are a company person, a member of the gang, or a person picked for the squad, the chances are that at home there is no cat curled up in front of the fire. The ambitious Yuppie, the aspiring politician, the professional athlete, these are not typical cat-owners. It is hard to picture football players with cats in their laps—much easier to envisage them taking their dogs for walks.

Those who have studied cat-owners and dog-owners as two distinct groups report that there is also a gender bias. The majority of cat lovers are female. This bias is not surprising in view of the division of labor evident in the development of human societies. Prehistoric males became specialized as group-hunters, while the females concentrated on food-gathering and childbearing. This difference contributed to a human male "pack mentality" that is far less marked in females. Wolves, the wild ancestors of domestic dogs, also became pack-hunters, so the modern dog has much more in common with the human male than with the human female.

The argument will always go on—feline self-sufficiency and individualism versus canine camaraderie and good-fellowship. But it is important to stress that in making a valid point I have caricatured the two positions. In reality there are many people who enjoy equally the company of both cats and dogs. And all of us, or nearly all of us, have both feline and canine elements in our personalities. We have moods when we want to be alone and thoughtful, and other times we wish to be in the center of a crowded, noisy room.

* bipedal: walking on two feet

16. The primary purpose of the passage is to

(A) show the enmity that exists between cats and dogs
(B) advocate dogs as making better pets than cats
(C) distinguish the different characteristics of dogs and cats
(D) show the inferiority of dogs because of their dependent nature
(E) emphasize the role that human society plays in the personalities of domestic pets

17. In line 15, the word "pseudoparents" means

(A) part-time parents who are only partially involved with their young
(B) individuals who act as parents of adults
(C) parents who neglect their young
(D) parents who have both the characteristics of humans and their pets
(E) adoptive parents who aren't related to their young

GO ON TO THE NEXT PAGE

18. The passage as a whole does all of the following EXCEPT

(A) use a statistic
(B) make parenthetical statements
(C) quote a knowledgeable individual
(D) restate an argument
(E) make a generalization

19. According to the passage, the domestic cat can be described as

(A) a biped because it possesses the characteristics of animals with two feet
(B) a pseudopet because it can't really be tamed and will always retain its wild habits
(C) a contradiction because although it lives comfortably with humans, it refuses to be dominated by them
(D) untamed because it preserves its independence
(E) dominant because although it plays the part of a pet, it acquires obedience from humans

20. The author suggests that an important difference between dogs and cats is that, unlike dogs, cats

(A) do not have complex social organizations
(B) obey mainly because of their obedient nature
(C) have a more creative nature
(D) do not regard their owners as the leader of their social group
(E) are not skilled hunters

21. It can be inferred from lines 18–36 that the social structure of dogs is

(A) flexible
(B) hierarchical
(C) abstract
(D) male-dominated
(E) somewhat exclusive

GO ON TO THE NEXT PAGE

22. The "ambitious Yuppie" mentioned in line 55 is an example of a person

(A) who lacks the ability to be self-sufficient
(B) who seeks group-oriented status
(C) who is a stereotypical pet-owner
(D) who has a weak personality
(E) who cares little for cat lovers

23. The fifth paragraph (lines 59–69) indicates that human females

(A) prefer the society of cats less than that of dogs
(B) developed independent roles that didn't require group behavior
(C) had to gather food because they were not strong enough to hunt
(D) are not good owners for the modern dog
(E) were negatively affected by the division of labor of human societies

24. The author uses lines 70–73 ("The argument . . . positions.") to

(A) show that the argument stated in the passage is ultimately futile and thus not worth continuing
(B) disclaim contradictions that are stated in the passage
(C) qualify the generalizations used to make the author's point
(D) ensure that the reader doesn't underestimate the crux of the passage
(E) highlight a difference between individualism and dependency

STOP

If you finish before time is called, you may check your work on this section only. Do not turn to any other section in the test.

SECTION 8
Time — 20 minutes
16 Questions

Turn to Section 8 of your answer sheet to answer the questions in this section.

Directions: For this section, solve each problem and decide which is the best of the choices given. Fill in the corresponding circle on the answer sheet. You may use any available space for scratchwork.

Notes

1. The use of a calculator is permitted.
2. All numbers used are real numbers.
3. Figures that accompany problems in this test are intended to provide information useful in solving the problems. They are drawn as accurately as possible EXCEPT when it is stated in a specific problem that the figure is not drawn to scale. All figures lie in a plane unless other wise indicated.
4. Unless otherwise specified, the domain of any function f is assumed to be the set of all real numbers x for which $f(x)$ is a real number.

Reference Information

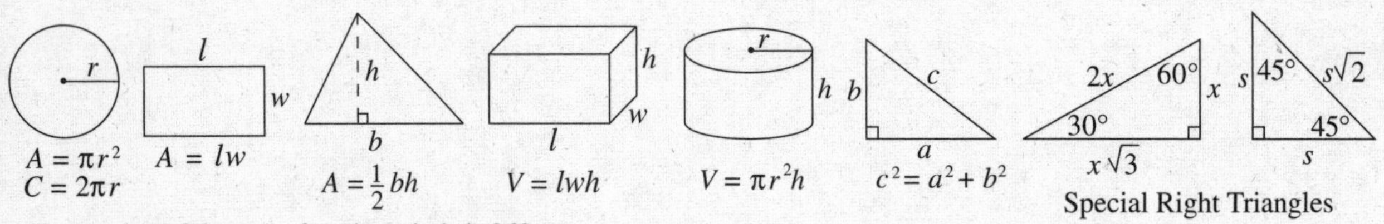

The number of degrees of arc in a circle is 360.

The sum of the measures in degrees of the angles of a triangle is 180.

1. If $3x - 5 = 4$, what is the value of $9x - 15$?

(A) 3
(B) 4
(C) 9
(D) 12
(E) 15

Price of Buttons in Store *X*

Color	Price
Black	\$2 per 5 buttons
Blue	\$2 per 6 buttons
Brown	\$3 per 8 buttons
Orange	\$4 per 12 buttons
Red	\$4 per 7 buttons

2. In Store *X*, which color costs the most per button?

(A) Black
(B) Blue
(C) Brown
(D) Orange
(E) Red

GO ON TO THE NEXT PAGE

3. In the *xy*-coordinate plane, which of the following ordered pairs is a point on the line $y = 2x - 6$?

(A) (6, 7)
(B) (7, 7)
(C) (7, 8)
(D) (8, 7)
(E) (8, 8)

4. For which of the following values of x is $\frac{x^2}{x^3}$ the least?

(A) 1
(B) –1
(C) –2
(D) –3
(E) –4

5. If $(a + b)^2 = 49$, and $ab = 10$, which of the following represents the value of b in terms of a ?

(A) $\frac{\sqrt{29}}{a}$

(B) $\sqrt{29 - a^2}$

(C) $\sqrt{39 - a}$

(D) $\sqrt[a]{\frac{49}{10}}$

(E) $a^2\sqrt{49}$

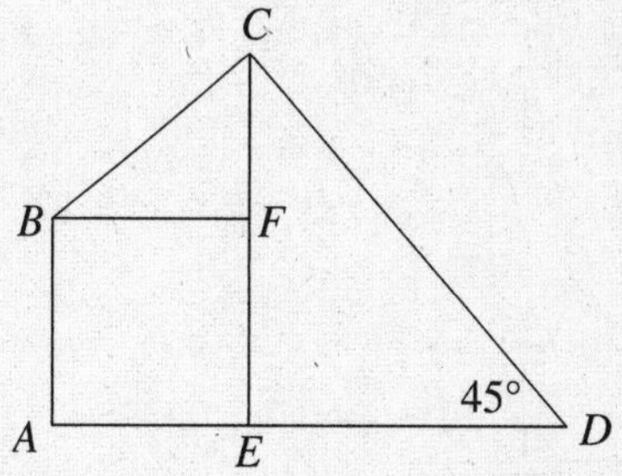

6. If the area of square $ABFE = 25$, and the area of $BCF = 10$, what is the length of $\overline{DE}$?

(A) 7
(B) 8
(C) 9
(D) 10
(E) 14

GO ON TO THE NEXT PAGE

7. If $x + 2y = 20$, $y + 2z = 9$, and $2x + z = 22$, what is the value of $x + y + z$?

(A) 10
(B) 12
(C) 17
(D) 22
(E) 51

8. If the sum of two numbers is 10, and one of these numbers is equal to the sum of 6 and twice the other number, what is the value of the larger number minus the smaller number?

(A) 2

(B) $5\frac{1}{4}$

(C) 6

(D) $7\frac{1}{3}$

(E) $8\frac{1}{2}$

9. For a given year, a mayor has $45,000 allotted to spend on the sanitation department, the police department, and the fire department. If $\frac{1}{5}$ of his money goes to the sanitation department, and $\frac{2}{3}$ of the remaining money goes to the police department, how much does the mayor have left for the fire department?

(A) $36,000
(B) $24,000
(C) $21,000
(D) $12,000
(E) $6,000

10. If the average measure of two angles in a parallelogram is y, what is the average degree measure of the other two angles?

(A) $180 - y$

(B) $180 - \frac{y}{2}$

(C) $360 - 2y$

(D) $360 + y$

(E) y

GO ON TO THE NEXT PAGE

11. If $m > 0$ and $b > 0$, which of the following could be a graph of $y = mx^2 + b$?

(A)

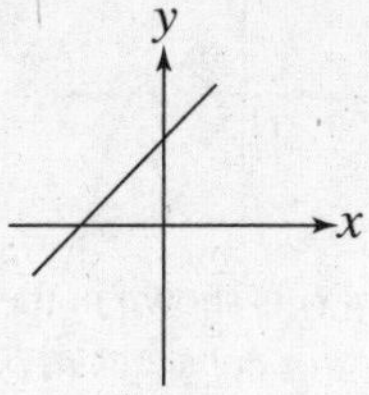

(B)

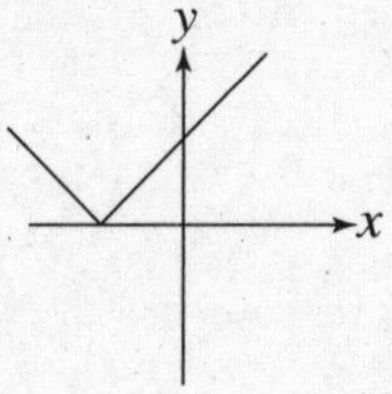

(C)

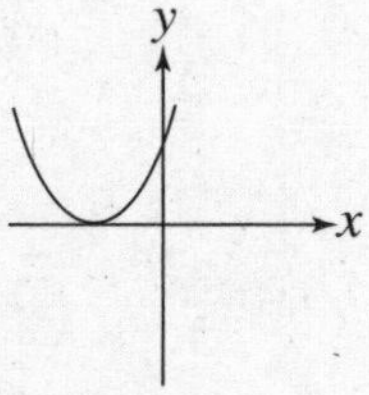

(D)

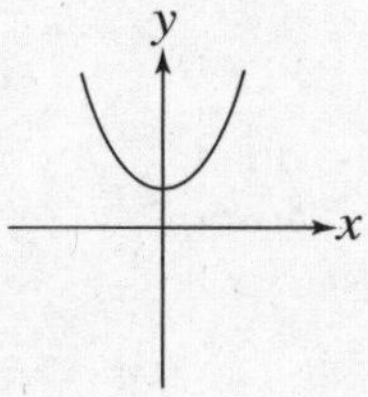

(E)

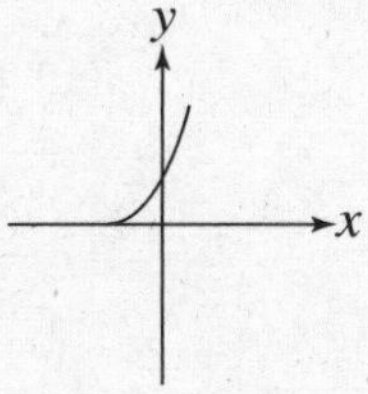

12. S is the set of all positive numbers n such that $n < 100$ and $\sqrt{n}$ is an integer. What is the median value of the members of set S ?

(A) 5
(B) 5.5
(C) 25
(D) 50
(E) 99

13. Point K lies outside the circle with center C such that $CK = 26$. $\overline{JK}$ is tangent to the circle at point J, and the distance from J to K is 2 less than the distance from K to C. What is the circumference of the circle?

(A) 10π
(B) 15π
(C) 20π
(D) 22π
(E) 24π

GO ON TO THE NEXT PAGE

14. On a map, 1 centimeter represents 6 kilometers. A square on the map with a perimeter of 16 centimeters represents a region with what area?

(A) 64 square kilometers
(B) 96 square kilometers
(C) 256 square kilometers
(D) 576 square kilometers
(E) 8,216 square kilometers

15. If 0.1% of m is equal to 10% of n, then m is what percent of $10n$?

(A) $\frac{1}{1{,}000}\%$

(B) 1%

(C) 10%

(D) 100%

(E) 1,000%

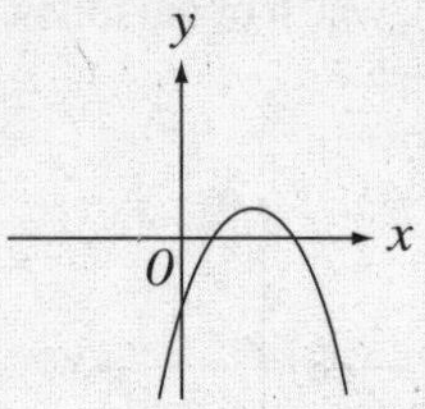

16. The graph of $y = g(x)$ is shown in the figure above. If $g(x) = ax^2 + bx + c$ for constants a, b, and c, and if $abc \neq 0$, then which of the following must be true?

(A) $ac > 1$
(B) $c > 1$
(C) $ac < 0$
(D) $a > 0$
(E) $ac > 0$

STOP

If you finish before time is called, you may check your work on this section only. Do not turn to any other section in the test.

NO TEST MATERIAL ON THIS PAGE.

SECTION 9
Time — 20 minutes
19 Questions

Turn to Section 9 of your answer sheet to answer the questions in this section.

Directions: For each question in this section, select the best answer from among the choices given and fill in the corresponding circle on the answer sheet.

Each sentence below has one or two blanks, each blank indicating that something has been omitted. Beneath the sentence are five words or sets of words labeled A through E. Choose the word or set of words that, when inserted in the sentence, best fits the meaning of the sentence as a whole.

Example:

Desiring to ------- his taunting friends, Mitch gave them taffy in hopes it would keep their mouths shut.

(A) eliminate (B) satisfy (C) overcome (D) ridicule (E) silence

Ⓐ Ⓑ Ⓒ Ⓓ ●

1. Max's grandmother seems -------; she is frequently observed behaving in an unconventional manner.

   (A) ordinary (B) eccentric (C) chronological (D) sociable (E) industrious

2. The antibiotic ointment was so effective on the infection in Molly's swollen finger that after only one application, the finger was no longer -------.

   (A) compressed (B) deflated (C) distended (D) fractured (E) disintegrated

3. Professor Cooligan told his class that since the Industrial Revolution, the global warming trend has been -------; human disregard for the environment precipitated many of the alterations in the earth's climate zones.

   (A) inevitable (B) malevolent (C) reciprocal (D) stagnant (E) guileless

4. After just one hour of study, Tyler unrealistically expected a ------- rise in his test scores, and was reluctant to work longer hours for steady, ------- score improvements.

   (A) repetitive . . swift
   (B) sudden . . interminable
   (C) trivial . . gradual
   (D) steep . . incremental
   (E) significant . . rapid

5. When participating in a yoga class, Katarina attains a ------- state; the soothing music and soft lighting invoke a serenity that is otherwise lacking in her frenzied existence.

   (A) euphonious (B) perspicuous (C) placid (D) prolific (E) supple

6. Dr. Schwartz's lecture on art, while detailed and scholarly, focused ------- on the pre-modern; some students may have appreciated his specialized knowledge, but those with more ------- interests may have been disappointed.

   (A) literally . . medieval
   (B) completely . . antediluvian
   (C) prodigiously . . germane
   (D) voluminously . . creative
   (E) utterly . . eclectic

GO ON TO THE NEXT PAGE

Directions: Each passage below is followed by questions based on its content. Answer the questions on the basis of what is <u>stated</u> or <u>implied</u> in each passage and in any introductory material that may be provided.

Questions 7–19 are based on the following passages.

The two passages below discuss the causes of deviant behavior and strategies for deterring it. The first passage is taken from a discussion of the classical perspective on deviance, while Passage 2 recounts a more recent interpretation of behavior.

Passage 1

Early attempts to understand what caused deviant behavior in society always centered on supernatural causes. People were criminals, it was assumed, because of some otherworldly influence, a demonic presence that tempted and manipulated otherwise good individuals into performing antisocial actions. But the arrival of the Enlightenment in Europe marked the end of this so-called demonic perspective and ushered in a new conception of the roots of deviant behavior, a viewpoint that came to be called the classical perspective.

The Enlightenment brought numerous changes to European culture. Foremost among them was an increased reliance on human rationality. Philosophers moved away from theologically centered debates and focused on such intellectual exercises as empiricism and the limits of human reason. Thus, it is no coincidence that the classical perspective on deviance describes criminal behavior not as the result of some supernatural entity but as the fruit of human rationality. Classicists maintain that a person chooses deviant behavior based on an intellectual "risk/reward" evaluation. The classicists start from the assumption that each individual wishes to maximize pleasure and minimize pain. Deviance occurs when an individual decides that the reward to be gained from an action outweighs the potential risk associated with the behavior. Thus, a person who decides to rob a bank has determined that the potential profits from the heist are worth the risk of incarceration.

Not surprisingly, adherents of the classical perspective advocate punishment as the best deterrent to deviant behavior. In order to prevent individuals from engaging in criminal activities, the risk associated with each activity must outstrip the reward. One classicist, Cesare Beccaria, even went so far as to maintain that a precise, mathematical system could be devised that would calculate the exact type of punishment necessary. However, arbitrary, excessive, or tyrannical punishments are not encouraged by the classical perspective. Because each deviant act arises from a rational calculation of pleasure versus pain, the appropriate punishment must merely exceed the expected pleasure in order to serve as a deterrent.

Passage 2

Just as people are able to influence and change society, society affects the behavior of its charges. It would be remiss to ascribe the emergence of deviant behavior solely to the perpetrator of that behavior. No individual exists in a vacuum; in order to understand the actions of an individual one must examine the society that produces the individual. Only by gaining an understanding of the relationship between individual and society can we begin to understand the causes of social deviance.

One way to begin to understand the existence of deviance is to imagine a "perfect" society. In this perfect society, each member shares common values and internalizes the norms of the group. In such a setting, each person is at peace because his or her re lationship to the society at large is in harmony. Furthermore, since each individual's goals and values are shared by the rest of the community, each participant in this perfect society feels actualized and secure, content that the needs of the individual are also the needs of the whole. Surely, deviant behavior would have no role in this utopia. The entire society would be coordinated by the predominance of shared mores, and each member's behavior would be bound by these common values. Unfortunately, perfect societies do not exist in the real world.

Consider now a realistic model of society. Change is constant; immigration brings new members to the society, urbanization uproots families, and technological advances offer new and different ways of living. Harmony and organization are not the norm. Instead, disorganization reigns supreme. With society in a state of flux, it is impossible for individuals to remain in harmony with the community, and it is this discord that breeds social deviance. Lacking the coordination of an overarching social consensus, individuals replace it with dissention. While in time particular changes in society might bring about new social norms, and thus new models of consensus, new changes will inevitably occur, giving rise to a new cycle of deviant behavior.

It follows, then, that in order to control deviant behavior, one must first look to stabilize the society that engenders it. When disorganization is replaced with organization and disparate values are supplanted by shared norms, deviant behavior will be eliminated.

7. The arrival of the Enlightenment in Europe shifted philosophers' focus from

(A) superstition to spirituality
(B) demons to angels
(C) criminals to law-abiding citizens
(D) classicists to modernists
(E) theology to intellectualism

GO ON TO THE NEXT PAGE

8. According to the classical perspective, deviant behavior is the result of

(A) a criminal act
(B) a demonic presence
(C) a rational decision based on intellectual evaluation
(D) a concept developed by philosophers
(E) rationale that minimizes pleasure and maximizes pain

9. Classicists did not encourage harsh, despotic punishments because

(A) risks must outstrip potential profits from a heist
(B) punishment can be meted out precisely and mathematically
(C) the demonic, otherworldly influence on actions will prevail
(D) the appropriate punishment must merely exceed the pain
(E) deviant acts arise from a reasoned assessment of pleasure versus pain

10. In line 42 of Passage 2, "ascribe" most nearly means

(A) reveal
(B) attribute
(C) describe
(D) distinguish
(E) explain

11. In lines 43–44 of Passage 2 ("No individual exists in a vacuum") suggests that

(A) society plays a key role in determining an individual's behavior
(B) an individual is accountable to those around him
(C) there is no relationship between individual behavior and society
(D) an individual can have a major impact on society
(E) without organized society, individuals would cease to exist

12. The author of Passage 2 uses the example of a "perfect" society to suggest that

(A) common values are necessary for a successful society
(B) it is a reflection of today's world
(C) society is obsessed with perfection
(D) people will never be happy in an imperfect society
(E) deviant behavior would not exist in such a society

13. In line 77, "engenders" most nearly means

(A) sexualizes
(B) publicizes
(C) enables
(D) advocates
(E) causes

14. In Passage 2, the author describes the realistic model of society in a tone that is

(A) nostalgic for the calmer days of society
(B) objectively summarizing a realistic society
(C) critical of disorganization in society
(D) reproachful of companies that promote technological growth
(E) approving of individuals who dissent from society

15. When change is constant, which of the following is LEAST likely to result, according to the author of the second passage?

(A) Immigration augments a society.
(B) Organization and harmony become the rule.
(C) Technological advancement spurs innovations.
(D) Disorganization reigns supreme.
(E) Social fluctuation is the norm.

GO ON TO THE NEXT PAGE

16. Both passages support which generalization about deviant behavior?

(A) Acts of deviance are ultimately the decision of the individual.
(B) Society is the main cause of deviant behavior.
(C) Deviant behavior can be eliminated only through severe punishment.
(D) Societal adjustments are the only way to eradicate deviance.
(E) The arrival of the Enlightenment in Europe promoted social deviance.

17. Which aspect of deviant behavior seems to matter a great deal in Passage 1, but not in Passage 2?

(A) The influence of demons on criminals
(B) The intellectual evaluation made by an individual
(C) The methods for calculating punishment
(D) The effects society has on the individual
(E) The act of robbing a bank

18. The passages differ in tone in that Passage 1 is

(A) enthusiastic while Passage 2 is cautious
(B) indignant while Passage 2 is nostalgic
(C) matter-of-fact while Passage 2 is sarcastic
(D) objective while Passage 2 is critical
(E) sensationalistic while Passage 2 is understated

19. Which statement best describes a significant difference between the two interpretations of how deviant behavior is propagated?

(A) Passage 1 emphasizes the individual's role; Passage 2 emphasizes society's role.
(B) Passage 1 explains the history of deviance; Passage 2 emphasizes the modern perspective.
(C) Passage 1 discusses the demonic perspective; Passage 2 discusses the role of disorganization.
(D) Each passage presents several reasons for deviant behavior.
(E) Each passage discusses society's role in deviant behavior.

STOP

If you finish before time is called, you may check your work on this section only.
Do not turn to any other section in the test.

SECTION 10
Time — 10 minutes
14 Questions

Turn to Section 10 of your answer sheet to answer the questions in this section.

Directions: For each question in this section, select the best answer from among the choices given and fill in the corresponding circle on the answer sheet.

The following sentences test correctness and effectiveness of expression. Part of each sentence or the entire sentence is underlined; beneath each sentence are five ways of phrasing the underlined material. Choice A repeats the original phrasing; the other four choices are different. If you think the original phrasing produces a better sentence than any of the alternatives, select choice A; if not, select one of the other choices.

In making your selection, follow the requirements of standard written English; that is, pay attention to grammar, choice of words, sentence construction, and punctuation. Your selection should result in the most effective sentence—clear and precise, without awkwardness or ambiguity.

EXAMPLE:

Bobby Flay baked his first cake and he was thirteen years old then.

(A) and he was thirteen years old then
(B) when he was thirteen
(C) at age thirteen years old
(D) upon the reaching of thirteen years
(E) at the time when he was thirteen Ⓐ●ⒸⒹⒺ

1. Weather vanes range in style from the practical to the fanciful, but in the end its purpose is still the same: to point out the direction of the wind.

(A) its purpose is still the same
(B) their purpose being the same
(C) the purpose is the same for every one of them
(D) they all share the same purpose
(E) the purpose is the same for all of them

2. The horrors of war and the experiences of a woman serving in the Woman's Royal Navy Service during the Second World War, which are stirringly chronicled in Edith Pargeter's novel *She Goes to War.*

(A) the Second World War, which are stirringly chronicled
(B) the Second World War are stirringly chronicled
(C) a stirring chronicle of the Second World War
(D) the Second World War, that appear in a stirring chronicle
(E) a chronicle of the Second World War that stirs the emotions

3. The commercial airliner flew too close to the military base, an act that the army viewed as a violation of its air space.

(A) as
(B) as if it was
(C) to be
(D) that it was
(E) for

4. Arvo Pärt is an Estonian composer, he is noted for his ethereal, unusual harmonies, and he will direct the symphony concert tonight.

(A) Arvo Pärt is an Estonian composer, he is noted for his ethereal, unusual harmonies, and he
(B) Arvo Pärt is an Estonian composer noted for his ethereal, unusual harmonies, he
(C) Arvo Pärt, an Estonian composer, and because he is noted for his ethereal, unusual harmonies, he
(D) Although Arvo Pärt is an Estonian composer, he is noted for his ethereal, unusual harmonies, and he
(E) Arvo Pärt, an Estonian composer noted for his ethereal, unusual harmonies,

GO ON TO THE NEXT PAGE

5. The lawyer for the plaintiff in the civil court case responded to the emotional appeals of the defendant she produced actual physical evidence of the defendant's culpability.

(A) defendant she produced
(B) defendant with the production of
(C) defendant, produced
(D) defendant; and produced
(E) defendant by producing

6. Sandeep could only objectively judge the results of the experiment after he realized that he could depend on expertise different from his own.

(A) could depend on expertise different from his own
(B) can depend on expertise different from his own
(C) could depend on expertise different from his expertise
(D) can depend on expertise different from his expertise
(E) would have the ability to depend on expertise different from his own

7. Dr. Kornstein's colleagues considered him not only a great surgeon but also being an inspiring teacher of innovative surgical techniques.

(A) being an inspiring teacher of
(B) having inspired the teaching of
(C) with inspiration teaching
(D) he was inspiring in his teaching of
(E) an inspiring teacher of

8. Many employees chose to switch to the new company insurance plan for the reasons that their monthly payments would be reduced.

(A) for the reasons that their monthly payments would be reduced
(B) because their monthly payments would be reduced
(C) because of their reductions in monthly payments
(D) because its monthly payments were to be reduced
(E) for the reason that they reduced their monthly payment

9. In spite of an appearance of no specific expression on its face, a squirrel sometimes plays clever games with anyone trying to view it, scrambling to the opposite side of a tree to elude a would-be observer.

(A) In spite of an appearance of no specific expression on its face, a squirrel
(B) Despite the fact of an appearance of no specific expression on its face, a squirrel
(C) Although the expression on the face of the squirrel is not specific in appearance, it
(D) Although a squirrel appears to have no specific expression on its face, it
(E) Although the face of a squirrel has no specific expression, it

10. Learning from recent field tests, the efficiency of the engine on which they would base next year's trucks was significantly increased by the designers.

(A) the efficiency of the engine on which they would base next year's trucks was significantly increased by the designers
(B) the designers based next year's truck engine on a significant increase in efficiency
(C) the designers significantly increased the efficiency of the engine on which they would base next year's trucks
(D) their efficiency was significant in designing the engine as a basis for next year's trucks
(E) the engine on which the designers would base next year's trucks was significantly increased in efficiency

GO ON TO THE NEXT PAGE

11. The crash of the Mars Climate Orbiter was caused by a lack of training among the members of the navigation team and failing to use metric units in the coding of the software.

(A) failing to use metric units
(B) a failure to use metric units
(C) by people which failed to use metric units
(D) because of the failure to use metric units
(E) because people failed to use metric units

12. Rory and I, starting to clear the snow away from the front door, we still have hours of work ahead of us.

(A) Rory and I, starting to clear the snow away from the front door
(B) Rory and I, starting to clear the snow away from the front door, however
(C) Rory and I have started to clear the snow away from the front door, and
(D) Even though starting from the front door to clear the snow away, Rory and I
(E) Even though Rory and I have started to clear the snow away from the front door

13. While rhododendron and cherry blossoms are both bright in color, the main difference being the size of the tree that grows them.

(A) the main difference being the size of the tree that grows them
(B) the main difference is that they grow on two trees that are different
(C) the two grow on trees of different sizes
(D) the main difference being they grow on different-size trees
(E) and the trees they grow on are different in size

14. Better known for *The Foreigner*, other works of Larry Shue, such as *The Nerd*, were of equal quality even though they were less famous.

(A) other works of Larry Shue, such as *The Nerd*,
(B) other works by Larry Shue, such as *The Nerd*,
(C) Larry Shue also created other works, such as *The Nerd*, that
(D) Larry Shue's other works, like *The Nerd*,
(E) Larry Shue wrote other stories, like *The Nerd*, that

NO TEST MATERIAL ON THIS PAGE.

PRACTICE TEST 1: ANSWER KEY

Section 2 Math	Section 3 Reading	Section 4 Math (Exp)	Section 5 Writing	Section 6 Math	Section 7 Reading	Section 8 Math	Section 9 Reading	Section 10 Writing
1. A	1. A	1. B	1. C	1. B	1. D	1. D	1. B	1. D
2. C	2. E	2. B	2. B	2. C	2. A	2. E	2. C	2. B
3. C	3. B	3. E	3. A	3. E	3. B	3. C	3. A	3. A
4. B	4. A	4. E	4. D	4. D	4. C	4. B	4. D	4. E
5. B	5. A	5. C	5. A	5. E	5. A	5. B	5. C	5. E
6. A	6. C	6. A	6. E	6. B	6. A	6. C	6. E	6. A
7. A	7. D	7. A	7. B	7. A	7. B	7. C	7. E	7. E
8. D	8. D	8. E	8. E	8. D	8. A	8. D	8. C	8. B
9. E	9. C	9. D	9. D	9. 2	9. E	9. D	9. E	9. D
10. B	10. B	10. B	10. D	10. 19, 39, 59, 79, 99	10. A	10. A	10. B	10. C
11. D	11. B	11. D	11. C	11. 145	11. C	11. D	11. A	11. B
12. D	12. C	12. E	12. B	12. 36	12. B	12. C	12. E	12. E
13. D	13. D	13. A	13. E	13. 130	13. D	13. C	13. E	13. C
14. E	14. D	14. D	14. A	14. 8	14. C	14. D	14. C	14. C
15. E	15. E	15. E	15. A	15. 12	15. B	15. E	15. B	
16. B	16. A	16. D	16. A	16. 4	16. C	16. E	16. A	
17. C	17. A	17. D	17. D	17. 3	17. E		17. B	
18. A	18. C	18. A	18. D	18. $\frac{6}{5}$ or 1.2	18. C		18. D	
19. C	19. E	19. C	19. E		19. C		19. A	
20. B	20. B	20. D	20. C		20. D			
	21. C		21. C		21. B			
	22. D		22. D		22. B			
	23. B		23. C		23. B			
	24. A		24. C		24. C			
			25. C					
			26. B					
			27. C					
			28. D					
			29. D					
			30. B					
			31. A					
			32. E					
			33. C					
			34. E					
			35. D					

SAT SCORING WORKSHEET

For directions on how to score your SAT practice test, see pages 389–390. Section 4 is the unscored, Experimental section.

SAT Writing Section

Total Writing Multiple-Choice Questions Correct from Sections 5 and 10: [ ]

−

Total Writing Multiple-Choice Questions Incorrect from Sections 5 and 10: ______ ÷ 4 = [ ]

Grammar Raw Score: [ ] — **Grammar Scaled Subscore!** [ ]

Compare the Grammar Raw Score to the Writing Multiple-Choice Subscore Conversion Table on the next page to find the Grammar Scaled Subscore.

+

Your Essay Score (2 – 12): ______ ÷ 2 = [ ]

Writing Raw Score: [ ]

Compare Raw Score to SAT Score Conversion Table on the next page to find the Writing Scaled Score.

Writing Scaled Score! [ ]

Be sure to register at **PrincetonReview.com/cracking** to gain access to our LiveGrader™ Service. Your essay can be scored by our graders there.

SAT Critical Reading Section

Total Critical Reading Questions Correct from Sections 3, 7, and 9: [ ]

−

Total Critical Reading Questions Incorrect from Sections 3, 7, and 9: ______ ÷ 4 = [ ]

Critical Reading Raw Score: [ ]

Compare Raw Score to SAT Score Conversion Table on the next page to find the Critical Reading Scaled Score.

Critical Reading Scaled Score! [ ]

SAT Math Section

Total Math Grid-In Questions Correct from Section 6: [ ]

+

Total Math Multiple-Choice Questions Correct from Sections 2, 6, and 8: [ ]

−

Total Math Multiple-Choice Questions Incorrect from Sections 2, 6, and 8: ______ ÷ 4 = [ ]

Don't include wrong answers from Grid-Ins!

Math Raw Score: [ ]

Compare Raw Score to SAT Score Conversion Table on the next page to find the Math Scaled Score.

Math Scaled Score! [ ]

SAT SCORE CONVERSION TABLE

Raw Score	Writing Scaled Score	Reading Scaled Score	Math Scaled Score	Raw Score	Writing Scaled Score	Reading Scaled Score	Math Scaled Score	Raw Score	Writing Scaled Score	Reading Scaled Score	Math Scaled Score
73	800			47	590–630	600–640	680–720	21	400–440	420–460	460–500
72	790–800			46	590–630	590–630	670–710	20	390–430	410–450	450–490
71	780–800			45	580–620	580–620	660–700	19	380–420	400–440	450–490
70	770–800			44	570–610	580–620	650–690	18	370–410	400–440	440–480
69	770–800			43	570–610	570–610	640–680	17	370–410	390–430	430–470
68	760–800			42	560–600	570–610	630–670	16	360–400	380–420	420–460
67	760–800	800		41	560–600	560–600	620–660	15	350–390	380–420	420–460
66	760–800	770–800		40	550–590	550–590	620–660	14	340–380	370–410	410–450
65	750–790	750–790		39	540–580	550–590	610–650	13	330–370	360–400	400–440
64	740–780	740–780		38	530–570	540–580	600–640	12	320–360	350–390	400–440
63	730–770	740–780		37	530–570	530–570	590–630	11	320–360	350–390	390–430
62	720–760	730–770		36	520–560	530–570	590–630	10	310–350	340–380	380–420
61	710–750	720–760		35	510–550	520–560	580–620	9	300–340	330–370	370–410
60	700–740	710–750		34	500–540	510–550	570–610	8	290–330	310–350	360–400
59	690–730	700–740		33	490–530	500–540	560–600	7	280–320	300–340	350–390
58	680–720	690–730		32	480–520	500–540	560–600	6	270–310	300–340	340–380
57	680–720	680–720		31	470–510	490–530	540–580	5	260–300	290–330	330–370
56	670–710	670–710		30	470–510	480–520	530–570	4	240–280	280–320	320–360
55	660–720	670–710		29	460–500	470–510	520–560	3	230–270	270–310	310–350
54	650–690	660–700	800	28	450–490	470–510	510–550	2	230–270	260–300	290–330
53	640–680	650–690	780–800	27	440–480	460–500	510–550	1	220–260	230–270	270–310
52	630–670	640–680	750–790	26	430–470	450–490	500–540	0	210–250	200–240	240–280
51	630–670	630–670	740–780	25	420–460	450–490	490–530	–1	200–240	200–230	220–260
50	620–660	620–660	730–770	24	410–450	440–480	480–520	–2	200–230	200–220	210–250
49	610–650	610–650	710–750	23	410–450	430–470	480–520	–3	200–220	200–210	200–240
48	600–640	600–640	700–740	22	400–440	420–460	470–510				

WRITING MULTIPLE-CHOICE SUBSCORE CONVERSION TABLE

Grammar Raw Score	Grammar Scaled Subscore	Grammar Raw Score	Grammar Scaled Subscore	Grammar Raw Score	Grammar Scaled Subscore	Grammar Raw Score	Grammar Scaled Subscore	Grammar Raw Score	Grammar Scaled Subscore	Grammar Raw Score	Grammar Scaled Subscore
49	79–80	40	70–74	31	61–65	22	52–56	13	43–47	4	33–37
48	78–80	39	69–73	30	60–64	21	52–56	12	42–46	3	31–35
47	78–80	38	68–72	29	59–63	20	51–55	11	41–45	2	28–32
46	77–80	37	67–71	28	58–62	19	50–54	10	40–44	1	26–30
45	76–80	36	66–70	27	57–61	18	49–53	9	39–43	0	23–27
44	75–79	35	65–69	26	56–60	17	48–52	8	37–41	–1	22–26
43	73–77	34	64–68	25	55–59	16	47–51	7	36–40	–2	21–25
42	72–76	33	63–67	24	54–58	15	46–50	6	35–39	–3	20–24
41	71–75	32	62–66	23	53–57	14	45–49	5	34–38		

Chapter 20
Answers and Explanations for Practice Test 1

SECTION 2

1. A Answer this question in bite-sized pieces. The first step is to use your calculator to compute the sum of the subscriptions: \$68.80. The down payment was half that amount, leaving \$34.40 to be paid in 4 installments of \$8.60 each. If you answered D or E, you may have misread the question.

2. C Try Plugging In the Answers. Starting with C, put in $\frac{1}{2}$ for x:

$$\frac{2\left(\frac{1}{2}\right)}{\left(\frac{1}{2}\right)^2+1}=\frac{2}{\frac{1}{2}+2}$$

$$\frac{1}{1\frac{1}{4}}=\frac{2}{2\frac{1}{2}}$$

Cross-multiply: $2\frac{1}{2}=2\left(1\frac{1}{4}\right)=2\frac{1}{2}$. So C is correct. Another way would be to cross-multiply first to get $2x^2+4x=2x^2+2$. Subtract $2x^2$ from both sides to get $4x=2$. Divide by 4 to get $x=\frac{1}{2}$.

3. C This is an excellent time to turn on your calculator. If 48,000 people live in Town X and each household has 3.2 people, you can determine the number of households: $48{,}000 \div 3.2 = 15{,}000$. And since each household has 1.2 televisions, you can now determine the number of televisions: $15{,}000 \times 1.2 = 18{,}000$.

4. B From the statement, you know that flour is necessary to make the cookies. You don't know that flour is the only thing necessary to make the cookies. For example, you may also need sugar and eggs. You cannot conclude A or E, because there may be other reasons for not making the cookies (maybe you didn't feel like it, or maybe you were out of sugar). Choice C is not necessarily true because there may be other things necessary besides flour. Answer choice D contradicts the original statement. Choice B must be true because you couldn't have made the cookies without the flour.

5. B Start by plugging in what you know into the function given. If $f(x) = x^2 - c$, and $f(-2) = 6$, then plug in -2 for x in the function: $f(-2) = (-2)^2 - c$. Solve and replace $f(-2)$ with 6: $6 = 4 - c$; $2 = -c$; and $c = -2$. If you picked answer choice (A), you forgot that $(-2)^2$ is positive 4, and if you picked answer choice (E) then you forgot about the minus sign in the original function.

6. A First solve for b. If $9b = 81$, then b must equal 9. Insert 9 for b into $\sqrt{b}\bullet\sqrt[3]{3b}$:
$\sqrt{9}\bullet\sqrt[3]{3\bullet9}=3\bullet\sqrt[3]{27}=3\bullet3=9$

7. A The formula for the circumference of a circle is $C = 2\pi r$ or $C = d\pi$. (If you forget the formula, you can look it up at the beginning of the section.) The circumference of the circle is 5, so $5 = \pi d$. Now, just solve for d, which equals $\frac{5}{\pi}$.

8. D If you got this question wrong, you either misread it or forgot the correct order of operations. Remember to do parentheses first. Translating the information to an equation, you'd get the following:

$$(1+2)(2+3)(3+4)=\frac{1}{2}(20+x)$$

$$3 \times 5 \times 7 = \frac{1}{2}(20 + x)$$
$$105 = \frac{1}{2}(20 + x)$$
$$210 = 20 + x$$
$$190 = x$$

9. E Approach the problem in bite-sized pieces. $\sqrt{x} = 2^2$, so $\sqrt{x} = 4$. Square both sides to get $x = 16$.

10. B We're solving for shirts and pants, which constitute 60% of total sales. Because shoes ($12,000) account for 15%, shirts and pants would be four times that amount, or $48,000. Another way to solve this is to find out the total value of sales and find 60% of that. If $20,000 represents 25% (or $\frac{1}{4}$) of sales, then the total must be $80,000. Using translation, you'll find that $\frac{60}{100} \times \$80{,}000 = \$48{,}000$.

11. D You should have noticed several things about this question. First, the figure was not drawn to scale. So a good first step would be to redraw the figure to comply with the condition ($\overline{AB} > \overline{CD}$). Second, the question asks which of the following *must* be true. *Must* is an important word—if it were *which of the following could be true,* you'd change your analysis completely. So, redrawing the figure, you'd get something like this:

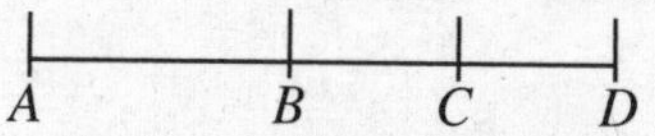

In this figure, $\overline{AB}$ is clearly larger than $\overline{CD}$. Because plugging in numbers makes the distance more concrete, you might have made $AB = 3$ and $CD = 2$, for example. Because you don't know the length of BD, however, you'd have to leave it alone. Now, let's check the conditions. Option I: Well, this could be true, but it doesn't have to be. So, option I is out. This allows you to eliminate A and E. Option II: If you let $AB = 3$ and $CD = 2$, $AC = 3 + BC$ while $BD = BC + 2$. No matter what BC is, $AC > BD$. Option II is true. This allows you to eliminate C, which does not include Option II. We still need to check one more. Option III: If $AB > CD$, and $AC > AB$, then $AC > CD$. Option III is true; therefore, D is the answer.

12. D Absolute value, a number's distance from zero on a number line, is always expressed as a positive number. Cross out A and B since both are negative. Solve the function with $x = 1$: $f(1) = |(|1| - 3)| = 2$.

13. D This geometric sequence can be expressed as 6×2^x, where x is the number of hours. So, after 9 hours, there will be $6 \times 2^9 = 6 \times 512 = 3{,}072$. Alternatively, you could just work out the problem each hour by doubling. So, after the 1st hour, there are $6 \times 2 = 12$. Then, after the 2nd hour, there are $12 \times 2 = 24$, and so on, until you get to the 9th hour.

14. E Because any value squared must be 0 or positive, the least possible value for x^2 is 0. This means the least possible value of $x^2 + 2$ is 2. So, A, B, C, and D are not possible values for $f(x)$. Only E is a possible value because when $x = 0$, $f(x) = 2$.

15. E Once again, the way *not* to solve an SAT question is to reason algebraically. Instead, use your calculator to start cubing integers and stop when you find an integer cubed that is greater than 200. 1^3, 2^3, 3^3, 4^3, and 5^3 are all less than 200. 6^3 is 216, so that's too large. Thus there are 5 numbers.

16. B Plug in! Because the values you choose for x and y must satisfy the equation, let x equal 6 and y equal 9. The perimeter p would then equal 6 + 6 + 9 + 9, or 30. The target is y, which is equal to 9. Plugging In 30 for p in each of the choices, you'd get B as the answer. Although some of you might have answered this question correctly by using algebra, doing so might have caused you to make a mistake without realizing it. Trust us. Plugging In is always the safer method for this type of problem. The Joe Bloggs choice, by the way, was C.

17. C And yet again, the slow way to solve a word problem like this is to set up equations. Letting w and l represent the number of wins and losses, respectively, the slow method of setting up equations would yield the following:

$$\frac{w}{l} = \frac{3}{1}$$

$$\frac{w+6}{l} = \frac{5}{1}$$

Then you'd have to substitute $\frac{3}{1}$ for $\frac{w}{l}$ in the second equation and solve for l and then go back to solve for w.

We can also plug in the answer choices, starting in the middle, C, and see which one works:

	Before		**After**	
	Wins	Losses	Wins	Losses
(A)	3			
(B)	6			
(C)	9	3 (3:1)	15	3 (5:1)
(D)	15			
(E)	24			

Bingo! We found the answer on the first try! If C didn't work, you'd move up or down depending on whether the result was too small or too big.

18. A This is a great opportunity to plug in. Make up a value for x—let's say 40. Then name the two other angles created by the lines that meet at vertex P— let's call the one to the left of x (within the same triangle as the angle labeled $a°$) angle y and the one to the right of x (within the same triangle as the angle labeled $b°$) angle z. Now make up values for these two angles so the sum of x, y, and z is 90. Let's say that $y = 30$ and $z = 20$. Because both of these triangles are right triangles, $a = 180 - 90 - 30 = 60$, and $b = 180 - 90 - 20 = 70$. Thus $a + b = 130$, which becomes our target. Only A yields this answer.

19. C First a little error avoidance: Because 5 is one of the numbers you see, 5^2, or 25, is not going to be the answer. It's a Joe Bloggs answer. So, eliminate A. Next, let's estimate the area before you try to solve directly. The length of the square's side is a little more than 5, so the area is going to be a little more than 5^2, or 25. E is too large, so before solving the problem, you've eliminated A and E. If you couldn't calculate the area exactly, you could guess from among the remaining choices. To determine the area, let's begin by assigning the variable s to indicate the length of the square's sides. The area is given by the formula: $A = s^2$. Notice the triangle formed by side $\overline{AB}$ and the x- and y-axes. The base of that triangle is 1 and the height is 5, so you can use the Pythagorean theorem to find the length of side $\overline{AB}$ or s:

$$1^2 + 5^2 = s^2$$
$$26 = s^2$$
$$s = \sqrt{26}$$
$$s^2 = 26$$

20. B Probability is the chance of something happening. In this case, to find the probability, find the area that is in the circle but not the square, divided by the area of the circle (which represents all possibilities). Plug in for the radius of the circle. Let's say $r = 5$. So, the area of the circle is $\pi \times 5^2 = 25\pi$. The area that is in the circle but not the square is the area of the circle minus the area of the square. Find the area of the square. The diagonal of the square is equal to the diameter of the circle: $2 \times 5 = 10$. The diameter creates a 45°-45°-90° triangle from the square. So, the side of the square is $\frac{10}{\sqrt{2}}$. That means the area of the square is $\left(\frac{10}{\sqrt{2}}\right)^2 = \frac{100}{2} = 50$. Therefore, the area within the circle but not the square is $25\pi - 50$. That means the probability is $\frac{25\pi - 50}{25\pi} \approx 0.36$. This is the target. Only B matches. After you've plugged in and realized that the probability is $\frac{(25\pi - 50)}{25\pi}$, you can also solve algebraically:

$$\frac{25\pi - 50}{25\pi} = \frac{25(\pi - 2)}{25\pi} = \frac{\pi - 2}{\pi}.$$

Another, even more complicated, approach would be to call the area of the circle πr^2, the diameter $2r$, and the area of the square $\left(\frac{2r}{\sqrt{2}}\right)^2 = \frac{4r^2}{2} = 2r^2$. The probability would be $\frac{\pi r^2 - 2r^2}{\pi r^2}$. This is simplified: $\frac{r^2(\pi - 2)}{\pi r^2} = \frac{\pi - 2}{\pi}$. It's much more confusing when you don't plug in numbers!

SECTION 3

1. **A** The clues *to prevent household fires* and *flammable liquids* make *flammable* a good word to recycle for the blank. A comes closest to this meaning. B, C, and D are unrelated. E means the opposite of the word needed.

2. **E** The semicolon is a same-direction trigger. Because Mark hates mistakes, he will review his papers "carefully." We can immediately eliminate B, C, and D. E means "very carefully." If you weren't sure what A meant, you had to guess. Give yourself a pat on the back if you guessed rather than leaving the question blank. Even if you got the question wrong, you did the right thing. And in the long run, that's how your score goes up.

3. **B** The clue for the first blank is *defends* and the trigger word is *nor*. A good word to use for the first blank will be one that is the opposite of *defends*, such as "disagrees with." This eliminates D and E. Now look at the second blank. According to the first part of the sentence, Jenkins doesn't do anything positive or negative, so a good word for the blank is "neutrality." This eliminates A and C.

4. **A** *Great thinkers* must have "great" *insights*, so the first blank is a positive word. The clues here are *voiced so often* and *mere*, which indicate something trivial or unimportant. Things that are voiced often can be called "repetitions," or some related negative word. The word *ironic* also suggests that the first and second blanks contrast in meaning. The only choice that has a positive word followed by a negative word is A. Remember to use POE to avoid words you don't know. Because *beliefs* is not negative, you can eliminate B, even if you do not know what *banal* means.

5. **A** The clue is *been taught to communicate*, and the trigger word *but* indicates that the *skeptics* doubt this. So the skeptics must be arguing that the apes have *not really been taught*; they may be "mimicking" (aping!) their trainers. A is the best choice. Even if you don't know what A, B, or E means, you should be able to use POE on C and D, and then guess.

6. **C** The clue is *technical difficulty and challenging counterpoint*, so good words for the blanks are *difficult* and *complex*, which agree with each other. This eliminates B and D, as both contain answers that disagree with each other. You can eliminate A because *diminutive* means small. Although *inscrutable* in E means "difficult to understand," the word *classical* does not mean "difficult" or "complex."

7. **D** The first and second blanks are both somewhat negative words. E is the only bad guess, since it doesn't make much sense to view a situation as *political* and be *perplexed* by it. A, B, C, and D are all good guesses because at least one of the words is somewhat negative. Guessing one of these choices would have been better than leaving the question blank. If you look closely, you'll notice that the trigger *since* tells you that the two blanks must be similar to each other. Eliminate A, as there is no evidence for how *obscure* or "little known" their situations are. B is close, but *bellicose* means "prone to fighting," which is not supported by the sentence. Eliminate C, as *sanguine* means "confident and positive," which does not agree with *acute* and is not negative.

8. **D** The clues in this sentence are *ancient ruins of marvelous bygone civilizations* and *sad*. What is sad about looking at the ruins of ancient civilizations? Seeing that, you can gather that human greatness doesn't last. This idea is reinforced by the time trigger—if an ETS sentence completion compares past and present, it is usually to show a change. Therefore, you can put "doesn't last" in the blank, and the best match is *transience*.

9. **C** After the second sentence, the passage shifts into information about *hypergraphia* and also suggests that if the cause of writer's block is found to be *neurological*, then different treatment techniques might

be appropriate. Therefore, we need an answer referring to a shift in meaning. A is not supported by the passage, which is not critical. B is too vague and doesn't really refer to anything, and D is too broad. E refers to two problems, although only one, *writer's block*, is mentioned in the passage.

10. **B** After a discussion of treatments for writer's block in the first half of the passage, the second half of the passage develops the idea that writer's block may have a *neurological* cause. A is incorrect because no comparison takes place. C is incorrect because some information is provided, but it is not detailed. D is incorrect since the passage doesn't question *current techniques.* E is incorrect because only one side effect of *temporal lobe epilepsy* is mentioned.

11. **B** B is correct, because the passage gives interesting historical information about a city like a travel guide does. A is incorrect, because the information given about the *arrondissements* is not detailed enough for a proposal, nor is the author recommending that other cities follow Paris's example. There is no evidence of *satire,* making C incorrect. The passage mentions Roman history only briefly, and does not mention art history, making both D and E incorrect.

12. **C** The passage states that Paris was protected by a wall. *New walls were built* that became the site of today's streets. The protective walls determined the shape of the city. A is incorrect, because an increase in population required expansion of the city's walls. There is no evidence for B or D. Although the passage mentions Romans, there is no reference to improving upon their architecture, making E incorrect.

13. **D** D is the best answer. A majority of the passage discusses the Zambesi River and its tributaries. Very little information is given on people, making A wrong. B is incorrect; color is mentioned in line 12 *(yellowish-green tinge)* but not again. No mention is made of C. E is mentioned only in the last line.

14. **D** The best choice is D. In lines 8–11, the passage states that Livingston explored the Zambesi and its tributaries in order to find if they could be used *for commerce.* A is not the primary reason for the expedition. Although refugees from Portuguese slavery are mentioned in passing at the end of the passage, contacting Portuguese settlers, B, is not mentioned at all in the passage. C is incorrect because it is not known if the way is safe or not. E is incorrect, because it is not stated that Livingston was the first to survey the land.

15. **E** The fish *screen* themselves from the *rays* of the *sun*—thus, E is the best answer. A is too positive; fish would not *screen themselves* from a *pleasant* sun. B is not supported by the passage. C is one definition of *torrid,* but it doesn't fit in this context. D does not refer to the sun but rather to the fish.

16. **A** The passage states that the Kongone is the *safest* branch for travel, because of the straight course and the depth of the water. The passage states that boats should not attempt the bar when the wind is from the south and south-east though. Thus, A is the best answer. B cannot be inferred since it is unknown if and when the beacon would be built. C is deceptive; the passage states that if the wind is from the *east or north* the bar would be smooth. D is too extreme; of the three rivers that Livingston explored, the Kongone is the best route. But that is not the same as being the best of all rivers in Africa. E is a misstating of the passage. East Luabo should not attempted unless the wind is from the north-east, not the Kongone.

17. **A** Although the Kongone is mentioned throughout the third paragraph, the passage describes the effects of the current in lines 39–41. B is too strong. The change of water level is not attributed to the current, eliminating C. D is not supported by the passage. E refers not to the Kongone, but refers instead to the situation on the Zambesi.

18. C Livingston indicates that the river he is charting may be the river described by de Gama. A is incorrect, because Livingston isn't certain that the river is the same one that de Gama referred to. B is not supported by the passage. D doesn't make any sense; mentioning de Gama does not explain the lack of Portuguese settlers. E is wrong; there is no pillar at the river. C is the best answer.

19. E E is the best answer; the passage presents factual information in an objective tone. A is incorrect; an author is not disinterested in his subject. B and C are too strong. D is wrong, as little personal information about Livingston is revealed.

20. B Lines 56–60 indicate that the natives had no interest in making contact with Livingston. A is extreme. No information is given about *most* of the inhabitants of Africa. C is not supported by the passage. Although Livingston saw few people, many people might have lived there. D is beyond the information given in the passage. E is incorrect because while the natives are not interested in making contact with Livingston, the passage never states they are *upset*.

21. C C is the best choice. The first paragraph gives some details about the beginnings of the journey, which is later described in greater detail. A is not correct because Livingston's private life is not described. B is wrong because no mention is made of characteristics or skills. D is incorrect; Livingston and his companions are not *lackadaisical*. E is wrong, because it doesn't actually explain why he was in Africa.

22. D In lines 54–56, the author describes how one can locate the Kongone by using Milambe and East Luabo. A is incorrect, because the current and wind can make it more difficult to travel on the Kongone. B is mentioned in the passage, but is not given as a reason that Livingston decided that the river was the "best" course for a boat. C is also not stated as a contributing factor. E is wrong; there is no beacon on Pearl Island.

23. B Lines 31–34 state that the water level of the Kongone is at *two fathoms* at low water, but during the spring tides rises by *12 to 14 feet* (*spring tides* refer to the rise and fall of the tides at or soon after a new or full moon). The *cuttlefish* referred to in A are not clearly part of the Kongone; they are mentioned as being observed when Livingston was still offshore. C is incorrect; the passage clearly states that the Milambe is the most westerly. D is wrong because the bar of the Kongone is not contrasted with the bars of the other tributaries. E refers to East Luabo, not to the Kongone.

24. A A is the best choice, because lines 43–44 state that the East Luabo is the easiest to spot. B is mentioned, but not as reason that East Luabo is favorable to navigators. C is contradicted by the passage, as the river is safe only when the wind is east or north-east. D is beyond the information given in the passage since no mention is given of *European navigators*. E is also not supported. The passage makes it clear that Livingston is not certain whether East Luabo is the same as the river described by de Gama.

SECTION 4

1. B This simple equation should present you with little difficulty, but beware: It is on precisely such questions that your guard might come down and you can become careless! Plugging In the answer choices is safest. Only B works:

$$2 + (0) = 2 - (0)$$

$$2 = 2$$

2. B As the directions at the beginning of every math section remind us, the area of a triangle is given by this formula: $A = \frac{1}{2}bh$. If the base is 4 and the height is 1, the area is 2. $A = \frac{1}{2} \times 4 \times 1 = 2$.

3. E If the area of square A is 16, the length of each side is 4, and the perimeter is 16. You are told that this is $\frac{2}{3}$ of B's perimeter, which you can calculate:

$$\frac{2}{3}x = 16$$

$$x = 16 \times \frac{3}{2} = 24$$

Now that you know the perimeter of B, you can calculate the perimeter of C:

$$\frac{2}{3}x = 24$$

$$x = 24 \times \frac{3}{2} = 36$$

If the perimeter of C is 36, each side is 9, and the area of C is 9^2, or 81. If you chose B, you need to read the question more carefully.

4. E According to the ratios given, you know that the mixture contains more wheat than rye; there must be more than 5 pounds of wheat. So let's eliminate A and B. Use the Ratio Box.

Corn	Wheat	Rye	Total
3	5	2	10
2.5	2.5	2.5	2.5
7.5	12.5	5	25

Because there is a total of 5 pounds of rye, the multiplier is 2.5. This allows you to solve for 12.5 pounds for the wheat.

5. C Because 135° is one of the middle angles of the circle, the triangles must each have a 45° angle, and are therefore both identical 45°-45°-90° triangles. Remember (or check the front page of the test) that the ratio of the sides in such a triangle is $x : x : \sqrt{2}x$. You know that the diameter of the circle is 12, so the hypotenuse (which is equal to the radius of the circle) of each triangle is 6. If 6 is the long side, the other side of each triangle must be $\frac{6}{\sqrt{2}}$. Now you can find the area of one of the triangles and double it. The area of a triangle is $\frac{1}{2}bh$, and both the base and height are equal to $\frac{6}{\sqrt{2}}$. So $\frac{1}{2} \times \frac{6}{\sqrt{2}} \times \frac{6}{\sqrt{2}} = \frac{36}{4} = 9$. You have found the area for one of the triangles, so double it to get 18, or C. Another way to solve this is to use the side of your answer sheet as a ruler and ballpark. If $XZ = 12$, the hypotenuse of each triangle is 6. Now mark off the length of 6 with your homemade ruler and compare that to a side of one of the triangles. You can guesstimate that the side is about 4. Using that approximation, calculate that since the base and height of both triangles is 4, the area of each triangle is $\frac{1}{2} \times 4 \times 4 = 8$. The area of both triangles together is 16, which is closest to 18, or C. ETS wants you to do complicated geometry, but all you care about is finding the answer.

6. A Translate each statement, piece by piece. The first part tells us that " the product of x and y is 76." Since *product* means multiplication, then the first equation must be $xy = 76$, so you can eliminate answers (C) and (D). The second part says that "x is twice the square of y," which translates to $x = 2y^2$, so eliminate answers (B) and (E), and (A) is the only answer left. Notice that only the y needs to be squared, which is why (B) is wrong. The second equation for (B) would be written as "the square of twice y," which is not what the problem stated.

7. A Try roughly plotting the data points, and then look at your graph. Find the answer that best fits your graph. Alternatively, notice that the number of customers increases as the temperature increases. The line of best fit will go up as you follow the graph from left to right, so eliminate B, D, and E. Notice that the number of customers does not increase by the same number for each 10-degree temperature increase. This is an exponential increase, not a linear increase. So, the graph will be curved. Eliminate C. Only A fits the data in the chart.

8. E Plug in 6 for c. The question is now asking what percent of 18 is 9. The answer would be 50. Whichever choice gives you 50 when 6 is plugged in for C is the answer. Therefore, E is the answer. Remember: Plugging in good numbers will make your life much easier!

9. D Draw the missing figures. When you sketch this out, you'll see that it's a right triangle with legs of lengths 4 and 5. Use the Pythagorean theorem: $4^2 + 5^2 = c^2$. Now solve for c. $c^2 = 41$ and $c = \sqrt{41}$. Remember that the question asked for perimeter, so add up the sides: $4 + 5 + \sqrt{41} = 9 + \sqrt{41}$, which is choice D.

10. B If 20% of the coins are either nickels or dimes, 80% are neither. 80% of 220 equals 176. Use your calculator or write it out and solve:

$$\frac{8}{10} \times 220 = 176$$

11. D Take out your calculator:

$$216{,}000 + 20\% \text{ of } 216{,}000 = 259{,}200$$
$$204{,}000 + 20\% \text{ of } 204{,}000 = 244{,}800$$
$$259{,}200 - 244{,}800 = 14{,}400$$

Another route to the answer is to take the difference immediately (216,000 – 204,000 = 12,000) and then increase that by 20%.

Watch out for partial answers. E is 20% of Springfield's population, and A is the difference between 20% of Springfield's population and 20% of Rockville's population.

12. E With algebraic answer choices, you should plug in numbers. Let's let $x = y = 2$, which makes $z = 4$. Plugging these values into the choices, you'd get the following:

(A) $2(2) + 2(2) = 2(4)$ [Yes]

(B) $2 - 2 = 0$ [Yes]

(C) $2 - 4 = 2 - 4$ [Yes]

(D) $2 = \frac{4}{2}$ [Yes]

(E) $4 - 2 = 2(2)$ [No]

The correct answer is E. Don't forget the EXCEPT!

13. A Do NOT try to figure out the seven numbers in the original list! The median is the middle number in a list of numbers. Because 8 is lower than every other number, and 43 is higher, they won't change the value of the median. This means that option II is wrong, so you can eliminate B, D, and E. Because A and C both include I, you know it must be true without even checking it. Let's focus on option III. The mode is the number repeated most often. Because 8 and 43 weren't in the original list, they can't change the mode. Eliminate C and pick A.

14. D There are variables in the answer choices, and the question asks you what *must be* true. This indicates that you will need to plug in values for x, possibly more than once. Try both –2 and 3. Only D remains true for both. Remember that the square of any nonzero number, either positive or negative, is always positive.

15. E The relationship is: the smaller the shoes, the greater the difficulty. This is an inverse relationship. So, look for an inverse function. Only E is an inverse function. If you weren't sure, try plugging in 8 and 10 for the s. The function should yield a greater D for 8 than it does for 10. Only E has $D(8) > D(10)$.

16. D Note first that this is an EXCEPT question. Now, since $a^2b = 12^2$, and b is an odd integer, let's see what you can come up with. Let's make b equal 1, so you get the following: $a^2 \times 1 = 12^2 = 144$, so $a = 12$. If a equals 12, it is divisible by 1, 2, 3, 4, 6, and 12. The only choice that remains is D.

17. D Since each side is a mysterious "x long," let's make up a value for x to make our lives a little easier. Let's use 10, just because it's nice and round. To find the area of the first triangle, you'll have to find the height, which is the middle side of a 30°-60°-90° triangle. If the entire base is 10, then the height is $5\sqrt{3}$. The area is then $A = \frac{1}{2}bh = \frac{1}{2}10(5\sqrt{3}) = 25\sqrt{3}$. The second triangle has side lengths of $2x$, which means each side is 20 long. We can find the area in the same way as the first one. We'll end up with a height of $10\sqrt{3}$, and the area is $\frac{1}{2}20(10\sqrt{3}) = 100\sqrt{3}$. Since the area of the second triangle is four times the area of the first one, the answer is (D), 1 : 4.

18. A Keep in mind that this figure is not drawn to scale. Because $\overline{BD} \parallel \overline{AE}$, you know that the following angles are equal: $\angle DCE, \angle CEA, \angle BCA, \angle CAE$. Because triangle ACE has two equal angles, it is isosceles and the sides opposite those angles are also equal. Therefore, $CE = AC = 3$.

19. C Plug in numbers. If $a = 10$ and $b = 10$, then the inequality doesn't work: $(10 – 5)(10 + 5) = (5)(15) = 75$, which is larger than 0, so eliminate answers (D) and (E). If $a = –5$ and $b = –10$ then the inequality also doesn't work: $(–5 – 5)(-10 + 5) = (–10)(–5)$, which is larger than 0, so eliminate answers (A) and (B), and (C) is the only answer left.

20. D Because 61 is the value of the *second* term in the sequence, plug in 2 for n: $a^{3(2)} – 3 = 61$. Therefore, $a^6 = 64$, and a must be equal to ±2. Make sure you read carefully; III would work if 61 were the value of the *first* term.

SECTION 5

1. C All versions of the underlined phrase except C are wordy or awkward.

2. B If something has been happening for the last two thousand years, it shouldn't be discussed in the present or future tense. Eliminate A, D, and E for that error. *Building technologies* continue to change, so it

would be better to use *have changed* rather than *had changed. Had changed* implies that the technologies will no longer change.

3. A The sentence is correct as it is written. B and E rewrite the verbs in *-ing* form, not the first choice for a clear sentence. C eliminates the cause-and-effect relationship present in the original. D adds the word *it,* which makes the sentence a run-on.

4. D D uses the correct idiom, *belief that.* Both A and E use an incorrect idiom, *belief of.* In B, the first *is* is unnecessary and makes the sentence awkward. C adds another unnecessary word, *which.*

5. A There is no error in the sentence as it is written.

6. E The beginning of the sentence is in the past tense, so get rid of anything that uses present tense in the underlined portion: A and C. B changes the meaning by using *second* in a different context. D changes the wording to *a miracle is what he needed,* which isn't parallel with the rest of the sentence.

7. B As written, A contains nonparallel structure. C misplaces the word *careful*; D mistakenly implies a cause-and-effect relationship; and E uses the word *yet,* implying a contradiction which does not exist, and splits the infinitive *to document.* Only B correctly uses the parallel structure *you should gather... and document,* without adding other errors.

8. E The sentence should compare the soil of Pennsylvania with the soil of the Rhine. Only E does so correctly: the phrase *that of* helps draw the proper comparison. Each of the other choices creates a faulty comparison.

9. D An *-ing* form of a verb cannot be the main verb of a sentence, as in A and C. Also, to avoid a misplaced modifier, the phrase *as one of the forward-looking, enlightened monarchs of Europe* should follow the word *reputation* as it does in D. B adds the word *however,* which is unnecessary, and E says *always,* which changes the meaning.

10. D Watch out for switches from the pronoun *you* to the pronoun *one.* Stick with one or the other. Both A and B switch between the two. C isn't a complete sentence, and E is awkward and somewhat changes the meaning.

11. C This sentence contains the ambiguous pronoun *it,* leaving the reader unsure which design movement *instigated* the paradigm shift. Eliminate A and B for this error. Both D and E use *and* instead of *however.* Because the second half of the sentence shows a difference between the two schools of design, and the first half shows a similarity, *however* is better, so eliminate D and E.

12. B Plural nouns must refer to plural nouns. There are two *characters* so they cannot be *an orphan*; they would be *orphans.*

13. E There is no error in the sentence as it is written.

14. A This sentence confuses subject with object. Because the speaker is the subject, *me* should be changed to *I.*

15. A An adverb, *completely,* is needed to modify the verb *exhausted.*

16. A To correct the error in subject-verb agreement, change *is* to *are* because *benefits* is plural.

17. D D creates an error in verb parallelism. The verbs in the list, *listening* and *reading,* do not agree with *she practiced.* It should be *practicing.*

18. D This sentence misuses an incorrect comparison modifier. Because more than two *jingoists* are mentioned (*all*), change *more* to the superlative *most.*

19. E There is no error in the sentence as it is written.

20. **C** The verbal phrase *brushing your teeth* acts as a singular noun (you could replace this phrase with *it*), which requires the singular verb *promotes.*

21. **C** In this sentence, the *trends* discussed *seem* to do two things: *show* and *indicating.* The verbs need to be parallel in form but are not. C should read *indicate* instead.

22. **D** The semicolon indicates that both clauses must be independent, so *being* creates a fragment. The correct form should be *was.*

23. **C** In C, *it* is a singular pronoun, which doesn't agree with the plural subject *species.* The sentence should read "they swing."

24. **C** This adjective should be in comparative form (*higher*) to parallel *shorter, lighter, or tighter.*

25. **D** This is a verb tense error; the father performed the action in the past tense, but not so far in the past as to require the past perfect tense. Therefore, *exercised* is better than *had exercised.*

26. **B** This sentence uses the wrong conjunction. Because the sentence contrasts two unlike things, replace *and* with *but* for greater logic and clarity.

27. **C** The sentence should read: "Saif knew that the other applicants weren't as good as he"; using *him* isn't correct. Some may even write the sentence as: "Saif knew that the other applicants weren't as good as he was"; however, the verb *was* isn't necessary.

28. **D** *She* is ambiguous in this sentence; it could refer either to Natalie or to Noelle. It should read *Natalie.*

29. **D** In D, *Branagh* sets up a faulty comparison. *Olivier's* performance should be compared to *Branagh's* performance, not to *Branagh* himself. It should read *to Kenneth Branagh's.*

30. **B** Although there are no big errors in the original version, it is longer and less straightforward than B. C and E change the meaning of the sentence, and D is as awkward as the original.

31. **A** B and C introduce a casual tone that doesn't flow with the rest of the passage. Deleting the word *another,* as D suggests, and deleting the entire sentence, as E suggests, would confuse the meaning and flow of the sentence and passage. A is best because it creates a transition between two examples that both support the author's main point.

32. **E** Only E retains the correct meaning of the sentence while using correct grammar. The original version, as given in A, uses a run-on sentence. B does not fix this original error just by adding a semicolon. Both C and D suggest that the employees will invest in the stock, the stock will plummet, and their savings will disappear. You need to retain the original meaning—that this is a possibility and not a definite occurrence.

33. **C** The first paragraph discusses one side of an issue: Protective legislation may limit freedom and be unnecessary. The second paragraph shows the other side of the debate: Some laws may be helpful. The third paragraph concludes that a compromise is best. Thus, sentence 10 should be the concluding sentence of the second paragraph, making C the best answer. B would upset the chronology of the second paragraph. A improperly creates a contrast with the preceding ideas. D destroys the agreement between *their* and *people.* Similarly, E's lack of noun agreement illogically implies that the employees all share one retirement account.

34. **E** Only E correctly uses the parallel construction *some people will think...others will complain.*

35. **D** With omission questions, read the sentence with the sentences immediately before and after it, then read those two sentences without the sentence in question. You are looking for a sentence with a piece

of information that is not relevant to the passage. Sentences 3, 7, 11, and 15 are all necessary parts of the passage; therefore you can eliminate them and choose D.

SECTION 6

1. B The best way to approach this problem is to plug in the answers. Start with C. When 6 is subtracted from 10, the result is 4. Divide 4 by 2 to see if it equals 3. It does not, so C can't be correct. Because our answer was too small, you need to subtract a smaller number from 10. Try B. When 4 is subtracted from 10, the result is 6. Divide by 2 to get 3; this is correct.

2. C The number of degrees in a line is 180. Therefore, $b + c = 180$. And since $a + 90 = 180$, $a = 90$. So $a + b + c = 270$. Note that E is the Joe Bloggs choice—"it cannot be determined" is rarely the correct answer.

3. E Use the formula for distance: *distance* = *rate* × *time.*

   Steve runs 12 miles at 8 miles per hour, which means that he runs for $1\frac{1}{2}$ hours (or 1.5 if you're using your calculator). Adam runs the same 12 miles at 6 miles per hour, which means that he runs for 2 hours. Adam takes half an hour longer to complete the race, and half an hour is 30 minutes.

4. D Because there are variables in the answers, try Plugging In! If $a = 2$, then $\frac{4a}{3} \times 6a = \frac{8 \times 12}{3} = 32$. Plug $a = 2$ into the answers to find that only D is 32. Another option is to rewrite the problem as $\frac{4a}{3} \times \frac{6a}{1}$. Reduce before you multiply by dividing the denominator of the first term and the numerator of the second term by 3 to get $\frac{4a}{1} \times \frac{2a}{1} = 8a^2$.

5. E To solve this problem, you need to figure out the ratio between the *x*- and *y*-values on line segment $\overline{AB}$. Looking at the figure, $\overline{AB}$ is the hypotenuse of a right triangle with a side of 12. You can see this is a multiple of one of ETS's favorite right triangles: 3:4:5. This is a 9:12:15 triangle, and the coordinates of point *B* are (9, 12). All the points on line segment $\overline{AB}$ are in a ratio of 9:12. Only E has a similar ratio.

6. B Because you aren't given the cost of any book, you can plug in our own values. Let's say that the average cost of the textbooks, excluding the anatomy textbook, is \$10. You can make all the books cost \$10 each to make the problem easier. The anatomy textbook would cost \$30. The total cost of all the textbooks would be \$130. The anatomy textbook would be $\frac{\$30}{\$130} = \frac{3}{13}$ of the total cost.

7. A The trick is to notice that this parallelogram is actually made of two equal triangles. By finding the area of the triangles, you can find the area of the parallelogram. The triangles are both right triangles, and the two sides given in the figure follow the 3:4:5 pattern. If you look at triangle *ACD* with $\overline{AC}$ as the base, the base is 3 and the height is 4. Now use the formula for area of a triangle:

$$A = \frac{1}{2} \times 3 \times 4 = 6$$

   That means the parallelogram is 2 × 6 = 12.
   Also, if you estimate the area, the base is 5 and the height is less than 3, so the area is less than 15. The only answer less than 15 is A!

8. **D** Plug in a value for b, the number of minutes the pie is baked. Let's say 52 minutes, because 52 is greater than 50, less than 60, and not 55 (which is in all the answer choices). The only answer choice that works is (D): $|52 - 55| = |-3| = 3$, which is less than 5.

9. **2**

Just simplify and solve for x:

$$\frac{x+2x+3x}{2}=6$$

$$\frac{6x}{2}=6$$

$$6x=12$$

$$x=2$$

Remember that the first grid-in question returns the difficulty meter to easy!

10. **19, 39, 59, 79, or 99**

The simplest way to solve this problem would be to find values of n that satisfy the first condition, and then to check which of those also satisfies the second condition. So, let's find some numbers that leave a remainder of 4 when divided by 5: {9, 14, 19, 24, 29}.

That should be enough. Now let's check which of these leaves a remainder of 3 when divided by 4:

$$9 \div 4 = 2\ R1$$

$$14 \div 4 = 3\ R2$$

$$19 \div 4 = 4\ R3$$

19 is one acceptable response.

11. **145**

Because the two lines are parallel, $110 + 2x = 180$. Solving this equation for x, you get $x = 35$. Looking at the triangle, the missing angle (m) can be found by solving the equation $110 + x + m = 180$. If $x = 35$, $m = 35$. If $m + y = 180$ and $m = 35$, $y = 145$.

12. **36**

If $x^2 = 16$ then $x = \pm 4$. If $y^2 = 4$ then $y = \pm 2$. To maximize $(x - y)^2$, you need to maximize the difference. The greatest difference is $(-4) - 2 = -6$ or $4 - (-2) = 6$, and both 6^2 and $(-6)^2$ equal 36.

13. **130**

First use a Ratio Box to find the number of males and females. If the ratio is 2 to 3, the total ratio is 5. The actual is 250, so the multiplier is 50. That means there are $50 \times 2 = 100$ males and $50 \times 3 = 150$ females. Set up a group grid (the bolded numbers are information from the problem):

	Males	Females	Total
French	**80**	20	**100**
Spanish	20	130	150
Total	100	150	250

You find that 20 females must be taking French, and because there 150 females total, 130 must be taking Spanish.

14. **8**

In the diagram, you can assume that the shorter ticks are evenly spaced, so each one must be 0.25 units long. Plugging the coordinates of the points into the given expression gives you $\frac{jk}{lmn} = \frac{(-2.5)(-1.5)}{(0.5)(0.75)(1.25)} = 8$. As you can see, canceling works well: The two negatives cancel each other out, and two of the numbers in the numerator are double the size of two of the numbers in the denominator. This leaves you with $\frac{jk}{lmn} = \frac{(2)(2)}{(0.5)} = 8$. You can also just plug the whole thing into your calculator, but make sure you use enough parentheses: You need to enclose the entire numerator in parentheses, and then the entire denominator in parentheses.

15. **12**

Start with the most restricted spots. There are 2 tools that can go in the first spot. Once you put 1 there, only 1 tool can go in the second spot. Once you've used these 2 tools, there are only 3 that can go in the third spot, then 2 in the fourth spot and 1 in the fifth spot. So, there are 2 × 1 × 3 × 2 × 1 = 12 ways to arrange the tools.

16. **4**

This question looks tough, so work it one step at a time, and start with what you know. Sector *AOB* is a quarter-circle (it covers an angle of 90 out of 360 degrees), so multiplying its area (π) by 4 gives you the area of the whole circle (4π). Plugging this into the equation for the area of a circle, $A = \pi r^2$, gives you $4\pi = \pi r^2$, and the radius must be a positive value, so $r = 2$. This means that the coordinates of point *A* must be (–2, 0). Because *A* is on both the circle and the parabola, you can plug its *x*- and *y*-coordinates into the given equation of the parabola, $y = x^2 - b$. This becomes $0 = (-2)^2 - b$, so $b = 4$.

17. **3**

The first step is to draw a diagram:

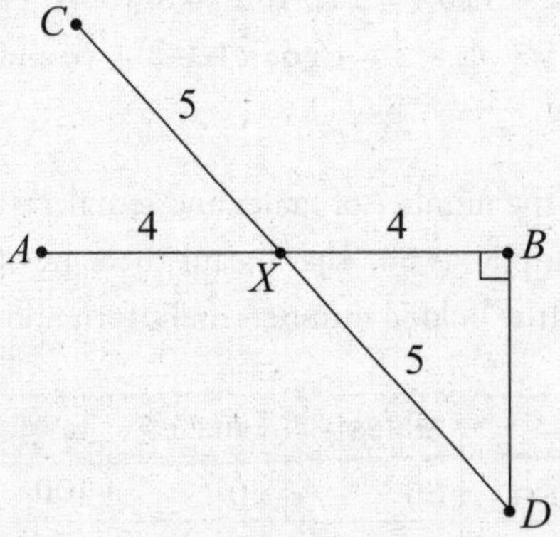

You should notice that *BD* is part of one of ETS's favorite right triangles: a 3:4:5 triangle. So *BD* = 3.

18. $\mathbf{\frac{6}{5}}$ **or 1.2**

Inversely proportional means $x_1y_1 = x_2y_2$ where *x* represents hours of sleep and *y* represents the number of errors: (2 hours)(3 errors) = (5 hours)(*y* hours). 6 = 5*y*, so $y = \frac{6}{5}$

SECTION 7

1. **D** Because *morality* is being linked with *religion*, you need a word along the lines of *erosion*; *collapse* is the only choice that fits.

2. **A** The clue in this sentence is *anarchy*, which means lack of order. If people have been shaken by the lack of order, they must be ready to buy "order" at any price. A comes closest to this meaning.

3. **B** You may have had trouble coming up with your own words on this question. This is because there is a relationship between the blanks. The phrase *external factors* is a clue. On the one hand, if animal behaviors are inherited, they would be relatively unaffected by external factors. On the other hand, if the animal behaviors are learned, they would be affected by external factors. B is the only one to preserve this relationship.

4. **C** We know the general's civilian life is simple, dignified, and *stoic*. The only blank that fits is C; B and D miss the clues. A and E, if you weren't sure what they mean, are good guesses, but incorrect.

5. **A** The clue is *cruel severity of some criminal penalties*. A judge (at least one that ETS likes) would probably want to avoid or to lessen *the cruel severity of some criminal penalties*. B and D miss the point completely. If you know what *condone* means, it also misses the point; if not, it's not a bad guess. E is a Joe Bloggs trap that contradicts the clue.

6. **A** *Hutton* and *Darwin* are used as examples of different scientists who contributed to geology. B is incorrect because the last sentence states that controversy surrounds many geologic theories and they are *constantly challenged*. C is incorrect because biological evolution expanded upon, rather than disproved, the theory of Uniformity. D is too negative an answer; though the science may be relatively new, it is not *inexact*. E is incorrect, because the passage mentions *seventeenth-century* attempts to date the earth.

7. **B** The best answer is B. Passage 1 does not attempt to *prove*, *contradict*, or *criticize* a theory. Therefore A, C, D, and E can all be eliminated.

8. **A** Both passages refer to Geological Evolution as a theory, which implies that it has not yet been proven to be a fact. B and D are mentioned only in Passage 2 whereas E is mentioned or implied only in Passage 1. C is not correct because the age of the theory is not discussed in Passage 2. A is the best answer.

9. **E** The best answer is E. *Confirmation*, *exception*, and *itemization* are too extreme or demanding to be accomplished in a short reading passage. Therefore, A, B and C can all be eliminated. D does not take into account the example of Heart Mountain, which appears to disprove the Geological Evolutionary theory.

10. **A** The lead words in this question are *the author's parents*. You learn about the author's parents in line 5: *my parents were at their wits' end*. The author mentions his parents again in lines 24–26: *My parents… agreed with the schoolmasters*. A paraphrases the answer well (*frustrated*). B is incorrect because the author's parents clearly knew that he had a problem. How could they be oblivious to the fact that he was expelled from several schools? C has nothing to do with the passage. You might be able to infer that the author's parents were wealthy because they sent him to a boarding school, but you cannot know their attitude toward the poor from the passage. D confuses several unconnected ideas mentioned in the passage. There is nothing in the passage to suggest that the author's parents were schoolmasters. The first paragraph states that the author's family lived together *in Bukovina*, so E is incorrect.

11. **C** According to lines 14–18, *An attempt to harmonize the imbalances in my character by means of strict discipline at a boarding school...nearly led to the same ignominious end*. Even if you don't know what *ignominious* means, it should still be clear that the attempt to straighten out the author had the same result as it did before—it didn't work. This idea is paraphrased in C, which says that *the tactics were failing*. A is extreme. Perhaps the author was a bit unstable, but there is nothing in the passage that suggests the author was a *danger to others*. Remember: If an answer choice is half bad, it's all bad. B is a trap. Maybe the author did poorly in school partly because the schools were too difficult. Or maybe not. The passage tells you nothing about the difficulty of the schools. All you know is that the author was having a really hard time. D is another trap. You have no way of knowing from the passage how well the author got along with his peers. In E, you know that his academic career is in bad shape, but does that mean he'll never finish school?

12. **B** The best answer is B. You are told that the author's people were once subjects of the Austro-Hungarian Empire. In a parenthetical aside he tells you that they still regard Austria as their cultural homeland. This is attached to the sentence in which you are told that he was sent to school in Styria, presumably a place in Austria.

13. **D** Go back to the passage, find the word *ignominious*, and cross it out. Then read the sentence and come up with your own word. According to lines 19–20, the author just barely escaped *final ostracism from the privileged ranks*. If he was about to get thrown out of the privileged ranks, the word that best describes that situation is *disgraceful* or something strongly negative. The other answers are incorrect because they don't accurately describe the author's situation as it is described in the passage.

14. **C** This is a general question, so you need to know only the main idea of the passage. You know that the author was not happy in the passage, because he says he felt *skushno*, a word that means *more than dreary boredom*. You can get rid of A and E because they're positive. D is too extreme; it is highly unlikely ETS would ever suggest that someone was suicidal. B is incorrect because the passage never says that the author had trouble with his friends.

15. **B** Your first clue to the author's attitude toward the aphorism is that he calls it *trivial*. After he quotes the aphorism, the author says, *this optimistic notion results more from wishful thinking than from practical experience*. The author clearly has a very negative opinion of it. B gives a perfect paraphrase of *wishful thinking* by saying that the author found the aphorism *unrealistic*. You can get rid of A as it is positive. D can be eliminated because the author wasn't confused (*bemused*), and you can eliminate E because it refers to his *faith in it*; the author clearly has no faith in the aphorism. C is incorrect because the author doesn't say anything about the aphorism working for others.

16. **C** This is a general question, so you only need to know the main idea of the passage. In simple terms, the passage talks about the difference between cats and dogs. This is exactly what choice C says. Notice that the author presents both sides of the issue and doesn't advocate one animal over the other. That's why B and D are wrong. A is way too extreme. If you don't know what *enmity* means, look it up and you'll see. E only covers one section of the passage, not the primary purpose of the passage as a whole.

17. **E** According to the passage, the cat treats its human owners as *pseudoparents* because they took over from the real mother at a sensitive stage of the kitten's development. That means the human owners are obviously not the kitten's real parents, but rather like adoptive parents that took over from the kitten's real mother. E says exactly that. A is wrong because *pseudo-* doesn't mean part-time. Human owners can be full-time parents to a cat, but that doesn't make them the cat's real parents. B misses the mark

because the passage is talking about the parents of cats, not the parents of adults. C is wrong because the passage doesn't say anything about neglect. D makes no sense. How can someone have the characteristics of both humans and cats?

18. **C** This is a general question, but it is also an EXCEPT question, so do it last. The only way to answer this question is to search through the passage for each of the answer choices. Remember: You're looking for the answer choice that is not there. The passage uses a statistic in line 61, makes a parenthetical statement in line 38, restates an argument in lines 70–73, and makes generalizations throughout the passage. C is the only one left.

19. **C** The lead words in this question are *the domestic cat*, which should lead you to the first paragraph. According to lines 11–12, *the young cat becomes bimental. It may be a cat physically, but mentally it is both feline and human.* To be both feline and human is definitely a contradiction. Common sense kills A because cats don't have two feet. B and D are incorrect because domestic cats are tame by definition. Otherwise, they would be wild. E doesn't make any sense. Do cats dominate humans? No way!

20. **D** The lead words in this question are *difference between dogs and cats*, which should lead you right to the beginning of the second paragraph. According to lines 27–33, the adult *pet dog sees its human family both as pseudoparents* and *dominant members of the pack....* On the other hand, cats *never hunt in packs*, and most of their day is spent in *solitary stalking*. So while dogs see their owners as leaders of the pack, cats do not, because they're solitary. This is paraphrased in D. A directly contradicts the passage. According to lines 30–31, *cats do have a complex social organization*. Read carefully. B has it backward. Dogs are obedient, not cats. C comes out of nowhere. Where does it say that cats are creative? E also contradicts the passage. According to lines 31–32, cats spend most of their time in solitary stalking, which means they're probably good hunters.

21. **B** According to the lines 23–25, *dogs live in packs with tightly controlled status relationships among the individuals. There are top dogs, middle dogs, and bottom dogs....* This describes a social structure that is *hierarchical*. (If you don't know what hierarchical means, look it up!) The other answers are incorrect because none of them accurately describes the social structure in the lines quoted above. There is nothing abstract C or flexible A about tightly controlled status relationships, nor is there any mention of male domination in the passage. And exclusivity E is certainly not the issue.

22. **B** According to the passage, an *ambitious Yuppie* is an example of someone who is *not a typical cat-owner*. Because *cat-owners are solitary* people, this means the *ambitious Yuppie* must be *a group-oriented person*. Accordingly, B is the answer. A and D are insulting to Yuppies, and ETS wants to avoid controversy. C might be tempting, but ETS likes to avoid stereotypes. E is not mentioned in the passage.

23. **B** You can immediately eliminate C and D because ETS would never say anything negative or overly stereotypical about women. According to the fifth paragraph, the differences between the roles of prehistoric men and women *contributed to a human male "pack mentality" that is far less marked in females*. This idea is paraphrased in B. A is the opposite of what is said in the passage, and E is not supported.

24. **C** To answer this question, you have to know what *caricature* means. A caricature is an exaggerated drawing, so the author is saying that he exaggerated in the passage. He is thus qualifying some of the generalizations he has made in the passage. A is too extreme. ETS would never suggest that the author of one of its passages made a futile argument. B misses the point of these lines, which refer to generalizations, not contradictions. D goes in the wrong direction. In the lines cited in the question, the author admits that he exaggerated in order to make his point, so he's trying to ensure that readers

don't overestimate what he said in the passage. E sounds like psychobabble; it also has nothing to do with what the author is saying at the end of the passage.

SECTION 8

1. D Use the first equation to solve for x: $3x - 5 = 4$, so $x = 3$. Plug in 3 for x: $9x - 15 = 27 - 15 = 12$.

2. E This is an excellent calculator question. Here are the costs per unit for each color:

$$\text{Black} = \frac{\$2.00}{5} = \$.40 \text{ per button}$$

$$\text{Blue} = \frac{\$2.00}{6} = .33 \text{ per button}$$

$$\text{Brown} = \frac{\$3.00}{8} = .375 \text{ per button}$$

$$\text{Orange} = \frac{\$4.00}{12} = .33 \text{ per button}$$

$$\text{Red} = \frac{\$4.00}{7} = .57 \text{ per button}$$

The red buttons are the most expensive.

3. C Plug the answers into the equation starting with C. The (x, y) point is (7, 8), so plug in 7 for x and 8 for y. Because $8 = 2(7) - 6$, C is the correct answer.

4. B Before you reach for your calculator, reduce the expression.

$$\frac{x^2}{x^3} = \frac{x \bullet x}{x \bullet x \bullet x} = x^{-1}$$

Then simply try each choice; At –1, B has the least value. If you selected E, you didn't work out each choice.

5. B One way to solve this problem is to plug in. First, simplify $(a + b)^2 = 49$ by taking the square root of both sides to find $a + b = 7$. Now, brainstorm some values for a and b that make $a + b = 7$ and $ab = 10$: let's say a is 2 and b is 5. So, find the answer that yields 5 when you plug in $a = 2$. Only B works. The second, more complicated, way is to FOIL out $(a + b)^2 = 49$ to get $a^2 + 2ab + b^2 = 49$. Plug in 10 for ab to get $a^2 + 2(10) + b^2 = 49$. That means, $a^2 + 20 + b^2 = 49$. Subtract 20 from both sides to get $a^2 + b^2 = 29$. Subtract a^2 from both sides to get $b^2 = 29 - a^2$. Take the square root of both sides to find $b = \sqrt{29 - a^2}$.

6. C First, you can estimate. Because square $ABFE$ has an area of 25, EF equals 5 and EC looks to be a little less than twice EF, or in the 7–9 range. Thus, since $CE = ED$, because they are the legs of a 45°-45°-90° triangle, you can eliminate D and E. You also know that the area of $\triangle BCF$ is 10, and that its base (BF) is 5. Using the formula for area, you can calculate FC, the height of the triangle: $10 = \left(\frac{1}{2}\right)(5) \times (h)$, $h = 4$. So $5(FE) + 4(FC) = 9$, which is the length of $\overline{CE}$ and $\overline{DE}$.

7. C Stack all three equations and add them together to get $3x + 3y + 3z = 51$. Factor out a 3 to get $3(x + y + z) = 51$. Divide both sides by 3 to get $x + y + z = 17$.

8. D Translate into algebra. *The sum of two numbers is 10* means $x + y = 10$. Next, *one number is equal to the sum of 6 and twice the other number* means $x = 6 + 2y$. Rearrange the second equation into $x - 2y = 6$. Subtract the second equation from the first to find $3y = 4$. Divide by 3 to find $y = \frac{4}{3}$. Plug that into the first equation to get $x + \frac{4}{3} = 10$. So, $x = 8\frac{2}{3}$. *The larger number minus the smaller number* is $8\frac{2}{3} - 1\frac{1}{3} = 7\frac{1}{3}$.

9. D Go through this problem one piece at a time. We know that $\frac{1}{5}$ of the \$45,000 goes to the sanitation department. Remember that "of" in math questions means to multiply, so $\frac{1}{5} \times 45{,}000 = \$9{,}000$. He now has (45,000 – 9,000) \$36,000 left. He spends $\frac{2}{3}$ of that \$36,000 remaining on the police department, which is $(\frac{2}{3} \times 36{,}000) = \$24{,}000$. He now has (36,000 – 24,000) \$12,000 left to spend, so the answer is (D).

10. A Let's begin by drawing a parallelogram and Plugging In a number for y, say 50, and calling the other two angles x:

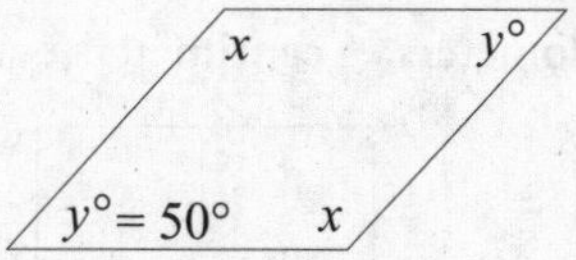

Because there are 360 degrees in a quadrilateral, you know that $2x + 100° = 360°$, which means $x = 130°$. So, you're looking for the choice that gives you 130 when $y = 50°$. You simply plug 50 into all of the answer choices to find that A is the only one that works.

11. D This is a parabola, because one of the two variables is squared. Eliminate A, B, and E, which are not parabolic graphs. Because the smallest possible value of mx^2 is 0, the smallest possible value of $mx^2 + b$ is b, so all of the curve must be above the x-axis. Only D works.

12. C First, you need to compute all possible values of n:

$\sqrt{n}$	n
1	1
2	4
3	9
4	16
5	25
6	36
7	49
8	64
9	81

Now, be careful! The median value for $\sqrt{n}$ is 5, but the median value for n is 25.

13. C Draw a picture! Look at triangle *CJK*. $\angle CJK$ is 90 because the radius of a circle is always perpendicular to a line tangent to that circle. Use the Pythagorean theorem, $(CJ)^2 + 24^2 = 26^2$, or your knowledge of right triangles (this is a multiple of a 5:12:13 triangle) to get $CJ = 10$, which represents the radius of the circle. So the circumference of the circle = $2\pi \times 10$ or 20π.

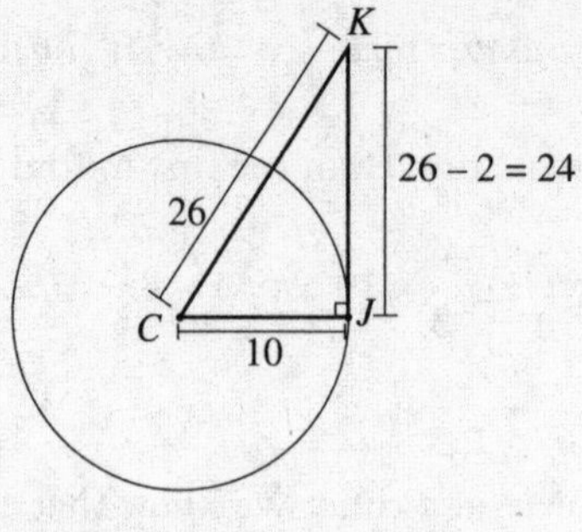

14. D This is a tricky question. Let's draw a picture:

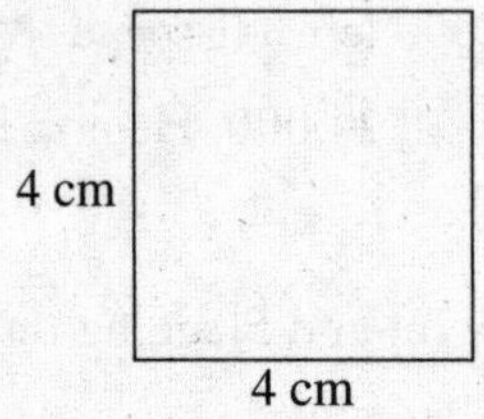

Because 1 centimeter equals 6 kilometers, 4 centimeters equals 24 kilometers:

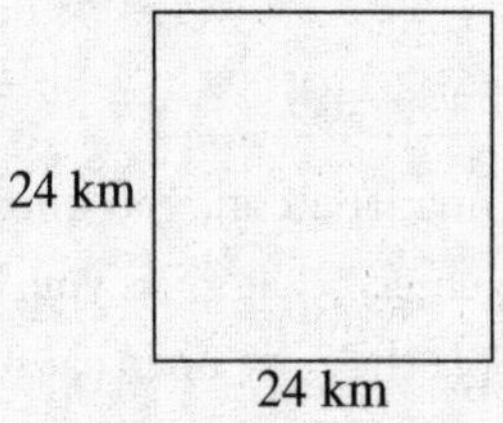

The area of this region is 24^2 or 576. In case you were wondering, B is the Joe Bloggs answer because $16 \times 6 = 96$.

15. E Plug in values for *m* and *n* and use translation to solve this percent problem. You're working with a small percent, so plug in a big number for *m*. Let's say *m* = 2,000. 0.1% of 2,000 = $\frac{0.1}{100} \times \frac{2{,}000}{1} = 2$. Therefore, 10% of *n* is 2; rewrite this as $\frac{10}{100} \times n = 2$. Solving for *n*, you get $n = 20$. Now translate the rest of the problem: *m* is what percent of 10*n* can be written as $2{,}000 = \frac{x}{100} \times 10 \times 20$. Solving for *x*, you get $x = 1{,}000$, so the answer is 1,000%.

16. E Remember your transformation rules. Whenever a parabola faces down, the quadratic equation has a negative sign in front of it. It always helps to plug in! Let's take an example. If your original equation was $(x + 2)^2$, putting a negative sign in front, $-(x + 2)^2$, would flip the parabola. If you expand out that equation, you get $-x^2 - 4x - 4$. Notice that a in this equation is –1. Also, notice that c in the equation is just the y-intercept, because if you plug in 0 for x you get $y = c$. On the graph, the y-intercept is negative. And a negative number times a negative number is always positive. Again, plug in if you like it better: $(-1)(-4) = +4$. The best answer is E.

SECTION 9

1. B The best choice is B. The clue is *unconventional*, which tells you that "out of the ordinary" is a good phrase for the blank. *Eccentric*, B, is closest in meaning. Even if you are not sure what B means, you can eliminate A as it is opposite from the meaning of the blank. C has to do with the order of events in time, not with a person's behavior; D, *friendly*, and E, *hardworking*, have nothing to do with behaving in an unusual manner.

2. C We can recycle the clue *swollen* into the blank, and immediately eliminate A and B, which have the opposite connotation. D and E do not mean *swollen*, so only C, *distended*, is left, making C the best answer.

3. A The best answer is A. The idea of human carelessness causing changes tells you that the blank should mean "bound to happen." You can eliminate B and E because "wishing evil" and "being honest" are human attributes. C, "equally shared," and D, "sluggish," do not mean "bound to happen," so you are left with A, *inevitable*.

4. D The clue *unrealistically* tells you that Tyler expected to improve his score greatly right away, so you can save B, D, and E, all of which could describe a great rise in his score. Thus you can eliminate A, "repeating," and C, "unimportant." Looking at the finalists, since the second blank should mean "slow and steady," you can cross out B, "endless," and E, "fast." You are left with D, which is the best answer.

5. C The clue is *invoke a serenity that is otherwise lacking in her frenzied existence.* A good word for the blank is "relaxed." Only C agrees with our word. If you guessed A because the root *eu-* means "good" as in *euphoria*, don't feel bad. That was a smart guess, and smart guesses mean more points overall.

6. E The clue for the second blank is *appreciated his specialized knowledge*, and the trigger word is *but*, which tells you that the second part of the sentence must mean the opposite of the clue. If some students didn't appreciate the specialized knowledge, then the *disappointed* students had "non-specialized" interests. The only word in the answer choices that means "non-specialized" is *eclectic*. The other word in E also makes sense because it fits the clue. You know that the professor *has specialized knowledge*, so if his lecture focused *utterly* on something, then it was very specialized.

7. E E is correct because Passage 1 states in the beginning of the second paragraph that philosophers shifted from theology to *intellectual exercises*. A is incorrect given the information in the passage. B is not supported, because there is not mention of angels anywhere in the passage. C is not supported because there is no mention of law-abiding citizens. D is a trap answer because the mention of *classicists* may make this look like an attractive answer choice.

8. **C** C is the credited choice because of lines 16–18 in Passage 1. A is incorrect because deviant behavior <u>is</u> a criminal act, not the result of one. B is incorrect because that would be according to the *demonic perspective.* D is not supported in the passage and E is incorrect because deviant behavior is the result of rationale that maximizes pleasure and minimizes pain, not the opposite.

9. **E** E is a close paraphrase of lines 37–38 in Passage 1, *each deviant act arises from a rational calculation of pleasure versus pain....* Every other answer choice contains expressions found in the passage, but not as a cause for avoiding arbitrary, tyrannical punishment. B might seem like an attractive choice, but the belief that punishment could be *meted out precisely and mathematically* is not cited as a reason for avoiding overly severe punishment.

10. **B** A, C, and E are incorrect because the author is not revealing, describing, or explaining the emergence of deviant behavior to the individual. The author says that it is wrong to attribute the behavior solely to the individual; D does not reflect this meaning, but B does.

11. **A** A is the credited choice because of the phrase that follows the semicolon: *society produces the individual.* B is not in the passage. C is the opposite of what is said in the passage. D is a stretch from line 43 and does not answer the question. E is extreme.

12. **E** The author states in line 58, *deviant behavior would have no role in this utopia.* A is too broad; while the author does place emphasis on having an organized society, the point of doing so was to show how the relationship between the individual and society produces deviant behavior. B is the opposite of what is stated by the passage, as it says that the utopia does not exist. C and D are extreme.

13. **E** A is a trap answer, because it relates gender to sexuality. B and D do not make sense. C means "allows." Between C and E, though, E is the better answer, because the disorganization in society is causing the deviance (lines 68–70).

14. **C** While ETS tends to be middle-of-the-road, the author's emphatic description of society's disorganization gives the third paragraph a distinctly critical tone. A is not mentioned in passage, as there is no indication that the calmer, utopian days ever existed. In B, the third paragraph is not objective. D is not mentioned in the passage. E is wrong because the author does not approve of the deviance.

15. **B** With constant change, there cannot be harmony and organization. A, C, D, and E can all result from change, but remember that the question asks which is the <u>least</u> likely to occur.

16. **A** According to both the third paragraph of Passage 2 and the main discussion in Passage 1, deviance is a choice made by an individual. B is not supported, since both authors discuss the individual causes of deviance. C is wrong because severe punishment is never advocated. D is true for 2 but not for 1. E is wrong because it contradicts information in Passage 1. The Enlightenment did not cause deviance; it only viewed it differently.

17. **B** Rationality is a central focus of Passage 1, but is not mentioned in Passage 2. A is not important in either. C is not the focus of 1 and is not mentioned at all in 2. D is important in the second passage, not the first. E is mentioned in the first, but as an act of deviant behavior, not an aspect of it, and even so, it does not matter a great deal to the passage.

18. **D** Passage 1 is presented very factually, while Passage 2 has a note of criticism in describing the disorganization of society. A is not true of either passage. B is wrong because Passage 1 is not indignant. C is wrong because Passage 2 is not sarcastic. E is not true of either passage.

19. **A** Passage 1 discusses the intellectual evaluation made by the individual, and Passage 2 discusses how deviance would not increase if it weren't for disharmony in society. B and C do not answer to the propagation aspect of the question because neither answer has any effect on how or why deviance is increased. D and E do not describe any difference between the interpretations.

SECTION 10

1. **D** *Weather vanes* is plural, so it's important to use a plural pronoun later in the sentence: get rid of A. B unnecessarily uses the word *being,* so eliminate it. Only D matches the sentence structure of the beginning of the sentence: *weather vanes* comes first, so in the second half *they* comes first.

2. **B** This sentence is a fragment. By eliminating the word *which,* the sentence becomes complete. In B the sentence says correctly, *horrors...and experiences...are...chronicled.* In C, D, and E, the verb is missing, so these versions of the sentence are also fragments.

3. **A** There is no error in this sentence as it is written.

4. **E** As written, A includes several words that make the sentence unnecessarily wordy. Because E omits the words *is, he is,* and *and he,* this version of the sentence becomes streamlined and correct. B is a run-on. C and D add *because* and *although,* changing the meaning of the sentence.

5. **E** Only E uses the correct idiom *responded...by.* In addition, the original sentence is a run-on. B is needlessly wordy. C and D both create fragments: C needs a conjunction to be correct; in D, the phrase that follows the semicolon lacks a grammatical subject.

6. **A** The original sentence is concise and uses the past tense required by *could* and *after* in the non-underlined portion. B and D use the present tense. C and E are wordy and redundant.

7. **E** The construction *not only...but also* achieves parallelism in E, since the noun *an inspiring teacher* matches *a great surgeon* in form. A unnecessarily uses the word *being.* B, C, and D violate parallelism.

8. **B** A is unnecessarily wordy. E is wordy and contains a noun agreement error; employees have monthly payments. C changes the meaning of the sentence, suggesting that they switched plans after their payments were reduced, which is not correct. D also changes the meaning, suggesting that the new plan's payments were being reduced from a higher price point to a lower one.

9. **D** Choices A and B are wordy and unidiomatic. C and E warp the intended meaning by (among other things) implying that *the expression,* C, or *the face,* E, *plays games.* Only D correctly and concisely expresses the idea that *the squirrel...plays games.*

10. **C** Only *the designers* can logically be modified by the phrase *learning from recent tests,* so eliminate A, D, and E. B changes the intended meaning, illogically saying that an *engine* can be based on an increase in efficiency.

11. **B** Parallelism requires a noun such as *a failure* to follow *a lack of training,* making B the only possible answer. Also, *which* in C is inappropriate, because you must use the pronoun *who* when referring to people. C also changes the intended meaning by implying that the *people,* rather than *a failure,* caused the crash. *Because,* in choices D and E, is redundant with *caused by* in the non-underlined portion of the sentence.

12. E Because the pronoun *we* is not underlined and therefore must remain in the sentence, beginning the sentence with *Rory and I* will make it a run-on. Kill A, B, and C. D ends with *Rory and I*, making the *we* that follows it unnecessary and incorrect. E provides a properly constructed subordinate clause and is correct.

13. C Always watch out for unnecessary use of the word *being*. It shows up incorrectly in both A and D, so eliminate both of those. The sentence should set up an opposite, since it starts with a way in which the two are similar, and ends with a way in which the two are different. E uses *and*, which doesn't accomplish this. Between B and C, C is more concise.

14. C Watch out for misplaced modifiers. The phrase *better known for* The Foreigner should describe *Larry Shue*, but in A, B, and D the phrase incorrectly describes something else. E incorrectly uses the word *like* instead of *such as*. *Like* should be used to compare two nouns; *such as* should be used to give an example.

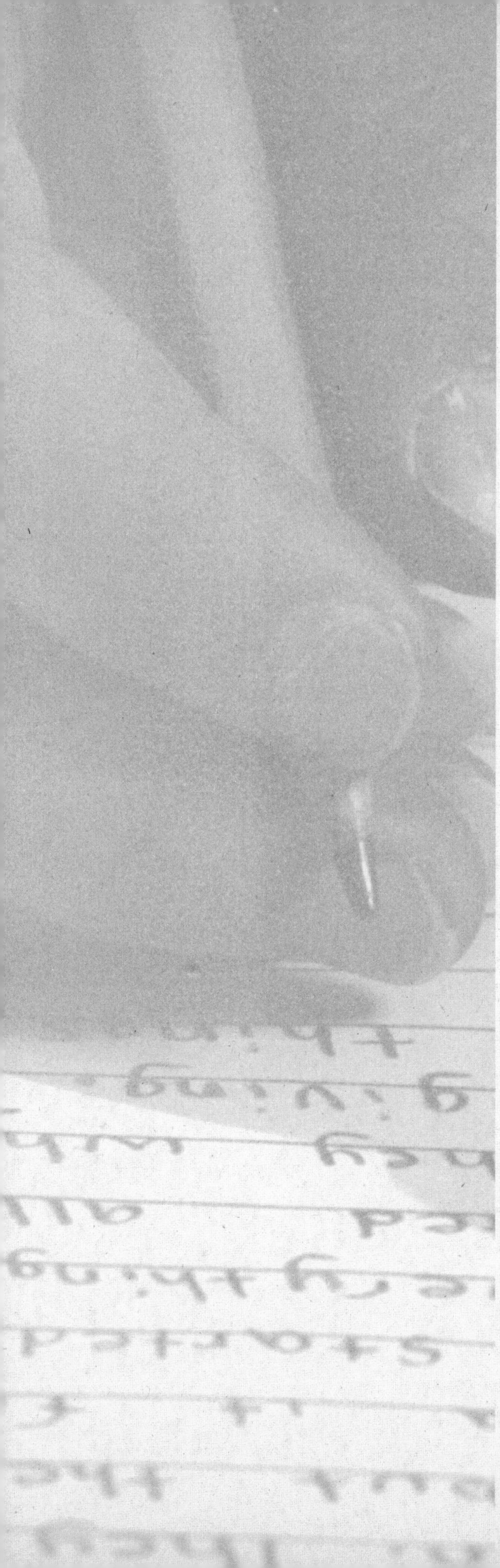

Chapter 21
Practice Test 2

SECTION 1
ESSAY
Time — 25 minutes

Turn to Section 1 of your answer sheet to write your essay.

The essay gives you an opportunity to show how effectively you can develop and express ideas. You should, therefore, take care to develop your point of view, present your ideas logically and clearly, and use language precisely.

Your essay must be written on the lines provided on your answer sheet—you will receive no other paper on which to write. You will have enough space if you write on every line, avoid wide margins, and keep your handwriting to a reasonable size. Remember that people who are not familiar with your handwriting will read what you write. Try to write or print so that what you are writing is legible to those readers.

You have twenty-five minutes to write an essay on the topic assigned below. DO NOT WRITE ON ANOTHER TOPIC. AN OFF-TOPIC ESSAY WILL RECEIVE A SCORE OF ZERO.

Think carefully about the issue presented in the following excerpt and the assignment below.

> The more critical reason dominates, the more impoverished life becomes. When reason is overvalued, the individual suffers a loss. Relying more on facts and rationality than on imagination and theory detracts from the quality of a person's intellectual life.
>
> Adapted from Carl Jung

Assignment: Is knowing facts as important as understanding ideas and concepts? Plan and write an essay in which you develop your point of view on this issue. Support your position with reasoning and examples taken from your reading, studies, experience, or observations.

DO NOT WRITE YOUR ESSAY IN YOUR TEST BOOK. You will receive credit only for what you write on your answer sheet.

BEGIN WRITING YOUR ESSAY ON PAGE 3 OF THE ANSWER SHEET (FOUND AT THE BACK OF THE BOOK).

STOP

If you finish before time is called, you may check your work on this section only. Do not turn to any other section in the test.

SECTION 2
Time — 25 minutes
24 Questions

Turn to Section 2 of your answer sheet to answer the questions in this section.

Directions: For each question in this section, select the best answer from among the choices given and fill in the corresponding circle on the answer sheet.

Each sentence below has one or two blanks, each blank indicating that something has been omitted. Beneath the sentence are five words or sets of words labeled A through E. Choose the word or set of words that, when inserted in the sentence, best fits the meaning of the sentence as a whole.

Example:

Desiring to ------- his taunting friends, Mitch gave them taffy in hopes it would keep their mouths shut.

(A) eliminate (B) satisfy (C) overcome (D) ridicule (E) silence

ⒶⒷⒸⒹ●

1. Nuclear power plants are some of the largest producers of ------- wastes, with each plant producing barrels of radioactive material that must be stored in special protective containers.

   (A) biodegradable (B) artificial (C) reasonable (D) durable (E) noxious

2. The scientific community was ------- when a living specimen of the coelacanth, thought to be no longer -------, was discovered by deep-sea fishermen.

   (A) perplexed . . common
   (B) overjoyed . . dangerous
   (C) unconcerned . . local
   (D) astounded . . extant
   (E) dismayed . . alive

3. After the governor's third trip overseas, voters complained that he was paying too little attention to ------- affairs.

   (A) intellectual (B) extraneous (C) specialized (D) aesthetic (E) domestic

4. The Roman Emperor Claudius was viewed with ------- by generations of historians until newly discovered evidence showed him to be ------- administrator.

   (A) suspicion . . a deficient
   (B) reluctance . . an inept
   (C) antagonism . . an eager
   (D) indignation . . an incompetent
   (E) disdain . . a capable

5. Communities in primitive areas where natural ------- is scarce must be resourceful in order to secure adequate nutrition.

   (A) development (B) competition (C) sustenance (D) augmentation (E) intervention

6. Morgan's interest was focused on ------- the division between theory and empiricism; she was convinced that a ------- of philosophy and applied science was possible and necessary.

   (A) eradicating . . synthesis
   (B) maintaining . . restoration
   (C) crossing . . stabilization
   (D) overlooking . . duplicity
   (E) refuting . . delineation

7. His style is best described as -------: his signature vivid colors and mixture of bold patterns, combined with his dramatic bearing, always make him the center of attention.

   (A) vehement (B) imperious (C) modest (D) flamboyant (E) stoic

8. Although at times Nikolai could be disagreeable and even -------, more often than not he was the most ------- person you could hope to meet.

   (A) contentious . . complaisant
   (B) disgruntled . . befuddled
   (C) contradictory . . disconcerted
   (D) misguided . . solicitous
   (E) curmudgeonly . . didactic

GO ON TO THE NEXT PAGE

Directions: Each passage below is followed by questions based on its content. Answer the questions on the basis of what is stated or implied in each passage and in any introductory material that may be provided.

Questions 9–10 are based on the following passage.

Though today Zora Neale Hurston is best known as an author, many readers overlook Hurston's contributions as an anthropologist. Drawn by the Harlem Renaissance, Hurston crafted both fiction and nonfiction that deconstructed the African American experience. Hurston also worked with noted anthropologist Franz Boas to debunk the claims of racist scientists. Her desire to disprove these eugenicists' claims led her to measure the skulls of African Americans on the streets of New York. Her cultural studies of Eatonville, Florida, still remain some of the richest anthropological writing about the African American South.

9. The term "deconstructed" in line 4 implies that Hurston

(A) participated fully in the Harlem Renaissance
(B) engaged in scientific experiments
(C) made a deliberate study of African American life
(D) cut herself off from Harlem to write about it objectively
(E) attempted to bring about sweeping changes to African-American communities

10. The passage LEAST supports which of the following statements about Zora Neale Hurston?

(A) She was influenced by the blossoming of the arts in Harlem.
(B) She was a widely acclaimed social anthropologist.
(C) She attempted to measure the cranial capacity of African Americans.
(D) She investigated the culture of a Southern town.
(E) She was an author highly skilled in several genres.

Questions 11–12 are based on the following passage.

Many modern naval vessels are equipped with a sophisticated new sonar system called SURTASS LFA. Environmentalists argue that the intensity of the sound bursts emitted by the system, measured at 215 decibels, poses a serious threat to marine wildlife. (In contrast, a rock concert reaching only 150 decibels is considered a health risk to humans.) They claim that the alarming number of whale carcasses found on beaches near areas where vessels use SURTASS LFA are evidence of its impact. Proponents of SURTASS LFA argue that no causal link between the use of the system and these whale deaths has been established, and contend that the system is safe.

11. The purpose of this passage is primarily to

(A) demonstrate that the claims of environmentalists are unfounded
(B) argue against further use of SURTASS LFA
(C) outline a controversy regarding the use of a new technology
(D) emphasize the danger humans pose to wildlife
(E) summarize the arguments of environmentalists who oppose SURTASS LFA

12. The example of the rock concert

(A) compares the way humans and whales are affected by sound
(B) bolsters the author's overall argument in favor of banning SURTASS LFA
(C) refutes environmentalists' claims about sonar's dangers
(D) provides a context from which to judge the intensity of SURTASS LFA emissions
(E) has nothing to do with the rest of the passage

GO ON TO THE NEXT PAGE

Questions 13–24 are based on the following passage.

The following passage was excerpted from a book called The Extraordinary Origins of Everyday Things, *which was published in 1987.*

Because early man viewed illness as divine punishment and healing as purification, medicine and religion were inextricably linked for centuries. This notion is apparent in the origin of our word "pharmacy," which comes from the Greek *pharmakon*, meaning "purification through purging."

By 3500 B.C., the Sumerians in the Tigris-Euphrates Valley had developed virtually all of our modern methods of administering drugs. They used gargles, inhalations, pills, lotions, ointments, and plasters. The first drug catalog, or pharmacopoeia, was written at that time by an unknown Sumerian physician. Preserved in cuneiform script on a single clay tablet are the names of dozens of drugs to treat ailments that still afflict us today.

The Egyptians added to the ancient medicine chest. The Ebers Papyrus, a scroll dating from 1900 B.C. and named after the German egyptologist George Ebers, reveals the trial-and-error know-how acquired by early Egyptian physicians. To relieve indigestion, a chew of peppermint leaves and carbonates (known today as antacids) was prescribed, and to numb the pain of tooth extraction, Egyptian doctors temporarily stupefied a patient with ethyl alcohol.

The scroll also provides a rare glimpse into the hierarchy of ancient drug preparation. The "chief of the preparers of drugs" was the equivalent of a head pharmacist, who supervised the "collectors of drugs," field workers who gathered essential minerals and herbs. The "preparers' aides" (technicians) dried and pulverized ingredients, which were blended according to certain formulas by the "preparers." And the "conservator of drugs" oversaw the storehouse where local and imported mineral, herb, and animal-organ ingredients were kept.

By the seventh century B.C., the Greeks had adopted a sophisticated mind-body view of medicine. They believed that a physician must pursue the diagnosis and treatment of the physical (body) causes of disease within a scientific framework, as well as cure the supernatural (mind) components involved. Thus, the early Greek physician emphasized something of a holistic approach to health, even if the suspected "mental" causes of disease were not recognized as stress and depression but interpreted as curses from displeased deities.

The modern era of pharmacology began in the sixteenth century, ushered in by the first major discoveries in chemistry. The understanding of how chemicals interact to produce certain effects within the body would eventually remove much of the guesswork and magic from medicine.

Drugs had been launched on a scientific course, but centuries would pass before superstition was displaced by scientific fact. One major reason was that physicians, unaware of the existence of disease-causing pathogens such as bacteria and viruses, continued to dream up imaginary causative evils. And though new chemical compounds emerged, their effectiveness in treating disease was still based largely on trial and error.

Many standard, common drugs in the medicine chest developed in this trial-and-error environment. Such is the complexity of disease and human biochemistry that even today, despite enormous strides in medical science, many of the latest sophisticated additions to our medicine chest shelves were accidental finds.

13. The author cites the literal definition of the Greek word *pharmakon* in line 5 in order to

(A) show that ancient civilizations had an advanced form of medical science
(B) point out that many of the beliefs of ancient civilizations are still held today
(C) illustrate that early man thought recovery from illness was linked to internal cleansing
(D) stress the mental and physical causes of disease
(E) emphasize the primitive nature of Greek medical science

14. It was possible to identify a number of early Sumerian drugs because

(A) traces of these drugs were discovered during archaeological excavations
(B) the ancient Egyptians later adopted the same medications
(C) Sumerian religious texts explained many drug-making techniques
(D) a pharmacopoeia in Europe contained detailed recipes for ancient drugs
(E) a list of drugs and preparations was compiled by an ancient Sumerian

15. The passage suggests that which of the following is a similarity between ancient Sumerian drugs and modern drugs?

(A) Ancient Sumerian drugs were made of the same chemicals as modern drugs.
(B) Like modern drugs, ancient Sumerian drugs were used for both mental and physical disorders.
(C) The different ways patients could take ancient Sumerian drugs are similar to the ways modern drugs are taken.
(D) Both ancient Sumerian drugs and modern drugs are products of sophisticated chemical research.
(E) Hierarchically organized groups of laborers are responsible for the preparation of both ancient Sumerian and modern drugs.

GO ON TO THE NEXT PAGE

16. According to the passage, the seventh-century Greeks' view of medicine differed from that of the Sumerians in that the Greeks

(A) discovered more advanced chemical applications of drugs
(B) acknowledged both the mental and physical roots of illness
(C) attributed disease to psychological, rather than physical, causes
(D) established a rigid hierarchy for the preparation of drugs
(E) developed most of the precursors of modern drugs

17. The "hierarchy" referred to in line 22 is an example of

(A) a superstitious practice
(B) the relative severity of ancient diseases
(C) the role of physicians in Egyptian society
(D) a complex division of labor
(E) a recipe for ancient drugs

18. In the final paragraph, the author makes which of the following observations about scientific discovery?

(A) Human biochemistry is such a complex science that important discoveries are uncommon.
(B) Chance events have led to the discovery of many modern drugs.
(C) Many cures for common diseases have yet to be discovered.
(D) Trial and error is the best avenue to scientific discovery.
(E) Most of the important discoveries made in the scientific community have been inadvertent.

19. Which of the following is NOT cited in the passage as a characteristic of ancient Egyptian medicine?

(A) Anesthesia
(B) Ointments
(C) Ingredients derived from animals
(D) Use of trial and error
(E) A workplace hierarchy

20. It can be inferred from the passage that some drugs commonly used in 1987

(A) were not created intentionally
(B) caused the very diseases that they were designed to combat
(C) were meant to treat imaginary causative evils
(D) were created in the sixteenth century
(E) are now known to be ineffective

21. Which of the following documents from seventh-century Greece, if discovered, would most support the author's characterization of ancient Greek medicine?

(A) A sophisticated formula for an antacid
(B) A scientific paper theorizing that stress causes disease
(C) A doctor's prescription that urges the patient to pray to Asclepius, the Greek god of healing
(D) An essay that details the ancient Egyptian influence upon Greek medicine
(E) A book in which the word "pharmacology" was used repeatedly

22. The passage implies that

(A) ancient Greek medicine was superior to ancient Egyptian medicine
(B) some maladies have supernatural causes
(C) a modern head pharmacist is analogous to an ancient Egyptian conservator of drugs
(D) most ailments that afflicted the ancient Sumerians still afflict modern human beings
(E) the ancient Egyptians made no major discoveries in the field of chemistry

23. In line 38, the word "holistic" most nearly means

(A) psychological
(B) modern
(C) physiological
(D) comprehensive
(E) homeopathic

24. The passage indicates that advances in medical science during the modern era of pharmacology may have been delayed by

(A) the lack of a clear understanding of the origins of disease
(B) primitive surgical methods
(C) a shortage of chemical treatments for disease
(D) an inaccuracy in pharmaceutical preparation
(E) an overemphasis on the psychological causes of disease

STOP

If you finish before time is called, you may check your work on this section only. Do not turn to any other section in the test.

SECTION 3
Time — 25 minutes
20 Questions

Turn to Section 3 of your answer sheet to answer the questions in this section.

Directions: For this section, solve each problem and decide which is the best of the choices given. Fill in the corresponding circle on the answer sheet. You may use any available space for scratchwork.

Notes

1. The use of a calculator is permitted.
2. All numbers used are real numbers.
3. Figures that accompany problems in this test are intended to provide information useful in solving the problems. They are drawn as accurately as possible EXCEPT when it is stated in a specific problem that the figure is not drawn to scale. All figures lie in a plane unless other wise indicated.
4. Unless otherwise specified, the domain of any function *f* is assumed to be the set of all real numbers *x* for which *f*(*x*) is a real number.

Reference Information

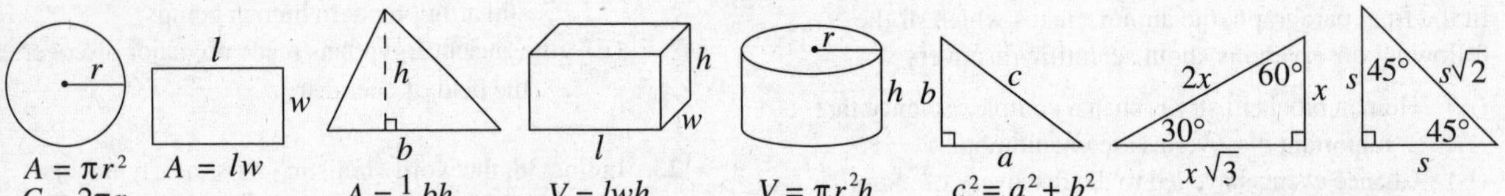

$A = \pi r^2$ $C = 2\pi r$ $A = lw$ $A = \frac{1}{2}bh$ $V = lwh$ $V = \pi r^2 h$ $c^2 = a^2 + b^2$

Special Right Triangles

The number of degrees of arc in a circle is 360.

The sum of the measures in degrees of the angles of a triangle is 180.

1. If $\frac{12}{4} = x$, what is the value of $4x + 2$?

(A) 2
(B) 3
(C) 4
(D) 12
(E) 14

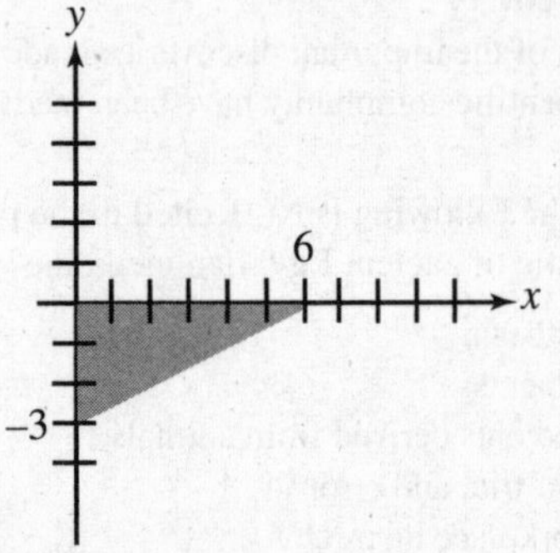

2. In the figure above, which of the following points lies within the shaded region?

(A) (−1, 1)
(B) (1, −2)
(C) (4, 3)
(D) (5, −4)
(E) (7, 0)

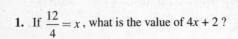

GO ON TO THE NEXT PAGE

3. Six cups of flour are required to make a batch of cookies. How many cups of flour are required to make enough cookies to fill 12 cookie jars, if each cookie jar holds 1.5 batches?

(A) 108
(B) 90
(C) 81
(D) 78
(E) 72

4. If n is an even integer, which of the following must be an odd integer?

(A) $3n - 2$

(B) $3(n + 1)$

(C) $n - 2$

(D) $\frac{n}{3}$

(E) n^2

5. In the coordinate plane, what is the midpoint of the line segment with endpoints at (3, 4) and (0, 0) ?

(A) (1.5, 2)
(B) (5, 0)
(C) (2.5, 0)
(D) (3.5, 3.5)
(E) (1.75, 1.75)

6. $x\sqrt{4} - x\sqrt{9} =$

(A) $-5x$
(B) $-x\sqrt{5}$
(C) $-x$
(D) x
(E) $3x$

GO ON TO THE NEXT PAGE

	Number Sold	Average Weight per Parrot (in pounds)
Red Parrots	5	2
Blue Parrots	4	3

7. The chart above shows the number of red and blue parrots Toby sold in May and the average weight of each type of bird sold. If Toby sold no other parrots, what was the average (arithmetic mean) weight, in pounds, of the parrots that Toby sold in May?

(A) 2

(B) $2\frac{4}{9}$

(C) $2\frac{1}{2}$

(D) 5

(E) 9

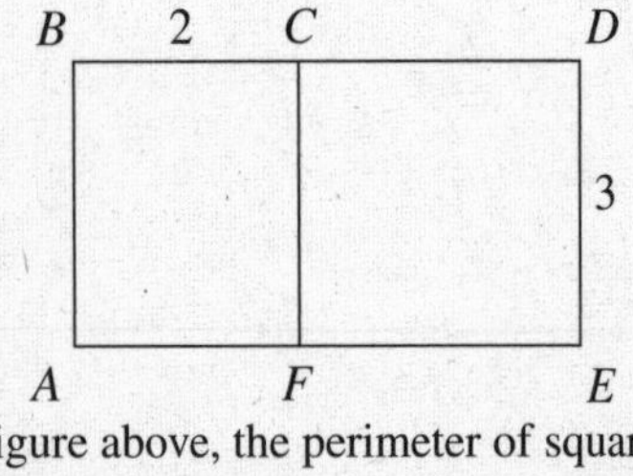

8. In the figure above, the perimeter of square *FCDE* is how much smaller than the perimeter of rectangle *ABDE* ?

(A) 2
(B) 3
(C) 4
(D) 7
(E) 16

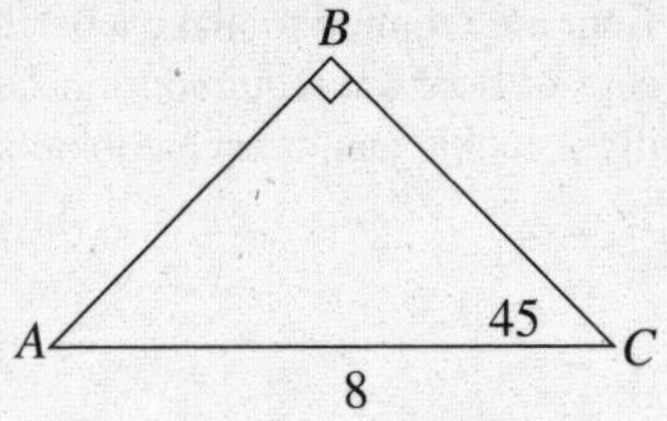

9. In $\triangle ABC$ above, if $AC = 8$, what is the length of $\overline{BC}$?

(A) $8\sqrt{2}$
(B) 8
(C) 6
(D) $4\sqrt{2}$
(E) $3\sqrt{2}$

10. If $\frac{\sqrt{x}}{2} = 2\sqrt{2}$, what is the value of x ?

(A) 4
(B) 16
(C) $16\sqrt{2}$
(D) 32
(E) 64

GO ON TO THE NEXT PAGE

11. If b equals 40% of a, then in terms of b, 40% of $4a$ is equal to which of the following?

(A) $\frac{b}{40}$

(B) $\frac{b}{4}$

(C) b

(D) $4b$

(E) $16b$

Questions 12–13 refer to the following definition.

For all real numbers x, let $f(x) = 2x^2 + 4$.

12. What is the value of $f(4)$?

(A) 16
(B) 18
(C) 20
(D) 36
(E) 72

13. Which of the following is equal to $f(3) + f(5)$?

(A) $f(4)$
(B) $f(6)$
(C) $f(8)$
(D) $f(10)$
(E) $f(15)$

14. If the circle with center O has a diameter of 9, then what is the area of the circle with center O ?

(A) 81π

(B) $\frac{9}{2}\pi$

(C) $\frac{81}{4}\pi$

(D) 18π

(E) 9π

GO ON TO THE NEXT PAGE

15. The graph of which of the following equations is parallel to the line with equation $y = -3x - 6$?

(A) $x - 3y = 3$

(B) $x - \frac{1}{3}y = 2$

(C) $x + \frac{1}{6}y = 4$

(D) $x + \frac{1}{3}y = 5$

(E) $x + 3y = 6$

16. How many solutions exist to the equation $|x| = |2x - 1|$?

(A) 0
(B) 1
(C) 2
(D) 3
(E) 4

17. There are k gallons of gasoline available to fill a tank. After d gallons have been pumped, in terms of k and d, what percent of the gasoline has been pumped?

(A) $\frac{100d}{k}\%$

(B) $\frac{k}{100d}\%$

(C) $\frac{100k}{d}\%$

(D) $\frac{k}{100(k-d)}\%$

(E) $\frac{100(k-d)}{k}\%$

18. Ray and Jane live 150 miles apart. Each drives toward the other's house along a straight road connecting the two, Ray at a constant rate of 30 miles per hour and Jane at a constant rate of 50 miles per hour. If Ray and Jane leave their houses at the same time, how many miles are they from Ray's house when they meet?

(A) 40

(B) $51\frac{1}{2}$

(C) $56\frac{1}{4}$

(D) 75

(E) $93\frac{1}{4}$

GO ON TO THE NEXT PAGE

19. A bag contains 4 red hammers, 10 blue hammers, and 6 yellow hammers. If three hammers are removed from the bag at random and no hammer is returned to the bag after removal, what is the probability that all three hammers will be blue?

(A) $\frac{1}{2}$

(B) $\frac{1}{8}$

(C) $\frac{3}{20}$

(D) $\frac{2}{19}$

(E) $\frac{3}{18}$

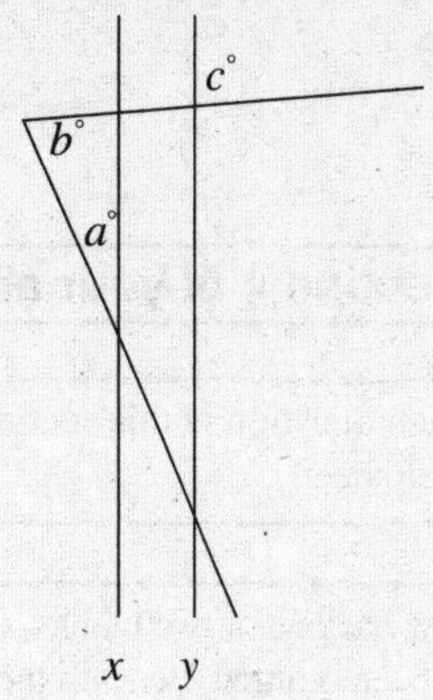

20. In the figure above, $x \parallel y$. What is the value of a in terms of b and c ?

(A) $b + c$
(B) $2b - c$
(C) $180 - b + c$
(D) $180 - b - c$
(E) $360 - b - c$

STOP

If you finish before time is called, you may check your work on this section only.
Do not turn to any other section in the test.

SECTION 4
Time — 25 minutes
24 Questions

Turn to Section 4 of your answer sheet to answer the questions in this section.

Directions: For each question in this section, select the best answer from among the choices given and fill in the corresponding circle on the answer sheet.

Each sentence below has one or two blanks, each blank indicating that something has been omitted. Beneath the sentence are five words or sets of words labeled A through E. Choose the word or set of words that, when inserted in the sentence, best fits the meaning of the sentence as a whole.

Example:

Desiring to ------- his taunting friends, Mitch gave them taffy in hopes it would keep their mouths shut.

(A) eliminate (B) satisfy (C) overcome (D) ridicule (E) silence

Ⓐ Ⓑ Ⓒ Ⓓ ●

1. Plants that grow in the desert or on high rocky ledges can survive long periods of ------- because they hoard water in their leaves, stems, and root systems.

(A) darkness (B) inactivity (C) dormancy (D) warmth (E) aridity

2. Thanks to his eloquence and logic, Liam spoke ------- and made it difficult for even his most bitter opponents to ------- his opinions.

(A) monotonously . . clash with
(B) charmingly . . yield to
(C) tediously . . contend with
(D) abhorrently . . concede to
(E) cogently . . disagree with

3. Some subatomic particles, ------- only through their effects on other bodies, have been compared to outer planets whose ------- was first deduced from eccentricities in other planets' orbits.

(A) feasible . . irregularity
(B) palpable . . creation
(C) perceptible . . fallacy
(D) discernable . . existence
(E) verifiable . . proximity

4. Miranda, in her desire to foster -------, often felt compelled to ------- readily to others in tense situations.

(A) cooperation . . object
(B) fortitude . . defer
(C) dissension . . surrender
(D) harmony . . acquiesce
(E) discourse . . appeal

5. Although detractors labeled Margaret Thatcher's policies -------, she asserted that her ideas ultimately helped bring about a period of prosperity in the United Kingdom.

(A) premature (B) autocratic (C) regressive (D) ingenious (E) seditious

GO ON TO THE NEXT PAGE

The passages below are followed by questions based on their content; questions following a pair of related passages may also be based on the relationship between the paired passages. Answer the questions on the basis of what is stated or implied in the passage and in any introductory material that may be provided.

Questions 6–9 are based on the following passages.

Passage 1

The War of 1812 between the United States and England is one of the least-known in American history. Ironically, this war cemented America's independence in Europe's eyes. Although lacking a clear winner, it proved to the Old World that the United States could hold its own against the mighty British navy, then in the heyday of its impressive power. The war was fought for several reasons: The declaration of war by the United States was ostensibly in response to British actions against American goods and sailors. Also, many Americans had their eyes on the rich Spanish territory of Florida and the vast land of Canada.

Passage 2

Curiously, one of the most important battles of the War of 1812 actually took place after the war was over. For three years, the United States and Britain were locked in a stalemate, with neither side emerging as a clear victor. While the Americans forced the British into Canada and defeated them at the Battle of the Thames, the British succeeded in burning Washington. Less than three weeks after signing the Treaty of Ghent on December 24, 1814, General Andrew Jackson defeated the British in a decisive battle at New Orleans, a victory that contributed greatly to the development of American confidence and nationalism.

6. According to Passage 1, which of the following contributed to the decision of the United States to declare war on England in 1812 ?

I. Expansionist tendencies among citizens and leaders of the United States
II. British actions taken against the interests of the United States
III. A desire to show the independence of the United States from England

(A) I only
(B) II only
(C) I and II
(D) I and III
(E) I, II, and III

7. Both passages support which of the following statements about the War of 1812 ?

(A) Neither side was able to score a decisive victory in the war.
(B) The war was important not just for the results of the battles but for its effect on the American psyche.
(C) It is likely that the United States would have won the war if it had continued on.
(D) The war was the most significant international engagement of the nineteenth century.
(E) The war was justified due to British injustices against the United States.

8. The authors of both passages would likely agree that

(A) from a military standpoint, neither the United States nor Britain could claim to have won the War of 1812
(B) the War of 1812 had a much greater impact on American citizens than it did on British citizens
(C) the British forces would most likely have won the War of 1812 if they had not lost the Battle of the Thames
(D) Andrew Jackson's victory at New Orleans was the most important battle of the War of 1812
(E) the War of 1812 is not well known among people in the United States and Britain

9. In Passage 2, the author most likely considers Andrew Jackson's victory the "most important" battle because

(A) it proved to the British that the American army was a force to be reckoned with
(B) the American forces had not won a battle since the burning of Washington
(C) without Jackson's victory, the British would have been less willing to sign a peace treaty
(D) it was the only battle in which the American forces had been able to defeat the British
(E) the victory at New Orleans carried a great symbolic value to the people of America

GO ON TO THE NEXT PAGE

Questions 10–15 are based on the following passage.

A parable is a symbolic story that, like a fable, teaches a moral lesson. The parable below was written by the Czech author Franz Kafka and was published in 1935.

Poseidon sat at his desk, doing figures. The administration of all the waters gave him endless work. He could have had assistants, as many as he wanted—and he did have very many—but since he took his job very seriously, he would in the end go over all the figures and calculations himself, and thus his assistants were of little help to him. It cannot be said that he enjoyed his work; he did it only because it had been assigned to him; in fact, he had already filed petitions for—as he put it—more cheerful work, but every time the offer of something different was made to him it would turn out that nothing suited him quite as well as his present position. And anyhow, it was quite difficult to find something different for him. After all, it was impossible to assign him to a particular sea; aside from the fact that even then the work with figures would not become less but only more petty, the great Poseidon could in any case occupy only an executive position. And when a job away from the water was offered to him he would get sick at the very prospect; his divine breathing would become troubled, and his brazen chest would begin to tremble. Besides, his complaints were not really taken seriously; when one of the mighty is vexatious, the appearance of an effort must be made to placate him, even when the case is most hopeless. In actuality, a shift of posts was unthinkable for Poseidon—he had been appointed God of the Sea in the beginning, and that he had to remain.

What irritated him most—and it was this that was chiefly responsible for his dissatisfaction with his job—was to hear of the conceptions formed about him: how he was always riding about through the tides with his trident when all the while he sat here in the depths of the world-ocean, doing figures uninterruptedly, with now and then a trip to Jupiter as the only break in the monotony—a trip, moreover, from which he usually returned in a rage. Thus he had hardly seen the sea—had seen it fleetingly in the course of hurried ascents to Olympus, and he had never actually traveled around it. He was in the habit of saying that what he was waiting for was the fall of the world; then, probably, a quiet moment would yet be granted in which, just before the end and after having checked the last row of figures, he would be able to make a quick little tour.

Poseidon became bored with the sea. He let fall his trident. Silently he sat on the rocky coast and a gull, dazed by his presence, described wavering circles around his head.

10. It can be inferred from the author's description of Poseidon's routine (lines 27–35) that

(A) Poseidon prefers performing his duties to visiting Jupiter
(B) Poseidon is too busy to familiarize himself with his kingdom
(C) Poseidon requires silence for the performance of his duties
(D) if the world falls, Poseidon will no longer be able to travel
(E) Poseidon's dissatisfaction with his job detracts from his efficiency

11. According to the passage, Poseidon's dissatisfaction with his job primarily stems from

(A) the constant travel that is required of him
(B) the lack of seriousness with which his complaints are received
(C) the constantly changing nature of his duties
(D) others' mistaken notions of his routine
(E) his assistants' inability to perform simple bookkeeping tasks

GO ON TO THE NEXT PAGE

12. The author of the passage portrays the god Poseidon as

(A) a dissatisfied bureaucrat
(B) a powerful deity
(C) a disgruntled vagabond
(D) a capable accountant
(E) a ruthless tyrant

13. Poseidon is unable to change occupations for all of the following reasons EXCEPT

(A) his appointment as God of the Sea is inherently unchangeable
(B) he has fallen into disfavor with the gods on Mount Olympus
(C) he cannot imagine a life away from the water
(D) nothing else suits him as well as his present position
(E) his job must be appropriate to his elevated status

14. In line 43 of the passage, the word "described" most nearly means

(A) soared
(B) conveyed
(C) imagined
(D) followed
(E) traced

15. Which of the following statements best characterizes the moral lesson that the parable is meant to impart?

(A) It is better to be an assistant than an executive.
(B) A bad job can be hazardous to one's health.
(C) Power can be a source of unhappiness.
(D) All careers inevitably lead to boredom.
(E) A job is not meant to be a source of amusement.

GO ON TO THE NEXT PAGE

Questions 16–24 are based on the following passage.

The role of women has historically been different in different cultures. The following passage presents an analysis of women in Frankish society by Suzanne Fonay Wemple.

Although the laws and customs in lands under Frankish domination emphasized the biological function and sexual nature of women, they did not deprive women of opportunities to find personal fulfillment in a variety of roles. Frankish women could sublimate their sexual drives and motherly instincts in ways not available to women in ancient societies. Their labor, moreover, was not as exploited as it had been in primitive tribal societies. Queens had access to power not only through their husbands but also through churchmen and secular officials whom they patronized. As widows, acting as regents for their sons, they could exercise political power directly. The wives of magnates issued donations jointly with their husbands, founded monasteries, endowed churches, cultivated interfamilial ties, transmitted clan ideology to their children, supervised the household, and administered the family's estates when their husbands were away. Whether they contracted a formal union or entered into a quasi-marriage, their children could inherit. As widows, they acted as guardians of their minor children, arranged their marriages, and in the absence of sons, wielded economic power as well. In the dependent classes, women shared their husbands' work, produced textiles and articles of clothing both for their family's and the lords' use, and were instrumental in bringing about the merger of the free and slave elements in society.

For those who wished to free their bodies, souls, and brains from male domination and devote their lives to the service of God, Christianity provided an alternative way of life. Although, in relation to the total population, women in religious life remained a small minority even in the seventh and eighth centuries, when many female communities were founded, their roles, social functions, and cultural contributions have an importance for the history of women that outweighs their numbers. This alternative way of life was available not only to the unmarried but also to widows. Monasteries served as places of refuge for married women as well. The rich and the poor, at least until the late eighth century, were accepted as members. Women from all walks of life, as well as relatives, friends, and dependents of the foundresses and abbesses, were invited to join the new congregations. Freed from the need to compete for the attention of men, women in these communities sustained each other in spiritual, intellectual, scholarly, artistic, and charitable pursuits. Writings by early medieval nuns reveal that female ideals and modes of conduct were upheld as the way to salvation and as models of sanctity in the monasteries led by women. By facilitating the escape of women from the male-dominated society to congregations where they could give expression to their own emotions, ascetic ideals, and spiritual strivings, Christianity became a liberating force in the lives of women. Historians have often overlooked these positive effects and concentrated instead on the misogynistic sentiments perpetuated by the male hierarchy.

16. The passage suggests that women under Frankish law were

(A) confined to narrow social roles
(B) cut off from religious communities
(C) exploited as slaves and servants
(D) defined in physical or biological terms
(E) valued but essentially powerless

17. It can be inferred from the passage that marriage in Frankish society

(A) was the only means of exchanging wealth
(B) could be entered into formally or informally
(C) always raised women to positions of greater influence
(D) held greater importance than in primitive societies
(E) was generally arranged by the bride's mother

18. The word "instrumental" as used in line 23 most nearly means

(A) profitable
(B) skilled
(C) harmonious
(D) resistant
(E) vital

GO ON TO THE NEXT PAGE

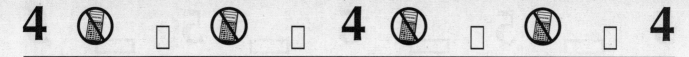

19. The passage suggests which of the following about women in religious life?

(A) Only unmarried women could participate in the religious lifestyle.
(B) Many women turned to the religious life to escape difficulties with their husbands.
(C) Writing by these women became the model for life in a monastery.
(D) The impact on society they had was not proportionate to the actual number of women engaged in religious life.
(E) Women in religious lifestyles were able to overcome the misogynistic tendencies of the male hierarchy.

20. The passage attributes women's ability to engage in "spiritual, intellectual, scholarly, artistic, and charitable pursuits" (lines 42–43) to

(A) the monastic lifestyle present in religious communities
(B) their freedom from the traditional duties ascribed to women
(C) the homogeneous nature of the religious communities
(D) the overthrow of the male dominated social hierarchy
(E) the sense of salvation the women experienced upon joining a religious community

21. The status of women in Frankish society can best be described as

(A) accorded different rights and responsibilities based on their social class and marital status
(B) able to exercise political power by acting in place of their sons
(C) having their marriages arranged for them by a widow
(D) necessary in order to bring about the peaceful merger of slaves and freemen
(E) free to divorce their husbands in order to enter into religious life

22. The primary purpose of the passage is to

(A) settle a dispute regarding the importance of religious communities in Frankish societies
(B) evaluate the position of women in Frankish society relative to that of women in other societies
(C) argue that Frankish women had more rights than women in any other society
(D) provide new evidence in the field of women's history
(E) detail the different roles and lifestyles of women of varying social position in Frankish society

23. The passage implies that Frankish women outside religious communities

(A) felt obliged to compete for male attention
(B) were not inclined to religious feeling
(C) had greatly diminished economic power
(D) did not contribute to Frankish culture
(E) relied on males for emotional support

24. According to the passage, Christianity facilitated the "escape of women from the male-dominated society" (lines 46–47) by doing all of the following EXCEPT

(A) permitting women self-expression
(B) providing refuge for widows
(C) putting pressure on women to study
(D) removing male social pressures
(E) diversifying women's social roles

STOP

If you finish before time is called, you may check your work on this section only. Do not turn to any other section in the test.

SECTION 5
Time — 25 minutes
18 Questions

Turn to Section 3 of your answer sheet to answer the questions in this section.

Directions: For this section, solve each problem and decide which is the best of the choices given. Fill in the corresponding circle on the answer sheet. You may use any available space for scratchwork.

Notes

1. The use of a calculator is permitted.
2. All numbers used are real numbers.
3. Figures that accompany problems in this test are intended to provide information useful in solving the problems. They are drawn as accurately as possible EXCEPT when it is stated in a specific problem that the figure is not drawn to scale. All figures lie in a plane unless other wise indicated.
4. Unless otherwise specified, the domain of any function f is assumed to be the set of all real numbers x for which $f(x)$ is a real number.

Reference Information

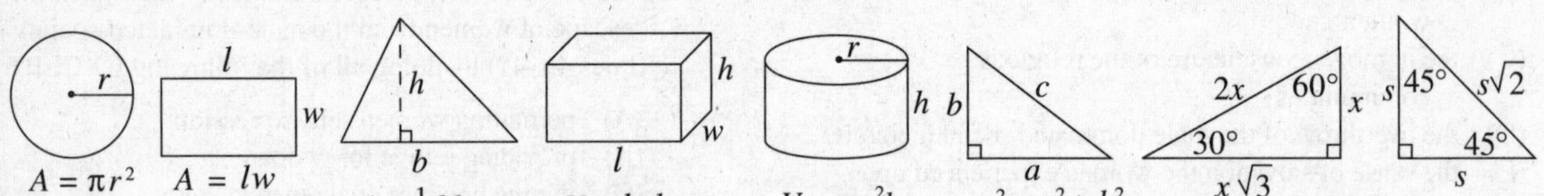

$A = \pi r^2$
$C = 2\pi r$
$A = lw$
$A = \frac{1}{2}bh$
$V = lwh$
$V = \pi r^2 h$
$c^2 = a^2 + b^2$
Special Right Triangles

The number of degrees of arc in a circle is 360.

The sum of the measures in degrees of the angles of a triangle is 180.

1. If $2x + 10 = 16$, what is the value of $2x - 10$?

(A) −4
(B) −3
(C) 3
(D) 4
(E) 6

2. The only way to purchase Brand *X* muffins is to buy one or more boxes that each contain 6 muffins. Each box costs \$1.50. If Alejandro needs at least 20 muffins, what is the least amount of money he could spend?

(A) \$3.00
(B) \$4.50
(C) \$6.00
(D) \$7.50
(E) \$30.00

GO ON TO THE NEXT PAGE

3. How many even integers are there between 2 and 100, not including 2 and 100 ?

(A) 98
(B) 97
(C) 50
(D) 49
(E) 48

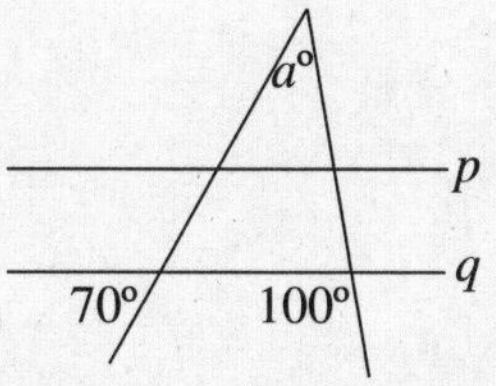

4. In the figure above, line p is parallel to line q. What is the value of a ?

(A) 10
(B) 30
(C) 35
(D) 40
(E) 70

5. If $f(3) = 6$ and $f(4) = 13$, then which of the following could be $f(x)$?

(A) $x + 3$
(B) $2x$
(C) $3x + 1$
(D) $x^2 - 2$
(E) $x^2 - 3$

6. In ΔABC, $\overline{AB} \cong \overline{BC}$ and $\overline{AB} \perp \overline{BC}$. If AC = 10, what is the area of the triangle?

(A) $10\sqrt{2}$
(B) 25
(C) 50
(D) $50\sqrt{2}$
(E) 100

GO ON TO THE NEXT PAGE

7. In 1998, Andrei had a collection of 48 baseball caps. Since then, he has given away 13 caps, purchased 17 new caps, and traded 6 of his caps to Pierre for 8 of Pierre's caps. Since 1998, what has been the net percent increase in Andrei's collection?

(A) 6%

(B) $12\frac{1}{2}\%$

(C) $16\frac{2}{3}\%$

(D) 25%

(E) $28\frac{1}{2}\%$

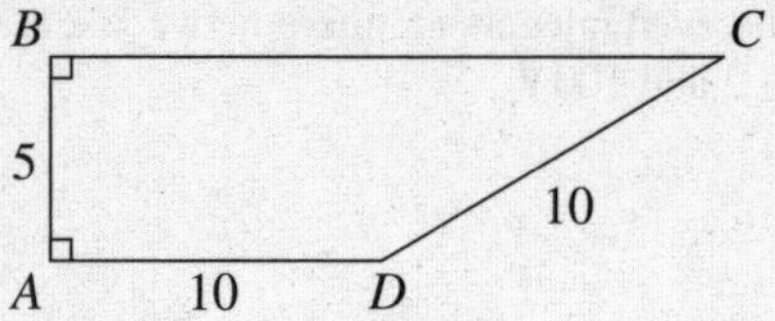

8. What is the area of quadrilateral *ABCD* in the figure above?

(A) 50

(B) $50+\frac{25\sqrt{2}}{2}$

(C) 70

(D) $50+\frac{25\sqrt{3}}{2}$

(E) 75

GO ON TO THE NEXT PAGE

Directions: For Student-Produced Response questions 9–18, use the grids to the right of the answer document page on which you have answered questions 1–8.

Each of the remaining 10 questions requires you to solve the problem and enter your answer by marking the circles in the special grid, as shown in the examples below. You may use any available space for scratch work.

Answer: $\frac{7}{12}$

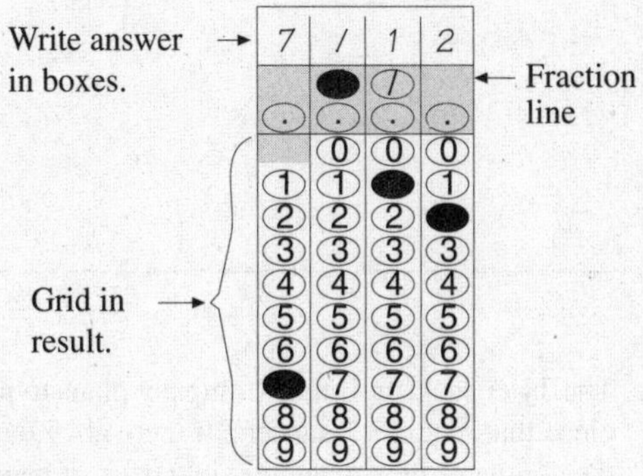

Answer: 2.5

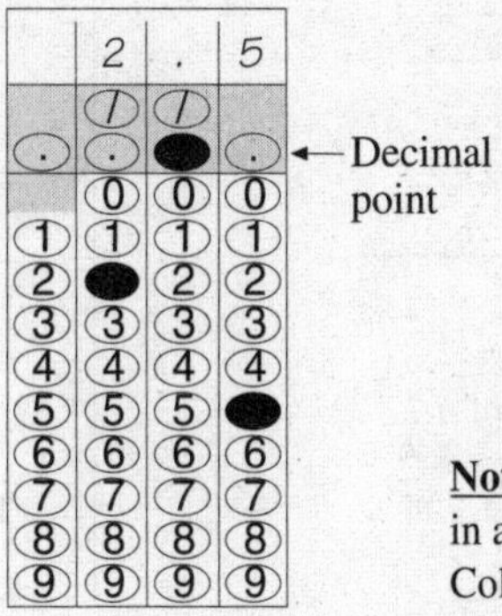

Answer: 201
Either position is correct.

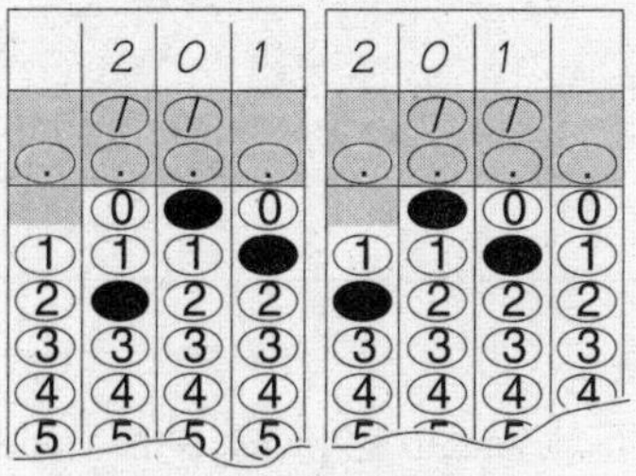

Note: You may start your answers in any column, space permitting. Columns not needed should be left blank.

- Mark no more than one circle in any column.
- Because the answer document will be machine-scored, **you will receive credit only if the circles are filled in correctly.**
- Although not required, it is suggested that you write your answer in the boxes at the top of the columns to help you fill in the circles accurately.
- Some problems may have more than one correct answer. In such cases, grid only one answer.
- No question has a negative answer.
- **Mixed numbers** such as $3\frac{1}{2}$ must be gridded as 3.5 or 7/2. (If 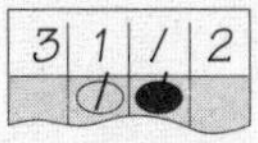 is gridded, it will be interpreted as $\frac{31}{2}$, not $3\frac{1}{2}$.)

- **Decimal Answers:** If you obtain a decimal answer with more digits than the grid can accommodate, it may be either rounded or truncated, but it must fill the entire grid. For example, if you obtain an answer such as 0.6666..., you should record your result as .666 or .667. **A less accurate value such as .66 or .67 will be scored as incorrect.**

Acceptable ways to grid $\frac{2}{3}$ are:

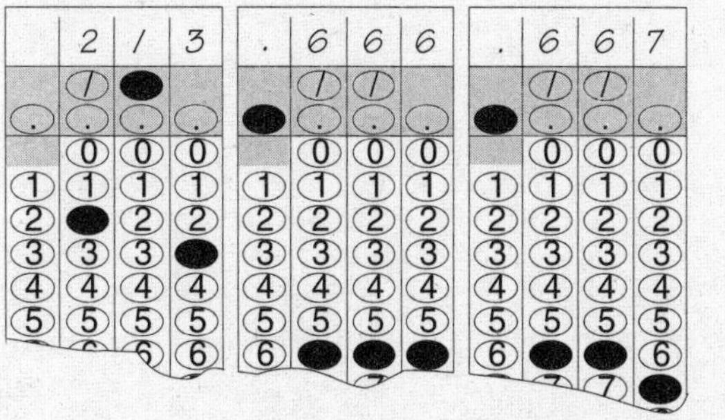

9. A certain clothing store sells only T-shirts, sweatshirts, and turtlenecks. On Wednesday, the store sells T-shirts, sweatshirts, and turtlenecks in a ratio of 2 to 3 to 5. If the store sells 30 sweatshirts on that day, what is the total number of garments that the store sells on Wednesday?

10. A rectangular box has a height of 4.5 inches and a base with an area of 18 square inches. What is the volume of the rectangular box in cubic inches?

GO ON TO THE NEXT PAGE

11. If $5x - 4 = x - 1$, what is the value of x ?

12. If $a^b = 4$, and $3b = 2$, what is the value of a ?

13. If b is a prime number such that $3b > 10 > \frac{5}{6}b$, what is one possible value of b ?

14. The Tyler Jackson Dance Company plans to perform a piece that requires 2 dancers. If there are 7 dancers in the company, how many possible pairs of dancers could perform the piece?

GO ON TO THE NEXT PAGE

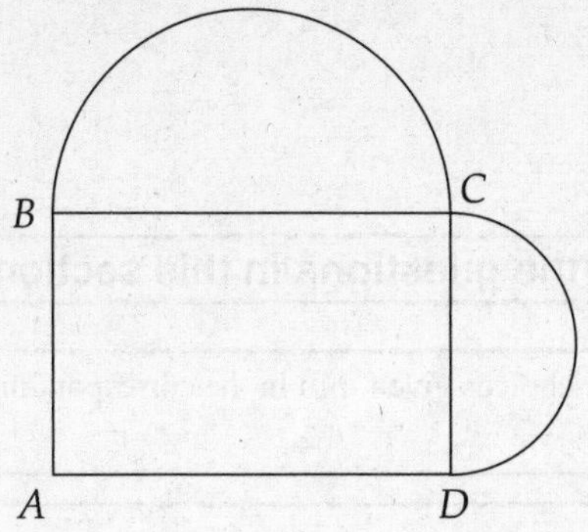

15. In the figure above, if semicircular arc BC has length 6π and semicircular arc CD has length 4π, what is the area of rectangle $ABCD$?

16. Let $f(x) = x^2 - 5$. If $f(6) - f(4) = f(y)$, what is $|y|$?

SPICE PRICES OF DISTRIBUTOR D	
Spice	**Price Per Pound**
Cinnamon	\$8.00
Nutmeg	\$9.00
Ginger	\$7.00
Cloves	\$10.00

17. The owner of a spice store buys 3 pounds each of cinnamon, nutmeg, ginger, and cloves from distributor D. She then sells all of the spices at \$2.00 per ounce. What is her total dollar profit (1 pound = 16 ounces)? (Disregard the \$ sign when gridding your answer.)

18. Points E, F, G, and H lie on a line in that order. If $EG = \frac{5}{3}EF$ and $HF = 5FG$, then what is $\frac{EF}{HG}$?

STOP

If you finish before time is called, you may check your work on this section only. Do not turn to any other section in the test.

SECTION 6
Time — 25 minutes
18 Questions

Turn to Section 2 of your answer sheet to answer the questions in this section.

Directions: For this section, solve each problem and decide which is the best of the choices given. Fill in the corresponding circle on the answer sheet. You may use any available space for scratchwork.

Notes

1. The use of a calculator is permitted.
2. All numbers used are real numbers.
3. Figures that accompany problems in this test are intended to provide information useful in solving the problems. They are drawn as accurately as possible EXCEPT when it is stated in a specific problem that the figure is not drawn to scale. All figures lie in a plane unless other wise indicated.
4. Unless otherwise specified, the domain of any function f is assumed to be the set of all real numbers x for which $f(x)$ is a real number.

Reference Information

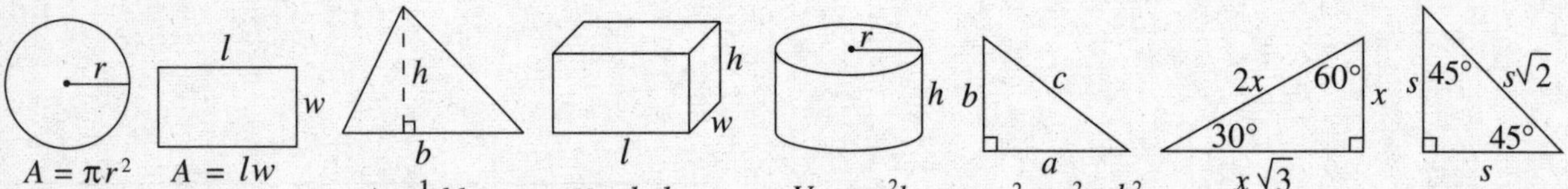

$A = \pi r^2$ $C = 2\pi r$ $A = lw$ $A = \frac{1}{2}bh$ $V = lwh$ $V = \pi r^2 h$ $c^2 = a^2 + b^2$

Special Right Triangles

The number of degrees of arc in a circle is 360.

The sum of the measures in degrees of the angles of a triangle is 180.

1. If $x + 6 > 0$ and $1 - 2x > -1$, then x could equal each of the following EXCEPT

(A) -6

(B) -4

(C) -2

(D) 0

(E) $\frac{1}{2}$

2. Elsa has a pitcher containing x ounces of root beer. If she pours y ounces of root beer into each of z glasses, how many ounces of root beer will remain in the pitcher?

(A) $\frac{x}{y} + z$

(B) $xy - z$

(C) $\frac{x}{yz}$

(D) $x - yz$

(E) $\frac{x}{y} - z$

GO ON TO THE NEXT PAGE

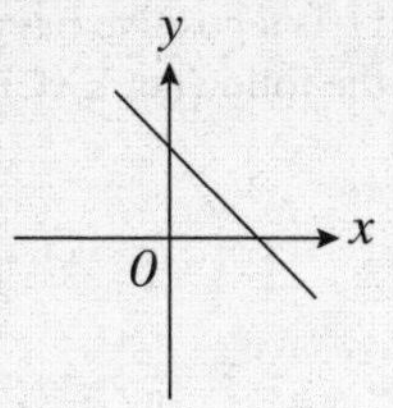

3. Which of the following could be the equation of the line represented in the graph above?

(A) $y = 2x + 4$
(B) $y = 2x - 4$
(C) $y = -2x - 1$
(D) $y = -2x - 4$
(E) $y = -2x + 4$

4. Starting with a blue light, a strand of colored lights contains lights in a repeating pattern of blue, orange, green, purple, red, and yellow. What is the color of the 53rd light?

(A) Blue
(B) Orange
(C) Green
(D) Purple
(E) Red

5. If $x = y + 1$ and $y \geq 1$, then which of the following is equal to $x^2 - y^2$?

(A) $(x - y)^2$
(B) $x^2 - y - 1$
(C) $x + y$
(D) $x^2 - 1$
(E) $y^2 + 1$

6. Triangle ABC has a perimeter of 10, and the lengths of its sides are all integers. If a is the length of side $\overline{BC}$, what is the difference between the largest and smallest possible values of a ?

(A) 1
(B) 2
(C) 3
(D) 4
(E) 7

GO ON TO THE NEXT PAGE

7. What is the greatest number of regions into which an equilateral triangle can be divided using exactly three straight lines?

(A) 4
(B) 6
(C) 7
(D) 8
(E) 9

8. If $a = 4b + 26$, and b is a positive integer, then a could be divisible by all of the following EXCEPT

(A) 2
(B) 4
(C) 5
(D) 6
(E) 7

GO ON TO THE NEXT PAGE

Directions: For Student-Produced Response questions 9–18, use the grids to the right of the answer document page on which you have answered questions 1–8.

Each of the remaining 10 questions requires you to solve the problem and enter your answer by marking the circles in the special grid, as shown in the examples below. You may use any available space for scratch work.

Answer: $\frac{7}{12}$

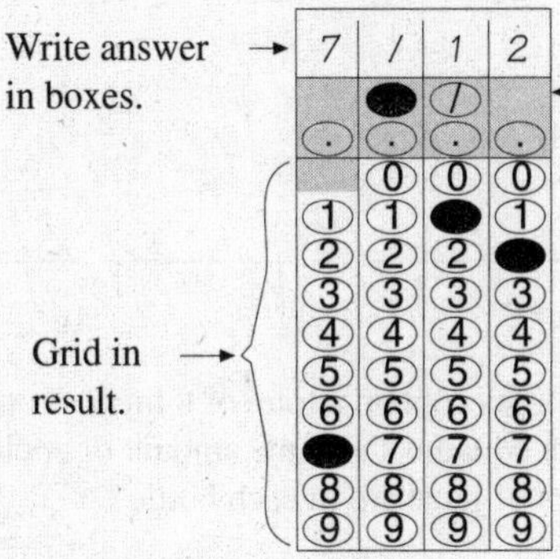

Answer: 2.5

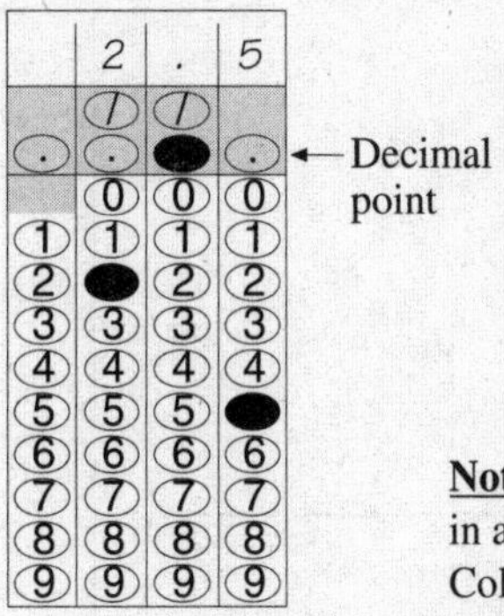

Answer: 201
Either position is correct.

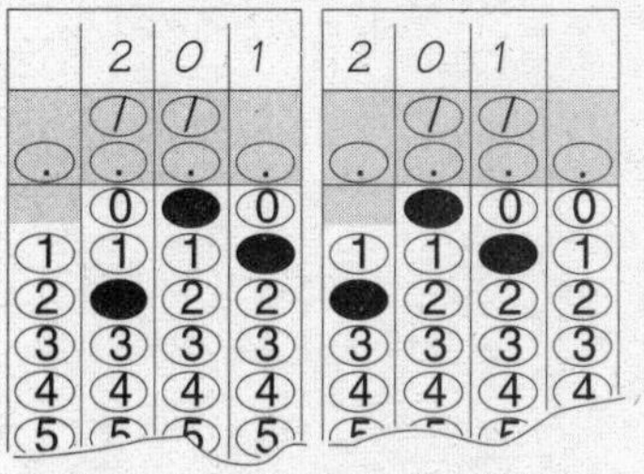

Note: You may start your answers in any column, space permitting. Columns not needed should be left blank.

- Mark no more than one circle in any column.
- Because the answer document will be machine-scored, **you will receive credit only if the circles are filled in correctly.**
- Although not required, it is suggested that you write your answer in the boxes at the top of the columns to help you fill in the circles accurately.
- Some problems may have more than one correct answer. In such cases, grid only one answer.
- No question has a negative answer.
- **Mixed numbers** such as $3\frac{1}{2}$ must be gridded as 3.5 or 7/2. (If 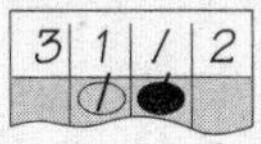 is gridded, it will be interpreted as $\frac{31}{2}$, not $3\frac{1}{2}$.)
- **Decimal Answers:** If you obtain a decimal answer with more digits than the grid can accommodate, it may be either rounded or truncated, but it must fill the entire grid. For example, if you obtain an answer such as 0.6666..., you should record your result as .666 or .667. **A less accurate value such as .66 or .67 will be scored as incorrect.**

Acceptable ways to grid $\frac{2}{3}$ are:

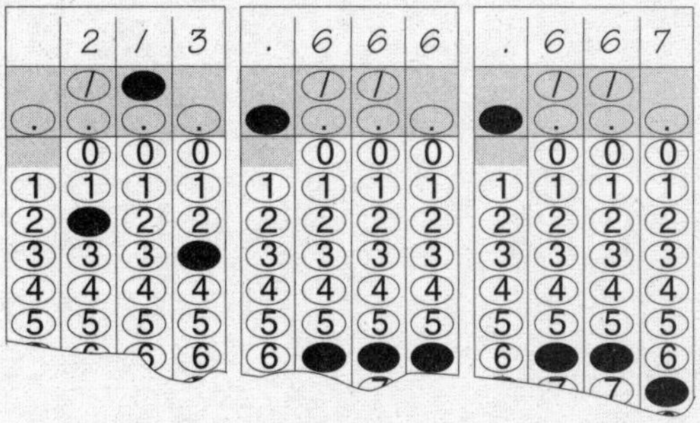

9. If $3x = 12$, what is the value of $\frac{8}{x}$?

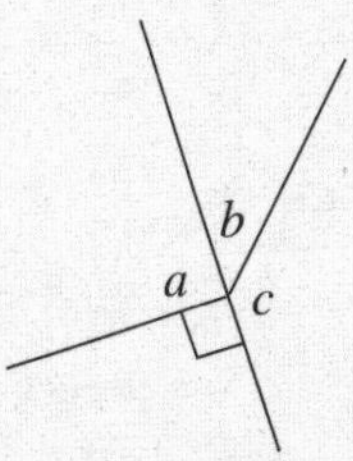

10. In the figure above, what is the value of $a + b + c$?

GO ON TO THE NEXT PAGE

11. *Y* is a point on $\overline{XZ}$ such that $XY = \frac{1}{2}XZ$. If the length of $\overline{YZ}$ is $4a + 6$, and the length of $\overline{XZ}$ is 68, what is the value of a ?

12. If $4x + 2y = 24$ and $\frac{7y}{2x} = 7$, what is the value of x ?

13. If $\frac{x^2 + x - 6}{x^2 - 8x + 12} = 4$, what is the value of x ?

14. Twenty bottles contain a total of 8 liters of apple juice. If each bottle contains the same amount of apple juice, how many liters of juice are in each bottle?

GO ON TO THE NEXT PAGE

15. The American Ballet Repertory Company will choose 4 new corps members from its apprentice program. The apprentice program is made up of 6 women and 6 men. If 3 women and 1 man are to be chosen for the corps, how many different groupings are possible?

16. The estimated population of rabbits in a certain forest is given by the function $P(t) = at + 120$ where t is an integer which represents the number of years after the rabbit population was first counted, $0 \leq t \leq 10$, and a is a constant. If there were 192 rabbits 3 years after the population was first counted, how many rabbits will there be 7 years after the population was first counted?

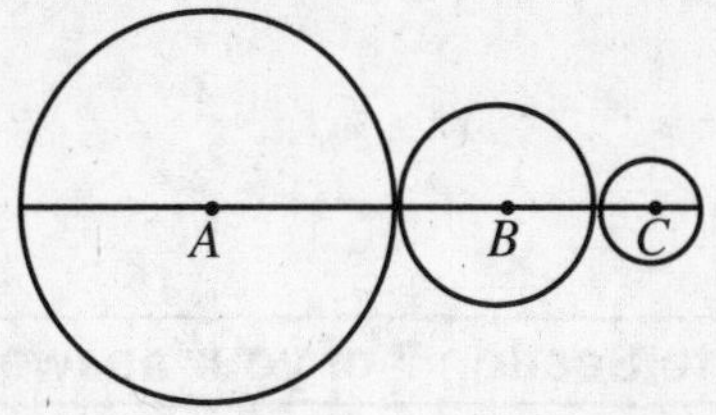

17. In the figure above, the radius of the circle with center A is twice the radius of the circle with center B and four times the radius of the circle with center C. If the sum of the areas of the three circles is 84π, what is the length of AC ?

18. One-fifth of the cars in a parking lot are blue and $\frac{1}{2}$ of the blue cars are convertibles. If $\frac{1}{4}$ of the convertibles in the parking lot are blue, then what percent of the cars in the lot are neither blue nor convertibles? (Disregard the % sign when gridding your answer.)

STOP

If you finish before time is called, you may check your work on this section only.
Do not turn to any other section in the test.

SECTION 7
Time — 25 minutes
35 Questions

Turn to Section 7 of your answer sheet to answer the questions in this section.

Directions: For each question in this section, select the best answer from among the choices given and fill in the corresponding circle on the answer sheet.

The following sentences test correctness and effectiveness of expression. Part of each sentence or the entire sentence is underlined; beneath each sentence are five ways of phrasing the underlined material. Choice A repeats the original phrasing; the other four choices are different. If you think the original phrasing produces a better sentence than any of the alternatives, select choice A; if not, select one of the other choices.

In making your selection, follow the requirements of standard written English; that is, pay attention to grammar, choice of words, sentence construction, and punctuation. Your selection should result in the most effective sentence—clear and precise, without awkwardness or ambiguity.

EXAMPLE:

Bobby Flay baked his first cake and he was thirteen years old then.
(A) and he was thirteen years old then
(B) when he was thirteen
(C) at age thirteen years old
(D) upon the reaching of thirteen years
(E) at the time when he was thirteen Ⓐ●ⒸⒹⒺ

1. Rotary phones, once the height of technology, are now so obsolete and rare as to be unknown to younger generations.

(A) are now so obsolete and rare as to be unknown to younger generations
(B) are now so obsolete and rare and unknown to younger generations
(C) are now unknown to younger generations stemming from their obsoleteness and rareness
(D) now are obsolete and rare, which means that younger generations are unaware of it
(E) now are unknown and younger generations think they are obsolete and rare

2. The hearings of the McCarthy era often cast doubt on the integrity of those brought to trial as well as anyone that had a relation to them, however distant.

(A) that had a relation to them, however distant
(B) with relationships to them, even distantly
(C) related to them, however distantly
(D) with a relationship to the defendants, however distantly
(E) related to them, however distant

3. When you look at a sixteenth-century painting of the Annunciation by Lorenzetti or Giotto, one may notice certain sartorial or architectural details outlined in gold leaf.

(A) one may notice
(B) people may notice
(C) you may notice
(D) one may be noticing
(E) one's thoughts are

4. Fats nicknamed "trans fats" cling to body cells for 57 days, and this is not true of unsaturated fats such as olive and canola oils, which nourish the body without damaging the cells.

(A) and this is not true of unsaturated fats such as olive and canola oils, which nourish
(B) not true of unsaturated fats such as olive and canola oils, which nourish
(C) as opposed to unsaturated fats such as olive and canola oils, nourishing
(D) unsaturated fats such as olive and canola oils nourish
(E) but unsaturated fats such as olive and canola oils nourish

GO ON TO THE NEXT PAGE

5. Knoll, known for their Scandinavian designs, sells the Barcelona chair that the architect Mies van der Rohe designed in the style of his own building in Barcelona.

(A) known for their Scandinavian designs
(B) known for its Scandinavian designs
(C) designing the Scandinavian furniture that it's known for
(D) though they're known for Scandinavian designs
(E) known to be Scandinavian designers

6. Towing companies face harsh new restrictions that detail where they can operate, which vehicles are off limits, and when they can begin; because of new legislation is why.

(A) because of new legislation is why
(B) new legislation being the reason
(C) with new legislation as the reason
(D) these restrictions are the result of new legislation
(E) all of those restrictions come from new legislation recently passed

7. The increase in hours they are required to work in an understaffed, unsupportive situation have angered the nurses at West Branch Rest Home and threatened a walkout.

(A) have angered the nurses at West Branch Rest Home and threatened a walkout
(B) has angered the nurses at West Branch Rest Home and caused them to threaten a walkout
(C) have angered the nurses at West Branch Rest Home, and a walkout is threatened
(D) has angered the nurses at West Branch Rest Home, which caused a threat to have a walkout
(E) has angered the nurses at West Branch Rest Home to have a walkout

8. Galleons, a sailing ship from the seventeenth century, were known for their large size, however they were unable to sail into the wind because of the design of their sails.

(A) a sailing ship from the seventeenth century, were known for their
(B) a sailing ship from the seventeenth century, was known for its
(C) a seventeenth-century sailing ship, was known for its
(D) seventeenth-century sailing ships, was known for its
(E) seventeenth-century sailing ships, were known for their

9. Just an hour after Evan and Ken reached the skate park, he fell and broke his wrist in two places.

(A) he fell and broke his wrist in two places
(B) his wrist broke when he fell in two places
(C) his wrist being broke in two places as a result of falling
(D) Evan fell and broke his wrist in two places
(E) Evan was falling and breaking two bones in his wrist

10. The Advanced Acting course requires neither a final exam or project other than the performance of a major role in the spring play.

(A) neither a final exam or project other than the performance of
(B) no final exam and assigns no project, but does expect each student to perform
(C) no other final exam or project excepting for the performing by students of
(D) no other final exam nor assigns any project other than to be performing
(E) neither a final exam or a major project other than performing

11. Many regard Sappho as the writer who originated the tradition of expressing tormented love in Western poetry.

(A) regard Sappho as
(B) regard Sappho to be
(C) regard Sappho to have been
(D) consider that Sappho is
(E) consider Sappho as being

GO ON TO THE NEXT PAGE

The following sentences test your ability to recognize grammar and usage errors. Each sentence contains either a single error or no error at all. No sentence contains more than one error. The error, if there is one, is underlined and lettered. If the sentence contains an error, select the one underlined part that must be changed to make the sentence correct. If the sentence is correct, select choice E. In choosing answers, follow the requirements of standard written English.

EXAMPLE:

The other players and her significantly improved
A B C

the game plan created by the coaches. No error
D E

Ⓐ●ⒸⒹⒺ

12. The object of the game of chess is to put the other
A B
player's king in a vulnerable position, so that you can
C
eventually capture them. No error
D E

13. In the author's latest novel, the hero traveled to Montana
A
where she finds a mysteriously deserted house and,
B
through a series of misunderstandings, becomes
C
embroiled in an international smuggling ring. No error
D E

14. Many biographers had claimed that Samuel Langhorne
A B
Clemens changed his name to Mark Twain to echo the
C
riverboat captain's call ascertaining the safe navigation
D
depth of the Mississippi River. No error
E

15. After having read numerous diet books, Charles
A
decided that the simplest plan would be the best: eat
B
fewer calories and exercise more. No error
C D E

16. A study showed that students prefer writing in pencil
A
more than writing in pen simply because fixing mistakes
B C
is less difficult. No error
D E

17. When learning how to paint, one should comply to
A
the teacher's instruction; with more experience, the
B
burgeoning painter can experiment with technique.
C D
No error
E

18. Not having traveled abroad before, John was both
A B C
apprehensive and excited about his upcoming trip to the
D
Galápagos Islands. No error
E

19. The field of consumer electronics have never been fixed;
A
DVDs have replaced VHS tapes, just as CDs replaced
B C
cassette tapes in the past. No error
D E

20. One should use parchment paper while baking cookies
A B
because the cookies won't stick to this lining and you
C D
won't have to scrub the pan. No error
E

GO ON TO THE NEXT PAGE

21. Salma and Raiza may be (A) identical twins, but (B) Salma is the more (C) athletic and Raiza the most (D) studious. No error (E)

22. Forest fires, long thought to be (A) a detriment to the environment, are (B) now understood not only (C) to be unavoidable but also to be a boon (D) to the forests. No error (E)

23. Superbowl commercials perfectly (A) target their (B) demographics because the advertisers regularly spent (C) exorbitant amounts of time and money designing (D) the ads. No error (E)

24. Although many people scoff at (A) superstitions, they (B) usually have some of their own, from (C) retrieving face-up pennies from the sidewalk to selecting (D) lucky numbers for the lottery. No error (E)

25. Returning (A) to school in September, Linnea told us in minute (B) detail how she had rode (C) her bike from our town in coastal New Jersey to Eugene, Oregon, entirely (D) on her own. No error (E)

26. The sculptor Rodin often departed (A) from traditional styles in his creations; unlike other sculptors (B), his creations made obvious (C) the materials from which they were built (D). No error (E)

27. Jane, who is known for (A) her diligence, smugly reminded Jason that if he would have planned (B) ahead instead of procrastinating (C), he would not have had (D) to write his entire research paper in just one weekend. No error (E)

28. Some words in the English language has (A) several meanings that are unrelated except through (B) their origins: *testudinate*, for example, can mean either (C) curved and vault-shaped, or extremely slow moving, since the word derives from (D) the Latin word for *turtle*. No error (E)

29. The woman whom (A) the board picked to design (B) the new building is a renowned (C) architect and has received (D) many awards. No error (E)

GO ON TO THE NEXT PAGE

Directions: The following passage is an early draft of an essay. Some parts of the passage need to be rewritten.

Read the passage and select the best answers for the questions that follow. Some questions are about particular sentences or parts of sentences and ask you to improve sentence structure or word choice. Other questions ask you to consider organization and development. In choosing answers, follow the requirements of standard written English.

Questions 30–35 are based on the following passage.

(1) When I agreed to stage-manage my school's production of *Guys and Dolls*, I really had no idea of what a stage manager actually did. **(2)** Still, I decided that it would be an interesting experience, and a way to get involved with theater, since I am definitely not an actor. **(3)** Besides, if there were already a director, a choreographer, and sets and lights to be built and run by technicians, how much could there be left for a stage manager to do? **(4)** I figured that I would spend a lot of time watching rehearsal and doodling into my script.

(5) My illusions were shattered by the first rehearsal. **(6)** I discovered that it was my responsibility to make sure that all of the actors were present, had scripts, and gave me their schedules before they left the room. **(7)** It became a nightmare. **(8)** I found that it was virtually impossible to get all twenty-five cast members together for a group scene, especially since actors kept calling me with emergency orthodontist appointments, and last-minute family gatherings. **(9)** When the actor who was playing Sky was sick one day and had to miss rehearsal, I had to walk through his part myself. **(10)** It was probably the first time in the history of American theater that Sky Masterson was ever wearing a miniskirt and leggings.

(11) I sat to the side of the stage, with my script open on a music stand in front of me. **(12)** "Standby, cue 1," I whispered into my headset. **(13)** "Cue 1: go." The lights came up, the show began, and I knew that it had all been worthwhile.

30. Which of the following words or phrases is unnecessary in sentence 1?

(A) production of
(B) actually did
(C) agreed to
(D) When
(E) really

31. In context, which version of the underlined part of sentence 3 (reproduced below) is the best?

Besides, if there were already a director, a choreographer, and sets and lights to be built and run by technicians, how much could there be left for a stage manager to do?

(A) (As it is now)
(B) and sets, lights, and technicians
(C) and the building and running of sets and lights by technicians
(D) and technicians to build the sets and run the lights
(E) and technicians who would run the lights and be building the sets

32. In context, the best version of the underlined portion of sentence 10 (reproduced below) is which of the following?

It was probably the first time in the history of American theater that Sky Masterson was ever wearing a miniskirt and leggings.

(A) (As it is now)
(B) had ever worn
(C) could have worn
(D) would ever be wearing
(E) had ever before worn

33. Which of the following sentences, if added at the beginning of the final paragraph, would provide the best transition?

(A) Luckily, the actor soon regained his health.
(B) We rehearsed for five weeks.
(C) Finally, it was opening night.
(D) Everyone was filled with nervous excitement.
(E) I communicated with the light and sound operators through a headset.

GO ON TO THE NEXT PAGE

34. The writer's story would be most improved if a paragraph were included on which of the following topics?

(A) The author's other extracurricular activities
(B) The author's responsibilities during different phases of rehearsal
(C) The historical background of *Guys and Dolls*
(D) The audition process
(E) The plays produced in previous years

35. In context, which is the best version of the underlined portion of sentence 11 (reproduced below) ?

I sat to the side of the <u>*stage, with my script open*</u> *on a music stand in front of me.*

(A) (As it is now)
(B) stage, my script being open
(C) stage, my script having been opened
(D) stage. With my script opened
(E) stage. My script open

STOP

If you finish before time is called, you may check your work on this section only. Do not turn to any other section in the test.

SECTION 8
Time — 20 minutes
16 Questions

Turn to Section 8 of your answer sheet to answer the questions in this section.

Directions: For this section, solve each problem and decide which is the best of the choices given. Fill in the corresponding circle on the answer sheet. You may use any available space for scratchwork.

Notes

1. The use of a calculator is permitted.
2. All numbers used are real numbers.
3. Figures that accompany problems in this test are intended to provide information useful in solving the problems. They are drawn as accurately as possible EXCEPT when it is stated in a specific problem that the figure is not drawn to scale. All figures lie in a plane unless other wise indicated.
4. Unless otherwise specified, the domain of any function f is assumed to be the set of all real numbers x for which $f(x)$ is a real number.

Reference Information

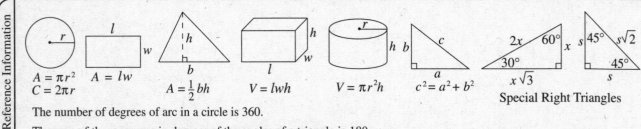

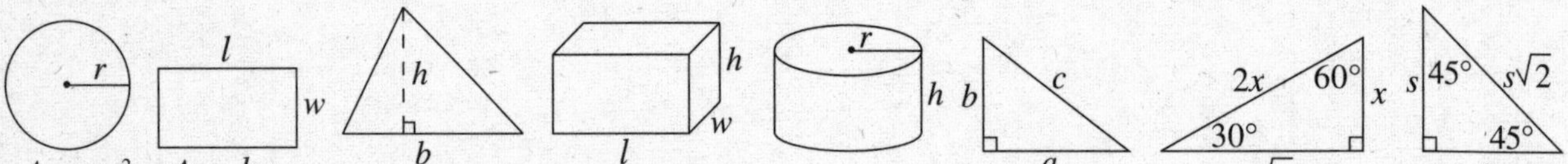

$A = \pi r^2$ $C = 2\pi r$ | $A = lw$ | $A = \frac{1}{2}bh$ | $V = lwh$ | $V = \pi r^2 h$ | $c^2 = a^2 + b^2$ | Special Right Triangles

The number of degrees of arc in a circle is 360.

The sum of the measures in degrees of the angles of a triangle is 180.

1. If $6 - y = 2y - 6$, what is the value of y ?

(A) 0
(B) 2
(C) 4
(D 6
(E) 12

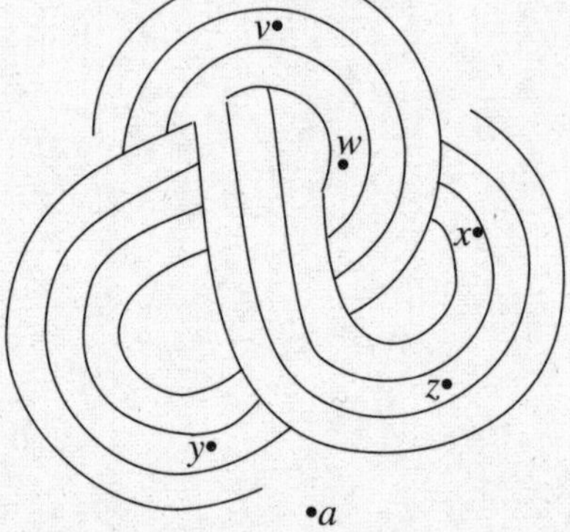

2. Which of the following points can be connected to point a by a continuous path without crossing any line or curve in the figure above?

(A) v
(B) w
(C) x
(D) y
(E) z

GO ON TO THE NEXT PAGE

	Computer Production	
	Morning Shift	Afternoon Shift
Monday	200	375
Tuesday	245	330
Wednesday	255	340
Thursday	250	315
Friday	225	360

3. Computer production at a factory occurs during two shifts, as shown in the chart above. If computers are produced only during the morning and afternoon shifts, on which of the following pairs of days is the greatest total number of computers produced?

(A) Monday and Thursday
(B) Tuesday and Thursday
(C) Tuesday and Wednesday
(D) Tuesday and Friday
(E) Monday and Friday

4. If a rectangular swimming pool has a volume of 16,500 cubic feet, a uniform depth of 10 feet, and a length of 75 feet, what is the width of the pool, in feet?

(A) 22
(B) 26
(C) 32
(D) 110
(E) 1,650

5. Cindy has a collection of 80 records. If 40% of her records are jazz records, and the rest are blues records, how many blues records does she have?

(A) 32
(B) 40
(C) 42
(D) 48
(E) 50

6. A science class has a ratio of girls to boys of 4 to 3. If the class has a total of 35 students, how many more girls are there than boys?

(A) 20
(B) 15
(C) 7
(D) 5
(E) 1

GO ON TO THE NEXT PAGE

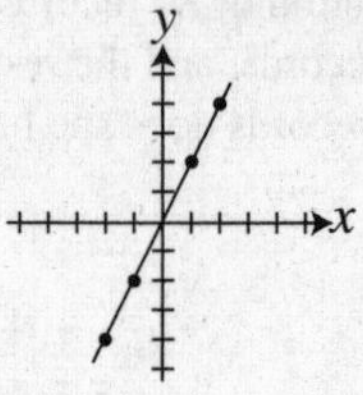

7. The graph above shows $y = 2x$. Which of the following graphs represents $y = |2x|$?

(A)

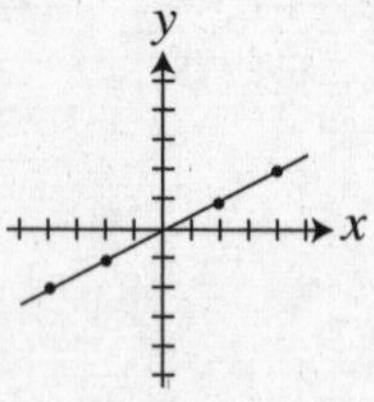

(B)

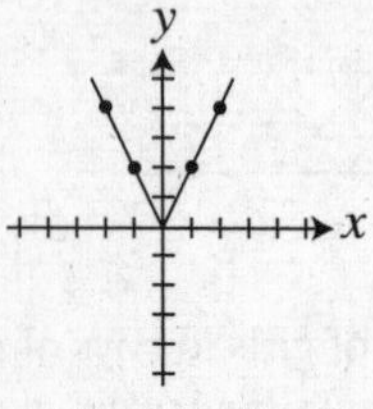

(C)

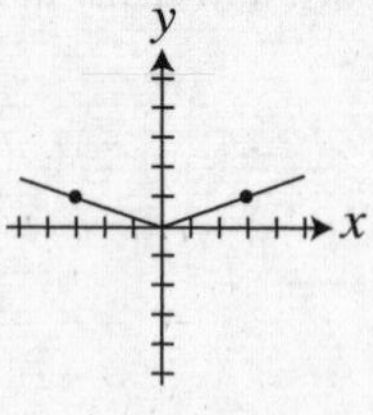

(D)

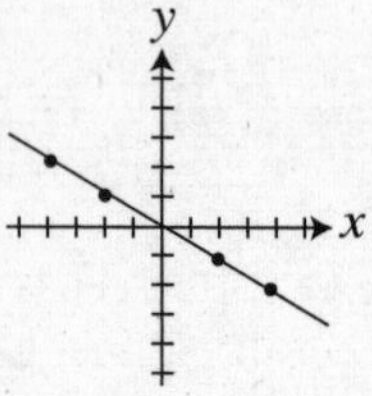

(E)

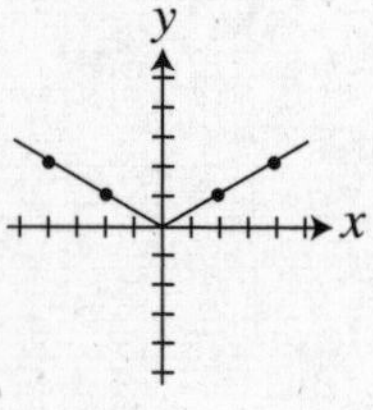

8. The length of a certain rectangle is twice the width. If the area of the rectangle is 128, what is the length of the rectangle?

(A) 4

(B) 8

(C) 16

(D) $21\frac{1}{3}$

(E) $42\frac{2}{3}$

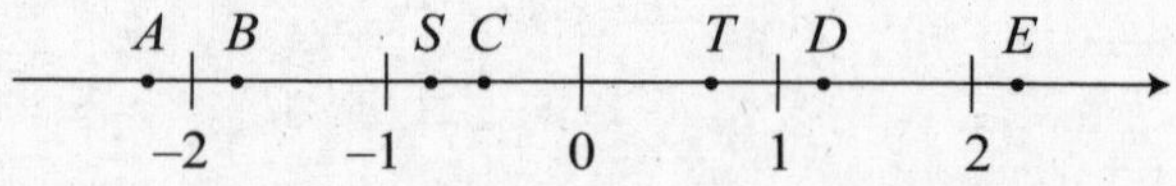

9. Which of the lettered points on the number line above could represent the result when the coordinate of point T is divided by the coordinate of point *S* ?

(A) *A*
(B) *B*
(C) *C*
(D) *D*
(E) *E*

GO ON TO THE NEXT PAGE

10. For positive integer x, 10 percent of x percent of 1,000 is equal to which of the following?

(A) x
(B) $10x$
(C) $100x$
(D) $1{,}000x$
(E) $10{,}000x$

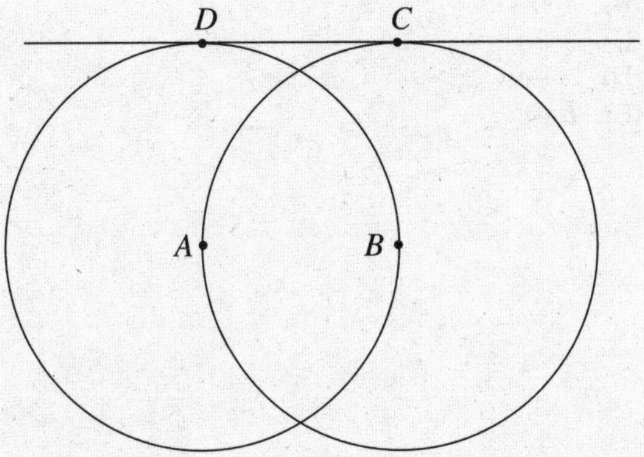

11. In the figure above, A and B are the centers of two circles of identical circumference. $\overleftrightarrow{CD}$ is tangent to both circles and parallel to $\overleftrightarrow{AB}$ (not shown). If r is the radius of the circle with center A, what is the area of quadrilateral $ABCD$ (not shown) in terms of r?

(A) $4r^2$
(B) $4r$
(C) $2r^2$
(D) $2r$
(E) r^2

12. Nails are sold in 8-ounce and 20-ounce boxes. If 50 boxes of nails were sold and the total weight of the nails sold was less than 600 ounces, what is the greatest possible number of 20-ounce boxes that could have been sold?

(A) 34
(B) 33
(C) 25
(D) 17
(E) 16

13. If $c = \frac{1}{x} + \frac{1}{y}$ and $x > y > 0$, then which of the following is equal to $\frac{1}{c}$?

(A) $x + y$

(B) $x - y$

(C) $\frac{x+y}{xy}$

(D) $\frac{xy}{x+y}$

(E) $\frac{1}{x} + \frac{1}{y}$

GO ON TO THE NEXT PAGE

14. In the xy-plane, which of the following is a point of intersection between the graphs of $y = x + 2$ and $y = x^2 + x - 2$?

(A) (0, –2)
(B) (0, 2)
(C) (1, 0)
(D) (2, 4)
(E) (3, 5)

15. If $f(g(a)) = 6$, $f(x) = \frac{x}{2} + 2$, and $g(x) = |x^2 - 10|$, which of the following is a possible value of a ?

(A) $\sqrt{2}$
(B) $\sqrt{3}$
(C) 2
(D) 6
(E) 18

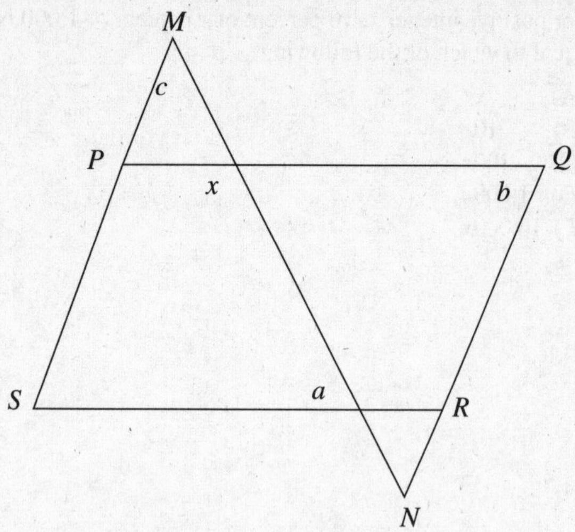

16. If $PQRS$ is a parallelogram, then which of the following must be equal to x ?

(A) $180 - b$
(B) $180 - c$
(C) $a + b$
(D) $a + c$
(E) $b + c$

STOP

If you finish before time is called, you may check your work on this section only. Do not turn to any other section in the test.

NO TEST MATERIAL ON THIS PAGE.

SECTION 9
Time — 20 minutes
19 Questions

Turn to Section 9 of your answer sheet to answer the questions in this section.

Directions: For each question in this section, select the best answer from among the choices given and fill in the corresponding circle on the answer sheet.

Each sentence below has one or two blanks, each blank indicating that something has been omitted. Beneath the sentence are five words or sets of words labeled A through E. Choose the word or set of words that, when inserted in the sentence, best fits the meaning of the sentence as a whole.

Example:

Desiring to ------- his taunting friends, Mitch gave them taffy in hopes it would keep their mouths shut.

(A) eliminate (B) satisfy (C) overcome (D) ridicule (E) silence

Ⓐ Ⓑ Ⓒ Ⓓ ●

1. The success of the school's book club is owed to the club's policy that the novels selected, authored by a ------- group, cover a broad array of subject matters and range of historical eras.

(A) scholarly (B) meritorious (C) diverse (D) erudite (E) sophisticated

2. The apparent ------- with which professional skiers descend the slopes is deceptive; this activity requires ------- effort and intense concentration.

(A) trepidation . . conscious
(B) motivation . . resolute
(C) nonchalance . . strenuous
(D) consideration . . unpredictable
(E) insouciance . . minimal

3. The children in the parade wore a range of costumes, some dressing in classic ghost or witch costumes, some as civic figures such as firefighters or police officers, and others as famous singers and other ------- of popular culture.

(A) monikers (B) diplomats (C) icons (D) pariahs (E) dupes

4. Mr. Planka's explanations were unnecessarily -------, incorporating entirely too many layers of trivial information that his students did not need.

(A) winsome (B) terse (C) convoluted (D) fallacious (E) deafening

5. Reflecting upon her vacation, Cecilia felt that it was both ------- and -------; she enjoyed visiting New York, but did not like all the traveling required to get there.

(A) arduous . . distressing
(B) realistic . . dramatic
(C) relaxing . . peaceful
(D) restful . . wearisome
(E) traditional . . consistent

6. Despite appearing stylistically -------, Pablo Picasso's paintings exhibit artistic ------- on multiple levels.

(A) superficial . . inaccuracy
(B) excessive . . abundance
(C) precise . . elegance
(D) unsophisticated . . complexity
(E) imaginative . . creativity

GO ON TO THE NEXT PAGE

Directions: Each passage below is followed by questions based on its content. Answer the questions on the basis of what is <u>stated</u> or <u>implied</u> in each passage and in any introductory material that may be provided.

Questions 7–19 are based on the following passages.

The discipline of physics has seen a number of changes in the last 100 years. The following passages discuss two of those changes.

Passage 1

It is mandatory to preface any discussion of atoms by paying homage to Democritus, an Ionian philosopher of the fifth century B.C., the earliest known proponent of an atomic theory. Though Democritus's ideas were in many ways strikingly modern and were promulgated by his more celebrated successor Epicurus, his theory never gained wide acceptance in Greek thought. It had largely been forgotten by the time of the late Renaissance rebirth of science. While the dramatic rise of the atomic theory over the last century and a half seems to have vindicated Democritus, only the Greek name atom ("indivisible") remains to establish his claim as the father of the theory.

Nonetheless, Democritus's thinking contained the seed of the idea that has dominated twentieth-century physical thought. He was one of the first to perceive that nature on a sufficiently small scale might be qualitatively different in a striking way from the world of our ordinary experience. And he was the first to voice the hope, today almost an obsession, that underlying all the complex richness, texture, and variety of our everyday life might be a level of reality of stark simplicity, with the turmoil we perceive representing only the nearly infinite arrangements of a smaller number of constituents.

Today, the notion that simplicity is to be found by searching nature on a smaller level is embedded in physical thought to the point that few physicists can imagine any other approach.

Democritus's ideas were popular among the philosophically sophisticated founders of modern physics. Galileo, Newton, and most of their contemporaries were atomists, but their beliefs were based more on intuition than on concrete evidence. Moreover, the invention of calculus had eliminated the difficulties with continuity that had in part motivated the Greek atomists, so the theory received little attention in the century following Newton's work. Still, the atomic theory remained a popular speculation among physicists, because it offered the hope that all the properties of matter might ultimately be explained in terms of the motion of the atoms themselves.

It remained for the chemists of the early nineteenth century to find the first solid empirical support for atomism. Without stretching the point too far, it is fair to say that in 1800 the atomic theory was something physicists believed but couldn't prove, while the chemists were proving it but didn't believe it.

Passage 2

The discovery that the universe is expanding was one of the great intellectual revelations of the twentieth century. With hindsight, it is easy to wonder why no one had thought of it before. Newton, and others, should have realized that a static universe would soon start to contract under the influence of gravity. But suppose instead the universe is expanding. If it were expanding fairly slowly, the force of gravity would cause it eventually to stop expanding and then to start contracting. However, if it were expanding at more than a certain critical rate, gravity would never be strong enough to stop it, and the universe would continue to expand forever. This is a bit like what happens when one fires a rocket upward from the surface of the earth. If it has a fairly low speed, gravity will eventually stop the rocket and it will start falling back. On the other hand, if the rocket has more than a certain critical speed (about seven miles per second), gravity will not be strong enough to pull it back, so it will keep going away from the earth forever. This behavior of the universe could have been predicted from Newton's theory of gravity at any time in the nineteenth, the eighteenth, or even the late seventeenth centuries. Yet so strong was the belief in a static universe that it persisted into the early twentieth century. Even Einstein, when he formulated the general theory of relativity in 1915, was so sure that the universe had to be static that he modified his theory to make this possible, introducing a so-called cosmological constant into his equations. Einstein introduced a new "antigravity" force, which, unlike other forces, did not come from any particular source, but was built into the very fabric of space-time. He claimed that space-time had an inbuilt tendency to expand, and this could be made to balance exactly the attraction of all the matter in the universe, so that a static universe would result.

7. In line 5, the word "promulgated" most nearly means

(A) plagiarized
(B) dismissed
(C) protected
(D) obscured
(E) promoted

GO ON TO THE NEXT PAGE

8. From the information presented in Passage 1, which of the following can be properly inferred about Democritus?

(A) Although his view was initially met with skepticism, Democritus was among the first to advocate an atomic theory.
(B) Although he was known more for his work in politics, Democritus also made important scientific discoveries.
(C) His ideas were incompatible with those of Galileo and Newton.
(D) Democritus was unduly credited with being the father of Greek atomism.
(E) Democritus was more known for his discovery of calculus than for his theory of atomism.

9. The "obsession" that the author describes in line 19 can best be described as

(A) Democritus' desire to see his ideas accepted by the scientific community
(B) physicists' search for Democritus' original writings on atoms
(C) the author's own search for the principles underlying matter
(D) modern scientists' quest for a simple unifying property of everyday matter
(E) early nineteenth-century chemists' search for the first solid evidence of atomism

10. The third paragraph of Passage 1 is used by the author to

(A) express dismay at the narrow-mindedness of early scientists
(B) highlight the ironic acceptance of a once spurned theory
(C) convey wonder for the inexplicableness of this obsession
(D) transition into a discussion of the usefulness of atomic theory
(E) show how modern physicists are unwilling to explore alternatives to atomic theory

11. The last paragraph of Passage 1 suggests that

(A) it was only after the physicists proved the existence of atoms that the chemists believed their claims
(B) chemistry was the first scientific field to take atomic theory seriously
(C) atomic theory did not strictly fall within the domain of any one scientific discipline
(D) while physicists first proved the theory, it was chemists who made the most practical use of atoms
(E) the recognition of chemistry and physics as separate disciplines is arbitrary and detrimental to the pursuit of knowledge

12. Which of the following can be inferred from Passage 2 about the expanding universe?

(A) It was incompatible with accepted nineteenth-century beliefs.
(B) Newton discovered it during his work with gravity.
(C) Most scientists believe that the idea is no longer tenable.
(D) The existence of gravity makes it impossible for the universe to expand.
(E) The expanding universe theory cannot be proven.

13. The author of Passage 2 mentions Newton in order to

(A) point out the ignorance of many physicists
(B) give one example of a proponent of the expanding universe theory
(C) illustrate the point that the expanding universe theory could have been discovered earlier
(D) provide evidence that the universe is not expanding
(E) show the consequences of a scientist's disregard for a new theory

14. The author's reference to a rocket (lines 57–63) serves to illustrate

(A) the implications of an expanding universe
(B) the forces governing the universe's gradual expansion
(C) the similarity of the energy released by the universe and that released by rockets
(D) the way in which gravity prevents the universe from expanding
(E) the theory of a static universe

15. In Passage 2, the author's description of Einstein's general theory of relativity serves to

(A) bolster the author's theory that the universe is expanding
(B) show that scientists were reluctant to abandon the theory of a static universe
(C) indicate the creativity that Einstein brought to his work
(D) question the validity of the theory of the expanding universe
(E) underscore Einstein's reliance on Newtonian physics

GO ON TO THE NEXT PAGE

16. The term "cosmological constant" (line 71) refers to

(A) a mathematical constant employed by Einstein to bring his theories in line with the idea of a static universe
(B) an equation used by Einstein to debunk Newton's ideas about universal expansion
(C) a theory developed by opponents of Einstein's general theory of relativity
(D) the mathematical model that was used to disprove Newtonian physics
(E) the theory that the mass of all matter in the universe must remain the same

17. In the last line of Passage 2, the word "static" most nearly means

(A) charged
(B) conflicting
(C) particulate
(D) unchanging
(E) dynamic

18. The authors of both passages would most probably agree with which of the following statements?

(A) Democritus and Newton both struggled to see their theories accepted by others.
(B) Neither Democritus nor Newton received credit for his theory.
(C) Newton, Einstein, and Democritus are all responsible in part for setting back modern physics.
(D) The atomic model of matter and the theory of the expanding universe cannot both be correct.
(E) Scientists may adopt particular theories in spite of weak or contradictory evidence.

19. Based on the information in both passages, a difference between atomism and the expanding universe theory is

(A) the idea of atomism can be traced to the ancient Greeks, while the model of the expanding universe is a relatively recent theory
(B) atomism is easier to understand and explore than the static universe theory
(C) atomism was developed for political reasons, while the static universe theory is purely scientific
(D) the theory of atomism has been thoroughly proven, while the static universe theory is now thought to be incorrect
(E) the static universe theory is more adaptable to modern science than is the atomistic theory

STOP

If you finish before time is called, you may check your work on this section only. Do not turn to any other section in the test.

SECTION 10
Time — 10 minutes
14 Questions

Turn to Section 10 of your answer sheet to answer the questions in this section.

Directions: For each question in this section, select the best answer from among the choices given and fill in the corresponding circle on the answer sheet.

The following sentences test correctness and effectiveness of expression. Part of each sentence or the entire sentence is underlined; beneath each sentence are five ways of phrasing the underlined material. Choice A repeats the original phrasing; the other four choices are different. If you think the original phrasing produces a better sentence than any of the alternatives, select choice A; if not, select one of the other choices.

In making your selection, follow the requirements of standard written English; that is, pay attention to grammar, choice of words, sentence construction, and punctuation. Your selection should result in the most effective sentence—clear and precise, without awkwardness or ambiguity.

EXAMPLE:

Bobby Flay baked his first cake and he was thirteen years old then.

(A) and he was thirteen years old then
(B) when he was thirteen
(C) at age thirteen years old
(D) upon the reaching of thirteen years
(E) at the time when he was thirteen

Ⓐ●ⒸⒹⒺ

1. Of the top investment firms, only the few that have complied with SEC guidelines should be trusted by investors looking for a good place to build capital.

(A) Of the top investment firms, only the few that have complied with SEC guidelines
(B) Of the top investment firms, only a few, those which have compliance with SEC guidelines,
(C) Only a few of the top investment firms, because of complying with SEC guidelines
(D) Only a few of the top investment firms, in which the SEC guidelines were complied by,
(E) Only a few of the top investment firms complied with SEC guidelines,

2. The audience, though still trying to appreciate the modern theater production, are getting restless and won't be able to sit still for much longer.

(A) production, are getting restless and won't be able to
(B) production is getting restless and aren't able to
(C) production, are getting restless and they won't be able to
(D) production is getting restless and they won't be able to
(E) production, is getting restless and won't be able to

3. Antique furniture can be worth a great deal of money, but so many fakes abound that it can be difficult to distinguish valuable and worthless pieces.

(A) valuable and worthless pieces
(B) valuable to worthless pieces
(C) between valuable and worthless pieces
(D) between valuable from worthless pieces
(E) valuable pieces from those that are worthless pieces

4. Unlike the Asian people that we now think of as Japanese, the first settlements in the Japanese Archipelago were established by Caucasians called the Ainu.

(A) the first settlements in the Japanese Archipelago were established by Caucasians called the Ainu
(B) the settling of the Japanese Archipelago was first done by the Ainu, who were Caucasians
(C) the Ainu, who established the first settlements in the Japanese Archipelago, were Caucasians
(D) the Ainu, as Caucasians, were the first to establish settlements in the Japanese Archipelago
(E) settling the Japanese Archipelago was first done by Caucasians called the Ainu

GO ON TO THE NEXT PAGE

5. A Mongol emperor associated with ancient Chinese splendor, the tiny Japanese fleet nevertheless managed to defeat Kublai Khan's huge, nearly invincible army.

(A) splendor, the tiny Japanese fleet nevertheless managed to defeat Kublai Khan's huge, nearly invincible army
(B) splendor, the tiny Japanese fleet nevertheless being the first to defeat Kublai Khan's huge nearly invincible army
(C) splendor, Kublai Khan's army was nevertheless defeated by the tiny, nearly invincible Japanese fleet
(D) splendor, Kublai Khan commanded a nearly invincible army that was nevertheless defeated by the tiny Japanese fleet
(E) splendor, the tiny, nearly invincible fleet of the Japanese nevertheless managing to defeat the huge army commanded by Kublai Khan

6. In 1666, the Great Fire of London, though it destroyed over 14,000 buildings and left 100,000 people homeless, actually ended the bubonic plague outbreak by incinerating the rats that carried the disease.

(A) homeless, actually ended
(B) homeless, actually ending
(C) homeless, actually it had ended
(D) homeless; actually ended
(E) homeless, and it ended

7. Though all of Dawn's Siamese kittens are descended from the same four progenitors, each kitten has its own distinct personality.

(A) each kitten has its own distinct personality
(B) each kitten has their own distinct personalities
(C) with each one there having distinct personalities
(D) which each has its own distinct personality
(E) each kitten is having a distinct personality of their own

8. Jenna was very self-assured about the upcoming audition, this confidence gave her the ability to continue performing her scene even after she forgot several lines.

(A) this
(B) and this
(C) however, her
(D) that
(E) because her

9. One of the deciding factors in Edward III's retreat from France in 1390 was a freak electrical hailstorm; killing scores of his horses and armored knights.

(A) hailstorm; killing
(B) hailstorm and it killed
(C) hailstorm, and killing
(D) hailstorm, being the death of
(E) hailstorm that killed

GO ON TO THE NEXT PAGE

10. The effects of the poliomyelitis that author Kyra Stanley contracted as a young child had been evident in her early stories.

(A) had been evident
(B) being evident
(C) was evident
(D) were evident
(E) and she was evident

11. During his semester of student teaching, the observation of several students copying from each other's papers without consequence gave Mr. Peters the impression that the school had no effective policy against cheating.

(A) the observation of several students copying from each other's papers without consequence gave Mr. Peters
(B) Mr. Peters observed several students copying from each other's papers without consequence; he formed
(C) observing several students copying from each other's papers without consequence gave Mr. Peters
(D) Mr. Peters, observing several students copying from each other's papers without consequence and forming
(E) the observation by Mr. Peters of several students copying from each other's papers without consequence gave him

12. When Jacques Lacan was developing his psychoanalytical theories, ideas from Freud, Heidigger, and even the structural linguists were used, but also original concepts were added by him.

(A) ideas from Freud, Heidigger, and even the structural linguists were used, but also original concepts were added by him
(B) ideas from Freud, Heidigger, and even the structural linguists were used, as well as original concepts were added by him
(C) he used not only ideas from Freud, Heidigger, and even the structural linguists, but also his original concepts
(D) he used not only ideas from Freud, Heidigger, and even the structural linguists and added original concepts, too
(E) ideas from Freud, Heidigger, the structural linguists, and original concepts were added by him

13. The nutrition guideline called the "Food Pyramid" has not been as effective in fighting obesity and heart disease as experts had anticipated; as a result, reduced levels of carbohydrate intake will be recommended by them.

(A) reduced levels of carbohydrate intake will be recommended by them
(B) experts now recommend eating fewer carbohydrates
(C) had recommended reduced levels of carbohydrate intake
(D) the recommendations for reduced carbohydrate intake will be made by them
(E) will be recommending reduced levels of carbohydrate intake

14. In contrast to them in New York and other American cities, Belgium's streets are not littered with fast food containers and discarded papers; however, pedestrians do need to watch out for dog droppings.

(A) In contrast to them in New York and other American cities, Belgium's streets
(B) Belgium's streets, in contrast to them in New York and other American cities,
(C) Belgium's streets, when in contrast to those in New York and other American cities,
(D) Belgium's streets, in contrast to those in New York and other American cities,
(E) Belgium's streets contrast to New York and American cities, they

STOP

If you finish before time is called, you may check your work on this section only. Do not turn to any other section in the test.

NO TEST MATERIAL ON THIS PAGE.

PRACTICE TEST 2: ANSWER KEY

Section 2 Reading	Section 3 Math	Section 4 Reading	Section 5 Math (Exp)	Section 6 Math	Section 7 Writing	Section 8 Math	Section 9 Reading	Section 10 Writing
1. E	1. E	1. E	1. A	1. A	1. A	1. C	1. C	1. A
2. D	2. B	2. E	2. C	2. D	2. C	2. B	2. C	2. E
3. E	3. A	3. D	3. E	3. E	3. C	3. C	3. C	3. C
4. E	4. B	4. D	4. B	4. E	4. E	4. A	4. C	4. C
5. C	5. A	5. C	5. E	5. C	5. B	5. D	5. D	5. D
6. A	6. C	6. C	6. B	6. B	6. D	6. D	6. D	6. A
7. D	7. B	7. B	7. B	7. C	7. B	7. B	7. E	7. A
8. A	8. C	8. A	8. D	8. B	8. E	8. C	8. A	8. B
9. C	9. D	9. E	9. 100	9. 2	9. D	9. C	9. D	9. E
10. B	10. D	10. B	10. 81	10. 270	10. B	10. A	10. B	10. D
11. C	11. D	11. D	11. .75 or $\frac{3}{4}$	11. 7	11. A	11. E	11. C	11. B
12. D	12. D	12. A	12. 8	12. 3	12. D	12. E	12. A	12. C
13. C	13. B	13. B	13. 5, 7, or 11	13. 9	13. A	13. D	13. C	13. B
14. E	14. C	14. E	14. 21	14. .4 or $\frac{2}{5}$	14. B	14. D	14. B	14. D
15. C	15. D	15. C	15. 96	15. 120	15. E	15. A	15. B	
16. B	16. C	16. D	16. 5	16. 288	16. B	16. E	16. A	
17. D	17. A	17. B	17. 282	17. 18	17. A		17. D	
18. B	18. C	18. E	18. .375 or $\frac{3}{8}$	18. 50	18. E		18. E	
19. B	19. D	19. D			19. A		19. A	
20. A	20. D	20. C			20. D			
21. C		21. A			21. D			
22. E		22. E			22. E			
23. D		23. A			23. C			
24. A		24. C			24. E			
					25. C			
					26. B			
					27. B			
					28. A			
					29. E			
					30. E			
					31. D			
					32. B			
					33. C			
					34. B			
					35. A			

SAT SCORING WORKSHEET

For directions on how to score your SAT practice test, see pages 389–390. Section 5 is the unscored, Experimental section.

SAT Writing Section

Total Writing Multiple-Choice Questions Correct from Sections 7 and 10: ______

−

Total Writing Multiple-Choice Questions Incorrect from Sections 7 and 10: ______ ÷ 4 = ______

Be sure to register at PrincetonReview.com/cracking to gain access to our LiveGrader™ Service. Your essay can be scored by our graders there.

Grammar Raw Score: ______ → **Grammar Scaled Subscore!** ______

Compare the Grammar Raw Score to the Writing Multiple-Choice Subscore Conversion Table on the next page to find the Grammar Scaled Subscore.

+

Your Essay Score (2 – 12): ______ × 2 = ______

Writing Raw Score: ______

Compare Raw Score to SAT Score Conversion Table on the next page to find the Writing Scaled Score. → **Writing Scaled Score!** ______

SAT Critical Reading Section

Total Critical Reading Questions Correct from Sections 2, 4, and 9: ______

−

Total Critical Reading Questions Incorrect from Sections 2, 4, and 9: ______ ÷ 4 = ______

Critical Reading Raw Score: ______

Compare Raw Score to SAT Score Conversion Table on the next page to find the Critical Reading Scaled Score. → **Critical Reading Scaled Score!** ______

SAT Math Section

Total Math Grid-In Questions Correct from Section 6: ______

+

Total Math Multiple-Choice Questions Correct from Sections 3, 6, and 8: ______

−

Total Math Multiple-Choice Questions Incorrect from Sections 3, 6, and 8: ______ ÷ 4 = ______

Don't include wrong answers from grid-ins!

Math Raw Score: ______

Compare Raw Score to SAT Score Conversion Table on the next page to find the Math Scaled Score. → **Math Scaled Score!** ______

SAT SCORE CONVERSION TABLE

Raw Score	Writing Scaled Score	Reading Scaled Score	Math Scaled Score	Raw Score	Writing Scaled Score	Reading Scaled Score	Math Scaled Score	Raw Score	Writing Scaled Score	Reading Scaled Score	Math Scaled Score
73	800			47	590–630	600–640	680–720	21	400–440	420–460	460–50
72	790–800			46	590–630	590–630	670–710	20	390–430	410–450	450–49
71	780–800			45	580–620	580–620	660–700	19	380–420	400–440	450–49
70	770–800			44	570–610	580–620	650–690	18	370–410	400–440	440–48
69	770–800			43	570–610	570–610	640–680	17	370–410	390–430	430–47
68	760–800			42	560–600	570–610	630–670	16	360–400	380–420	420–46
67	760–800	800		41	560–600	560–600	620–660	15	350–390	380–420	420–46
66	760–800	770–800		40	550–590	550–590	620–660	14	340–380	370–410	410–45
65	750–790	750–790		39	540–580	550–590	610–650	13	330–370	360–400	400–44
64	740–780	740–780		38	530–570	540–580	600–640	12	320–360	350–390	400–44
63	730–770	740–780		37	530–570	530–570	590–630	11	320–360	350–390	390–43
62	720–760	730–770		36	520–560	530–570	590–630	10	310–350	340–380	380–42
61	710–750	720–760		35	510–550	520–560	580–620	9	300–340	330–370	370–41
60	700–740	710–750		34	500–540	510–550	570–610	8	290–330	310–350	360–40
59	690–730	700–740		33	490–530	500–540	560–600	7	280–320	300–340	350–39
58	680–720	690–730		32	480–520	500–540	560–600	6	270–310	300–340	340–38
57	680–720	680–720		31	470–510	490–530	540–580	5	260–300	290–330	330–37
56	670–710	670–710		30	470–510	480–520	530–570	4	240–280	280–320	320–36
55	660–720	670–710		29	460–500	470–510	520–560	3	230–270	270–310	310–35
54	650–690	660–700	800	28	450–490	470–510	510–550	2	230–270	260–300	290–33
53	640–680	650–690	780–800	27	440–480	460–500	510–550	1	220–260	230–270	270–31
52	630–670	640–680	750–790	26	430–470	450–490	500–540	0	210–250	200–240	240–28
51	630–670	630–670	740–780	25	420–460	450–490	490–530	–1	200–240	200–230	220–26
50	620–660	620–660	730–770	24	410–450	440–480	480–520	–2	200–230	200–220	210–25
49	610–650	610–650	710–750	23	410–450	430–470	480–520	–3	200–220	200–210	200–24
48	600–640	600–640	700–740	22	400–440	420–460	470–510				

WRITING MULTIPLE-CHOICE SUBSCORE CONVERSION TABLE

Grammar Raw Score	Grammar Scaled Subscore	Grammar Raw Score	Grammar Scaled Subscore	Grammar Raw Score	Grammar Scaled Subscore	Grammar Raw Score	Grammar Scaled Subscore	Grammar Raw Score	Grammar Scaled Subscore	Grammar Raw Score	Grammar Scaled Subscore
49	79–80	40	70–74	31	61–65	22	52–56	13	43–47	4	33–37
48	78–80	39	69–73	30	60–64	21	52–56	12	42–46	3	31–35
47	78–80	38	68–72	29	59–63	20	51–55	11	41–45	2	28–32
46	77–80	37	67–71	28	58–62	19	50–54	10	40–44	1	26–30
45	76–80	36	66–70	27	57–61	18	49–53	9	39–43	0	23–27
44	75–79	35	65–69	26	56–60	17	48–52	8	37–41	–1	22–26
43	73–77	34	64–68	25	55–59	16	47–51	7	36–40	–2	21–25
42	72–76	33	63–67	24	54–58	15	46–50	6	35–39	–3	20–24
41	71–75	32	62–66	23	53–57	14	45–49	5	34–38		

Chapter 22
Answers and Explanations for Practice Test 2

SECTION 2

1. **E** The blank in this sentence is a word that describes the wastes produced by nuclear power plants. What do you know about the wastes? The wastes are *radioactive materials that have to be stored in protective containers*, which means they must be dangerous, so "dangerous" would be a good word for the blank. E, *noxious*, is the best match for dangerous.

2. **D** Let's start with the second blank. The clues for this blank are *living specimen* and *thought to be no longer*. If a *living specimen* was found, and it affects the *scientific community*, then the creature must have been thought to be no longer *living*—a good word for the second blank. Only D and E have second blank words that match *living*. For the first blank, a word that means "surprised" is needed, because you'd certainly be surprised if something you thought was dead turned out to be alive. There is nothing in the sentence to indicate disappointment, so E, *dismayed*, can be eliminated. *Astounded* comes closest to the meaning of surprised.

3. **E** The clues here are *third trip overseas* and *voters complained*. Why would the voters complain about the governor taking a lot of trips abroad? If he's always away in a foreign country, then he probably isn't paying a lot of attention to the affairs of his own country. So you can put "his own country" in the blank. Looking to the answer choices, *domestic* is the best match; it means the opposite of foreign.

4. **E** For this question you need to figure out the relationship between the blanks. Claudius *was viewed* one way by *generations of historians*, until *newly discovered evidence* changed everyone's mind. So the words in the blanks must be somewhat opposite in meaning. You can get rid of A, B, and D because the words aren't opposites. In C and E, the first word is negative and the second is positive, so they are both possibilities. To narrow it down, let's look at the second blank, which describes Claudius's ability as an administrator. Would it make sense to call him an *eager* administrator? Not really, so get rid of C.

5. **C** The clues in this sentence are *scarce* and *nutrition*. In these primitive areas, something is scarce, so they have to be *resourceful* to find nutrition. What is scarce? It must be *nutrition*; that's why they have to be resourceful to find it. So you can recycle the clue and put *nutrition* in the blank. Looking at the answer choices, *sustenance* is the best match for *nutrition*.

6. **A** Let's start with the first blank. The first clue in the sentence is *division between*. Morgan wants to do something with the *division between theory and empiricism*. In the second part of the sentence, you learn that she thinks doing something with philosophy and applied science is possible and necessary. If doing something with both things together is possible and necessary, then she must be against the division, so the word in the first blank must mean "against." Eliminate B and C. Because Morgan is against the division, she must be convinced that a combination is possible and necessary, so you can put "combination" in the second blank. Eliminate D and E, neither of which contains a second word meaning "combination."

7. **D** The colon is a same-direction trigger telling you that the clue for the blank is *vivid colors and mixture of bold patterns* and *center of attention*. A good word to use for the blank is "showy." *Flamboyant* comes closest in meaning to "showy."

8. **A** Let's start with the second blank. The clue in this sentence is *disagreeable*, and the trigger word for the second blank is *although*, which means that the word in the second blank is the opposite of *disagreeable*. Therefore you can put "agreeable" in the second blank. Looking at the answer choices, the only word that matches "agreeable" is *complaisant*, and *contentious* is close in meaning to *disagreeable*.

9. **C** Hurston consciously wrote about the lives of African Americans. In A, although Hurston did participate in the Harlem Renaissance, the term *deconstructed* refers to her writing, not her participation. B is too literal: Hurston's writing is not about actual scientific experimentation. D is incorrect because there is no evidence that Hurston was *cut off* from Harlem. Finally, E is too extreme; there's no support for Hurston trying to make *sweeping changes.*

10. **B** This is the only statement that is not implied or stated in the passage: Although she was indeed an anthropologist, *widely acclaimed* is too extreme and makes this statement inaccurate. All the other choices are supported by information in the passage and therefore are the incorrect answers.

11. **C** C is correct, because it says that the author merely relates the arguments of both sides without adding his own opinion. This also explains why A and B are incorrect. D is too broad and not discussed in the passage, and E is only partially correct. While the passage does touch upon some arguments of opponents to SURTASS LFA, he also discusses the views of *proponents,* and thus this is not the author's main point.

12. **D** D is correct because the example demonstrates how harmful sounds at 150 decibels can be, and this allows the reader to appreciate how dangerous sounds at 215 decibels would be. A is incorrect because the author is comparing different sound levels, not humans and whales. B and C are both incorrect because the author neither supports nor attacks either side in the argument. E is unsupported by the text.

13. **C** According to the first paragraph, *early man viewed...healing as purification,* and this notion is apparent in the *origin of our word "pharmacy."* The passage then gives the meaning of the Greek word *pharmakon*, which is *purification through purging.* Therefore, the literal definition is cited to give an example of how early man thought of healing as purging, or internal cleansing, as is paraphrased in C. Remember: The answer to most specific questions will be an exact paraphrase of what the passage says. Choice A doesn't make any sense. Did ancient civilization have an advanced form of medical science? No way. Don't forget to use your common sense. B doesn't answer the question, and it is irrelevant. You're talking about ancient medicine, not ancient beliefs in general. D is wrong because the passage doesn't say anything in the first paragraph about the mental and physical causes of diseases. This is mentioned much later in the passage. Make sure you're reading in the right place. E is too extreme, and it actually contradicts the passage. In lines 32–33, the passage says that *the Greeks had adopted a sophisticated mind-body view of medicine*, so they were certainly not primitive.

14. **E** The lead words in this question are *early Sumerian drugs*, which should lead you back to the second paragraph. According to lines 9–13, *the first drug catalog, or pharmacopoeia, was written...by an unknown Sumerian physician. Preserved in cuneiform script on a single clay tablet are the names of dozens of drugs to treat ailments that still afflict us today.* So it was possible to identify a number of early Sumerian drugs because somebody back then wrote them all down, which is exactly what E says. A is wrong because the passage doesn't say anything at all about traces of the drugs being found in archeological excavations. If it's not in the passage, then it's not ETS's answer. B is wrong because the passage says in line 14 that the Egyptians added to the ancient knowledge of medicine. The passage doesn't say that they used the same medications as the Sumerians. C is wrong because the passage doesn't say anything at all about Sumerian religious texts. D is way off the topic. The passage is about ancient civilizations, not about Europe. Modern Europe didn't even exist back then. Read the answer choices carefully.

15. **C** This question asks about Sumerian drugs again, so you need to go back to the second paragraph. This time the question is looking for a similarity between Sumerian drugs and modern drugs. According to lines 6–8, *the Sumerians in the Tigris-Euphrates Valley had developed virtually all of our modern methods of administering drugs.* So the similarity between Sumerian and modern drugs is in the methods of administering drugs, which is paraphrased in C as the delivery of drugs. The answer to most specific questions will be an exact paraphrase of what the passage says. A is wrong because the passage says that the Sumerians had the same methods of administering drugs, not that they used the same chemicals. Besides, it doesn't make any sense to say that an ancient civilization had the same chemicals that you do now. They didn't have penicillin, or anything like that, did they? Don't forget about common sense. B is wrong because the passage doesn't talk about mental and physical disorders until much later in the passage. Use the lead words to make sure you are reading in the right place. D doesn't make any sense at all. Were ancient Sumerian drugs the products of sophisticated chemical research? No way! Use common sense. E is wrong because a hierarchy of drug producers was part of Egyptian society, not Sumerian society.

16. **B** The lead words in this question are *the seventh-century Greeks*, which should lead you to the fifth paragraph. The question asks how the view of medicine differed between the Greeks and the Sumerians. According to lines 32–33, *By the seventh century B.C., the Greeks had adopted a sophisticated mind-body view of medicine.* If this view were newly adopted by the Greeks, it must have been different from what the Sumerians thought. So the difference is that the Greeks had a mind-body view. "Mind-body" is paraphrased in B as *the mental and physical roots of illness.* A is wrong because the passage doesn't say anything about advanced chemical applications. Read carefully. C contradicts the passage. The Greeks believed that it was necessary to treat the mind and the body. That is the point of the fifth paragraph. Go back and read it again. D is wrong because a hierarchy of drug producers was part of Egyptian society, not Greek society. E is wrong because the word *most* makes it an extreme answer. The Greeks didn't develop *most* of the precursors of modern drugs. What about the Egyptians and the Sumerians?

17. **D** For this question, you should read before and after the word *hierarchy* to give yourself some context. In the fourth paragraph, the passage talks about the *hierarchy of ancient drug preparation*. In lines 22–31, the passage describes the different people involved in the process of making drugs, including the *chief of the preparers of drugs*, the *collectors of drugs*, the *preparers*, the *preparers' aides*, and the *conservator of drugs*. With all these different jobs, the *hierarchy* must be an example of a *division of labor*. A is wrong because the fourth paragraph doesn't say anything about superstitious practices. B is wrong because the passage doesn't say anything about the severity of ancient diseases. C is close, but the fourth paragraph is about the people who *made drugs* in ancient Egypt, not the doctors who administered the drugs. E is also wrong because the fourth paragraph is about the people who made the drugs, not the recipes for the drugs themselves. Read carefully.

18. **B** To answer this question, you just need to read the final paragraph and find out what the passage says about *scientific discovery*. According to the last paragraph, *many of the latest sophisticated additions to our medicine chest shelves were accidental finds.* In other words, many modern drugs were discovered by accident. B paraphrases the idea of *accidental finds* as *chance events*. A doesn't make any sense. Are discoveries in biochemistry *uncommon*? Most biochemists would probably disagree. Don't forget to use common sense. C may actually be true, but the passage doesn't mention it, so it can't be ETS's

answer. ETS's answers come right out of the passage. You don't need any outside knowledge. D is wrong because the word *best* makes this a *must* answer. How do you know that trial and error is the *best* way to make scientific discoveries? The passage never says that it's the best way. E is wrong because it is also a *must* answer. Is it really true that *most* of the important scientific discoveries have been accidents? Besides, you're talking only about *drugs* here!

19. **B** The best answer is B. Ointments are mentioned in the passage as a characteristic of *Sumerian,* not Egyptian, medicine (line 9). Each of the other answer choices is cited as a characteristic of Egyptian medicine: anesthesia (lines 20–21, in which ethyl alcohol is used to *numb the pain of tooth extraction*), ingredients derived from animals (line 30), use of trial-and-error (lines 16–17), and a workplace hierarchy (lines 22–31).

20. **A** According to the last paragraph of the passage, many drugs common in 1987 *were accidental finds*; this supports A. B is not only a bit wacky, but it's also unsupported by the passage. C and D use deceptive language—they quote directly from the passage, but they don't answer the question. Neither choice refers to drugs used in 1987. D is especially tricky, because the *modern era of pharmacology* (line 42) began in the sixteenth century, which does *not* necessarily mean that any modern *drugs* were created then. E may well be true, but this idea is not discussed in the passage and therefore it is not correct.

21. **C** The best answer is C. Seventh-century Greek medicine is discussed in the fifth paragraph. The author contends that the seventh-century Greeks had a *mind-body view of medicine* (line 33) in which mental maladies were *interpreted as curses from displeased deities* (lines 40–41). Evidence that a seventh-century Greek doctor's prescription urged a patient to pray to a Greek deity would support this contention. A is incorrect because in the passage, the author discusses the Egyptian, not Greek, use of antacids. In the fifth paragraph, the author states that *the suspected "mental" causes of disease were* not [*emphasis added*] *recognized as stress* (lines 39–40), so B is incorrect. There is no discussion in the passage of the Egyptian influence on Greek medicine, or of Greek use of the term *pharmacology,* so choices D and E are incorrect as well. Note that most of the incorrect answer choices for this question contain a word or phrase that is used in the passage (e.g., *sophisticated*). Remember that the use of a word or phrase from the passage in an answer choice does not ensure that the choice is correct. In fact, such an inclusion is often a trap! The right answer often contains a paraphrase of material in the passage, instead of the exact wording.

22. **E** The best answer is E. The language in E can be characterized as extreme, but that language is supported by the passage. In lines 42–43, the author states that the first major discoveries in chemistry occurred in the sixteenth century. This statement supports choice E, because the ancient Egyptians lived long before the sixteenth century. A is an extreme statement that is not supported by the passage. B is tricky—the author states that throughout history, many people have *believed* that diseases can have supernatural causes, but nowhere does the author state that this belief is in fact true. C is wrong because, according to the passage, a modern head pharmacist is analogous to the Egyptian *chief of preparers of drugs* (lines 23–24), not to the conservator of drugs. D would be correct if you substituted the word *some* for *most.* As written, however, it is an extreme answer choice that is unsupported by the passage.

23. **D** Go back to the passage, find the word *holistic,* and cross it out. Then read the sentence and come up with your own word. The paragraph is talking about how the Greeks had a *mind-body view of medicine,* meaning they believed it was important to treat the mind as well as the body. Because

they believed in treating the whole person, that means they emphasized an approach to health that included everything. So you use "included everything" in place of *holistic.* The best match in the answer choices is *comprehensive.* A and C are wrong because *holistic* doesn't just describe the psychological perspective or just the physiological perspective, but both together. B gets the time frame wrong. The Greeks were ancient, not modern. E is a trap answer, because it is a type of medicine.

24. **A** The lead words in this sentence are *modern era of pharmacology,* which should lead you to the sixth paragraph. This paragraph talks about how the modern era of pharmacology began, but the question asks what delayed advances in medical science during the modern era. So you need to keep reading into the next paragraph to find the answer: *physicians, unaware of the existence of disease-causing pathogens such as bacteria and viruses, continued to dream up imaginary causative evils.* So the problem was that doctors didn't really know what caused diseases, and that is exactly what A says. The other answer choices are wrong because none of them is mentioned anywhere in the passage. Go back and read the second to last paragraph carefully.

SECTION 3

1. **E** If you divide 12 by 4, you'll see that $x = 3$. When you plug $x = 3$ into the term, you'll see that $4(3) + 2 = 12 + 2 = 14$.

2. **B** The shaded region lies in the quadrant where x is positive and y is negative. Given this, you can get rid of A, C, and E. If you plot answers B and D, you'll find that (1, –2) is inside the shaded region, while (5, –4) is not.

3. **A** You need to take this question one step at a time. First, figure out how many batches there are in 12 jars of cookies. If one jar holds 1.5 batches, then 12 jars will hold 12×1.5, or 18 batches. Now you need to figure out how much flour is needed for 18 batches. If you need 6 cups of flour for 1 batch, then for 18 batches you will need 18×6, or 108 cups.

4. **B** There are variables in the answers, so this is a plug-in question. If $n = 2$, then answer choice B is the only answer choice that gives you an odd integer: $3(n + 1) = 3(2 + 1) = 3(3) = 9$. Plugging In makes this problem much easier.

5. **A** Use the midpoint formula $\left(\frac{x_1 + x_2}{2}, \frac{y_1 + y_2}{2}\right)$: Take the average of the x-coordinates of the two points to get the x-coordinate of the midpoint, and do the same for the y-coordinates. The midpoint between (3, 4) and (0, 0) is therefore $\left(\frac{3+0}{2}, \frac{4+0}{2}\right) = (1.5, 2)$.

6. **C** This question is much easier if you work out the square roots first. You know that $\sqrt{4} = 2$ and $\sqrt{9} = 3$, so you can rewrite the question like this: $2x - 3x = -x$.

7. **B** Use average pies:

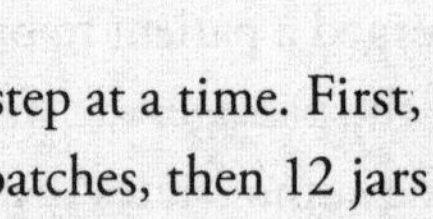

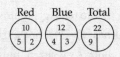

In the first pie you have the number of red parrots sold, which is 5, and the average weight, which is 2. That gives you a total weight of 10 pounds. In the second pie you have the number of blue parrots, which is 4, and the average weight, which is 3. That gives you a total weight of 12. To find the average weight of all the parrots, you need to find the total weight of all the parrots. This is simply the total of the red plus the total of the blue. In the last pie you have the total number of parrots, which is 9, and the total weight of all the parrots, which is 22. This gives you an average weight of $\frac{22}{9} = 2\frac{4}{9}$.

8. C Remember that the perimeter is the sum of all the sides. *FCDE* is a square, so all the sides are equal. Because $\overline{DE} = 3$, each side of the square is 3, so you know that $\overline{CD}$, $\overline{CF}$, and $\overline{EF}$ are all 3. *ABDE* is a rectangle, which means that the opposite sides are equal. $\overline{BC} = 2$, so $\overline{AF} = 2$ also. Along the same lines $\overline{DE}$ equals 3, so that means the opposite side, $\overline{AB}$, also equals 3. Add up all the sides of *ABDE* to find the perimeter: 2 + 2 + 3 + 3 + 3 + 3 = 16. To find out how much smaller the perimeter of *FCDE* is, just subtract: 16 – 12 = 4.

9. D The sides of a 45°-45°-90° triangle have a special pattern, which you can find in the gray box at the beginning of every Math section. Each leg of a 45°-45°-90° triangle is equal to the hypotenuse divided by $\sqrt{2}$. Because the hypotenuse in triangle *ABC* is 8, $\overline{BC}$ must be equal to $\frac{8}{\sqrt{2}}$. You can't have a square root on the bottom of a fraction; so multiply the top and the bottom by $\sqrt{2}$. That gives you $\frac{8\sqrt{2}}{2} = 4\sqrt{2}$. Meanwhile, you can use Ballparking to eliminate A and B. Because the hypotenuse of a right triangle is always the longest of the three sides, $\overline{BC}$ must be less than 8.

10. D Multiply both sides by 2 to get $\sqrt{x} = 4\sqrt{2}$. Square both sides to get $x = 16 \times 2$. Therefore, $x = 32$. You could also have plugged in the answer choices. For D, put 32 in for *x* and ask, does $\frac{\sqrt{32}}{2} = 2\sqrt{2}$? Then does $\sqrt{32} = 4\sqrt{2}$? Square both sides to find that it does, so D is correct.

11. D If there are variables in the answer choices you should…plug in! First, cross out that phrase *in terms of b*, because you don't need it. Next, let's plug in a number for *a*. This is a percent question, so let $a = 100$. Because *b* is 40% of *a*, that means $b = 40$. If $a = 100$, then $4a = 400$. Use your calculator to find 40% of 400, which is 160. That's your target answer. When $b = 40$, D gives you 160.

12. D According to the function, $f(x) = 2x^2 + 4$. To find the value of $f(4)$, just substitute 4 for *x*: $f(4) = 2(4)^2 + 4 = 32 + 4 = 36$.

13. B To find the value of $f(3) + f(5)$, find the values of $f(3)$ and $f(5)$ separately: $f(3) = 2(3)^2 + 4 = 22$ and $f(5) = 2(5)^2 + 4 = 54$. So $f(3) + f(5) = 76$. You already know that $f(4) = 36$ from question 12, so you can cross out A. C is the Joe Bloggs answer because Joe simply adds 3 and 5, and it can't be that easy. If you ballpark D and E, putting 10 or 15 in the function will give you a number bigger than 100, and you're looking for 76, so D and E are too big. That means the answer is B by POE.

14. C The formula for the area of a circle is πr^2, so you need to find the radius, *r*, of the circle. You know that the diameter is 9, and the radius is half of the diameter, so the radius is $\frac{9}{2}$. Because there are fractions in the answer choices, you might as well keep the radius as a fraction. Now you replace *r* with $\frac{9}{2}$ in the formula for area of a circle: $A = \pi\left(\frac{9}{2}\right)^2 = \frac{81}{4}\pi$.

15. **D** Lines that are parallel have the same slope. In the form $y = mx + b$, m is the slope. So, the slope is -3. Find the line that has a slope of -3 when you rewrite it in the form $y = mx + b$. Only D works when you rewrite it: Subtract x from both sides to get $\frac{1}{3}y = 5 - x$, then multiply both sides by 3 to get $y = 15 - 3x$ or $y = -3x + 15$.

16. **C** If $|x| = |2x - 1|$ this means that either $x = 2x - 1$ or $-x = 2x - 1$. The solutions to these equations are 1 and $\frac{1}{3}$, respectively. However, you need to recognize only that the equation has two different solutions to establish that the answer is C.

17. **A** Variables in the answer choices? Plug in! This is a percent question, so make $k = 100$ and $d = 40$. If 40 out of the 100 gallons have been pumped, that equals 40%. So 40% is your target answer. When you plug $k = 100$ and $d = 40$ into the answers, only A gives you 40. Plugging In turns a hard question into a much easier question.

18. **C** For this question you need to know the distance formula: $d = r \times t$. There are two good ways to solve this question. One is Plugging In the Answers. The question asks how far Ray and Jane will be from Ray's house when they meet. Start with C: If they are $56\frac{1}{4}$ miles away from Ray's house, and Ray traveled from home at 30 miles per hour, then you can figure out the time he traveled using the $d = r \times t$ formula (and your calculator): $56\frac{1}{4} = 30 \times t$, $t = 1\frac{7}{8}$. In this case Ray has traveled for $1\frac{7}{8}$ hours. If Jane has traveled $93\frac{3}{4}$ miles and Ray has traveled $56\frac{1}{4}$ miles, then they have traveled a total of 150 miles when they meet. Bingo! You're done. An even easier way is to think about how fast Ray and Jane are traveling put together. You can simply add the rates. Together they are traveling at 80 miles per hour. Therefore you can figure out the time by setting 150 miles = $80 \times t$. The time is $1\frac{7}{8}$ hours. To find how far Ray has traveled, use the formula one last time: $d = 30 \times 1\frac{7}{8} = 56\frac{1}{4}$.

19. **D** To figure out probability, you need to work with fractions; the total number of possible outcomes goes on the bottom, and the number of desired outcomes goes on the top. To figure out the probability of selecting three blue hammers, you need to figure out the probability of getting a blue hammer each time a hammer is selected. The first time, there are a total of 20 hammers and 10 of them are blue, so the probability of getting a blue hammer is $\frac{10}{20} = \frac{1}{2}$. When the second hammer is selected, there are only 19 hammers left, and only 9 of them are blue. So the probability of getting a blue hammer the second time is $\frac{9}{19}$. When the third hammer is selected, there are a total of 18 hammers left and 8 are blue, so the probability of getting a blue hammer on the third try is $\frac{8}{18} = \frac{4}{9}$. To find the probability of selecting three blue hammers, you need to multiply the three separate probabilities: $\frac{1}{2} \times \frac{9}{19} \times \frac{4}{9} = \frac{2}{19}$. By the way, A and C are Joe Bloggs answers because he doesn't consider how the probability changes with each event.

20. D Don't forget that you can plug in on geometry questions. Let's make $b = 70°$ and $a = 30°$. So the third angle in the triangle is 80°. You know that c would be 80°, because it is opposite an 80° angle. Your target answer is a = 30°, so plug in 80° and 70° to find it. The only possible answer is D.

SECTION 4

1. E The clue in this sentence is *they hoard water in their leaves.* If the plants are hoarding water, they must be doing it to survive long periods without water. So you can put "without water" in the blank, in which case the best match is *aridity.*

2. E The clue for this sentence is *eloquence and logic.* If Liam is eloquent and logical, he must speak "very well"; therefore, you can eliminate A, C, and D because they're negative. Liam's eloquence and logic probably made it difficult for his *most bitter opponents* to contradict his opinions. The best match for "contradict" is *disagree with,* in E. It also makes sense that Liam's eloquence and logic made him speak *cogently.*

3. D The clue in this sentence is *first deduced from eccentricities in other planets' orbits.* If subatomic particles are being compared to the outer planets, then these particles must have been deduced through their effects on other particles. If you put "deducible" (recycle the clues!) in the first blank, you can get rid of A. What was deduced about the outer planets and subatomic particles? That they existed. So you can put "existence" in the second blank, which means D must be the answer. Notice that it would not make sense to talk about the outer planets' *proximity,* or their *creation*; they are not close by and you really can't deduce creation.

4. D The clues in this sentence are *foster* and *in tense situations.* Because *foster* is a positive word, meaning to care for or nurture, a good phrase for the first blank must be positive; you can get rid of C because *dissension* is a negative word and E because *discourse* is neither positive nor negative. If Miranda wants to foster something good, then in tense situations she is probably compelled to give in to others. You can use "give in" for the second blank, which means you can eliminate A. Between B and D, you can eliminate B because *fortitude* doesn't make any sense in the first blank. Remember: It's often easier to figure out which answer is wrong than to figure out which one is right.

5. C The clue in this sentence is *helped bring about a period of prosperity in the United Kingdom,* and the trigger word is *although,* which means the blank must be the opposite of *helped.* If you put "harmful" in the blank, the best match is *regressive.*

6. C I and II are both true. The author tells you that the war was fought for several reasons. The reasons that are mentioned are a desire for Florida and Canada on the part of the United States—i.e., *expansionist tendencies*—and as a response to *British actions taken against the United States.* Statement III is mentioned as an unexpected result of the war, which means it couldn't have been a reason for starting the war.

7. B Choice B is the best answer. Passage 1 states that the war was in effect a second War of Independence. Passage 2 states that American confidence and nationalism increased after the war. A is wrong because Passage 2 mentions battles that each side won. The passage does not give you any information to support C. D may be true, but neither passage speaks about other international conflicts. E is more closely related to Passage 1 than Passage 2.

8. **A** In the first passage, the author says the war lacked a *clear winner.* Passage 2 says that there was no *clear victor.* B, while perhaps true, is incorrect because the impact on British citizens is not mentioned in the passages. C can't be supported anywhere in Passage 2. D is more relevant to Passage 2 than Passage 1. E is incorrect because the second passage doesn't mention how well known the war is in either the United States or Britain. A is the best answer.

9. **E** Choice E is the best answer. Passage 2 states that although the war was over, Jackson's victory contributed greatly to American confidence and nationalism. A contains information from Passage 1 and so is incorrect. B is not clearly supported by Passage 2 because no other battles are mentioned. C is incorrect because Jackson's victory took place after the treaty was signed. D is directly contradicted by the passage which says that the Americans defeated the British at the Battle of the Thames.

10. **B** In lines 33–35, the passage says, *Thus he had hardly seen the sea—had seen it fleetingly...and he had never actually traveled around it.* If you read further, you also learn that Poseidon was waiting for the fall of the world so he would have a quiet moment to make a quick little tour of the sea. From that you can infer that Poseidon is too busy to see his own kingdom. A gets it backward. The passage says that Poseidon's trips to visit Jupiter are the only break in the monotony of his job, so if anything, he prefers the trips to his duties, not the other way around. C is wrong because the passage doesn't say anything about Poseidon needing silence. D contradicts the passage. Poseidon is waiting for the fall of the world so that he can finally get out and make a quick little tour of his domain, which he has never had a chance to see. E is wrong because the passage doesn't say anything to suggest that Poseidon is inefficient.

11. **D** The lead word for this question is *dissatisfaction*, so you should go back to the passage and find where it mentions Poseidon's dissatisfaction. Lines 26–28 describe what is chiefly responsible for his dissatisfaction. He does not like to hear the conceptions formed about him: *how he was always riding about through the tides with his trident.* According to the passage, Poseidon doesn't actually get out much at all, so people have the wrong idea about what he actually does. This is exactly what D says. A contradicts the passage. Poseidon was so irritated by the false idea people had that he was always riding around with his trident. B is a trap. The question asks what is primarily responsible for Poseidon's dissatisfaction. Although something similar to B is mentioned earlier in the passage, it's not *chiefly responsible for his dissatisfaction* (lines 26–27). Use the lead words to make sure you are reading in the right place. C contradicts the passage. Poseidon does the exact same thing every day. That's why he's so bored and unhappy. E is incorrect because the passage says that Poseidon actually did most of the bookkeeping tasks himself, leaving little for his assistants to do (lines 4–6).

12. **A** This is a general question, so you need to know only the main idea of the passage. The passage portrays Poseidon as someone who sits around working out figures all day and doesn't go out much. Poseidon is also clearly unhappy (as you learned in questions 10 and 11), so he is best described as a *dissatisfied bureaucrat.* The other answer choices are wrong because they don't fit the main idea of the passage. Poseidon may be a deity, but the passage doesn't characterize him as being *powerful.* Poseidon is definitely not a *vagabond*, and he's definitely not a *tyrant.* D is half-wrong, which means that it's all wrong. Although the description of Poseidon's duties make him sound like an *accountant*, the passage focuses on his unhappiness, not his capabilities as an accountant.

13. **B** This is an EXCEPT question, so it will probably be time consuming to answer. You need to know why Poseidon is unable to change his job, so you need to go back to the passage and find where that is discussed. Remember: You're looking for the reason that is not mentioned, so you can eliminate answer choices that are mentioned. The passage mentions A in lines 24–25: *he had been appointed God of the Sea in the beginning, and that he had to remain.* C is in lines 17–18: *when a job away from the water was offered to him he would get sick at the very prospect.* D is in lines 11–12: *nothing suited him quite as well as his present position*, and E is in lines 16–17: *Poseidon could in any case occupy only an executive position*. Therefore B must be the answer.

14. **E** The best answer is E. This is a Vocab In Context (VIC) question, so you should work it like a sentence completion. Go back to the passage, cross out the word *described*, and fill in your own word based on the context of the passage. In this case, a good word to put in the blank is "formed." The only answer choice that is close to "formed" is *traced*, in E. Choice A is tempting, because it seems to describe something that a gull would do, but it does not make sense in context. (Is it possible to *soar* circles? Nope.) B is also tempting, because it refers to a more common meaning of the word *described*, but that is not the meaning that is used in the passage. Remember: When a VIC question asks you about a commonly known word, such as *described*, the primary meaning of the word is almost always a trap. Eliminate it! C is wrong, because the gull was not *imagining* circles. (This passage is not about the inner lives of animals!) There is no evidence in the passage to support choice D, which does not match up with "formed."

15. **C** The main idea of the passage is that Poseidon's power, in the form of his job as *God of the Sea*, caused him to be unhappy. Choice C matches this idea the best. A is never implied by the passage. B is incorrect because Poseidon's sickness results from a job *offer,* not from a job itself. D and E are extreme answer choices unsupported by the passage.

16. **D** The lead words in this question are *Frankish law*, which should lead you to the beginning of the passage. According to lines 1–3, *the laws and customs in lands under Frankish domination emphasized the biological function and sexual nature of women....* These lines are perfectly paraphrased in D, which says that women were *defined in physical or biological terms*. A contradicts the passage. Frankish society *did not deprive women of opportunities to find personal fulfillment in a variety of roles* (lines 3–4). B completely contradicts the second half of the passage, which is all about women in religious communities. Always keep in mind the main idea of the passage. C contradicts lines 7–8, which tell you that Frankish society did not exploit women's labor. E is wrong because lines 8–24 say that women had access to power in several different ways.

17. **B** The lead word in this question is *marriage*, which should lead to lines 16–18. According to these lines, in Frankish society people either *contracted a formal union or entered into a quasi-marriage.* B paraphrases this sentence by saying that marriage could be entered into formally or informally. A is wrong because the word *only* makes this a must answer, and not likely to be right. Besides, does it make sense to say that marriage *was the only means of exchanging wealth*? C implies that marriage *always* raised women to positions of power, which is definitely not the case. D is wrong because there is no comparison made in the passage between marriage in primitive society and marriage within Frankish society. Read carefully. E is wrong because the passage doesn't say anything about whose mother—the bride's or the groom's—arranged a marriage.

18. E Go back to the passage, find the word *instrumental*, and cross it out. Then read the sentence and come up with your own word. According to the passage, women *were instrumental in bringing about the merger of the free and slave elements in society* (lines 23–24); therefore, they were *vital* to the process. C is a trap answer because it refers to the word *instrument* and because instruments remind you of harmony. The other choices are wrong because they don't make any sense in context.

19. D D is supported by lines 30–33. A is contradicted by the passage, which states that widows were also able to participate. B is incorrect. The passage states that monasteries were a refuge for married women, but doesn't say that *many* women sought refuge or why. C is not stated. The writings of medieval nuns are mentioned, but not as a model for *life in a monastery*. E is beyond the information in the passage.

20. C C is the best answer. Once the women were *freed from the need to compete for the attention of men* (lines 40–41), they were able to engage in the pursuits mentioned in lines 42–43. A and B may be true, but are not explicitly stated in the passage as reasons. D is not stated in the passage. E is beyond the information provided.

21. A Lines 8–24 detail the different rights and roles of queens, the wives of magnates, and the wives of members of the working classes. B, C, and D are wrong because they do not answer the question. They all refer to specific classes of women, not *women in Frankish society*. E is never mentioned. A is the best answer.

22. E Based on the blurb and the passage, E is the best answer. The passage lists the role of women in Frankish society, giving information on the queen, the working class, and the religious population. A can be eliminated because there is no dispute in the passage. B cannot be correct because no other societies are mentioned. C is too extreme and, additionally, no other societies are presented. D is incorrect because there is no indication that the passage provides new information.

23. A The only answer choice that comes from something stated in the passage is A. According to lines 40–43, women outside the communities must have had to compete for the attention of men. B doesn't make any sense. How can it be true that women outside the religious community were not inclined to any religious feeling at all? Just because they weren't nuns doesn't mean they weren't religious. C is wrong because it makes no sense to say that women outside the religious community had less economic power. If anything, the opposite would be true. D is too extreme and offensive. ETS would never say that women outside religious communities did not contribute to Frankish culture. E is wrong because ETS would never suggest that women had to rely on men for emotional support. Besides, the passage never says that. Read carefully.

24. C This is an EXCEPT question. ETS is asking how Christianity allowed women to escape from male-dominated society, so you have to go back to the passage and find where that is discussed. You are looking for the answer choice that is not mentioned. A is mentioned in line 48; B is mentioned in lines 35–36; D is mentioned in lines 40–43; E is mentioned in lines 25–28. That leaves C.

SECTION 5

1. **A** Subtract 10 from both sides to find $2x = 6$, then substitute 6 for $2x$. $6 - 10 = -4$. You could also solve for x, and then plug that into the expression. If $2x = 6$, then $x = 3$. So, $2(3) - 10 = 6 - 10 = -4$.
2. **C** If he bought 3 boxes of muffins at $4.50, he would have $3 \times 6 = 18$ muffins. That's not enough muffins. So, he needs to buy 4 boxes of muffins. Each box costs $1.50; so, the cost is $4 \times \$1.50 = \$6.00$.
3. **E** From 1 to 100, there are 50 even integers. If you don't include 2 and 100, then there are only 48.
4. **B** Fill in the angles of the small triangle. The lower left angle is 70° and the lower right angle is 80°. Because the angles in a triangle must add up to 180°, $a = 180 - 70 - 80 = 30$.
5. **E** Plug 3 into each answer choice, and try to get 6. Eliminate C and D. Now plug 4 into each remaining answer choice, and try to get 13. Eliminate A and B.
6. **B** This is a right triangle with two equal sides, so it is a 45°-45°-90° triangle. $\overline{AC}$ must be the hypotenuse, so the legs are each $\frac{10}{\sqrt{2}}$. The legs are also the height and base of the triangle. $A = \frac{1}{2}bh$, so $A = \frac{1}{2} \times \frac{10}{\sqrt{2}} \times \frac{10}{\sqrt{2}} = \frac{100}{2 \times 2} = 25$.
7. **B** This question has several steps, so don't try to do it all at once. Take it one step at a time. Andrei starts out with 48 baseball caps. In the first step, Andrei gives away 13 caps, so he has 35 left. In the next step, he buys 17 new caps, so now he has 52. Then Andrei gives Pierre 6 caps (46 left) and gets 8 caps in return. In the end, Andrei has 54 baseball caps, which is 6 more caps than he had originally. The percent increase is $\frac{change}{original} \times 100 = \frac{6}{48} \times 100 = \frac{100}{8} = 12.5$. You can also change $\frac{6}{48}$ to a percent by typing it into your calculator and multiplying by 100.
8. **D** Draw a line straight up from D to divide the shape into a rectangle and a triangle. The area of a 5-by-10 rectangle is 50. To get the area of the triangle, find the length of the base; you already know the height is 5. Use the Pythagorean theorem, or to save time, recognize that this is a 30°-60°-90° triangle because the hypotenuse is twice as long as the shortest side. The base is therefore $5\sqrt{3}$. The area of the triangle is therefore $\frac{1}{2} \times 5 \times 5\sqrt{3} = 12.5\sqrt{3}$. The total area of $ABCD$ is therefore $50 + 12.5\sqrt{3}$.
9. **100**

Use a Ratio Box:

T-Shirts	Sweatshirts	Turtlenecks	Total
2	3	5	10
10	10	10	10
20	30	50	100

You need to work out only the *total* column to figure out the total number of garments that the store sold, which is 100.

10. **81**

The formula for the volume of a box is length × width × height. But the question gives you the area of the base of the crate, so you already know that length × width = 18. The volume of the crate, then, is simply the area of the base times the height: 18 × 4.5 = 81.

11. **.75 or $\frac{3}{4}$**

All you have to do is solve for x:

$$5x - 4 = x - 1$$
$$5x = x + 3$$
$$4x = 3$$
$$x = \frac{3}{4} \text{ or } .75$$

12. **8**

Using $3b = 2$, solve for b by dividing both sides by 3 to get $b = \frac{2}{3}$. That means $a^{\frac{2}{3}} = 4$. Fractional exponents tell you to use the denominator as the root and use the numerator as a regular exponent. So, $\sqrt[3]{a^2} = 4$. First, cube both sides to find $a^2 = 4^3 = 64$. Next, take the square root of both sides to find $a = 8$.

13. **5, 7, or 11**

First, think of a prime number that will make $3b$ greater than 10. How about 5? To see if that fits the other side of the inequality, you need to find the value of $\frac{5}{6} \times 5 = \frac{25}{6}$ which is less than 10, so 5 is one possible value of b. Remember: You need to find only *one* possible value of b.

14. **21**

Let's say you have seven dancers: A, B, C, D, E, F, and G. How many different ways can you pair them up? This is a combination question, because A and B is the same pair as B and A, and you don't want to count them twice. Start by finding the number of possible *permutations*: 7 × 6 = 42. Finally, divide this number by 2 × 1 = 2 (we're looking to fill 2 positions) to eliminate redundant combinations. There are 21 possible combinations.

15. **96**

You know that arc BC is a semicircle, which means it's half a circle. So the circumference of the entire circle would be $6\pi \times 2 = 12\pi$. Therefore, the diameter of that circle is 12. Because $\overline{BC}$ is also a side of the rectangle you know that the length of rectangle $ABCD$ is 12. You can also use the same method to find the width. If the length of semicircle CD is 4π, then the circumference of the entire circle would be 8π and the diameter is 8. Because $\overline{CD}$ is the width of the rectangle, you can find the area: length × width = 12 × 8 = 96.

16. **5**

$f(6) = 6^2 - 5 = 31$. $f(4) = 4^2 - 5 = 11$. So $f(6) - f(4) = 20$. You then find y such that $y^2 - 5 = 20$. $y^2 = 25$, so $y = 5$ or -5, and the absolute value of $y = 5$.

17. **282**

This is a hard question, so you have to stay on your toes. If the owner buys 3 pounds of each spice, that means she pays the following amounts for each spice:

cinnamon: $8 × 3 = $24
nutmeg: $9 × 3 = $27
ginger: $7 × 3 = $21
cloves: $10 × 3 = $30

So she pays a total of 24 + 27 + 21 + 30, or $102 for 12 pounds of spices. She then sells the spices per *ounce*, so you have to figure out first how many ounces of spices she has. If 1 pound is 16 ounces, then 12 pounds is 12 × 16, or 192 ounces. She sells all the spices at $2 per ounce, so she makes 192 × $2, or $384. To figure out her profit, subtract the amount she paid for the spices from the amount she made selling them: $384 – $102 = $282.

18. **.375 or $\frac{3}{8}$**

Because the question doesn't give you a figure, you should draw one. Then plug in some values.

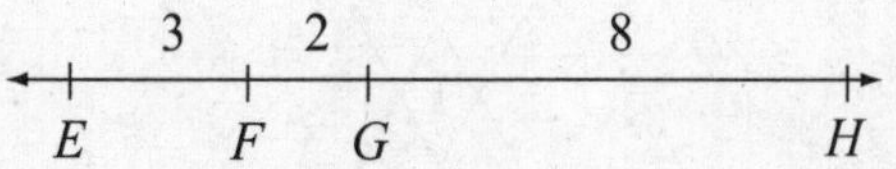

If $EG = \frac{5}{3}EF$, then you can make $EF = 3$ and $EG = 5$. That means FG must be 2. If $HF = 5FG$, then $HF = 5(2) = 10$. If $HF = 10$ and $FG = 2$, then $HG = 8$. So $\frac{EF}{HG} = \frac{3}{8}$ or .375 .

SECTION 6

1. **A** The question is essentially asking which of the answers cannot be a value of x. So just try each answer one at a time by plugging the number into each of the two inequalities in the question, and see which one doesn't fit. If $x = -6$, is $-6 + 6 > 0$? No, because zero is not greater than zero. So –6 is the exception.

2. **D** Whenever there are variables in the answers, you should always plug in. Let's say $x = 20$, which means there are 20 ounces of root beer in the pitcher. Next, let's make $y = 3$ and $z = 4$. That means Elsa pours 3 ounces into each of 4 glasses, so she pours a total of 12 ounces. The question asks how much root beer remains in the pitcher, so your target answer is 20 – 12, or 8. Go to the answer choices and plug in $x = 20$, $y = 3$, and $z = 4$. In answer choice D: $x - yz = 20 - (3)(4) = 20 - 12 = 8$.

3. **E** Remember that the equation of a line is $y = mx + b$, where m is the slope and b is the y-intercept. POE! The line in the graph has negative slope, so you can eliminate A and B, and it has a positive y-intercept, so you can eliminate C and D.

4. **E** Start by writing out the pattern: blue is the 1st light, orange is 2nd, green is 3, purple is 4, red is 5, and yellow is 6. Then the pattern starts over again, so the 7th light is blue, orange is 8, green is 9, purple is 10, red is 11, and yellow is 12. Notice that the yellow lights go by multiples of 6? The 18th light will also be yellow, as will the 24th, 30th, and so on. We want to know the 53rd, so the closest light we know to 53 is the 54th light, which is yellow. If the 54th is yellow, then the light immediately before is the 53rd, which must be red, answer (E).

5. **C** Whenever there are variables in the answer choices, you should plug in. Because $x = y + 1$ and $y \geq 1$, you can make $x = 5$ and $y = 4$. In that case, $x^2 - y^2 = 25 - 16 = 9$, so 9 is your target answer. When you plug $x = 5$ and $y = 4$ into the answer choices, only C gives you 9. Plugging In turns a hard question into a much easier question.

6. **B** The "Third Side Rule" states that any side must be less than the sum of the other two sides, and greater than the difference between the other two sides. In other words, if the sides are a, b, and c, $|b - c| < a < b + c$. Find the smallest possible value of a. If $a = 1$, then $b + c = 9$. For example, $b = 4$ and $c = 5$. This is illegal, as $|b - c| = a$. If $a = 2$, then $b = 4$ and $c = 4$, so 2 is okay. The largest a can be is 4, because if $a = 5$, then $a = b + c$ and you have violated the Third Side Rule. Thus, the difference between the largest possible value of a and the smallest possible value of a is $4 - 2 = 2$.

7. **C** The Joe Bloggs answer is E because Joe simply chooses the greatest number. If you draw three straight, intersecting lines through the center of the triangle, you get 6 regions, so you know that you can have at least 6. Therefore, you can eliminate A. But that was too easy. That means the answer must be 7 or 8. If you don't have time, you can guess between C and D. Here's how you can actually get 7 regions:

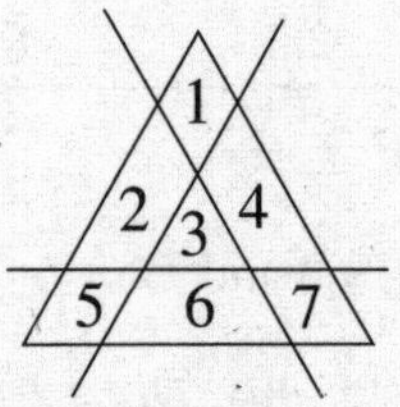

8. **B** To find out what numbers a could be divisible by, you need to try different values of b. If $b = 1$, then $a = 4(1) + 26 = 30$. In this case, a is divisible by 2, 5, and 6, so you can cross out A, C, and D. If $b = 4$, then $a = 42$, which is divisible by 7, so cross out E. That leaves only B, which must be the answer.

9. 2

First, solve for x. Divide both sides of the equation by 3, and you get $x = 4$. Then divide 8 by 4, which gives you 2.

10. 270

The trick here is that ETS is not asking for the value of a, b, or c. It just wants to know what they add up to. ETS is testing only the Rule of 360. All the angles in the figure make up a circle, so they all add up to 360. The right angle is 90 degrees, so $90 + a + b + c = 360$. Therefore $a + b + c = 270$.

11. 7

It would definitely help to draw out this question:

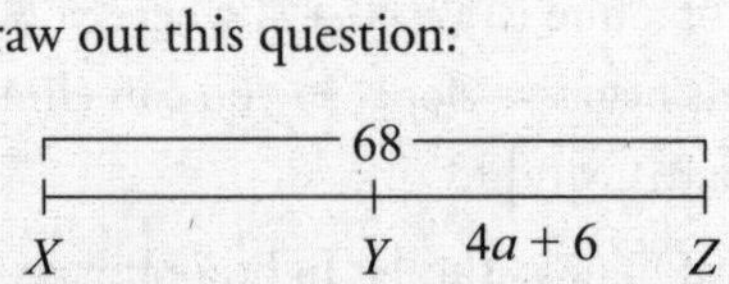

$XY = \frac{1}{2}XZ$, which means Y is the midpoint of $\overline{XZ}$. So $XY = YZ$, and therefore $YZ = \frac{1}{2}XZ$.

If $YZ = 4a + 6$ and $XZ = 68$, then $4a+6=\frac{1}{2}(68)$. Now just solve for a:

$$4a+6=\frac{1}{2}(68)$$

$$4a + 6 = 34$$

$$4a = 28$$

$$a = 7$$

12. **3**

You can solve this question using simultaneous equations because you have two equations with two variables. First, you need to rearrange the equations a bit: $4x + 2y = 24$ divided by 2 on both sides becomes $2x + y = 12$. $\frac{7y}{2x}=7$, multiplied by $2x$ on both sides, becomes $7y = 14x$. This, divided by 7 on both sides, becomes $y = 2x$, which can be manipulated into $2x - y = 0$. Now you can add the equations:

$$\begin{array}{r} 2x+y=12 \\ +\ 2x-y=0 \\ \hline 4x=12 \end{array}$$

So $x = 3$.

13. **9**

Factor the numerator and the denominator into $\frac{(x-2)(x+3)}{(x-2)(x-6)}=4$. The $(x-2)$ cancels out of the top and bottom to leave $\frac{(x+3)}{(x-6)}=4$. Multiply both sides by $(x - 6)$ to get $x + 3 = 4x - 24$. Subtract x from both sides: $3 = 3x - 24$. Add 24 to both sides: $27 = 3x$. Divide by 3 to get $x = 9$.

14. **.4 or $\frac{2}{5}$**

You can solve this question by setting up a proportion. There are 8 liters in 20 bottles of juice, and you need to find out how many liters are in one bottle. Here's what the proportion looks like: $\frac{8}{20}=\frac{x}{1}$. Solve for x, and your answer is $\frac{2}{5}$ or 0.4.

15. **120**

There are 6 women total to choose from and the company needs 3, so you would do $6 \times 5 \times 4 = 120$. However, because order doesn't matter we need to get rid of duplicates. Mathematically this is done by dividing your answer by the factorial of the number of spaces you need to fill. Because we need 3, we divide by 3! or 6, which leaves us with 20. Now, on to the men. There are 6 men to choose and we need only 1. So there are 6 ways to choose that. Now we have to count our women (20) and our men (6). Remember in probability that *and* means multiply. $20 \times 6 = 120$, which is the answer.

16. **288**

We can't figure out how many rabbits there were after 7 years until we know the constant a. To find it, let's use one of the data points that we're given. We know that after 3 years ($t = 3$) there were 192 rabbits ($P(t) = 192$). Plug both of those into the equation and we get $192 = a(3) + 120$, which we can solve to find $a = 24$. Now plug that into our original equation, and we have $P(t) = 24t + 120$. To find out how many rabbits there were after 7 years, plug in $t = 7$: $P(t) = 24(7) + 120 = 288$.

17. **18**

To answer this question you have to set up an equation. If the radius of C is r, then the radius of B is $2r$ and the radius of A is $4r$. The formula for the area of a circle is πr^2. Because 84π is the sum of the areas of the circles, this is your equation:

$$\pi r^2 + \pi(2r)^2 + \pi(4r)^2 = 84\pi$$
$$r^2 + 4r^2 + 16r^2 = 84$$
$$21r^2 = 84$$
$$r^2 = 4$$
$$r = 2$$

If $r = 2$, then the radius of C is 2, the radius of B is 4, and the radius of A is 8. $\overline{AC}$ consists of the radius of A, the diameter of B, and the radius of C, so $AC = 8 + 4 + 4 + 2 = 18$.

18. **50**

You don't know how many cars are in the parking lot, so you can plug in a number. Let's say there are 40 cars in the parking lot. Now read through the question; if $\frac{1}{5}$ of the cars are blue, there are 8 blue cars. If $\frac{1}{2}$ of the blue cars are convertibles, there are 4 blue convertibles. If $\frac{1}{4}$ of all the convertibles are blue, and there are 4 blue convertibles, that means there are 16 convertibles all together. The question asks what percent of the cars are neither blue nor convertibles. At this point, the question becomes a group question, and you have a formula for solving such questions: total = group 1 + group 2 – both + neither. In this question, the total is 40 cars, group 1 is the 8 blue cars, and group 2 is the 16 convertibles. You also know that 4 cars are both blue and convertibles. Now just plug those values into the formula: $40 = 16 + 8 - 4 + n$. Then solve for n, which equals 20. So 20 out of the total 40 cars are neither blue nor convertibles: $\frac{20}{40} = \frac{1}{2} = 50\%$.

SECTION 7

1. A Take care of the answers one by one for this sentence. B is not a complete sentence. C uses the ambiguous pronoun *their*, D uses the ambiguous pronoun *it*, and E changes the meaning by suggesting rotary phones are unknown in general.
2. C C correctly modifies the verb *related* with the adverb *distantly*. A is incorrect because in general, *anyone* is a "who" and not a "that." In B and D, to modify *relationships* (a noun) you need *distant* (an adjective) and not *distantly* (an adverb). In E, to modify *related* (a verb) you need *distantly* (an adverb) and not *distant* (an adjective).
3. C The pronoun *you* refers to the person viewing the paintings, and so the next pronoun which refers to that person should also be *you* rather than *people*, as in B or *one*, as in A, D, and E.
4. E In the original sentence A, *and* does not imply the contrast between the two types of fat; you need the conjunction *but*, which is used in E. B and D, each missing a conjunction, are run-on sentences. C uses the *-ing* form of the verb, which is not the first choice for a clear sentence.

5. **B** *Knoll* isn't clearly singular or plural, so look for its verb: *sells*. Because *sells* is singular, so too is *Knoll* (neither is underlined). Eliminate A, D, and E because all are plural. Between B and C, B is much more concise and clear.
6. **D** Because there is a semicolon in this sentence, there should be a complete sentence on each side of it. Eliminate C because it is not a complete sentence. B unnecessarily uses the word *being*, so eliminate it. E uses the word *those*, but because it is referring to something in the same sentence it should have been *these*. Between A and D, A is redundant, using both *because* and *is why*.
7. **B** A singular noun needs a singular verb (*Increase... has)*, so this eliminates choices A and C. In D, the word *which* follows the name of the rest home, implying that the home caused the nurses to threaten. In E, *angered the nurses...to have a walkout* sounds awkward and makes little sense.
8. **E** *Galleons* is plural, so eliminate anything that tries to describe them singularly: A, B, and C. D also uses the singular pronoun *its*, and so should be eliminated.
9. **D** In both B and the original sentence, the pronoun *he* is unclear in its reference: It could mean either Evan or Ken. Only D and E correct this error, but E needlessly uses the *-ing* form of the verbs.
10. **B** The error in the original, A, and E uses the incorrect construction *neither...or.* E also puts the final verb in the awkward *-ing* form. C and D unnecessarily add the word *other.* B uses the correct parallel structure: *requires...assigns...does expect.*
11. **A** There is no error in this sentence as written. The idiom, *regard...as,* is the proper construction.
12. **D** The pronoun in D disagrees with the noun it replaces: *King* is singular; *them* is plural.
13. **A** *Traveled* is in the wrong tense. The rest of the sentence describes the plot in the present tense, so it should read *travels.*
14. **B** The verb should be *claim* or *have claimed.* There is no reason to use the past perfect, as there is no action occuring after it to warrant this tense.
15. **E** There is no error in the sentence as it is written.
16. **B** The phrase "more than" is the wrong idiomatic phrase here. The correct phrase is "prefer something to something."
17. **A** This sentence has an idiom error: *comply to* should be *comply with.*
18. **E** There is no error in the sentence as it is written.
19. **A** The subject *field* is singular and the verb *have* is plural. Watch out for prepositional phrases that follow nouns: *of consumer electronics* is only a description of *field.* It is the *field* that *has never been fixed*, not *consumer electronics.*
20. **D** The pronouns shift from *one* to *you.* Correct this error by changing both words to *one* or changing both words to *you.*
21. **D** When comparing two people, you must always use the comparative form *the more* rather than the superlative form *the most,* which is used only with three or more things.
22. **E** There is no error in the sentence as it is written.
23. **C** To correct the verb-tense problem in this sentence, change *spent* to *spend* because *target* is in the present tense.
24. **E** There is no error in the sentence as it is written.
25. **C** This sentence contains an error in verb tense: C should say *had ridden.* The simple past tense, *rode,* is always used without a helping verb (*has, had, is, was,* for example).
26. **B** You cannot compare *other sculptors* to Rodin's *creations.* It should be: unlike other sculptors' creations, or unlike those of other sculptors.

27. B When making a contrary-to-fact statement (Jason did not, in fact, plan ahead), never use a *would* in an *if* clause. Thus, if he *had planned,...he would not have had to write.*

28. A The subject is *words*, which is plural, so the verb needs to be plural, as well. Trim the fat—cross out the inessential words, such as prepositional phrases—to find the basics of the sentence: *words... have...meanings.*

29. E There is no error in the sentence as it is written.

30. E If you try to remove the words *production of* in A and *actually did* in B, you will see that the sentence makes no sense without these words. Likewise, if you remove *agreed to* in C, the sentence loses an important verb. Removing *when* in D creates a run-on sentence. E is the only available choice.

31. D The sentence uses a list of items and all items in that list should be parallel. Only D does this correctly. B changes the meaning. C is in the passive voice, and E is awkward with the use of *be building.*

32. B The tense *was ever wearing* is used incorrectly in the original sentence. In C, the use of *could* makes no sense in context. Likewise, in D, the uses of *would ever be* makes no sense and is awkward. E is also awkward and makes no sense.

33. C The last paragraph talks of the opening night, and only C uses a transition word, *finally,* and introduces the topic of the paragraph.

34. B With addition questions, always stick to the main topic. Only B does so by discussing the author's responsibilities during the rehearsal. This goes well with the discussion of the production and opening night. In A, the author's other activities are not applicable to a passage about a theater production. C is too broad as this is a personal account of a production. Likewise, D and E are too broad.

35. A The sentence is acceptable as it is now, and therefore A is the best choice. B and C are inferior because the words *being* and *having* are rarely the verb forms found in the best version of an SAT sentence. D and E each create a sentence that lacks a verb.

SECTION 8

1. C To solve for *y*, begin by adding *y* to both sides of the equation, which gives you $6 = 3y - 6$. Then add 6 to both sides, which gives you $12 = 3y$. Now divide both sides by 3, and you find that $y = 4$. You can also plug in the answer choices for any question that asks you to solve for a variable: $6 - 4 = 2(4) - 6$.

2. B This is what is called a visual perception problem. It's like a maze. Just put your pencil on *a* and see which other letter you can connect to *a* without crossing any lines. The only letter you can reach directly is *w*, all the way in the middle.

3. C This is a perfect calculator question. Just add the morning shift and the afternoon shift for each day and see which total is the greatest. The total for both Tuesday and Wednesday (the greatest) is $575 + 595 = 1{,}170$.

4. A For this question, you need to know that volume equals *length* × *width* × *height*. You know that the volume is 16,500, the depth, or height, is 10, and the length is 75. Just put those numbers in the formula: $16{,}500 = 75 \times w \times 10$. Use your calculator to solve for *w*, which equals 22.

5. **D** The idea of *the rest* in this question can save you from doing unnecessary arithmetic. If 40% of the records are jazz, then *the rest*, or 60%, are blues. Because there are 80 records, just use your calculator to find 60% of 80, which is 48.

6. **D** Use a Ratio Box:

Girls	**Boys**	**Total**
4	3	7
5	5	5
20	15	35

There are 20 girls and 15 boys, so there are 5 more girls than boys.

7. **B** Try Plugging In some values for x and see if the graphs include that point. If $x = 0$, then $y = 0$, so, (0, 0) should be a point on the graph. Unfortunately this doesn't eliminate anything. If $x = 1$, then $y = 2$, so, (1, 2) should be a point on the graph. Eliminate A, C, D, and E.

8. **C** Plug in the answers starting with C. If the length is 16, the width is half of that. $16 \div 2 = 8$. Area is length × width. So, does $128 = 16 \times 8$? Yes, so C is correct. Alternatively, write an equation. The equation is area = $w \times 2w$. So, $128 = 2w^2$. Divide by 2 to get $64 = w^2$. Take the square root of both sides to find $w = 8$. The length is twice this width, so length = $2 \times 8 = 16$, so the answer is C.

9. **C** Plug in! Let's make $T = .5$ and $S = -.8$. Because a positive number divided by a negative number is negative, eliminate D and E. $.5 \div -.8 = -.625$, which is closest to C.

10. **A** Once again, plug in: Let's say $x = 50$. Now you can translate the question:

$$\frac{10}{100} \times \frac{50}{100} \times 1{,}000 =$$

If you work this out on your calculator, you should get 50 as your target answer. If $x = 50$, the only answer that works is A.

11. **E** Because A is the center of one circle and B is a point on the circumference, $\overline{AB}$ is r. $\overline{AD}$ and $\overline{BC}$ are also r. Whenever a line is tangent to a circle, the radius drawn to the point of tangency is perpendicular to the line. So, $\overline{AD}$ and $\overline{BC}$ are perpendicular to $\overline{CD}$. That means $ABCD$ is a square. Plug in for the radius, say $r = 6$. The area of a square is the square of a side, so the area is 36. Plug 6 into the answer choices to see which agrees with 36. Only E is 36!

12. **E** This is a perfect question for PITA (Plugging In the Answers). The question asks for the greatest possible number of 20-ounce boxes. Start with C. If there are twenty-five 20-ounce boxes, then there are twenty-five 8-ounce boxes because a total of 50 boxes were purchased. In this case, the twenty-five 20-ounce boxes weigh 500 ounces, and the twenty-five 8-ounce boxes weigh 200 ounces; the total is 700 ounces. This is too big because the question says the total weight was less than 600. If C is too big, A and B must also be too big; eliminate all three. If you try D, the total weight is 604 ounces, which is still too big. So the answer must be E.

13. D Here's yet another chance to plug in because of the variables in the answer choices. In this case, you have several variables. You should start by plugging in values for x and y, and then work out c. Because $x > y > 0$, let's say $x = 6$ and $y = 3$. Therefore, $c = \frac{1}{6} + \frac{1}{3}$, which equals $\frac{1}{2}$. The question asks for the value of $\frac{1}{c}$, which is the reciprocal of $\frac{1}{2}$, or 2. This is your target answer. If you plug $x = 6$ and $y = 3$ into all of the answer choices, you'll find that only D equals 2.

14. D Test the answer choices. The first number in each pair represents x, and the second number represents y. The ordered pair should work in both functions. Try C in the first equation: Does $0 = (1) + 2$? No. So, C is not the answer. Try D in the first equation: Does $4 = (2) + 2$? Yes. So, try D in the second equation: Does $4 = (2)^2 + 2 - 2$? Yes. Because D works in both equations, it is the correct answer.

15. A This a great opportunity to Plug In The Answers! Start with C, and plug into $g(x)$ first: $|2^2 - 10| = 6$. Now plug that value into $f(x)$: $\frac{6}{2} + 2 = 5$. Cross out C. Now the tough decision is whether or not a bigger or smaller value of a is needed. If you aren't sure which way to go, then just try another answer. For instance, plug D into $g(x)$: $|6^2 - 10| = 26$. Now into $f(x)$: $\frac{26}{2} + 2 = 15$. You got a lot further away from the answer, and using D resulted in a number much too big! Cross out E as well, and try one of the first two answers. Plug A into $g(x)$: $\left|\sqrt{2}^2 - 10\right| = 8$. Now into $f(x)$: $\frac{8}{2} + 2 = 6$! A is the correct answer.

16. E There are variables in the answer choices, so plug in. However, you can't plug in a value for all the variables at once because you must follow the rules of geometry. (Makes sense, right? It's the last question in the section.) Let's start by saying $a = 70$ and $b = 60$. Because $PQRS$ is a parallelogram, angle Q must equal angle S, so angle S also equals 60. If you look at the big triangle that contains a and c, you already know that two of the angles are 60 and 70, so the third angle, c, must be 50. You know that PQ and SR are parallel and, you can see that x is a big angle and a is a small angle. So $a + x = 180$. Because $a = 70$, that means $x = 110$. Therefore, your target answer is 110. Plug your values for a, b, and c into the answers and you'll find that E equals 110.

SECTION 9

1. C In this sentence, the clue is *cover a broad array of subject matters and range of historical eras.* A good word or phrase to use for the blanks would be "varied" or "all different." *Diverse* comes closest to this meaning. Remember to use word roots to help you eliminate answers. *Meritorious* shares the same root as *merit*, and merit means something of worth. So *meritorious* probably means something similar and does not match our word for the blank.

2. C The clues in this sentence are *apparent* and *deceptive.* Professional skiers descend the slopes with apparent "ease," but this apparent ease is deceptive. Therefore, it must actually be difficult to ski well. The best way to complete the second part of the sentence is to say that skiing *requires great effort and intense concentration.* So you can put "great" in the second blank. That gets rid of E. Then you have "ease" in the first blank, and the best match among the remaining answers is *nonchalance.*

3. C The missing word here needs to describe the role of *famous singers* in *popular culture.* Therefore "famous people" would fit well here. C is the best choice, because an *icon* is an idol or person who is the object of great attention.

4. **C** The clues here are *unnecessarily, trivial information*, and *did not need*. A good word for the blank is "wordy." A is incorrect as *winsome* means "charming." B is incorrect as *terse* means "concise." E is incorrect as *deafening* means "loud." D is incorrect as *fallacious* means "wrong." So the best answer is C, which means "complicated."

5. **D** The blanks here are related to each other, but the clues tell you in what manner. The clues *enjoyed visiting New York* and *did not like all the traveling* indicate that Cecilia had two contradictory feelings— one good, one bad. Look for a contradictory relationship between the blanks. A and C include two similar words. Cross them off. B and E have answers that are not really related at all. Only D includes two answers that are contradictory, involving both rest and work.

6. **D** In this sentence, putting a word in one blank affects the word in the other blank, so the relationship between the blanks should be determined first. The trigger *despite* suggests that the two blanks have an opposite relationship. A, B, C, and E can be eliminated because the words in those choices do not comply with the trigger, thus D is the best answer.

7. **E** Go back to the passage, find the word *promulgated*, and cross it out. Then read the sentence and come up with your own word. The first part of the sentence is saying something very positive about Democritus's ideas, so you need a positive word. That means you can eliminate A, B, and D. It doesn't make sense to say that Democritus's ideas were protected, so you can cross out C. E is the only choice left.

8. **A** The best way to find the answer to this question is to use POE. B says that Democritus was *known for his work in politics,* but this is not mentioned anywhere in the passage. C says that *his ideas were incompatible with those of Galileo and Newton,* which contradicts lines 30–32. D says that *Democritus was unduly credited*, but the passage is all about giving him proper credit. E says that Democritus was *known for his discovery of calculus,* which is not said anywhere in the passage, and it also happens to be completely false. That leaves only A.

9. **D** The obsession referred to in Passage 1 (lines 18–23) is the search for a level of stark simplicity *underlying all the complex richness, texture, and variety of our everyday life.* This idea is paraphrased perfectly in D, which says that scientists are on a *quest for a simple unifying property of everyday matter.* The passage is talking about something that is today almost an obsession, so A and E are wrong because they are not about modern science. B and C are wrong because they aren't mentioned anywhere in the passage. If it's not in the passage, then it's not the right answer.

10. **B** For this question you need to understand the main idea of Passage 1; Democritus's ideas were way ahead of his time. The first passage states, *his theory never gained wide acceptance in Greek thought.* The third paragraph tells you that now his ideas are so *embedded in physical thought to the point that few physicists can imagine any other approach.* You know that Democritus's ideas were once not accepted but now they are, making B a good answer. You can also use POE on this question. A is wrong because the word *dismay* is extreme and the author never says that the early scientists were *narrow-minded.* You can get rid of C because the author does not tell you he is surprised or confused by the modern acceptance of Democritus's ideas. Eliminate D, because the passage does not go on to talk about the uses of atomic theory. E is close, but not close enough. The author does not say that they are unwilling to explore other theories, but rather that they cannot even think of them.

11. **C** This is an inference question, because it uses the word *suggests*, which tells you that the author did not directly state the right answer but gave you enough information to draw a conclusion. On inference questions, look for an answer that you can definitely say is right. C is supported by the paragraph, because you know that both chemists and physicists dealt with it and its implications. There is no support in the passage for A, B, D, or E.

12. **A** According to the first sentence of Passage 2, *the discovery that the universe is expanding was one of the great intellectual revelations of the twentieth century.* B is wrong because it says that Newton *should have realized*, not that he did. C isn't right because the idea was discovered, and is still accepted, by modern physicists. You can eliminate D because it's too extreme and contradicts the passage. E is also too extreme. That leaves only A.

13. **C** Go back to Passage 2 and find where Newton is mentioned. According to lines 48–51, *With hindsight, it is easy to wonder why no one had thought of it before. Newton, and others, should have realized that a static universe would soon start to contract under the influence of gravity.* So the passage uses Newton as an example of a scientist who might have come up with the idea of an expanding universe before it was actually discovered in the twentieth century. This idea is paraphrased in C. A is wrong because ETS would never suggest that many physicists are ignorant. Remember: ETS has great respect for scientists. Newton wasn't a proponent of the expanding-universe theory, so you can discount B. D contradicts the main idea of the passage. According to the author, the universe is expanding. Go back and read the first sentence of the passage. E is wrong because Newton didn't disregard the expanding-universe theory. There was no such theory back then!

14. **B** According to lines 54–58, if the universe was *expanding at more than a certain critical rate, gravity would never be strong enough to stop it.... This is a bit like what happens when one fires a rocket upward from the surface of the earth.* So the rocket is being used as an example of how the force of gravity applies to the idea of an expanding universe. B paraphrases this nicely. A is wrong because the rocket example is not an implication of the expanding universe. The rocket is simply an example used to illustrate the implications of gravity on the expanding-universe theory. C makes no sense. Is the energy released by a rocket similar to the energy released by an entire universe? No way! D and E contradict the main idea of the author, that the universe is expanding.

15. **B** The lead words for this question are *Einstein's general theory of relativity*, which should lead you back to lines 67–70. According to these lines, *Even Einstein, when he formulated the general theory of relativity in 1915, was so sure that the universe had to be static that he modified his theory to make this possible.* So the passage is showing you that, among modern scientists, even Einstein wanted to maintain the idea that the universe is static. He even changed his famous theory of relativity to make this possible. This idea is perfectly paraphrased in B. A is wrong because the expanding-universe theory is not the author's theory. C is incorrect because the passage says nothing about Einstein's creativity. The point is that Einstein disagreed with the expanding-universe theory. D is wrong because the passage never suggests that the expanding-universe theory may not be valid. Just because Einstein didn't agree with the theory doesn't mean it's wrong. E strays too far from the main idea. Remember: The passage is about the expanding-universe theory, not about Einstein's relation to Newton.

16. **A** According to lines 66–77, Einstein wanted so much to maintain the idea of the static universe that he *modified his theory [of relativity] to make this possible.* The change he made was to introduce the *so-called cosmological constant.* That is exactly what A says. B is wrong because Newton didn't have any ideas about the expanding-universe theory. The theory didn't exist back in Newton's time! C is off the mark because the cosmological constant is part of Einstein's theory of relativity, not an idea developed by his opponents. Read more carefully. You can't pick D, either, because Newtonian physics has never been disproved, and this is not suggested anywhere in the passage. The passage is about the expanding-universe theory. Don't forget the main idea. E is incorrect because the passage is not about the mass of all matter. Again, everything in the passage relates to the expanding-universe theory.

17. D Go back to Passage 2, find the word *static*, and cross it out. Then read the sentence and come up with your own word. According to the passage, Einstein and many other modern scientists were against the idea of an expanding universe. That means they must have believed in a universe that wasn't expanding. So you can put "not expanding" in place of static. The best match for "not expanding" in the answer choices is *unchanging*. The other answers are wrong because they don't make any sense in context.

18. E Because this question involves both passages, you should definitely do it last. The easiest way to answer this question is to use POE. A is only about Passage 1, so you can eliminate it. Newton certainly received credit for his theories, so you can eliminate B. C is wrong because the passages discuss the contribution of the three scientists mentioned, so you can eliminate it. Between D and E, choice E is better because it's a *may* answer, and ETS likes wishy-washy answers.

19. A According to the passages, Democritus, an ancient Greek scientist, first came up with the theory of atomism, while the expanding-universe theory was first put forth in the twentieth century. That is one clear difference between the two theories, and it also happens to be exactly what A says. B is wrong because the passages never suggest that atomism is easier to understand than the static universe theory. The comparison is never made. C is way off base. There is no mention of politics anywhere in either passage. D is too extreme. The passage never says that the theory of atomism had been proven. Remember that it's just a theory. E contradicts the main idea of the passage. Modern science has rejected the static universe theory in favor of the expanding-universe theory.

SECTION 10

1. A Always check the answer choices to determine if any work with the part of the sentence that is not underlined. B is wordy and choppy because of all the phrases that are set off by commas. The phrase *because of complying* in C would be stronger if it were *because they comply*. D uses *complied by*, which is not the correct idiom. E is a run-on. A is the strongest choice.

2. E Collective nouns, such as *audience*, are singular, so make sure to use singular pronouns and verbs with them. A and C use *are*—a plural verb. D uses the plural *they*. B contains a plural verb, *aren't*.

3. C There are two idioms at work in this sentence and the answer choices: *distinguish...from* and *between...and*. A, B, and D all use the idioms incorrectly. E is wordier than C and fails to maintain parallelism in comparing the two things.

4. C As written, the sentence creates a faulty comparison. It states that something is *unlike the Asian people*. Only another people can be contrasted with the Asian people. But this sentence says that the *settlements* were unlike the Asian people, so A is incorrect. B and E have this error as well. D fixes the faulty comparison by placing *the Ainu* right after the comma, but *as Caucasians* makes no sense here.

5. D An introductory phrase (in this case, *A Mongol emperor associated with ancient Chinese splendor*) must directly precede the noun to which it refers. Only D does this by placing Kublai Khan's name right after the comma. C is deceptive because it uses his name as a modifier: The noun is actually *army*. In the other three answer choices, the noun is *fleet*, which is not what the introductory phrase is referring to.

6. **A** The sentence is correct as it stands. B turns the sentence into a fragment. C unnecessarily changes the verb tense by adding *had*. D incorrectly changes the comma to a semicolon, which is used only when the word group on each side of it expresses a complete thought. In this case, the phrase following the semicolon is missing a subject. In E, *and it* is redundant. Therefore, A is the best answer.

7. **A** This sentence is correct as it stands. The word *each* is singular, and is therefore correctly referred to by the pronoun *its*. In B and E, the word *their* is plural and therefore incorrect. C says each kitten has personalities (plural), and D unnecessarily adds the word *which*. Thus, A is the best answer.

8. **B** B is the best answer. The clause that precedes the comma and the one after the comma can stand as complete sentences and must therefore be separated by a period, a semicolon, or a comma followed by a conjunction. B correctly uses this last option. Both A and D create comma splices, while C and E add unnecessary words that change the meaning of the sentence.

9. **E** E correctly uses the word *that* to introduce a description of what the storm did. The semicolon is incorrect in A because the words following it are missing a subject and therefore express an incomplete thought. In B, *and it* is an unnecessary addition. Answers containing *-ing* verbs, such as C and D, are rarely the best choice, leaving E as the best answer.

10. **D** The best choice is D. The subject is *effects*, so the verb must be plural (*were*). A uses the past perfect for no reason; the simple past tense D is sufficient here. The verb in C is singular and so does not agree with the subject. The word *being* in choice B makes the sentence a fragment. E uses the wrong pronoun, thereby changing the meaning of the second part of the sentence.

11. **B** B is the best answer. *Mr. Peters* has to follow the comma, because the opening modifier describes him, not *the observation*, as in A and E, or the act of *observing*, as in C. Choice D doesn't actually contain a main verb.

12. **C** The best answer is C. A, B, and E are passive. C also correctly uses the construction *not only…but also*, while D incorrectly says *not only…and…too.*

13. **B** The original sentence, A, and the sentence in D are written in the passive voice. In C, the verb is in the past tense but needs to be in the future. E uses the future progressive tense, which unnecessarily adds *–ing*. Only B is clearly worded.

14. **D** The pronoun *them* is incorrect in the original, A, and in B. The pronoun *those* should refer to the streets in Belgium: This appears in both C and D, although C unnecessarily adds the word *when*. E is a comma splice, a form of run-on sentence.

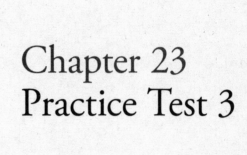

Chapter 23
Practice Test 3

SECTION 1
ESSAY
Time — 25 minutes

Turn to Section 1 of your answer sheet to write your essay.

The essay gives you an opportunity to show how effectively you can develop and express ideas. You should, therefore, take care to develop your point of view, present your ideas logically and clearly, and use language precisely.

Your essay must be written on the lines provided on your answer sheet—you will receive no other paper on which to write. You will have enough space if you write on every line, avoid wide margins, and keep your handwriting to a reasonable size. Remember that people who are not familiar with your handwriting will read what you write. Try to write or print so that what you are writing is legible to those readers.

You have twenty-five minutes to write an essay on the topic assigned below. DO NOT WRITE ON ANOTHER TOPIC. AN OFF-TOPIC ESSAY WILL RECEIVE A SCORE OF ZERO.

Think carefully about the issue presented in the following excerpt and the assignment below.

> Whenever any form of government becomes destructive to these ends [the natural rights of men], it is the right of the people to alter or to abolish it, and to institute new government, laying its foundation on such principles and organizing its powers in such form, as to them shall seem most likely to effect their Safety and Happiness.
> The Declaration of Independence

Assignment: Does questioning authority make a society stronger? Plan and write an essay in which you develop your point of view on this issue. Support your position with reasoning and examples taken from your reading, studies, experience, or observations.

DO NOT WRITE YOUR ESSAY IN YOUR TEST BOOK. You will receive credit only for what you write on your answer sheet.

BEGIN WRITING YOUR ESSAY ON PAGE 3 OF THE ANSWER SHEET (FOUND AT THE BACK OF THE BOOK).

STOP

If you finish before time is called, you may check your work on this section only. Do not turn to any other section in the test.

SECTION 2
Time — 25 minutes
20 Questions

Turn to Section 2 of your answer sheet to answer the questions in this section.

Directions: For this section, solve each problem and decide which is the best of the choices given. Fill in the corresponding circle on the answer sheet. You may use any available space for scratchwork.

Notes

1. The use of a calculator is permitted.
2. All numbers used are real numbers.
3. Figures that accompany problems in this test are intended to provide information useful in solving the problems. They are drawn as accurately as possible EXCEPT when it is stated in a specific problem that the figure is not drawn to scale. All figures lie in a plane unless other wise indicated.
4. Unless otherwise specified, the domain of any function f is assumed to be the set of all real numbers x for which $f(x)$ is a real number.

Reference Information

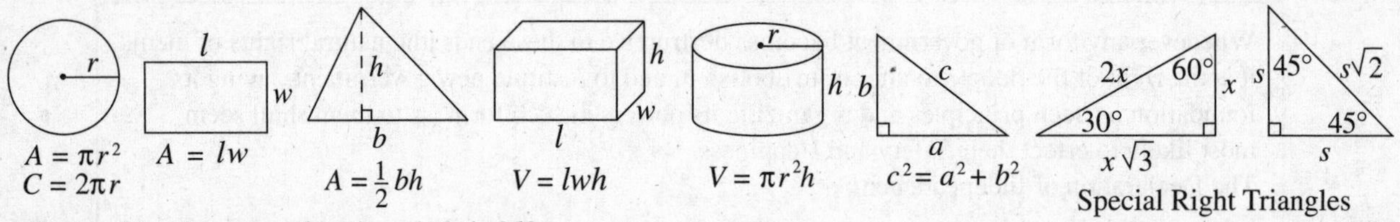

The number of degrees of arc in a circle is 360.

The sum of the measures in degrees of the angles of a triangle is 180.

1. If $4y + 8 = 12y + 24$, then $y =$

(A) -2
(B) -1
(C) 1
(D) 2
(E) 4

2. If $f(2) = 10$ and $f(4) = 44$, which of the following could be $f(x)$?

(A) $2x + 6$
(B) $2x^2 + 12$
(C) $2x^3 + 2$
(D) $2x^3 - 4x$
(E) $3x^2 - x$

GO ON TO THE NEXT PAGE

3. A jar contains a number of jelly beans of which 58 are red, 78 are green, and the rest are blue. If the probability of choosing a blue jelly bean from this jar at random is $\frac{1}{5}$, how many blue jelly beans are in the jar?

(A) 34
(B) 56
(C) 78
(D) 102
(E) 152

4. If the nth term in a sequence is $3 \times 2n$, what is the 10th term in the sequence?

(A) 60
(B) 1,024
(C) 1,536
(D) 3,072
(E) 6,144

5. If 3 more than x is 2 more than y, what is x in terms of y ?

(A) $y - 5$
(B) $y - 1$
(C) $y + 1$
(D) $y + 5$
(E) $y + 6$

6. ABCD is a quadrilateral such that $AB = BC$, $AD = \frac{1}{2}CD$, and $AD = \frac{1}{4}AB$. If $BC = 12$, what is the perimeter of ABCD ?

(A) 44
(B) 42
(C) 40
(D) 36
(E) 33

GO ON TO THE NEXT PAGE

7. If a, b, c, and d are consecutive multiples of 5, and $a < b < c <$ d, what is the value of $(a - c)(d - b)$?

(A) −100
(B) −25
(C) 0
(D) 50
(E) 100

8. Which of the following is equivalent to $-9 \leq 3b + 3 \leq 18$?

(A) $-4 \leq b \leq 5$
(B) $-4 \leq b \leq 6$
(C) $-3 \leq$ b ≤ 5
(D) $3 \leq b \leq 5$
(E) $4 \leq b \leq 6$

9. A store sells boxes of 6 lightbulbs for $30 each, and boxes of 12 lightbulbs for $48 each. The price per bulb is what percent less when purchased in a box of 12 than in a box of 6 ?

(A) 80%
(B) 75%
(C) 50%
(D) 25%
(E) 20%

10. A cartographer is measuring the straight-line distance between five different towns. The towns are arranged in such a way that any given line connecting two of the towns will not pass through any of the other towns. How many such straight-line distances must she measure?

(A) 4
(B) 5
(C) 7
(D) 10
(E) 25

GO ON TO THE NEXT PAGE

Questions 11–12 refer to the following table, which shows the amount of rain that fell during a 30-day period in 1998.

Rainfall	
Rainfall (in inches)	Number of Days
0	17
1	5
2	3
3	3
4	2

11. What is the mode of the amount of rainfall, in inches, over these 30 days?

(A) 0
(B) 1
(C) 2
(D) 3
(E) 4

12. If 200 inches of rainfall were expected to fall during all of 1998, what percent of the expected yearly rainfall was reached during this 30-day period?

(A) 56%
(B) 42%
(C) 28%
(D) 14%
(E) 7%

13. Line *l* contains points (3, 2) and (4, 5). If line *m* is perpendicular to line *l*, then which of the following could be the equation of line *m* ?

(A) $y=-\frac{1}{5}x+3$

(B) $y=-\frac{1}{3}x+5$

(C) $y=-3x+5$

(D) $y=5x+\frac{1}{3}$

(E) $y=\frac{1}{3}x+5$

GO ON TO THE NEXT PAGE

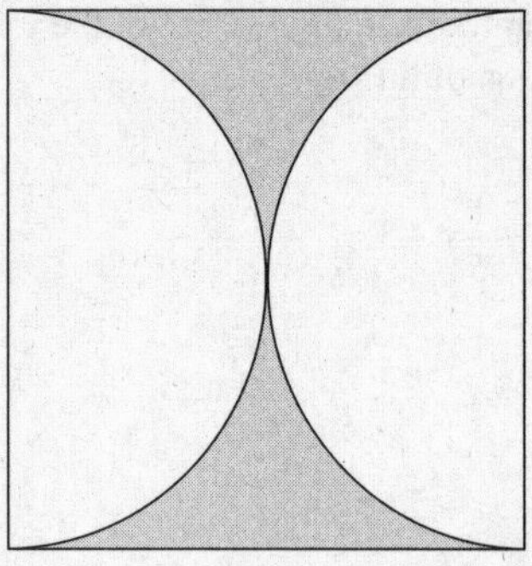

14. In the figure above, *ABCD* is a square with sides of length 2. The square contains two semicircles with diameters $\overline{AB}$ and $\overline{CD}$. What is the sum of the areas of the two shaded regions?

(A) $2-\frac{\pi}{2}$

(B) $2-\pi$

(C) $4-\pi$

(D) $4-2\pi$

(E) $4-\frac{\pi}{4}$

15. Jennifer ran from her house to school at an average speed of 6 miles per hour and returned along the same route at an average speed of 4 miles per hour. If the total time it took her to run to the school and back was one hour, how many minutes did it take her to run from her house to school?

(A) 16
(B) 18
(C) 20
(D) 22
(E) 24

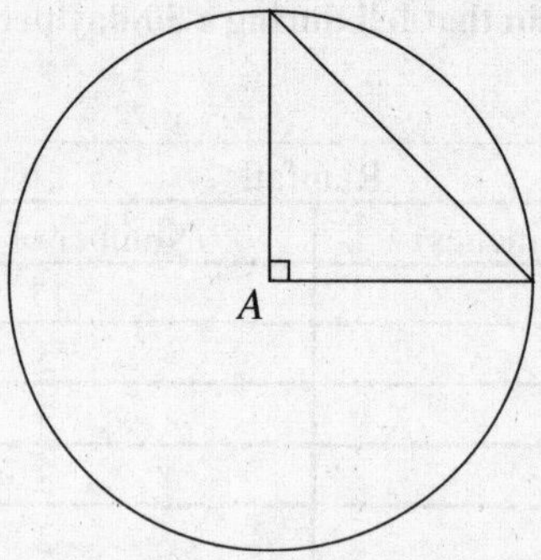

16. In the figure above, $\overline{AC}$ and $\overline{AB}$ are radii of the circle with center *A*. If $\triangle ABC$ has area 18, what is the circumference of the circle?

(A) 6π
(B) 9π
(C) 12π
(D) 18π
(E) 36π

17. If a circle has an area that is half its circumference, what is its radius?

(A) $\frac{1}{2}$

(B) 1

(C) 4

(D) π

(E) 2π

GO ON TO THE NEXT PAGE

18. If Marta is assigned to Project A, then the project will be completed on time. Which of the following can be concluded?

(A) If Project A is completed on time, then Marta must have been assigned to Project A.
(B) If Marta was assigned to Project B, then Project A will not be completed on time.
(C) If Project A is not completed late, then no one other than Marta was assigned to Project A.
(D) If Marta is not assigned to Project A, then Project A will be completed late.
(E) If the project is completed one week late, then Marta was not assigned to Project A.

19. The lengths of two sides of a triangle are 5 and 7. If the length of the third side is an integer, what is the least possible perimeter of the triangle?

(A) 12
(B) 13
(C) 14
(D) 15
(E) 17

20. If $x^2 - x = 12$ and $y^2 - y = 12$, what is the greatest possible value of $x - y$?

(A) 0
(B) 4
(C) 7
(D) 12
(E) 24

STOP

If you finish before time is called, you may check your work on this section only.
Do not turn to any other section in the test.

SECTION 3
Time — 25 minutes
24 Questions

Turn to Section 3 of your answer sheet to answer the questions in this section.

Directions: For each question in this section, select the best answer from among the choices given and fill in the corresponding circle on the answer sheet.

Each sentence below has one or two blanks, each blank indicating that something has been omitted. Beneath the sentence are five words or sets of words labeled A through E. Choose the word or set of words that, when inserted in the sentence, best fits the meaning of the sentence as a whole.

Example:

Desiring to ------- his taunting friends, Mitch gave them taffy in hopes it would keep their mouths shut.

(A) eliminate (B) satisfy (C) overcome (D) ridicule (E) silence

Ⓐ Ⓑ Ⓒ Ⓓ ●

1. While Sarah may have been rather quiet, she was by no means a -------, for she often spent evenings with other people and considered that time to be quite -------.
   (A) recluse . . enjoyable
   (B) conservative . . worthless
   (C) reformer . . irritating
   (D) barbarian . . confusing
   (E) critic . . demanding

2. One of the serious ------- of meteorology is that natural weather patterns cannot be ------- in the laboratory for investigation.
   (A) successes . . achieved
   (B) complexities . . broadened
   (C) premises . . accredited
   (D) limitations . . recreated
   (E) advantages . . analyzed

3. The playwright ------- realism and fantasy in her work so well that the audience is never sure whether the characters' experiences are ------- or imaginary.
   (A) integrates . . actual
   (B) mingles . . congenial
   (C) combines . . apparent
   (D) delineates . . indistinct
   (E) exposes . . verifiable

4. The improvements made on the new automobile are largely -------; although the exterior has been changed, the engine has remained unchanged.
   (A) mechanical (B) superficial (C) economical (D) redundant (E) expensive

5. Some educators view television as an entirely ------- presence in society, virtually disregarding the idea that television has the potential to be -------.
   (A) pernicious . . understood
   (B) auxiliary . . discontinued
   (C) deleterious . . beneficial
   (D) cohesive . . informative
   (E) stabilizing . . veiled

6. Zora Neale Hurston's talent at convincing her readers to believe in the world as she describes it in her novels is due to her ability to create extremely ------- characters.
   (A) unsavory (B) demonstrative (C) ambiguous (D) unilateral (E) credible

7. It is often said that seventeenth-century literature is ------- to today's readers, especially when compared with more recent works, which introduce fewer problems of -------.
   (A) significant . . interpretation
   (B) impractical . . tradition
   (C) inscrutable . . comprehension
   (D) opaque . . contemplation
   (E) instructional . . agreement

8. Drew was a ------- boss, one who gave generous holiday bonuses and often overlooked minor lapses in judgment.
   (A) miserly (B) supercilious (C) disingenuous (D) munificent (E) gregarious

GO ON TO THE NEXT PAGE

Directions: Each passage below is followed by questions based on its content. Answer the questions on the basis of what is stated or implied in each passage and in any introductory material that may be provided.

Questions 9–10 are based on the following passage.

The theory that a meteor struck the Earth 65 million years ago, blanketing the earth in dust and killing the dinosaurs, has recently been challenged. A layer of iridium has been identified in sites worldwide and linked with this event. Scientists concluded that the meteor that caused a large crater in Mexico also wiped out the dinosaurs. New evidence suggests otherwise. Current researchers note that many fossils that contain glass globules from the meteor were deposited immediately after impact, but are separated by a layer of shale and limestone from the iridium. Recent estimates that the shale and limestone would take 300,000 years to form suggest, instead, a second, later iridium-laden meteor.

9. The structure of the passage could best be described in what way?

(A) A theory is explained in depth and supported by additional information.
(B) A theory is explained and discredited based on inaccurate data.
(C) A theory is explained, a flaw is exposed, and another theory espoused.
(D) A theory is explained and its many flaws are exposed.
(E) A theory is explained and the proponents of that theory are then criticized.

10. The primary purpose of the passage is to

(A) estimate the time when the dinosaurs became extinct
(B) systematically debunk alternatives to the current theory explaining dinosaurs' extinction
(C) note the contents of meteors, particularly iridium and glass globules
(D) explain conclusively what caused the extinction of the dinosaurs
(E) propose a possible cause of the extinction of the dinosaurs

Questions 11–12 are based on the following passage.

The author of the Pledge of Allegiance was not an American political icon such as Thomas Jefferson or Benjamin Franklin, but rather an employee of Youth's Companion magazine named Francis Bellamy. Written in 1892, the Pledge was part of a larger program to commemorate the arrival of Christopher Columbus in the Americas, thereby inspiring allegiance in a country recuperating from the horrors of civil war. Later revisions added the words "under God" as a reaction to "godless" communism. In historical perspective, then, the Pledge of Allegiance assumes a surprisingly fluid meaning considering it has been recited for more than one hundred years.

11. The author of the passage mentions Thomas Jefferson and Benjamin Franklin in order to

(A) suggest authors who might have written a better Pledge of Allegiance
(B) emphasize the relative obscurity of the author of the Pledge of Allegiance
(C) provide more information about the origin of the Pledge of Allegiance
(D) commemorate their contributions to American political writings
(E) imply that they inspired Francis Bellamy to write the Pledge of Allegiance

12. It can be most reasonably inferred from the passage that

(A) the Pledge of Allegiance unified Americans after the Civil War
(B) the Pledge of Allegiance has not retained the original phrasing as written by Francis Bellamy
(C) Francis Bellamy would have supported the addition of "under God" to the Pledge of Allegiance
(D) the phrase "under God" sparked great controversy about reciting the Pledge of Allegiance
(E) an earlier version of the Pledge of Allegiance referred to the arrival of Christopher Columbus

GO ON TO THE NEXT PAGE

Questions 13–24 are based on the following passage.

In this excerpt from a book written in 1984, Dr. Richard M. Restak discusses two different schools of thought in brain research: those who believe there is a strong relationship between the brain and the mind, and those who do not. By citing various neuroscientists, Restak conveys the struggle many scientists have with the issue.

Two years before his death at age eighty-four, neurosurgeon Wilder Penfield was writing his final book, *The Mystery of the Mind*. During moments away from his desk, Penfield continued to ponder the theme of his book: the relationship of mind, brain, and science.

One weekend while at his farm outside of Montreal, Penfield began painting on a huge rock. On one side, he painted a Greek word for "spirit" along with a solid line connecting it to an Aesculapian torch, which represented science. The line continued around the rock to the other side, where he drew an outline of a human head with a brain drawn inside, which contained, at its center, a question mark. At this point, Penfield was satisfied: brain studies, if properly conducted, would lead inevitably to an understanding of the mind.

But as Penfield progressed with his book, he became less certain that the study of the brain, a field in which he had done pioneering work earlier in his career, would ever lead to an understanding of the mind. Finally, six months before he died, he reached a conclusion.

Donning six sweaters to protect himself from the harsh Canadian wind, Penfield returned to the rock and, with shaking hands, converted the solid line connecting the spirit and brain into an interrupted one. This alteration expressed, in a form for all to see, Penfield's doubts that an understanding of the brain would ever lead to an explanation of the mind.

Among neuroscientists, Penfield is not alone in undergoing, later in life, a change in belief about the relationship of the mind to the brain. Sir John Eccles, a Nobel Prize winner, has teamed up in recent years with Karl Popper. Together they have written *The Self and Its Brain*, an updated plea for dualism: the belief that the mind and the brain are distinct entities. Brain researcher Karl Pribram is currently collaborating with physicist David Bohm in an attempt to integrate mind and consciousness with ideas drawn from quantum physics. Together they are searching for a model capable of integrating matter and consciousness into a holistic worldview.

Why should these brain researchers have a change of heart late in their careers about the adequacy of our present knowledge of the brain to provide an "explanation" for mind and consciousness? What compels them toward a mystical bent?

Interest and enthusiasm regarding the brain can't be the only explanations why neuroscientists are susceptible to a mystical bent, since only a small number of them end up waxing philosophical. But the nature of their research and the kinds of questions asked undoubtedly contribute to later "conversions." Penfield's work involved neurosurgical explorations into the temporal lobes. In response to Penfield's electrical probe, his patients reported familiar feelings and vivid memories. In essence, these patients reported experiences that did not correspond to actual events in the operating theater, but rather were the result of direct stimulation of neural tissues. Does this mean that our conscious experience can be understood solely in terms of electrical impulses?

Researchers like Wilder Penfield and Roger Sperry are examples of brain researchers who have become disillusioned with claims that the mind can "be explained" in terms of brain functioning. They have revolted against what another neuroscientist calls the "Peter Pan school of neuroscience" with its "bloodless dance of action potentials" and its "hurrying to and fro of molecules."

Common to all these brain scientists is a willingness to adapt innovative attitudes as well as pursue unorthodox lines of inquiry. They have also been open to transcendental influences. Eccles, for instance, had a "sudden overwhelming experience" at age eighteen that aroused an intense interest in the mind-brain problem. He attributes his choice of career in the neurosciences to this experience.

Brain researchers with a "mystical bent" have also been comfortable sharing their findings and ideas with specialists in other fields. Penfield's book, *The Mystery of the Mind*, was encouraged by Charles Hendle, professor of philosophy at Yale. It was a much-needed encouragement, since the other neuroscientists to whom Penfield had shown his early draft discouraged him from proceeding with the project. To them, Penfield's speculative leap from neurophysiologist to philosopher was "unscientific." At Hendle's urging, Penfield proceeded to detail "how I came to take seriously, even to believe, that the consciousness of man, the mind, is something not to be reduced to brain mechanisms."

13. The "solid line" painted by Penfield (line 8) represents

(A) Penfield's desire to link art and science within one discipline
(B) Penfield's reluctance to make any connections between the mind and the brain
(C) Penfield's conclusion that experiments had proven the link between the brain and the mind
(D) an example of Penfield's mental confusion
(E) Penfield's confidence that the mind would eventually be understood through study of the brain

GO ON TO THE NEXT PAGE

14. It can be inferred from the passage that Pribram and Bohm decided to collaborate because

(A) they felt that a holistic world view could explain quantum physics
(B) they felt that consciousness might better be understood by unorthodox avenues of inquiry
(C) they wanted to expand on the findings of Eccles and Popper
(D) new findings in the field of quantum physics had convinced them that there is no relationship between matter and consciousness
(E) Penfield's book contained factual errors that they felt they must correct

15. The word "bent" in line 44 most nearly means

(A) inclination
(B) distortion
(C) determination
(D) talent
(E) revelation

16. It can be inferred that skeptics believe that advocates of the "Peter Pan school of neuroscience"

(A) succeed in creating a definitive technique for neurosurgeons to follow
(B) fail to take brain study seriously as a field of endeavor
(C) misunderstand the importance of brain waves in the study of the mind
(D) rely too much on the physiological to explain the workings of the mind
(E) believe that abstract aspects of the mind cannot be explained scientifically

17. The main distinction between orthodox and unorthodox neuroscientists is that

(A) the former believe in enlarging the pool of research topics, while the latter tend to stay within their own field
(B) the latter seek out alternative sources for research, while the former regard only those with a mystical bent as worthy
(C) the former encourage "unscientific" research, while the latter concern themselves primarily with mystical phenomena
(D) the latter regard the former with contempt, while the former consider the latter to be colleagues
(E) the former tend to ignore research that is not based in science, while the latter support exploration that calls on various sources

18. In line 48, "waxing" most nearly means

(A) shining
(B) waning
(C) becoming
(D) increasing
(E) sealing

19. Penfield's doubts about the validity of the brain-mind connection were tangibly represented by

(A) an Aesculapian torch
(B) a broken line
(C) a Greek word
(D) a large painted rock
(E) a solid line

GO ON TO THE NEXT PAGE

20. Which of the following statements is NOT supported by the information in the passage?

(A) Speculation about the mind-brain connection extends across disciplines.
(B) Some brain scientists are not unwilling to try avant-garde approaches.
(C) It is not unusual for brain researchers to have a late-in-life change of heart.
(D) Penfield expressed deep doubts about the correctness of his early conclusions.
(E) Properly executed brain studies lead to a full understanding of the mind.

21. According to the passage, during neurosurgical exploration, Penfield's patients

(A) behaved like victims of brain traumas
(B) asked their doctor probing questions
(C) followed their impulses while under sedation
(D) perceived events that had never happened
(E) clearly recalled things unrelated to their surroundings

22. The author mentions Eccles and Popper (lines 30 and 31) in order to

(A) prove definitively that neuroscience is incapable of explaining the mind
(B) give examples of other neuroscientists who altered their convictions about the brain-mind link
(C) indicate that only through teamwork can dualism be fully explained
(D) contrast their beliefs about the relation between the brain and the mind with those of Penfield
(E) present concrete evidence that the brain and the mind are distinct entities

23. An orthodox neuroscientist is most likely of the opinion that

(A) consciousness can be understood in terms of electrical impulses
(B) the Greeks were correct about the relation of the spirit to scientific inquiry
(C) mysticism and philosophy are useful disciplines for scientists
(D) transcendentalist concepts are influential in brain research
(E) quantum physics has great potential in the study of consciousness

24. Which of the following statements is NOT supported by information in the passage?

(A) Penfield gradually lost the convictions that had earlier satisfied him.
(B) Pribram and Bohm worked together to investigate the relation of physics to neuroscience.
(C) There may be more to the workings of the body and the mind than can be explained by science.
(D) Charles Hendle was Penfield's teacher when the latter was an undergraduate.
(E) Penfield used the results of brain experiments to try to form a theory of the mind.

STOP

If you finish before time is called, you may check your work on this section only. Do not turn to any other section in the test.

NO TEST MATERIAL ON THIS PAGE.

SECTION 4
Time — 25 minutes
35 Questions

Turn to Section 4 of your answer sheet to answer the questions in this section.

Directions: For each question in this section, select the best answer from among the choices given and fill in the corresponding circle on the answer sheet.

The following sentences test correctness and effectiveness of expression. Part of each sentence or the entire sentence is underlined; beneath each sentence are five ways of phrasing the underlined material. Choice A repeats the original phrasing; the other four choices are different. If you think the original phrasing produces a better sentence than any of the alternatives, select choice A; if not, select one of the other choices.

In making your selection, follow the requirements of standard written English; that is, pay attention to grammar, choice of words, sentence construction, and punctuation. Your selection should result in the most effective sentence—clear and precise, without awkwardness or ambiguity.

EXAMPLE:

Bobby Flay baked his first cake and he was thirteen years old then.

(A) and he was thirteen years old then
(B) when he was thirteen
(C) at age thirteen years old
(D) upon the reaching of thirteen years
(E) at the time when he was thirteen

Ⓐ●ⒸⒹⒺ

1. Radio broadcasts once were the most popular form of entertainment; families used to gather around the radio at night for their favorite programs.

(A) gather around the radio at night for their favorite programs
(B) gather around to listen to its favorite programs
(C) gather around the radio at night for they're favorite programs
(D) gather around to listen to it's favorite programs
(E) gather around the radio at night for there favorite programs

2. Concluding the final session of the communications class, speak slowly and enunciate clearly while making eye contact was the recommendation Ms. Benton gave her students.

(A) speak slowly and enunciate clearly while making eye contact was the recommendation Ms. Benton gave her students
(B) speaking slowly and enunciating clearly while making eye contact were what Ms. Benton told her students to do
(C) her students were advised by Ms. Benton to speak slowly and enunciate clearly while making eye contact
(D) speak slowly and enunciate clearly while making eye contact, recommendations made by Ms. Benton, were what her students should do
(E) Ms. Benton recommended that her students speak slowly and enunciate clearly while making eye contact

3. First president George Washington is credited to breed the first mules in the United States using a jack and a jennet presented to him by the King of Spain in 1786.

(A) to breed
(B) since he bred
(C) by breeding
(D) with breeding
(E) having bred

4. Classical composers who influenced the genre of the string quartet range from Haydn's credit for its invention in the eighteenth century, as well as Shostakovich.

(A) Haydn's credit for its invention in the eighteenth century, as well as
(B) Haydn, who in the eighteenth century was inventing it, and
(C) Haydn, who is credited with its invention in the eighteenth century, to
(D) Haydn's invention in the eighteenth century, for which he received the credit, and
(E) its invention by Haydn, who received the credit in the eighteenth century, to

GO ON TO THE NEXT PAGE

5. A major cause of stress in school is where seniors must manage not only academic requirements and sports schedules, but also standardized testing and college applications, during the first semester.

(A) where seniors must manage not only academic requirements and sports schedules, but also
(B) seniors need to manage not only academic requirements and sports schedules, but also
(C) where seniors must manage not only academic requirements and sports schedules, and also
(D) when seniors must manage both academic requirements and sports schedules, but also
(E) the management by seniors of not only academic requirements and sports schedules, but also

6. Alaska, the largest state by far with nearly 2.5 times the land area of the next largest state, which has one of the smallest populations with only 650 thousand residents.

(A) state, which has one of the smallest populations
(B) state, that has one of the smallest populations
(C) state and has one of the smallest populations
(D) state, has one of the smallest populations
(E) state, will have one of the smallest populations

7. Stars other than our sun, astronomers have discovered, have planets the size of Jupiter in orbit about them.

(A) astronomers have discovered, have
(B) which, astronomers have discovered, have
(C) having possibly, according to the discovery of many astronomers
(D) there are some astronomers who have discovered that they may have
(E) astronomers are discovering they have

8. She was one of the most famous mystery writers of the century, and Dorothy L. Sayers also built one of her most famous novels around the question of higher education for women in the pre-war era.

(A) She was one of the most famous mystery writers of the century, and Dorothy L. Sayers
(B) One of the most famous mystery writers of the century, Dorothy L. Sayers
(C) Famous mystery writer of the century that she was, Dorothy L. Sayers
(D) Dorothy L. Sayers has been one of the most famous mystery writers of the century, and she
(E) Being one of the most famous mystery writers of the century, Dorothy L. Sayers

9. In addition to having more natural resources, the land area of the United States is significantly larger than most other countries.

(A) the land area of the United States is significantly larger than most other countries
(B) the land area is significantly larger than most other countries for the United States
(C) the United States also has significantly more land area than most other countries
(D) the United states has more land area also than most other significant countries
(E) the land area of other countries is less than that of the United States

10. Carrie, Tanya, and Alex were shopping when, after trying to buy shoes, she realized she didn't have her wallet.

(A) when, after trying to buy shoes, she realized she didn't have her wallet
(B) and then she realized she didn't have her wallet after trying to buy shoes
(C) when Tanya realized she didn't have her wallet since she tried to buy shoes
(D) and, since Tanya tried to buy shoes, she realized she didn't have her wallet
(E) when Tanya realized she didn't have her wallet after trying to buy shoes

11. Clifton Chenier became known as the "King of Zydeco" because of his spending much of his life in the popularizing of zydeco music.

(A) of his spending much of his life in the popularizing of
(B) he spent much of his life popularizing it,
(C) of his popularization for much of his life of
(D) he spent much of his life in the popularizing of
(E) he spent much of his life popularizing

GO ON TO THE NEXT PAGE

The following sentences test your ability to recognize grammar and usage errors. Each sentence contains either a single error or no error at all. No sentence contains more than one error. The error, if there is one, is underlined and lettered. If the sentence contains an error, select the one underlined part that must be changed to make the sentence correct. If the sentence is correct, select choice E. In choosing answers, follow the requirements of standard written English.

EXAMPLE:

The other players and her significantly improved
A B C

the game plan created by the coaches. No error
D E

Ⓐ●ⒸⒹⒺ

12. Celestial navigation, the ancient practice of using
A
heavenly bodies to guide a ship's course, has becoming a
B C
dying art since the advent of modern global positioning
D
systems. No error
E

13. The artist's repeated use of pale colors and amorphous
A
forms, intended to imbue his paintings with a
B
sense of ambiguity, only makes the paintings look weakly.
C D
No error
E

14. Excessive sugar intake can lead to addiction, obesity, and
A B C
to diabetes. No error
D E

15. During late summer evenings, we would sit on
A B
the porch swing and rock very slow in time to the
C
sound of the cicadas. No error
D E

16. Popping corn is possible because of the tiny amount
of water present in dried kernels; when the kernels are
A
heated, the water expands until it bursts the seams of the
B C D
kernels. No error
E

17. The improvements people make in how they eat and
A
exercise pay off in that individuals have more energy and
B
are happier after becoming more healthier. No error
C D E

18. *Fortuitous* means "happening by chance," but since so
A
many have used it to mean "lucky," this malapropism has
B C
been added to dictionaries as a secondary definition.
D
No error
E

19. After I realized last summer that no one could see through
A B
my mirrored sunglasses, I wear them everywhere.
C D
No error
E

20. During the Triassic period, there was only one huge land
mass, Pangaea, which encompassed all the present-day
A B
continents; some of the plants and trees familiar to us
C
today also grew on Pangaea. No error
D E

GO ON TO THE NEXT PAGE

21. Many of the students which were chosen for the National
A
Student Leadership Conference opted for the U.S. Politics
B
and Policies program; they spent several days attending
Congressional events and touring the capitol's sights.
C D
No error
E

22. If you do not enjoy fearless pigeons landing on yourself
A B
for food, you should avoid St. Mark's Square in Venice.
C D
No error
E

23. Some books contend that, as a student familiarizes
A
himself with early American history, one must
B
keep in mind that certain parts of history are recounted by
C D
those who lived it and are therefore subjective. No error
E

24. Some people, independent from their approval of citizen
A B
participation in government, dislike performing jury duty
C
themselves. No error
D E

25. They say comedians face a difficult task: they must
A B
challenge and mock the status quo without alienating
C D
their audiences who represent the status quo. No error
E

26. Upon reviewing a map of his property, John realized
A
that he could not build the barn where he had intended
B
because it belonged to a neighboring farmer. No error
C D E

27. Most art critics agree that of the two painters, Elena
A B
is more skilled at conveying the inner emotions of her
C D
subjects. No error
E

28. The viewers will have the opportunity to make
A
their preference clear, as the station plans to conduct an
B C D
extensive voter survey. No error
E

29. In many offices, the use of halogen light bulbs is more
A B C
popular than fluorescent bulbs, even though fluorescent
D
bulbs save more energy than
halogen bulbs. No error
E

GO ON TO THE NEXT PAGE

Directions: The following passage is an early draft of an essay. Some parts of the passage need to be rewritten.

Read the passage and select the best answers for the questions that follow. Some questions are about particular sentences or parts of sentences and ask you to improve sentence structure or word choice. Other questions ask you to consider organization and development. In choosing answers, follow the requirements of standard written English.

Questions 30–35 are based on the following passage.

(1) John Graham had been taking pre-law courses at Yale in hopes of becoming a lawyer. **(2)** In 1980 his career path took a major turn when he decided to be a professional football player. **(3)** Graham is always enthusiastic about sports, and so his change of path was not a total surprise. **(4)** When he was growing up in Sayville, New York, he played varsity football in high school.

(5) His father was the Sayville High School football coach. **(6)** When Graham was playing on the Yale football team, a professional football scout discovered him. **(7)** Because of this, upon graduating from college, Graham became a part of the New York Jets. **(8)** After a highly successful football career, he began to receive offers from the major networks for sports commentary jobs. **(9)** Jobs that relied upon his keen insight and understanding of the workings of football.

(10) Now he is one of the most respected football commentators in the country, frequently compared to Howard Cosell. **(11)** One might assume that any well-known sports broadcaster would be satisfied enough with his success. **(12)** A highly compassionate person, Graham cares very much about the assistance he gives to charities that help seriously ill children. **(13)** Because of the work he has done, he was named "Sportsman of the Year" on two occasions. **(14)** As an athlete, broadcaster, and philanthropist, John Graham is certainly someone to look up to.

30. In the context of the passage, which of these words would be most logical to insert at the beginning of sentence 2 ?

(A) Certainly,
(B) Of course,
(C) Furthermore,
(D) However,
(E) Predictably,

31. Which of the following changes is most needed in sentence 3 ?

(A) Change "Graham" to "He"
(B) Change "is always" to "had always been"
(C) Omit "and so"
(D) Replace "path" with "paths"
(E) Replace "change of" with "changing"

32. Which of the following is the best revision of the underlined portion of sentence 9 (reproduced below)?

Jobs that relied upon his keen insight and understanding of the workings of football.

(A) These jobs relied
(B) Such jobs were relying
(C) Jobs like these ones relied
(D) In them, he relied
(E) These were relying

GO ON TO THE NEXT PAGE

33. Which of the following would be the best way to combine sentences 11 and 12 (reproduced below)?

One might assume that any well-known sports broadcaster would be satisfied enough with his success. A highly compassionate person, Graham cares very much about the assistance he gives to charities that help seriously ill children.

(A) Like any well-known sport broadcaster satisfied with his success, Graham is a highly compassionate person, assisting charities that help seriously ill children.
(B) A well-known sports broadcaster, Graham assists charities that help seriously ill children, and is a highly compassionate person.
(C) Graham is a highly compassionate person, which means assisting charities that help seriously ill children as well as being a well-known sports broadcaster.
(D) Graham has shown his compassionate nature, assisting charities which help seriously ill children, and is a well-known sports broadcaster.
(E) Not satisfied with his success as a well-known sports broadcaster, Graham has shown his compassionate nature by assisting charities that help seriously ill children.

34. Which of the following would be the best way to conclude the passage?

(A) (As it is now)
(B) Add the phrase "Of course," at the beginning of sentence 14.
(C) Omit sentence 14.
(D) Place sentence 13 after sentence 14.
(E) Add the sentence "He too had many accomplishments." after sentence 14.

35. In context, which of the following is the best sentence to insert between sentences 11 and 12 ?

(A) But not for Graham.
(B) Graham became too well-known for his own good.
(C) For Graham, though, success is not enough.
(D) Graham is a great admirer of Howard Cosell.
(E) Graham, having qualities of success and of caring.

STOP

If you finish before time is called, you may check your work on this section only.
Do not turn to any other section in the test.

SECTION 5
Time — 25 minutes
18 Questions

Turn to Section 5 of your answer sheet to answer the questions in this section.

Directions: For this section, solve each problem and decide which is the best of the choices given. Fill in the corresponding circle on the answer sheet. You may use any available space for scratchwork.

Notes

1. The use of a calculator is permitted.
2. All numbers used are real numbers.
3. Figures that accompany problems in this test are intended to provide information useful in solving the problems. They are drawn as accurately as possible EXCEPT when it is stated in a specific problem that the figure is not drawn to scale. All figures lie in a plane unless other wise indicated.
4. Unless otherwise specified, the domain of any function f is assumed to be the set of all real numbers x for which $f(x)$ is a real number.

Reference Information

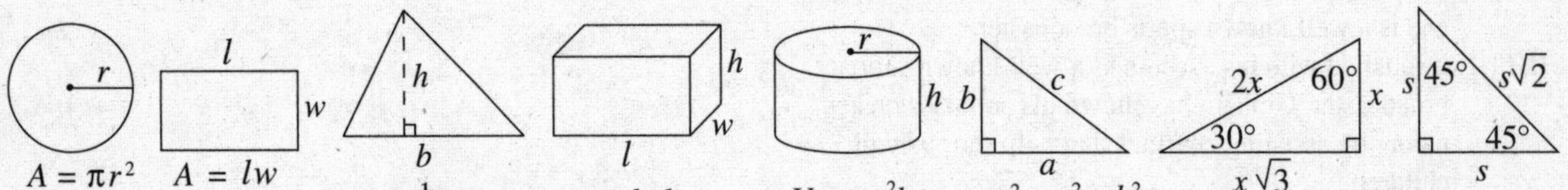

$A = \pi r^2$ $C = 2\pi r$ $A = lw$ $A = \frac{1}{2}bh$ $V = lwh$ $V = \pi r^2 h$ $c^2 = a^2 + b^2$

Special Right Triangles

The number of degrees of arc in a circle is 360.

The sum of the measures in degrees of the angles of a triangle is 180.

1. If x and y are both integers, and $xy \neq 0$, which of the following MUST be true of $|xy|$?

(A) It is greater than zero.
(B) It is less than zero.
(C) It is an even number.
(D) It is an odd number.
(E) It is a prime number.

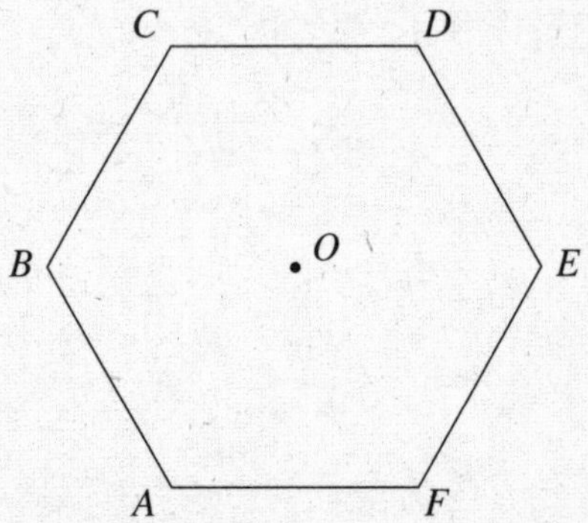

2. O is the center of equilateral hexagon $ABCDEF$, shown above. What is the degree measure of $\angle FOD$ (not shown) ?

(A) 60
(B) 72
(C) 110
(D) 120
(E) 150

GO ON TO THE NEXT PAGE

3. Which of the following points lies the greatest distance from the origin in the xy coordinate system?

(A) $\left(-\frac{3}{2},-\frac{3}{2}\right)$

(B) (–1, –1)

(C) $\left(-\frac{1}{2},0\right)$

(D) (0, 1)

(E) $\left(2,-\frac{1}{2}\right)$

4. If one worker can pack 15 boxes every two minutes, and another can pack 15 boxes every three minutes, how many minutes will it take these two workers, working together, to pack 300 boxes?

(A) 10
(B) 12
(C) 15
(D) 24
(E) 30

5. If the remainder when x is divided by 5 equals the remainder when x is divided by 4, then x could be any of the following EXCEPT

(A) 20
(B) 21
(C) 22
(D) 23
(E) 24

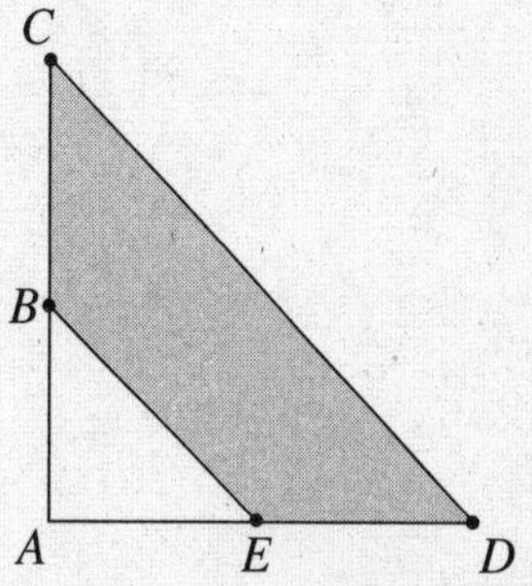

Note: Figure not drawn to scale.

6. If B is the midpoint of $\overline{AC}$ and E is the midpoint of $\overline{AD}$, what fraction of $\triangle ACD$ is shaded?

(A) $\frac{1}{4}$

(B) $\frac{1}{3}$

(C) $\frac{1}{2}$

(D) $\frac{2}{3}$

(E) $\frac{3}{4}$

GO ON TO THE NEXT PAGE

7. If $x > 0$ and $(3-\sqrt{x})(3+\sqrt{x}) = 7$, what is the value of x?

(A) 4
(B) 3
(C) 2
(D) 1
(E) 0

8. The product of integers x and y is divisible by 36. If x is divisible by 6, which of the following must be true?

I. y is divisible by x.

II. y is divisible by 6.

III. $\frac{y}{6}$ is divisible by 6.

(A) None
(B) I only
(C) II only
(D) I and III only
(E) II and III only

GO ON TO THE NEXT PAGE

Directions: For Student-Produced Response questions 9–18, use the grids to the right of the answer document page on which you have answered questions 1–8.

Each of the remaining 10 questions requires you to solve the problem and enter your answer by marking the circles in the special grid, as shown in the examples below. You may use any available space for scratch work.

Answer: $\frac{7}{12}$

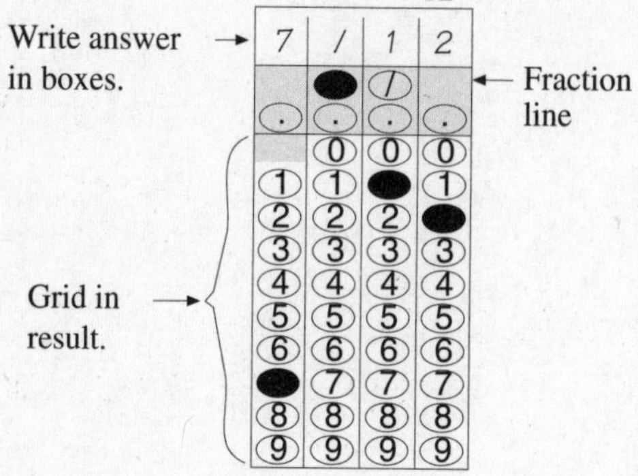

Answer: 2.5

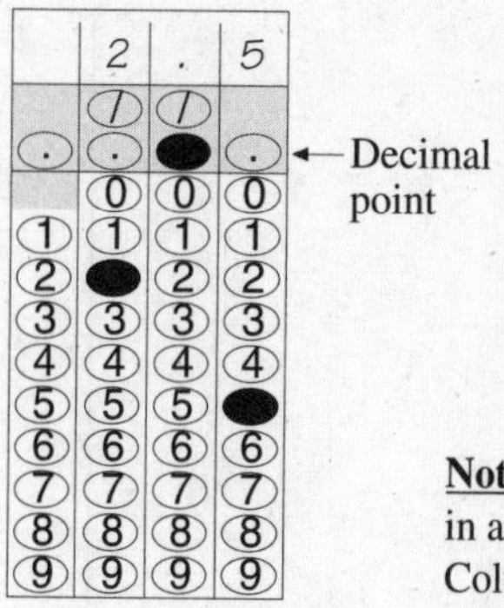

Answer: 201
Either position is correct.

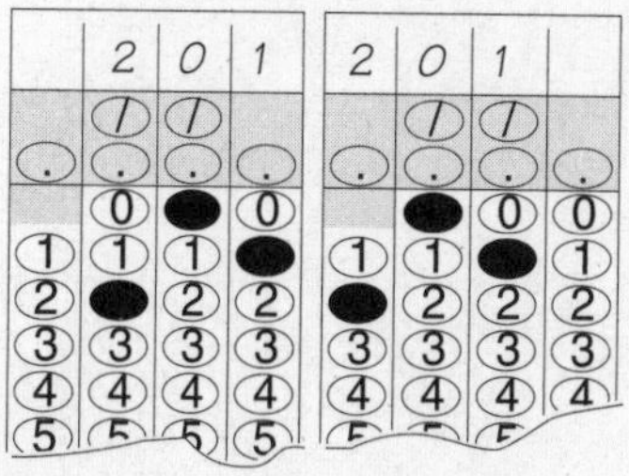

Note: You may start your answers in any column, space permitting. Columns not needed should be left blank.

- Mark no more than one circle in any column.
- Because the answer document will be machine-scored, **you will receive credit only if the circles are filled in correctly.**
- Although not required, it is suggested that you write your answer in the boxes at the top of the columns to help you fill in the circles accurately.
- Some problems may have more than one correct answer. In such cases, grid only one answer.
- No question has a negative answer.
- **Mixed numbers** such as $3\frac{1}{2}$ must be gridded as 3.5 or 7/2. (If 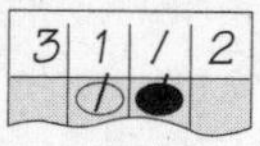 is gridded, it will be interpreted as $\frac{31}{2}$, not $3\frac{1}{2}$.)

- **Decimal Answers:** If you obtain a decimal answer with more digits than the grid can accommodate, it may be either rounded or truncated, but it must fill the entire grid. For example, if you obtain an answer such as 0.6666..., you should record your result as .666 or .667. **A less accurate value such as .66 or .67 will be scored as incorrect.**

Acceptable ways to grid $\frac{2}{3}$ are:

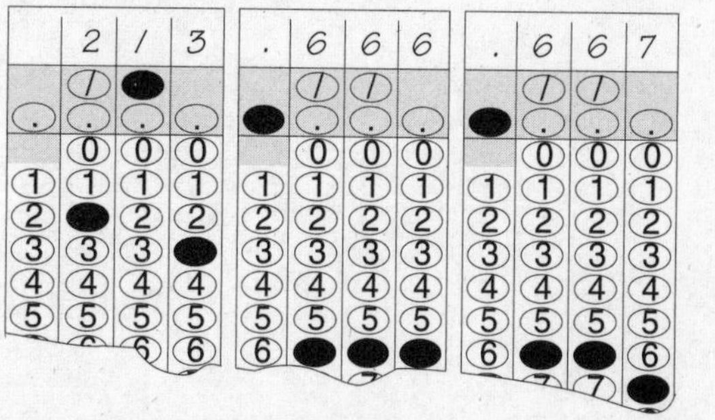

9. If $9^{-2} = \left(\frac{1}{3}\right)^x$, then $x =$

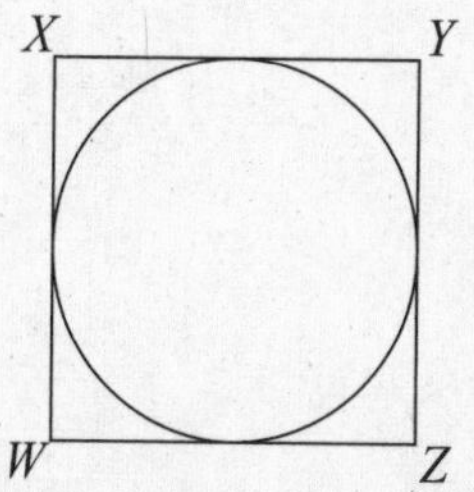

10. In the figure above, a circle is inscribed in square *WXYZ*. If the area of the circle is 400π, what is the area of *WXYZ* ?

GO ON TO THE NEXT PAGE

11. There were 320 students at a school assembly attended only by juniors and seniors. If there were 60 more juniors than seniors and if there were 30 more female juniors than male juniors, how many male juniors were at the assembly?

12. A rectangle of width 5 has a diagonal of length 13. What is the perimeter of the rectangle?

13. Jeannette's average (arithmetic mean) score for six tests was 92. If the sum of the scores of two of her tests was 188, then what was her average score for the other four tests?

14. If Alexandra pays $56.65 for a table, and this amount includes a tax of 3% on the price of the table, what is the amount, in dollars, that she pays in tax? (Ignore the dollar sign when gridding your answer.)

GO ON TO THE NEXT PAGE

15. Tiles numbered 1 through 25 are placed in a bag. If one tile is removed at random, what is the probability that the number on the tile is a prime number?

16. Alan and Ben each run at a constant rate of 7.5 miles per hour. Carla runs at a constant rate of 10 miles per hour. Debby runs at a constant rate of 12 miles per hour. In a relay race with these four runners as a team running one right after the other, Alan runs 0.3 miles, then Ben runs 0.3 miles, then Carla runs 0.5 miles, then Debby runs 0.24 miles. What is the team's average speed in miles per hour?

17. If the distance from (2, 6) to (1, b) is a, $a = (|-1| + 16)^{\frac{1}{2}}$, and $b < a$, what is the value of b ?

18. If $-1 \le a \le 2$ and $-3 \le b \le 2$, what is the greatest possible value of $(a + b)(b - a)$?

STOP

If you finish before time is called, you may check your work on this section only. Do not turn to any other section in the test.

SECTION 6
Time — 25 minutes
24 Questions

Turn to Section 6 of your answer sheet to answer the questions in this section.

Directions: For each question in this section, select the best answer from among the choices given and fill in the corresponding circle on the answer sheet.

Each sentence below has one or two blanks, each blank indicating that something has been omitted. Beneath the sentence are five words or sets of words labeled A through E. Choose the word or set of words that, when inserted in the sentence, best fits the meaning of the sentence as a whole.

Example:

Desiring to ------- his taunting friends, Mitch gave them taffy in hopes it would keep their mouths shut.

(A) eliminate (B) satisfy (C) overcome
(D) ridicule (E) silence

Ⓐ Ⓑ Ⓒ Ⓓ ●

1. The fireworks display created so much ------- that the night sky was completely -------, almost as if it were the middle of the day.

(A) heat . . exploded
(B) gunpowder . . polluted
(C) color . . decorated
(D) refuse . . detonated
(E) light . . illuminated

2. In speech and in action, she was never haughty or -------; she was always willing to ------- any recommendations, even if she did not agree with them at first.

(A) arrogant . . deny
(B) conceited . . consider
(C) ornery . . oppose
(D) lenient . . embrace
(E) accommodating . . ignore

3. Presidents of large companies have traditionally been very -------; they rarely suggest radical new ideas unless all other options have been investigated and found to be impossible.

(A) inventive (B) conservative (C) gentrified
(D) ingenuous (E) gratuitous

4. Although it has begun to garner -------, until recently, African drum music was virtually ------- by all but those with the most esoteric tastes.

(A) acclaim . . overlooked
(B) respect . . praised
(C) criticism . . ignored
(D) recognition . . played
(E) censure . . disregarded

5. While many health-conscious individuals have stopped eating eggs, dietitians say that in appropriate quantities, eggs can be quite -------.

(A) injurious (B) erudite (C) convenient
(D) perfunctory (E) salubrious

GO ON TO THE NEXT PAGE

Directions: Each passage below is followed by questions based on its content. Answer the questions on the basis of what is stated or implied in each passage and in any introductory material that may be provided.

Questions 6–9 are based on the following passages.

Passage 1

The most striking outgrowths of the expansion of the Internet over the past few years have been the numerous legal questions regarding copyright laws and the right to privacy. For many consumers, these two issues create a surprising paradox. Jane Doe wants to freely download music and movies without fear of retribution for violation of copyright laws. Simultaneously, she opposes companies acquiring her personal information to sell to advertisers. Activist groups, whose presence will play a major role in legal decisions, are still considering the issue. In the meantime, Ms. Doe pays for her new CDs with an unusual currency: a list of the sites she frequents each week and an e-mail address with lenient filters.

Passage 2

In the days of the Victorian operetta-creators Gilbert and Sullivan, artists learned that "pirates" in American audiences transcribed songs and lyrics during shows and rushed away afterwards to produce cribbed versions of the play. The artists' outrage helped to spark the first American copyright law. However, with the advent of low-tech home recording equipment, new measures needed to be taken. In response to the rapid increase in copyright infringement, Congress has aided copyright holders, imposing draconian punishments to discourage breach of the laws. Today's casual Internet users should take care to avoid getting caught in the crossfire between consumers and copyright owners.

6. The statements about Jane Doe in the third and fourth sentences (lines 5–8)

(A) exacerbate an already controversial issue
(B) argue for more lenient copyright laws
(C) illustrate the contradiction identified in the previous sentence
(D) contradict the paradox explained earlier in the paragraph
(E) apply the theory from the previous sentence to a specific case

7. The content of both passages suggests that Jane Doe and the "pirates" in American audiences would not be averse to

(A) divulging personal details
(B) protecting intellectual property
(C) appealing to the activist groups to support their claims
(D) having open access to others' creative yield
(E) seeking retribution for copyright violations

8. It is implied in both passages that

(A) in earlier times, singers and songwriters were glad to share their works freely
(B) existing copyright laws on intellectual property are not always effectual
(C) civic activist organizations deserve more respect than the law
(D) unusual currency is an equitable exchange for intellectual property
(E) artists and songwriters should be more defensive of their property

9. In the context of the passage, the meaning of "draconian" (line 22) is closest to

(A) high-tech
(B) dragon-like
(C) illicit
(D) legal
(E) severe

GO ON TO THE NEXT PAGE

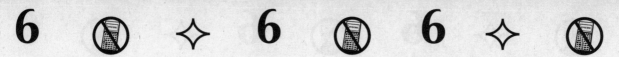

Questions 10–15 are based on the following passage.

The following passage is about the art and recreation of Southeastern Indians.

The ceremonies and rituals of the Southeastern Indians seem bizarre, outlandish, even irrational, until viewed against the background of their belief system. When seen in their original context, the ceremonies and rituals of the Southeastern Indians are no more irrational than are our own. We encounter the same sort of problem in understanding the art forms and games of the Southeastern Indians, and likewise we find the solution to be similar. Our best road to understanding the Indians' artistic and recreational forms is to view them as the outward expressions of their belief system.

In some ways the task of understanding the artistic and recreational forms of the Southeastern Indians is more difficult than understanding their ceremonial life. One problem is that the Indians reached their highest artistic development in the late prehistoric and early historic period. De Soto saw architectural forms and artistic creations that surpassed anything witnessed by the Europeans who came after him, and because many of these creations were made of perishable materials, they did not survive. Hence, perhaps the best Southeastern Indian art is irretrievably gone.

A further difficulty in dealing with the artistic and recreational forms of the Southeastern Indians is that all of these are intimately imbedded in other social and cultural institutions. They are neither as self-contained nor as separable from other institutions as are the art forms and games in our own culture. For instance, the Southeastern Indians placed a high value on men who could use words skillfully. Jack and Anna Kilpatrick have discussed the condensed poetry in some of the Cherokee magical formulas, some of them containing a single word, compound in form, which might be likened to tiny imagist poems. Another form of verbal artistry was oratory, the words of a gifted speaker that could move contentious men to reach consensus or the timid and hesitant to go against the enemy. And yet oratory can hardly be separated from the political institutions of the Southeastern Indians.

In looking at the art and recreation of the Southeastern Indians, we will often wish that we knew more about underlying social factors. For example, even though we know much about the Southeastern Indian ball game, we do not know the precise nature of the social and political forces that led them to play it with such ferocity. To a lesser extent, we know the basic rules of chunkey, but what we do not understand is why the Indians would sometimes bet the last thing they owned on the outcome of a game. In general, we sense that the players of these games were motivated by social factors that lie outside the playing field, but we cannot often be specific about what these factors were.

10. The main purpose of the passage is to

(A) show how bizarre certain Southeastern Indian ceremonies and rituals are
(B) explain the rules of several games played by the Southeastern Indians
(C) describe the difficulties inherent in appreciating the Southeastern Indians' artistic and recreational forms
(D) explore the mysticism of the ceremonies and rituals in the Southeastern Indians' belief system
(E) delineate the difference between the artistic forms of the Southeastern Indians and the Cherokee Indians

11. Which of the following best describes the "problem" mentioned in line 6?

(A) The belief system of the Southeastern Indians was irrational and therefore impossible to understand.
(B) It is difficult to comprehend the artistic and recreational expression of the Southeastern Indians without understanding their belief system.
(C) A superficial examination of the ceremonies and rituals of the Southeastern Indians makes them appear similar to our own.
(D) Since we have virtually no understanding of the beliefs of the Southeastern Indians, it is unlikely we will ever understand the significance of their art.
(E) Scholars are unwilling to acquaint themselves sufficiently with the artistic and recreational forms of the Southeastern Indians.

GO ON TO THE NEXT PAGE

12. According to the passage, which of the following was an advantage of skilled oratory?

(A) It was effective in enhancing one's athletic ability.
(B) An orator was responsible for composing the magical formulas used in spiritual rituals.
(C) Orators were usually the most powerful warriors among the Southeastern Indians.
(D) Timid and hesitant speakers could soothe anxious tempers.
(E) A skilled speaker could mend differences between opposing parties.

13. The author mentions the game "chunkey" in line 44 primarily in order to

(A) prove that the Southeastern Indians were more concerned with politics than with organized competition
(B) show how social politics and ferocious violence were interconnected in the lives of the Southeastern Indians
(C) explain how the Southeastern Indians' interest in competition and artistic endeavor was dictated by separate social factors
(D) provide an example of how the Southeastern Indians' competitive nature was motivated by social influences
(E) describe the unusual and ambiguous rules of a little-known competition

14. Our difficulties in understanding the recreational and artistic systems of the Southeastern Indians can be ascribed to which of the following causes?

I. All instances of original Southeastern Indian art are unavailable to us.
II. We do not know to what degree Indian poetic and rhetorical output was political, and to what extent it was artistic.
III. We are unclear about the exact significance of certain forms of Indian recreation.

(A) I
(B) III
(C) I and II
(D) II and III
(E) I, II, and III

15. The author mentions the loss of many of the Indians' artistic and architectural creations as a parallel to

(A) the Indian art seen by later European explorers
(B) our own irrational rituals and ceremonies
(C) poetry expressed by Cherokee magical formulas
(D) contentious men rallying against attackers
(E) the reason the Indians wagered heavily on chunkey

GO ON TO THE NEXT PAGE

Questions 16–24 are based on the following passage.

The following passage discusses the history and some of the characteristics of jazz.

Like the blues, jazz emphasizes individualism. The performer is at the same time the composer, shaping the music into style and form. A traditional melody or harmonic framework may serve as the takeoff point for improvisation, but it is the personality of the player and the way he or she improvises that produce the music. Performances of the same work differ from player to player, for each recreates the music in his or her own individual way. Jazz is learned through oral tradition, as is folk song, and those who would learn to play it do so primarily by listening to others playing jazz.

Although improvisational in nature, jazz nonetheless contains recognizable elements that derive from older musical traditions. The influence of ragtime is represented in jazz by the emphasis on syncopation and the presence of the piano in the ensemble. The influence of the brass band reveals itself in the jazz instrumentation,* in the roles assigned to each instrument, and in the resulting musical texture. In the classic New Orleans band, for example, three instruments are given melodic roles; the cornet typically plays the lead, the clarinet plays a counter melody, and the trombone plays the lower voice of the trio. The other instruments—the drums, banjos, guitars, and basses—function as the rhythm section. Although pianos were added to jazz bands from the beginning, and often a second cornet as well, the instruments remained basically the same as in brass bands. Later, trumpets took the place of cornets and saxophones were added or used in place of clarinets. The addition of saxophones suggests the influence of the syncopated dance orchestra, which used saxophones early in its development.

The brass band emphasized the ensemble sound, as distinguished from solo music, and this tradition, too, passed over into the performances of early jazz bands. In many jazz performances of the early 1920s, for example, all of the instruments played throughout the piece, the cornet always retaining the lead melody. In performances that included solo passages, the other instruments typically gave firm support, particularly the rhythm section. The ensemble sound of the brass band was basically polyphonic in nature, not chordal. As many as two or three clearly defined melodic lines dominated the texture, and frequently the rhythm instruments furnished little counter melodies.

The polyphonic texture of the music was a result of "collective improvisation" with each melody player improvising his or her part in such a way that the parts combined into a balanced, integrated whole. The concept of jazz improvisation changed its implications over the years. In this early period, the performer embellished the melody, adding extra tones and altering note values, but in such a manner as to retain the essential shape of the original melody.

The most salient features of jazz derive directly from the blues; its soloists approximate the voice with their instruments, but try to recreate its singing style and blue notes by using scooping, sliding, whining, growling, and falsetto effects. Finally, jazz uses the call-and-response style of the blues, by employing an antiphonal relationship between two solo instruments or between solo and ensemble.

Jazz is created from the synthesis of certain elements in the style of its precursors. Its most striking feature is its exotic sound, which is produced not only by the kinds of instruments used in the orchestra, but also by the manner in which intonation is used. Instead of obtaining exact pitches, the players glide freely from one note to another (or through long series of notes in glissandos) and frequently fluctuate the pitches (i.e., use a wide vibrato).

* Instrumentation refers to the choice of instruments within a musical group.

16. The main purpose of the passage is to show that

(A) three instrument melodies were not the dominant style of jazz
(B) the call-and-response style of the blues was highly successful
(C) blues was a uniquely American form of music with a completely original style
(D) the New Orleans band was the single greatest influence on the evolution of jazz
(E) jazz is a complex musical form with a complicated history

17. The author uses the examples of ragtime and brass bands to illustrate

(A) that jazz is not entirely an original creation
(B) the diversity of elements that jazz has passed on to other styles
(C) the origins of certain jazz compositions
(D) the relative growth in popularity of modern jazz
(E) the long, illustrious history that led to the creation of jazz

GO ON TO THE NEXT PAGE

18. The influence of the brass band on jazz performance includes all of the following EXCEPT

(A) the playing of the lead melody by the cornet
(B) emphasis on the ensemble sound
(C) polyphonic music rather than chordal music
(D) the playing of all the instruments throughout the song
(E) the complete lack of solo passages

19. One of the "salient features" of jazz (line 50) would be that

(A) the instruments mimic human voices
(B) jazz is dominated by singers
(C) music lovers prefer the blues to jazz
(D) the music is composed with singers in mind
(E) every jazz musician is also a jazz singer

20. The word "striking" in line 58 most nearly means

(A) removing
(B) pounding
(C) thoughtful
(D) remarkable
(E) believable

21. The exotic sound of jazz is primarily a result of

(A) the use of syncopated rhythms
(B) the influences of ragtime and brass bands
(C) the selection of instruments and the ways in which sounds are manipulated
(D) the addition of extra tones and the replacement of one note with another
(E) the first and third beat percussion work

22. According to the passage, the development of jazz was influenced by all of the following EXCEPT

(A) ragtime bands
(B) dance orchestras
(C) brass bands
(D) folk instrumentation
(E) blues singing

23. Which of the following statements is NOT supported by the information in the passage?

(A) Jazz is sometimes considered to be the only original American art form.
(B) Learning jazz takes place through the ear more so than through the eye.
(C) Jazz is more contrapuntal than harmonic.
(D) Jazz compositions do not always observe strict rhythms.
(E) The clarinet was the precursor to the saxophone in the jazz band.

24. It can be inferred from the passage that

(A) music composed or performed before the advent of jazz was not polyphonic
(B) the first known instance of a jazz performance was in 1920
(C) the classic New Orleans jazz band consisted of three categories of instruments
(D) a clear and exact sound is characteristic of instruments playing jazz
(E) a jazz composition may not sound exactly the same from one performance to the next

STOP

**If you finish before time is called, you may check your work on this section only.
Do not turn to any other section in the test.**

SECTION 7

Time — 25 minutes
24 Questions

Turn to Section 7 of your answer sheet to answer the questions in this section.

Directions: For each question in this section, select the best answer from among the choices given and fill in the corresponding circle on the answer sheet.

Each sentence below has one or two blanks, each blank indicating that something has been omitted. Beneath the sentence are five words or sets of words labeled A through E. Choose the word or set of words that, when inserted in the sentence, best fits the meaning of the sentence as a whole.

Example:

Desiring to ------- his taunting friends, Mitch gave them taffy in hopes it would keep their mouths shut.

(A) eliminate (B) satisfy (C) overcome (D) ridicule (E) silence

Ⓐ Ⓑ Ⓒ Ⓓ ●

1. Their daughter's story that she was robbed of her homework by wandering gypsies was so entirely implausible that the parents believed it to be -------.

   (A) an explanation (B) an intimidation (C) a fabrication (D) a rationalization (E) a confirmation

2. While industry in the late twentieth century believed itself to be ------- in its treatment of laborers, Cesar Chavez made a career of revealing the ------- experienced by farm workers.

   (A) generous . . injustices
   (B) just . . satisfaction
   (C) vindictive . . challenges
   (D) superior . . relationships
   (E) immutable . . consistency

3. The two teams reached an agreement that was -------: they promised to exchange players of comparable talent.

   (A) equitable (B) variable (C) hypocritical (D) inconvenient (E) extended

4. Professor Yang's article was unusually -------, but its brevity did not conceal the importance of Yang's discovery.

   (A) intricate (B) coherent (C) irrelevant (D) terse (E) ambitious

5. The Black Plague was so ------- that in a few short years it had reduced the population of medieval Europe substantially.

   (A) lenient (B) susceptible (C) suppressed (D) maudlin (E) virulent

6. Her promotional tour was ------- by missteps, but the increasing appreciation for her works suggests that the effects of these blunders were -------.

   (A) enervated . . destructive
   (B) avoided . . ancillary
   (C) surrounded . . astute
   (D) beleaguered . . negligible
   (E) besmirched . . indubitable

7. While the ambassador was not ------- about the path that his country was taking, he did not believe that its economic politics would cause a significant amount of -------.

   (A) pragmatic . . affluence
   (B) sanguine . . distress
   (C) impartial . . ambivalence
   (D) despondent . . despair
   (E) agitated . . tumult

8. Lisa was known for her ------- speeches in which she rambled for a long time with frequent repetitions about trivial topics.

   (A) eloquent (B) hoarse (C) garrulous (D) terse (E) compelling

GO ON TO THE NEXT PAGE

Directions: Each passage below is followed by questions based on its content. Answer the questions on the basis of what is stated or implied in each passage and in any introductory material that may be provided.

Questions 9–10 are based on the following passage.

A procedure known as a cochlear implant can allow people who exhibit certain kinds of deafness to detect and interpret sounds. Although the procedure does not restore the natural hearing mechanism, it does permit the interpretation of speech and a high level of interaction with the "hearing world." Despite its possible benefits, the procedure remains controversial. In addition to concerns regarding the risk of surgery to correct a non-fatal disorder, opponents of the procedure cite a moderately high proportion of cases in which the procedure is not effective. Moreover, deaf individuals often value their deafness as an integral part of their identity; cochlear implants may jeopardize that identity.

9. The author's primary purpose is to

(A) argue for the universal implementation of cochlear implants
(B) introduce the cochlear implant procedure and illustrate some of its drawbacks
(C) soundly condemn doctors who perform cochlear implants
(D) admonish those who do not value an individual's unique identity
(E) describe the scientific basis for a certain type of hearing loss

10. Which of the following most accurately describes the purpose of the final three sentences of the passage?

(A) To illustrate important points about the nature of identity
(B) To discuss possible objections to a potentially beneficial procedure
(C) To offer alternatives to a controversial surgery
(D) To provide factual evidence in support of a disputed theory
(E) To question the appropriateness of surgical interventions in non-fatal maladies

GO ON TO THE NEXT PAGE

Questions 11–12 are based on the following passage.

When Igor Stravinsky's *Le Sacre du Printemps* (*The Rite of Spring*) premiered in Paris in 1913, the ballet sparked violent riots for over three days. Although the composer blamed the dancers, choreography, and theater's management for causing the melee, contemporary reports suggest that it may have been the composer's use of unconventional harmonies that provoked the crowd. The resulting violence may remind modern audiences of the riots sometimes associated with sporting events. While the public's propensity for rioting seems to have remained constant over the last century, the nature of the events that trigger public violence has certainly changed.

11. Which of the following was NOT mentioned as a possible cause of the riots in 1913 ?

(A) Theater management
(B) Ballet dancers
(C) Unconventional harmonies used in the ballet
(D) Choreography used in *Le Sacre du Printemps*
(E) Dissatisfied audience members

12. Which of the following can be properly inferred from the information above?

(A) Before 1913, people did not riot over public performances.
(B) No prior rioting event had been as long or as widespread as was the 1913 Paris incident.
(C) Stravinsky had hoped to spark violence in support of the arts.
(D) The catalyst of the modern riot may be different from that of its antecedents.
(E) Violence is never justified, regardless of the provocation.

Questions 13–24 are based on the following passage.

The following passage written in 1989 is taken from A Year in Provence *by Peter Mayle. In this excerpt, we follow a family's first exposure to the French district.*

The proprietor of Le Simiane wished us a happy new year and hovered in the doorway as we stood in the narrow street, blinking into the sun.

"Not bad, eh?" he said, with a flourish of one velvet-clad arm which took in the village. "One is fortunate to be in Provence."

Yes indeed, we thought, one certainly was. If this was winter, we wouldn't be needing all the foul-weather paraphernalia—boots and coats and inch-thick sweaters—that we had brought over from England. We drove home, warm and well fed, making bets on how soon we could take the first swim of the year, and feeling a smug sympathy for those poor souls in harsher climates who had to suffer real winters.

Meanwhile, a thousand miles to the north, the wind that had started in Siberia was picking up speed for the final part of its journey. We had heard stories about the mistral. It drove people, and animals, mad; it was an extenuating circumstance in crimes of violence. It blew for fifteen days on end, uprooting trees, overturning cars, smashing windows, tossing old ladies into the gutter, splintering telegraph poles, moaning through houses like a cold and baleful ghost—every problem in Provence that couldn't be blamed on the politicians was the fault of the *sacre vent*[1] which the Provençeaux spoke about with a kind of masochistic pride.

Typical Gallic exaggeration, we thought. If they had to put up with the gales that come off the English Channel and bend the rain so that it hits you in the face almost horizontally, then they might know what a real wind was like. We listened to their stories and, to humor the tellers, pretended to be impressed.

And so we were poorly prepared when the first mistral of the year came howling down the Rhône valley, turned left, and smacked into the west side of the house with enough force to skim roof tiles into the swimming pool and rip a window that had carelessly been left open off its hinges. The temperature dropped twenty degrees in twenty-four hours. It went to zero, then six below. Readings taken in Marseilles showed a wind speed of 180 kilometers an hour. And then one morning, with the sound of branches snapping, the pipes burst one after the other under the pressure of water that had frozen in them overnight.

They hung off the wall, swollen and stopped up with ice, and Monsieur Menicucci studied them with his professional plumber's eye.

"Oh là là," he said. *"Oh là là."* He turned to his young apprentice, whom he invariably addressed as *jeune homme*[2] or *jeune*. "You see what we have here, *jeune*. Naked pipes. No insulation. Côte d'Azur plumbing. In Cannes, in Nice, it would do, but here . . ."

GO ON TO THE NEXT PAGE

He made a clucking sound of disapproval and wagged his finger under *jeune's* nose to underline the difference between the soft winters of the coast and the biting cold in which we were now standing, and pulled his woolen bonnet firmly down over his ears. He was short and compact, built for plumbing, as he would say, because he could squeeze himself into constricted spaces that more ungainly men would find inaccessible. While we waited for *jeune* to set up the blowtorch, Monsieur Menicucci delivered the first of a series of lectures and collected *pensées* which I would listen to with increasing enjoyment throughout the coming year. Today, we had a geophysical dissertation on the increasing severity of Provençal winters.

For three years in a row, winters had been noticeably harder than anyone could remember—cold enough, in fact, to kill ancient olive trees. But why? Monsieur Menicucci gave me a token two seconds to ponder this phenomenon before warming to his thesis, tapping me with a finger from time to time to make sure I was paying attention.

It was clear, he said, that the winds which brought the cold down from Russia were arriving in Provence with greater velocity than before, taking less time to reach their destination and therefore having less time to warm up en route. And the reason for this—Monsieur Menicucci allowed himself a brief but dramatic pause—was a change in the configuration of the earth's crust. *Mais oui*.[3] Somewhere between Siberia and Ménerbes the curvature of the earth had flattened, enabling the wind to take a more direct route south. It was entirely logical. Unfortunately, part two of the lecture ("Why the Earth Is Becoming Flatter") was interrupted by a crack of another burst pipe, and my education was put aside for some virtuoso work with the blowtorch.

[1] French for "sacred wind"

[2] French for "young man"

[3] French for "But, of course"

13. The author's comment about the family "making bets on how soon we could take the first swim of the year" (lines 11–12) refers to

(A) the vain desire to partake of the French waters
(B) the longing for real pleasure on an otherwise dull French vacation
(C) the hope that a return to the British shore would cure their homesickness
(D) the faith that the powerful mistral would soon vanish and allow them to swim happily once again
(E) the anticipation of warm weather that would make it conceivable to swim, despite the season

14. The word "poor" in line 12 most nearly means

(A) humble
(B) unfortunate
(C) inferior
(D) destitute
(E) underprivileged

15. The author describes the mistral as "an extenuating circumstance in crimes of violence" in lines 17–18 in order to

(A) explain the problems attributed to the judicial system
(B) illustrate that the primary cause of problems in Provence is natural disasters beyond human control
(C) explain how the mistral is blamed for damage caused by politicians
(D) emphasize that damage caused by the mistral is negligible compared to that caused by the English gale winds
(E) illustrate the severity of the effects of the mistral on people

16. The word "baleful" in line 21 most nearly means

(A) lonely
(B) ambitious
(C) sprightly
(D) menacing
(E) rambunctious

17. In line 26 the author implies that "the gales that come off the English Channel"

(A) prevent most nautical vessels from reaching their destination
(B) can combine with a mistral and cause unimaginable havoc across the European countryside
(C) have greater force than their French counterparts
(D) bend the rain into horizontal streams only under certain storm conditions
(E) cause damage only around the English Channel

GO ON TO THE NEXT PAGE

18. The "clucking sound of disapproval" (line 50) made by Monsieur Menicucci signifies his

(A) belief that the plumbing installation was inappropriate for the climate conditions
(B) disdain for the English visitors
(C) opinion of his assistant's work ethic
(D) preference for the warmer winters of the coast
(E) sense that the plumbing in Cannes and Nice is superior to that in Provence

19. The author implies that Monsieur Menicucci offers the "token two seconds" (line 66)

(A) as an effrontery to the author whose opinion was not regarded with sufficient consideration
(B) in sincere hope that the author might be able to shed some light on the mystery
(C) simply as a courtesy, since Menicucci believes he can provide the definitive theory on the phenomenon's cause
(D) in confusion, momentarily forgetting what he had been discussing
(E) to reveal his own respect for the mistral's capacity for destruction

20. Which of the following best describes Menicucci's theory about the earth's crust?

(A) The burst pipes were the result of the increased velocity of the mistral.
(B) Siberia is gradually moving closer to Provence.
(C) The presence of wind in most regions is completely determined by the curvature of the earth.
(D) Wind slows down across a flat plain, since it wants to change directions.
(E) A deviation in the earth's shape results in changes in weather patterns.

21. The author's comment *"Mais oui"* suggests the author regards Menicucci as a

(A) highly educated thinker whose theory is provocative
(B) confused character who cannot adequately articulate his ideas
(C) plumber whose grasp of the English language is impressive
(D) slightly pompous comic figure who perceives himself to be overly knowledgeable
(E) deceitful man interested in misleading the author into believing fanciful tales

22. Which of the following can be inferred from the passage?

I. The author's house in Provence had a swimming pool.
II. The author was born in England.
III. The first mistral that the author experienced lasted for fifteen days.

(A) None of the above
(B) I only
(C) III only
(D) I and II only
(E) I, II, and III

23. The tone of the passage can best be described as

(A) passionate
(B) exasperated
(C) anecdotal
(D) argumentative
(E) sentimental

24. Which of the following does the passage imply about Cannes?

(A) It is a coastal city.
(B) It shares a border with Nice.
(C) It is a popular tourist destination.
(D) It typically has harsher winters than does Provence.
(E) It is the hometown of Monsieur Menicucci.

STOP

If you finish before time is called, you may check your work on this section only. Do not turn to any other section in the test.

NO TEST MATERIAL ON THIS PAGE.

GO ON TO THE NEXT PAGE

SECTION 8
Time — 20 minutes
19 Questions

Turn to Section 8 of your answer sheet to answer the questions in this section.

Directions: For each question in this section, select the best answer from among the choices given and fill in the corresponding circle on the answer sheet.

Each sentence below has one or two blanks, each blank indicating that something has been omitted. Beneath the sentence are five words or sets of words labeled A through E. Choose the word or set of words that, when inserted in the sentence, best fits the meaning of the sentence as a whole.

Example:

Desiring to ------- his taunting friends, Mitch gave them taffy in hopes it would keep their mouths shut.

(A) eliminate (B) satisfy (C) overcome (D) ridicule (E) silence

Ⓐ Ⓑ Ⓒ Ⓓ ●

1. Upon learning that she had won the grand prize instead of just any prize, her initial joy turned into -------.

   (A) apathy (B) euphoria (C) spontaneity (D) contention (E) misery

2. The increased humidity coupled with oppressively high temperatures made us feel ------- at the beach this summer.

   (A) earnest (B) animated (C) resilient (D) exotic (E) listless

3. Anthropologists had long assumed that hunter-gatherers moved continually in their search for food; however, recent findings indicate that during the Mesolithic period, such groups were often quite -------.

   (A) prudent (B) credulous (C) industrious (D) indigent (E) sedentary

4. Since none of the original doors or windows of the Mayan Indian homes have survived, restoration work on these portions of the buildings has been largely -------.

   (A) exquisite (B) impertinent (C) speculative (D) decorous (E) abstract

5. The council was divided into such strong factions that it was almost impossible to garner ------- support to pass the bill.

   (A) biased (B) strenuous (C) bureaucratic (D) bipartisan (E) unnecessary

6. The boys expected to be admonished for their -------, so it was no surprise when they were severely ------- by their parents.

   (A) proficiency . . censured
   (B) magnanimity . . beguiled
   (C) dilemma . . esteemed
   (D) roguery . . nonplussed
   (E) impishness . . castigated

GO ON TO THE NEXT PAGE

Directions: Each passage below is followed by questions based on its content. Answer the questions on the basis of what is stated or implied in each passage and in any introductory material that may be provided.

Questions 7–19 are based on the following passages.

The following passages deal with the question of air pollution. Passage 1 gives a broad historical overview, and Passage 2 discusses one type of pollutant.

Passage 1

Even before there were people, there were cases of air pollution. Volcanoes erupted, spewing ash and poisonous gases into the atmosphere. There were dust storms. Gases collected over marshes. When people appeared on the scene and began their conquest of nature, they also began to pollute the air. They cleared land, which made possible even larger dust storms. They built cities, and the soot from their hearths and the stench from their waste filled the air. The Roman author Seneca wrote in A.D. 61 of the "stink, soot and heavy air" of the imperial city. In 1257, the Queen of England was forced to move away from the city of Nottingham because the heavy smoke was unendurable.

The Industrial Revolution brought even worse air pollution. Coal was burned to power factories and to heat homes. Soot, smoke, and sulfur dioxide filled the air. The good old days? Not in the factory towns. But there were large rural areas unaffected by air pollution.

With increasing population, the entire world is becoming more urban. It is the huge megalopolises that are most affected by air pollution. But rural areas are not unaffected. In the neighborhoods around smoky factories, there is evidence of increased rates of spontaneous abortion and of poor wool quality in sheep, decreased egg production and high mortality in chickens, and increased food and care required for cattle. The giant Ponderosa pines are dying over a hundred miles from the smog-plagued Los Angeles basin. Orbiting astronauts visually traced drifting blobs of Los Angeles smog as far east as western Colorado. Other astronauts, more than 100 kilometers up, were able to see the plume of smoke from the Four Corners power plant near Farmington, New Mexico. This was the only evidence from that distance that Earth is inhabited.

Traffic police in Tokyo have to wear gas masks and take "oxygen breaks"—breathing occasionally from tanks of oxygen. Smog in Athens at times has forced factory closings and traffic restrictions. Acid rain in Canada is spawned by air pollution in the United States, contributing to strained relationships between the two countries. Sydney, Rome, Tehran, Ankara, Mexico City, and most other major cities in the world have had frightening episodes of air pollution.

Passage 2

One of the two major types of smog—consisting of smoke, fog, sulfur dioxide, sulfuric acid, ash, and soot—is called London smog. Indeed, the word smog is thought to have originated in England in 1905 as a contraction of the words "smoke" and "fog."

Probably the most notorious case of smog in history started in London on Thursday, 4 December, 1952. A large cold air mass moved into the valley of the Thames River. A temperature inversion placed a blanket of warm air over the cold air. With nightfall, a dense fog and below-freezing temperatures caused the people of London to heap coal into their small stoves. Millions of these fires burned throughout the night, pouring sulfur dioxide and smoke into the air. The next day, Friday, the people continued to burn coal when the temperature remained below freezing. The factories added their smoke and chemical fumes to the atmosphere.

Saturday was a day of darkness. For twenty miles around London, no light came through the smog. The air was cold and still. And the coal fires continued to burn throughout the weekend. On Monday, 8 December, more than one hundred people died of heart attacks while trying desperately to breathe. The city's hospitals were overflowing with patients with respiratory diseases.

By the time a breeze cleared the air on Tuesday, 9 December, more than 4,000 deaths had been attributed to the smog. This is more people than were ever killed in any single tornado, mine disaster, shipwreck, or airplane crash. This is more people than were killed in the attack on Pearl Harbor in 1941. Air pollution episodes may not be as dramatic as other disasters, but they can be just as deadly.

Soot and ash can be removed by electrostatic precipitators. These devices induce an electric charge on the particles, which then are attracted to oppositely charged plates and deposited. Unfortunately, electrostatic precipitators use large amounts of electricity, and the electrical energy has to come from somewhere. Fly ash removed from the air has to be put on the land or water, although it could be used in some way. Increasingly, fly ash is being used to replace part of the clay in making cement.

The elimination of sulfur dioxide is more difficult. Low-sulfur coal is scarce and expensive. The most plentiful fuel that exists is low-grade, high-sulfur coal. Pilot runs have shown that sulfur can be washed from finely pulverized coal, but the process is expensive. There are also processes for converting dirty coal to clean liquid and gaseous fuels. These processes may hold promise for the future, but they are too expensive to compete economically with other fuels at present. They also waste a part of the coal's energy.

GO ON TO THE NEXT PAGE

7. Passage 1 implies that air pollution
   (A) was originally caused by the Industrial Revolution
   (B) affects only urban areas
   (C) has natural as well as manmade causes
   (D) will never be eliminated through the use of better fuels because they are too expensive
   (E) seriously affects the nervous systems of both people and animals

8. The author of Passage 1 uses both the Roman author Seneca and the Queen of England (lines 9–12) as evidence that
   (A) civilization has necessarily caused air pollution
   (B) air pollution has always existed in cities
   (C) urban air pollution is not just a modern problem
   (D) humanity disregards its environment
   (E) recently, the level of air pollution has risen dramatically

9. According to the author of Passage 1, air pollution problems of today differ from those of the Industrial Revolution and before in that
   (A) remote communities may now feel the effects of air pollution regardless of their proximity to the source of the pollution
   (B) today's polluted factory towns were once clean rural communities unaffected by urban air pollution
   (C) modern urban areas are no longer more polluted than the suburban and rural communities that surround them
   (D) the use of coal as fuel has greatly increased the number of cities and megalopolises that are contributing to the world's air pollutants
   (E) modern disasters caused by incidents of extreme air pollution cause far more damage than they did hundreds of years ago

10. The orbiting astronauts are discussed by the author (lines 26–32) in order to
   (A) demonstrate the increased urbanization of modern civilization
   (B) prove that air pollution is an inevitable consequence of human progress
   (C) support the claim that pollution has become the defining characteristic of modern society
   (D) provide evidence that pollution is no longer restricted to urban areas
   (E) further the argument that large urban areas are most affected by air pollution

11. The last paragraph of Passage 1 suggests that air pollution causes all of the following EXCEPT
   (A) difficulties in international relations
   (B) otherwise unnecessary closings of businesses
   (C) changes in the quality of some water
   (D) changes in work habits
   (E) high levels of lung disease

12. The author of Passage 2 discusses the 1952 outbreak of London smog in order to
   (A) demonstrate that smog has serious effects that are not controllable by human action
   (B) point out that air pollution is a major threat to human health only over a long period of time
   (C) describe an example of the lethal potential of air pollution
   (D) support the claim that air pollution must be controlled
   (E) prove that the toxic effects of air pollution are far worse in Europe than in the United States

13. According to Passage 2, London smog can best be described as
   (A) a deadly type of air pollution that cannot be completely eliminated
   (B) a phenomenon responsible for more deaths than from any other natural cause
   (C) a threat to human health that we are often unaware of
   (D) a combination of fog conditions and heavy accumulations of smoke from fossil fuel fires
   (E) a new, mostly uninvestigated, type of air pollution

14. The statistics cited in lines 64–70 imply that
   (A) any effects of a serious air pollution episode cannot be seen until some time after the episode
   (B) in the short run, air pollution produces more traumatic health problems than other disasters
   (C) most of the fatalities from air pollution do not occur during an air pollution episode
   (D) air pollution episodes can be among the most devastating types of disasters
   (E) it is impossible to know the total death rate from a given episode of air pollution

GO ON TO THE NEXT PAGE

15. Passage 2 suggests that electrostatic precipitators work by a process in which

(A) electricity is attracted to particles
(B) charged particles are attracted to plates with the opposite charge
(C) a large amount of electricity ionizes the air
(D) induction acts on charged particles
(E) ash and soot are naturally charged particles

16. The author of Passage 2 believes that the removal of sulfur dioxide from air pollution is difficult because

(A) the technology to remove sulfur dioxide is only currently in development
(B) any successful process utilizes more natural resources than it produces
(C) sulfur is made up of very resilient molecules that cannot be broken down easily
(D) sulfur is a basic compound in all fuels that are currently used
(E) the available methods are costly and involve some waste

17. It can be inferred that the author of Passage 1 would agree with which statement about the cost of pollution control discussed in Passage 2?

(A) Society must be prepared to spend whatever it takes to eliminate all forms of air pollution.
(B) The cost of pollution control is too high to make it economically efficient with current technology.
(C) The more we are concerned with limiting the effects of pollution, the less we will be able to eliminate the sources of pollution.
(D) Dealing with pollution can be a significant challenge for urban populations.
(E) The cost of pollution control is much higher than the cost of changing to better energy sources.

18. Which factor mentioned in Passage 1 most likely contributed to the environmental disaster described in Passage 2?

(A) The Industrial Revolution
(B) Natural sources of air pollution
(C) Land clearing
(D) Heavy smoke from Nottingham
(E) Improper disposal of solid waste

19. Which of the following is NOT a difference that exists between the two passages?

(A) Passage 1 views air pollution as a timeworn problem and gives historical contexts to show its permanence in human society past and present while Passage 2 focuses only on the modern era.
(B) Passage 2 focuses on the effect of air pollution on urban populations while Passage 1 discusses the effect it has had on both urban and rural areas.
(C) Passage 2 uses one historical example to illustrate the dangers of air pollution while Passage 1 uses several historical examples.
(D) Passage 1 recognizes the Industrial Revolution as a major factor in air pollution while Passage 2 contends that it was no worse than other factors.
(E) Passage 2 provides the reader with possible methods for preventing or treating polluted air while Passage 1 does not.

STOP

If you finish before time is called, you may check your work on this section only. Do not turn to any other section in the test.

SECTION 9
Time — 20 minutes
16 Questions

Turn to Section 9 of your answer sheet to answer the questions in this section.

Directions: For this section, solve each problem and decide which is the best of the choices given. Fill in the corresponding circle on the answer sheet. You may use any available space for scratchwork.

Notes

1. The use of a calculator is permitted.
2. All numbers used are real numbers.
3. Figures that accompany problems in this test are intended to provide information useful in solving the problems. They are drawn as accurately as possible EXCEPT when it is stated in a specific problem that the figure is not drawn to scale. All figures lie in a plane unless other wise indicated.
4. Unless otherwise specified, the domain of any function f is assumed to be the set of all real numbers x for which $f(x)$ is a real number.

Reference Information

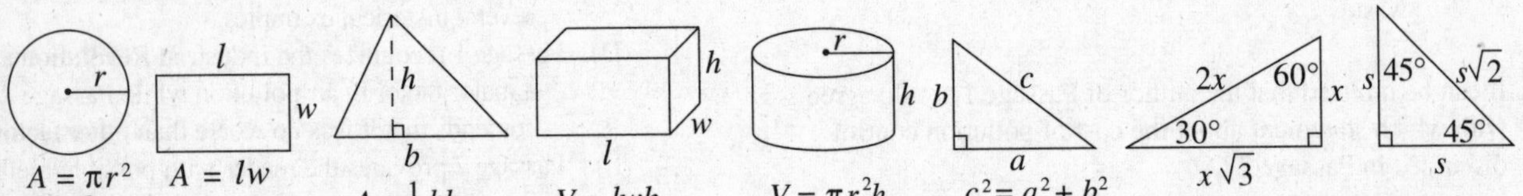

$A = \pi r^2$ $\quad C = 2\pi r$ $\quad A = lw$ $\quad A = \frac{1}{2}bh$ $\quad V = lwh$ $\quad V = \pi r^2 h$ $\quad c^2 = a^2 + b^2$

Special Right Triangles

The number of degrees of arc in a circle is 360.

The sum of the measures in degrees of the angles of a triangle is 180.

1. Which of the following represents the statement "the sum of the squares of x and y is equal to the square root of the difference of x and y"?

(A) $x^2 + y^2 = \sqrt{x - y}$

(B) $x^2 - y^2 = \sqrt{x + y}$

(C) $(x + y)^2 = \sqrt{x} - \sqrt{y}$

(D) $\sqrt{x + y} = (x - y)^2$

(E) $\sqrt{x} + \sqrt{y} = x^2 - y^2$

2. If $3a + 2b + c = 22$, $b + c = 8$, and $c = 6$, what is the value of $a + b + c$?

(A) 4
(B) 8
(C) 12
(D) 18
(E) 36

GO ON TO THE NEXT PAGE

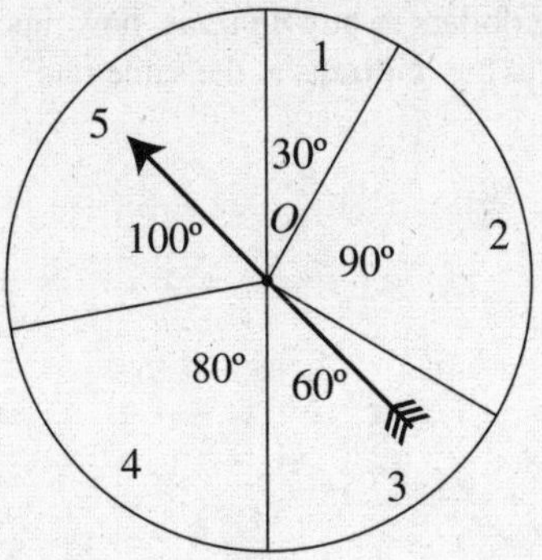

3. In the ABC board game, the circular spinner centered at *O* shown in the figure above is used to determine how far a player's piece will advance on the board during a given turn. After each spin, the arrow points in a random direction, and the number printed in the region where the arrow points gives the number of spaces a piece will advance. What is the probability that Kim's piece will advance 3 or 4 spaces during her turn?

(A) $\frac{11}{18}$

(B) $\frac{7}{18}$

(C) $\frac{2}{9}$

(D) $\frac{1}{6}$

(E) $\frac{1}{18}$

4. If x and y are integers such that $4x - 8 > 0$ and $4y + 8 < 0$, then which of the following must be true?

(A) xy is even.
(B) xy is odd.
(C) xy is negative.
(D) xy is positive.
(E) xy is equal to zero.

5. A rectangle with length 16 and width 6 has an area that is 3 times the area of a triangle with height 8. What is the length of the base of the triangle?

(A) 4
(B) 8
(C) 12
(D) 16
(E) 22

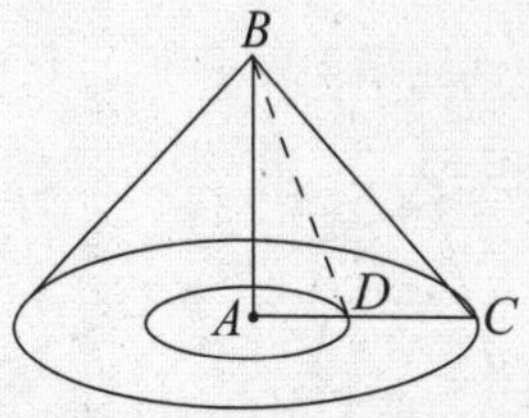

Note: Figure not drawn to scale.

6. A right circular cone is drawn above, with two circles centered at *A* on its base as shown. *AB* is the height of the cone, the measure of $\angle ABC$ is 60°, and $\overline{BC}$ has a length of *y*. If $\overline{BD}$ bisects $\angle ABC$, which of the following gives the area of the smaller circle in terms of *y* ?

(A) $8\pi\sqrt{y}$

(B) $4\pi\sqrt{y}$

(C) $y\pi$

(D) $\frac{\pi}{4}y^2$

(E) $\frac{\pi}{12}y^2$

GO ON TO THE NEXT PAGE

7. During the past week, a factory produced 10,000 computer disks, of which 30 were found to be defective. At this rate, if the factory produced 1,000,000 computer disks, approximately how many would be defective?

(A) 3
(B) 30
(C) 300
(D) 3,000
(E) 30,000

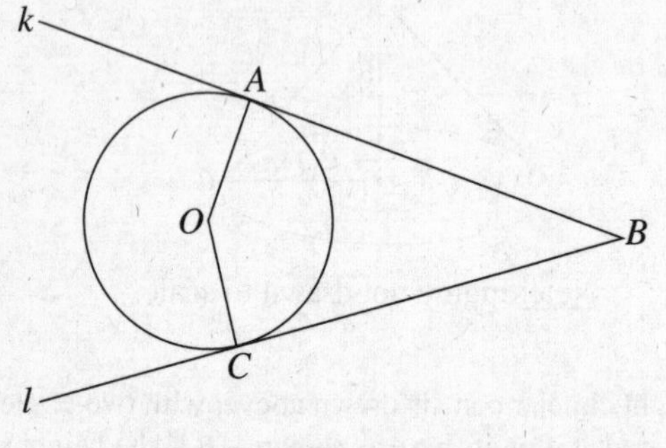

Note: Figure not drawn to scale.

8. In the figure above, lines k and l are tangent to the circle with center O at points A and C, respectively. If $OB = 4$, $OA = AB$, $AB = BC$, and $\overline{OA} \perp \overline{OC}$ then $OA =$

(A) $\sqrt{2}$
(B) 2
(C) $2\sqrt{2}$
(D) 4
(E) $4\sqrt{2}$

9. If it costs z dollars to buy n pizzas, how much will it cost, in dollars, to buy b pizzas at the same rate?

(A) $\frac{zb}{n}$

(B) $\frac{b}{zn}$

(C) $\frac{nb}{z}$

(D) $\frac{zn}{b}$

(E) znb

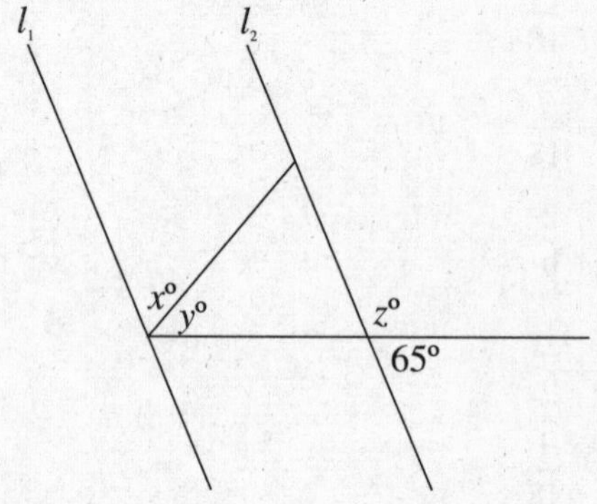

10. In the figure above, if $l_1 \parallel l_2$ and $x = 55$, then $y + z =$

(A) 120
(B) 145
(C) 175
(D) 180
(E) 195

GO ON TO THE NEXT PAGE

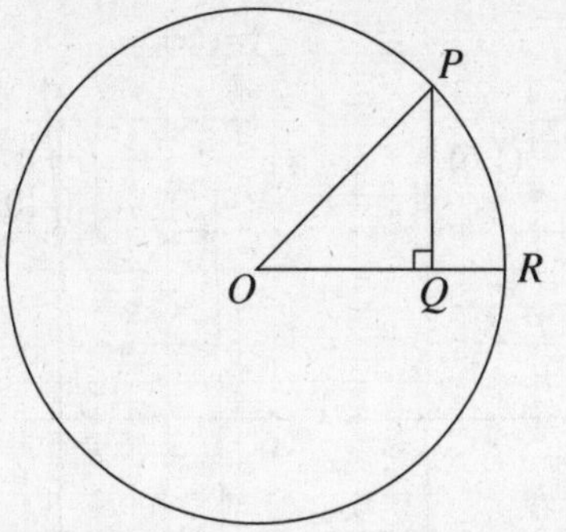

Note: Figure not drawn to scale.

11. In the circle above with center O, $OQ = QR$. If the radius of the circle is 8, what is the area of $\triangle OPQ$?

(A) 4
(B) $4\sqrt{3}$
(C) 8
(D) $8\sqrt{3}$
(E) 16

12. Eighty students went on a class trip. If there were fourteen more boys than girls on the trip, how many girls were on the trip?

(A) 26
(B) 33
(C) 40
(D) 47
(E) 66

13. For all x, let $f(x) = (10 - x)^2$. If $p = f(6)$, which of the following is equal to $4p$?

(A) $f(24)$
(B) $f(18)$
(C) $f(12)$
(D) $f(8)$
(E) $f(4)$

14. If b is a positive number not equal to 1, which of the following must also be positive?

(A) $\frac{b}{b+1}$

(B) $\frac{b+6}{b-3}$

(C) $\frac{1}{2b-2}$

(D) $2 - b$

(E) $2b - 1$

GO ON TO THE NEXT PAGE

15. What is the distance between the x-intercept and the y-intercept of the line $y = \frac{2}{3}x - 6$?

(A) 9

(B) 15

(C) $\sqrt{89}$ (approximately 9.43)

(D) $\sqrt{117}$ (approximately 10.82)

(E) $15 + \sqrt{117}$ (approximately 25.82)

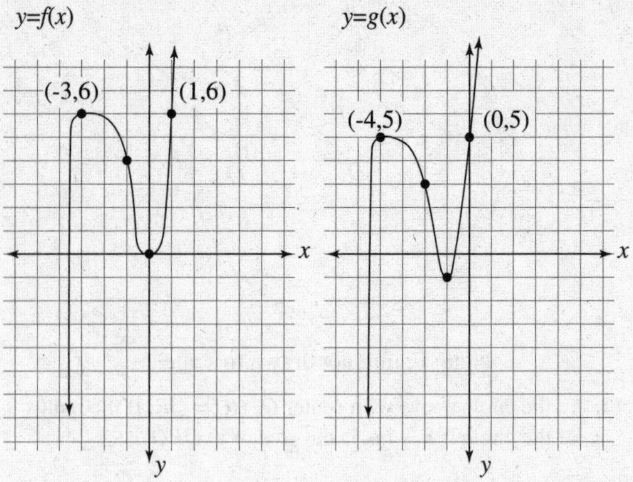

16. The figures above show the graphs of the functions f and g. The function f is defined by $f(x) = 2x^3 + 5x^2 - x$. The function g is defined by $g(x) = f(x - h) - k$, where h and k are constants. What is the value of hk ?

(A) –2
(B) –1
(C) 0
(D) 1
(E) 2

STOP

If you finish before time is called, you may check your work on this section only.
Do not turn to any other section in the test.

NO TEST MATERIAL ON THIS PAGE.

SECTION 10
Time — 10 minutes
14 Questions

Turn to Section 10 of your answer sheet to answer the questions in this section.

Directions: For each question in this section, select the best answer from among the choices given and fill in the corresponding circle on the answer sheet.

The following sentences test correctness and effectiveness of expression. Part of each sentence or the entire sentence is underlined; beneath each sentence are five ways of phrasing the underlined material. Choice A repeats the original phrasing; the other four choices are different. If you think the original phrasing produces a better sentence than any of the alternatives, select choice A; if not, select one of the other choices.

In making your selection, follow the requirements of standard written English; that is, pay attention to grammar, choice of words, sentence construction, and punctuation. Your selection should result in the most effective sentence—clear and precise, without awkwardness or ambiguity.

EXAMPLE:

Bobby Flay baked his first cake and he was thirteen years old then.
(A) and he was thirteen years old then
(B) when he was thirteen
(C) at age thirteen years old
(D) upon the reaching of thirteen years
(E) at the time when he was thirteen — Ⓐ ● Ⓒ Ⓓ Ⓔ

1. Theater doesn't allow much extra time, a fact with which Ryan is familiar being as he was in many different productions.

(A) being as he was
(B) as he has been
(C) seeing as how he will be
(D) being that he was
(E) because he will be

2. In order to follow the building code for commercial construction, all doors should be at least 3 feet wide and swing outward to allow wheelchair access.

(A) at least 3 feet wide and swing outward to allow wheelchair access
(B) at least 3 feet wide and swung outward to allow wheelchair access
(C) at least 3 feet wide and should be made to swing outward to allow wheelchair access
(D) at least 3 feet wide or wider and swing outward to allow wheelchair access
(E) at least 3 feet wide or wider and swung outward to allow wheelchair access

3. *On a Sunday Afternoon on the Island of the Grande Jatte*, a nineteenth-century pointillism masterpiece by Seurat, is one of the better examples of paintings created in this unique style.

(A) a nineteenth-century pointillism masterpiece by Seurat, is one of the better examples
(B) Seurat's pointillism masterpiece of the nineteenth-century can be one of the best examples
(C) a nineteenth-century pointillism masterpiece by Seurat, is to be one of the better examples
(D) Seurat's pointillism masterpiece, is one of the best examples in the nineteenth century
(E) a nineteenth-century pointillism masterpiece by Seurat, is one of the best examples

4. American etiquette is different from other countries in that it requires the recipients of compliments to accept them with thanks, rather than turn them aside with protest.

(A) other countries
(B) other countries are
(C) that of another country
(D) what another country is
(E) that of other countries

GO ON TO THE NEXT PAGE

5. Dr. Eglise's students were required to do a certain amount of preparation for each class: this being that they had to read an article he gave them and brainstorm ideas for an essay on the same topic.

(A) class: this being that they had to
(B) class, including
(C) class: they had to
(D) class, however having to
(E) class, and they had to not only

6. Renowned for her writing across several subjects and genres, Barbara Kingsolver's poems are impassioned denunciations of violence in Central America.

(A) genres, Barbara Kingsolver's poems are impassioned denunciations of
(B) genres; Barbara Kingsolver wrote poems that are impassioned denunciations of
(C) genres, Barbara Kingsolver writes poems which passionately denounce
(D) genres, the poems of Barbara Kingsolver poems passionately denounce
(E) genres; passionately denouncing is what Barbara Kingsolver's poems do to

7. The scientist allowed very few of his experiments to be published because his exacting standards caused him to question whether his findings were complete and able to be shown to the scientific community.

(A) because his exacting standards caused him to question
(B) as a result of his standards being exacting, he questioned
(C) having exacting standards causing him to question
(D) his standards being so exacting that he questioned
(E) because of his exacting standards, which causing him to question

8. Although the badger has a reputation as a fierce animal, it has a gentler side which is shown in several works of literature, these include *Cold Moons* by Aeron Clement and *Incident at Hawk's Hill* by Allen Eckert.

(A) literature, these include
(B) literature, two of these are
(C) literature, these being
(D) literature, such as
(E) literature, like

9. A majority of the girls in Toria's class wore sandals even on wintry days, however there was a great effort made by teachers and parents to discourage them from doing so.

(A) however there was a great effort made by teachers and parents
(B) along with great efforts made by the teachers and parents
(C) when even parents and teachers are making the effort
(D) despite great efforts made by teachers and parents
(E) even though great efforts by teachers and parents

10. After polling the parish, the church's roof committee voted to replace the slate tiles with asphalt shingles and they did this to save thousands of dollars.

(A) and they did this to
(B) and so it could
(C) they wanted to
(D) in order that they might
(E) in order to

11. A truck collided with Emma's car and, although she was uninjured, she could hardly stop trembling with fright.

(A) uninjured, she could hardly stop
(B) uninjured; she couldn't hardly stop
(C) uninjured, she couldn't hardly stop
(D) uninjured, since she couldn't stop
(E) uninjured, she could, however, hardly stop

12. Because of the danger of rabies within the state, this is the reason for the ban on transporting skunks and raccoons to open spaces across town lines.

(A) this is the reason for the ban on transporting skunks and raccoons to open spaces across town lines
(B) there is a ban on transporting skunks and raccoons to open spaces across town lines
(C) a ban on skunks and raccoons in open spaces across town lines has been declared
(D) a ban has been declared on skunks and raccoons openly across town lines
(E) it is the reason for the open ban to transport skunks and raccoons to spaces across town lines

GO ON TO THE NEXT PAGE

13. The population of Las Vegas, the fastest growing city in the United States, has increased by more than three times in the past hundred years.

(A) has increased by more than three times
(B) increased by more than three times
(C) was more than tripled
(D) has more than tripled
(E) had more than tripled

14. Several recent studies have indicated that a student's ability to seek help from their teachers predicts college success as well as a standardized test score does.

(A) to seek help from their teachers predicts
(B) in seeking help from their teachers and predicting
(C) to seek help from teachers predicts
(D) to seek help from his or her teachers always predicts
(E) to not only seek the help of teachers but also predict

STOP

If you finish before time is called, you may check your work on this section only.
Do not turn to any other section in the test.

NO TEST MATERIAL ON THIS PAGE.

PRACTICE TEST 3: ANSWER KEY

Section 2 Math	Section 3 Reading	Section 4 Writing	Section 5 Math	Section 6 Reading	Section 7 Reading (Exp)	Section 8 Reading	Section 9 Math	Section 10 Writing
1. A	1. A	1. A	1. A	1. E	1. C	1. B	1. A	1. B
2. E	2. D	2. E	2. D	2. B	2. A	2. E	2. C	2. A
3. A	3. A	3. D	3. A	3. B	3. A	3. E	3. B	3. E
4. D	4. B	4. C	4. D	4. A	4. D	4. C	4. C	4. E
5. B	5. C	5. B	5. E	5. E	5. E	5. D	5. B	5. C
6. E	6. E	6. D	6. E	6. C	6. D	6. E	6. E	6. C
7. A	7. C	7. A	7. C	7. D	7. B	7. C	7. D	7. A
8. A	8. D	8. B	8. A	8. B	8. C	8. C	8. C	8. D
9. E	9. C	9. C	9. 4	9. E	9. B	9. A	9. A	9. D
10. D	10. E	10. E	10. 1,600	10. C	10. B	10. D	10. C	10. E
11. A	11. B	11. E	11. 80	11. B	11. E	11. E	11. D	11. A
12. D	12. B	12. C	12. 34	12. E	12. D	12. C	12. B	12. B
13. B	13. E	13. D	13. 91	13. D	13. E	13. D	13. B	13. D
14. C	14. B	14. D	14. 1.65	14. D	14. B	14. D	14. A	14. C
15. E	15. A	15. C	15. $\frac{9}{25}$ or .36	15. E	15. E	15. B	15. D	
16. C	16. D	16. E	16. 8.93	16. E	16. D	16. E	16. B	
17. B	17. E	17. D	17. 2	17. A	17. C	17. D		
18. E	18. C	18. E	18. 9	18. E	18. A	18. A		
19. D	19. B	19. D		19. A	19. C	19. D		
20. C	20. E	20. E		20. D	20. E			
	21. E	21. A		21. C	21. D			
	22. B	22. B		22. D	22. B			
	23. A	23. B		23. A	23. C			
	24. D	24. B		24. E	24. A			
		25. A						
		26. C						
		27. E						
		28. B						
		29. D						
		30. D						
		31. B						
		32. A						
		33. E						
		34. A						
		35. C						

SAT SCORING WORKSHEET

For directions on how to score your SAT practice test, see pages 389–390. Section 7 is the unscored, Experimental section.

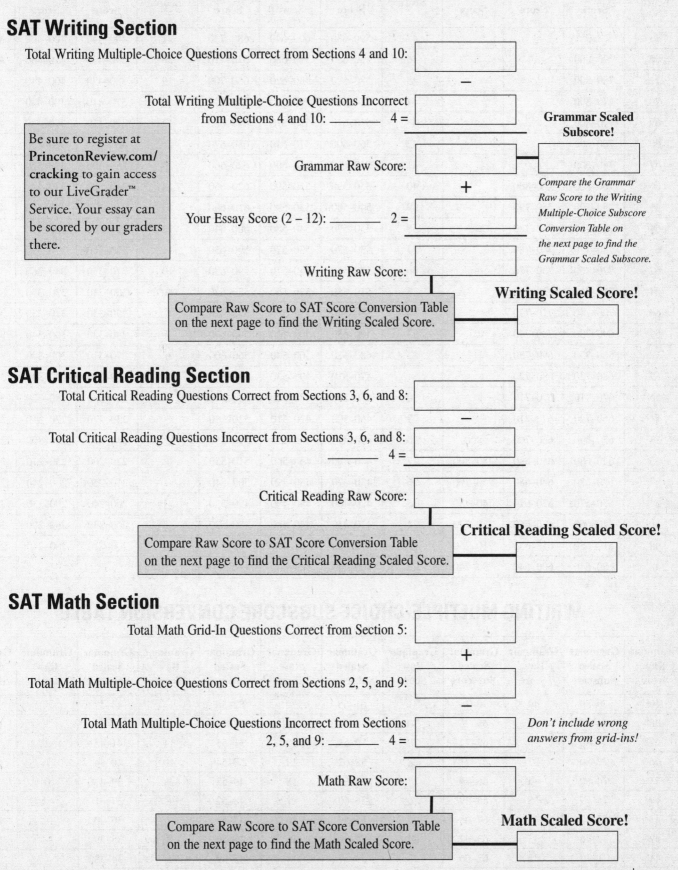

SAT Writing Section

Total Writing Multiple-Choice Questions Correct from Sections 4 and 10: ☐

−

Total Writing Multiple-Choice Questions Incorrect from Sections 4 and 10: ______ ÷ 4 = ☐

Be sure to register at **PrincetonReview.com/cracking** to gain access to our LiveGrader™ Service. Your essay can be scored by our graders there.

Grammar Raw Score: ☐

Grammar Scaled Subscore! ☐

Compare the Grammar Raw Score to the Writing Multiple-Choice Subscore Conversion Table on the next page to find the Grammar Scaled Subscore.

+

Your Essay Score (2 – 12): ______ × 2 = ☐

Writing Raw Score: ☐

Compare Raw Score to SAT Score Conversion Table on the next page to find the Writing Scaled Score.

Writing Scaled Score! ☐

SAT Critical Reading Section

Total Critical Reading Questions Correct from Sections 3, 6, and 8: ☐

−

Total Critical Reading Questions Incorrect from Sections 3, 6, and 8: ______ ÷ 4 = ☐

Critical Reading Raw Score: ☐

Compare Raw Score to SAT Score Conversion Table on the next page to find the Critical Reading Scaled Score.

Critical Reading Scaled Score! ☐

SAT Math Section

Total Math Grid-In Questions Correct from Section 5: ☐

+

Total Math Multiple-Choice Questions Correct from Sections 2, 5, and 9: ☐

−

Total Math Multiple-Choice Questions Incorrect from Sections 2, 5, and 9: ______ ÷ 4 = ☐

Don't include wrong answers from grid-ins!

Math Raw Score: ☐

Compare Raw Score to SAT Score Conversion Table on the next page to find the Math Scaled Score.

Math Scaled Score! ☐

SAT SCORE CONVERSION TABLE

Raw Score	Writing Scaled Score	Reading Scaled Score	Math Scaled Score	Raw Score	Writing Scaled Score	Reading Scaled Score	Math Scaled Score	Raw Score	Writing Scaled Score	Reading Scaled Score	Math Scaled Score
73	800			47	590–630	600–640	680–720	21	400–440	420–460	460–50
72	790–800			46	590–630	590–630	670–710	20	390–430	410–450	450–49
71	780–800			45	580–620	580–620	660–700	19	380–420	400–440	450–49
70	770–800			44	570–610	580–620	650–690	18	370–410	400–440	440–48
69	770–800			43	570–610	570–610	640–680	17	370–410	390–430	430–47
68	760–800			42	560–600	570–610	630–670	16	360–400	380–420	420–46
67	760–800	800		41	560–600	560–600	620–660	15	350–390	380–420	420–46
66	760–800	770–800		40	550–590	550–590	620–660	14	340–380	370–410	410–45
65	750–790	750–790		39	540–580	550–590	610–650	13	330–370	360–400	400–44
64	740–780	740–780		38	530–570	540–580	600–640	12	320–360	350–390	400–44
63	730–770	740–780		37	530–570	530–570	590–630	11	320–360	350–390	390–43
62	720–760	730–770		36	520–560	530–570	590–630	10	310–350	340–380	380–42
61	710–750	720–760		35	510–550	520–560	580–620	9	300–340	330–370	370–41
60	700–740	710–750		34	500–540	510–550	570–610	8	290–330	310–350	360–40
59	690–730	700–740		33	490–530	500–540	560–600	7	280–320	300–340	350–39
58	680–720	690–730		32	480–520	500–540	560–600	6	270–310	300–340	340–38
57	680–720	680–720		31	470–510	490–530	540–580	5	260–300	290–330	330–37
56	670–710	670–710		30	470–510	480–520	530–570	4	240–280	280–320	320–36
55	660–720	670–710		29	460–500	470–510	520–560	3	230–270	270–310	310–35
54	650–690	660–700	800	28	450–490	470–510	510–550	2	230–270	260–300	290–33
53	640–680	650–690	780–800	27	440–480	460–500	510–550	1	220–260	230–270	270–31
52	630–670	640–680	750–790	26	430–470	450–490	500–540	0	210–250	200–240	240–28
51	630–670	630–670	740–780	25	420–460	450–490	490–530	–1	200–240	200–230	220–26
50	620–660	620–660	730–770	24	410–450	440–480	480–520	–2	200–230	200–220	210–25
49	610–650	610–650	710–750	23	410–450	430–470	480–520	–3	200–220	200–210	200–24
48	600–640	600–640	700–740	22	400–440	420–460	470–510				

WRITING MULTIPLE-CHOICE SUBSCORE CONVERSION TABLE

Grammar Raw Score	Grammar Scaled Subscore	Grammar Raw Score	Grammar Scaled Subscore	Grammar Raw Score	Grammar Scaled Subscore	Grammar Raw Score	Grammar Scaled Subscore	Grammar Raw Score	Grammar Scaled Subscore	Grammar Raw Score	Grammar Scaled Subscore
49	79–80	40	70–74	31	61–65	22	52–56	13	43–47	4	33–37
48	78–80	39	69–73	30	60–64	21	52–56	12	42–46	3	31–35
47	78–80	38	68–72	29	59–63	20	51–55	11	41–45	2	28–32
46	77–80	37	67–71	28	58–62	19	50–54	10	40–44	1	26–30
45	76–80	36	66–70	27	57–61	18	49–53	9	39–43	0	23–27
44	75–79	35	65–69	26	56–60	17	48–52	8	37–41	–1	22–26
43	73–77	34	64–68	25	55–59	16	47–51	7	36–40	–2	21–25
42	72–76	33	63–67	24	54–58	15	46–50	6	35–39	–3	20–24
41	71–75	32	62–66	23	53–57	14	45–49	5	34–38		

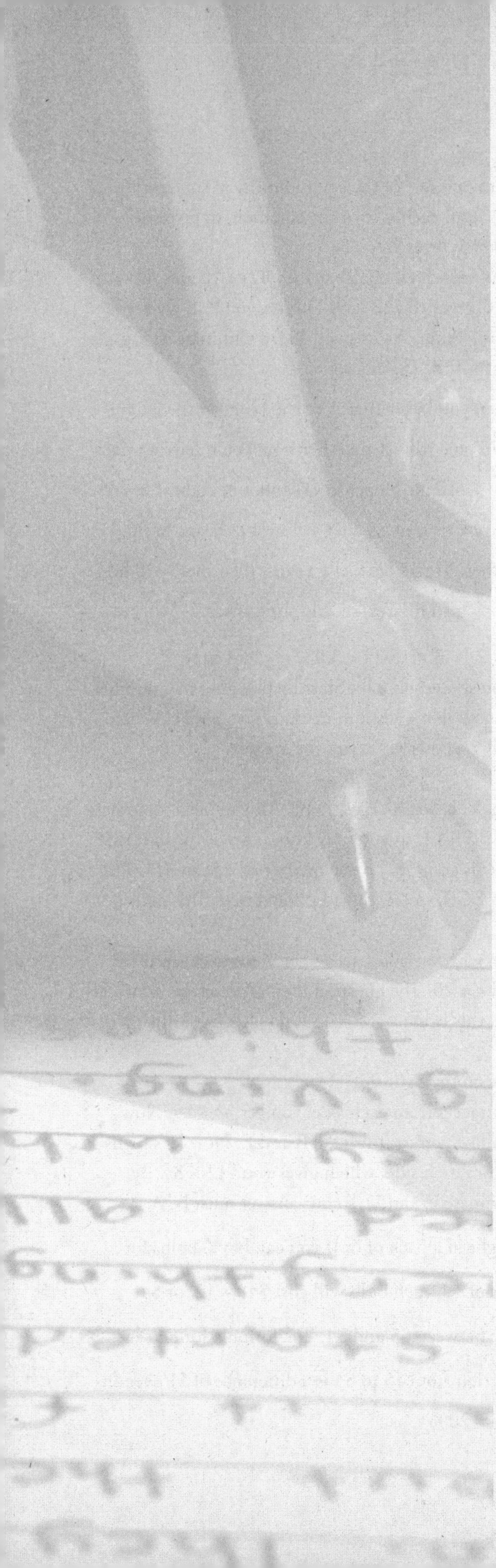

Chapter 24 Answers and Explanations for Practice Test 3

SECTION 2

1. **A** To solve for y, you should start by moving all the y's to one side of the equation. If you subtract $4y$ from each side, you get $8 = 8y + 24$. Now subtract 24 from each side of the equation, to give you $-16 = 8y$. Finally, you should divide each side by 8, which gives you $-2 = y$.

2. **E** Let's plug $x = 2$ and $x = 4$ into the answer choices, and see which choice makes $f(2) = 10$ and $f(4) = 44$. If you plug 2 into A, you get 10. B gives you 20. C gives you 18, and D gives you 8. E gives you 10; leave it in. Now plug in $x = 4$ into the choices that remain. A gives you 14, so eliminate it. E gives you 44. Only E works for both of our numbers, so it must be the answer.

3. **A** If the probability of picking a blue jelly bean is $\frac{1}{5}$, then you know that $\frac{1}{5}$ of the beans in the jar are blue. Let's try Plugging In the Answers. If there are 78 blue jelly beans, then you would have a total of $58 + 78 + 78 = 214$ beans in the jar. Is 78 equal to $\frac{1}{5}$ of 214? Nope, so C cannot be right. Let's try B. If there are 56 blue jelly beans, then you would have a total of $58 + 78 + 56 = 192$ beans in the jar. Is 56 equal to $\frac{1}{5}$ of 192? Nope. So let's try A. If there are 34 blue jelly beans, then there will be a total of $58 + 78 + 34 = 170$ jelly beans. Is 34 equal to $\frac{1}{5}$ of 170? Yes, so A is our answer.

4. **D** To find the 10th term of 3×2^n, plug 10 in for n: $3 \times 2^{10} = 3 \times 1{,}024 = 3{,}072$.

5. **B** Whenever you see variables in the answer choices, you should plug in. Start by plugging in a number for x. If $x = 10$, then 3 more than x is 13. Now you know that 13 is 2 more than y, so $y = 11$. When you plug in 11 for y in all of the answers, B is the only one that gives you the answer $x = 10$, your target answer.

6. **E** Don't assume that the figure $ABCD$ must be a rectangle; it doesn't have to be. All you need to do here is follow the rules: You know that $AB = BC$ and that $BC = 12$, so you now know two of the four sides (sides AB and BC) are equal to 12. You know that AD is going to be one quarter of AB, so AD must be equal to 3. Finally, you know that AD is one half of CD, so CD must be equal to 6. This makes the total perimeter $12 + 12 + 3 + 6$, or 33.

7. **A** Because it is much easier working with numbers than with variables, let's plug in some consecutive multiples of 5. Let's say that $a = 5$, $b = 10$, $c = 15$, and $d = 20$. The question then asks for the value of $(a - c)(d - b)$. Using the numbers you just plugged in, this becomes $(5 - 15)(20 - 10)$, or $(-10)(10)$, which equals -100.

8. **A** Let's take this one step at a time. First, just concentrate on the right side: $3b + 3 \leq 18$. You can simply treat this like an equation: If you subtract 3 from each side, you get $3b \leq 15$. Now you can divide each side by 3 to get $b \leq 5$. This will allow you to eliminate B and E. Now let's focus on the left side: $-9 \leq 3b + 3$. Again, let's subtract 3 from each side, which gives you $-12 \leq 3b$. By dividing each side by 3, you get $-4 \leq b$. This will eliminate C and D, so our answer must be A.

9. **E** Let's start by finding the amount per bulb when bought in a pack of 6: If you can buy 6 bulbs for \$30, then each bulb will cost \$30 ÷ 6, or \$5. In a box of 12, each bulb will cost \$48 ÷ 12, or \$4.

   Now you need to figure out the percentage difference between \$5 and \$4. The formula for percentage difference is $\frac{\textit{difference}}{\textit{original}} \times 100$. In this case, a reduction from \$5 to \$4 is a difference of \$1 over an original price of \$5. So the percentage difference is $\frac{1}{5} = 20\%$.

10. D Start by drawing out the towns. Let's call the towns *V, W, X, Y,* and *Z*. The problem states that the towns can't all be in a straight line, so draw them in a pentagon. Now connect the towns together. From the first town, *V*, the cartographer would have to measure 4 distances: *VW, VX, VY,* and *VZ*. From town *W*, she would have to measure only 3 distances, because she has already measured the distance from *V* to *W*: *WX, WY,* and *WZ*. From town *X* she would have to measure 2 distances: *XY* and *XZ*, and from town *Y* should have to measure the last distance, *YZ*. In total, she measured 10 distances between towns.

11. A Remember that the mode is the number that appears most often in a list. The number that appears most often (17 times) in the rainfall chart is 0.

12. D If you add up the amount of rainfall accounted for in the chart, you get:

5 days of 1 inch = 5 total inches of rain
3 days of 2 inches = 6 total inches of rain
3 days of 3 inches = 9 total inches of rain
2 days of 4 inches = 8 total inches of rain

for a grand total of 28 inches. If you expect 200 inches in a year, what percent of 200 is 28 inches? Translate this into algebra as $\frac{x}{100} \bullet 200 = 28$, and you get $x = 14\%$.

13. B First, find the slope of line *l* by using the slope formula: $\frac{y_1 - y_2}{x_1 - x_2} = \frac{5-2}{4-3} = \frac{3}{1}$. A line perpendicular to line *l* must have a slope that is the negative reciprocal of *l*'s slope. So, its slope should be $-\frac{1}{3}$. In the standard line equation $y = mx + b$, m is the slope. Only B has a slope of $-\frac{1}{3}$. If you didn't remember the rule about the slope of perpendicular lines, you could have sketched out each of the lines and looked for the answer that looked perpendicular to *l*.

14. C Choices B and D have negative values, so you can eliminate them right away. Start with the area of the whole figure. The square has sides of 2, so its area is 4. Now let's remove the area of the two semicircles (which is the same as the area of one whole circle). These semicircles have a radius of 1, so the area of one whole circle will be π. So the area of the shaded region will be $4 - \pi$.

15. E Let's plug in the answer choices, starting with C. twenty minutes is $\frac{1}{3}$ of an hour, so (using *rate × time = distance*) Jennifer ran $6 \times \frac{1}{3} = 2$ miles to school. If she returned at 4 miles per hour, you can find the time for her return trip using the formula $4 \times t = 2$. Her return time is $\frac{1}{2}$ hour, or 30 minutes. Her total time is supposed to be one hour, but here it's only 50 minutes. Eliminate A, B, and C because they're too small. Let's skip to E; that multiple of 6 looks like it will work better with time units than 22. Twenty-four minutes is $\frac{2}{5}$ of an hour, so Jennifer ran $6 \times \frac{2}{5} = 2.4$ miles to school. If she returned at 4 miles per hour, you can find the time for her return trip using $4 \times t = 2.4$. Her return time is $\frac{3}{5}$ of an hour, or 36 minutes. Her total time is indeed one hour, so E is the answer.

16. C Because $\overline{AC}$ and $\overline{AB}$ are each radii of the circle, you know they are equal in length. This means that the triangle ABC must be isosceles, and the base and the height are equal. What base and height would give the triangle an area of 18? The base and height would each have to equal 6, because $\frac{1}{2} \times 6 \times 6 = 18$. Because the circumference of the circle is equal to $2\pi r$, the circumference will be equal to 12π.

17. B Plugging In the Answers is the easiest way to solve this problem. If the radius is 4, then the area, πr^2, is 16π, and the circumference, $2\pi r$, is 8π. The area using the value in C is *twice* the circumference, not half. In order to make the area smaller, try B. If the radius is 1, then the area is π and the circumference is 2π. This is what the problem asks for! B must be the correct answer.

18. E The statement tells you that Marta will get the project completed on time. You don't know if other people could get the project done on time. You cannot conclude A, B, C, or D because there could be other people that also get projects completed on time. Also, for B, Marta could be assigned to both Project B and Project A. You can conclude E: If the project is not on time, then Marta could not have been assigned to it because if Marta were assigned to it, the project would be on time.

19. D You know that any two sides of a triangle must add up to be larger than the third side. This means that whatever the third side of the triangle is, its value + 5 must be larger than 7. This means that the third side must be larger than 2. Because the question specifies that the third side has an integer value, the smallest integer larger than 2 is 3. So the third side will measure 3, and the perimeter will be $3 + 5 + 7 = 15$.

20. C A good rule of thumb on the SAT is: If it looks like a quadratic equation, try to make it into a quadratic equation. If you try to solve for x, the best way is to move 12 to the same side of the equation, and then factor. $x^2 - x - 12 = 0$ will factor as $(x - 4)(x + 3)$. This means that x could be 4 or -3. You can factor for y in the same way, so y could also be 4 or -3. The greatest value for $x - y$ will be if $x = 4$ and $y = -3$, which is a difference of 7.

SECTION 3

1. A For the second blank, a good clue is *rather quiet* combined with the trigger *while.* This tells you that whatever comes in the second blank must mean that she was the opposite of *rather quiet*; in fact, she must have liked being around people. You can eliminate B, C, D, and E, leaving only A.

2. D Even if you can't find an exact word for the first blank, you can probably tell that it's going to be a negative word because of the clues *serious* and *natural weather patterns cannot.* This makes it likely that the first blank is discussing a problem with meteorology. This will allow you to eliminate A, C, and E. What might be a problem with meteorology? Probably if natural weather patterns cannot be "studied" or "created" in a lab. This will eliminate B, and makes D our best answer.

3. A In this sentence the second blank has a better clue, so you should start there. The clue is *imaginary* and the trigger *or* tells you that the blank is the opposite of *imaginary.* A good word for the blank is "real" or "not imaginary." You can eliminate B, C, and D. For the first blank, what kind of word would describe what a playwright could do to make the audience uncertain? That playwright might combine realism and fantasy. Conversely, if the playwright *exposed realism* and *fantasy,* why would you be unable to tell fantasy from reality? Therefore, eliminate E; A is our best answer.

4. **B** The key to this question is the semicolon; this trigger tells you that whatever follows the semicolon describes the word in the blank. What follows says that the exterior of the car is different but the interior is the same. A good phrase for the blank is "on the surface." B is the closest.

5. **C** This sentence may seem to lack a good clue. That is because the clue is the relationship between the two blanks. In this case, *virtually disregarding the idea that* indicates that they need to be opposites; either educators view it as bad while it actually has the power to be good, or educators view it as good while ignoring the fact that it can be bad. Knowing this, you can eliminate any answer pairs whose words are not strongly opposed—choices such as A, B, D, and E. The only answer that contains two strongly opposed words is C.

6. **E** In this sentence, the clue is *convincing her readers to believe.* This means that she must be able to create extremely "believable" characters. E comes closest to this meaning.

7. **C** From the clue that *more recent works…introduce fewer problems*, you know that the first blank should describe a problem of seventeenth-century literature—a word like "difficult" for readers. This eliminates A and E. For the second blank, you will need to say that the *more recent works* are not difficult for readers. B and D don't really have anything to do with reading, so our best answer is C.

8. **D** The clue in this sentence is *who gave generous holiday bonuses and often overlooked minor lapses in judgment.* A word to describe someone like this is "kind" or "generous." This easily eliminates A, B, and C, which are negative words. *Gregarious* and *munificent* come close, as both are positive words, but *gregarious* means social and *munificent* means generous, making D the best choice.

9. **C** With questions that ask you about the structure of a passage, try to match the description to the specifics of the passage. For A, the meteor theory is not explained in depth. How much depth can you have in one paragraph? Remember to watch out for extreme words or answer choices that don't make common sense. Eliminate A. There is no mention of *inaccurate data,* as mentioned in B, so you can eliminate it. Only one flaw of the first theory is mentioned in the paragraph, so you need to eliminate D because it talks about *many flaws.* The people who support the first theory are barely mentioned and never criticized, so eliminate E. The structure of the passage is most similar to C.

10. **E** Before answering a main idea question, always state the main idea in your own words. The author's main point is that there is a flaw in the current theory of dinosaur extinction leading to a revised theory. A and C are too narrow and not about *why* the dinosaurs died out. Eliminate them. D is too extreme; you do not know if this *conclusively* explains *what caused the extinction of the dinosaurs.* Eliminate it. You now have two choices, B and E. When you have it down to two, look for what makes one of the answers wrong. The author never says that the original theory is totally wrong, but rather that there is a flaw in it. This makes B extreme because it says that the passage thoroughly disproves the current theory. Eliminate B and choose E.

11. **B** The author introduces Jefferson and Franklin as examples of famous American figures whom you might have thought had written the Pledge of Allegiance, whereas the Pledge's true author is not well known. A is close, but says that Jefferson and Franklin could have written a *better* pledge, and the author never says that. Eliminate it. C, D, and E are not supported by the passage and were not the point of the sentence that mentions Franklin and Jefferson.

12. **B** Remember that in an inference question you need to find an answer that is supported by the passage. B is supported by the sentence that mentions that there were *later revisions* that *added the words "under God."* You have no information on A, C, or E, so eliminate them. D is true, but is never mentioned in the passage. Don't use outside information to answer the questions on this test.

13. **E** This is a line reference question, so you should read these lines in context to find the answer. You know that Penfield believed *brain studies...would lead inevitably to an understanding of the mind.* The correct answer is a paraphrase of this idea. E says exactly this.

14. **B** Pribram's and Bohm's collaboration is discussed in paragraph 5. Reread the paragraph and then use POE. A, C, D, and E may sound tempting but none of them are actually stated. B is a nice, general choice, which sums up the scientists' intentions.

15. **A** For a vocab-in-context question like this one, you should cross out the word *bent,* reread the sentence, and put your own word in the blank. In this sentence, you would probably insert a word like "belief" or "inclination." The word that best fits this idea is A.

16. **D** *Peter Pan school of neuroscience* is mentioned in paragraph 8. If you read the rest of the paragraph for context, you see that the point of the paragraph is that researchers become disillusioned with claims that the mind can *be explained* in terms of brain functioning. Which choice best paraphrases this idea? D does.

17. **E** Unorthodox research is mentioned at the beginning of paragraph 9. There it states that unorthodox researchers were open to *innovative attitudes* and *transcendental influences.* E paraphrases this idea.

18. **C** The best answer is C. If you replace the word *waxing* with a blank, the sentence says *a small number of them end up ------- philosophical* and "becoming" is the only choice that fits sensibly into the sentence. The other words all relate to the word *waxing* but do not make sense in this context.

19. **B** In paragraph 4, Dr. Penfield changes *the solid line connecting the spirit and brain into an interrupted one.* A, C, and E were all painted on the rock mentioned in D but did not signify his doubts. B is the best answer.

20. **E** The best answer is E. The wording in this choice is too extreme and thus appropriate for a NOT answer; the passage focuses on scientists who came to believe that brain studies could NOT explain fully the mind's workings. A appears in lines 73–75, and in B, *not unwilling* means willing; the passage focuses on scientists willing to *adapt innovative attitudes as well as pursue unorthodox lines of inquiry.* In C, the five scientists mentioned in the first half of this article are *brain researchers [who] have a change of heart late in their careers.* D appears in lines 24-27.

21. **E** Brain-injured patients such as those in A are not mentioned in the passage, nor are the type of questions patients asked Penfield. *Impulses* in the passage refers to electrical impulses applied to parts of the brain, C, not to actions. Patients reported experiences that were not happening at the time, not ones that had never taken place, D. The best answer is E..

22. **B** The best answer is B, as stated in lines 32–34. The wordings in answer choices A, *prove definitively,* C, *fully explained,* and E, *concrete evidence,* are too extreme. D is incorrect because these scientists are in agreement, not in contrast, with Penfield.

23. **A** The key word here is *orthodox*: An orthodox scientist does not believe anything out of the ordinary in his field, and the scientists mentioned in the article did indeed believe that the mind could be understood through study of its physical functioning—until they had a change of heart. Orthodox scientists have not changed their views from the original one. A Greek word is mentioned in the second paragraph, but not a Greek belief about science, so B can be eliminated. C, D, and E are unorthodox approaches to scientific inquiry, as detailed throughout the paragraph. A is the best answer.

24. **D** The best answer is D. Hendle is mentioned as a professor of philosophy at Yale, but not necessarily as Penfield's former teacher. A appears in lines 24–27, B in 34–37, C throughout the passage, and E in lines 51–58.

SECTION 4

1. A There are no errors in the sentence as it is written. B, C, D, and E all introduce pronouns that are incorrect: In B, *its* is singular but *families* is plural; in C, *they're* has the wrong meaning; in D, *it's* has the wrong meaning and is singular; and in E, *there* isn't even a pronoun.
2. E The original sentence is in the passive voice, rarely the best choice. B, C, and D are also in the passive voice; B and D are also rewritten awkwardly. E is the most streamlined version of the sentence, and avoids having a misplaced modifier.
3. D The original sentence contains an idiom error. D avoids the unidiomatic phrasing of the original by linking an appropriate prepositional phrase *with breeding* to the verb *credited.*
4. C Because the subject is *classical composers,* the examples must be the composers themselves; not *Haydn's credit*, but *Haydn*. That eliminates all but B and C. B does not use the *from...to* construction that describes a *range* and it changes the meaning by eliminating mention of *credit.*
5. B A *cause* cannot be *where,* as in A and C, or *when*, as in D. E is a very awkward passive phrase, *the management by seniors of.*
6. D The original sentence would be fine if the word *which* was just taken out, which D does. The word *which* makes this sentence a fragment, as does *that* in B. *And* in C simply does not make sense as a sentence. E incorrectly uses the future tense; the sentence should be in the present.
7. A This sentence is correct as it stands. Adding *which* in B makes it a fragment. Both C and D are wordy, and E, with the addition of *-ing*, makes little sense.
8. B B is the clearest, most concise choice. As written in A, *she was* is redundant. C is awkward. D changes the verb tense so it no longer agrees with the non-underlined part of the sentence. E uses the word *being*, which on the SAT usually indicates unnecessary wordiness.
9. C This sentence contains a misplaced modifier: *In addition to having more natural resources* should be describing *the United States.* This eliminates A, B, and E. C and D both properly place *the United States* directly after the comma, but D moves the words *also* and *significantly,* changing the meaning.
10. E The original sentence contains an ambiguity error. We don't know who doesn't have her wallet. Eliminate A and B. Only E fixes the error without adding other errors to the sentence.
11. E The original sentence is awkward and wordy, as are C and D. B contains an unnecessary and awkward pronoun, *it.* E provides the most clear and concise phrasing.
12. C C, which uses the *-ing* form, creates a problem in verb construction. *Has become* is the correct phrasing.
13. D *Weakly* is describing the appearance of the paintings, not the painting's sense of vision, and so it should be an adjective (describing a noun), not an adverb. It should read *look weak.*
14. D Parallelism is the problem in this sentence. To keep the list parallel, omit *to.*
15. C Because *rock* is a verb, the modifying word *slow* should be an adverb. Change *slow* to *slowly.*
16. E There is no error in the sentence as it is written.
17. D In D, *more* is redundant; *healthier,* all by itself, is the proper phrasing.
18. E There is no error in the sentence as it is written.
19. D This is a verb tense error. Because *realized* is in the past tense and the sentence mentions the previous summer, *wear* should be the past tense *wore.*
20. E There is no error in the sentence as it is written.
21. A The pronoun refers to people, and thus should read, *the students who*; the word *which* is appropriate in this context for anything else except humans.

22. **B** There is a pronoun agreement error here. Because the subject is *you*, change *yourself* to *you*.
23. **B** The sentence contains a pronoun agreement error. The word *one* doesn't agree with *himself.*
24. **B** This sentence has an idiom error; *independent from* should be *independent of.*
25. **A** To correct this ambiguous pronoun, name the people who make this statement or, if none exist, remove *they say.*
26. **C** In C, *it* is an ambiguous pronoun; it is unclear whether *it* refers to the *barn,* the *property,* or *where he had intended.*
27. **E** There is no error in this sentence as it is written.
28. **B** Because *viewers* is plural, *preference* should also be plural. It should read *their preferences.*
29. **D** The sentence contains a faulty comparison. The phrase *use of* can't be compared to *fluorescent bulbs.*
30. **D** The use of the word *however* in D best reflects the shift in the meaning of the two sentences. The first sentence discusses Graham's hope of becoming a lawyer and the second sentence shows a change in this plan. None of the other answers emphasizes this transition.
31. **B** The first two sentences make it clear that you are discussing the past. The use of the present tense verb *is* in sentence 3 is therefore incorrect, and needs to be changed to the past tense.
32. **A** The original sentence is a fragment. A is short and correctly uses the past tense. B incorrectly uses the verb *were relying,* which is not in the simple past tense. C is unnecessarily wordy and subtly changes the meaning. D also changes the meaning by saying that it is Graham and not the *jobs* that relied on his keen insight. E incorrectly uses the verb *were relying.*
33. **E** When combining two sentences, determine how their content should be linked. The first sentence discusses what you would expect of most people, while the second sentence discusses how Graham's behavior differs. Only E shows that contrasting relationship between the two sentences.
34. **A** There is no reason to include the phrase *of course* at the beginning of the last sentence, as the passage does not give you a reason to think this is an obvious fact. Eliminate B. C and D would make the end of the passage awkward, and E does not agree with the author's opinion of Graham's accomplishments as expressed throughout the passage.
35. **C** C is the best bridge between the two sentences, linking Graham's success with his compassion. A and E are fragments; B and D are not indicated in the passage.

SECTION 5

1. **A** If both x and y are integers, it doesn't matter if they are positive or negative, odd or even; when the absolute value of their product is taken, by definition, it will be positive. (None of the other answer choices need *necessarily* be true, although C, D, and E *could* be.)
2. **D** If you draw the lines from the center of a hexagon to its six vertices, you create six equilateral triangles. All the interior angles must add up to 360. $\angle FOD$ comprises two of them. The answer is 120, or D.
3. **A** The easiest way to find the lengths is to create triangles and use the hypotenuses. A becomes about 2.12; B is $\sqrt{2}$ (or 1.4); C is .5; D is 1; and E is 2.06. The distance farthest from the origin is 2.12.
4. **D** The easiest way to solve this problem is to get to a common rate. You know that one packer packs 15 boxes every 2 minutes, and the other packs 15 boxes every 3 minutes. If you put these in terms of 6-minute intervals, the first packer will pack 45 boxes in 6 minutes, while the other packs 30 every 6 minutes. This means that together they will pack 75 boxes in 6 minutes, 150 boxes in 12 minutes, and 300 boxes in 24 minutes.

5. E One of the safest ways to solve this problem is by Plugging In the Answers. While you normally start with C, you don't want to forget that this is an EXCEPT question, so let's just start with A and go straight through to E. Assume $x = 20$. Is the remainder when 20 is divided by 5 the same as the remainder when 20 is divided by 4? Sure, the remainder is 0 in each case. So you can cross off A. (This is an EXCEPT question, don't forget!) How about B? If $x = 21$, is the remainder the same? Yes, the remainder is 1 when 21 is divided by 4 and when it is divided by 5. How about C? If $x = 22$, the remainder is 2 when divided by 4 and when divided by 5. How about D? If $x = 23$, then the remainder is 3 when divided by 4 and when divided by 5. If $x = 24$, however, the remainder when 24 is divided by 4 is 0, while the remainder when 24 is divided by 5 is 4. Therefore, E is our answer.

6. E Plug in numbers for the base and height of triangle *ACD*. For example, $AC = 10$ and $AD = 8$. The area of *ACD* is therefore $\frac{1}{2}(10)(8) = 40$. The area of *ABE* is $\frac{1}{2}(5)(4) = 10$. The area of the shaded region is therefore $40 - 10 = 30$, so the fraction of *ACD* that is shaded is $\frac{30}{40} = \frac{3}{4}$.

7. C Let's multiply out what you have in parentheses using FOIL. This gives you $9 + 3\sqrt{x} - 3\sqrt{x} - x$, or $9 - x$. So our equation now reads $9 - x = 7$. This makes $x = 2$.

8. A Let's try Plugging In some numbers for this problem. Start by choosing 18 for x and 2 for y. This makes their product 36, which is divisible by 36. You also made sure to pick a value for x that is divisible by 6. Using these numbers, let's look at statements I, II, and III. Are they true? Statement I is not true, because 2 cannot be evenly divided by 18; because statement I is not true, you can eliminate B and D. Now what about statement II? It's also false, so you can cross off C and E. This means our answer must be A.

9. **4**

Negative exponents mean to take the reciprocal and raise it to the power. So $9^{-2} = \left(\frac{1}{9}\right)^2 = \frac{1}{81}$. Now find what power of $\frac{1}{3} = \frac{1}{81}$. Because $3^4 = 81$, $\left(\frac{1}{3}\right)^4 = \frac{1}{81}$, and x must be 4.

10. **1,600**

If the area of the circle is 400π, then you can figure out its radius. $A = \pi r^2$ so $400 = \pi r^2$, and the radius is 20. The diameter of the circle is twice the radius, or 40. Because this circle is inscribed in the square, you know that the diameter of the circle is equal to one side of the square, so you know that each side is equal to 40. The area of the square is $40 \times 40 = 1{,}600$.

11. **80**

You know that the total number of students is 320. Because you know that there are 60 more juniors than seniors, the easy way to find out how many of each there are is to take half of 320 (which is 160) and then add half of 60 to get the number of juniors, and subtract half of 60 to get the number of seniors. This means that the number of juniors is 190 and the number of seniors is 130. (Their difference is 60 and their sum is 320.) Therefore, there are 190 juniors. Knowing that there are 30 more female juniors than male juniors, you can find the number of male juniors the same way—take half of 190 (which is 95) and subtract half of 30: $95 - 15 = 80$.

12. **34**

If a rectangle has a width of 5 and a diagonal of 13, this means that its other side must be 12, because 5:12:13 is a Pythagorean triple. Therefore, the perimeter of the rectangle will be $5 + 12 + 5 + 12 = 34$.

13. **91**

Let's begin by using our Average Pie. If Jeanette's average on 6 tests was 92, then you know that her total score on all six tests must be 92 × 6 = 552. Two of those test scores add up to 188; if you remove those two tests, the other four tests must have a sum that adds up to 552 – 188, or 364. So the average of these four tests will be 364 ÷ 4, or 91.

14. **1.65**

The best way to approach this problem is to set up an equation. There is some price such that if you add 3% of the price to the price itself, you get \$56.65. This means that you can set up an equation: $x + 3\%$ of $x = 56.65$, or $x + 0.03x = 56.65$. Now you can just solve for x, and you get the original price, which was \$55. Subtract this from \$56.65 to get the tax \$1.65.

15. $\mathbf{\frac{9}{25}}$ **or .36**

Probability in this case is the number of prime numbers divided by the total number of possibilities (25 numbers). The prime numbers between 1 and 25 are 2, 3, 5, 7, 11, 13, 17, 19, and 23. So, there are 9 prime numbers. The probability is $\frac{9}{25}$.

16. **8.93**

To solve this problem, it is important to remember the formula distance = rate × time. Here, to get the overall average speed, you need to know the total distance and total time. The total distance is found by adding all of the distances given: 0.3 + 0.3 + 0.5 + 0.24 = 1.34. To find the time for each, rewrite the rate formula as follows: time = $\frac{\text{dist.}}{\text{rate}}$, thus time = $\frac{0.3}{7.5} = 0.04$ hours for both Alan and Ben. For Carla, time = $\frac{0.5}{10} = 0.05$ hours, and for Debby, time = $\frac{0.24}{12} = 0.02$ hours. The total time is 0.04 + 0.04 + 0.05 + 0.02 = 0.15 hours. Thus the average rate is $\frac{1.34 \text{ miles}}{0.15 \text{ hours}} = 8.93$ miles per hour.

17. 2

Absolute value is the distance from zero to the number on the number line, or in other words, the positive version of the number. So, $\left(|-1|+16\right)^{\frac{1}{2}} = (17)^{\frac{1}{2}}$. A fractional exponent means the denominator is used as a root, so this is $\sqrt{17}$. Next, use the distance formula: distance = $\sqrt{(x_1 - x_2)^2 + (y_1 - y_2)^2}$. Thus, $\sqrt{17} = \sqrt{(2-1)^2 + (6-b)^2}$. Square both sides: $17 = (2 - 1)^2 + (6 - b)^2$. So, $17 = 1 + (6 - b)^2$. Subtract 1 from both sides to get $16 = (6 - b)^2$. Take the square root of both sides to get $4 = 6 - b$. Subtract 6 from both sides to find $-2 = -b$. So, $b = 2$.

18. **9**

This looks suspiciously like a quadratic equation, and if you multiply it out, its equivalent is $b^2 - a^2$. You want to make this as large as possible, so you want b^2 to be large and a^2 to be small. If b = –3, $b^2 = 9$; if $a = 0$, $a^2 = 0$. So $b^2 - a^2$ can be as large as 9.

SECTION 6

1. **E** The clue here is *almost as if it were the middle of the day.* This tells you that the second blank must be a term such as "lit up" and the first word something like "light." This makes E our best choice.
2. **B** A good clue for the first blank is *haughty.* You know that the first blank has to be a negative word that goes along with haughty—a word like "stubborn" or "arrogant." This will eliminate D and E. The second blank needs to be an opposing idea, something like "willing to listen." This eliminates A and C, which leaves you with B.
3. **B** In this sentence you have a punctuation trigger (the semicolon) that tells you that the word in the blank will mean *rarely suggest radical new ideas.* B, *conservative,* fits the bill.
4. **A** The trigger word *although* tells you that the words in the blanks should have opposite meanings. B, C, D, and E are all pairs that have similar meanings, so they can be eliminated. This leaves you with A.
5. **E** The trigger word *while* combined with *health-conscious individuals have stopped eating eggs* means that the word in the blank must be a word that means "healthful" (or at least "not unhealthful"). E means exactly this.
6. **C** The statements about Jane Doe demonstrate the author's assertion that *For many consumers, these two issues* (right to privacy and copyright rules) *create a surprising paradox* (lines 4–5). C best summarizes this. A is incorrect because no controversy is clearly identified in the passage. B is an almost word-for-word paraphrase of the first sentence. However, the statements about Jane Doe demonstrate the paradox (or conflict), not the legal and ethical questions. Be wary of choosing answers that seem to come straight from the passage. The sentences do not contradict the paradox mentioned in the first two sentences, making D incorrect. Finally, E sounds okay until you look at it closely. First, the previous two sentences provide you with an assertion or statement about the Internet and its users, not a theory. Second, Jane Doe is an example of the average user mentioned in the second sentence, not a real, specific case.
7. **D** D is the best answer. Because "not averse" means willing, you see that in Jane Doe's case, she is willing to download others' creations at no cost, and likewise, the "pirates" of Victorian times "cribbed" what they could of new operettas and produced them on their own without paying the creators. The subjects of A and C do not appear in both passages. B and E would impede the copying that Ms. Doe and the pirates did or would like to do.
8. **B** Although copyright laws regarding intellectual property have existed for years, evolving technology makes it possible for individuals to circumvent the protection they offer, so the laws are not always effective or immediately enforceable. A says the opposite of what the Gilbert and Sullivan passage says. C is not correct because respect for laws and organizations is not mentioned in either passage. D cannot work because while the Jane Doe passage says that she pays for her downloads in *unusual currency,* the passage does not imply whether she or the author thinks this is a fair exchange. Neither passage implies that artists should be more self-protective as in E. The best answer is B.
9. **E** If you cross out the word *draconian* and fill in your own word, in the context of the sentence (*imposing ------- punishments*), the blank should mean something like "harsh." *Severe,* E, is closest to this meaning. There is a similarly spelled word (*dragonian*) which means "dragon-like," as in B, but it is not the same as *draconian.* The concepts in A, C, and D all appear in the passages, but they are not used to describe punishments. Therefore, E is the best answer.

10. **C** From the introductory blurb, you know that the passage is about the *art and recreation of Southeastern Indians.* A is too extreme and slightly offensive. Eliminate it. B isn't the main purpose of the passage. D doesn't mention art and recreation; eliminate it. For E, the Cherokee Indians were mentioned only as a detail. This makes our best choice C.

11. **B** If you read about the problem in context, the passage says that you need to view the art and games as the *outward expressions of their belief system.* That is, you need to understand their beliefs to understand their art and recreation. B states this best. A is extreme and offensive. The passage never states that the belief system is *impossible to understand.* Eliminate it. C and E are never mentioned in the passage so you can safely eliminate them. Finally, D isn't mentioned and contradicts the passage. You do have some understanding of the beliefs of Southeastern Indians. Eliminate it.

12. **E** Use the lead words *advantage of skilled oratory* to locate the right reference. In lines 33–34 the passage says that *the words of a gifted speaker...could move contentious men to reach consensus.* E is a paraphrase of these lines. None of the other answers are supported and D twists the reference. It says that *timid,* not skilled, speakers could soothe anxious tempers.

13. **D** In lines 40–43 the author says *even though we know much about the Southeastern Indian ball game, we do not know the precise nature of the social and political forces that led them to play it with such ferocity.* This best supports D. There is no support for the other four answers.

14. **D** D is the best answer. Statement II is true, because the third paragraph discusses the fact that poetry and public speaking were both artistic and political, but you do not know which aspect was more important. Likewise, III is supported in the passage: *we do not know the precise nature of the social and political forces that led them to play...with such ferocity.* Statement I is unsupported because it is too extreme: While the second paragraph says *many of these creations* and *the best Southeastern Indian art* is gone, it does not state that all of it is gone.

15. **E** The important part of the question asks for a parallel instance to *the loss of many of the Indians' artistic and architectural creations.* The final paragraph states that *we do not understand...why the Indians would sometimes bet the last thing they owned on the outcome of a game* [*of chunkey*]. Both the instances of art and the reasons for the game's importance have been lost in the centuries that have passed because they were central to the Indian culture, and are therefore parallel examples. A is incorrect because this art was seen by explorers and is therefore mentioned in contrast, not in parallel; B is incorrect because our rituals are not mentioned as being irrational. Poetic magical formulas are mentioned in the passage, but not in relation to our lack of knowledge about them, therefore C is wrong. The *contentious men* need to reach consensus, not fight the enemy, thus D can be eliminated.

16. **E** From the introductory blurb, you know that this passage is primarily about jazz. This means that B and C can't be the answer, so eliminate them. A is just too narrow to be correct; the passage is not primarily about three instrument melodies. Likewise, the New Orleans band is a detail of the passage, but not the main idea. After crossing off A and D, you are left with E.

17. **A** The lead words here are *ragtime and brass bands.* You can find these mentioned on the first lines of the second paragraph. There it says that jazz contains *elements that derive from older musical traditions.* A is a paraphrase of this idea.

18. **E** This could be a time-consuming question, so you may want to skip it and come back to it if you have time. From answering the previous question, you know that the answers may be found starting in the second paragraph. You can find support for A in line 19, B in line 30, C in line 38, and D in lines 33–34. This means our answer must be E.

19. **A** Because this question has a line reference, let's go to that line and read it in context. There, the passage says that jazz tries to imitate blues by recreating its singing style. This best supports A.

20. **D** For a vocab-in-context question, cross out the word you're being asked about, reread the sentence, and come up with a word you think fits the blank. You'll probably pick a word like "interesting" or "distinctive." Which choice comes closest to this idea? D does.

21. **C** The lead words here are *exotic sound*. You can find these in the beginning of the final paragraph of the passage, which says that the kinds of instruments used and the manner in which intonation is used are characteristic of jazz. Choice C is the best paraphrase of this idea. A, B, D, and E are too specific and do not paraphrase the reference.

22. **D** Because this question will take a lot of time, you may want to go for easier, quicker questions first. You can find evidence in the second paragraph that jazz was heavily influenced by ragtime, brass bands, and dance orchestras. In the next-to-last paragraph you see evidence that it was heavily influenced by blues. This allows you to eliminate A, B, C, and E, which leaves D as our best answer.

23. **A** A is the best answer, because while the statement is true, it is mentioned nowhere in the passage. The other answer choices are all supported by the passage. B is found in lines 8–10; counterpoint, C, is mentioned in line 20; syncopation (lack of strict rhythm), D, is found in line 28; and the clarinet-saxophone connection is mentioned in lines 26–27.

24. **E** Because of the information about improvisation in the fourth paragraph, E is the best answer. None of the other answer choices contain statements supported by the passage.

SECTION 7

1. **C** The clue is *entirely implausible*. A good word for the blank might be "falsehood." Only C means falsehood.

2. **A** This sentence starts with the trigger *while*. So you know that the two blanks need to be contrasting ideas. The only pair that has a strong opposite relationship is A.

3. **A** The clue is *exchange players of comparable talent*. Therefore, as the colon is a same-direction trigger, the agreement was "equal." A best expresses this meaning.

4. **D** A good clue for this blank is *brevity*—the sentence says that the article's brevity didn't detract from its importance, so you know that the article was brief. What is another word for brief? *Terse*!

5. **E** Here you have a great clue: *reduced the population substantially*. So you need a word that means "very deadly." The choice that most nearly means this is E.

6. **D** The clue for the first blank is *by missteps*. Because *missteps* is another word for "mistakes" you know that the blank must be something like "affected negatively." A and B do not match this meaning. Eliminate them. The clues for the second blank are the trigger words *but* and *increasing appreciation*. Therefore you know the *missteps* have not done permanent damage to the author's reputation. A good word for the second blank is "unimportant." D best matches this meaning.

7. **B** Let's look at the relationship between the blanks. You could be looking for a pair of words like "happy" and "harm," or you could be looking for a pair like "sad" and "good." So you're looking for words that are somewhat opposite. Eliminate A, C, D, and E.

8. **C** C is the best answer because the clue is *rambled for a long time with frequent repetitions about trivial topics*. Therefore, words like "rambling" or "boring" would work well in the blank. Because the words in A, B, D, and E do not agree with the clue, they can be eliminated.

9. **B** B best states the main idea of the passage. A and C are both too extreme; the passage does not argue for or against the procedure. D and E are not supported by the passage; neither deaf culture nor the scientific basis for hearing loss are discussed at length in the passage.

10. **B** B specifically describes the purpose of all three of the final sentences. A and E are not correct because they refer to only one sentence of the final three. C is incorrect because no alternatives are provided. D is not correct because there is no disputed theory to support.

11. **E** Remember to check the passage for each item and not rely on memory. E is correct, because it is the only choice not mentioned in the passage as a possible cause of the riots in 1913. All the remaining answers are mentioned in the second sentence.

12. **D** D is the best answer because it can be proven with information from the passage. Because you know that both ballet and sporting events have caused riots, D must be true. A is incorrect because you have no information about the nature of prior riots. B and C are unsupported by the passage. E is a nice thought, but has nothing in the passage to back it up.

13. **E** Just following these lines the author says that his family felt *a smug sympathy for those poor souls in harsher climates who had to suffer real winters.* This means that he was discussing the warmth of the weather he was used to. E is the best paraphrase of this idea.

14. **B** For a vocab-in-context question, you should cover the word in question, reread the line, and put your own word into the blank. In this case, you'd probably use a word like "unhappy." The closest choice is B.

15. **E** If you read these lines in context, you see that they are followed by a list of problems that the wind causes: *uprooted trees, overturned cars,* and the like. These all illustrate how powerful and destructive the wind is, which best supports E.

16. **D** Here you have another vocab-in-context question. If you cover up the word *baleful* and try to use your own word in its place, you'd probably choose a word like "scary." Which choice comes closest to this idea? D does.

17. **C** In the previous lines, the author discusses how certain people complained about the wind in Provence, and that they would think differently *if they had to put up with the gales that come off the English Channel.* The author is thereby saying that the gales off the English Channel are worse than anything in Provence. This best supports C.

18. **A** For this question you know from lines 39–41 that Menicucci was concerned that *the pipes burst... under the pressure of water that had frozen in them overnight.* You also know that Menicucci was a plumber (so he would naturally be working on the pipes). This best supports A.

19. **C** In the first lines of the last paragraph, you find Menicucci clearly expounding on his theory of why the winds were so bitterly cold. He therefore thinks he knows the answer, which allows you to eliminate B, D, and E. Choice A is extreme, so you should avoid it as well. This leaves you with C as the best choice.

20. **E** This is a tough question, so your best bet is to use POE. From the last paragraph you know that Menicucci thinks that the harsher wind was caused by a flattening of the curvature of the earth, which enabled the wind to take a more direct route south from Siberia to Provence. Because the pipes have nothing to do with this question, A should be crossed off. B, C, and D look tempting, but if you reread the paragraph, you'll see that Menicucci never said any of these things. E sounds just like his theory and is the best answer.

21. **D** Remember that every question will have some support in the passage. Immediately prior to saying *mais oui,* the passage says that Menicucci *allowed himself a brief but dramatic pause.* This indicates that he was being somewhat theatrical and pompous. This best supports D.

22. **B** The best answer is B. You can infer Statement I from the mention of the author's swimming pool in line 34. Because Statement I must be in the correct answer, eliminate A and C. You cannot infer Statement II. You know that the author and his family came to Provence from England, but the author's birthplace is never mentioned in the passage. Eliminate D and E, because they include Statement II. *Voila!* You're done without having to check Statement III. But just for the record—you cannot infer Statement III either. People tell the author stories about the mistral lasting days on end (line 18), but the length of the first mistral that the author actually experienced is not mentioned in the passage.

23. **C** This passage is a first-person narrative, told in an informal and humorous manner. An anecdote is a short account of an interesting or humorous incident, so C is the best answer. None of the other answer choices fits. E is the second best answer, but the author's humor is far too dry to be accurately characterized as sentimental.

24. **A** The best answer is A. In lines 50–53, the author states that Monsieur Menicucci *wagged his finger under* jeune's *nose to* underline [emphasis added] *the difference between the soft winters of the coast and the biting cold in which we were now standing. Underline*, as used here, means to emphasize, so this sentence is emphasizing the point made in the previous paragraph, which was that pipes without insulation can freeze and burst in Provence but are far less likely to do so in Cannes or Nice. Thus, it is implied that Cannes and Nice are coastal cities. None of the other answer choices are implied by the passage. D is a trap answer, because it says the opposite of what the passage implies.

SECTION 8

1. **B** B is the best answer, because the clue is *she had won the grand prize instead of just any prize.* This suggests that her joy would increase, so a good phrase for the blank is "more joy." None of the other answer choices agrees with the clue; therefore, each can be eliminated.

2. **E** The clue is *increased humidity coupled with oppressively high temperatures*, which describes a rather unpleasant situation. A word with a negative connotation would work well in the blank, like "bad." Because *listless* in E means lacking energy, it is the best answer.

3. **E** Our clue here is *had...assumed that hunter-gatherers moved* combined with the trigger *however.* So you need a word in the blank that means the opposite of moving—a word that means "staying in one place." The word that best fits this idea is E.

4. **C** The clue here is *none of the original doors or windows...survived.* In that case, the restoration is largely guesswork. C is the best choice.

5. **D** The clues from the sentence are *divided into strong factions, impossible to garner,* and *support to pass the bill.* A good phrase to describe the support that would be needed to pass the bill is "from both sides," and *bipartisan* in D means exactly that. Because none of the answer choices agree with the clues, all are incorrect.

6. **E** Start with the first blank. If they were expecting to be *admonished*, then the boys were probably up to "something bad," or "mischief." Eliminate the answers that don't mean something close to "mischief," so (A), (B), and (C) are gone. The second phrase tells us what the parents did, which is "yell at them," as we know from *admonished* in the earlier part of the sentence. Eliminate (D), leaving (E).

7. **C** According to the first paragraph, some of the causes of pollution included the eruption of volcanoes, dust storms, and marsh gases. In the following lines, the passage states that humans were also responsible for pollution. C restates these ideas.

8. **C** Let's go back to the passage and read the lines in question. They mention ancient cities that had pollution problems. This sounds a lot like either B or C. Both of these are plausible, so you should pick the one that is more general and defendable based on what the passage says. Earlier in the passage, the author tells you that people early on *began to pollute the air.* The passage doesn't say that the air pollution *always existed in cities.* Beware of extreme words; they are often wrong. This makes C a better choice than B.

9. **A** Using the lead words *air pollution* and *Industrial Revolution,* and knowing that the answer to the last question was found in the first paragraph, you can find the relevant reference. The second paragraph tells you that *The Industrial Revolution brought even worse air pollution* and *there were large rural areas unaffected by air pollution.* In the beginning of the third paragraph, the passage tells you that today *rural areas are not unaffected* (line 20). A best summarizes this difference. B uses words from the passage but says something the passage didn't. You don't know what the factory towns were before they were factory towns. C, D, and E are never mentioned and are therefore incorrect.

10. **D** If you read these lines in context, you find in lines 27–28 that the *astronauts…traced drifting blobs of Los Angeles smog as far east as western Colorado.* This means that the smog has spread from a big city to the countryside. This is paraphrased by D. B and C, while tempting, are much too extreme to be correct.

11. **E** This is an EXCEPT question, so the correct answer choice is *not* mentioned in the passage. The final paragraph of Passage 1 mentions strained relationships between the United States and Canada, factory closings, and acid rain. This means you can eliminate A, B, and C. The passage also mentions a change in the work habits of traffic police, so D can be eliminated. This leaves E as our best answer.

12. **C** Remember to look back to the passage for evidence to support your answer. A is quite extreme, so you should avoid it. B is tempting, but the passage never really talks about the long run. Instead, it mentions only a particular historical event. Lines 65–66 say that *more than 4,000 deaths had been attributed to the smog,* which makes C our best answer.

13. **D** The lead words here are *London smog.* You can find London smog described in the first paragraph of Passage 2, where you are told it was a combination of *smoke, fog, sulfur dioxide, sulfuric acid, ash, and soot.* This is best paraphrased by D.

14. **D** The opening lines of this paragraph say that air pollution has killed *more people than were ever killed in any single tornado.* In other words, air pollution is extremely dangerous and deadly. D is a paraphrase of this idea.

15. **B** For a detail question like this one, be sure to look back to find the answer in the passage. Lines 72–74 say that electrostatic precipitators *induce an electric charge on the particles, which then are attracted to oppositely charged plates and deposited.* This makes B the best choice.

16. **E** Again, let's look back to the passage. In lines 80–81 you find that the processes to remove sulfur dioxide from air pollution are expensive and waste a part of the coal's energy. E says exactly this.

17. D A and B are extreme, so you should avoid them. Neither author discusses eliminating the sources of pollution, so you can also cross off C. Finally, neither author says that the cost of pollution control is much higher than the cost of changing to better energy sources, so you can eliminate E as well. D is a nice SAT-type answer, because it's fairly general and hard to argue with.

18. A In lines 13–15, the first passage says *The Industrial Revolution brought even worse air pollution….Soot, smoke, and sulfur dioxide filled the air.* This explains why sulfur dioxide and soot created London smog. This makes A our answer.

19. D Because the passage asks you to choose the one that is NOT a difference and therefore not mentioned in the passages, let's look for what is mentioned and cross them off. Whatever is left must be right. A is true; Passage 1 discusses pollution from Seneca's time to today, while Passage 2 talks only of the past 100 years. Cross it off. B is also true because Passage 2 discusses the problem of smog in London, while Passage 1 talks about a range of affected areas. Cross it off. C is mentioned as well; Passage 1 brings up Seneca, Queen Elizabeth, and Tokyo while Passage 2 focuses solely on London. E is also true, because Passage 2 discusses some methods employed in treating air pollution, while Passage 1 offers no solutions to the problems it discusses.

SECTION 9

1. A Take it one phrase at a time. The "sum" means you will add two things. The "squares of x and y" means to square x and square y, or x^2 and y^2. Add these to get $x^2 + y^2$. Cross out any answer that does not have $x^2 + y^2$ as the first part of the equation. Only A is left.

2. C If $c = 6$ and $b + c = 8$, then you know that $b = 2$. Because you know that $c = 6$ and $b = 2$, you can solve for a: If $3a + 2b + c = 22$, then $3a + 4 + 6 = 22$, so $3a = 12$, and $a = 4$. Therefore, $a + b + c = 4 + 2 + 6$, or 12.

   Or try stacking:

$$\begin{aligned} 3a + 2b + c &= 22 \\ b + c &= 8 \\ +c &= 6 \\ 3a + 3b + 3c &= 36 \\ 3(a + b + c) &= 36 \\ a + b + c &= 12 \end{aligned}$$

3. B Because probability = # of outcomes fulfilling the requirements over the total # of outcomes, you need to find the total area of sectors that are labeled 3 and 4 over the total area of the circular spinner. Even though you don't know the area of the circle, you know that this fraction is the same part of the whole as the total degree measure of central angles that enclose 3 and 4 over the total degree measure of the circular spinner, which is the total area of sectors that are labeled 3 and 4 over the total area of the circular spinner. This gives you $\frac{60° + 80°}{360°}$, or $\frac{140°}{360°} = \frac{7}{18}$.

4. C Let's start by figuring out what the values of x and y could be. You know that $4x - 8 > 0$. If you add 8 to each side of the equation, you get $4x > 8$, which means that $x > 2$. So x could be 3, 4, or any integer larger than 2. Likewise, you know that $4y + 8 < 0$. If you subtract 8 from each side of this equation, you get $4y < -8$, which means that $y < -2$. So y could be -3, -4, or any integer less than -2. Neither x nor y can be zero, so the product xy cannot be zero. This means you can eliminate E. And because you don't know whether x and y are odd or even you can also eliminate A and B. You do know, though, that x will always be positive and y will always be negative, so whatever numbers x and y are, you know their product will always be negative.

5. B If a rectangle has length 16 and width 6, then its area will be the length times the width, or 16×6, which equals 96. If this is 3 times the area of a triangle, then the triangle will have an area of 32. If a triangle with area 32 has height of 8, you can use the triangle formula for area of a triangle to find the base: $\frac{1}{2} \times$ base $\times$ height = area. $32 = \frac{1}{2}b \times 8$, so base $\times$ 4 = 32. This means that the base is equal to 8.

6. E Plug in! There are two 30°-60°-90° triangles imbedded in this problem, so that is the best way to tackle this. Plug in for y, and go on from there. If you were to use 18 for y, the height of the cone would be 9. The base of the smaller triangle would be $\frac{9}{\sqrt{3}}$. That is also the radius of the circle, so square that number and get 27, and then multiply by π to get the area of the circle, which is 27π. This is the target. Plug your original value into the answer choices. If $y = 18$, the only answer that works out to 27π is E. Algebraically, the height is $\frac{y}{2}$, and the base of the smaller triangle is $\frac{y}{2\sqrt{3}}$ (using the 30°-60°-90°). Square that and multiply by π, and you get E.

7. D You can set up a proportion, or simply notice that 1,000,000 is $10,000 \times 100$. So if you multiply 30 by 100 you get 3,000.

8. C Because lines k and l are tangent to the circle, they form right angles with the radii. Angles OAB, AOC, and OCB in quadrilateral $OABC$ are all 90°, and all four angles must add to 360°, so the remaining angle must also be 90°, which makes $OABC$ a rectangle. Because $\overline{OA}$ and $\overline{OC}$ are radii, they are equal, and you are told that $\overline{OA}$ is the same length as the other two sides. Thus, all four sides are equal. So $OABC$ is actually a square. Draw in $\overline{OB}$ and you'll see that it bisects the square, forming two 45°-45°-90° triangles (see the reference information at the beginning of any SAT Math section). So $OB = 4 = s\sqrt{2}$. Solving for s gives you $2\sqrt{2}$, which is the length of each side of the square.

9. A This is a great problem for Plugging In. Let's try using $z = 2$, $n = 5$, and $b = 15$. If \$2 will buy 5 pizzas, then how much will 15 pizzas cost? Three times the number of pizzas will have three times the cost, so \$6. Now you just need to figure out which choice will give you \$6. Try calculating each of the answer choices, and you'll find that only A equals \$6.

10. C Because you have parallel lines, let's identify the big and small angles. The small angles measure 65°, so the big angles measure 115°. So $x + y = z = 115$. If you add everything together and substitute $x = 55$, you get $55 + y + z = 230$, so $y + z = 175$.

11. D Because $\overline{OP}$ is a radius of the circle, $OP = 8$. Because $\overline{OR}$ is a radius of the circle, $OR = OQ + QR$, and $OQ = QR$, therefore $OQ = 4$. Using the Pythagorean theorem—or recognizing the ratio of sides in a 30°-60°-90° triangle—will give you the value of PQ: $4\sqrt{3}$. Because area $= \frac{1}{2}bh$, the area is $\frac{1}{2} \times 4 \times 4\sqrt{3} = 8\sqrt{3}$.

12. B This is a great problem to solve by Plugging In the Answers. Let's start with C. Could the number of girls on the trip be 40? If there are 14 more boys than girls, then there must be 40 + 14 = 54 boys. But that makes a total of 94 students; that's too much because there are only 80 students. So you can cross off C, D, and E because they are all too big. Let's try B. Could there be 33 girls? In this case there will be 33 + 14 = 47 boys, and 33 + 47 equals 80. So B is the answer.

13. B Let's start by solving for p. You know that $p = f(6)$, which means that it will be equal to $(10 - 6)^2$, or 16. So $4p$ will be equal to 4(16), or 64. Now you simply have to figure out which choice gives you 64. $p(18)$ will equal $(10 - 18)^2$, which is 64. So, B is the answer.

14. A Be sure to read the question carefully; the key here is *must be positive.* Let's try Plugging In an easy number for b. If you make $b = 2$, then let's see which of the choices is positive. A becomes $\frac{2}{3}$. B becomes $\frac{8}{-1}$, so you can eliminate it. C becomes $\frac{1}{2}$. D becomes 0, so you can eliminate it, and E becomes 3. Now let's try making $b = \frac{1}{2}$. In this case, A becomes $\frac{1}{3}$. C becomes –1, so you eliminate it. E becomes 0; eliminate. That leaves you with A.

15. D First find the x- and y-intercepts. The y-intercept is (0, –6). To find the x-intercept, replace y with 0: $0 = \frac{2}{3}x - 6$; $6 = \frac{2}{3}x$; and $x = 9$. So, the x-intercept is (9, 0). Now create a triangle and use the Pythagorean theorem: $6^2 + 9^2 = 117$. The distance between the x- and y-intercepts is $\sqrt{117}$.

16. B The second graph moves down 1 and to the left 1. Remember that when a graph moves to the left it is represented by $(x + h)$, which would be the same as $x - (-1)$. So $h = -1$. Because a negative k represents moving down, $k = 1$. $1 \times (-1) = -1$.

SECTION 10

1. B Avoid the word *being* if possible, which eliminates A and D. Also, watch out for verb tense. The non-underlined part of the sentence is in the present tense, so eliminate C and E because they are both in the future tense.

2. A There are no errors in the sentence as it is written. Both D and E use the phrase *at least 3 feet wide or wider,* which is redundant. B incorrectly uses *swung* instead of *swing,* and C is unnecessarily wordy.

3. E The original sentence, A, has the comparative adjective *better,* which is incorrect when comparing more than two things. B uses *can be,* which changes the meaning of the sentence. C uses future tense, which doesn't really make sense. In D, switching the adjective *nineteenth-century* into a modified noun changes the meaning of the sentence.

4. E E correctly compares American etiquette with the etiquette of other countries. This answer choice includes the phrase *that of* and thus uses the correct form of comparison. The rest of the choices all have a faulty comparison. A and B are missing the phrase *that of* and do not correctly establish a comparison. C is closer, but you need to compare American etiquette with the etiquette of other countries (plural). In D, the comparison is not properly drawn. The word *what* doesn't do the job.

5. **C** The problem with the original sentence is that it uses the long-winded and awkward phrase *this being that they had to* instead of a concise one. B is very concise, but the phrase *including read an article* is grammatically incorrect. C, on the other hand, is both concise and grammatically correct, so get rid of A, because there is a better alternative. D and E are no less awkward than the original sentence, so eliminate them. C is the remaining choice.

6. **C** The best choice is C. Only a person can be *renowned for her writing*, and thus *Barbara Kingsolver* should follow the comma. However, A follows the comma with *Barbara Kingsolver's poems*, while D follows it with *the poems of Barbara Kingsolver*. B and E incorrectly insert a semicolon in place of the comma, turning the initial modifier into a fragment.

7. **A** There is no error in the sentence as it is written. Choice B creates a run-on sentence (in particular, a comma splice). Choice C is awkward and wordy because of all the -ing words and states that the experiments have the exacting standards. Choice D is also awkwardly worded because of *being*. Choice E can be eliminated because of improper verb tense.

8. **D** A and B both contain comma splices. C tries to rephrase the sentence using the word *being*, which is seldom desirable, and also suggests that the works that follow are the only two examples in the history of literature. D offers a concise way to introduce examples. E is even more concise, but improperly uses the word *like* to introduce examples.

9. **D** The original sentence is awkward, wordy, and incorrectly uses *however* as a substitute for *but* or *though*. B uses *along with* to join the two halves of the sentence, failing to signal that there is a conflict between the adults and the girls. In C, the word *even* is unnecessary. E is missing a verb. This leaves D as the best answer.

10. **E** E is the most concise answer, and because it introduces no grammatical errors, it is correct. A, C, and D all refer to the singular committee as *they*, while B is unnecessarily wordy and awkward compared to E.

11. **A** The best choice is A. The sentence is correct as it stands. Eliminate B and C because, with or without the semicolon, a double negative (*not hardly*) is considered incorrect. The word *since* in D is unnecessary: It means "because" here and does not make sense in the sentence. The addition of *however* in E is redundant, because the sentence already uses the word *although*.

12. **B** The original sentence contains the word *because*, so adding *the reason* is redundant; eliminate A and E. C and D wrongly imply that the ban is on the animals, not on transporting them. This leaves you with B as the best answer.

13. **D** In D, the present perfect *has tripled* agrees with the present tense of *the past hundred years* to indicate a time frame from one point until now, and is the most concise way of stating this idea. A and B are wordy. In C, *was tripled* is passive—when possible, choose the active voice on the SAT. E has the incorrect verb tense; *had tripled* is the past perfect while the sentence is discussing something that started in the past, but has not finished.

14. **C** This sentence's error is in pronoun agreement: *Student* is singular, but *their* is plural in both A and B. D corrects this error but adds *always*, which changes the meaning. E unnecessarily adds *not only...but also*. In C, the corrected phrase reads *to seek help from teachers*, eliminating the pronoun and, thus, the error.

Chapter 25
Practice Test 4

SECTION 1
ESSAY
Time — 25 minutes

Turn to Section 1 of your answer sheet to write your essay.

The essay gives you an opportunity to show how effectively you can develop and express ideas. You should, therefore, take care to develop your point of view, present your ideas logically and clearly, and use language precisely.

Your essay must be written on the lines provided on your answer sheet—you will receive no other paper on which to write. You will have enough space if you write on every line, avoid wide margins, and keep your handwriting to a reasonable size. Remember that people who are not familiar with your handwriting will read what you write. Try to write or print so that what you are writing is legible to those readers.

You have twenty-five minutes to write an essay on the topic assigned below. DO NOT WRITE ON ANOTHER TOPIC. AN OFF-TOPIC ESSAY WILL RECEIVE A SCORE OF ZERO.

Think carefully about the issue presented in the following excerpt and the assignment below.

> Thomas Jefferson believed that the will of the majority is "the only legitimate foundation of any government," and that the protection of the public's right to free expression is of primary importance in a democracy. However, there are those who look back through the pages of history and note that when great changes have occurred in history—particularly when great principles are involved—as a rule the majority are wrong.

Assignment: What is your view of the claim that the opinion of the majority is not always right? In an essay, support your position by discussing an example (or examples) from literature, the arts, science and technology, history, current events, or your own experience or observation.

DO NOT WRITE YOUR ESSAY IN YOUR TEST BOOK. You will receive credit only for what you write on your answer sheet.

BEGIN WRITING YOUR ESSAY ON PAGE 3 OF THE ANSWER SHEET
(FOUND AT THE BACK OF THE BOOK).

STOP

If you finish before time is called, you may check your work on this section only.
Do not turn to any other section in the test.

SECTION 2
Time — 25 minutes
18 Questions

Turn to Section 2 of your answer sheet to answer the questions in this section.

Directions: For this section, solve each problem and decide which is the best of the choices given. Fill in the corresponding circle on the answer sheet. You may use any available space for scratchwork..

Notes

1. The use of a calculator is permitted.
2. All numbers used are real numbers.
3. Figures that accompany problems in this test are intended to provide information useful in solving the problems. They are drawn as accurately as possible EXCEPT when it is stated in a specific problem that the figure is not drawn to scale. All figures lie in a plane unless other wise indicated.
4. Unless otherwise specified, the domain of any function f is assumed to be the set of all real numbers x for which $f(x)$ is a real number.

Reference Information

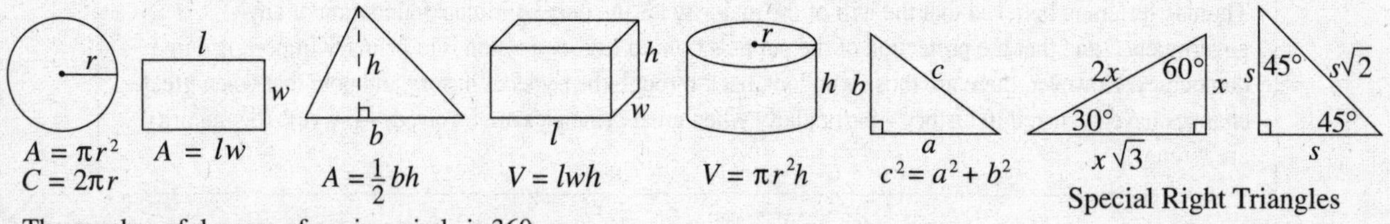

The number of degrees of arc in a circle is 360.

The sum of the measures in degrees of the angles of a triangle is 180.

1. Which of the following is equal to $3x + 9y + 12$?

(A) $3(x + 3y + 9)$
(B) $3(x + 3y) + 12$
(C) $3(x + 3y) + 4$
(D) $3(x + 6y + 9)$
(E) $3x(3y + 4)$

2. To ship boxes of books, Luis charges $4.95 per box plus a one-time service fee of $7.00 per order. If he receives an order for 12 boxes of books, how much will Luis charge?

(A) $11.95
(B) $23.95
(C) $66.40
(D) $84.00
(E) $143.40

GO ON TO THE NEXT PAGE

3. If $f(x) = \sqrt{3x-2}$, what is the smallest possible value of $f(x)$?

(A) There is no such value.

(B) 0

(C) $\frac{2}{3}$

(D) 1

(E) 2

Questions 4–5 refer to the following chart.

Grade	Activity	Price per item	Funds Raised from Activity
9th	Car Wash	$5.00 per car	$255.00
10th	Bake Sale	$2.00 per cookie	$360.00
11th	Magazine Sales	$2.50 per magazine	$337.50
12th	Bake Sale	$1.50 per cookie	$180.00

4. How many cars did the 9th grade class wash during the car wash?

(A) 5
(B) 51
(C) 122
(D) 180
(E) 255

5. How many more cookies were sold by the 10th grade than were sold by the 12th grade?

(A) 60
(B) 90
(C) 120
(D) 150
(E) 180

$$\begin{array}{r} 1D7C \\ \times \quad 6 \\ \hline 94C8 \end{array}$$

6. If C and D represent digits in the correctly worked multiplication problem above, then $C + D =$

(A) 2
(B) 7
(C) 8
(D) 13
(E) 15

GO ON TO THE NEXT PAGE

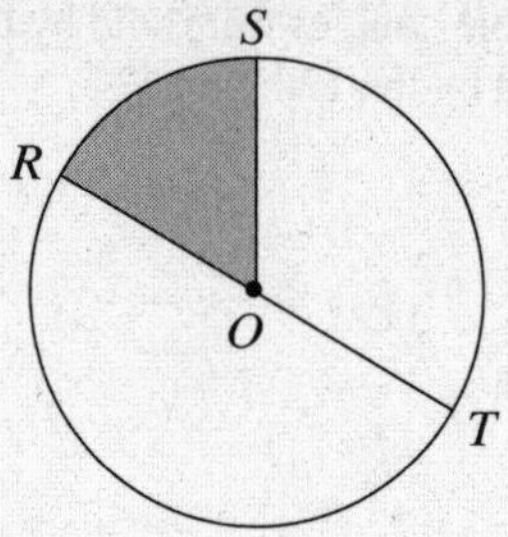

7. In the figure above, $\overline{RT}$ is the diameter of the circle with center O. The shaded portion of the figure has an area of 25π and is $\frac{1}{9}$ the area of the entire circle. What is the length of arc RST ?

(A) 15π
(B) 25π
(C) 30π
(D) 112.5π
(E) 125π

8. If $x^2 - |5x| = -6$, then what is one possible value of x ?

(A) 5
(B) 2
(C) 0
(D) 5
(E) 6

GO ON TO THE NEXT PAGE

Directions: For Student-Produced Response questions 9–18, use the grids to the right of the answer document page on which you have answered questions 1–8.

Each of the remaining 10 questions requires you to solve the problem and enter your answer by marking the circles in the special grid, as shown in the examples below. You may use any available space for scratch work.

Answer: $\frac{7}{12}$

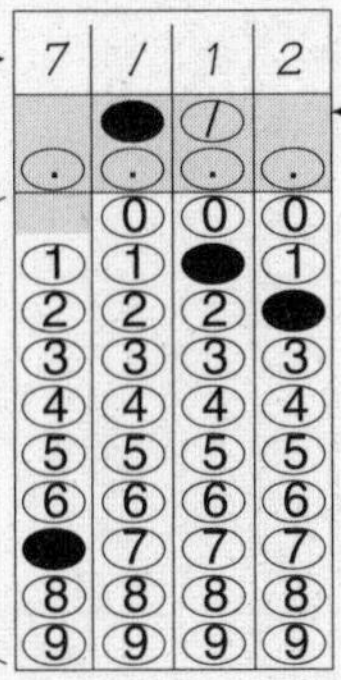

Answer: 2.5

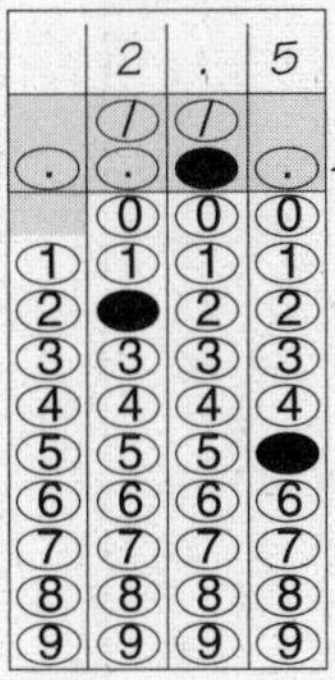

Answer: 201
Either position is correct.

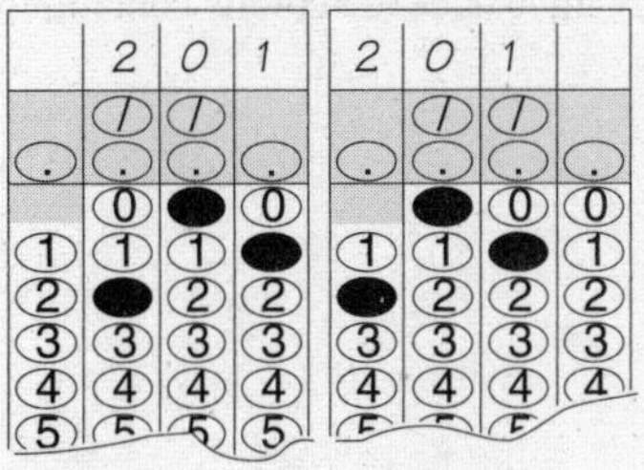

Note: You may start your answers in any column, space permitting. Columns not needed should be left blank.

- Mark no more than one circle in any column.
- Because the answer document will be machine-scored, **you will receive credit only if the circles are filled in correctly.**
- Although not required, it is suggested that you write your answer in the boxes at the top of the columns to help you fill in the circles accurately.
- Some problems may have more than one correct answer. In such cases, grid only one answer.
- No question has a negative answer.
- **Mixed numbers** such as $3\frac{1}{2}$ must be gridded as 3.5 or 7/2. (If 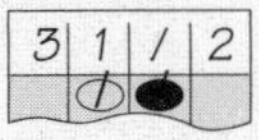 is gridded, it will be interpreted as $\frac{31}{2}$, not $3\frac{1}{2}$.)

- **Decimal Answers:** If you obtain a decimal answer with more digits than the grid can accommodate, it may be either rounded or truncated, but it must fill the entire grid. For example, if you obtain an answer such as 0.6666..., you should record your result as .666 or .667. **A less accurate value such as .66 or .67 will be scored as incorrect.**

Acceptable ways to grid $\frac{2}{3}$ are:

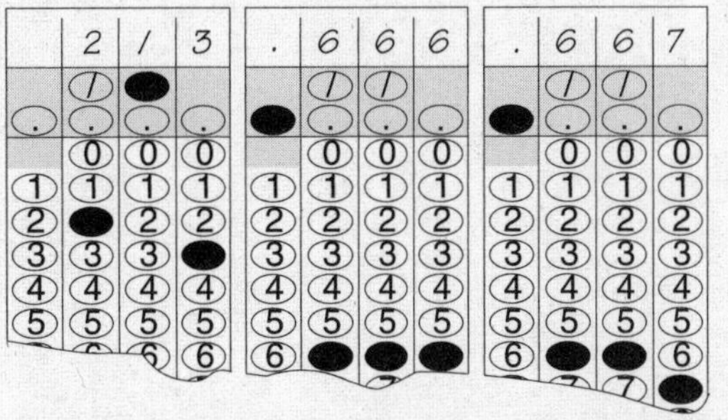

9. If $3(y - 2) = 24$, then what does $5(y - 2)$ equal?

10. Twelve tomatoes are checked, and four of them are found to be rotten. What is the probability that one tomato chosen at random will not be rotten?

GO ON TO THE NEXT PAGE

$$n = 12 \times 2^{\frac{t}{3}}$$

11. The number of mice in a certain colony is shown by the formula above, such that n is the number of mice and t is the time, in months, since the start of the colony. If 2 *years* have passed since the start of the colony, how many mice does the colony contain now?

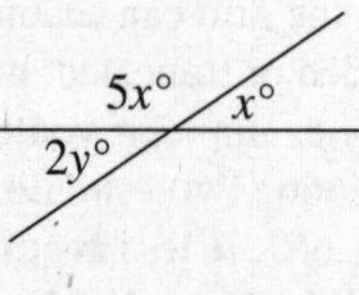

12. In the figure above, what is the value of y ?

13. Squaring a certain number is equivalent to multiplying the number by 10 and then taking one-half the result. What is one possible value of the number?

14. If b is 9 more than c, c is 4 more than a, and d is 3 more than a, then what is the positive difference between b and d ?

GO ON TO THE NEXT PAGE

15. On Thursday, Jeanine drove 20 miles to work, at an average speed of 40 miles per hour. She then drove home along the same route at an average speed of 50 miles per hour. How many hours did she spend driving to and from work on Thursday?

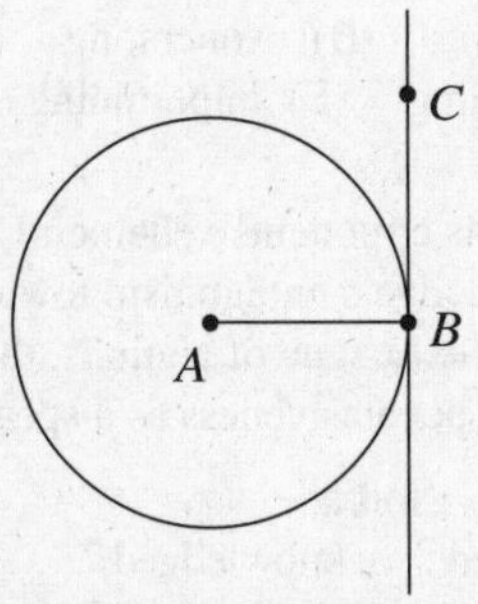

Note: Figure not drawn to scale.

16. In the figure above, $\overline{BC}$ is tangent to circle with center A at B. If the length of $\overline{AC}$ (not shown) is $10\sqrt{3}$, and $AC = 2AB$, what is the length of $\overline{BC}$?

17. Set X consists of twelve numbers. The average (arithmetic mean) of the first six numbers is 15. The sum of the last six numbers is 24. What is the average of all twelve numbers in set X?

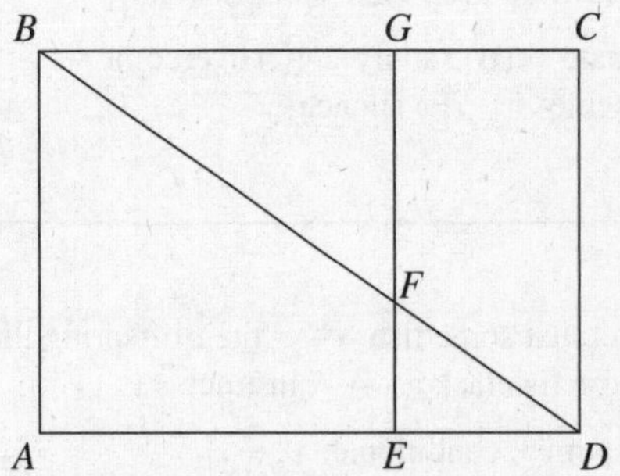

Note: Figure not drawn to scale.

18. In the figure above, the area of rectangle $ABCD$ is 120. If $\overline{AD} \perp \overline{EG}$, $CD = 6$, and $AE = 12$, what is the length of $\overline{EF}$?

STOP

If you finish before time is called, you may check your work on this section only. Do not turn to any other section in the test.

SECTION 3
Time — 25 minutes
24 Questions

Turn to Section 3 of your answer sheet to answer the questions in this section.

Directions: For each question in this section, select the best answer from among the choices given and fill in the corresponding circle on the answer sheet.

Each sentence below has one or two blanks, each blank indicating that something has been omitted. Beneath the sentence are five words or sets of words labeled A through E. Choose the word or set of words that, when inserted in the sentence, best fits the meaning of the sentence as a whole.

Example:

Desiring to ------- his taunting friends, Mitch gave them taffy in hopes it would keep their mouths shut.

(A) eliminate (B) satisfy (C) overcome (D) ridicule (E) silence

Ⓐ Ⓑ Ⓒ Ⓓ ●

1. The fact that some fish ------- their offspring illustrates that these fish lack a ------- instinct.

(A) spurn . . conditional
(B) mesmerize . . visual
(C) consume . . predatory
(D) devour . . nurturing
(E) protect . . maternal

2. Because the company was forced to ------- the faulty product and stop distribution, it soon had ------- of useless inventory.

(A) examine . . a market
(B) challenge . . a mass
(C) explain . . an oversupply
(D) release . . a backlog
(E) recall . . an abundance

3. Every previous attempt to force the mayor from office had failed, yet his critics ------- in their impeachment efforts.

(A) foundered (B) persevered (C) lagged (D) condensed (E) receded

4. When Jerome awoke from the nightmare, he had difficulty ------- whether his memory was of an amorphous dream or of an actual reality.

(A) ascertaining (B) exonerating (C) disputing (D) concealing (E) importuning

5. Even though his opponents vehemently ------- Senator Henry Cabot Lodge's antagonism toward the United Sates joining the League of Nations, they still ------- his eloquence and persuasiveness as a speaker.

(A) deplored . . forbade
(B) repudiated . . acknowledged
(C) sustained . . admired
(D) understood . . bewildered
(E) slandered . . overlooked

GO ON TO THE NEXT PAGE

Directions: Each passage below is followed by questions based on its content. Answer the questions on the basis of what is stated or implied in each passage and in any introductory material that may be provided.

Questions 6–9 are based on the following passages.

The following paragraphs discuss the invention of the mechanized cotton gin by Eli Whitney in the eighteenth century.

Passage 1

Eli Whitney is generally credited with the invention of the cotton gin, which he patented in 1794, but some historians question the extent of Whitney's authorship. Some studies conclude that Georgia plantation owner Catharine Greene contributed key elements of the design. Another study shows that slaves working on Greene's plantation devised the first cotton gins but were not allowed to register a patent. Still other theories maintain that primitive "roller gins" had been used for centuries before Whitney, who only mechanized and improved the process. It's not hard to imagine that one or all of these parties made unacknowledged contributions, since the United States Patent and Trademark Office will not issue a patent if the inventor concedes outside influences.

Passage 2

History books observe that Eli Whitney invented and patented the cotton gin in 1794, but most texts don't give proper credit to Catharine Greene, who made significant contributions to Whitney's original model. Greene hired Whitney to live on her plantation and tutor her, and it was there that Whitney heard planters complain about manually removing the seeds from the cotton. Whitney began to develop his cotton gin, while Greene provided food, shelter, and encouragement. Greene's contribution was more than symbolic, however: when Whitney's initial gins kept clogging, Greene suggested he use a comb-like device to separate the pulled cotton fibers from the machine. It was this device that elevated Whitney's gin above the other primitive and inept tools already available.

6. The author of Passage 1 mentions the detail about the United States Patent and Trademark Office in the last sentence in order to

(A) condemn Whitney for his decision to seek a patent
(B) further clarify why slaves could not seek a patent
(C) deny that others made unacknowledged contributions
(D) demonstrate how Whitney inadvertently ignored outside contributions
(E) offer a possible reason why Whitney claimed sole authorship

7. The author of Passage 2 claims all of the following about Catharine Greene EXCEPT

(A) she provided physical and mental support for Whitney
(B) she explained the need for the invention
(C) she suggested a key design element
(D) some of her contributions were responses to problems
(E) she did not initially employ Whitney in order to develop the cotton gin

8. The conclusions about Catharine Greene in Passages 1 and 2 differ in that Passage 1 is

(A) uncertain, while Passage 2 is unequivocal
(B) inquisitive, while Passage 2 is uncertain
(C) biased, while Passage 2 is objective
(D) confident, while Passage 2 is skeptical
(E) ignorant, while Passage 2 is informed

9. Which of the following can be inferred from BOTH passages?

(A) Catharine Greene used "roller gins" on her plantation.
(B) The contributions of slaves were instrumental in the original design of the cotton gin.
(C) Certain design features of Whitney's gin may have been suggested by outside influences.
(D) The United States Patent Office refused to issue patents for all gins before Whitney's.
(E) The most popular tool to prepare cotton before Whitney's gin was the "roller gin."

GO ON TO THE NEXT PAGE

Questions 10–18 are based on the following passage.

The following passage was taken from the autobiography of Helen Keller, who was stricken with an illness that left her deaf and blind as a young child.

I guessed vaguely from my mother's signs and from the hurrying to and fro in the house that something unusual was about to happen, so I went to the door and waited on the steps. The afternoon sun penetrated the mass of honeysuckle that covered the porch, and fell on my upturned face. My fingers lingered almost unconsciously on the familiar leaves and blossoms which had just come forth to greet the sweet southern spring. I did not know what the future held of marvel or surprise for me. Anger and bitterness had preyed upon me continually for weeks and a deep languor had succeeded this passionate struggle.

Have you ever been at sea in a dense fog, when it seemed as if a tangible white darkness shut you in, and the great ship, tense and anxious, groped her way toward the shore with plummet and sounding-line, and you waited with beating heart for something to happen? I was like that ship before my education began, only I was without compass or sounding-line, and had no way of knowing how near the harbour was. "Light! Give me light!" was the wordless cry of my soul, and the light of love shone on me in that very hour.

I felt approaching footsteps, I stretched out my hand as I supposed to my mother. Someone took it, and I was caught up and held close in the arms of her who had come to reveal all things to me, and, more than all things else, to love me.

The morning after my teacher came she led me into her room and gave me a doll. When I had played with it a little while, Miss Sullivan slowly spelled into my hand the word "d-o-l-l." I was at once interested in this finger play and tried to imitate it. When I finally succeeded in making the letters correctly I was flushed with childish pleasure and pride. Running downstairs to my mother I held up my hand and made the letters for doll. I did not know that I was spelling a word or even that words existed; I was simply making my fingers go in monkey-like imitation. But my teacher had been with me several weeks before I understood that everything has a name.

One day, while I was playing with my new doll, Miss Sullivan put my big rag doll into my lap also, spelled "d-o-l-l" and tried to make me understand that "d-o-l-l" applied to both. Earlier in the day we had had a tussle over the words "m-u-g" and "w-a-t-e-r." Miss Sullivan had tried to impress it upon me that "m-u-g" is mug and that "w-a-t-e-r" is water, but I persisted in confounding the two. In despair she had dropped the subject for the time, only to renew it at the first opportunity. I became impatient at her repeated attempts and, seizing the new doll, I dashed it upon the floor. I was keenly delighted when I felt the fragments of the broken doll at my feet. Neither sorrow nor regret followed my passionate outburst. I had not loved the doll. In the still, dark world in which I lived there was no strong sentiment or tenderness.

We walked down the path to the well-house, attracted by the fragrance of the honeysuckle with which it was covered. Someone was drawing water and my teacher placed my hand under the spout. As the cool stream gushed over one hand she spelled into the other the word water, first slowly, then rapidly. I stood still, my whole attention fixed upon the motions of her fingers. Suddenly I felt a misty consciousness as of something forgotten—a thrill of returning thought; and somehow the mystery of language was revealed to me. I knew then that "w-a-t-e-r" meant the wonderful cool something that was flowing over my hand. That living word awakened my soul, gave it light, hope, joy, set it free! There were barriers still, it is true, but barriers that could in time be swept away.

I left the well-house eager to learn. Everything had a name, and each name gave birth to a new thought. As we returned to the house every object which I touched seemed to quiver with life. That was because I saw everything with the strange, new sight that had come to me. On entering the door I remembered the doll I had broken. I felt my way to the hearth and picked up the pieces. I tried vainly to put them together. Then my eyes filled with tears; for I realized what I had done, and for the first time I felt repentance and sorrow.

10. According to the passage, the narrator views language as

(A) a necessary but impractical part of life
(B) the key to her appreciation of the world around her
(C) a phenomenon that remains shrouded in mystery
(D) the only method that she can use to express her feelings
(E) a barrier to understanding her own thoughts

11. The word "succeeded " in line 10 most nearly means

(A) accomplished
(B) split
(C) followed
(D) broken
(E) performed

12. The analogy to "being at sea in a dense fog" (lines 12–18) is used to show that the author felt

(A) scared, because she felt like she was sinking in her dark, still life
(B) angry, because she could not control her life
(C) adventurous, because she knew that learning could be like a journey
(D) lost, because she had difficulty communicating with the world
(E) confused, because her new teacher was trying to accomplish too much

GO ON TO THE NEXT PAGE

13. The author's reference to "finger play" in line 28 emphasizes her

(A) childish need to learn by playing games with dolls and toys
(B) teacher's technique for teaching her grammar
(C) initial inability to understand that she was spelling words with her hands
(D) opinion that learning sign language was as easy as a child's game
(E) mother's helplessness in teaching her to communicate with her teacher

14. The narrator 's attitude toward breaking the doll changes from

(A) sorrow to understanding
(B) excitement to disgust
(C) anger to joy
(D) pleasure to regret
(E) indifference to enjoyment

15. The author implies that, prior to the arrival of her teacher, she

(A) experienced feelings of resentment, followed by a time of inactivity
(B) had never felt loved before
(C) did not expect anything good to happen in her future
(D) was eager to learn about the world but lacked the means to
(E) was not dominated by sentimentalism and tenderness

16. The passage suggests that the author broke the doll in order to

(A) express her frustration at her inability to understand her teacher's lesson
(B) lash out at her teacher for her teacher's failure to instruct her properly
(C) reveal the extent to which she felt enraged by her situation
(D) see if her teacher would become angry at her childish actions
(E) compare her teacher's reaction to her behavior to her mother's reaction

17. It can be inferred from the passage that the author would most likely agree with which of the following statements?

(A) Without language, humans are destined to feel anger and bitterness.
(B) In order for people to overcome their flaws, they must open themselves up to new situations.
(C) People often destroy treasured objects without fully realizing the consequences of their actions.
(D) Learning can free a person from the barriers they construct around themselves.
(E) Children need positive role models to help shape their lives.

18. The difference between the author's experience in lines 29–34 ("When I...imitation") and in lines 59–63 ("I knew...away") can best be characterized as the difference between

(A) pride and humility
(B) physical sensation and mental facility
(C) memorization and comprehension
(D) truth and mystery
(E) childishness and maturity

GO ON TO THE NEXT PAGE

Questions 19–24 are based on the following passage.

Discovering a previously unknown plant or animal is not an unusual occurrence in the scientific community. Biologists are constantly in the process of identifying and classifying new species. The following passage describes one recently discovered animal, Nanaloricus mysticus, which lives in the sand on the ocean floor.

In 1983, a previously unknown creature, *Nanaloricus mysticus*, which vaguely resembles an ambulatory pineapple, was described as a new species, new genus, new family, new order, and new phylum of animals. Barrel-shaped, a quarter of a millimeter long (one-hundredth of an inch), sheathed in neat rows of scales and spines, it possesses a snout up front and, when young, a pair of flippers like penguin wings at the rear. Almost nothing is known about its ecology and behavior, but we can guess from its body shape and armament that it burrows like a mole in search of microscopic prey.

To place a species in its own phylum, the decision made in this case by the Danish zoologist Reinhardt Kristensen, is a bold step. He said—and other zoologists agreed—that *Nanaloricus mysticus* is anatomically distinct enough to deserve placement alongside major groups such as the phylum Mollusca, comprising all the snails and other mollusks, and phylum Chordata, consisting of all the vertebrates and their close relatives. Kristensen named the new phylum Loricifera, from the Latin *lorica* (corset) and *ferre* (to bear). The "corset" in this case is the cuticular sheath that encases most of the body.

The Loriciferans—now a larger group, since about thirty other species have been discovered in the past decade—live among a host of other tiny, bizarre animals found in the spaces between grains of sand and gravel on the ocean bottom. This Lilliputian fauna is so poorly known that most of the species lack a scientific name. They are nevertheless cosmopolitan and extremely abundant. And they are almost certainly vital to the healthy functioning of the ocean's environment.

The existence of Loriciferans and their submicroscopic associates is emblematic of how little we know of the living world, even that part necessary for our existence. We dwell on a largely unexplored planet. Large numbers of new species continue to be discovered every year. And of those already discovered, more than 99 percent are known only by a scientific name, a handful of specimens in a museum, and a few scraps of anatomical description in scientific journals. It is a myth that scientists break out champagne when a new species is discovered. Our museums are glutted with new species. We don't have time to describe more than a small fraction of those pouring in each year. How many more unknown pieces of the ecological puzzle remain to be found? No one has the faintest idea; it is one of the great unsolved problems of science.

19. The passage serves primarily to

(A) describe one of the ways in which scientists categorize formerly undiscovered species
(B) encourage zoologists to be bolder when making classifications
(C) reveal the extent of scientific ignorance concerning the life forms that inhabit the ocean floor
(D) point out the abundance of undiscovered life forms through the discussion of a new phylum
(E) express approval for the scientists who discovered *Nanaloricus mysticus*

20. The passage suggests that new species are classified according to their

(A) position in the food chain
(B) reproductive behavior
(C) geographical location
(D) relationships to other animals
(E) physical characteristics

21. In describing the *Nanaloricus mysticus*, the author provides all of the following EXCEPT

(A) precise measurements
(B) an evolutionary explanation
(C) a literal description
(D) a physical comparison
(E) speculations about function

22. The word "cosmopolitan" (line 28) most nearly means

(A) tiny
(B) important
(C) bizarre
(D) unknown
(E) widespread

GO ON TO THE NEXT PAGE

23. It can be inferred that the author states "It is a myth... discovered" (lines 39–40) because

(A) scientists no longer care about the discovery of new species
(B) new species are evolving at a faster rate than that at which scientists can discover them
(C) each new species discovered represents new knowledge about the world
(D) it is true that scientists view the discovery of a new species as a significant event
(E) the number of species that remain unstudied is staggering

24. The passage implies that one consideration that goes into the placement of a new species into a phylum is

(A) the relative abundance of the new species in the ecosystem
(B) the structural characteristics of the newly discovered species
(C) the importance of the new species to the ecosystem as a whole
(D) the geographical distribution of the new species
(E) the name given to the new species by its discoverer

STOP

If you finish before time is called, you may check your work on this section only.
Do not turn to any other section in the test.

SECTION 4
Time — 25 minutes
35 Questions

Turn to Section 4 of your answer sheet to answer the questions in this section.

Directions: For each question in this section, select the best answer from among the choices given and fill in the corresponding circle on the answer sheet.

The following sentences test correctness and effectiveness of expression. Part of each sentence or the entire sentence is underlined; beneath each sentence are five ways of phrasing the underlined material. Choice A repeats the original phrasing; the other four choices are different. If you think the original phrasing produces a better sentence than any of the alternatives, select choice A; if not, select one of the other choices.

In making your selection, follow the requirements of standard written English; that is, pay attention to grammar, choice of words, sentence construction, and punctuation. Your selection should result in the most effective sentence—clear and precise, without awkwardness or ambiguity.

EXAMPLE:

Bobby Flay baked his first cake and he was thirteen years old then.
(A) and he was thirteen years old then
(B) when he was thirteen
(C) at age thirteen years old
(D) upon the reaching of thirteen years
(E) at the time when he was thirteen

Ⓐ●ⒸⒹⒺ

1. The tornado, a great swirling mass of violently rotating air, causes tremendous destruction whether it touches down on the earth.
   (A) The tornado, a great swirling mass of violently rotating air, causes tremendous destruction whether it touches down on the earth.
   (B) The tornado, a great mass of violently rotating air, causes tremendous destruction when it touches down on the earth.
   (C) A great swirling mass of violently rotating air, the tornado causes tremendous destruction because of its touching down on the earth.
   (D) When it touches down the earth, the tornado, a great swirling mass of violently rotating air, tremendous destruction is caused.
   (E) Causing tremendous destruction when touching down to the earth, a great swirling mass of violently rotating air is a tornado.

2. *Abe Lincoln in Illinois* is a historical film about Abraham Lincoln's where his life as a shopkeeper, suitor, lawyer, legislator, and president.
   (A) Lincoln's where his life
   (B) Lincoln where he lives his life
   (C) Lincoln in which he lives
   (D) Lincoln's life
   (E) Lincoln about his life

3. Some argue that talking on a cell phone while driving is no more distracting than eating a sandwich or looking at a map.
   (A) eating a sandwich or looking at a map
   (B) sandwich eating or looking at a map
   (C) when compared to eating or looking at a sandwich or a map
   (D) when you eat a sandwich or look at a map
   (E) the acts of eating a sandwich or looking at a map

4. Vanessa took a leisurely lunch on Friday; walking through the park, the grass tickling her feet.
   (A) walking through the park, the grass tickling her feet
   (B) the grass tickled her feet while walking through the park
   (C) finding the grass tickled her feet, walking through the park
   (D) finding that walking through the park, made the grass tickle her feet
   (E) the grass tickled her feet as she walked through the park

GO ON TO THE NEXT PAGE

5. As soon as the minister declared Anders and Siri husband and wife, the seven bells in the church tower ringing, and the spectators waiting outside the church sent up a rousing cheer.

(A) Anders and Siri husband and wife, the seven bells in the church tower ringing
(B) Anders and Siri to be husband and wife, the seven bells in the church tower ring
(C) Anders and Siri being husband and wife, the seven bells in the church tower rang
(D) that since Anders and Siri husband and wife, the seven bells in the church tower had rung
(E) Anders and Siri husband and wife, the seven bells in the church tower rang

6. After his election to the town council, Randy announced that, clearly, there were many promises that he would be unable to keep.

(A) Randy announced that, clearly, there were many promises that he would be unable to keep
(B) Randy announced that there was many promises that he would be unable to keep clearly
(C) Randy announced that there were many promises that he would clearly be unable to keep
(D) clearly, Randy would be unable to keep his many promises
(E) Randy clearly announced that there is many promises that he would be unable to keep

7. It is often assumed that women do not care for "violent" sports, such as football or boxing; however, this assumption overlooks the fact that many women are not only fans of these sports, but also participants in them.

(A) such as football or boxing; however, this assumption overlooks the fact that many women are not only fans of these sports, but also participants in them
(B) like football or boxing; it overlooks the women who are not only fans but will be participating in them
(C) such as football or boxing, whereas this assumption, which overlooks the facts, misses that many women are not only fans of these sports, but also participants in them
(D) like football or boxing; however, the fact that many women are not only fans of these sports, but also participants in them is overlooked through this assumption
(E) such as football or boxing, assuming wrongly that many women are not only fans of these sports, but also participants in them

8. Never before in the course of human conflict has so much been owed by so many to so few.

(A) has so much been owed
(B) have we been so deeply in debt
(C) has a large quantity been owed
(D) is so much being owed
(E) in which so much was owed

9. Many people assume that all aspiring singers strive to work on Broadway, in opera, or in the popular music industry, though many vocalists building successful careers at theme parks, performing on cruise ships, or working as backup singers.

(A) though many vocalists building successful careers at theme parks, performing on cruise ships, or working as backup singers
(B) still many vocalists are building successful careers at theme parks, performing on cruise ships, or working as backup singers
(C) but in truth many vocalists build successful careers singing at theme parks, performing on cruise ships, or working as backup singers
(D) despite the fact that many vocalists build successful careers at theme parks, or on cruise ships, or working as backup singers
(E) even though many vocalists, building successful careers, sing at theme parks, performing on cruise ships, or backup singers

10. The Maginot Line proved itself to be worthless at defending France in wartime furthermore its construction cost drained French resources.

(A) wartime furthermore its
(B) wartime; furthermore, it's
(C) wartime, furthermore, it's
(D) wartime; furthermore, its
(E) wartime, furthermore its

11. In the story *Peter Pan*, Wendy, along with John and Michael, fly to Never-Neverland beside Peter Pan to confront the dread Captain Hook.

(A) along with John and Michael, fly to Never-Neverland beside Peter Pan
(B) along with John and Michael, flies to Never-Neverland beside Peter Pan
(C) along with John and Michael, is about to fly to Never-Neverland beside Peter Pan
(D) besides John, Michael, and Peter Pan flying to Never-Neverland
(E) John, and Michael flies to Never-Neverland, while beside Peter Pan

GO ON TO THE NEXT PAGE

The following sentences test your ability to recognize grammar and usage errors. Each sentence contains either a single error or no error at all. No sentence contains more than one error. The error, if there is one, is underlined and lettered. If the sentence contains an error, select the one underlined part that must be changed to make the sentence correct. If the sentence is correct, select choice E. In choosing answers, follow the requirements of standard written English.

EXAMPLE:

The other (A) players and **her** (B) **significantly** (C) improved the game plan **created by** (D) the coaches. **No error** (E)

Ⓐ ● Ⓒ Ⓓ Ⓔ

12. Martha's high SAT score caused many of her classmates to feel jealous **for** (A) her, but **they** (B) should have **prepared themselves** (C) for the test as thoroughly as she **had**. (D) **No error** (E)

13. **Despite** (A) their urban upbringing, the campers wanted **to have** (B) the most natural experience possible, and **therefore** (C) did not pack any utensils, sleeping bags, or **no** (D) prepackaged food. **No error** (E)

14. Kimberly had mixed **success** (A) in her attempt **to grow** (B) cacti and geraniums; while some died, **the other** (C) thrived because **she** (D) failed to water them regularly. **No error** (E)

15. **Throughout** (A) the fashion industry, both designers of shoes **and** (B) **purse designers** (C) often choose to expand **their** (D) brands into other accessories. **No error** (E)

16. One of the **most** (A) amusing aspects of *The Iliad* **is** (B) that, despite the immense size of the two clashing armies, **everyone** (C) knew everyone else's **name**. (D) **No error** (E)

17. **It is** (A) **common knowledge** (B) that adding spices to tofu always **make** (C) it taste **better**. (D) **No error** (E)

18. Bats, **much like** (A) honeybees, sometimes have **specific** (B) roles in the cave, **such as** (C) guarding the entrance and **scouting** (D) for new caves. **No error** (E)

19. Alan **should of** (A) known **that** (B) his sister **would try** (C) to blame the damaged headlight on **him**. (D) **No error** (E)

20. Susie, despite **having dated** (A) John for only one month, **was** (B) convinced that **she and him** (C) **were** (D) the perfect couple. **No error** (E)

GO ON TO THE NEXT PAGE

21. While it was different from all of the other classes
A B
he had ever taken, Erik was still unhappy with his
C D
psychology class. No error
E

22. By the time she finishes her last final exam next
A B
week, Jen has spent eighteen hours consolidating,
C
outlining, and studying her class notes. No error
D E

23. The success of a new computer company lies in its
A
ingenuity; the machines must have a clever design, be
efficient in a unique way, and generally they provide
B
the consumer with previously unknown but now vital
C D
features. No error
E

24. Nothing prepared the country for the brutal civil war
A
it faced at the end of the century, even though they saw
B C D
several wars previously. No error
E

25. To talk with one's grandparents about their lives when
A B C
they were young is having a real understanding of history.
D
No error
E

26. Most of the exchange students which were working
A
in the shore area could barely make enough money to
B
support themselves during the summer months. No error
C D E

27. Either Jack or Ashlee are volunteering at the shelter this
A
weekend, but she won't go if he is going. No error
B C D E

28. As its popularity has grown, the Weimaraner, like other
A
popular breeds, have run the increasing risk of over-
B C D
breeding. No error
E

29. There was a time where it was common practice for men
A
to surrender their seats to women, but that era seems to
B C D
have passed. No error
E

GO ON TO THE NEXT PAGE

Directions: The following passage is an early draft of an essay. Some parts of the passage need to be rewritten.

Read the passage and select the best answers for the questions that follow. Some questions are about particular sentences or parts of sentences and ask you to improve sentence structure or word choice. Other questions ask you to consider organization and development. In choosing answers, follow the requirements of standard written English.

Questions 30–35 are based on the following student essay.

(**1**) Last month I visited a sanctuary for birds of prey. (**2**) There were 30 outdoor cages, they were all large. (**3**) Each cage held between one and four birds of prey: hawks, eagles, owls, or vultures. (**4**) Besides each cage was information on the species of bird in the cage: range, habitat, size, rarity, and other interesting information. (**5**) The bird sanctuary takes birds which have been injured. (**6**) It tries to heal the birds. (**7**) The birds which are fully healed are released back into the wild. (**8**) Sadly, about half of the birds which arrive at the sanctuary can not be fully healed. (**9**) This was necessary, as birds of prey, which are unable to fly or see well, would not survive in the wild. (**10**) These birds are the ones in the cages. (**11**) I felt sad for the birds: their cages were large and they had good food, but it was clear that they wanted to fly free. (**12**) They would never be able to fly free again.

(**13**) The birds, which came from all over the United States, had been injured many ways, but there were two which were by far the most common. (**14**) Many birds had been hit by cars, and many others had been shot. (**15**) It is illegal to shoot birds of prey in the United States. (**16**) Seeing these hawks and even bald eagles which would never fly again made me angry. (**17**) It also convinced me to drive at a reasonable speed and watch out for animals. (**18**) On a happier note, I now feel a special thrill whenever I look up and see a bird of prey flying free.

30. The first paragraph is to be split into two smaller paragraphs. The most appropriate place to begin a new paragraph would be between

(A) sentences 3 and 4
(B) sentences 4 and 5
(C) sentences 7 and 8
(D) sentences 8 and 9
(E) sentences 10 and 11

31. In context, which revision to sentence 4 is most needed?

(A) Change "Besides" to "Beside"
(B) Eliminate "species of"
(C) Change "cage" to "cages"
(D) Replace the colon with a comma
(E) Change "and other interesting information" to "and so forth"

32. Which of the following, in context, is the best way to combine sentences 5 and 6, reproduced below?

The bird sanctuary takes birds which have been injured. It tries to heal the birds.

(A) The sanctuary takes birds which have suffered an injury and tries to heal it.
(B) The sanctuary takes injured birds, and yet it tries to heal them.
(C) Birds are tried to be healed when injured at the sanctuary.
(D) Injured birds are healed when the sanctuary takes them.
(E) The sanctuary takes injured birds and tries to heal them.

33. Which of the following pairs of sentences should be switched with each other in order to improve the flow of the passage?

(A) Sentences 2 and 3
(B) Sentences 9 and 10
(C) Sentences 11 and 12
(D) Sentences 13 and 14
(E) Sentences 16 and 17

GO ON TO THE NEXT PAGE

34. Sentences 14 and 15, reproduced below, can best be combined in which of the following ways?

Many birds had been hit by cars, and many others had been shot. It is illegal to shoot birds of prey in the United States.

(A) Many birds had been hit by cars despite the fact that many others in the United States had been illegally shot.
(B) Many birds had been hit and shot by cars in the United States; it is not legal.
(C) Many birds had been hit by cars, and many others had been shot, even though it is illegal in the United States to shoot birds of prey.
(D) Many birds had been hit by cars, and many others had been shot; while it is illegal to shoot birds of prey in the United States.
(E) Many birds had been hit by cars, and many others had been shot; it is illegal in the United States.

35. Which of the following sentences can be eliminated without harming the meaning or flow of the passage?

(A) Sentence 10
(B) Sentence 15
(C) Sentence 6
(D) Sentence 4
(E) Sentence 18

STOP

If you finish before time is called, you may check your work on this section only.
Do not turn to any other section in the test.

SECTION 5
Time — 25 minutes
18 Questions

Turn to Section 5 of your answer sheet to answer the questions in this section.

Directions: This section contains two types of questions. You have 25 minutes to complete both types. For questions 1-8, solve each problem and decide which is the best of the choices given. Fill in the corresponding circle on the answer sheet. You may use any available space for scratchwork.

Notes

1. The use of a calculator is permitted.
2. All numbers used are real numbers.
3. Figures that accompany problems in this test are intended to provide information useful in solving the problems. They are drawn as accurately as possible EXCEPT when it is stated in a specific problem that the figure is not drawn to scale. All figures lie in a plane unless other wise indicated.
4. Unless otherwise specified, the domain of any function f is assumed to be the set of all real numbers x for which $f(x)$ is a real number.

Reference Information

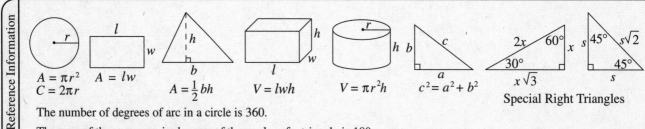

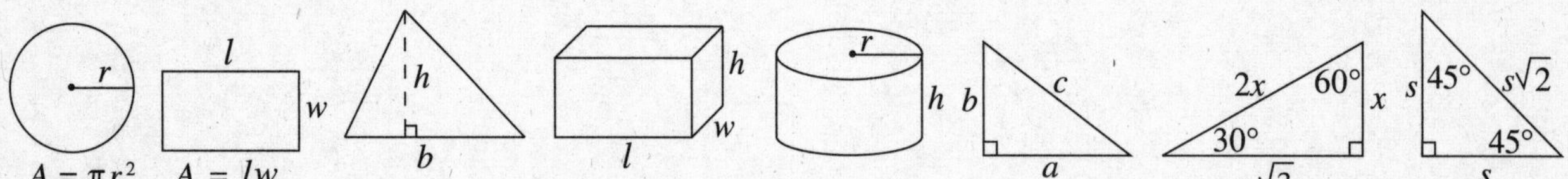

$A = \pi r^2$
$C = 2\pi r$

$A = lw$

$A = \frac{1}{2}bh$

$V = lwh$

$V = \pi r^2 h$

$c^2 = a^2 + b^2$

Special Right Triangles

The number of degrees of arc in a circle is 360.

The sum of the measures in degrees of the angles of a triangle is 180.

1. If 7 times a number is 84, what is 4 times the number?

(A) 16
(B) 28
(C) 48
(D) 52
(E) 56

2. A painter drains 4 gallons of turpentine from a full 16-gallon jug. What percent of the turpentine remains in the jug?

(A) 33%
(B) 45%
(C) 50%
(D) 67%
(E) 75%

GO ON TO THE NEXT PAGE

3. If each number in the following sum were increased by t, the new sum would be 4.22. What is the value of t ?

$$\begin{array}{r} 0.65 \\ 0.85 \\ 0.38 \\ +\underline{0.86} \\ 2.74 \end{array}$$

(A) 0.24
(B) 0.29
(C) 0.33
(D) 0.37
(E) 0.43

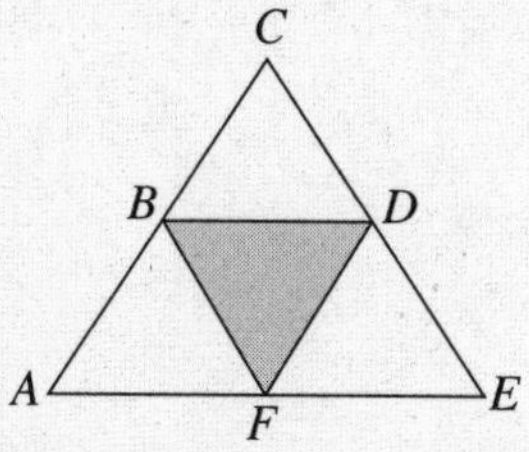

4. In the figure above, ΔACE is equilateral, and B, D, and F are the midpoints of $\overline{AC}$, $\overline{CE}$, and $\overline{AE}$, respectively. If the area of ΔACE is 24, what is the area of the shaded region?

(A) 4
(B) 6
(C) 8
(D) 12
(E) 16

5. If $p=-\frac{1}{q}$, $q=-\frac{1}{r}$, $r=-\frac{1}{s}$, and $s=-\frac{1}{4}$, what is the value of p ?

(A) -4
(B) $-\frac{1}{4}$
(C) 0
(D) $\frac{1}{4}$
(E) 4

6. When 23 is divided by 3, the remainder is x. What is the remainder when 23 is divided by $2x$?

(A) 1
(B) 2
(C) 3
(D) 4
(E) 5

GO ON TO THE NEXT PAGE

7. A monthly Internet service costs d dollars for the first 10 hours, and e dollars per hour for each hour after the first ten. Which of the following could represent the cost of the service, if h represents the total number of hours the service was used this month?

(A) $d + e(h - 10)$
(B) $d + 10eh$
(C) $eh + 10d$
(D) $eh(d - 10)$
(E) $h(d + 10e)$

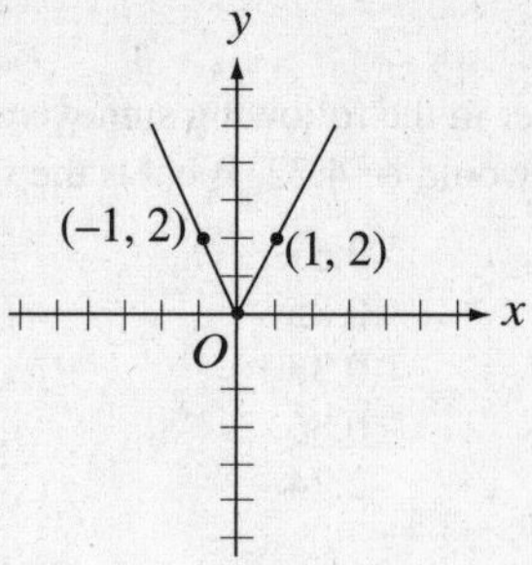

8. The graph of $y = f(x)$ is shown above. Which of the following could be the equation for $f(x)$?

(A) $f(x) = 2x$
(B) $f(x) = x^2$
(C) $f(x) = 2x^2$
(D) $f(x) = x - 2$
(E) $f(x) = |2x|$

GO ON TO THE NEXT PAGE

Directions: For Student-Produced Response questions 9–18, use the grids to the right of the answer document page on which you have answered questions 1–8.

Each of the remaining 10 questions requires you to solve the problem and enter your answer by marking the circles in the special grid, as shown in the examples below. You may use any available space for scratch work.

Answer: $\frac{7}{12}$

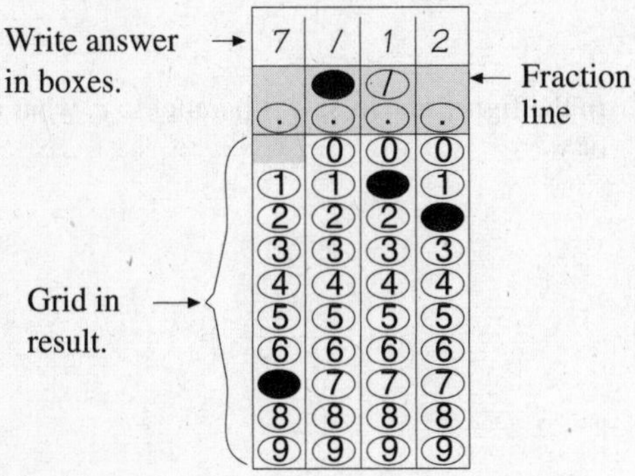

Answer: 2.5

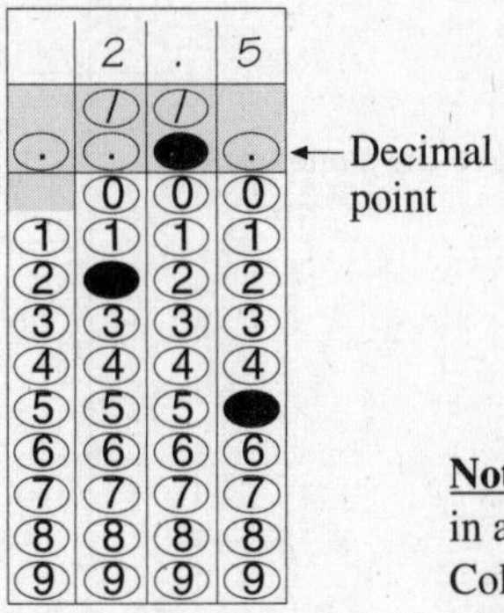

Answer: 201
Either position is correct.

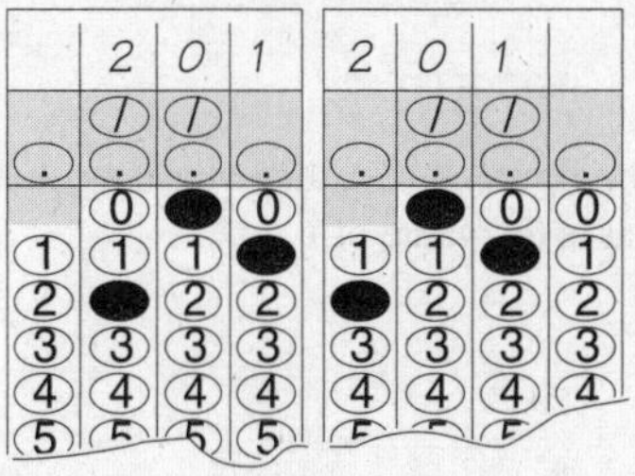

Note: You may start your answers in any column, space permitting. Columns not needed should be left blank.

- Mark no more than one circle in any column.
- Because the answer document will be machine-scored, **you will receive credit only if the circles are filled in correctly.**
- Although not required, it is suggested that you write your answer in the boxes at the top of the columns to help you fill in the circles accurately.
- Some problems may have more than one correct answer. In such cases, grid only one answer.
- No question has a negative answer.
- **Mixed numbers** such as $3\frac{1}{2}$ must be gridded as 3.5 or 7/2. (If 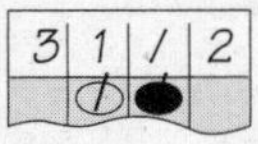 is gridded, it will be interpreted as $\frac{31}{2}$, not $3\frac{1}{2}$.)

- **Decimal Answers:** If you obtain a decimal answer with more digits than the grid can accommodate, it may be either rounded or truncated, but it must fill the entire grid. For example, if you obtain an answer such as 0.6666..., you should record your result as .666 or .667. **A less accurate value such as .66 or .67 will be scored as incorrect.**

Acceptable ways to grid $\frac{2}{3}$ are:

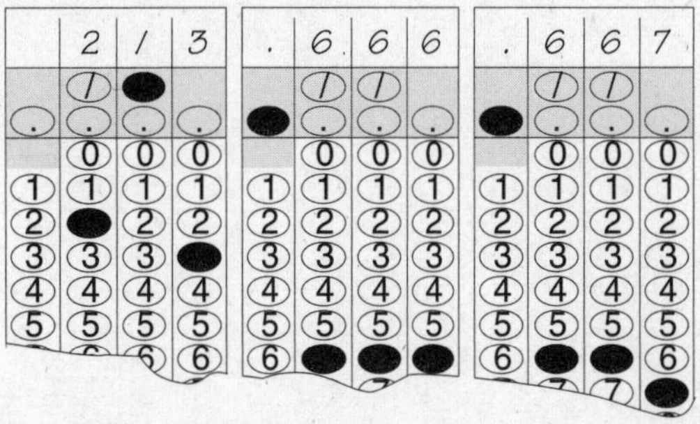

9. If $\sqrt{x} + 22 = 38$, $x =$

10. Set A contains all odd integers from 0 to 10 that are not prime. If y is a member of set A, what is one possible value of y ?

GO ON TO THE NEXT PAGE

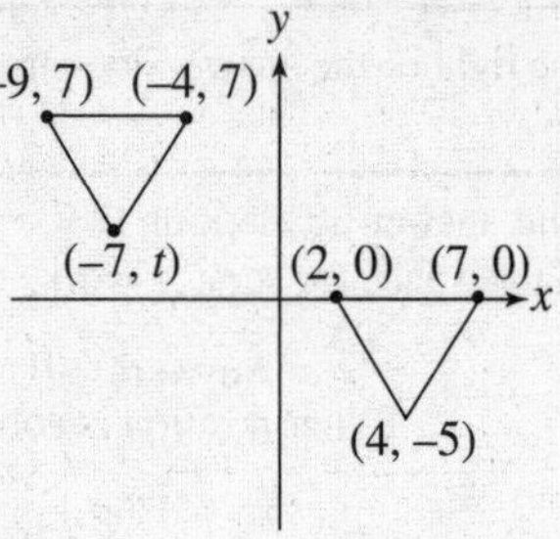

11. In the figure above, the two triangles have the same area. What is the value of t ?

12. If q is an integer between 50 and 70 and can be expressed as $7j + 3$ where j is an integer, what is one possible value of q ?

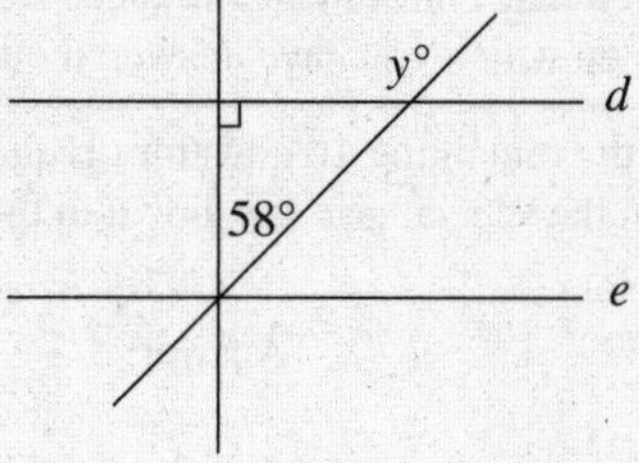

13. In the figure above, if d is parallel to e, what is the value of y ?

14. Nine people in an investment club purchased $114 worth of stock x. Each of five people bought a share of stock x. Each of three people bought $\frac{4}{5}$ of a share. One person bought $\frac{1}{5}$ of a share. How much did a share of stock x cost?

GO ON TO THE NEXT PAGE

15. If $4^x \bullet n^2 = 4^{x+1} \bullet n$ and x and n are both positive integers, what is the value of n ?

16. If $f(x) = \frac{x^2 + 108}{9}$ and $f(3a) = -7a$, then what is the product of all possible real values of a ?

FOREIGN LANGUAGES STUDIED BY STUDENTS AT LAWRENCE HIGH SCHOOL

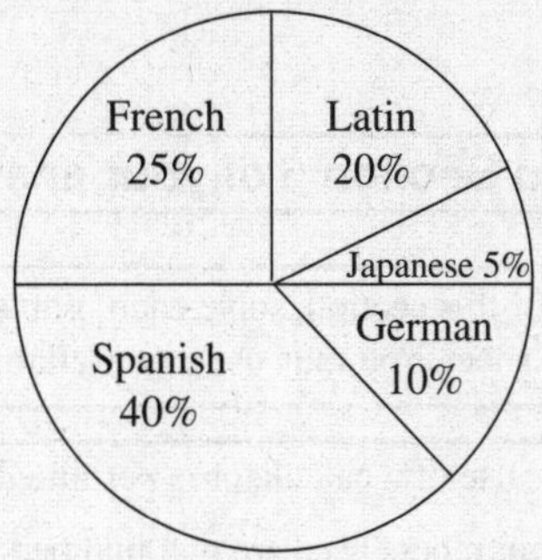

17. The graph above shows the foreign languages studied by 500 students during the 1996–1997 academic year. At the beginning of the 1997–1998 academic year, the number of students studying a foreign language increased by 20, and the same number of students studied Spanish, Latin, and German as did during the previous year. If the percentage of students who studied Japanese increased to 10% during the 1997–1998 academic year, how many students studied French that year? (Assume that no student studied more than one foreign language at a time.)

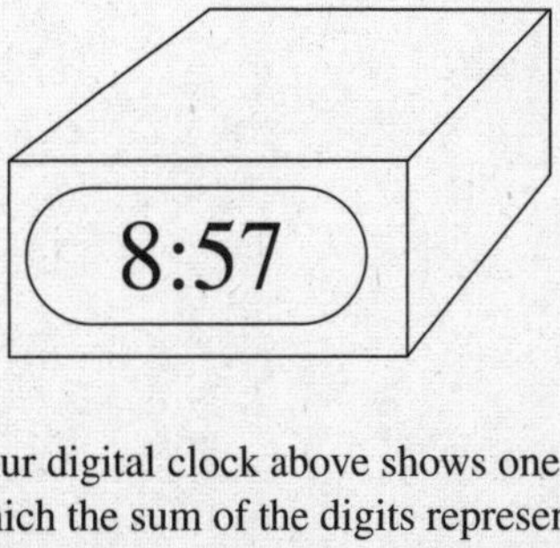

18. The 12-hour digital clock above shows one example of a time at which the sum of the digits representing the time is equal to 20. During a twelve-hour period, starting at noon, for how many minutes would the sum of the digits displayed be greater than or equal to 20 ?

STOP

If you finish before time is called, you may check your work on this section only. Do not turn to any other section in the test.

SECTION 6
Time — 25 minutes
20 Questions

Turn to Section 6 of your answer sheet to answer the questions in this section.

Directions: For this section, solve each problem and decide which is the best of the choices given. Fill in the corresponding circle on the answer sheet. You may use any available space for scratchwork.

Notes

1. The use of a calculator is permitted.
2. All numbers used are real numbers.
3. Figures that accompany problems in this test are intended to provide information useful in solving the problems. They are drawn as accurately as possible EXCEPT when it is stated in a specific problem that the figure is not drawn to scale. All figures lie in a plane unless other wise indicated.
4. Unless otherwise specified, the domain of any function f is assumed to be the set of all real numbers x for which $f(x)$ is a real number.

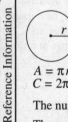

Reference Information

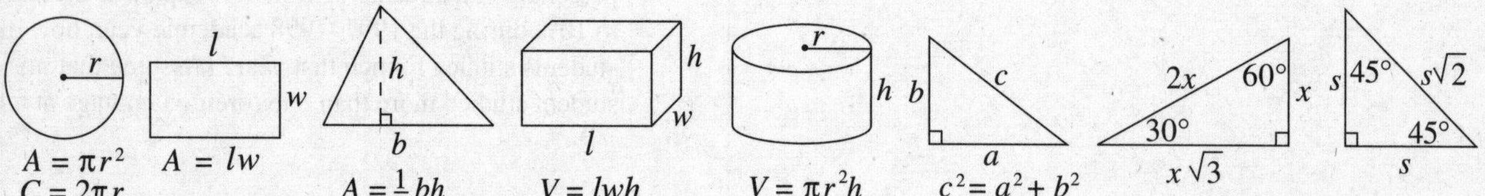

$A = \pi r^2$ $C = 2\pi r$ | $A = lw$ | $A = \frac{1}{2}bh$ | $V = lwh$ | $V = \pi r^2 h$ | $c^2 = a^2 + b^2$ | Special Right Triangles

The number of degrees of arc in a circle is 360.

The sum of the measures in degrees of the angles of a triangle is 180.

1. A bookcase with 6 shelves has 20 books on the top shelf and 30 books on each of the remaining shelves. How many books are there on all 6 shelves of the bookcase?

(A) 120
(B) 130
(C) 150
(D) 160
(E) 170

2. If $a + b = 14$, $b = \frac{c}{4}$, and $c = 24$, then $a =$

(A) 4
(B) 6
(C) 8
(D) 10
(E) 12

GO ON TO THE NEXT PAGE

3. A pack of ten baseball cards costs \$3. A pack of twelve basketball cards costs \$3. If Karim spends \$15 on packs of one type of card, then at most how many more basketball cards than baseball cards could he purchase?

(A) 5
(B) 10
(C) 12
(D) 15
(E) 18

4. A fleet of 5 trucks must make deliveries. Each truck is loaded with k cartons. Each carton contains 60 boxes. If there are a total of 900 boxes, what is the value of k ?

(A) 3
(B) 5
(C) 7
(D) 9
(E) 10

5. If 35% of p is equal to 700, what is 40% of p ?

(A) 98
(B) 245
(C) 280
(D) 800
(E) 2,000

6. The total cost to hold a party at a banquet hall is the result when the product of the number of guests and the cost of food per person is added to the product of the hourly cost to rent the hall and the number of hours the party will last. One hundred guests have been invited, the food costs a total of two hundred dollars, and the hall charges fifty dollars per hour. To save money, the organizers would like to reduce the length of the party from 4 hours to 2 hours. How much money would the organizers save by reducing the length of the party?

(A) \$400
(B) \$300
(C) \$200
(D) \$100
(E) The price will not change.

GO ON TO THE NEXT PAGE

7. If $a \;- b \; = 119$ and $a - b = 7$, what is the value of a ?

(A) 5
(B) 12
(C) 14
(D) 17
(E) 21

8. $\left(-\frac{1}{3}a^5b^2c^7\right)^3 =$

(A) $-\frac{1}{9}a^8b^5c^{10}$

(B) $-\frac{1}{9}a^{15}b^6c^{21}$

(C) $\frac{1}{9}a^{15}b^5c^{21}$

(D) $-\frac{1}{27}a^{15}b^6c^{21}$

(E) $\frac{1}{27}a^8b^5c^{10}$

9. At a track meet, Brian jumped a distance of 14 feet, 9 inches. If Mike jumped exactly $2\frac{1}{2}$ feet farther than Brian, how far did Mike jump?

(1 foot = 12 inches.)

(A) 17 feet, 6 inches
(B) 17 feet, 5 inches
(C) 17 feet, 3 inches
(D) 17 feet, 2 inches
(E) 17 feet, 1 inch

x	y
–3	–7
–1	–3
2	3

10. Based on the chart above, which of the following could express the relationship between x and y ?

(A) $y = x - 4$
(B) $y = x - 2$
(C) $y = 2x - 1$
(D) $y = 2x + 2$
(E) $y = 3x - 3$

GO ON TO THE NEXT PAGE

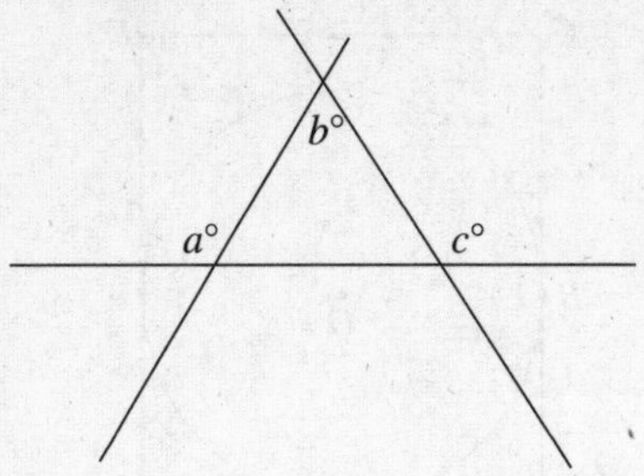

11. Based on the figure above, which of the following expressions is equal to b ?

(A) $a - c$
(B) $180 - (a + c)$
(C) $(a + c) - 90$
(D) $(a + c) - 180$
(E) $360 - (a + c)$

12. If $12(10m + 8)(6m + 4)(2m) = 0$, then how many different possible values of m exist?

(A) One
(B) Two
(C) Three
(D) Four
(E) Five

1	2	3	4	5

13. In a certain game, a red marble and a blue marble are dropped into a box with five equally-sized sections, as shown above. If each marble lands in a different section of the box, how many different arrangements of the two marbles are possible?

(A) 5
(B) 20
(C) 25
(D) 40
(E) 100

14. If a square lies completely within a circle, which of the following must be true?

I. The radius of the circle is equal in length to one side of the square.
II. The area of the square is less than the area of the circle.
III. All four corners of the square touch the circle.

(A) I only
(B) II only
(C) I and II only
(D) II and III only
(E) I, II, and III

GO ON TO THE NEXT PAGE

15. Which of the following could be the units digit of the cube of an integer?

I. 2
II. 6
III. 8

(A) I only
(B) II only
(C) I and II only
(D) I and III only
(E) I, II, and III

---

16. What is the remainder when the sum of three consecutive even integers is divided by 6 ?

(A) 0
(B) 1
(C) 2
(D) 3
(E) 4

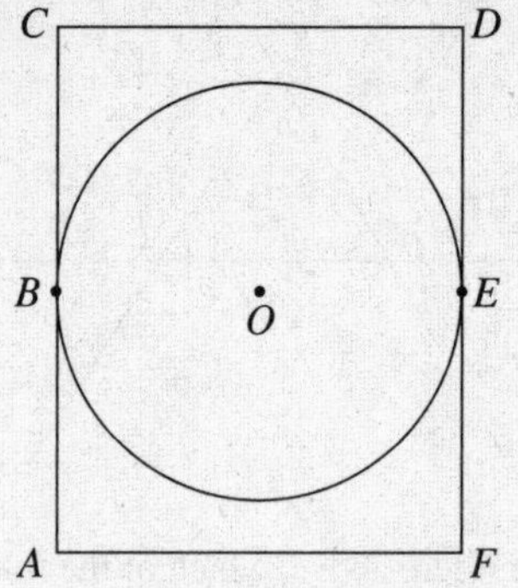

Note: Figure not drawn to scale.

17. In the figure above, *ACDF* is a rectangle and the circle with center *O* has a radius of *r*. $\overline{AC}$ is tangent to the circle at point *B*, $\overline{DF}$ is tangent to the circle at point *E*, and *COE* measures 120 . If $\overline{CF}$ (not shown) passes through *O*, then what is the length of $\overline{CF}$ in terms of *r* ?

(A) $2\pi r$
(B) $2r\sqrt{2}$
(C) $2r\sqrt{3}$
(D) $4\pi r$
(E) $4r$

GO ON TO THE NEXT PAGE

18. Which of the following is the graph of a line perpendicular to the line defined by the equation $2x + 5y = 10$?

(A)

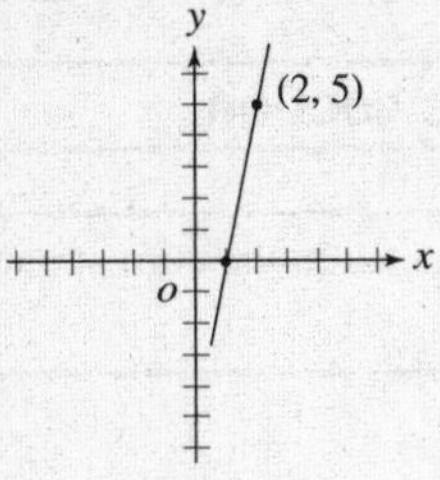

(B)

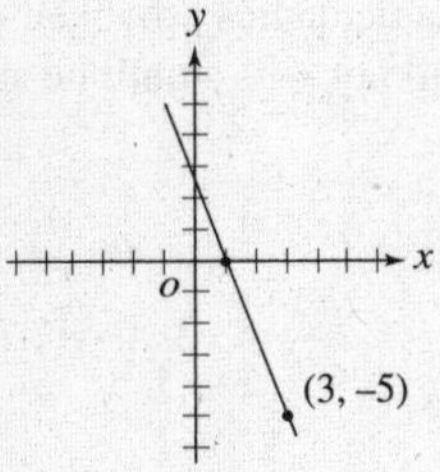

(C)

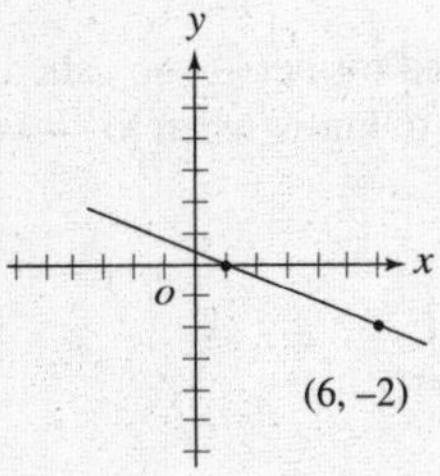

(D)

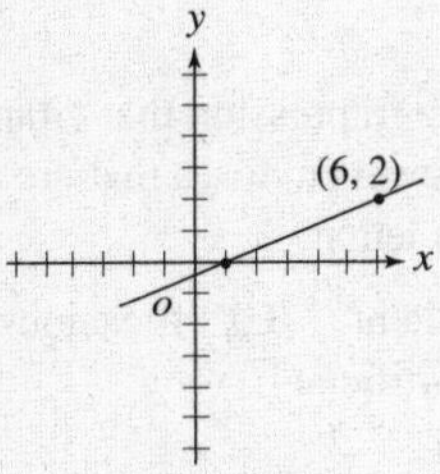

(E)

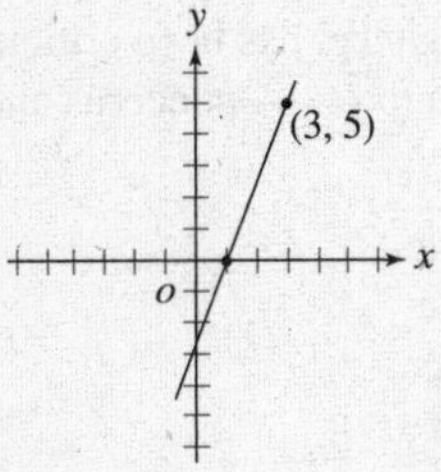

19. If y is directly proportional to the square of x, then which of the following tables could represent values of x and y ?

(A)

x	y
2	4
3	6
4	8

(B)

x	y
1	2
4	8
9	18

(C)

x	y
2	3
4	9
16	27

(D)

x	y
1	3
2	12
3	27

(E)

x	y
1	4
2	5
3	6

20. In a group of 300 mice, 75% are male and 20% are albino. What is the greatest number of mice in the group that could be both female and not albino?

(A) 45
(B) 60
(C) 75
(D) 225
(E) 240

STOP

If you finish before time is called, you may check your work on this section only.
Do not turn to any other section in the test.

SECTION 7

Time — 25 minutes

24 Questions

Turn to Section 7 of your answer sheet to answer the questions in this section.

Directions: For each question in this section, select the best answer from among the choices given and fill in the corresponding circle on the answer sheet.

Each sentence below has one or two blanks, each blank indicating that something has been omitted. Beneath the sentence are five words or sets of words labeled A through E. Choose the word or set of words that, when inserted in the sentence, best fits the meaning of the sentence as a whole.

Example:

Desiring to ------- his taunting friends, Mitch gave them taffy in hopes it would keep their mouths shut.

(A) eliminate (B) satisfy (C) overcome (D) ridicule (E) silence

Ⓐ Ⓑ Ⓒ Ⓓ ●

1. As a person who would never ------- animals, Amelia takes extra care to avoid hitting squirrels while driving.

(A) maltreat (B) accept (C) placate (D) discern (E) entreat

2. Bacteria that cause illness in patients can be ------- by antibiotics, but these drugs can be made less ------- by prescribing them in excessive amounts.

(A) combated . . effective
(B) cultivated . . available
(C) diminished . . profitable
(D) repelled . . weak
(E) digested . . preventative

3. Once rumors of Amy's lack of propriety were substantiated, the bookstore ------- its job offer to her.

(A) fortified (B) cogitated (C) tempered (D) rescinded (E) regulated

4. Although Mr. Skillman had surreptitiously embezzled a considerable sum of money during his career, he was surprisingly ------- when he ultimately professed his guilt to his superiors.

(A) conspiratorial (B) dull (C) forthright (D) horrified (E) evasive

5. The supervisor's questionable tactics provoked ------- among the workers that did not ------- until he stepped down.

(A) tranquility . . appear
(B) devotion . . vanish
(C) conflict . . emerge
(D) revolution . . develop
(E) dissent . . subside

6. Just as Higgins is respected for her ------- , she is also recognized for her ability to know when to ------- her responsibilities.

(A) lethargy . . transfer
(B) productivity . . hoard
(C) initiative . . delegate
(D) integrity . . overlook
(E) impartiality . . ignore

7. Many people are under the impression that vitamin supplements are -------; however, doses that are not carefully regulated can be lethal.

(A) innocuous (B) virulent (C) efficacious (D) capricious (E) artificial

8. The architect, whose work has been described as functional but lacking elegance, has been criticized for paying too much attention to ------- concerns and not enough to ------- detail.

(A) financial . . decorative
(B) utilitarian . . aesthetic
(C) decisive . . pragmatic
(D) pedestrian . . opulent
(E) practical . . lucrative

GO ON TO THE NEXT PAGE

Directions: Each passage below is followed by questions based on its content. Answer the questions on the basis of what is <u>stated</u> or <u>implied</u> in each passage and in any introductory material that may be provided.

Questions 9–10 are based on the following passage.

An excess of carbon dioxide—a chemical produced in great quantities by automobiles, manufacturing, and human beings—is thought to cause global warming and a host of other environmental problems. To combat the effects of this compound, some scientists have suggested that the government simply plant more trees. Because trees and other green plants consume carbon dioxide and produce oxygen, a greater number of trees could reduce the amount of carbon dioxide in the air, thus decreasing the negative impact on the environment. Unfortunately, trees cannot lessen the concentration of other harmful pollutants such as carbon monoxide. Therefore, planting more trees is not by itself an effective solution to air pollution.

9. The author's tone can best be described as

(A) derisive
(B) admiring
(C) dismissive
(D) objective
(E) sentimental

10. The third sentence (lines 6–10) serves primarily to

(A) provide an explanation for a proposed course of action
(B) contradict an earlier assertion
(C) illustrate a contrasting point of view
(D) points out flaws in an opposing argument
(E) offers a restatement of a previous point

Questions 11–12 are based on the following passage.

When the United States entered World War II, thousands of women filled professional positions that had long been held almost exclusively by men. One of these women was Gertrude Elion, who would become one of America's foremost medical researchers. While a few women had become notable scientists prior to Elion, she was one of the first to gain widespread recognition during her lifetime. Although Elion never completed a doctoral degree, she developed treatments for several types of cancer and other diseases. In 1957, Elion invented a drug that made the first organ transplants possible. In her lifetime, Elion acquired, among other honors, 45 patents, 23 honorary degrees, and a Nobel Prize for medicine in 1988.

11. It can be reasonably inferred that Gertrude Elion

(A) was one of the first American women to receive a doctoral degree
(B) was instrumental to the success of the first organ transplants
(C) is considered the greatest female scientist of the twentieth century
(D) would not have entered the medical field had it not been for World War II
(E) was the first woman in a male-dominated field

12. According to the passage, all of the following are true statements EXCEPT

(A) Elion invented treatments for a variety of diseases
(B) Elion was active in her field during the 1950s
(C) because of her gender, Elion's efforts were not recognized by her peers
(D) women had been engaged in scientific research fields prior to Elion
(E) a doctoral degree was not then a prerequisite to becoming a successful scientist

GO ON TO THE NEXT PAGE

Questions 13–24 are based on the following passage.

Lyndon Johnson served as President of the United States from 1963 to 1968. In this passage, a noted historian presents one analysis of his administration.

Robert McNamara once said to a friend that he would "never work with a more complicated man than Lyndon Johnson." McNamara's words appropriately described both the man and the administration he presided over. Rarely had any one individual, or any single administration aspired to so much, generated so many expectations, raised so many hopes, and ultimately suffered so many setbacks. Like the state he came from, Texas, Johnson represented a giant presence in American society. He brought the "liberal consensus" to its fullest expression in post–World War II history. Yet simultaneously, and through it all, he also exhibited the limitations, the tragic flaws, and the inherent contradictions of all that he embodied.

No one could gainsay Johnson's achievement. He wanted to be "the greatest of them all, the whole bunch of them," and in many ways, he succeeded. In the areas of education, Medicare, urban development, social welfare, and above all, civil rights, he had achieved what few could even envision. As one civil rights leader noted at the time of Johnson's death, "When the forces demanded and the mood permitted, for once an activist, human-hearted man had his hands on the levers of power ... [Lyndon Johnson] was there when we and the nation needed him, and oh my God, do I wish he was there now."

Yet in the very course of attempting to realize his dreams, Johnson exhibited fatal flaws of personality and political philosophy that contributed to his undoing. If egomania is an occupational disease of most politicians and virtually all presidents, Johnson carried the illness to its most extreme form. He personally was going to save the nation, right all the wrongs, emulate and then eclipse his mentors. He alone would make it all happen, rising above the conflicts he had been seeking to escape since childhood and imprinting, through personal will, his own brand of dominance on the entire nation. Fantasizing about his role as president, he told Doris Kearns, "If only I could take the next step and become dictator of the whole world, then I could really make things happen. Every hungry person would be fed, every ignorant child educated, every jobless man employed."

In retrospect, it is difficult to separate Johnson's quest for dominance from his desire to correct injustice. Indeed, helping others often seemed to be the instrument by which he could most directly satisfy his own ego. Johnson desperately wanted to overshadow his political father, F.D.R.*, and the way to do that was to even more effectively uplift the downtrodden. If Johnson could achieve what had eluded F.D.R., then he would occupy the place in history reserved for the noblest and best leaders. Significantly, his moment of greatest triumph came after his landslide victory in 1964 when, he told Doris Kearns, "for the first time in all my life I truly felt loved by the American people."

The tragedy of Lyndon Johnson was that both his personality and his political assumptions proved inadequate to the dimensions of the foreign policy and domestic tensions that would emerge during his presidency. This final irony, perhaps, was that the man who did more than anyone else to bring to perfection the politics of the liberal consensus ended up presiding over a fragmented nation. At the height of his success, his own commitment to aggressive anticommunism abroad —while seeking to maintain unity at home —would lead to the most severe division in American society since the Civil War.

*Franklin Delano Roosevelt, president of the United States from 1933–1945.

13. The main purpose of this passage is to

(A) link Johnson's personality with his presidential performance
(B) provide a history of Johnson's administration
(C) prove that Johnson was our noblest and best leader
(D) celebrate Johnson's civil rights achievements
(E) document Johnson's dangerous mental instability

14. The author suggests that Johnson achieved his most remarkable success in the area of

(A) education
(B) health care
(C) urban development
(D) fighting communism
(E) civil rights

15. The author quotes the civil rights leader (lines 20–24) in order to

(A) provide an example of one of Johnson 's many character flaws
(B) strengthen his contention that Johnson was successful in the area of civil rights
(C) prove that Johnson was considered a leader of the civil rights movement
(D) demonstrate how Johnson abused the power of his office
(E) show that whatever his failings, Johnson was a kind man

16. Johnson's "illness," mentioned in line 29, refers to

(A) his fantasies of himself as world dictator
(B) his debilitating and ultimately fatal heart disease
(C) the self-centeredness common to politicians
(D) the inner conflicts that had haunted him since childhood
(E) the societal racism that he was never able to eliminate

GO ON TO THE NEXT PAGE

17. As used in line 31, the word "eclipse" most nearly means

(A) block
(B) surpass
(C) darken
(D) dominate
(E) personify

18. According to the author, Johnson's desire to help others

(A) served to bolster his self-esteem
(B) led to his foreign policy failures
(C) was distinct from his desire for dominance
(D) grew from his involvement in the civil rights movement
(E) resulted in his landslide victory in 1964

19. According to the author, what is ironic about Johnson's legacy?

(A) Though a humble man, his administration is renowned for its arrogance.
(B) The policies of a consensus builder proved to be politically divisive.
(C) It has never been acknowledged that he accomplished more than F.D.R.
(D) Despite his personal failings, as President he was unusually successful.
(E) Although he was physically large, Johnson was quite frail.

20. The author implies that Johnson's failures as a President could primarily be attributed to

(A) the complications that arose after America's involvement in the Vietnam War
(B) Johnson's failure to emulate the governing style of Franklin Delano Roosevelt
(C) the fragmented state of the nation that existed during Johnson's presidency
(D) Johnson's tendency to believe that he could single handedly right all the wrongs of society
(E) a combination of Johnson's character and his myopic beliefs about politics

21. The author's attitude toward Johnson is one of

(A) scholarly detachment
(B) mild disappointment
(C) intense regret
(D) measured sympathy
(E) tragic realization

22. It can be inferred from the passage that Doris Kearns

(A) was privy to Johnson's most personal thoughts and moments
(B) served as a member of Johnson's presidential cabinet
(C) was at times a confidante of Johnson
(D) was romantically involved with Johnson
(E) recorded Johnson's words for later use in a biography

23. The author included the quote from Robert McNamara most probably to

(A) support his argument with testimony from a close friend of Johnson
(B) foreshadow the coming discussion of Johnson's presidency and character
(C) demonstrate that his view of Johnson is shared by many of Johnson's contemporaries
(D) forestall an objection to his argument by providing documentary evidence
(E) lend an air of authority to his argument by quoting an appropriate expert

24. The author's contentions about Johnson's presidency would be most weakened if it could be shown that

(A) Johnson's statements to Doris Kearns were not entirely truthful
(B) most historians consider Johnson one of America's greatest presidents
(C) Johnson's policy decisions often incorporated ideas and plans proposed by his staff members
(D) Johnson seldom thought of himself as suffering from egomania
(E) the years of the Johnson presidency were some of the most prosperous in American history

STOP

If you finish before time is called, you may check your work on this section only. Do not turn to any other section in the test.

SECTION 8
Time — 20 minutes
19 Questions

Turn to Section 8 of your answer sheet to answer the questions in this section.

Directions: For each question in this section, select the best answer from among the choices given and fill in the corresponding circle on the answer sheet.

Each sentence below has one or two blanks, each blank indicating that something has been omitted. Beneath the sentence are five words or sets of words labeled A through E. Choose the word or set of words that, when inserted in the sentence, best fits the meaning of the sentence as a whole.

Example:

Desiring to ------- his taunting friends, Mitch gave them taffy in hopes it would keep their mouths shut.

(A) eliminate (B) satisfy (C) overcome (D) ridicule (E) silence

Ⓐ Ⓑ Ⓒ Ⓓ ●

1. Jamal's efforts to ------- his spending habits hit a snag every time he walked by a used bookstore because it seemed that he could always ------- buying more books.

(A) emphasize . . understand
(B) exaggerate . . mandate
(C) curb . . justify
(D) control . . reject
(E) undermine . . imagine

2. To the theater critic, having a CD player on stage during a play about the 1950s was as ridiculously ------- as featuring a cellular phone in a performance set in ancient Rome.

(A) anachronistic (B) antiquated (C) naive (D) timorous (E) muddled

3. Detectives often solve crimes not through sudden dramatic inspiration, but rather through a gradual investigative approach that ------- all possibilities until only one explanation remains.

(A) foretells (B) redistributes (C) exhausts (D) entraps (E) disrupts

4. The students in the ballroom dancing class stood in awe of their teachers, a ------- pair that twirled with effortless grace around the dance floor.

(A) menacing (B) fractious (C) lithe (D) contemptuous (E) deceptive

5. After a sudden ------- in popularity, the director's unique compositional method is now experiencing a mild renaissance among fans of experimental film.

(A) blandishment (B) disparity (C) transgression (D) ebb (E) elevation

6. It was clear from the ------- in his voice that the contractor was truly sorry for the massive delays in the project and was hoping for ------- for causing the couple such inconvenience.

(A) strain . . adulation
(B) contrition . . clemency
(C) remorse . . justification
(D) gratification . . remediation
(E) jubilance . . amelioration

GO ON TO THE NEXT PAGE

Directions: Each passage below is followed by questions based on its content. Answer the questions on the basis of what is stated or implied in each passage and in any introductory material that may be provided.

Questions 7–19 are based on the following passages.

In the 1940s, a musical form called "bop" or "be-bop" evolved out of traditional jazz music. Some of its great proponents were Dizzy Gillespie, Charlie Parker, and Thelonius Monk. The first passage was written in 1987 by a contemporary of Dizzy Gillespie's, and the second is an analysis of be-bop written in 1991.

Passage 1

In Philadelphia in 1940 or 1941—just before I got drafted, anyway—I had a concert going on in the Academy of Music. I don't remember who was playing, but it must have been an authentic New Orleans jazz band, with maybe a Chicagoan or two thrown in. I'm sure Joe Sullivan was on piano. A local entrepreneur named Nat Segal, who owned a club called the Downbeat in South Philadelphia, asked me if I would, as a favor to him, permit a young trumpet player and a girl singer to participate. In those days there weren't any major music controversies going on in the business. We were still saying, in our sublime ignorance, "It's all jazz." So I agreed to have Nat's people on stage briefly, to give them an opportunity to be exposed to a concert audience. The skinny little girl singer, whom I judged to be about sixteen, told me her name was Sarah Vaughan. And the trumpeter, whom I had met before in Minton's in New York where he had seemed to be only fooling around with the other musicians on the stand, Thelonious Monk and Charlie Parker and, I think, Slim Gaillard (it's hard to remember for sure—after all, it was more than forty years ago), was Dizzy Gillespie.

So, anyway, he played in one or two sets at the Academy, and he still seemed to be just fooling around. I talked to him for a while backstage, and it struck me that he was far more personable and intelligent than most of the musicians I had been associated with in the world of authentic jazz. On reflection, I admitted to myself that most of these younger musicians playing that strange music they were calling "be-bop" were superior folks, generally better educated, more civilized. Their manners were better, they were more polite, more considerate of each other. I found what they were playing to be very boring, and the more I heard it and understood it, the less I liked it. I said all that to young Dizzy, and he said, "Everything moves along, man. It's not a question of whether it's better or worse, it just keeps movin'. There's no reason musicians, especially young ones, shouldn't experiment with the instruments—find out how far they can go."

Passage 2

In the early 1940s, an alternative direction in jazz was congealing in the styles of altoist Charlie "Bird" Parker and trumpeter John "Dizzy" Gillespie with more than a little assistance from pianist/composer/arranger Thelonious Monk. Parker, an alumnus of the Kansas City–styled big band of Jay McShann, had been "goofing around" with upper harmonics— ninths, elevenths, and thirteenths—since about 1939. At a Harlem club called Minton's Playhouse, Gillespie and Monk were also looking for something. When they all came together in 1944 and 1945, be-bop was born.

Put as simply as possible, be-bop was swing music turned inside out. If a swing drummer played beats one and three, the bop drummer would emphasize two and four—or any beats that took his fancy, if that's what he felt like. Since swing drummers laid heavy emphasis on the bass drum and tom-toms, the bop drummer played mostly high up, on the snares and cymbals. Because swing bands usually played reeds versus brass, the bop bands mixed sections. Solos tended to be more frantic, with plenty of sixteenth and thirty-second notes, exploring variations on the harmony rather than the melody. At such high speeds they also altered the concept of rhythm, moving away from uneven ("swinging") pairs of notes to even ("bopping") figures. And last, the boppers tried to reject or at least alter the regular Tin Pan Alley tunes that swing musicians played. Their compositions, though based on changes of some early songs, had more unusual chording, and melodies that were in themselves authentic jazz compositions (for instance, Dizzy Gillespie's "Groovin' High" as an improvisation on the chord pattern of "Whispering"). I am not altogether convinced that bop was a better or more creative way of playing jazz—it was simply different, more harmonically advanced, and inevitably more difficult to do well. This is one reason why the great interpreters of bop during the period from 1945 to 1955 amount to fewer than two dozen, whereas there were scores of excellent jazz musicians working in older idioms.

In 1945, a small label called Musicraft became the first to record and issue the "new music" commercially. Gillespie's quintet made "Groovin' High," included on *Jazz Vol. 11*, and others that first confused and then influenced many others. The first Gillespie group wasn't all bop; the band had a somewhat mixed style. Nevertheless, the 1945 Musicrafts are the first bop records.

After this initial stage of togetherness, however, the bop pioneers went essentially different ways. Gillespie formed the first bop big band, one that enjoyed unusual popular success for so experimental a group (possibly due to a general public interest in "new" things, as well as the pioneering of Kenton). Despite the fact that Monk was an arranger for a time, both he and Parker tended to prefer the intimacy of small groups.

GO ON TO THE NEXT PAGE

7. It can be most reasonably inferred from the author's reference to "music controversies" (lines 9–10) that

(A) the jazz industry would not always remain free of controversy
(B) jazz had been divided by fierce disagreements amongst musicians since its inception
(C) the narrator is ignorant of the wild popularity of be-bop
(D) rock-and-roll musicians often sparked controversies in the media
(E) music was undergoing a radical change in the early 1940s

8. In Passage 1, the author uses the expression "It's all jazz" (line 11) to mean that

(A) different types of jazz were musically identical to non-musicians
(B) the jazz music business was crippled by controversy
(C) all music was derived from a form of jazz
(D) any type of jazz music was worthy of attention
(E) the jazz community was ignorant of other musical styles

9. According to the author of Passage 1, bop musicians tended to differ from other jazz musicians in that

(A) they were better educated and more polite
(B) they were less concerned with making their music popular
(C) their music was more refined
(D) they were strongly influenced by swing music
(E) they had a better understanding of different types of music

10. Which of the following best describes the attitude toward be-bop music expressed by the author of Passage 1?

(A) He considered it an inferior imitation of traditional jazz forms.
(B) He found it intriguing but extremely difficult to understand.
(C) Although he came to understand the form, he found it uninteresting.
(D) He disliked it initially but grew to appreciate it.
(E) He considered it an important and inevitable link in the evolution of jazz.

11. Which of the following best expresses the idea conveyed by Dizzy Gillespie in lines 33–34 ?

(A) Musicians must experiment with different instruments to perfect jazz.
(B) Musicians most easily achieve fame by developing new types of music.
(C) The evolution of musical forms inevitably leads to richer, more complex musical styles.
(D) Music, including jazz, is in a constant state of evolution.
(E) The future of jazz lies in the hands of young musicians.

12. In Passage 2, the phrase "be-bop was swing music turned inside out" (lines 48–49) serves to

(A) highlight the interchangeable roles of pianist, composer, and arranger
(B) accord bop musicians greater respect than swing musicians
(C) contrast the rhythmic, instrumental, and harmonic elements of swing and bop
(D) compare the work of Charlie "Bird" Parker to that of Jay McShann
(E) contrast the uses of upper and lower harmonic scales

13. Which of the following is not given in Passage 2 as a style element of be-bop music?

(A) De-emphasis of the beats one and three
(B) Increased use of snares and cymbals
(C) Riffs based on variations of the harmony
(D) Solos composed of more sixteenth and thirty-second notes
(E) Heavy dependence on Tin Pan Alley tunes

14. The author of Passage 2 uses "Groovin' High" as an example of which of the following?

(A) A swing piece upon which bop musicians improvised
(B) One of Dizzy Gillespie's early solo works
(C) A Tin Pan Alley piece rejected by bop musicians
(D) A swing piece written by a musician who later became involved in bop
(E) A bop piece based in part upon an earlier swing piece

15. In line 70, the word "interpreters" is closest in meaning to

(A) composers
(B) performers
(C) translators
(D) critics
(E) inventors

GO ON TO THE NEXT PAGE

16. According to lines 67–70, which of the following is true of bop music?

(A) It is a more creative form than swing music.
(B) It emphasizes uneven note pairing.
(C) It was first recorded by Jay McShann's big band.
(D) It was a more harmonically sophisticated form of jazz music than swing was.
(E) It was the earliest form of jazz music.

17. The author of Passage 2 states that "there were scores of excellent jazz musicians working in older idioms" (lines 72–73) to emphasize that

(A) the public did not come to appreciate and support bop music until the 1950s
(B) fewer performers were able to master the demanding form of bop
(C) traditional forms could be appreciated by a larger group
(D) most jazz musicians preferred the greater discipline and complexity of traditional forms
(E) bop was a style that major record labels were initially reluctant to carry

18. In discussing Dizzy Gillespie, both the author of Passage 1 and the author of Passage 2

(A) express personal affection for him
(B) state that he was the most influential bop musician
(C) explore the significance of his compositions
(D) argue his importance to the evolution of jazz
(E) refer to his music in a discussion of be-bop

19. Which of the following best summarizes the difference in perspective between the two passages?

(A) Passage 1 considers the origins of a musical form, while Passage 2 is concerned with the future of the form.
(B) Passage 1 expresses ambivalence, while Passage 2 expresses a strong opinion.
(C) Passage 1 presents a specific incident, while Passage 2 offers a historical overview.
(D) Passage 1 discusses the evolution of jazz, while Passage 2 focuses on musical theory.
(E) Passage 1 presents an emotional argument, while Passage 2 is primarily factual.

STOP

If you finish before time is called, you may check your work on this section only. Do not turn to any other section in the test.

SECTION 9
Time — 20 minutes
16 Questions

Turn to Section 9 of your answer sheet to answer the questions in this section.

Directions: For this section, solve each problem and decide which is the best of the choices given. Fill in the corresponding circle on the answer sheet. You may use any available space for scratchwork.

Notes

1. The use of a calculator is permitted.
2. All numbers used are real numbers.
3. Figures that accompany problems in this test are intended to provide information useful in solving the problems. They are drawn as accurately as possible EXCEPT when it is stated in a specific problem that the figure is not drawn to scale. All figures lie in a plane unless other wise indicated.
4. Unless otherwise specified, the domain of any function f is assumed to be the set of all real numbers x for which $f(x)$ is a real number.

Reference Information

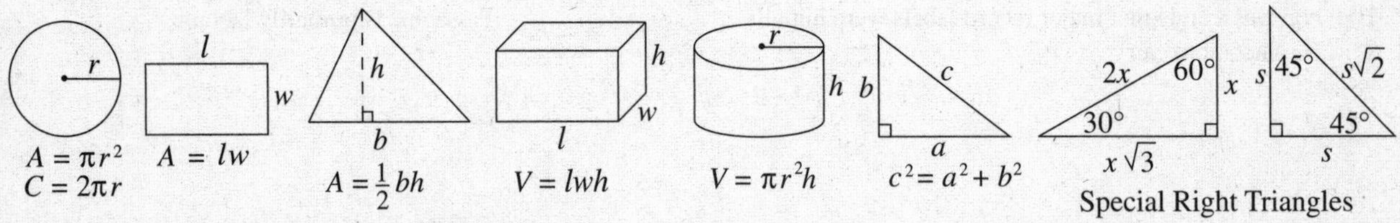

$A = \pi r^2$ $C = 2\pi r$ $A = lw$ $A = \frac{1}{2}bh$ $V = lwh$ $V = \pi r^2 h$ $c^2 = a^2 + b^2$

Special Right Triangles

The number of degrees of arc in a circle is 360.

The sum of the measures in degrees of the angles of a triangle is 180.

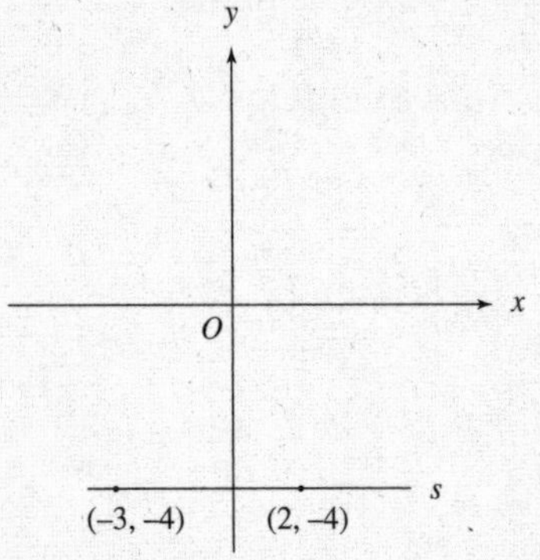

1. In the figure above, what is the slope of line s ?

(A) -1

(B) $-\frac{1}{2}$

(C) 0

(D) $\frac{1}{2}$

(E) 2

2. A local theater group sold tickets to a performance. The group sold 100 adult tickets and 50 child tickets. If the group made exactly \$800 in ticket sales, which of the following pairs (a, c) could represent the price of an adult ticket, a, and the price of a child ticket, c ?

(A) (9, 1)
(B) (8, 2)
(C) (7, 3)
(D) (6, 4)
(E) (5, 5)

GO ON TO THE NEXT PAGE

3. Out of 10,000 computer chips, 38 are found to be defective. At this rate, how many chips would be defective out of a million?

(A) 380
(B) 3,800
(C) 38,000
(D) 380,000
(E) 3,800,000

$$\frac{1}{8}+\frac{1}{10}=\frac{a}{b}$$

4. In the equation above, if a and b are positive integers and $\frac{a}{b}$ is in its simplest reduced form, what is the value of a ?

(A) 2
(B) 9
(C) 18
(D) 36
(E) 40

5. Juanita bought five items at the store. The prices of the first four items were \$6, \$11, \$14, and \$19. All five items were taxed at a rate of 5%, and the total cost of all five items, including tax, was \$63. What was the price of the fifth item?

(A) \$3
(B) \$5
(C) \$6
(D) \$8
(E) \$10

6. If $a = -2$, then $a + a^2 - a^3 + a^4 - a^5 =$

(A) −32
(B) −18
(C) 0
(D) 32
(E) 58

GO ON TO THE NEXT PAGE

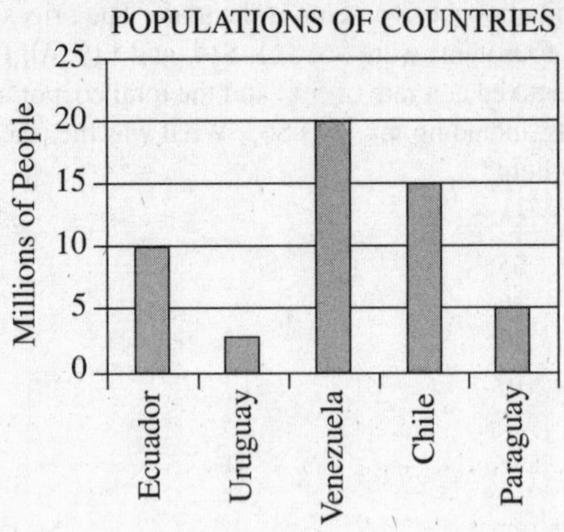

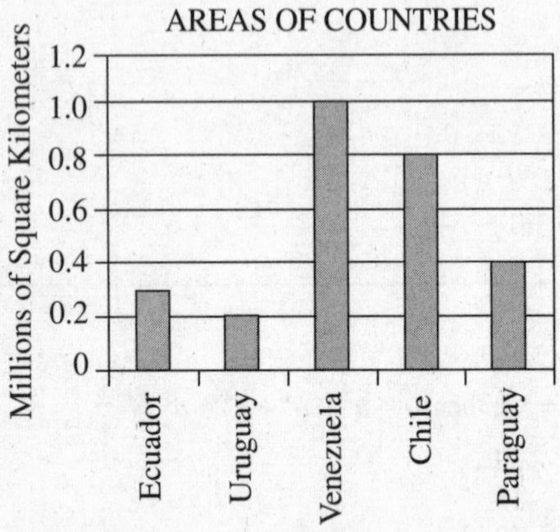

7. The populations and areas of five countries are shown in the graphs above. If population density is defined as $\frac{\text{population}}{\text{area}}$, which of the five countries has the highest population density?

(A) Ecuador
(B) Uruguay
(C) Venezuela
(D) Chile
(E) Paraguay

$$n = \frac{12}{p}$$

8. The number of bananas a fruit stand sells per day, n, varies inversely as the dollar price per banana that day, p, as shown in the formula above. On Tuesday, the stand sold 60 bananas. What was the price per banana on Tuesday?

(A) \$0.20
(B) \$0.25
(C) \$0.50
(D) \$2.00
(E) \$5.00

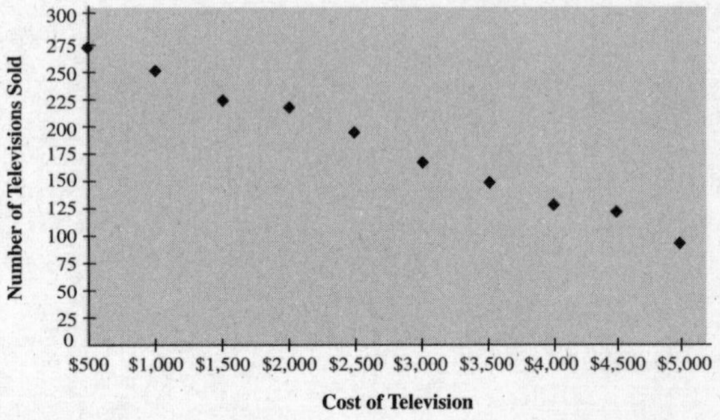

9. A certain store sells televisions ranging in price from \$500 to \$5,000 in increments of \$500. The graph above shows the total number of televisions sold at each price during the last 12 months. Approximately how much more revenue did the store collect from the televisions it sold priced at \$3,500 than it did from the televisions it sold priced at \$1,000 ?

(A) \$175,000
(B) \$250,000
(C) \$275,000
(D) \$350,000
(E) \$525,000

GO ON TO THE NEXT PAGE

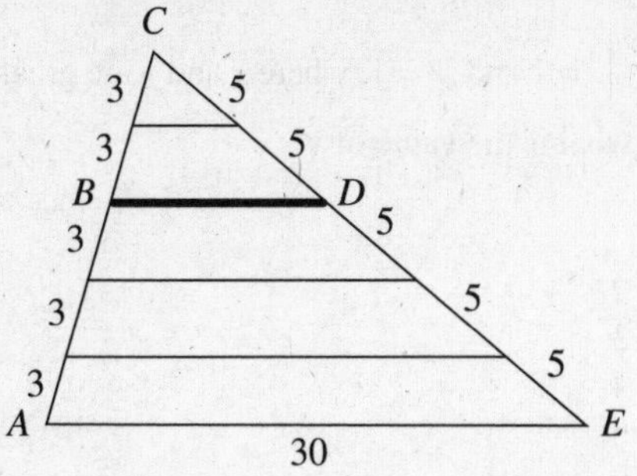

10. In the figure above, what is the length of $\overline{BD}$?

(A) 8
(B) 9
(C) 12
(D) 15
(E) 16

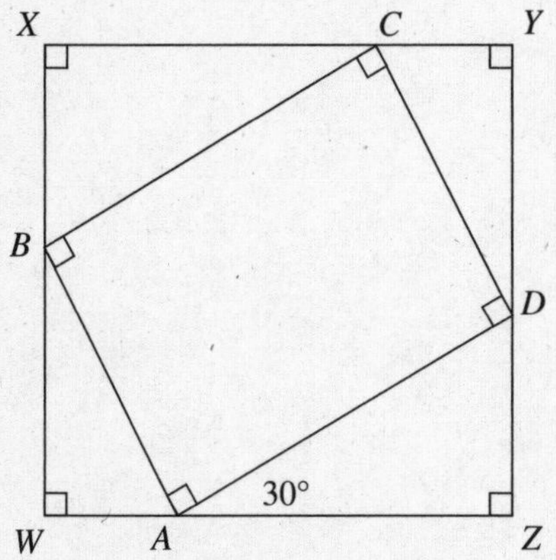

11. In the figure above, *ABCD* is a rectangle. If $YD = 4$ and $DZ = 3$, what is the area of *ABCD* ?

(A) $3\sqrt{3}$
(B) 7
(C) $8\sqrt{3}$
(D) $16\sqrt{3}$
(E) 49

12. Amy, Ben, and Dave are each flying to different cities. One of them is flying to Seattle, one of them is flying to London, and one of them is flying to St. Louis. Each flight is next week on one of three different days—Wednesday, Thursday, or Friday. Amy's flight is before Dave's, but after the flight to London. Dave is not flying to Seattle. For what day and to which city is Amy's flight?

	Day	City
(A)	Thursday	Seattle
(B)	Thursday	St. Louis
(C)	Wednesday	London
(D)	Wednesday	Seattle
(E)	Tuesday	St. Louis

GO ON TO THE NEXT PAGE

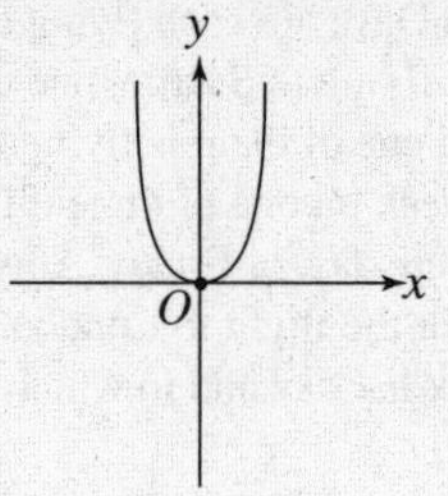

13. The graph of $y = x^2$ is shown in the figure above. Which of the following is the graph of $y = -(x+3)^2 - 4$?

(A)

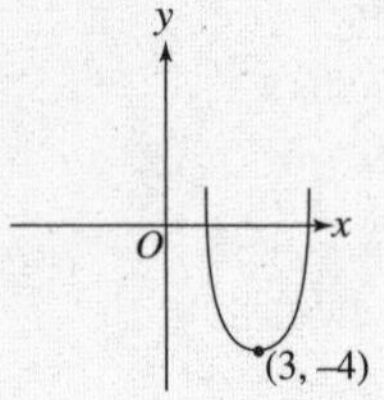

(B)

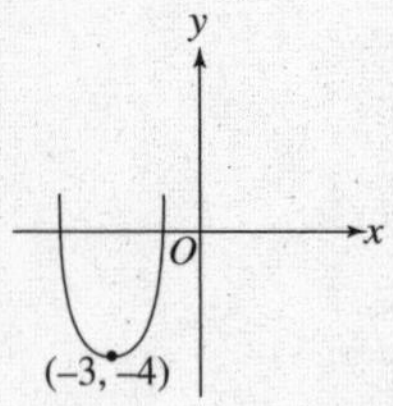

(C)

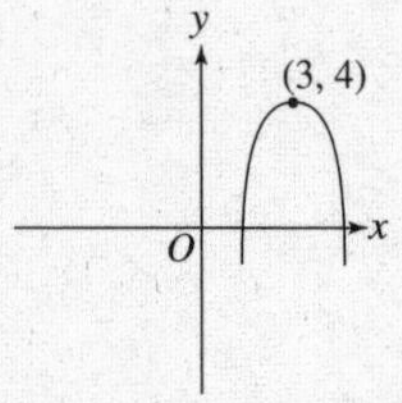

(D)

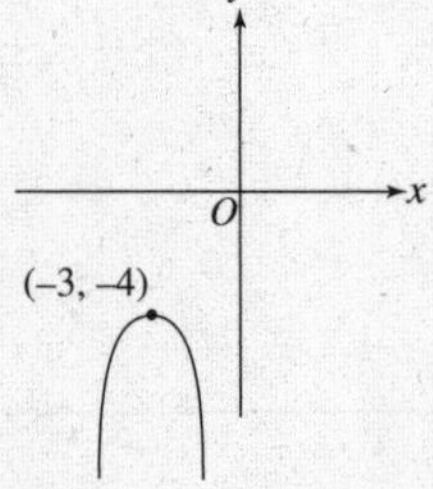

(E)

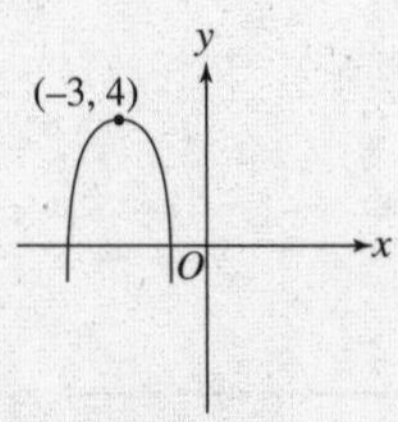

14. If $\left(\frac{xy}{2}\right)^x = 1$ and $x^y = 1$, where x and y are greater than zero, what is the value of y?

(A) 2
(B) 3
(C) 4
(D) 5
(E) 6

GO ON TO THE NEXT PAGE

15. In a list of seven integers, 13 is the smallest member, 37 is the largest member, the mean is 23, the median is 24, and the mode is 18. If the numbers 8 and 43 are then added to the list, which of the following will change?

I. The mean
II. The median
III. The mode

(A) I only
(B) I and II only
(C) I and III only
(D) II and III only
(E) I, II, and III

16. What is the area of a circle centered at (4, 3) that passes through the origin?

(A) 9π
(B) 12π
(C) 16π
(D) 25π
(E) 49π

STOP

If you finish before time is called, you may check your work on this section only. Do not turn to any other section in the test.

SECTION 10
Time — 10 minutes
14 Questions

Turn to Section 10 of your answer sheet to answer the questions in this section.

Directions: For each question in this section, select the best answer from among the choices given and fill in the corresponding circle on the answer sheet.

The following sentences test correctness and effectiveness of expression. Part of each sentence or the entire sentence is underlined; beneath each sentence are five ways of phrasing the underlined material. Choice A repeats the original phrasing; the other four choices are different. If you think the original phrasing produces a better sentence than any of the alternatives, select choice A; if not, select one of the other choices.

In making your selection, follow the requirements of standard written English; that is, pay attention to grammar, choice of words, sentence construction, and punctuation. Your selection should result in the most effective sentence—clear and precise, without awkwardness or ambiguity.

EXAMPLE:

Bobby Flay baked his first cake and he was thirteen years old then.

(A) and he was thirteen years old then
(B) when he was thirteen
(C) at age thirteen years old
(D) upon the reaching of thirteen years
(E) at the time when he was thirteen

Ⓐ●ⒸⒹⒺ

1. Having made significant contributions to the field of nursing Clara Barton.

(A) Having made significant contributions to the field of nursing Clara Barton.
(B) Significant contributions to the field of nursing were made by Clara Barton.
(C) Clara Barton made significant contributions to the field of nursing.
(D) Clara Barton having made significant contributions to the field of nursing.
(E) Clara Barton contributed significantly to nursing, her field.

2. Allergy season begins with the release of pollen spores in the spring and ends with the first frost in the late fall.

(A) begins with the release of pollen spores in the spring and ends
(B) that begins with the release of pollen spores in the spring and ends
(C) have begun with the release of pollen spores in the spring and ending
(D) beginning with the release of pollen spores in the spring and ending
(E) are begun with the release of pollen spores in the spring and ended

3. Millions of silkworms to produce the raw material needed to meet the worldwide demand for high-quality silk, over half of which is manufactured in just two countries.

(A) to produce the raw material
(B) produce the raw material
(C) would have produced what raw material was
(D) for producing the raw material was
(E) producing the raw material

4. My best friend, who moved to the United States from Guatemala at the age of ten, has, in recent years, spoken English fluently but still encounters seemingly basic words he does not know the meaning of.

(A) who moved to the United States from Guatemala at the age of ten, has, in recent years, spoken English fluently
(B) who moved to the United States from Guatemala while being ten years old, has spoken English fluently
(C) moving to the United States from Guatemala when he was ten years old, now is speaking English fluently
(D) who moved to the United States from Guatemala at the age of ten years, now speaking English fluently in recent years
(E) who moved to the United States from Guatemala at the age of ten, now speaks English fluently

GO ON TO THE NEXT PAGE

5. Believe it or not, although he is only 15, Sanjay is considered as one of the best soccer players in the entire league.

(A) considered as
(B) considered to be
(C) regarded to be
(D) regarded as being
(E) regarded as having been

6. Although he is fond of the music of both composers, Mr. Gomez prefers the compositions of Mozart to Beethoven.

(A) the compositions of Mozart to Beethoven
(B) the compositions of Mozart to Beethoven's compositions
(C) Mozart's compositions to Beethoven
(D) compositions by Mozart to compositions by Beethoven
(E) Mozart's compositions to Beethoven's

7. In the stage adaptation of *The Three Musketeers*, D'Artagnan asks Constance to flee the country with Artemis and he after their escapades are discovered.

(A) D'Artagnan asks Constance to flee the country with Artemis and he after their escapades are discovered
(B) D'Artagnan asks Constance to flee the country with he and Artemis after their escapades are discovered
(C) Constance is being asked by D'Artagnan and he to flee the country before Artemis discovers their escapades
(D) D'Artagnan asks Constance to flee the country with Artemis and him after their escapades are discovered
(E) their escapades being discovered and Constance having been invited by Artemis and him to flee the country

8. I am one of the few whom can rub my belly and pat my head at the same time.

(A) I am one of the few whom can
(B) I am one of the few who can
(C) I am one of the few that can
(D) I am one of the few people whom can
(E) I was one of the few that can

9. The number of players injured during football games could be minimized if coaches made sure their players always wear protective gear, maintain hydration, and learn proper technique for tackling other players.

(A) learn proper technique
(B) they learned proper technique
(C) by learning proper technique
(D) if proper technique is learned
(E) if there was proper technique learned

10. Despite its primitive technology, the mill runs this way for over 100 years.

(A) the mill runs this way for over 100 years
(B) the mill has ran this way for over 100 years
(C) for over 100 years, the mill runs this way
(D) the mill has run this way for over 100 years
(E) for over 100 years, the mill was to run this way

GO ON TO THE NEXT PAGE

11. The Franklin Institute of Philadelphia, opened in 1824 and named after Benjamin Franklin, remains a popular destination for school children on class trips.

(A) The Franklin Institute of Philadelphia, opened in 1824 and named after Benjamin Franklin, remains a popular destination for school children on class trips.
(B) Remaining a popular destination for school children on class trips, the Franklin Institute of Philadelphia opened in 1824 and named after Benjamin Franklin.
(C) The Franklin Institute of Philadelphia, a popular destination for children on school trips opened in 1824 and named after Benjamin Franklin.
(D) A popular destination for school children on class trips, the Franklin Institute of Philadelphia was opened and had been named after Benjamin Franklin in 1824.
(E) A popular destination for school children on class trips, in 1824 the Franklin Institute was opened and named after Benjamin Franklin.

12. Only after significant debate did the board of trustees adopt the new resolution, the changes to the university's structure would have a major impact on nearly every aspect of its budget.

(A) Only after significant debate did the board of trustees adopt the new resolution,
(B) Only after significant debate did the board of trustees adopt the new resolution, nevertheless
(C) Although only after significant debate did the board of trustees adopt the new resolution,
(D) Only after significant debate did the board of trustees adopt the new resolution, since
(E) Since only after significant debate did the board of trustees adopt the new resolution,

13. My friend ran a farm but refused to kill the animals he raised nor otherwise selling them for food.

(A) raised nor otherwise selling
(B) had raised nor otherwise did they sell
(C) have raised or otherwise to have sold
(D) raised or otherwise sold
(E) had raised or otherwise to sell

14. The selection of gifts at Joanne's Flower Shop, including vases, balloons, and cards, is far superior to Brian.

(A) is far superior to Brian
(B) are far superior to Brian
(C) is far superior to Brian's shop
(D) are far superior to Brian's shop
(E) is far superior to that of Brian's shop

STOP

If you finish before time is called, you may check your work on this section only.
Do not turn to any other section in the test.

NO TEST MATERIAL ON THIS PAGE.

GO ON TO THE NEXT PAGE

PRACTICE TEST 4: ANSWER KEY

Section 2 Math	Section 3 Reading	Section 4 Writing	Section 5 Math	Section 6 Reading	Section 7 Reading	Section 8 Reading	Section 9 Math	Section 10 Writing
1. B	1. D	1. B	1. C	1. E	1. A	1. C	1. C	1. C
2. C	2. E	2. D	2. E	2. C	2. A	2. A	2. D	2. A
3. B	3. B	3. A	3. D	3. B	3. D	3. C	3. B	3. B
4. B	4. A	4. E	4. B	4. A	4. C	4. C	4. B	4. E
5. A	5. B	5. E	5. E	5. D	5. E	5. D	5. E	5. B
6. C	6. E	6. C	6. C	6. D	6. C	6. B	6. E	6. E
7. A	7. B	7. A	7. A	7. B	7. A	7. A	7. A	7. D
8. B	8. A	8. A	8. E	8. D	8. B	8. D	8. A	8. B
9. 40	9. C	9. C	9. 256	9. C	9. D	9. A	9. C	9. A
10. .666	10. B	10. D	10. 1 or 9	10. C	10. A	10. C	10. C	10. D
11. 3072	11. C	11. B	11. 2	11. D	11. B	11. D	11. D	11. A
12. 15	12. D	12. A	12. 52, 59, or 66	12. C	12. C	12. C	12. A	12. D
13. 0 or 5	13. C	13. D	13. 148	13. B	13. A	13. E	13. D	13. E
14. 10	14. D	14. C	14. 15	14. B	14. E	14. E	14. A	14. E
15. .9	15. A	15. C	15. 4	15. E	15. B	15. B	15. A	
16. 15	16. A	16. E	16. 12	16. A	16. C	16. D	16. D	
17. 9.5	17. D	17. C	17. 118	17. E	17. B	17. B		
18. 2.4	18. C	18. E	18. 20	18. E	18. A	18. E		
	19. D	19. A		19. D	19. B	19. C		
	20. E	20. C		20. C	20. E			
	21. B	21. E			21. D			
	22. E	22. C			22. C			
	23. E	23. B			23. B			
	24. B	24. D			24. C			
		25. D						
		26. A						
		27. A						
		28. B						
		29. A						
		30. B						
		31. A						
		32. E						
		33. B						
		34. C						
		35. A						

SAT SCORING WORKSHEET

For directions on how to score your SAT practice test, see pages 389–390. Section 7 is the unscored, Experimental section.

SAT Writing Section

Total Writing Multiple-Choice Questions Correct from Sections 4 and 10: [ ]

−

Total Writing Multiple-Choice Questions Incorrect from Sections 4 and 10: ______ ÷ 4 = [ ]

Grammar Raw Score: [ ] — **Grammar Scaled Subscore!** [ ]

Compare the Grammar Raw Score to the Writing Multiple-Choice Subscore Conversion Table on the next page to find the Grammar Scaled Subscore.

+

Your Essay Score (2 – 12): ______ ÷ 2 = [ ]

Writing Raw Score: [ ]

Compare Raw Score to SAT Score Conversion Table on the next page to find the Writing Scaled Score.

Writing Scaled Score! [ ]

Be sure to register at **PrincetonReview.com/cracking** to gain access to our LiveGrader™ Service. Your essay can be scored by our graders there.

SAT Critical Reading Section

Total Critical Reading Questions Correct from Sections 3, 6, and 8: [ ]

−

Total Critical Reading Questions Incorrect from Sections 3, 6, and 8: ______ ÷ 4 = [ ]

Critical Reading Raw Score: [ ]

Compare Raw Score to SAT Score Conversion Table on the next page to find the Critical Reading Scaled Score.

Critical Reading Scaled Score! [ ]

SAT Math Section

Total Math Grid-In Questions Correct from Section 5: [ ]

+

Total Math Multiple-Choice Questions Correct from Sections 2, 5, and 9: [ ]

−

Total Math Multiple-Choice Questions Incorrect from Sections 2, 5, and 9: ______ ÷ 4 = [ ]

Don't include wrong answers from grid-ins!

Math Raw Score: [ ]

Compare Raw Score to SAT Score Conversion Table on the next page to find the Math Scaled Score.

Math Scaled Score! [ ]

SAT SCORE CONVERSION TABLE

Raw Score	Writing Scaled Score	Reading Scaled Score	Math Scaled Score	Raw Score	Writing Scaled Score	Reading Scaled Score	Math Scaled Score	Raw Score	Writing Scaled Score	Reading Scaled Score	Math Scaled Score
73	800			47	590–630	600–640	680–720	21	400–440	420–460	460–500
72	790–800			46	590–630	590–630	670–710	20	390–430	410–450	450–490
71	780–800			45	580–620	580–620	660–700	19	380–420	400–440	450–490
70	770–800			44	570–610	580–620	650–690	18	370–410	400–440	440–480
69	770–800			43	570–610	570–610	640–680	17	370–410	390–430	430–470
68	760–800			42	560–600	570–610	630–670	16	360–400	380–420	420–460
67	760–800	800		41	560–600	560–600	620–660	15	350–390	380–420	420–460
66	760–800	770–800		40	550–590	550–590	620–660	14	340–380	370–410	410–450
65	750–790	750–790		39	540–580	550–590	610–650	13	330–370	360–400	400–440
64	740–780	740–780		38	530–570	540–580	600–640	12	320–360	350–390	400–440
63	730–770	740–780		37	530–570	530–570	590–630	11	320–360	350–390	390–430
62	720–760	730–770		36	520–560	530–570	590–630	10	310–350	340–380	380–420
61	710–750	720–760		35	510–550	520–560	580–620	9	300–340	330–370	370–410
60	700–740	710–750		34	500–540	510–550	570–610	8	290–330	310–350	360–400
59	690–730	700–740		33	490–530	500–540	560–600	7	280–320	300–340	350–390
58	680–720	690–730		32	480–520	500–540	560–600	6	270–310	300–340	340–380
57	680–720	680–720		31	470–510	490–530	540–580	5	260–300	290–330	330–370
56	670–710	670–710		30	470–510	480–520	530–570	4	240–280	280–320	320–360
55	660–720	670–710		29	460–500	470–510	520–560	3	230–270	270–310	310–350
54	650–690	660–700	800	28	450–490	470–510	510–550	2	230–270	260–300	290–330
53	640–680	650–690	780–800	27	440–480	460–500	510–550	1	220–260	230–270	270–310
52	630–670	640–680	750–790	26	430–470	450–490	500–540	0	210–250	200–240	240–280
51	630–670	630–670	740–780	25	420–460	450–490	490–530	–1	200–240	200–230	220–260
50	620–660	620–660	730–770	24	410–450	440–480	480–520	–2	200–230	200–220	210–250
49	610–650	610–650	710–750	23	410–450	430–470	480–520	–3	200–220	200–210	200–240
48	600–640	600–640	700–740	22	400–440	420–460	470–510				

WRITING MULTIPLE-CHOICE SUBSCORE CONVERSION TABLE

Grammar Raw Score	Grammar Scaled Subscore	Grammar Raw Score	Grammar Scaled Subscore	Grammar Raw Score	Grammar Scaled Subscore	Grammar Raw Score	Grammar Scaled Subscore	Grammar Raw Score	Grammar Scaled Subscore	Grammar Raw Score	Grammar Scaled Subscore
49	79–80	40	70–74	31	61–65	22	52–56	13	43–47	4	33–37
48	78–80	39	69–73	30	60–64	21	52–56	12	42–46	3	31–35
47	78–80	38	68–72	29	59–63	20	51–55	11	41–45	2	28–32
46	77–80	37	67–71	28	58–62	19	50–54	10	40–44	1	26–30
45	76–80	36	66–70	27	57–61	18	49–53	9	39–43	0	23–27
44	75–79	35	65–69	26	56–60	17	48–52	8	37–41	–1	22–26
43	73–77	34	64–68	25	55–59	16	47–51	7	36–40	–2	21–25
42	72–76	33	63–67	24	54–58	15	46–50	6	35–39	–3	20–24
41	71–75	32	62–66	23	53–57	14	45–49	5	34–38		

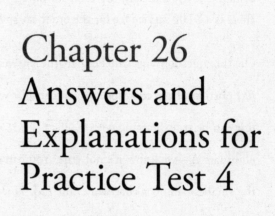

Chapter 26
Answers and Explanations for Practice Test 4

SECTION 2

1. **B** Although all three parts of $3x + 9y + 12$ are divisible by 3, the expression $3(x + 3y + 4)$ is not among the answers, so your best bet is to try each of the answers. A is out, because if 3 is factored out of the expression, The last number should be a 4, not a 9. Putting brackets around only part of the expression, such as $(3x + 9y)$, does not change the value of the entire expression. Since $(3x + 9y) + 12 = 3(x + 3y) + 12$, B is correct. You're done! There is no need to try out any further answer choices.

2. **C** Take this word problem in bite-sized pieces. We want to find the total cost of the order of 12 boxes of books. First multiply the total number of boxes by the price of 1 box: 12 × \$4.95 = \$59.40. There is a \$7.00 service fee for the order, so \$59.40 + \$7.00 = \$66.40.

3. **B** On this question you can Plug In the answers. The numbers in the answer choices replace the $f(x)$ portion of the equation, so you can just write out the rest of it, $\sqrt{3x-2}$, next to each to see if it can be true. Starting with C, if $\frac{2}{3} = \sqrt{3x-2}$, then $\frac{4}{9} = 3x - 2$, and $x = \frac{22}{3}$. Since C works, eliminate A—we know it's not true. You can also eliminate D and E because we are looking for the smallest number that works for $f(x)$. Now let's try B: If $0 = \sqrt{3x-2}$, then $0 = 3x - 2$, and $x = \frac{2}{3}$. $\frac{22}{3}$ is bigger than $\frac{2}{3}$, so cross out C. B is correct.

4. **B** To find out how many cars the 9th graders washed, take the *Funds Raised* and divide by the *Price per item* in the row for the 9th graders. $\frac{255.00}{5.00} = 51$, answer B.

5. **A** First find the number of cookies sold by 10th graders, again dividing *Funds Raised* by *Price per item*. $\frac{360.00}{2.00} = 180$. Now find the number of cookies sold by 12th graders: $\frac{180.00}{1.50} = 120$. Now subtract to find out how many more cookies the 10th graders sold: $180 - 120 = 60$, answer A.

6. **C** This is a multiplication problem, so to find C we need to find out what digit times 6 results in a product that ends in 8. The multiples of 6 that end in 8 are 18 and 48. If C is 3, then 6×3 is 18, and we carry the 1. The C in answer 94C8 also must be 3: $6 \times 7 = 42$, plus the 1 we carried, is 43. This gets a 3 into the C spot, (using 8 as a multiplier does not lead to an 8 in the C spot in the product). Now we need to find the value of D. Since we are carrying the 4 from the last multiplication, $6 \times D$ must result in a product of 0. Only $6 \times 5 = 30$ fits, so $D = 5$. Finally, find the sum of $C + D$: $3 + 5 = 8$, answer C.

7. **A** Arc *RST* is half the circumference of the circle. Finding the radius is key to any circle question. The question states that the area of the shaded portion of the circle is 25π and is $\frac{1}{9}$ of the circle, so we know that the whole circle has an area of $9(25\pi)$ or 225π. Now we can use the area formula to get the radius: $\pi r^2 = 225\pi$, so $r = 15$. The formula for the circumference of a circle is $2\pi r$, so the circumference of the whole circle is 30π, and since arc *RST* is half the circumference, its length is 15π, answer A.

8. **B** Here is a chance to Plug In the answer choices. Start with the middle value in C and see which makes the equation true: It is not possible for x to be 0, because $0^2 - |0| \neq -6$. The larger values don't equal –6 either: D gives 0 while E gives positive 6. B is correct: $(-2)^2 - |-10| = 4 - 10 = -6$.

9. **40** Divide both sides of the equation by three to find that $(y - 2) = 8$. There's no need to find y, since we need only to find five times the value of $(y - 2)$. Multiply both sides of the equation to find that $5(y - 2) = 40$.

10. $\mathbf{\frac{2}{3}}$ **or .666 or .667**

Out of the 12 tomatoes, we know 4 are rotten, but the question asks for the probability of choosing a *not rotten* tomato. If 4 tomatoes are rotten, 8 must not be rotten so the probability is $\frac{8}{12}$. You could grid in the fraction as is, reduced to $\frac{2}{3}$, or transform it into a decimal.

11. **3072** Because the t in $n = 12 \times 2^{\frac{t}{3}}$ represents the number of months, we cannot use the 2 *years* time frame given in the question in place of t. The colony has been growing for 24 months, which is evenly divisible by the 3 in the fractional exponent. The equation is much easier now that the fractional exponent is gone. $n = 12 \times 2^{\frac{24}{3}} = 12 \times 2^8 = 12 \times 256 = 3072$.

12. **15** We can't find the value of y without first finding the value of x. A straight line is 180°, so $5x + x = 180$, and $6x = 180$. Divide both sides by 6 to find that $x = 30$. Vertical angles are equal, so $2y = x$, or $2y = 30$, so $y = 15$.

13. **0 or 5** Translate this word problem into math: $x^2 = \frac{10x}{2}$. Simplify to $2x^2 = 10x$, then $x^2 = 5x$ and finally $x = 5$. There is another possibility: if x is replaced by 0 in the equation at any stage, it creates a true equation. $0^2 = \frac{10(0)}{2} = 0$.

14. **10** Here is another translation problem. The first sentence can be translated to $b = c + 9$, the second sentence as $c = a + 4$, the third sentence as $d = a + 3$. The question at the end is really asking for the value of $b - d$. Plug in a value for a in the third equation and it will give the value of d that we need. If $a = 2$, then $d = 2 + 3 = 5$. Use the same value for a in the second equation to find a value for c: $c = 2 + 4$, so $c = 6$. Plug this into the first equation to get the b value we need in order to find $b - d$. $b = 6 + 9 = 15$, so $b - d = 15 - 5 = 10$.

15. $\mathbf{\frac{9}{10}}$ **or .9**

This is a rate question, so we can use the formula $rate = \frac{distance}{time}$. Putting the information for Jeanine's trip to work into this form gives $40 = \frac{20}{t}$. Isolate t to find that $t = \frac{20}{40}$ so $t = \frac{1}{2}$. Coming from work, Jeanine drives faster, so the rate is different, but the mileage is the same: $50 = \frac{20}{t}$, so $t = \frac{20}{50}$, and $t = \frac{2}{5}$. Add the two together: $\frac{5}{10} + \frac{4}{10} = \frac{9}{10}$

16. **15** A line that is tangent to a circle forms a 90° angle with a radius or diameter. Radius $\overline{AB}$ and line $\overline{BC}$ form the legs of right triangle ABC, and the hypotenuse is $\overline{AC}$. We know that $AC = 10\sqrt{3}$, and that $AB = \frac{AC}{2}$, or one-half of AC, so $AB = 5\sqrt{3}$. When the hypotenuse is twice the length of the shortest side, we have a 30-60-90 triangle. The ratio of this special right triangle (as shown in the front of every math section on the SAT) is $x : x\sqrt{3} : 2x$, where x is the length of the side opposite the 30° angle. So $BC = 5\sqrt{3} \times \sqrt{3} = 5 \times 3 = 15$.

17. $\mathbf{\frac{19}{2}}$ **or 9.5**

Use an average pie every time the question uses the word *average*. In this case we end up with the following average pies that use the information in the question:

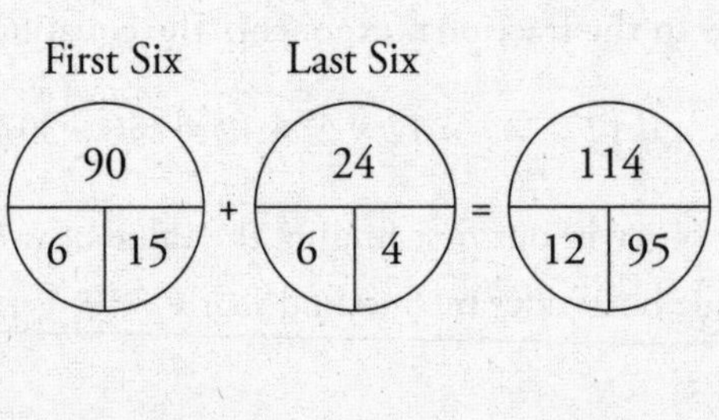

We need an average pie for the first six numbers: the six numbers' average is 15, so the total of those six numbers is $15 \times 6 = 90$. The last six have an average of 4, so the total of those six numbers is $4 \times 6 = 24$. Now take the two totals and add them together for the final mention of the word *average.* The total for all 12 numbers is 114, so to find the average, divide 114 by 12, which gives 9.5. You could also reduce the fraction $\frac{114}{12}$, since numerator and denominator are both divisible by 6, to $\frac{19}{2}$.

18. $\mathbf{\frac{12}{5}}$ **or 2.4**

Write the information from the question onto the figure given:

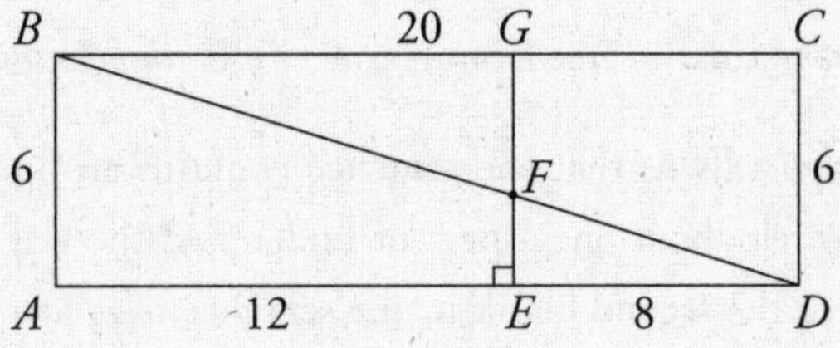

CD = 6, so *AB* = 6 because *ABCD* is a rectangle. Since the area of the rectangle is 120, we can find the length by using what we know in the area formula. *Area* = *lw*, so 120 = *l*(6), and 20 = *l*. Side *AD* = 20, and we know that *AE* = 12, so *ED* must equal 8. Now we have enough information to find the length of $\overline{EF}$. The perpendicular $\overline{EG}$ means that triangle *ABD* and triangle *EFD* are similar, so their sides are in proportion to each other: $\frac{6}{20} = \frac{EF}{8}$, so $20 \times EF = 48$, and $EF = 2.4$ or $\frac{12}{5}$.

SECTION 3

1. **D** The words *their offspring* indicate that the *instinct* must be about how these fish care for their young. The word "parental" is a good word for the second blank, which is pretty close to the second words in D (*nurturing*) and E (*maternal*), but not A, B, or C. Because the fish *lack* this instinct, we need a negative word for the first blank, which describes how the fish treat *their offspring.* Only *spurn* and *devour* are negative, and the second word in A does not fit; only the words in D match the meanings of both blanks.

2. **E** The trigger *and* indicates that two similar ideas are connected, so the first blank must mean something like *stop production.* Only E, *recall,* works well in the blank. But wait! Don't just bubble in E right away; make sure that the second word works too, because a word for the blank that is too narrow might eliminate the correct answer. The second blank describes the *useless inventory* which they could not distribute. The company must have had "a lot of" inventory, and *an abundance* is indeed a match.

3. **B** The word *yet* indicates a relationship that is opposite or unexpected. *Every previous attempt* to get rid of the mayor failed, and these attempts are the *impeachment efforts*. The continuous failure should stop the *critics* from trying any more, but the *yet* means that we need the opposite of stop, something like "continued." A, foundered, is a synonym for failed. B, *persevered,* means "persisted, maintained, or continued steadfastly," a good match. C and D mean the opposite of *continued.* D, *condensed,* does not relate at all to the sentence. B is correct.

4. **A** The word *whether* tells us that Jerome has a decision to make. He needs to "figure out" whether one thing or another is the truth. Eliminate C and D; these are not close to "figure out." There is some tough vocab in the answers: A, *ascertaining,* means "finding out definitely" which is the closest match. In B, *exonerate* means "to free from blame." In E, *importuning* means "begging."

5. **B** The trigger *Even though* tells us that the sentence contains an opposite relationship between the way Lodge's *opponents* felt about one aspect of Lodge and the way they felt about another aspect. We get a better clue for the second blank in the sentence: *eloquence and persuasiveness* are positive qualities in a speaker. Eliminate A, D, and E, which all have negative words in both blanks. We need a negative word for only the first blank, and "opposed" fits well with *opponents.* We can get rid of only C and D, but that leaves just B as a good match for both blanks.

6. **E** This question is asking "Why does the author mention the Patent Office?" The word *since* in line 11 is a sign of an explanation, and it explains that the *contributions* made by the people mentioned in the passage were *unacknowledged* because the *Patent and Trademark Office will not issue a patent to an inventor* if there are any *outside influences.* Eliminate A; it doesn't mention anything about not issuing patents to *outside influences.* B is out because slaves are not discussed in this part of the passage. C is the opposite of what we are looking for, which is that others did make contributions, but could not be acknowledged. D is not correct; the people were purposely left off the patent. E is the best paraphrase of the information in the passage.

7. **B** To answer an EXCEPT question, find evidence in the passage for each answer. This does take a long time, so save this one for after you finish easier questions. The question is asking "What does Passage 2 say about Greene?" The evidence for A is in lines 21–22, for C is in lines 24–25, for D is in lines 22–25, and for E is in lines 17–18. There is no evidence in the passage for B, so B is the answer.

8. **A** This question is asking "What's the difference in opinion about Greene?" Passage 1 states that *Some studies* give her credit for *key elements* but *Another study* and *still other studies* do not credit her. Passage 2 mentions that *proper credit* should go to her. Passage 1 is hesitant to credit her, while Passage 2 is confident that she deserves credit. Only A contains this relationship. The description of Passage 2 in B is the opposite of what we're looking for. While in D the description of Passage 1 is the opposite of what it should be. Both C and E lack words that describe either passage.

9. **C** An inference question on the SAT still needs to be proved by evidence you can find in the passage. In this case, we need to find evidence in both passages for an answer to be correct. A and E are out because *roller gins* is only in Passage 1. Eliminate D because it is not mentioned in either passage. Eliminate B because only Passage 1 mentions *slaves.* Only C is represented in both passages.

10. **B** The question is asking "What's the narrator's view on language?" The lead word *language* turns up in line 59, and is part of a description of how the author finally connected words to the sensations and objects around her. The passage states that when the *mystery of language was revealed* to her, it *awakened* her *soul* and made her *eager to learn* about her environment. The author definitely feels that language has affected her in a positive way, so eliminate A: *impractical* is the opposite of the author's feelings. B is correct because she had a new interest in the *world around her* when she realized that each thing had a name. The passage is about the authors *awakening* to understanding language, not a *mystery,* as in C. Eliminate D because *only* is extreme. E is the opposite of what is stated in the passage.

11. **C** This is a Vocab In Context (VIC) question, so you should treat it like a sentence completion. Go back to the passage, cross out the word described, and fill in your own word based on the context of the passage. In this case, a good phrase for the blank is "came after." The only answer choice that is close to "came after" is *followed,* in C. Choice A is tempting, because it is a definition for *succeeded,* but does not fit this context. Whenever a VIC question asks you about a commonly known word, such as *succeeded,* the primary meaning of the word is almost always a trap. B may be tempting because of the two distinct moods described, but *split* does not fit as a replacement for *succeeded* in the sentence.

12. **D** We need to find out how the author felt, so go to the passage and read the section of the passage near the analogy to find evidence of her feelings. In lines 13–20 she feels *shut in, tense and anxious* and *has no way of knowing* how to find her way. Choice A may be tempting because *scared* is a good match, but *sinking* is not mentioned in the analogy. There is no evidence for *anger* in B. The word *adventurous* in C is too positive a spin of the author's description. D is correct because *lost* fits the situation of having *no way of knowing* one's position. E is incorrect because this part of the passage describes a time before the teacher came.

13. **C** This question is really asking, "What does *finger play* tell us about the author?" The phrase describes the author's desire to imitate her teacher's movements, but in lines 32–33 she describes that she didn't know she was spelling a word. There is no mention of words in A. The author is just learning that words exist: *grammar* is not mentioned in the passage so eliminate B. C is a good paraphrase of the description in the passage. The author did not yet understand that she was using language, so D is out. E is too extreme.

14. **D** The passage states that the author was *keenly delighted* when she broke the doll. Eliminate A, C and E because none of those answers have a first word that is close to *delighted.* After the author's breakthrough in language, she feels *repentance and sorrow.* This matches the second word in D, *regret.* B is out because *disgust* is too strong.

15. **A** We need to find out what the author did before the teacher arrived. At the end of the first paragraph we read that the author's state of mind *for weeks* was *anger and bitterness,* replaced by a feeling of *languor,* or laziness. This is best paraphrased by *resentment* and *inactivity* in A. There is no indication that the author was unloved, as in B. C may be tempting, but the author states that she *did not know . . . what marvel or surprise* was in store for her, but that does not mean that she *did not expect anything good* ever to occur in her life. There is no evidence for D in the passage. The passage indicates that she was sentimental and tender in the description of the *familiar leaves and blossoms*, so E is out.

16. **A** The sentence that depicts the author breaking the doll states that the author *became impatient at her repeated attempts*, and then describes breaking the doll. In A, *frustration* matches the feeling of *impatience.* There is no evidence in the passage for any of the other answers. E may seem close, but *enraged* is a different emotion from *impatience*: frustration is a much closer match.

17. **D** An inference question must be proved by evidence in the passage. A is extreme. In B the word *flaws* is not supported by the passage: the passage is about one person's process of learning that language exists. C may be tempting, because of the example of the doll, but questions that ask about an author's agreement or disagreement are usually supported by the main idea of the passage. D is supported in lines 61–62 in which the author describes being *awakened* by the *living word,* and that *there were barriers still,* indicating that prior to learning language there were even more barriers. E may be true, but it is not mentioned in the passage.

18. **C** The experience in lines 28–34 is imitation without knowing. Later in the passage lines 57–61 describes the moment that the author really understood what language was. The answer that best matches "imitation" and "understanding" is *memorization and comprehension* in C.

19. **D** This question is asking about the primary purpose of the passage. What is the author's goal in writing the passage? A is a detail, not the primary reason for the passage. While the classification is described as a *bold step*, the main idea of the passage is not to *encourage bolder* classifications, so B is out. The *ignorance* mentioned in C is contradicted by the passage, which describes a lot of knowledge about the life forms. D is correct: *abundance of undiscovered life forms* is supported from the blurb at the top (*not an unusual occurrence*) and is supported throughout the passage in phrases such as *glutted with new species.* The *new phylum* is the *Nanaloricus mysticus.* There is no *approval* as in E.

20. **E** Lines 14–15 describes how the *Nanaloricus mysticus is anatomically distinct enough* to be its own group. Only E, *physical characteristics* matches *anatomically.*

21. **B** Beware of EXCEPT, NOT, or LEAST questions: They tend to be time consuming to answer. You're looking for the quality of the *Nanaloricus mysticus* that is not mentioned in the passage, so you can eliminate answer choices that are mentioned. The passage gives a *measurement* in lines 4–5—*a quarter of a millimeter*—so eliminate A. A description, *Barrel-shaped*, is given in line 4, so eliminate C. There is a comparison *like penguin wings* in line 7, so eliminate D. The *speculations about function* are seen in the *guess from its body shape and armament* that the creature *burrows like a mole*, so E is out. Therefore B, evolutionary explanation, must be the answer.

22. **E** Go back to the passage, find the word *cosmopolitan*, and cross it out. Then read the sentence and come up with your own word. The sentence has the trigger *and* between *cosmopolitan* and *extremely abundant*, so we need a word that matches the meaning of *abundant*. B may be tempting because another meaning of *cosmopolitan* is "worldwide scope or bearing," but that's not as close to *abundant* as E, *widespread*. The other choices are wrong because they don't make any sense in context.

23. **E** The word *inferred* tells you that the author did not directly state the right answer but gave you enough information to draw a conclusion. On inference questions, look for an answer that you can definitely support with evidence in the passage. Only E is supported by the passage, because the *myth* is that scientists get excited about new species: the reality is that *museums are glutted* with too many new species. A goes against common sense. There is no evidence for *evolving* as in B. C is true, but not mentioned in the passage. D is the opposite of what is stated in the passage.

24. **B** The second paragraph is where *phylum* is discussed. The question is asking "Why is a species placed in a phylum?" The reason given in lines 14–18 by the zoologist and other scientists is that the *Naniloricus mysticus is anatomically distinct enough* to be its own group. Only the *structural characteristics* come close to describing anatomy. A may be tempting because the *abundance* of new species is mentioned in the passage, but has nothing to do with placing of new species into a phylum.

SECTION 4

1. **B** The word *whether* indicates a choice between two options, but the sentence as written is unclear about what the second option would be. Since *tremendous destruction* is caused, the common *whether . . . or not* construction is not appropriate. Changing the word to *when*, as in B, clarifies the sentence. C changes the meaning of the entire sentence; D and E are both passive and awkward.

2. **D** The adverb *where* is only used for specific, physical locations. It cannot be used with *Lincoln's . . . life*. The film is about *Lincoln's life*, as seen in D: any additional words between are unnecessary and cause other errors.

3. **A** The sentence is correct as written. The list of actions is in parallel form. B and D are not parallel, C changes the meaning and E is wordy.

4. **E** The sentence as written is incomplete: it lacks a verb in the portion of the sentence after the semicolon, which must be able to stand on its own as a sentence. B indicates that the *grass walked*—not possible! C creates an unclear, incomplete sentence. The comma in D sets off an incomplete thought. Only E replaces the *ing* words from the original with verbs that make the sentence complete.

5. **E** In the sentence as written *ringing* is not parallel to the verbs *declared* and *sent.* In B the verb *ring* is in the present tense. In C *being* makes the sentence too wordy. D becomes unclear, and *had rung* is the incorrect tense. Only E uses the correct tense *rang* without adding any other errors.

6. **C** The sentence as written is choppy and the adverb *clearly* should modify a verb. B contains a subject-verb agreement error between *was* and *promises.* C is correct because *clearly* modifies the verb *be.* In D it is unclear what *clearly* is supposed to be modifying.

7. **A** The sentence is correct as written. There is an ambiguous pronoun *it* in B, and the rest of the answers rearrange the elements of the sentence in ways that make the sentence unclear.

8. **A** The sentence is correct as written. B is wordy, C is not parallel to the other parts of the sentence. D uses *being,* which usually makes a sentence unnecessarily passive and wordy, as it does here. E creates an incomplete sentence.

9. **C** Any *ing* construction, such as *building* is not as active as ETS prefers, so you can probably cross off A, B, and E right away. While what follows *despite,* in D, is a contrast; it should not be the *vocalists* themselves, but an opposite action to *strive* that should be set up as the contrast. B also contrasts *strive* with *vocalists,* and *are building* is not parallel with the verbs in the rest of the sentence. C is correct because but is the correct conjunction, *build* is parallel to *strive,* and the sentence is more active. The repeated use of *or* is inappropriate in D. E sets up *vocalists* as the contrast and uses *building* rather than the active *build.*

10. **D** The lack of punctuation between *wartime* and *furthermore* creates a run-on sentence. Each part could stand on its own as a sentence, so they should be joined by a semicolon, as in D. B and C use *it's* which means *it is* rather than the necessary possessive pronoun *its.* A comma is not strong enough to link two complete sentences, so E creates a comma splice.

11. **B** The sentence as written contains a subject-verb error. The subject of the sentence is *Wendy.* The other people mentioned in that part of the sentence, John and Michael, are enclosed by the two commas in a phrase that is non-essential to the sentence. B uses the correct verb *flies* without adding any errors to the sentence. C uses the wrong verb tense. In D *besides* should link the children and Peter Pan, and *flying* creates an incomplete sentence. E uses *flies,* but creates a plural subject by listing all three children.

12. **A** The preposition *for* in A creates an idiom error. The correct idiom is *jealous of.*

13. **D** The word *no* creates a double negative and disrupts the parallel structure in the list of what was *not* packed.

14. **C** There is an agreement problem in the sentence: the plural *some* does not agree with the singular *the other,* which should be *the others.*

15. **C** There is a parallelism error. The phrase in C should be in the same form as *designers of shoes* so *designers of purses* would be the parallel way to phrase C.

16. **E** There is no error in this sentence.

17. **C** The action of *adding spices* is singular, which is not in agreement with the plural verb *make*. The verb should be *makes*.

18. **E** There is no error in this sentence.

19. **A** There is an idiom error in A, which should read *should have*. This may be a tricky question because in speech, the contraction *should've* often sounds like *should of*.

20. **C** There is an agreement problem with the pronouns in C: *she* is a subject pronoun while *him* is an object pronoun. Because "they" *were the perfect couple*, both pronouns should be subject pronouns, as "they" is.

21. **E** There is no error in this sentence.

22. **C** The sentence is discussing a future time *next week*. The verb in C is incorrect because *has spent* is in a tense for an action that happened in the past and is continuing into the present. It should be *will have spent*.

23. **B** There is a parallelism error in the sentence because of the pronoun *they*. To be parallel with *be* and *have*, B should simply read *provide*.

24. **D** There is a pronoun agreement between the singular *it* and *they* in D. A *country* is singular.

25. **D** The use of *having* in D creates an idiom as well as a parallelism error. The construction should be "To *x* is to *y*." D should be *to have*.

26. **A** When referring to people, the pronoun *which* is incorrect; A should be *who*.

27. **A** When the *either . . . or* construction is used, we need a singular verb, because we are referring only to *Jack* or *Ashlee* but not both. The plural verb *are* in A should be *is*.

28. **B** There is a subject-verb agreement problem between the singular *the Weimaraner* and the plural verb *have* in B.

29. **A** The adverb *where* should be used only for physical locations. The sentence refers to time, so A should be *when it*.

30. **B** A paragraph break would best be added between sentences 4 and 5 because sentences 1–4 describe the sanctuary itself, while sentences 5–12 describe the birds that are treated at the sanctuary.

31. **A** The word *besides* means "furthermore," while *beside* refers to a physical location next to or near something. This second meaning fits with the context while the first does not, so A is correct.

32. E A contains an ambiguous pronoun *it.* The contrasting relationship indicated by *and yet* in B does not fit the context of the sentence. C is unclear. The lack of *tries* makes D too absolute. E concisely combines the two sentences and retains the original meaning.

33. B Go to the passage and see what happens when each pair of sentences is switched. B is the best option, because as is, the pronoun *this* in sentence 9 does not refer to anything in sentence 8, but if sentences 9 and 10 are switched, *this* would refer to the situation of the caged birds. Sentence 9 also explains why the birds are in cages. The rest of the pairs of sentences are in proper chronological order.

34. C Answer C best combines the sentences because it uses *even though* to link the idea of the birds that *had been shot* to the legality of *shooting birds.* The conjunction *despite* does not fit the relationship between the phrases. In B *shot by cars* makes little sense. There is an incomplete sentence after the semicolon in D. E contains an ambiguous pronoun *it.*

35. A Of the sentences listed, all provide essential information in the passage as it is written except sentence 10. Its information is redundant with that in sentence 11. As mentioned in the explanation for question 33, the unsupported *this* in sentence 9 is a problem, and switching 9 with 10 fixed that error. However, placing sentence 9 after 11 would fix the issue in 9, and make sentence 10 completely unnecessary.

SECTION 5

1. C Translate the words into math: $7 \times n = 84$, and we want to know the value of $4n$. $7n = 84$, so $n = 12$, and $4n = 48$, answer C.

2. E Out of the initial 16 gallons, 4 are removed, so 12 gallons remain. The fraction $\frac{12}{16}$ can be reduced to $\frac{3}{4}$, which is 75%, answer E.

3. D We can use PITA for this question. First use C, 0.33, for t. If we must add t to each of the four values, we will have $4t$. $4 \times 0.33 = 1.32$. When 1.32 is added to the sum in the question of 2.74, the total is 4.06, which is less than the 4.22 we were looking for. Eliminate A, B, and C and try a larger number. In D, $0.37 \times 4 = 1.48$, and $1.48 + 2.74 = 4.22$, just what we were looking for.

4. B Because the triangle is equilateral, and each of the three sides is cut in half, all of the short segments in the triangle are equal. This means that all four triangles within the larger triangle are equilateral and congruent. Since one of the four triangles is shaded, the shaded area is $\frac{1}{4}$ of the area of the larger triangle. $\frac{1}{4} \times 24 = 6$, answer B.

5. **E** Only s is equal to a number without a variable, so plug that into the equations in the question. The value of s is negative. The variable r is positive, because $r = -\frac{1}{s}$, and when $-\frac{1}{4}$ takes the place of s, the negative signs cancel out: $r = \frac{-1}{-\frac{1}{4}}$ and $r = 4$. Because r is positive, q is negative: $q = -\frac{1}{r}$ becomes $q = -\frac{1}{4}$. Finally, because q is negative, p is positive: $p = -\frac{1}{q}$, then $p = \frac{-1}{-\frac{1}{4}}$ and $p = 4$.

6. **C** First find the value of x: 3 goes into 23 7 times, with 2 left over, so $x = 2$. $2x = 4$ so divide 23 by 4: 4 goes into 23 evenly 5 times and there are 3 left over, so the answer is C, 3.

7. **A** This is a great Plugging In question. Make $d = 2$, so the first ten hours cost \$2.00, and $e = 3$, so service costs \$3.00 an hour. Pick a number above 10 for h to make your math easier: If $h = 20$, it can be split into two parts: The first 10 hours cost \$2.00, and the second ten hours cost $10 \times \$3.00 =$ \$30.00. Altogether that's \$32.00, the number we're looking for in the answers. Plug in the values for d, e, and h. The expression in A becomes $2 + 3(20 - 10) = 2 + 3(10) = 32$. A works, but always check all the answers just in case: B gives 602, C gives 80, D gives –480, and E gives 640. A is correct.

8. **E** In the graph, y is always positive. E is correct because absolute value is always positive. One way to answer this question is to plug in points from the graph into the equations in the answers. Using point (1, 2), A works because $2 = 2(1)$. Eliminate B because 2 does not equal 1^1; also, because of x^2, this is a parabola, not a line. Although the point works in C, $2x^2$ indicates a parabola, so eliminate C. Eliminate D because 2 does not equal $1 - 2$. In E $2 = 2$ does work. Now try the other point from the graph just on equations A and E. A is out because 2 does not equal –2.

9. **256** To solve this equation, get $\sqrt{x}$ by itself. $\sqrt{x} = 16$, so square both sides: $(\sqrt{x})^2 = 16^2$, so $x = 256$.

10. **1 or 9** List the numbers described: All the odd integers from 0 to 10 are 1, 3, 5, 7, 9. Of these numbers, 3, 5, and 7 are prime, leaving only 1 or 9.

11. **2** Because the two triangles have the same area and each have a base with length 5, their heights must be equal as well. For a triangle, $Area = \frac{1}{2}bh$. The bottom triangle has a height of 5 because the base is on the x-axis and the tip is at –5. This means that $t = 7 - 5 = 2$.

12. **52, 59 or 66**

One way to solve this problem is to Plug In numbers for j until you get a result that is between 50 and 70. Another way is to list the multiples of 7 that are close to the range given, such as 49, 56, and 63, and add 3 to each one, which gives 52, 59, and 66 respectively. Any one of these three numbers will get you the credit for the question. You need to come up with only *one possible value.*

13. **148** Use Fred's Theorem: A line crossing two parallel lines creates big angles and small angles. The big angle that matches y is split by a line perpendicular to d and e. The big angle is $58 + 90 = 148$, which is also the value for y. Another way to solve this is to find the third angle of the triangle: $180 - 90 - 58 = 32$. The 32° angle and the y° angle make up a straight line, so $180 - 32 = 148$.

14. **15** We need to find the cost of a single share of stock *x*. Of the nine people, 5 bought a share each, so if cost = *c*, then that is 5*c*. There are also 3 people who each bought $\frac{4}{5}$ of a share, so that's $3(\frac{4}{5}c)$. There is one more person, who bought $\frac{1}{5}$ of a share. Since the club spent $114, we can create the equation $5c + 3(\frac{4}{5}c) + 1(\frac{1}{5}c) = 114$. This simplifies to $\frac{25}{5}c + \frac{12}{5}c + \frac{1}{5}c = \frac{38}{5}c = 114$. Multiply both sides by $\frac{5}{38}$ to get *c* by itself, and $c = 114(\frac{5}{38}) = 15$.

15. **4** First simplify the equation $4x \bullet n^2 = 4^{x+1} \bullet n$, to $4x \bullet n = 4^{x+1}$, then Plug In. If $x = 2$, then $4^2 \bullet n = 4^{2+1}$. Since $16n = 4^3$, then $16n = 64$ and $n = 4$.

16. **12** Plug In the value we are given for *x* into the function. $\frac{(3a)^2 + 108}{9} = -7a$. Now we can solve for all possible values of *a* as the question asks: $\frac{9a^2 + 108}{9} = -7a$, and the fraction can be further simplified: $\frac{9(a^2 + 12)}{9} = a^2 + 12$. Since $a^2 + 12 = -7a$ can be rearranged into a quadratic equation, we can find two possible values for *a*: $a^2 + 7a + 12 = 0$, so $(a + 3)(a + 4) = 0$, and *a* can either be –3 or –4. The answer is 12 because we need the product of the possible answers and $(-3)(-4) = 12$.

17. **118** Based on the numbers for the 1996–1997 academic year and the percents shown in the graph, the 500 students are broken down into:

$$\text{Spanish} = \frac{40}{100}(500) = 200$$

$$\text{French} = \frac{25}{100}(500) = 125$$

$$\text{Latin} = \frac{20}{100}(500) = 100$$

$$\text{Japanese} = \frac{5}{100}(500) = 25$$

$$\text{German} = \frac{10}{100}(500) = 50$$

In the 1997–1998 school year, there were 20 more students, for a total of 520. The percent of students studying Japanese is now 10% of this, so there are 52 Japanese students and the same number of Spanish, Latin and German students as in the previous year. The number of French students (*f*) is the only unknown now: $520 = (52 + 200 + 100 + 50) + f$, and $520 = 402 + f$, so $f = 118$.

18. **20** This is a pattern question in disguise: Write it out, and be methodical! For the four spaces for digits, the first can be only 1, the second could be any digit 0 through 9, the third can be only 0 through 5, and the last digit can be any digit 0 through 9. When the last two spaces have the highest possible digits, showing :59, if the hour is 5 or below, the total is less than 19. This includes the hour of 12, because the hour does not count as 12, it is 1 + 2 = 3. In the next hour, the digits in 6:59 add

to 20. In the next hour, the digits in 7:59 add up to 21. If the middle digit is one less, 7:49 adds up to 20. If instead the last digit was one less, 7:58 also adds up to 20. In the 8 o' clock hour, we have, 8:39, 8:48, 8:49, 8:57, 8:58, and 8:59. In the 9 o' clock hour we have 9:29, 9:38, 9:39, 9:47, 9:48, 9:49, 9:56, 9:57, 9:58, and 9:59. There will be none in the 10 or 11 o' clock hours because their hour digits add up to 1 and 2 respectively and are too small. Count up the times that work: there are a total of 20 times during the 12 hours that add up to 20 or more.

SECTION 6

1. **E** Of the 6 shelves of the bookcase, one shelf has 20 books and the rest have 30 books each. $20 + 5(30) = 20 + 150 = 170$, answer E.

2. **C** The question gives the value for c, so we know that $b = \frac{24}{4} = 6$. Since $a + b = 14$, then $a + 6 = 14$ and $a = 8$, answer C.

3. **B** For \$15, Karim could buy 5 packs of either type of card. Baseball cards are 10 to a pack: $5 \times 10 = 50$ baseball cards. Basketball cards are 12 to a pack: $5 \times 12 = 60$. The difference between 50 and 60 is 10, answer B.

4. **A** Translate this problem into math and solve. The number of trucks times the number of cartons times the number of boxes within the carton is equal to the total number of boxes: $5k \times 60 = 900$. Now solve for k: $5k = 15$, so $k = 3$. You could also PITA (Plug In The Answers).

5. **D** To solve this problem, use percent translation. The first part of the sentence translates to $\frac{35}{100}p = 700$, and $p = 2000$. Now use the value for p and translate the last part of the question: $\frac{40}{100} \times 2{,}000 = 800$, answer D.

6. **D** Use Bite-Sized Pieces with a wordy question like this. To paraphrase, the question states that total cost = (food cost × number of people) + (hourly cost × number of hours). We are given the <u>total</u> cost of the food, so we don't need to use the number of people we are given. We are also told the hourly cost in the question, but need to find the difference in cost for a two-hour and a four-hour party: $200 + (50 \times 2) = 300$ and $200 + (50 \times 4) = 400$, so there is a difference in cost of \$100.

7. **B** We've got some quadratic equations here. The expression $a^2 - b^2$ can be factored into $(a + b)(a - b)$. The question tells us that $a - b = 7$, so we can replace that quantity in the factored equation: $(a + b) \times 7 = 119$, so $a + b = 17$. We need to find the value of a, and we can use simultaneous equations. If we stack and add the equations, the b-values cancel out:

$$\begin{array}{r} a + b = 17 \\ \underline{+\ a - b = 7} \\ 2a = 24 \end{array}$$

so $a = 12$, as seen in B.

8. **D** The exponent outside the parentheses must be distributed to every part within. Remember MADSPM: An exponent outside the *P*arentheses is *M*ultiplied by the exponents within. We end up with $\left(-\frac{1}{3}\right)^3 a^{15}b^6c^{21}$. This is not in the answers as is, but $\left(-\frac{1}{3}\right)^3 = -\frac{1}{27}$, which does match D.

9. **C** We need to have all the quantities in the same form of measure, so convert both into inches. Brian jumped 14 ft., 9 in., which is (12 × 14) + 9 = 177. Mike jumped $2\frac{1}{2}$ feet further, which is 30 inches further: 177 + 30 = 207. Look at the answers—all of them mention the distance of 17 feet: 17 × 12 = 204 inches, which is 3 inches less than the total of 207. Mike therefore jumped 17 feet, 3 inches, as in C.

10. **C** Plug In the values from the chart! Use the pair (–3, –7) from the top of the chart and eliminate answers that are not true: A becomes –7 = –3 – 4, which is true. Keep it. B becomes –7 = –3 – 2, so since –7 does not equal –5, eliminate it. Keep C: –7 = 2(–3) – 1 is true. Get rid of D, which becomes –7 = 2(–3) + 2: –7 does not equal –4. Get rid of E: –7 = 3(–3) – 3. –7 does not equal –9. Now use another pair just to test A and C. Using (–1, –3), A gives –3 = –1 – 4, which is not true, so eliminate it, leaving only C. The values (–1, –3) work: –3 = 2(–1) – 1.

11. **D** Plug In on geometry if there are variables in the equation. In the figure, the angle marked $a°$ looks bigger than 90° so make a = 150. The value of c should be something different, such as c = 140. Now we have information to figure out two of the angles of the triangle in which we find b. There are 180° in a straight line, so the angle on the left is 180 – 150 = 30 and the angle on the right is 180 – 140 = 40. There are 180° in a triangle, so 180 = b + 30 + 40, and b = 110, which is our target number. After replacing a and c in the answers with 150 and 140, respectively, only D equals 110. A gives 10; B gives –110; C gives 200; E gives 70.

12. **C** Each of the three expressions in parentheses could create a value that makes the equation equal 0.

Check to make sure that the three parentheses each have a distinct value for m before you bubble anything in. In the first parentheses, if $10m + 8 = 0$, then $10m = -8$, and $m = -\frac{8}{10}$. In the second parentheses, if $16m + 4 = 0$, then $16m = -4$, and $m = -\frac{4}{16}$. Check the third parentheses: If $2m = 0$, then $m = 0$. Those are three distinct values, so C is correct.

13. **B** This is a pattern question, so write it out: If the red marble lands in section 1, the possible red-blue pairs are 1 and 2, 1 and 3, 1 and 4, and 1 and 5. That's 4 possibilities. If the red marble lands in section 2, the possible red-blue pairs are 2 and 1, 2 and 3, 2 and 4, and 2 and 5. We count all four pairs, because though it seems like 1 and 2 is the same as 2 and 1, in both cases we dropped the red marble first, and red and blue is a different arrangement than blue and red. If the red marble lands in 3, the possibilities are 3 and 1, 3 and 2, 3 and 4, and 3 and 5: another 4 possibilities. A red marble in section 4 will give 4 possibilities, and in section 5 will also give 4 possibilities. 4 + 4 + 4 + 4 + 4 = 20, answer B.

14. **B** Draw a figure if one is described in the question but not shown. In this case, we know a square lies in a circle, and the way we draw these shapes depends on what is in each of the statements above the answers. Since the question wants to know what *must be true*, try to draw a figure to disprove each statement. Statement I can be disproved with a drawing such as

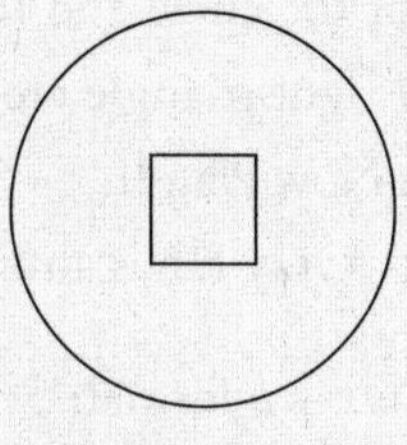

Eliminate A, C, and E because they all contain I. B and D both contain II, so it must be true. Check out statement III. The circle above disproves III, so get rid of D. Only B can be correct. Skipping statement II saves time: To prove it true you'd need to make the biggest possible square inside the circle, such as

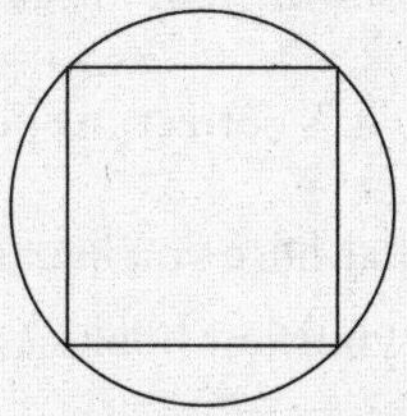

The diameter of the circle is the same as the diagonal of the square. If the diameter were 10, then the radius would be 5, and the area of the circle would be 25π. To find the area of the square, we can use the diagonal as the hypotenuse of a 45-45-90 triangle. The legs and hypotenuse have a ratio of $x : x : x\sqrt{2}$. In this case, the value of $10 = x\sqrt{2}$. Solve for x to find the side of the square: $x = \frac{10}{\sqrt{2}}$. The area of the square is $\left(\frac{10}{\sqrt{2}}\right)^2 = \frac{100}{2} = 50$. This is less than 25π, which is a little over 75.

15. **E** To answer this question, list some cubes of integers and see whether any of the digits in the statements turn up: $2^3 = 8$, so we know that statement III is true. Eliminate A, B, and C because none of them contain III. Both of the remaining answers contain I, so it must be true. We need to check only statement II. List cubes until a 6 comes up in the unit's digit or until the unit's digit begins repeating: $3^3 = 27$, $4^3 = 64$, $5^3 = 125$, $6^3 = 216$ so II is true. Pick E.

16. **A** Plug In! Come up with a list of three consecutive even integers, and divide by 6 to determine the remainder: 2 + 4 + 6 = 12. When 12 is divided by 6, the remainder is 0. If you are not sure, you can try with a different set of consecutive even integers: 10 + 12+ 14 = 36, and 36 is evenly divided by 6. The remainder will always be 0, answer A.

17. E The phrase *in terms of* means that this is a Plugging In question. The figure above the question is not drawn to scale, so redraw or add to the figure based on information in the question. Because $\overline{AC}$ and $\overline{DF}$ are tangent to the circle, they form a 90° angle with a radius or diameter of the circle. Draw in diameter $\overline{BE}$ and mark the right angles. Draw the diagonal of the rectangle $\overline{CF}$. The question states that $\angle COE = 120°$ so $\angle COB = 60°$. We have a 30-60-90 triangle, *COB,* in which $\overline{OB}$ is the radius of the circle and the shortest side of the triangle. Time to Plug In! If $r = 5$, the sides of this special right triangle are $5 : 5\sqrt{3} : 10$. So $CO = 10$, which is half the length of *CF*, which must equal 20. Now Plug In $r = 5$ in the answers: A results in 10π; B results in $10\sqrt{2}$; C gives $10\sqrt{3}$; D gives 20π. Only E has a result of 20.

18. E Convert the equation into the $y = mx + b$ format: $5y = -2x + 10$. Simplified, this is $y = -\frac{2}{5}x + 2$. The slope in this equation is $-\frac{2}{5}$. A line that is perpendicular will have a slope that is the negative reciprocal of this, or $\frac{5}{2}$. Right away you can eliminate B and C because their slopes are negative. Use points in the graph to find the slope of each answer. Eliminate A; it has points at (1, 0) and (2, 5), for a slope of 5—too steep. Eliminate D, because its points, (1, 0) and (6, 2), give a slope of $\frac{2}{5}$, the reciprocal of what we want. E is correct; its points, (1, 0) and (3, 5), give a slope of $\frac{5}{2}$.

19. D The term *direct proportion* means that once you square *x*, the ratio between x^2 and *y* should be the same for all pairs in the table. Use your test booklet as scratch paper and write the value for x^2 for each pair to check the ratios. In A, $2^2 = 4$, for a ratio of 1 : 4. This does not match the 9 : 6 ratio of the next pair, so eliminate A. The first ratio in B is 1 : 2, but the second is 16 : 8, so eliminate B. In C the first ratio is 4 : 3, but the second is 16 : 9, so eliminate C. Only D is a match: 1 : 3, 4 : 12, and 9 : 27 are all equivalent ratios.

20. C Out of the 300 mice, if 75% are male, 25% must be female, so translate: $\frac{25}{100} \times 300 = 75$ females. Eliminate D and E, because there are no more than 75 females of any sort. Because 20% of the mice are albino, and 25% of the mice are female, both groups are small enough not to overlap at all. There are 80% non-albino mice, so $\frac{80}{100} \times 300 = 240$ non-albino mice, so all 75 females could be non-albinos.

SECTION 7

1. A In this sentence, the clue is *takes extra care to avoid hitting squirrels.* A good word to use for the blank would be "hit." You can probably eliminate B and C pretty easily, but the rest of the words may be less familiar. *Maltreat* comes closest to the harm caused by hitting. *Placate* means "to allay the anger of" and *entreat* means "to plead."

2. A The first blank describes what is done to *bacteria* by *antibiotics.* A good word for the first blank is "killed." Eliminate B and E since the first words do not come close to "killed." The trigger *but*

indicates that the second blank should indicate that the antibiotics are *less* "able to kill." The word *effective* in A is a good match, while *profitable* and *weak* do not fit the sentence.

3. **D** The clue *lack of propriety* indicates that Amy was doing improper things. You can see the root *prop* is shared by these two words. Even without looking at that word, you know that *rumors* are typically bad things, so this would negatively impact how the bookstore would feel about hiring Amy. A good phrase for the blank is "took back." Only D *rescinded* matches this meaning. A is incorrect as *fortified* means "strengthened." B is incorrect as *cogitated* means "pondered." C is incorrect as *tempered* means "softened." E is incorrect as *regulated* means "controlled."

4. **C** The clue in this sentence is *surreptitiously embezzled a considerable sum of money*, and the trigger word is *although*, which means the blank must be the opposite of *surreptitious* or sneaky. If you put "not sneaky" or "honest" in the blank, the best match is *forthright*. E *evasive* is a synonym for sneaky, so it's the opposite of what we're looking for.

5. **E** The *questionable tactics* led to the supervisor's stepping down. Thus, the workers were probably unhappy about the *tactics*, so "unhappiness" is a good word for the first blank. Eliminate A and B because they are positive words. The second blank is about how the workers felt *until he stepped down*. Their unhappiness probably lasted the whole time the supervisor was there, so it probably *did not* "end" until he left. Of the three answers left, only *subside* matches "end."

6. **C** The phrase *respected for*, along with *Just as* and *also*, indicates that the words in the blank are both positive. The relationship between the blanks is an opposite, however, because in the first blank she is praised for how she does her job, the clue *ability to know when* indicates that circumstances differ at certain times. A, B, and E all have similar relationships. D has an opposite relationship, but *overlook* is negative. C is correct because *initiative* is a positive description of taking action and to *delegate* is to give *responsibility* to someone else.

7. **A** The semicolon trigger is like an equal sign between the two parts of the sentence. The second part of the sentence has the clue *can be lethal*, but also has the trigger *however*, which indicates an opposite meaning from the first part. A good phrase for the blank is "not lethal." The best match is A, *innocuous*. Eliminate B because *virulent* means "harmful," the opposite of what we are looking for. C is incorrect: *efficacious* means "effective." D is incorrect: *capricious* means "impulsive." E, *artificial*, has nothing to do with whether something is *lethal*.

8. **B** The sentence describes the work with a pair of opposites linked by the trigger *but*: *functional but lacking elegance*. The blanks are also opposites, linked by the *too much . . . not enough* construction. Recycle "functional" and "elegant" for the blanks. There is no mention of money in the sentence, so A, *financial*, and E, *lucrative*, should be eliminated. In B, *utilitarian . . aesthetic* is a good match. In C, *pragmatic* means "practical" which would be good as a first blank word, but is not a match for "elegant." Eliminate D because *pedestrian* means "everyday," and is not a synonym for "functional."

9. **D** The passage is informational: it states a problem and potential cause (*global warming, excess of carbon dioxide*), describes a response (*plant trees*), gives a reason for that particular response (*consume

carbon dioxide), provides a reason that the response is not completely successful (*other harmful pollutants*) and concludes that trees are not enough to fix all the pollution. This even-handed treatment of different sides of the issue is best described as *objective*. The other answers are too positive or negative.

10. **A** The phrase *serves primarily to* means that you need to find out why the author included the sentence. The third sentence starts with the word *Because*, which usually indicates that we're about to hear the reason for something. This matches the *explanation* mentioned in A. The opposite is indicated by words like *contradict, contrasting* and *flaws*. In E, a *restatement* would be indicated by a phrase such as "in other words" not *Because*.

11. **B** Although the question say *inferred*, you need to find the answer that is backed up by what is stated in the passage. There is no evidence of a *doctoral degree*, so eliminate A. B is supported in lines 10–11, in which the drug that *Elion invented . . . made the first organ transplant possible*. In C, *greatest* is extreme. There is no evidence in the passage for D or E.

12. **C** This is an EXCEPT question, so it will probably be time consuming to answer. You need to know which statement is not true, so you need to go back to the passage and find where each answer is discussed. Remember: You're looking for something that is not mentioned, so you can eliminate answer choices that are mentioned. The passage mentions A in lines 8–10: *she developed treatments for several . . . diseases*. B is in the date given in line 10: 1957. D is in lines 5–6: *a few women had become notable scientists*, and E is in line 8: *Elion never completed a doctoral degree* but she developed numerous medical innovations.

13. **A** A main purpose question asks "Why did the author write this?" A is correct. The purpose of the passage as a whole can be found by looking at the main ideas of each paragraph: The first paragraph discusses Johnson's personality (*complicated*). The second discusses his *achievement*. The third paragraph begins with the word *Yet*, which connects *his dreams* to Johnson's achievements, and the sentence also discusses Johnson's *flaws of personality*. We have a theme here: achievements and personality. Only A mentions these two aspects in *personality* and *performance*. This is not a straightforward, chronological *history* so B is incorrect. C and E are incorrect because they are extreme. D refers to a detail of the passage, not the passage as a whole.

14. **E** The word *achieved* should lead you to the second paragraph, which details the achievements. The phrase *above all* in line 17 indicates the *most remarkable* of these, which is *civil rights* as in E. The rest of the answers are not supported by the passage.

15. **B** Why did the author use the quote? The phrase *As one civil rights leader noted* tells you that the quote is an illustration of the author's previous statement the author, which is that Johnson accomplished more that anyone else could even imagine. The quote supports the author's contention that Johnson did a lot for civil rights. This is best paraphrased in B. The quote praises Johnson, and does not *point out flaws*, so A is incorrect. In C, *prove* is extreme. D is negative, and not supported by the passage. There are no *failings* mentioned in the quote, and *kind* is too mild for the praise in the quote.

16. **C** Look in the passage around the mention of *illness* to figure out what it is. Lines 27–28 mention that *egomania is an occupational disease*, and *the illness* refers back to *disease*. You need to find a word in the answers that is close to *egomania*. There is no mention of *fantasies* as mentioned in A until later in the passage, out of context of the discussion of *illness*. B is too literal, and there is no mention of *heart disease*. C is correct because *self-centeredness* is close in meaning to *egomania*. There is no evidence for *inner conflicts* or *societal racism* in the context of that paragraph.

17. **B** Go back to the passage, find the word *eclipse*, and cross it out. Then read the sentence and come up with your own word. The paragraph is talking about Johnson's belief that *he alone* could fix everything, *emulate* or copy the actions of his *mentors*, and then eclipse or "do even better than" them since only he could fill the role. B *surpass* fits the context of the sentence best. C may be tempting as *darken* describes a physical *eclipse*, but the word is used figuratively in the passage. D is close, but doesn't indicate a "better" quality, as one can *dominate* by force.

18. **A** Go back to the passage and find out what *Johnson's desire to help others* did. The lead word *help others* should take you to lines 42–43 *helping others . . . he could most satisfy his own ego*. Eliminate any answers that do not mention this. Only A mentions *self-esteem*, a synonym for *ego,* and *bolster* or "boost" is a positive word that fits with *satisfy*.

19. **B** The lead word in this question is *ironic*, which takes you to *irony* in line 55. The irony described is that Johnson's work for *consensus* led only to a *fragmented nation*. This is best paraphrased in B. There is no evidence in the passage for any of the other answers.

20. **E** This question is asking "Why did Johnson fail as President?" The answer is in the final paragraph, between *tragedy* in line 52 and *presidency* in line 55. The passage states that *both his personality and his political assumptions proved inadequate*. E is correct because it mentions both personality and *beliefs* which is similar in meaning to assumptions. A is too specific a detail and does not mention personality or beliefs. B is incorrect because there is no mention of Roosevelt in the context of Johnson's failures. C is a result of Johnson's failure, not the cause of it. D is too specific: it is only one example of Johnson's overall inadequate political assumptions.

21. **D** The author criticizes Johnson's personality, but mentions his many accomplishments. In the final paragraph the author mentions *tragedy* and that Johnson *did more than anyone else* for unity, but things turned out exactly the opposite of what he intended. D is correct because *measured sympathy* means that the author has a small or limited amount of sympathy. The list of ironies in the final paragraph makes it seem that the author recognizes the effort Johnson put into his presidency, and feels a little sorry that things turned out badly for Johnson. The author is not objective or *detached*: he does criticize, so A is out. In B *disappointment* is a little personal. C and E are extreme.

22. **C** The lead word in this question is *Doris Kearns*, and her name appears twice. In line 35, Johnson is sharing his *Fantasizing* with her, and in lines 50–51 he is sharing another personal feeling with her. The correct answer should mention sharing feelings. A is incorrect because *most* is too extreme;

Johnson could have had *personal thoughts* that the passage doesn't mention that are even more personal than the ones mentioned. There is no evidence in the passage for B. C is correct because a *confidant* is someone to confide in, and the use of *at times* makes it the opposite of extreme: on the SAT wishy-washy is a good thing. There is no evidence for D. E is not necessarily true; there is no evidence of *recording*.

23. **B** Go back to the passage and read a little bit above or below the quote to find why the author included it. Line 1 of the passage mentions McNamara, who describes Johnson as *complicated*. After the quote, the passage states that this *appropriately describes both the man and the administration*. From answering other questions, you may see that *man and the administration* fits with the *personality and accomplishments* theme of the passage, which is also seen in B in *Johnson's presidency and character*. A and C are incorrect because the passage starts with a quote: there is no *argument* or *view* yet. D is incorrect because no *objection* is raised. E is incorrect because no *authority* is needed: the blurb does more to provide authority with its mention of *noted historian*.

24. **C** In order to weaken an author's argument, pick the answer that is the most opposite of the main idea of the passage. The author's argument is that Johnson had a lot of ambition and talent, but his egomaniac personality got in his way and led to the opposite of what he envisioned. Use POE to get rid of as many answers as possible. A mentions a minor point: not too much would change if he were *not entirely truthful*. B does not address personality at all. C does the most to weaken the argument, because if Johnson is using his staff's ideas, he is not an egomaniac, and any problems are not necessarily his fault, so it's not just Johnson's personality that caused all the trouble. D does nothing, because most egomaniacs do not think they are egomaniacs, they just think they are right. E may be true, but does not relate to the author's argument.

SECTION 8

1. **C** The trigger *because* tells us that *buying more books* causes Jamal's *efforts* to *hit a snag*, so he must be trying to "slow" his spending habits. Eliminate A, B, and E because their words for the first blank do not agree with "slow." A good word for the second blank is something like "excuse" since he thinks buying books is worth going against his efforts. Only C, *curb . . . justify* matches for both blanks.

2. **A** There are two clues: *a CD player . . . in the 1950s* and *a cellular phone . . . in ancient Rome*. These make "out of place in time" a good phrase for the blank. A is correct: the root *chron* refers to time, and *ana* indicates an opposite or negative. B may be tempting because *antiquated* means old, but this doesn't reflect the out-of-place element of the clues.

3. **C** The clue *not through sudden inspiration* is linked by the trigger *but rather* to the description of a *gradual investigative approach*. A good word for the blank is "eliminates" since eventually *only one explanation remains*. Only C, *exhausts* has this meaning.

4. **C** The clues *stood in awe* and *twirled with effortless grace* make something like either "awesome" "graceful" good words for the blank. Eliminate A, B, D, and E because these are negative and we need something more positive, such as *lithe* which means "flexible and agile," similar to "graceful" and good qualities for dancers.

5. **D** There is a time trigger in this sentence, indicated by *After* and *now*. The clue *experiencing a mild renaissance* means that the work is more popular now than before, so "drop" is a good word for the blank. Only D, *ebb*, which means "a decline," matches. A is incorrect because *blandishment* means "flattering actions or speech." B is incorrect because *disparity* means "an inequality." C is incorrect because *transgression* means "a bad deed." E is incorrect because *elevation* is the opposite of "drop."

6. **B** The clue for the first blank is *the contractor was truly sorry*, so "sorrow" is a good word to describe *his voice*. Eliminate D and E because *gratification* and *jubilance* are positive, happy emotions. The clue for the second blank is *hoping for* and needs to relate to being *sorry for causing inconvenience*. A word like "forgiveness" works for the second blank. In the answers that are left, only C *clemency* fits. The second word in the answers we eliminated both mean "correcting or making better," which may be tempting, but remember that their first words are the opposite of what we need.

7. **A** A question that asks what can be *inferred* needs to be supported by evidence in the passage, so go back and see what the *author's reference to "music controversies"* tells us. The passage states that *In those days there weren't any major music controversies*. So we can infer that eventually there were some. This is reflected best in A. There is no evidence in the passage for the rest of the answers. C may be tempting because *ignorance* is mentioned in the passage, but is not an answer to this question. D may be true, but is not mentioned in the passage at all.

8. **D** We need to answer the question, "What does *it's all jazz* mean?" The passage states that the narrator was willing to have some unknown performers participate because *It's all jazz*—differences didn't matter. This is best paraphrased in D. Eliminate A because it lacks common sense. B is not supported by the passage. C is extreme: the word *all* is easy to prove false. There is no evidence for E, although *ignorant* may be tempting because the word *ignorance* is mentioned in the passage; this does not answer the question asked.

9. **A** Go back to the passage to see what it says about the lead words *bop musicians* to find out how bop musicians differ from other jazz musicians. In lines 28–29, the passage states that the author thought *"be-bop" musicians were superior folks, better educated, more civilized*. This is best paraphrased in A: *better educated and more polite*. B is not stated in the passage. C is not supported. D is incorrect because jazz musicians were also influenced by swing music. There is no evidence of the *better understanding* mentioned in E.

10. **C** The author's attitude toward be-bop in Passage 1 is negative: in lines 31–32, he states that he found it *boring*. And *the more I heard it and understood it, the less I liked it*. Only C *uninteresting* reflects *boring*. Eliminate A: there is no evidence in the passage of *inferior imitation*. B is contradicted by the passage: the author *understood* it, he just didn't like it. D reverses the chronology of emotions. E is too positive.

11. **D** Go back to the passage and summarize what Gillespie means by lines 33–34. Gillespie is responding to the author's criticism of be-bop. The passage states that he said *It's not a question of . . . better or worse, it just keeps movin'*, indicating that young musicians should *experiment with the instruments,* so that music keeps changing. A is incorrect because to *perfect jazz* is not mentioned (or possible!). B is incorrect because the quote is not about *fame.* C contradicts the statement that it's not about being *better or worse.* E is not mentioned in lines 33–34. Only D reflects this *experimentation* and change without contradicting the passage.

12. **C** To answer this question go back to the passage to find the specific reason that the author uses the phrase. The paragraph is about the differences between be-bop and swing music. This *contrast* is best captured in C. A and B are too specific in their focus on *musicians*; the comparison is about the characteristics of the music in general. D is tempting because these musicians are mentioned in Passage 2, but not in this comparison of musical styles. E is much too specific.

13. **E** This is a NOT question, so it will probably be time consuming to answer. You need to find where in Passage 2 each answer choice is discussed. Remember: You're looking for the reason that is not mentioned, so you can eliminate answer choices that are mentioned. The passage mentions A in lines 49–50: *If a swing drummer played beats one and three, the bop drummer would emphasize two and four.* B is in lines 53–54: *the bop drummer played mostly . . . on the snares and cymbals.* C is in lines 57–58: *exploring variations on the harmony rather than the melody.* D is in lines 55–57: *Solos tended to be more frantic, with plenty of sixteenth and thirty-second notes.* E is contradicted by information in lines 60–63, therefore E must be the answer.

14. **E** You need to go back to the passage and find out what *Groovin' High* is used as an example of. *Groovin' High* appears in line 65, and the phrase *for instance* indicates that this is an example of what is mention right before *for instance*, namely that it was based on *changes of some early songs.* A and D are incorrect because the *swing* piece is *Whispering* (line 66) while *Groovin' High* is a *bop* piece. Eliminate B because it is not about *solo works.* There is no evidence of *rejected* in C. Only E summarizes what is stated in the passage in lines 62–66.

15. **B** The best answer is B. This is a Vocab In Context (VIC) question, so you should work it like a sentence completion. Go back to the passage, cross out the word *interpreters,* and fill in your own word based on the context of the passage. In this case, a good word to put in the blank is "players." The only answer choice that is close to "players" is *performers,* in B. Choice A is tempting, because it seems to describe musicians, but someone can *compose* without playing. C is also tempting, because it refers to a more common meaning of the word *interpreters,* but that is not the meaning that is used in the passage. Remember: When a VIC question asks you about a commonly known word, such as *interpreters,* the primary meaning of the word is almost always a trap. Eliminate it! D and E are wrong, because these words don't match *players.*

16. **D** Go back to the passage and see what lines 67–70 say about bop. The passage says that the author is not convinced that bop is better, it's *just different* in that it is *more harmonically advanced.* This is best paraphrased in D, *more harmonically sophisticated.* A and B are mentioned in the passage,

but not in lines 67–70. C is not true, although *McShann* is mentioned elsewhere in the passage. E is incorrect because it is not true at all, and more important, there is no evidence in the passage to support it.

17. **B** To find out why the author of Passage 2 makes this statement, go back to the passage. The word *whereas* in line 72 indicates a contrast between the statement you need to find out about and the information before *whereas.* The gist is that there were few bop musicians but there were many *jazz musicians working in older idioms* because bop was *more difficult to do well* (lines 69–70). This is best paraphrased in B. A is incorrect because public appreciation is not the point of the contrast. C is incorrect because it does not mention the musicians. D contradicts the passage, which states that bop was more complicated. E is true, but not the point of the contrast.

18. **E** Go back to the passages and find out what is similar in their mentions of Dizzy Gillespie. Passage 1 mentions him as an example of a be-bop musician and supporter. Passage 2 also mentions Gillespie's influence in be-bop, stating in the first paragraph that he was part of when *be-bop was born.* A is incorrect; there is no *personal affection.* B is incorrect because *most influential* is extreme. C and D are incorrect because *explore the significance* and *argue his importance* are too strong and do not reflect the point of the passages.

19. **C** Another question about the two passages together, but this time you need to find out what is different between them. Passage 1 is about a personal experience of a specific concert that took place in 1940 or 1941. Passage 2 is more generally about the history of music and how it changed over a period of time: *early 1940s . . . in 1945 be-bop was born . . . the period from 1945 to 1955.* This is best paraphrased in C. A is incorrect because the passages are both historical, not about *the future.* B is incorrect because there is no *ambivalence.* There is no *musical theory* in Passage 2, so D is incorrect. There is no *emotional argument* in Passage 1, so eliminate E.

SECTION 9

1. **C** The slope of any horizontal line is 0, so right away you should know that the answer is C. Remember: Slope is $\frac{rise}{run}$, and there is no rise when the y-value doesn't change. The slope formula

$$\frac{y_2 - y_1}{x_2 - x_1} \text{ gives } \frac{-4-(-4)}{-3-2} = \frac{-0}{-5} = 0$$

2. **D** This is a great question for PITA. The question gives the number of adult and child tickets sold, and we know the total price is \$800. The answer choices list a price for each kind of ticket, so start with C and find $a(100) + c(50)$: C gives $7(100) + 3(50) = 850$, which is too big. It's hard to determine which direction will give a lower total cost. A and B turn out to be too big, but D is just right: $6(100) + 4(50) = \$800$.

3. **B** To solve this rate problem, set up two equivalent fractions: We know that 38 out of every 10,000 are defective and want to find how many defective chips there would be out of 1,000,000: $\frac{38}{10{,}000} = \frac{n}{1{,}000{,}000}$. You could cross-multiply or see that 1,000,000 has two more zeros than 10,000, so n should have two more zeros after 38 to become 3,800, as in answer B.

4. **B** The lowest number that both 8 and 10 are factors of is 40. Convert the fractions to a denominator of 40: $\frac{5}{40} + \frac{4}{40} = \frac{9}{40}$. There is no factor that 9 and 40 have in common, so the fraction cannot be reduced. The number in place of a in $\frac{a}{b}$ is 9. Be careful! E has the value of b.

5. **E** The numbers in the answer choices mean this is a great PITA question: we can try out the numbers in the answers as the price of Juanita's fifth item. First break the wordy question into bite-sized pieces—there is a lot of information to sort through. The cost of the four known items is 6 + 11 + 14 + 19 = \$50. We want to find the price that, when added to \$50 and then multiplied by 1.05 (for the total cost and 5% tax), should result in \$63. Start with C. \$6 + \$50 = \$56; \$56 × 1.05 = \$58.80—too small, so eliminate A, B, and C. Now try D: \$8 + \$50 = \$58; \$58 × 1.05 = \$60.90—too small, so eliminate D. Only E is left: \$10 + \$50 = \$60; \$60 × 1.05 = \$63.00.

6. **E** Plug in the number given for a in the expression to find the value: $-2 + (-2)^2 - (-2)^3 + (-2)^4 - (-2)^5$. Remember PEMDAS, the order of operations: The first thing to do here is deal with the *E*xponents, then we can take care of the *A*ddition and *S*ubtraction: $-2 + 4 - (-8) + 16 - (-32)$, which simplifies to $-2 + 4 + 8 + 16 + 32 = 58$, answer E.

7. **A** The top graph is of the countries' populations, and the bottom graph is of the countries' areas. Find the population density, $\frac{\textit{population}}{\textit{area}}$, for each country by taking its number from the top graph and dividing that by its number from the bottom graph:

$$\text{Ecuador} = \frac{10}{0.3}\text{, which equals 33.33}$$

$$\text{Uruguay} = \frac{2.5}{0.2}\text{, which equals 12.5}$$

$$\text{Venezuela} = \frac{20}{1.0}\text{, which equals 20}$$

$$\text{Chile} = \frac{15}{0.8}\text{, which equals 18.75}$$

$$\text{Paraguay} = \frac{5}{0.4}\text{, which equals 12.5}$$

The highest value among the countries is that of Ecuador, answer A.

8. A Plug In the number of bananas sold on Tuesday into the equation in place of n in order to find the value of p, the price per banana: $60 = \frac{12}{p}$, so $60p = 12$ and $p = 0.2$. Since the price is in dollars, that's \$0.20, as seen in A.

9. C The revenue is the *cost of television* × *number of televisions sold.* We only need the information from the graph for the television that costs \$3,500 and the television that costs \$1,000 in order to determine how much more revenue the \$3,500 television produced. There were 150 of the \$3,500 televisions sold, for a revenue of \$525,000. There were 250 of the \$1,000 televisions sold, for a revenue of \$250,000. The difference between the two is \$525,000 – \$250,000 = \$275, 000, as seen in C.

10. C The 5 equal lengths that make up the two sides of the largest triangle tell us that we are dealing with 5 similar triangles. The largest triangle has sides 15 : 25 : 30, and the sides of all 5 triangles will have an equivalent ratio. Reduced, the ratio is 3 : 5 : 6, which happens to be the dimensions of the smallest triangle. We want to find the length of *BD,* the base of a triangle with sides of 6 and 10. This is twice as big as the smallest triangle, so the base *BD* must be 6 × 2 =12, answer C.

11. D Label the figure with any information provided by the question. We know that $YD = 4$ and $DZ = 3$. First focus on triangle *ADZ*: because we have an angle of 30° and a right angle symbol, we are working with a 30-60-90 triangle. The length of *AD* is the hypotenuse of the triangle and one of the dimensions we need to find the area of rectangle ABCD. The ratio of sides in triangle *ADZ* is $x : x\sqrt{3} : 2x$, where x is the length of the side opposite the 30° angle and $2x$ is the hypotenuse So $AD = 2x = 6$. To find the other dimension of the rectangle, look at triangle *CYD.* This too is a 30-60-90 triangle, $\angle CDY = 30°$ because it forms a straight line with the 90° of the rectangle and the 60° from triangle ADZ. The question states that $DY = 4$, and this is opposite the 60° angle. Using the ratio, $4 = x\sqrt{3}$, and $x = \frac{4}{\sqrt{3}}$, and the hypotenuse, CD, must be $\frac{8}{\sqrt{3}}$. Now we have enough information to find the area of the rectangle: $6 \times \frac{8}{\sqrt{3}} = \frac{48}{\sqrt{3}}$. Multiply the top and bottom of the fraction by $\sqrt{3}$ to get $16\sqrt{3}$, as seen in answer D.

12. A Let's start with the fact that Amy's flight is before Dave's, which means she must be flying on Wednesday or Thursday. Her flight is after the flight to London, which means it has to be Thursday, and the flight to London is on Wednesday. Eliminate (C), (D), and (E). We also know that she is not flying to London, because the flight to London is the day before her flight, so she must be flying to either Seattle or St. Louis. Since Dave is not flying to Seattle, that means that Amy must be flying to Seattle, answer choice (A).

13. **D** The answer choices are split between those that are oriented like the original graph of $y = x^2$ and those that are flipped upside down. In the equation $y = -(x + 3)^2 - 4$, the negative sign flips the graph upside down, so eliminate the right-side up ones in A and B. Any number inside the parentheses added to x moves the graph to the left. Eliminate C because it has moved to the right. Any number outside the parentheses moves the graph up or down: when the number is subtracted from the expression in parentheses, the graph moves down, which makes D correct; E is the result that would happen if 4 were added instead of subtracted.

14. **A** Start with the second equation, $x^y = 1$. The only way for this to equal 1 would be if $y = 0$ or $x = 1$. The problem states that x and y are both greater than zero, which means that it must be that $x = 1$. Plugging that into the first equation gives us $\left(\frac{1y}{2}\right)^1 = 1$, so $\frac{y}{2} = 1$, and $y = 2$.

15. **A** Come up with a list of numbers that fits the description in the question. We know the smallest, largest, and middle numbers out of 7 spots:

13, __, __, 24, __, __, 37

Because the mode is 18, there must be more than one 18 in the list, and there is only one place they would fit:

13, 18, 18, 24, __, __, 37

The last piece of information we have is that the mean, or average, is 23. Since there are 7 numbers, the total sum is $7 \times 23 = 161$. The numbers we already know from the list add up to $13 + 18 + 18 + 24 + 37 = 110$. The last two integers must equal 51 when added together, so only 25 and 26 fit in the two spaces left in our list. Now add 8 and 43 to the list and evaluate statements I, II, and III. The mode will not change: 18 still occurs the most, so III is not true. Eliminate C, D, and E for containing III. The numbers 8 and 43 are lower and higher, respectively, than anything on the original list, so the median stays the same, so II is not true. Eliminate B because it contains II, leaving only A.

16. **D** Whenever a question describes a geometric figure but doesn't show it, draw it out. The center is at (4, 3), and the circle passes through the origin. The key to any circle is knowing the radius, which in this case is a line between the center at (4, 3) and the origin, such as:

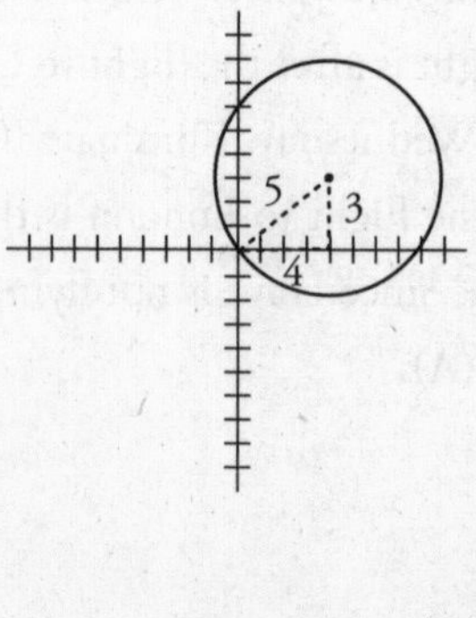

This makes it clear that the radius is the hypotenuse of a right triangle that has legs of 3 and 4. You can use the Pythagorean theorem or remember that 3:4:5 is a Pythagorean triplet. Since the radius has length 5, Area = $\pi r^2 = \pi 5^2 = 25\pi$, answer D.

SECTION 10

1. C As written, the sentence is incomplete: *Having* is not a verb. B is passive, which we don't want. C is correct because it is a complete sentence and is active. D lacks a verb and so is a sentence fragment. E is choppy and awkward.

2. A There is no error in the sentence as written. The words *begins* and *ends* are in parallel form. The word *that* is unnecessary in B. C contains an agreement problem between *have begun* and *ending.* D creates an incomplete sentence because the *ing* words do not function as verbs. E contains an agreement problem between *are begun* and *ended.*

3. B The sentence as written contains a fragment: *to produce* should simply be *produce* as it is in B. C is wordy and unclear. D contains an agreement problem between the past tense *was* and the present tense in the rest of the sentence. The *ing* word in E creates a sentence fragment.

4. E The verb construction *has . . . spoken* indicates an action that is no longer continuing, which does not make sense in relation to speaking English fluently. In B, *while being* is unnecessarily wordy. The *ing* word *moving* in C indicates something currently happening, while *now* lets you know that the *moving* happened in the past. D contains the redundant word *years.* Only E correctly places *moved* in the past tense, and *speaks fluently* in the present.

5. B There is an idiom error in the sentence as written. The correct idiom is *considered to be*, as in B. The meaning of the sentence changes in C, and D and E use *ing* words that do not fit with the rest of the sentence.

6. E There is a comparison error between *compositions of Mozart* and *Beethoven,* the person. B is awkward because the comparison is not in parallel form. C compares *compositions* to *Beethoven.* D is wordier than it needs to be, though it does make a proper comparison. E is the most concise proper comparison.

7. D There is a pronoun error in the sentence as written: the subject pronoun *he* should be the object pronoun *him.* If we take *Artemis* out of the sentence, it is clearer that Constance would *flee the country with* <u>him</u>, as in D. B uses the incorrect pronoun. C and E are passive and confusing due to the *ing* word *being.*

8. B The sentence as written contains a pronoun error. This time we have the object pronoun *whom* when we need the subject pronoun *who.* This correction is seen in B. C and E are incorrect because the pronoun *that* should not be used for people. D uses the subject pronoun.

9. **A** The sentence is correct as written. The verb *learn* is parallel with the other verbs in the list, *wear* and *maintain.* None of the other answers is parallel.

10. **D** The sentence has a verb tense error, because *runs* indicates the simple present tense, which does not fit with the continuous action of *over 100 years.* In B the construction *has ran* is incorrect. C and E contain misplaced modifiers. D is correct because it uses the correct construction *has run* without introducing any new errors.

11. **A** The sentence is correct as it stands. The descriptive phrase is set off from the present tense part of the sentence by a pair of commas and uses consistent past tense verbs within it to describe the history of the *Institute* discussed in the sentence. B and C require the use of *was* before *named.* D contains agreement problems between *was opened* and *had been.* E has a misplaced modifier.

12. **D** The sentence as written contains a comma splice. We need a transition at the end of the underlined portion. B uses the opposite direction transition, *nevertheless,* when we need a same direction transition. C changes the meaning of the sentence. D is correct because it uses the same direction transition *since* without introducing any other errors. E is unclear and changes the meaning of the sentence.

13. **E** There is a parallelism error between *to kill* and *otherwise selling* in the sentence as written. B uses the plural pronoun *they* that should refer to the singular *friend.* The plural verb *have* does not agree with *my friend.* D uses the simple past tense when we need the past perfect for *raised.* E contains the correct *had raised* and the construction *to sell* is parallel to *to kill.*

14. **E** The sentence as written contains a comparison error between *the gifts* and *Brian.* B contains the same error and adds a subject-verb agreement error. C creates an improper comparison between the *gifts* and the *shop.* D has a subject-verb error between the singular *selection* and the plural verb *are.* E is correct because *that of* refers to *The selection* and *Joanne's . . . Shop* is parallel to *Brian's shop.*

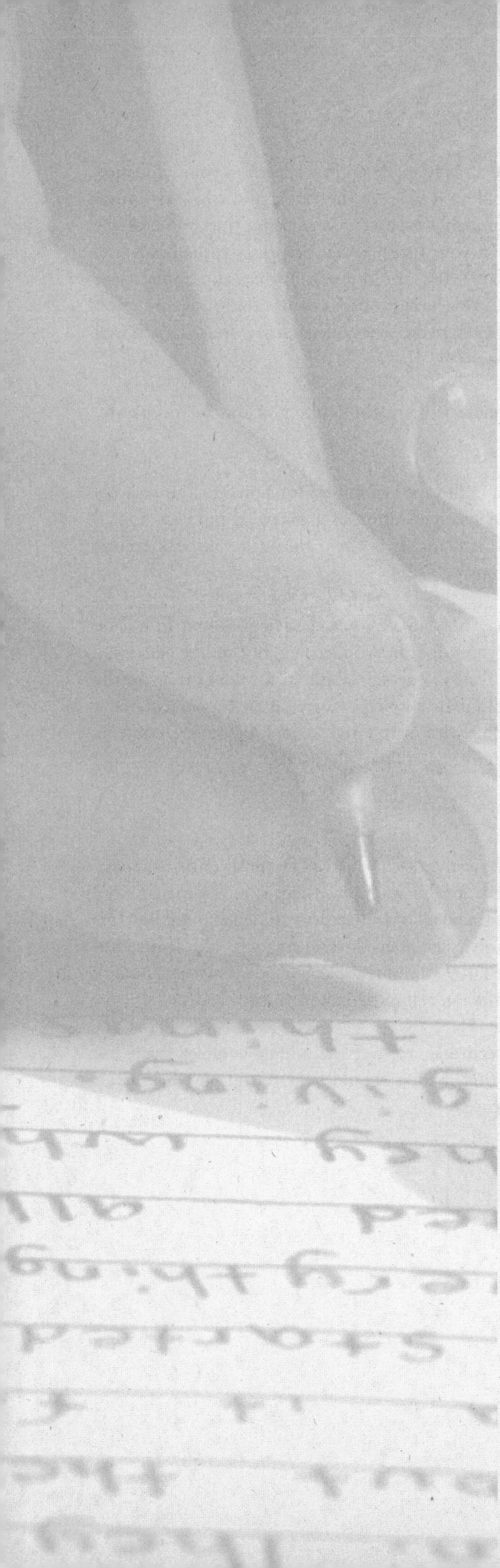

Paying For College 101

If you're reading this book, you've already made an investment in your education. You may have shelled out some cold hard cash for this book, and you've definitely invested time in reading it. It's probably even safe to say that this is one of the smaller investments you've made in your future so far. You put in the hours and hard work needed to keep up your GPA. You've paid test fees and applications fees, perhaps even travel expenses. You have probably committed time and effort to a host of extracurricular activities to make sure colleges know that you're a well-rounded student.

But after you get in, there's one more issue to think about: How do you pay for college?

More Great Titles from The Princeton Review
Paying for College Without Going Broke
The Best 373 Colleges

Let's be honest, college is not cheap. The average tuition for a private four-year college is about \$25,000 a year. The average tuition of a four-year public school is about \$6,500 a year. And the cost is rising. Every year the sticker price of college education bumps up about 6 percent.

Like many of us, your family may not have 25 grand sitting around in a shoebox. With such a hefty price tag, you might be wondering: "Is a college education really worth it? The short answer: Yes! No question about it. A recent survey by the College Board showed that people with a college degree earn 60 percent more than people who enter the workforce with only a high school diploma. Despite its steep price tag, a college education ultimately pays for itself.

Still, the cost of college is no joke.

Here's the good news. Even in the wake of the current financial crisis, financial aid is available to almost any student who wants it. There is an estimated \$143 billion—that's right, billion!—in financial aid offered to students annually. This comes in the form of federal grants, scholarships, state financed aid, loans, and other programs. Furthermore, the 2009 stimulus package made it easier to qualify for government aid, and lowered the interest rates on government loans.

We know that financial aid can seem like an overwhelmingly complex issue, but the introductory information in this chapter should help you grasp what's available and get you started in your search.

How Much Does College Really Cost?

When most people think about the price of a college education, they think of one thing and one thing alone: tuition. It's time to get that notion out of your head. While tuition is a significant portion of the cost of a college education, you need to think of all the other things that factor into the final price tag.

Let's break it down.

- Tuition and fees
- Room and board
- Books and supplies
- Personal expenses
- Travel expenses

Collectively, these things contribute to your total Cost of Attendance (COA) for one year at a college or university.

Understanding the distinction between tuition and COA is crucial because it will help you understand this simple equation:

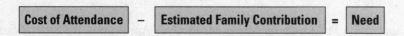

Cost of Attendance – **Estimated Family Contribution** = **Need**

When you begin the financial aid process, you will see this equation again and again. We've already talked about the COA, so let's talk about the Estimated Family Contribution, or EFC. The EFC simply means, "How much you and your family can afford to pay for college." Sounds obvious right?

Here's the catch: What you think you can afford to pay for college, what the government thinks you can afford to pay for college, and what a college or university thinks you can afford to pay for college are, unfortunately, three different things. Keep that in mind as we discuss financing options later on.

The final term in the equation is self-explanatory. Anything that's left after what you and your family have contributed, still needs to be covered. That's where financial aid packages come in.

Check out our Financial Aid Library
PrincetonReview.com/FinancialAidAdvice.aspx

WHAT'S IN A FINANCIAL AID PACKAGE?

A typical financial aid package contains money—from the school, federal government, or state—in various forms: grants, scholarships, work-study programs, and loans.

Let's look at the non-loan options first. Non-loan options include grants, scholarships, and work-study programs. The crucial thing about them is that they involve monetary assistance that you won't be asked to pay back. They are as close as you'll get to "free money."

Grants

Grants are basically gifts. They are funds given to you by the federal government, state agencies, or individual colleges. They are usually need-based, and you are not required to pay them back.

One of the most important grants is the Pell Grant. Pell Grants are provided by the federal government but administered through individual schools. Under the 2009 stimulus package, the maximum award one can receive through the Pell Grant is $4,800 dollars a year.

You apply for a Pell Grant by filling out the Free Application for Federal Student Aid (FAFSA). Remember that acronym because you'll be seeing it again. Completing the FAFSA is the first step in applying for any federal aid. The FAFSA can be found online at www.fafsa.ed.gov.

There are several other major federal grant programs that hand out grants ranging from $100 to $4,000 dollars annually. Some of these grants are given to students entering a specific field of study and others are need-based, but all of them amount to money that you never have to pay back. Check out the FAFSA website for complete information about qualifying and applying for government grants.

Believe It or Not...
The Chick and Sophie Major Memorial Duck Calling Contest, held annually by the Chamber of Commerce of Stuggart, Arkansas, gives out a $1,500 scholarship to any high school senior who can master hailing, feeding, comeback, and mating duck calls.

The federal government isn't the only source of grant money. State governments and specific schools also offer grants. Use the Internet, your guidance counselor, and your library to see what non-federal grants you might be eligible for.

Scholarships

Like grants, you never have to pay a scholarship back. But the requirements and terms of a scholarship might vary wildly. Most scholarships are merit- or need-based, but they can be based on almost anything. There are scholarships based on academic performance, athletic achievements, musical or artistic talent, religious affiliation, ethnicity, and so on.

When hunting for scholarships, one great place to start is the Department of Education's free "Scholarship Search," available at https://studentaid2.ed.gov/getmoney/scholarship. This database asks you a handful of questions about your academic history, interests, and future plans. It then uses this data to report on scholarships that you might be interested in pursuing. It's a free service and a great resource.

There is one important caveat about taking scholarship money. Some, but not all, schools think of scholarship money as income and will reduce the amount of aid they offer you accordingly. Know your school's policy on scholarship awards.

Check out the Scholarship Search Page
PrincetonReview.com/scholarships-financial-aid.aspx

Federal Work-Study (FWS)

One of the ways Uncle Sam disperses aid money is by subsidizing part-time jobs, usually on campus, for students who need financial aid. Because your school will administer the money, they get to decide what your work-study job will be. Work-study participants are paid by the hour, and federal law requires that they cannot be paid less than the federal minimum wage.

One of the benefits of a work-study program is that you get a paycheck just like you would at a normal job. The money is intended to go towards school expenses, but there are no controls over exactly how you spend it.

Colleges and universities determine how to administer work-study programs on their own campuses, so you must apply for a FWS at your school's financial aid office.

The Bottom Line? Not So Fast!
It is possible to appeal the amount of the financial aid package a school awards you. To learn more about how to do that, check out "Appealing Your Award Package" at PrincetonReview.com/appealing-your-award.aspx

LOANS

Most likely, your entire COA won't be covered by scholarships, grants, and work-study income. The next step in gathering the necessary funds is securing a loan. Broadly speaking, there are two routes to go: federal loans and private loans. Once upon a time, which route to choose might be open for debate. But these days the choice is clear: *Always* try to secure federal loans first. Almost without exception, federal loans provide unbeatable low fixed-interest rates; they come with generous repayment terms; and, although they have lending limits, these limits are quite generous and will take you a long way toward your goal. We'll talk about the benefits of private loans later, but they really can't measure up to what the government can provide.

Stafford Loans

The Stafford loan is the primary form of federal student loan. There are two kinds of Stafford loans: direct Stafford loans, which are administered by the Department of Education; and Federal Family Education Loans (FFEL), which are administered by a private lender bound by the terms the government sets for Stafford loans (FFEL loans are sometimes referred to as indirect Stafford loans, as well). Both direct and FFEL loans can be subsidized or unsubsidized. Students with demonstrated financial need may qualify for subsidized loans. This means that the government pays interest accumulated during the time the student is in school. Students with unsubsidized Stafford loans are responsible for the interest accumulated while in school. You can qualify for a subsidized Stafford loan, an unsubsidized Stafford loan, or a mixture of the two.

Stafford loans are available to all full-time students and most part-time students. Though the terms of the loan are based on demonstrated financial need, lack of need is not considered grounds for rejection. No payment is expected while the student is attending school. The interest rate on your Stafford loan will depend on when your first disbursement is. The chart below shows the fixed rates set by the government.

First disbursement made on or after	Interest rate on unpaid balance
July 1, 2011 to July 1, 2012	3.4 percent
July 1, 2012 to July 1, 2013	6.8 percent

Finally, depending on the amount owed and the payment plan agreed upon by the borrower and lender, students have between 10 and 25 years to pay off their loan.

As with grants, you must start by completing the Free Application for Federal Student Aid (FAFSA) to apply for a Stafford loan.

PLUS Loans

Another important federal loan is the PLUS loan. This loan is designed to help parents and guardians put dependent students through college. Like the Stafford loan, a PLUS loan might be a direct loan from the government, administered by your school's financial aid office, or it might be administered by a private lender who is bound to federal guidelines. Unlike the Stafford loan, the PLUS has no fixed limits or fixed interest rates. The annual limit on a PLUS loan is equal to your COA minus any other financial aid you are already receiving. It may be used on top of a Stafford loan. The interest rates on PLUS loans are variable though often comparable to, or even lower than, the interest rates on Stafford loans. Borrowers can choose when they will start paying the loan back: starting either 60 days from the first disbursement or six months after the dependent student has finished school.

To apply for a PLUS loan, your guardians must apply to the financial aid office of your school or with a FFEL private lender.

Perkins Loans

A third and final federal loan you should be aware of is the Perkins loan. Intended to help out students in extreme need, the Perkins loan is a government-subsidized loan that is administered only through college and university financial aid offices. Under the terms of a Perkins loan, you may borrow up to $5,500 a year of undergraduate study, up to $27,500. The Perkins loan has a fixed interest rate of just 5 percent. Payments against the loan don't start until nine months after you graduate. Apply for Perkins loans through your school's financial aid office.

Private Lenders

If this section had been written two years ago, we'd have started off with a discussion of common criticisms of the federal loan system. Then we would have mentioned a few private lenders who were fighting what they believed was the good fight against a government-subsidized monopoly. Whether or not this critique was valid, the sudden collapse of the housing bubble, spurred on in no small part by shoddy lending practices from major banks, has made the argument irrelevant.

We said it before, and we'll say it again: DO NOT get a private loan until you've exhausted all other options.

Before the crisis, many private lenders could offer competitive interest rates and relatively generous qualification standards. Now, for the most part, that's no longer the case. Private lenders are growing increasing selective of the borrowers they lend to, and the average interest rate for private loans hovers around 13 percent.

Still, there are some benefits to securing a private loan. First off, many students find that non-loan and federal loan options don't end up covering the entire bill. If that's the case, then private lenders might just save the day. Second, loans from private sources generally offer you greater flexibility with how you use the funds. Third, private loans can be taken out at anytime during your academic career. Unlike most non-loan and government-backed financial options, you can turn to private lenders whenever you need them.

All private lenders are not the same! As the old song says, "You better shop around." Every lender is going to offer you a different package of terms. What you need to do is find the package that best fits your needs and plans. Aside from low interest rates, which are crucially important, there other terms and conditions you will want to look out for.

Low origination fees Origination fees are fees that lenders charge you for taking out a loan. Usually the fee is simply deducted automatically from your loan checks. Obviously, the lower the origination fee, the better.

Minimal guaranty fees A guaranty fee is an amount you pay to a third-party who agrees to insure your loan. That way, if the borrower—that is you—can't pay the loan back, the guarantor steps in and pays the difference. Again, if you can minimize or eliminate this fee, all the better.

Interest rate reductions Some lenders will reduce your interest rates if you're reliable with your payments. Some will even agree to knock a little off the interest rate if you agree to pay your loans through a direct deposit system. When shopping for the best loan, pay careful attention to factors that might help you curb your interest rates.

Flexible payment plans One of the great things about most federal loans is the fact that you don't have to start paying them off until you leave school. In order to compete, many private lenders have been forced to adopt similarly flexible payment plans. Before saying yes to a private loan, make sure that it comes with a payment timetable you can live with.

WHERE THERE'S A WILL THERE'S A WAY

No matter what the state of the economy, going to college will always make good financial sense. This is especially true today, with the wealth of low-interest federal assistance programs available to you. There are plenty of excellent financing options out there. With a little effort (and a lot of form-filling!) you'll be able to pay your way through school without breaking the bank.

About the Authors

Adam Robinson was born in 1955 and lives in New York City.

John Katzman was born in 1959. He graduated from Princeton University in 1980. After working briefly on Wall Street, he founded The Princeton Review in 1981. Having begun with nineteen high school students in his parents' apartment, Katzman now oversees courses that prepare millions of high school and college students annually for tests, including the SAT, GRE, GMAT, and LSAT. He lives in New York City.

Have you gone online yet!?

Go online to PrincetonReview.com/cracking to type in your answers for these tests and get a score report.

The score report will tell you what areas you need to work on the most. After learning about these topics in the book, you can use your online lessons and drills to reinforce what you've learned.

You can also take a practice test online and enjoy the luxury of automatic grading!

Why are you still here? Go online!

princetonreview.com/cracking

Diagnostic Test Form

Use a No. 2 pencil only. Be sure each mark is dark and completely fills the intended oval. Completely erase any errors or stray marks.

1 **Your Name:**
(Print)

Last First M.I.

Signature: Date / /

Home Address:
Number and Street City State Zip Code

E-Mail: School: Class:
(Print)

2 YOUR NAME
Last Name (First 4 Letters) | FIRST INIT | MID INIT

A B C D E F G H I J K L M N O P Q R S T U V W X Y Z

3 PHONE NUMBER

0 1 2 3 4 5 6 7 8 9

IMPORTANT: Fill in items 6 and 7 exactly as shown on the preceding page.

6 TEST FORM
(Copy from back of test book)

7 TEST CODE

0 1 2 3 4 5 6 7 8 9

4 DATE OF BIRTH

MONTH	DAY		YEAR	
JAN				
FEB				
MAR	0	0		0
APR	1	1		1
MAY	2	2		2
JUN	3	3		3
JUL		4		4
AUG		5	5	5
SEP		6	6	6
OCT		7	7	7
NOV		8	8	8
DEC		9	9	9

8 OTHER

1 A B C D E
2 A B C D E
3 A B C D E

5 SEX

MALE
FEMALE

OpScan *i*NSIGHT™ forms by Pearson NCS EM-253760-3:654321 Printed in U.S.A.

PLEASE DO NOT WRITE IN THIS AREA

SERIAL #

THIS PAGE INTENTIONALLY LEFT BLANK

The Princeton Review Diagnostic Test Form

ESSAY

SECTION 1

Begin your essay on this page. If you need more space, continue on the next page. Do not write outside of the essay box.

Continue on the opposite side if necessary.

PLEASE DO NOT WRITE IN THIS AREA

SERIAL #

Continuation of ESSAY Section 1 from previous page. Write below only if you need more space.

Start with number 1 for each new section. If a section has fewer questions than answer spaces, leave the extra answer spaces blank. Be sure to erase any errors or stray marks completely.

SECTION 2

1 Ⓐ Ⓑ Ⓒ Ⓓ Ⓔ	11 Ⓐ Ⓑ Ⓒ Ⓓ Ⓔ	21 Ⓐ Ⓑ Ⓒ Ⓓ Ⓔ	31 Ⓐ Ⓑ Ⓒ Ⓓ Ⓔ
2 Ⓐ Ⓑ Ⓒ Ⓓ Ⓔ	12 Ⓐ Ⓑ Ⓒ Ⓓ Ⓔ	22 Ⓐ Ⓑ Ⓒ Ⓓ Ⓔ	32 Ⓐ Ⓑ Ⓒ Ⓓ Ⓔ
3 Ⓐ Ⓑ Ⓒ Ⓓ Ⓔ	13 Ⓐ Ⓑ Ⓒ Ⓓ Ⓔ	23 Ⓐ Ⓑ Ⓒ Ⓓ Ⓔ	33 Ⓐ Ⓑ Ⓒ Ⓓ Ⓔ
4 Ⓐ Ⓑ Ⓒ Ⓓ Ⓔ	14 Ⓐ Ⓑ Ⓒ Ⓓ Ⓔ	24 Ⓐ Ⓑ Ⓒ Ⓓ Ⓔ	34 Ⓐ Ⓑ Ⓒ Ⓓ Ⓔ
5 Ⓐ Ⓑ Ⓒ Ⓓ Ⓔ	15 Ⓐ Ⓑ Ⓒ Ⓓ Ⓔ	25 Ⓐ Ⓑ Ⓒ Ⓓ Ⓔ	35 Ⓐ Ⓑ Ⓒ Ⓓ Ⓔ
6 Ⓐ Ⓑ Ⓒ Ⓓ Ⓔ	16 Ⓐ Ⓑ Ⓒ Ⓓ Ⓔ	26 Ⓐ Ⓑ Ⓒ Ⓓ Ⓔ	36 Ⓐ Ⓑ Ⓒ Ⓓ Ⓔ
7 Ⓐ Ⓑ Ⓒ Ⓓ Ⓔ	17 Ⓐ Ⓑ Ⓒ Ⓓ Ⓔ	27 Ⓐ Ⓑ Ⓒ Ⓓ Ⓔ	37 Ⓐ Ⓑ Ⓒ Ⓓ Ⓔ
8 Ⓐ Ⓑ Ⓒ Ⓓ Ⓔ	18 Ⓐ Ⓑ Ⓒ Ⓓ Ⓔ	28 Ⓐ Ⓑ Ⓒ Ⓓ Ⓔ	38 Ⓐ Ⓑ Ⓒ Ⓓ Ⓔ
9 Ⓐ Ⓑ Ⓒ Ⓓ Ⓔ	19 Ⓐ Ⓑ Ⓒ Ⓓ Ⓔ	29 Ⓐ Ⓑ Ⓒ Ⓓ Ⓔ	39 Ⓐ Ⓑ Ⓒ Ⓓ Ⓔ
10 Ⓐ Ⓑ Ⓒ Ⓓ Ⓔ	20 Ⓐ Ⓑ Ⓒ Ⓓ Ⓔ	30 Ⓐ Ⓑ Ⓒ Ⓓ Ⓔ	40 Ⓐ Ⓑ Ⓒ Ⓓ Ⓔ

SECTION 3

1 Ⓐ Ⓑ Ⓒ Ⓓ Ⓔ	11 Ⓐ Ⓑ Ⓒ Ⓓ Ⓔ	21 Ⓐ Ⓑ Ⓒ Ⓓ Ⓔ	31 Ⓐ Ⓑ Ⓒ Ⓓ Ⓔ
2 Ⓐ Ⓑ Ⓒ Ⓓ Ⓔ	12 Ⓐ Ⓑ Ⓒ Ⓓ Ⓔ	22 Ⓐ Ⓑ Ⓒ Ⓓ Ⓔ	32 Ⓐ Ⓑ Ⓒ Ⓓ Ⓔ
3 Ⓐ Ⓑ Ⓒ Ⓓ Ⓔ	13 Ⓐ Ⓑ Ⓒ Ⓓ Ⓔ	23 Ⓐ Ⓑ Ⓒ Ⓓ Ⓔ	33 Ⓐ Ⓑ Ⓒ Ⓓ Ⓔ
4 Ⓐ Ⓑ Ⓒ Ⓓ Ⓔ	14 Ⓐ Ⓑ Ⓒ Ⓓ Ⓔ	24 Ⓐ Ⓑ Ⓒ Ⓓ Ⓔ	34 Ⓐ Ⓑ Ⓒ Ⓓ Ⓔ
5 Ⓐ Ⓑ Ⓒ Ⓓ Ⓔ	15 Ⓐ Ⓑ Ⓒ Ⓓ Ⓔ	25 Ⓐ Ⓑ Ⓒ Ⓓ Ⓔ	35 Ⓐ Ⓑ Ⓒ Ⓓ Ⓔ
6 Ⓐ Ⓑ Ⓒ Ⓓ Ⓔ	16 Ⓐ Ⓑ Ⓒ Ⓓ Ⓔ	26 Ⓐ Ⓑ Ⓒ Ⓓ Ⓔ	36 Ⓐ Ⓑ Ⓒ Ⓓ Ⓔ
7 Ⓐ Ⓑ Ⓒ Ⓓ Ⓔ	17 Ⓐ Ⓑ Ⓒ Ⓓ Ⓔ	27 Ⓐ Ⓑ Ⓒ Ⓓ Ⓔ	37 Ⓐ Ⓑ Ⓒ Ⓓ Ⓔ
8 Ⓐ Ⓑ Ⓒ Ⓓ Ⓔ	18 Ⓐ Ⓑ Ⓒ Ⓓ Ⓔ	28 Ⓐ Ⓑ Ⓒ Ⓓ Ⓔ	38 Ⓐ Ⓑ Ⓒ Ⓓ Ⓔ
9 Ⓐ Ⓑ Ⓒ Ⓓ Ⓔ	19 Ⓐ Ⓑ Ⓒ Ⓓ Ⓔ	29 Ⓐ Ⓑ Ⓒ Ⓓ Ⓔ	39 Ⓐ Ⓑ Ⓒ Ⓓ Ⓔ
10 Ⓐ Ⓑ Ⓒ Ⓓ Ⓔ	20 Ⓐ Ⓑ Ⓒ Ⓓ Ⓔ	30 Ⓐ Ⓑ Ⓒ Ⓓ Ⓔ	40 Ⓐ Ⓑ Ⓒ Ⓓ Ⓔ

CAUTION **Use the answer spaces in the grids below for Section 2 or Section 3 only if you are told to do so in your test book.**

Student-Produced Responses

ONLY ANSWERS ENTERED IN THE OVALS IN EACH GRID WILL BE SCORED. YOU WILL NOT RECEIVE CREDIT FOR ANYTHING WRITTEN IN THE BOXES ABOVE THE OVALS.

Grids 9, 10, 11, 12, 13, 14, 15, 16, 17, 18 (each grid identical):

	/	/	
.	.	.	.
	0	0	0
1	1	1	1
2	2	2	2
3	3	3	3
4	4	4	4
5	5	5	5
6	6	6	6
7	7	7	7
8	8	8	8
9	9	9	9

Start with number 1 for each new section. If a section has fewer questions than answer spaces, leave the extra answer spaces blank. Be sure to erase any errors or stray marks completely.

SECTION 4

1 Ⓐ Ⓑ Ⓒ Ⓓ Ⓔ	11 Ⓐ Ⓑ Ⓒ Ⓓ Ⓔ	21 Ⓐ Ⓑ Ⓒ Ⓓ Ⓔ	31 Ⓐ Ⓑ Ⓒ Ⓓ Ⓔ
2 Ⓐ Ⓑ Ⓒ Ⓓ Ⓔ	12 Ⓐ Ⓑ Ⓒ Ⓓ Ⓔ	22 Ⓐ Ⓑ Ⓒ Ⓓ Ⓔ	32 Ⓐ Ⓑ Ⓒ Ⓓ Ⓔ
3 Ⓐ Ⓑ Ⓒ Ⓓ Ⓔ	13 Ⓐ Ⓑ Ⓒ Ⓓ Ⓔ	23 Ⓐ Ⓑ Ⓒ Ⓓ Ⓔ	33 Ⓐ Ⓑ Ⓒ Ⓓ Ⓔ
4 Ⓐ Ⓑ Ⓒ Ⓓ Ⓔ	14 Ⓐ Ⓑ Ⓒ Ⓓ Ⓔ	24 Ⓐ Ⓑ Ⓒ Ⓓ Ⓔ	34 Ⓐ Ⓑ Ⓒ Ⓓ Ⓔ
5 Ⓐ Ⓑ Ⓒ Ⓓ Ⓔ	15 Ⓐ Ⓑ Ⓒ Ⓓ Ⓔ	25 Ⓐ Ⓑ Ⓒ Ⓓ Ⓔ	35 Ⓐ Ⓑ Ⓒ Ⓓ Ⓔ
6 Ⓐ Ⓑ Ⓒ Ⓓ Ⓔ	16 Ⓐ Ⓑ Ⓒ Ⓓ Ⓔ	26 Ⓐ Ⓑ Ⓒ Ⓓ Ⓔ	36 Ⓐ Ⓑ Ⓒ Ⓓ Ⓔ
7 Ⓐ Ⓑ Ⓒ Ⓓ Ⓔ	17 Ⓐ Ⓑ Ⓒ Ⓓ Ⓔ	27 Ⓐ Ⓑ Ⓒ Ⓓ Ⓔ	37 Ⓐ Ⓑ Ⓒ Ⓓ Ⓔ
8 Ⓐ Ⓑ Ⓒ Ⓓ Ⓔ	18 Ⓐ Ⓑ Ⓒ Ⓓ Ⓔ	28 Ⓐ Ⓑ Ⓒ Ⓓ Ⓔ	38 Ⓐ Ⓑ Ⓒ Ⓓ Ⓔ
9 Ⓐ Ⓑ Ⓒ Ⓓ Ⓔ	19 Ⓐ Ⓑ Ⓒ Ⓓ Ⓔ	29 Ⓐ Ⓑ Ⓒ Ⓓ Ⓔ	39 Ⓐ Ⓑ Ⓒ Ⓓ Ⓔ
10 Ⓐ Ⓑ Ⓒ Ⓓ Ⓔ	20 Ⓐ Ⓑ Ⓒ Ⓓ Ⓔ	30 Ⓐ Ⓑ Ⓒ Ⓓ Ⓔ	40 Ⓐ Ⓑ Ⓒ Ⓓ Ⓔ

SECTION 5

1 Ⓐ Ⓑ Ⓒ Ⓓ Ⓔ	11 Ⓐ Ⓑ Ⓒ Ⓓ Ⓔ	21 Ⓐ Ⓑ Ⓒ Ⓓ Ⓔ	31 Ⓐ Ⓑ Ⓒ Ⓓ Ⓔ
2 Ⓐ Ⓑ Ⓒ Ⓓ Ⓔ	12 Ⓐ Ⓑ Ⓒ Ⓓ Ⓔ	22 Ⓐ Ⓑ Ⓒ Ⓓ Ⓔ	32 Ⓐ Ⓑ Ⓒ Ⓓ Ⓔ
3 Ⓐ Ⓑ Ⓒ Ⓓ Ⓔ	13 Ⓐ Ⓑ Ⓒ Ⓓ Ⓔ	23 Ⓐ Ⓑ Ⓒ Ⓓ Ⓔ	33 Ⓐ Ⓑ Ⓒ Ⓓ Ⓔ
4 Ⓐ Ⓑ Ⓒ Ⓓ Ⓔ	14 Ⓐ Ⓑ Ⓒ Ⓓ Ⓔ	24 Ⓐ Ⓑ Ⓒ Ⓓ Ⓔ	34 Ⓐ Ⓑ Ⓒ Ⓓ Ⓔ
5 Ⓐ Ⓑ Ⓒ Ⓓ Ⓔ	15 Ⓐ Ⓑ Ⓒ Ⓓ Ⓔ	25 Ⓐ Ⓑ Ⓒ Ⓓ Ⓔ	35 Ⓐ Ⓑ Ⓒ Ⓓ Ⓔ
6 Ⓐ Ⓑ Ⓒ Ⓓ Ⓔ	16 Ⓐ Ⓑ Ⓒ Ⓓ Ⓔ	26 Ⓐ Ⓑ Ⓒ Ⓓ Ⓔ	36 Ⓐ Ⓑ Ⓒ Ⓓ Ⓔ
7 Ⓐ Ⓑ Ⓒ Ⓓ Ⓔ	17 Ⓐ Ⓑ Ⓒ Ⓓ Ⓔ	27 Ⓐ Ⓑ Ⓒ Ⓓ Ⓔ	37 Ⓐ Ⓑ Ⓒ Ⓓ Ⓔ
8 Ⓐ Ⓑ Ⓒ Ⓓ Ⓔ	18 Ⓐ Ⓑ Ⓒ Ⓓ Ⓔ	28 Ⓐ Ⓑ Ⓒ Ⓓ Ⓔ	38 Ⓐ Ⓑ Ⓒ Ⓓ Ⓔ
9 Ⓐ Ⓑ Ⓒ Ⓓ Ⓔ	19 Ⓐ Ⓑ Ⓒ Ⓓ Ⓔ	29 Ⓐ Ⓑ Ⓒ Ⓓ Ⓔ	39 Ⓐ Ⓑ Ⓒ Ⓓ Ⓔ
10 Ⓐ Ⓑ Ⓒ Ⓓ Ⓔ	20 Ⓐ Ⓑ Ⓒ Ⓓ Ⓔ	30 Ⓐ Ⓑ Ⓒ Ⓓ Ⓔ	40 Ⓐ Ⓑ Ⓒ Ⓓ Ⓔ

CAUTION Use the answer spaces in the grids below for Section 4 or Section 5 only if you are told to do so in your test book.

Student-Produced Responses ONLY ANSWERS ENTERED IN THE OVALS IN EACH GRID WILL BE SCORED. YOU WILL NOT RECEIVE CREDIT FOR ANYTHING WRITTEN IN THE BOXES ABOVE THE OVALS.

Grids 9, 10, 11, 12, 13, 14, 15, 16, 17, 18 (each grid):

	/	/	
.	.	.	.
	0	0	0
1	1	1	1
2	2	2	2
3	3	3	3
4	4	4	4
5	5	5	5
6	6	6	6
7	7	7	7
8	8	8	8
9	9	9	9

PLEASE DO NOT WRITE IN THIS AREA

SERIAL #

Start with number 1 for each new section. If a section has fewer questions than answer spaces, leave the extra answer spaces blank. Be sure to erase any errors or stray marks completely.

SECTION 6

1 Ⓐ Ⓑ Ⓒ Ⓓ Ⓔ	11 Ⓐ Ⓑ Ⓒ Ⓓ Ⓔ	21 Ⓐ Ⓑ Ⓒ Ⓓ Ⓔ	31 Ⓐ Ⓑ Ⓒ Ⓓ Ⓔ
2 Ⓐ Ⓑ Ⓒ Ⓓ Ⓔ	12 Ⓐ Ⓑ Ⓒ Ⓓ Ⓔ	22 Ⓐ Ⓑ Ⓒ Ⓓ Ⓔ	32 Ⓐ Ⓑ Ⓒ Ⓓ Ⓔ
3 Ⓐ Ⓑ Ⓒ Ⓓ Ⓔ	13 Ⓐ Ⓑ Ⓒ Ⓓ Ⓔ	23 Ⓐ Ⓑ Ⓒ Ⓓ Ⓔ	33 Ⓐ Ⓑ Ⓒ Ⓓ Ⓔ
4 Ⓐ Ⓑ Ⓒ Ⓓ Ⓔ	14 Ⓐ Ⓑ Ⓒ Ⓓ Ⓔ	24 Ⓐ Ⓑ Ⓒ Ⓓ Ⓔ	34 Ⓐ Ⓑ Ⓒ Ⓓ Ⓔ
5 Ⓐ Ⓑ Ⓒ Ⓓ Ⓔ	15 Ⓐ Ⓑ Ⓒ Ⓓ Ⓔ	25 Ⓐ Ⓑ Ⓒ Ⓓ Ⓔ	35 Ⓐ Ⓑ Ⓒ Ⓓ Ⓔ
6 Ⓐ Ⓑ Ⓒ Ⓓ Ⓔ	16 Ⓐ Ⓑ Ⓒ Ⓓ Ⓔ	26 Ⓐ Ⓑ Ⓒ Ⓓ Ⓔ	36 Ⓐ Ⓑ Ⓒ Ⓓ Ⓔ
7 Ⓐ Ⓑ Ⓒ Ⓓ Ⓔ	17 Ⓐ Ⓑ Ⓒ Ⓓ Ⓔ	27 Ⓐ Ⓑ Ⓒ Ⓓ Ⓔ	37 Ⓐ Ⓑ Ⓒ Ⓓ Ⓔ
8 Ⓐ Ⓑ Ⓒ Ⓓ Ⓔ	18 Ⓐ Ⓑ Ⓒ Ⓓ Ⓔ	28 Ⓐ Ⓑ Ⓒ Ⓓ Ⓔ	38 Ⓐ Ⓑ Ⓒ Ⓓ Ⓔ
9 Ⓐ Ⓑ Ⓒ Ⓓ Ⓔ	19 Ⓐ Ⓑ Ⓒ Ⓓ Ⓔ	29 Ⓐ Ⓑ Ⓒ Ⓓ Ⓔ	39 Ⓐ Ⓑ Ⓒ Ⓓ Ⓔ
10 Ⓐ Ⓑ Ⓒ Ⓓ Ⓔ	20 Ⓐ Ⓑ Ⓒ Ⓓ Ⓔ	30 Ⓐ Ⓑ Ⓒ Ⓓ Ⓔ	40 Ⓐ Ⓑ Ⓒ Ⓓ Ⓔ

SECTION 7

1 Ⓐ Ⓑ Ⓒ Ⓓ Ⓔ	11 Ⓐ Ⓑ Ⓒ Ⓓ Ⓔ	21 Ⓐ Ⓑ Ⓒ Ⓓ Ⓔ	31 Ⓐ Ⓑ Ⓒ Ⓓ Ⓔ
2 Ⓐ Ⓑ Ⓒ Ⓓ Ⓔ	12 Ⓐ Ⓑ Ⓒ Ⓓ Ⓔ	22 Ⓐ Ⓑ Ⓒ Ⓓ Ⓔ	32 Ⓐ Ⓑ Ⓒ Ⓓ Ⓔ
3 Ⓐ Ⓑ Ⓒ Ⓓ Ⓔ	13 Ⓐ Ⓑ Ⓒ Ⓓ Ⓔ	23 Ⓐ Ⓑ Ⓒ Ⓓ Ⓔ	33 Ⓐ Ⓑ Ⓒ Ⓓ Ⓔ
4 Ⓐ Ⓑ Ⓒ Ⓓ Ⓔ	14 Ⓐ Ⓑ Ⓒ Ⓓ Ⓔ	24 Ⓐ Ⓑ Ⓒ Ⓓ Ⓔ	34 Ⓐ Ⓑ Ⓒ Ⓓ Ⓔ
5 Ⓐ Ⓑ Ⓒ Ⓓ Ⓔ	15 Ⓐ Ⓑ Ⓒ Ⓓ Ⓔ	25 Ⓐ Ⓑ Ⓒ Ⓓ Ⓔ	35 Ⓐ Ⓑ Ⓒ Ⓓ Ⓔ
6 Ⓐ Ⓑ Ⓒ Ⓓ Ⓔ	16 Ⓐ Ⓑ Ⓒ Ⓓ Ⓔ	26 Ⓐ Ⓑ Ⓒ Ⓓ Ⓔ	36 Ⓐ Ⓑ Ⓒ Ⓓ Ⓔ
7 Ⓐ Ⓑ Ⓒ Ⓓ Ⓔ	17 Ⓐ Ⓑ Ⓒ Ⓓ Ⓔ	27 Ⓐ Ⓑ Ⓒ Ⓓ Ⓔ	37 Ⓐ Ⓑ Ⓒ Ⓓ Ⓔ
8 Ⓐ Ⓑ Ⓒ Ⓓ Ⓔ	18 Ⓐ Ⓑ Ⓒ Ⓓ Ⓔ	28 Ⓐ Ⓑ Ⓒ Ⓓ Ⓔ	38 Ⓐ Ⓑ Ⓒ Ⓓ Ⓔ
9 Ⓐ Ⓑ Ⓒ Ⓓ Ⓔ	19 Ⓐ Ⓑ Ⓒ Ⓓ Ⓔ	29 Ⓐ Ⓑ Ⓒ Ⓓ Ⓔ	39 Ⓐ Ⓑ Ⓒ Ⓓ Ⓔ
10 Ⓐ Ⓑ Ⓒ Ⓓ Ⓔ	20 Ⓐ Ⓑ Ⓒ Ⓓ Ⓔ	30 Ⓐ Ⓑ Ⓒ Ⓓ Ⓔ	40 Ⓐ Ⓑ Ⓒ Ⓓ Ⓔ

CAUTION Use the answer spaces in the grids below for Section 6 or Section 7 only if you are told to do so in your test book.

Student-Produced Responses

ONLY ANSWERS ENTERED IN THE OVALS IN EACH GRID WILL BE SCORED. YOU WILL NOT RECEIVE CREDIT FOR ANYTHING WRITTEN IN THE BOXES ABOVE THE OVALS.

Grids 9, 10, 11, 12, 13, 14, 15, 16, 17, 18 (each grid identical):

	/	/	
.	.	.	.
	0	0	0
1	1	1	1
2	2	2	2
3	3	3	3
4	4	4	4
5	5	5	5
6	6	6	6
7	7	7	7
8	8	8	8
9	9	9	9

Start with number 1 for each new section. If a section has fewer questions than answer spaces, leave the extra answer spaces blank. Be sure to erase any errors or stray marks completely.

SECTION 8

1 Ⓐ Ⓑ Ⓒ Ⓓ Ⓔ	11 Ⓐ Ⓑ Ⓒ Ⓓ Ⓔ	21 Ⓐ Ⓑ Ⓒ Ⓓ Ⓔ	31 Ⓐ Ⓑ Ⓒ Ⓓ Ⓔ
2 Ⓐ Ⓑ Ⓒ Ⓓ Ⓔ	12 Ⓐ Ⓑ Ⓒ Ⓓ Ⓔ	22 Ⓐ Ⓑ Ⓒ Ⓓ Ⓔ	32 Ⓐ Ⓑ Ⓒ Ⓓ Ⓔ
3 Ⓐ Ⓑ Ⓒ Ⓓ Ⓔ	13 Ⓐ Ⓑ Ⓒ Ⓓ Ⓔ	23 Ⓐ Ⓑ Ⓒ Ⓓ Ⓔ	33 Ⓐ Ⓑ Ⓒ Ⓓ Ⓔ
4 Ⓐ Ⓑ Ⓒ Ⓓ Ⓔ	14 Ⓐ Ⓑ Ⓒ Ⓓ Ⓔ	24 Ⓐ Ⓑ Ⓒ Ⓓ Ⓔ	34 Ⓐ Ⓑ Ⓒ Ⓓ Ⓔ
5 Ⓐ Ⓑ Ⓒ Ⓓ Ⓔ	15 Ⓐ Ⓑ Ⓒ Ⓓ Ⓔ	25 Ⓐ Ⓑ Ⓒ Ⓓ Ⓔ	35 Ⓐ Ⓑ Ⓒ Ⓓ Ⓔ
6 Ⓐ Ⓑ Ⓒ Ⓓ Ⓔ	16 Ⓐ Ⓑ Ⓒ Ⓓ Ⓔ	26 Ⓐ Ⓑ Ⓒ Ⓓ Ⓔ	36 Ⓐ Ⓑ Ⓒ Ⓓ Ⓔ
7 Ⓐ Ⓑ Ⓒ Ⓓ Ⓔ	17 Ⓐ Ⓑ Ⓒ Ⓓ Ⓔ	27 Ⓐ Ⓑ Ⓒ Ⓓ Ⓔ	37 Ⓐ Ⓑ Ⓒ Ⓓ Ⓔ
8 Ⓐ Ⓑ Ⓒ Ⓓ Ⓔ	18 Ⓐ Ⓑ Ⓒ Ⓓ Ⓔ	28 Ⓐ Ⓑ Ⓒ Ⓓ Ⓔ	38 Ⓐ Ⓑ Ⓒ Ⓓ Ⓔ
9 Ⓐ Ⓑ Ⓒ Ⓓ Ⓔ	19 Ⓐ Ⓑ Ⓒ Ⓓ Ⓔ	29 Ⓐ Ⓑ Ⓒ Ⓓ Ⓔ	39 Ⓐ Ⓑ Ⓒ Ⓓ Ⓔ
10 Ⓐ Ⓑ Ⓒ Ⓓ Ⓔ	20 Ⓐ Ⓑ Ⓒ Ⓓ Ⓔ	30 Ⓐ Ⓑ Ⓒ Ⓓ Ⓔ	40 Ⓐ Ⓑ Ⓒ Ⓓ Ⓔ

SECTION 9

1 Ⓐ Ⓑ Ⓒ Ⓓ Ⓔ	11 Ⓐ Ⓑ Ⓒ Ⓓ Ⓔ	21 Ⓐ Ⓑ Ⓒ Ⓓ Ⓔ	31 Ⓐ Ⓑ Ⓒ Ⓓ Ⓔ
2 Ⓐ Ⓑ Ⓒ Ⓓ Ⓔ	12 Ⓐ Ⓑ Ⓒ Ⓓ Ⓔ	22 Ⓐ Ⓑ Ⓒ Ⓓ Ⓔ	32 Ⓐ Ⓑ Ⓒ Ⓓ Ⓔ
3 Ⓐ Ⓑ Ⓒ Ⓓ Ⓔ	13 Ⓐ Ⓑ Ⓒ Ⓓ Ⓔ	23 Ⓐ Ⓑ Ⓒ Ⓓ Ⓔ	33 Ⓐ Ⓑ Ⓒ Ⓓ Ⓔ
4 Ⓐ Ⓑ Ⓒ Ⓓ Ⓔ	14 Ⓐ Ⓑ Ⓒ Ⓓ Ⓔ	24 Ⓐ Ⓑ Ⓒ Ⓓ Ⓔ	34 Ⓐ Ⓑ Ⓒ Ⓓ Ⓔ
5 Ⓐ Ⓑ Ⓒ Ⓓ Ⓔ	15 Ⓐ Ⓑ Ⓒ Ⓓ Ⓔ	25 Ⓐ Ⓑ Ⓒ Ⓓ Ⓔ	35 Ⓐ Ⓑ Ⓒ Ⓓ Ⓔ
6 Ⓐ Ⓑ Ⓒ Ⓓ Ⓔ	16 Ⓐ Ⓑ Ⓒ Ⓓ Ⓔ	26 Ⓐ Ⓑ Ⓒ Ⓓ Ⓔ	36 Ⓐ Ⓑ Ⓒ Ⓓ Ⓔ
7 Ⓐ Ⓑ Ⓒ Ⓓ Ⓔ	17 Ⓐ Ⓑ Ⓒ Ⓓ Ⓔ	27 Ⓐ Ⓑ Ⓒ Ⓓ Ⓔ	37 Ⓐ Ⓑ Ⓒ Ⓓ Ⓔ
8 Ⓐ Ⓑ Ⓒ Ⓓ Ⓔ	18 Ⓐ Ⓑ Ⓒ Ⓓ Ⓔ	28 Ⓐ Ⓑ Ⓒ Ⓓ Ⓔ	38 Ⓐ Ⓑ Ⓒ Ⓓ Ⓔ
9 Ⓐ Ⓑ Ⓒ Ⓓ Ⓔ	19 Ⓐ Ⓑ Ⓒ Ⓓ Ⓔ	29 Ⓐ Ⓑ Ⓒ Ⓓ Ⓔ	39 Ⓐ Ⓑ Ⓒ Ⓓ Ⓔ
10 Ⓐ Ⓑ Ⓒ Ⓓ Ⓔ	20 Ⓐ Ⓑ Ⓒ Ⓓ Ⓔ	30 Ⓐ Ⓑ Ⓒ Ⓓ Ⓔ	40 Ⓐ Ⓑ Ⓒ Ⓓ Ⓔ

SECTION 10

1 Ⓐ Ⓑ Ⓒ Ⓓ Ⓔ	11 Ⓐ Ⓑ Ⓒ Ⓓ Ⓔ	21 Ⓐ Ⓑ Ⓒ Ⓓ Ⓔ	31 Ⓐ Ⓑ Ⓒ Ⓓ Ⓔ
2 Ⓐ Ⓑ Ⓒ Ⓓ Ⓔ	12 Ⓐ Ⓑ Ⓒ Ⓓ Ⓔ	22 Ⓐ Ⓑ Ⓒ Ⓓ Ⓔ	32 Ⓐ Ⓑ Ⓒ Ⓓ Ⓔ
3 Ⓐ Ⓑ Ⓒ Ⓓ Ⓔ	13 Ⓐ Ⓑ Ⓒ Ⓓ Ⓔ	23 Ⓐ Ⓑ Ⓒ Ⓓ Ⓔ	33 Ⓐ Ⓑ Ⓒ Ⓓ Ⓔ
4 Ⓐ Ⓑ Ⓒ Ⓓ Ⓔ	14 Ⓐ Ⓑ Ⓒ Ⓓ Ⓔ	24 Ⓐ Ⓑ Ⓒ Ⓓ Ⓔ	34 Ⓐ Ⓑ Ⓒ Ⓓ Ⓔ
5 Ⓐ Ⓑ Ⓒ Ⓓ Ⓔ	15 Ⓐ Ⓑ Ⓒ Ⓓ Ⓔ	25 Ⓐ Ⓑ Ⓒ Ⓓ Ⓔ	35 Ⓐ Ⓑ Ⓒ Ⓓ Ⓔ
6 Ⓐ Ⓑ Ⓒ Ⓓ Ⓔ	16 Ⓐ Ⓑ Ⓒ Ⓓ Ⓔ	26 Ⓐ Ⓑ Ⓒ Ⓓ Ⓔ	36 Ⓐ Ⓑ Ⓒ Ⓓ Ⓔ
7 Ⓐ Ⓑ Ⓒ Ⓓ Ⓔ	17 Ⓐ Ⓑ Ⓒ Ⓓ Ⓔ	27 Ⓐ Ⓑ Ⓒ Ⓓ Ⓔ	37 Ⓐ Ⓑ Ⓒ Ⓓ Ⓔ
8 Ⓐ Ⓑ Ⓒ Ⓓ Ⓔ	18 Ⓐ Ⓑ Ⓒ Ⓓ Ⓔ	28 Ⓐ Ⓑ Ⓒ Ⓓ Ⓔ	38 Ⓐ Ⓑ Ⓒ Ⓓ Ⓔ
9 Ⓐ Ⓑ Ⓒ Ⓓ Ⓔ	19 Ⓐ Ⓑ Ⓒ Ⓓ Ⓔ	29 Ⓐ Ⓑ Ⓒ Ⓓ Ⓔ	39 Ⓐ Ⓑ Ⓒ Ⓓ Ⓔ
10 Ⓐ Ⓑ Ⓒ Ⓓ Ⓔ	20 Ⓐ Ⓑ Ⓒ Ⓓ Ⓔ	30 Ⓐ Ⓑ Ⓒ Ⓓ Ⓔ	40 Ⓐ Ⓑ Ⓒ Ⓓ Ⓔ

PLEASE DO NOT WRITE IN THIS AREA

SERIAL #

Diagnostic Test Form

Use a No. 2 pencil only. Be sure each mark is dark and completely fills the intended oval. Completely erase any errors or stray marks.

1 **Your Name:**
(Print)

Last First M.I.

Signature: Date / /

Home Address:
Number and Street City State Zip Code

E-Mail: School: Class:
(Print)

2 YOUR NAME
Last Name
(First 4 Letters) FIRST INIT MID INIT

– ’ A B C D E F G H I J K L M N O P Q R S T U V W X Y Z

3 PHONE NUMBER

0 1 2 3 4 5 6 7 8 9

IMPORTANT: Fill in items 6 and 7 exactly as shown on the preceding page.

6 TEST FORM
(Copy from back of test book)

7 TEST CODE

0 1 2 3 4 5 6 7 8 9

4 DATE OF BIRTH

MONTH	DAY		YEAR	
JAN				
FEB				
MAR	0	0		0
APR	1	1		1
MAY	2	2		2
JUN	3	3		3
JUL		4		4
AUG		5	5	5
SEP		6	6	6
OCT		7	7	7
NOV		8	8	8
DEC		9	9	9

8 OTHER
1 A B C D E
2 A B C D E
3 A B C D E

5 SEX
MALE
FEMALE

PLEASE DO NOT WRITE IN THIS AREA

SERIAL #

THIS PAGE INTENTIONALLY LEFT BLANK

The Princeton Review Diagnostic Test Form

ESSAY

SECTION

1

Begin your essay on this page. If you need more space, continue on the next page. Do not write outside of the essay box.

Continue on the opposite side if necessary.

PLEASE DO NOT WRITE IN THIS AREA

SERIAL #

Continuation of ESSAY Section 1 from previous page. Write below only if you need more space.

Start with number 1 for each new section. If a section has fewer questions than answer spaces, leave the extra answer spaces blank. Be sure to erase any errors or stray marks completely.

SECTION 2

1 Ⓐ Ⓑ Ⓒ Ⓓ Ⓔ	11 Ⓐ Ⓑ Ⓒ Ⓓ Ⓔ	21 Ⓐ Ⓑ Ⓒ Ⓓ Ⓔ	31 Ⓐ Ⓑ Ⓒ Ⓓ Ⓔ
2 Ⓐ Ⓑ Ⓒ Ⓓ Ⓔ	12 Ⓐ Ⓑ Ⓒ Ⓓ Ⓔ	22 Ⓐ Ⓑ Ⓒ Ⓓ Ⓔ	32 Ⓐ Ⓑ Ⓒ Ⓓ Ⓔ
3 Ⓐ Ⓑ Ⓒ Ⓓ Ⓔ	13 Ⓐ Ⓑ Ⓒ Ⓓ Ⓔ	23 Ⓐ Ⓑ Ⓒ Ⓓ Ⓔ	33 Ⓐ Ⓑ Ⓒ Ⓓ Ⓔ
4 Ⓐ Ⓑ Ⓒ Ⓓ Ⓔ	14 Ⓐ Ⓑ Ⓒ Ⓓ Ⓔ	24 Ⓐ Ⓑ Ⓒ Ⓓ Ⓔ	34 Ⓐ Ⓑ Ⓒ Ⓓ Ⓔ
5 Ⓐ Ⓑ Ⓒ Ⓓ Ⓔ	15 Ⓐ Ⓑ Ⓒ Ⓓ Ⓔ	25 Ⓐ Ⓑ Ⓒ Ⓓ Ⓔ	35 Ⓐ Ⓑ Ⓒ Ⓓ Ⓔ
6 Ⓐ Ⓑ Ⓒ Ⓓ Ⓔ	16 Ⓐ Ⓑ Ⓒ Ⓓ Ⓔ	26 Ⓐ Ⓑ Ⓒ Ⓓ Ⓔ	36 Ⓐ Ⓑ Ⓒ Ⓓ Ⓔ
7 Ⓐ Ⓑ Ⓒ Ⓓ Ⓔ	17 Ⓐ Ⓑ Ⓒ Ⓓ Ⓔ	27 Ⓐ Ⓑ Ⓒ Ⓓ Ⓔ	37 Ⓐ Ⓑ Ⓒ Ⓓ Ⓔ
8 Ⓐ Ⓑ Ⓒ Ⓓ Ⓔ	18 Ⓐ Ⓑ Ⓒ Ⓓ Ⓔ	28 Ⓐ Ⓑ Ⓒ Ⓓ Ⓔ	38 Ⓐ Ⓑ Ⓒ Ⓓ Ⓔ
9 Ⓐ Ⓑ Ⓒ Ⓓ Ⓔ	19 Ⓐ Ⓑ Ⓒ Ⓓ Ⓔ	29 Ⓐ Ⓑ Ⓒ Ⓓ Ⓔ	39 Ⓐ Ⓑ Ⓒ Ⓓ Ⓔ
10 Ⓐ Ⓑ Ⓒ Ⓓ Ⓔ	20 Ⓐ Ⓑ Ⓒ Ⓓ Ⓔ	30 Ⓐ Ⓑ Ⓒ Ⓓ Ⓔ	40 Ⓐ Ⓑ Ⓒ Ⓓ Ⓔ

SECTION 3

1 Ⓐ Ⓑ Ⓒ Ⓓ Ⓔ	11 Ⓐ Ⓑ Ⓒ Ⓓ Ⓔ	21 Ⓐ Ⓑ Ⓒ Ⓓ Ⓔ	31 Ⓐ Ⓑ Ⓒ Ⓓ Ⓔ
2 Ⓐ Ⓑ Ⓒ Ⓓ Ⓔ	12 Ⓐ Ⓑ Ⓒ Ⓓ Ⓔ	22 Ⓐ Ⓑ Ⓒ Ⓓ Ⓔ	32 Ⓐ Ⓑ Ⓒ Ⓓ Ⓔ
3 Ⓐ Ⓑ Ⓒ Ⓓ Ⓔ	13 Ⓐ Ⓑ Ⓒ Ⓓ Ⓔ	23 Ⓐ Ⓑ Ⓒ Ⓓ Ⓔ	33 Ⓐ Ⓑ Ⓒ Ⓓ Ⓔ
4 Ⓐ Ⓑ Ⓒ Ⓓ Ⓔ	14 Ⓐ Ⓑ Ⓒ Ⓓ Ⓔ	24 Ⓐ Ⓑ Ⓒ Ⓓ Ⓔ	34 Ⓐ Ⓑ Ⓒ Ⓓ Ⓔ
5 Ⓐ Ⓑ Ⓒ Ⓓ Ⓔ	15 Ⓐ Ⓑ Ⓒ Ⓓ Ⓔ	25 Ⓐ Ⓑ Ⓒ Ⓓ Ⓔ	35 Ⓐ Ⓑ Ⓒ Ⓓ Ⓔ
6 Ⓐ Ⓑ Ⓒ Ⓓ Ⓔ	16 Ⓐ Ⓑ Ⓒ Ⓓ Ⓔ	26 Ⓐ Ⓑ Ⓒ Ⓓ Ⓔ	36 Ⓐ Ⓑ Ⓒ Ⓓ Ⓔ
7 Ⓐ Ⓑ Ⓒ Ⓓ Ⓔ	17 Ⓐ Ⓑ Ⓒ Ⓓ Ⓔ	27 Ⓐ Ⓑ Ⓒ Ⓓ Ⓔ	37 Ⓐ Ⓑ Ⓒ Ⓓ Ⓔ
8 Ⓐ Ⓑ Ⓒ Ⓓ Ⓔ	18 Ⓐ Ⓑ Ⓒ Ⓓ Ⓔ	28 Ⓐ Ⓑ Ⓒ Ⓓ Ⓔ	38 Ⓐ Ⓑ Ⓒ Ⓓ Ⓔ
9 Ⓐ Ⓑ Ⓒ Ⓓ Ⓔ	19 Ⓐ Ⓑ Ⓒ Ⓓ Ⓔ	29 Ⓐ Ⓑ Ⓒ Ⓓ Ⓔ	39 Ⓐ Ⓑ Ⓒ Ⓓ Ⓔ
10 Ⓐ Ⓑ Ⓒ Ⓓ Ⓔ	20 Ⓐ Ⓑ Ⓒ Ⓓ Ⓔ	30 Ⓐ Ⓑ Ⓒ Ⓓ Ⓔ	40 Ⓐ Ⓑ Ⓒ Ⓓ Ⓔ

CAUTION Use the answer spaces in the grids below for Section 2 or Section 3 only if you are told to do so in your test book.

Student-Produced Responses

ONLY ANSWERS ENTERED IN THE OVALS IN EACH GRID WILL BE SCORED. YOU WILL NOT RECEIVE CREDIT FOR ANYTHING WRITTEN IN THE BOXES ABOVE THE OVALS.

Grids 9, 10, 11, 12, 13, 14, 15, 16, 17, 18 (each grid):

	/	/	
.	.	.	.
	0	0	0
1	1	1	1
2	2	2	2
3	3	3	3
4	4	4	4
5	5	5	5
6	6	6	6
7	7	7	7
8	8	8	8
9	9	9	9

Start with number 1 for each new section. If a section has fewer questions than answer spaces, leave the extra answer spaces blank. Be sure to erase any errors or stray marks completely.

SECTION 4

1 A B C D E	11 A B C D E	21 A B C D E	31 A B C D E
2 A B C D E	12 A B C D E	22 A B C D E	32 A B C D E
3 A B C D E	13 A B C D E	23 A B C D E	33 A B C D E
4 A B C D E	14 A B C D E	24 A B C D E	34 A B C D E
5 A B C D E	15 A B C D E	25 A B C D E	35 A B C D E
6 A B C D E	16 A B C D E	26 A B C D E	36 A B C D E
7 A B C D E	17 A B C D E	27 A B C D E	37 A B C D E
8 A B C D E	18 A B C D E	28 A B C D E	38 A B C D E
9 A B C D E	19 A B C D E	29 A B C D E	39 A B C D E
10 A B C D E	20 A B C D E	30 A B C D E	40 A B C D E

SECTION 5

1 A B C D E	11 A B C D E	21 A B C D E	31 A B C D E
2 A B C D E	12 A B C D E	22 A B C D E	32 A B C D E
3 A B C D E	13 A B C D E	23 A B C D E	33 A B C D E
4 A B C D E	14 A B C D E	24 A B C D E	34 A B C D E
5 A B C D E	15 A B C D E	25 A B C D E	35 A B C D E
6 A B C D E	16 A B C D E	26 A B C D E	36 A B C D E
7 A B C D E	17 A B C D E	27 A B C D E	37 A B C D E
8 A B C D E	18 A B C D E	28 A B C D E	38 A B C D E
9 A B C D E	19 A B C D E	29 A B C D E	39 A B C D E
10 A B C D E	20 A B C D E	30 A B C D E	40 A B C D E

CAUTION Use the answer spaces in the grids below for Section 4 or Section 5 only if you are told to do so in your test book.

Student-Produced Responses ONLY ANSWERS ENTERED IN THE OVALS IN EACH GRID WILL BE SCORED. YOU WILL NOT RECEIVE CREDIT FOR ANYTHING WRITTEN IN THE BOXES ABOVE THE OVALS.

Grids 9, 10, 11, 12, 13, 14, 15, 16, 17, 18 (each grid identical):

	/	/	
.	.	.	.
	0	0	0
1	1	1	1
2	2	2	2
3	3	3	3
4	4	4	4
5	5	5	5
6	6	6	6
7	7	7	7
8	8	8	8
9	9	9	9

PLEASE DO NOT WRITE IN THIS AREA

SERIAL #

Start with number 1 for each new section. If a section has fewer questions than answer spaces, leave the extra answer spaces blank. Be sure to erase any errors or stray marks completely.

SECTION 6

1 Ⓐ Ⓑ Ⓒ Ⓓ Ⓔ	11 Ⓐ Ⓑ Ⓒ Ⓓ Ⓔ	21 Ⓐ Ⓑ Ⓒ Ⓓ Ⓔ	31 Ⓐ Ⓑ Ⓒ Ⓓ Ⓔ
2 Ⓐ Ⓑ Ⓒ Ⓓ Ⓔ	12 Ⓐ Ⓑ Ⓒ Ⓓ Ⓔ	22 Ⓐ Ⓑ Ⓒ Ⓓ Ⓔ	32 Ⓐ Ⓑ Ⓒ Ⓓ Ⓔ
3 Ⓐ Ⓑ Ⓒ Ⓓ Ⓔ	13 Ⓐ Ⓑ Ⓒ Ⓓ Ⓔ	23 Ⓐ Ⓑ Ⓒ Ⓓ Ⓔ	33 Ⓐ Ⓑ Ⓒ Ⓓ Ⓔ
4 Ⓐ Ⓑ Ⓒ Ⓓ Ⓔ	14 Ⓐ Ⓑ Ⓒ Ⓓ Ⓔ	24 Ⓐ Ⓑ Ⓒ Ⓓ Ⓔ	34 Ⓐ Ⓑ Ⓒ Ⓓ Ⓔ
5 Ⓐ Ⓑ Ⓒ Ⓓ Ⓔ	15 Ⓐ Ⓑ Ⓒ Ⓓ Ⓔ	25 Ⓐ Ⓑ Ⓒ Ⓓ Ⓔ	35 Ⓐ Ⓑ Ⓒ Ⓓ Ⓔ
6 Ⓐ Ⓑ Ⓒ Ⓓ Ⓔ	16 Ⓐ Ⓑ Ⓒ Ⓓ Ⓔ	26 Ⓐ Ⓑ Ⓒ Ⓓ Ⓔ	36 Ⓐ Ⓑ Ⓒ Ⓓ Ⓔ
7 Ⓐ Ⓑ Ⓒ Ⓓ Ⓔ	17 Ⓐ Ⓑ Ⓒ Ⓓ Ⓔ	27 Ⓐ Ⓑ Ⓒ Ⓓ Ⓔ	37 Ⓐ Ⓑ Ⓒ Ⓓ Ⓔ
8 Ⓐ Ⓑ Ⓒ Ⓓ Ⓔ	18 Ⓐ Ⓑ Ⓒ Ⓓ Ⓔ	28 Ⓐ Ⓑ Ⓒ Ⓓ Ⓔ	38 Ⓐ Ⓑ Ⓒ Ⓓ Ⓔ
9 Ⓐ Ⓑ Ⓒ Ⓓ Ⓔ	19 Ⓐ Ⓑ Ⓒ Ⓓ Ⓔ	29 Ⓐ Ⓑ Ⓒ Ⓓ Ⓔ	39 Ⓐ Ⓑ Ⓒ Ⓓ Ⓔ
10 Ⓐ Ⓑ Ⓒ Ⓓ Ⓔ	20 Ⓐ Ⓑ Ⓒ Ⓓ Ⓔ	30 Ⓐ Ⓑ Ⓒ Ⓓ Ⓔ	40 Ⓐ Ⓑ Ⓒ Ⓓ Ⓔ

SECTION 7

1 Ⓐ Ⓑ Ⓒ Ⓓ Ⓔ	11 Ⓐ Ⓑ Ⓒ Ⓓ Ⓔ	21 Ⓐ Ⓑ Ⓒ Ⓓ Ⓔ	31 Ⓐ Ⓑ Ⓒ Ⓓ Ⓔ
2 Ⓐ Ⓑ Ⓒ Ⓓ Ⓔ	12 Ⓐ Ⓑ Ⓒ Ⓓ Ⓔ	22 Ⓐ Ⓑ Ⓒ Ⓓ Ⓔ	32 Ⓐ Ⓑ Ⓒ Ⓓ Ⓔ
3 Ⓐ Ⓑ Ⓒ Ⓓ Ⓔ	13 Ⓐ Ⓑ Ⓒ Ⓓ Ⓔ	23 Ⓐ Ⓑ Ⓒ Ⓓ Ⓔ	33 Ⓐ Ⓑ Ⓒ Ⓓ Ⓔ
4 Ⓐ Ⓑ Ⓒ Ⓓ Ⓔ	14 Ⓐ Ⓑ Ⓒ Ⓓ Ⓔ	24 Ⓐ Ⓑ Ⓒ Ⓓ Ⓔ	34 Ⓐ Ⓑ Ⓒ Ⓓ Ⓔ
5 Ⓐ Ⓑ Ⓒ Ⓓ Ⓔ	15 Ⓐ Ⓑ Ⓒ Ⓓ Ⓔ	25 Ⓐ Ⓑ Ⓒ Ⓓ Ⓔ	35 Ⓐ Ⓑ Ⓒ Ⓓ Ⓔ
6 Ⓐ Ⓑ Ⓒ Ⓓ Ⓔ	16 Ⓐ Ⓑ Ⓒ Ⓓ Ⓔ	26 Ⓐ Ⓑ Ⓒ Ⓓ Ⓔ	36 Ⓐ Ⓑ Ⓒ Ⓓ Ⓔ
7 Ⓐ Ⓑ Ⓒ Ⓓ Ⓔ	17 Ⓐ Ⓑ Ⓒ Ⓓ Ⓔ	27 Ⓐ Ⓑ Ⓒ Ⓓ Ⓔ	37 Ⓐ Ⓑ Ⓒ Ⓓ Ⓔ
8 Ⓐ Ⓑ Ⓒ Ⓓ Ⓔ	18 Ⓐ Ⓑ Ⓒ Ⓓ Ⓔ	28 Ⓐ Ⓑ Ⓒ Ⓓ Ⓔ	38 Ⓐ Ⓑ Ⓒ Ⓓ Ⓔ
9 Ⓐ Ⓑ Ⓒ Ⓓ Ⓔ	19 Ⓐ Ⓑ Ⓒ Ⓓ Ⓔ	29 Ⓐ Ⓑ Ⓒ Ⓓ Ⓔ	39 Ⓐ Ⓑ Ⓒ Ⓓ Ⓔ
10 Ⓐ Ⓑ Ⓒ Ⓓ Ⓔ	20 Ⓐ Ⓑ Ⓒ Ⓓ Ⓔ	30 Ⓐ Ⓑ Ⓒ Ⓓ Ⓔ	40 Ⓐ Ⓑ Ⓒ Ⓓ Ⓔ

CAUTION Use the answer spaces in the grids below for Section 6 or Section 7 only if you are told to do so in your test book.

Student-Produced Responses

ONLY ANSWERS ENTERED IN THE OVALS IN EACH GRID WILL BE SCORED. YOU WILL NOT RECEIVE CREDIT FOR ANYTHING WRITTEN IN THE BOXES ABOVE THE OVALS.

Grids 9, 10, 11, 12, 13, 14, 15, 16, 17, 18 (each grid identical):

	/	/	
.	.	.	.
	0	0	0
1	1	1	1
2	2	2	2
3	3	3	3
4	4	4	4
5	5	5	5
6	6	6	6
7	7	7	7
8	8	8	8
9	9	9	9

Start with number 1 for each new section. If a section has fewer questions than answer spaces, leave the extra answer spaces blank. Be sure to erase any errors or stray marks completely.

SECTION 8

1 Ⓐ Ⓑ Ⓒ Ⓓ Ⓔ	11 Ⓐ Ⓑ Ⓒ Ⓓ Ⓔ	21 Ⓐ Ⓑ Ⓒ Ⓓ Ⓔ	31 Ⓐ Ⓑ Ⓒ Ⓓ Ⓔ
2 Ⓐ Ⓑ Ⓒ Ⓓ Ⓔ	12 Ⓐ Ⓑ Ⓒ Ⓓ Ⓔ	22 Ⓐ Ⓑ Ⓒ Ⓓ Ⓔ	32 Ⓐ Ⓑ Ⓒ Ⓓ Ⓔ
3 Ⓐ Ⓑ Ⓒ Ⓓ Ⓔ	13 Ⓐ Ⓑ Ⓒ Ⓓ Ⓔ	23 Ⓐ Ⓑ Ⓒ Ⓓ Ⓔ	33 Ⓐ Ⓑ Ⓒ Ⓓ Ⓔ
4 Ⓐ Ⓑ Ⓒ Ⓓ Ⓔ	14 Ⓐ Ⓑ Ⓒ Ⓓ Ⓔ	24 Ⓐ Ⓑ Ⓒ Ⓓ Ⓔ	34 Ⓐ Ⓑ Ⓒ Ⓓ Ⓔ
5 Ⓐ Ⓑ Ⓒ Ⓓ Ⓔ	15 Ⓐ Ⓑ Ⓒ Ⓓ Ⓔ	25 Ⓐ Ⓑ Ⓒ Ⓓ Ⓔ	35 Ⓐ Ⓑ Ⓒ Ⓓ Ⓔ
6 Ⓐ Ⓑ Ⓒ Ⓓ Ⓔ	16 Ⓐ Ⓑ Ⓒ Ⓓ Ⓔ	26 Ⓐ Ⓑ Ⓒ Ⓓ Ⓔ	36 Ⓐ Ⓑ Ⓒ Ⓓ Ⓔ
7 Ⓐ Ⓑ Ⓒ Ⓓ Ⓔ	17 Ⓐ Ⓑ Ⓒ Ⓓ Ⓔ	27 Ⓐ Ⓑ Ⓒ Ⓓ Ⓔ	37 Ⓐ Ⓑ Ⓒ Ⓓ Ⓔ
8 Ⓐ Ⓑ Ⓒ Ⓓ Ⓔ	18 Ⓐ Ⓑ Ⓒ Ⓓ Ⓔ	28 Ⓐ Ⓑ Ⓒ Ⓓ Ⓔ	38 Ⓐ Ⓑ Ⓒ Ⓓ Ⓔ
9 Ⓐ Ⓑ Ⓒ Ⓓ Ⓔ	19 Ⓐ Ⓑ Ⓒ Ⓓ Ⓔ	29 Ⓐ Ⓑ Ⓒ Ⓓ Ⓔ	39 Ⓐ Ⓑ Ⓒ Ⓓ Ⓔ
10 Ⓐ Ⓑ Ⓒ Ⓓ Ⓔ	20 Ⓐ Ⓑ Ⓒ Ⓓ Ⓔ	30 Ⓐ Ⓑ Ⓒ Ⓓ Ⓔ	40 Ⓐ Ⓑ Ⓒ Ⓓ Ⓔ

SECTION 9

1 Ⓐ Ⓑ Ⓒ Ⓓ Ⓔ	11 Ⓐ Ⓑ Ⓒ Ⓓ Ⓔ	21 Ⓐ Ⓑ Ⓒ Ⓓ Ⓔ	31 Ⓐ Ⓑ Ⓒ Ⓓ Ⓔ
2 Ⓐ Ⓑ Ⓒ Ⓓ Ⓔ	12 Ⓐ Ⓑ Ⓒ Ⓓ Ⓔ	22 Ⓐ Ⓑ Ⓒ Ⓓ Ⓔ	32 Ⓐ Ⓑ Ⓒ Ⓓ Ⓔ
3 Ⓐ Ⓑ Ⓒ Ⓓ Ⓔ	13 Ⓐ Ⓑ Ⓒ Ⓓ Ⓔ	23 Ⓐ Ⓑ Ⓒ Ⓓ Ⓔ	33 Ⓐ Ⓑ Ⓒ Ⓓ Ⓔ
4 Ⓐ Ⓑ Ⓒ Ⓓ Ⓔ	14 Ⓐ Ⓑ Ⓒ Ⓓ Ⓔ	24 Ⓐ Ⓑ Ⓒ Ⓓ Ⓔ	34 Ⓐ Ⓑ Ⓒ Ⓓ Ⓔ
5 Ⓐ Ⓑ Ⓒ Ⓓ Ⓔ	15 Ⓐ Ⓑ Ⓒ Ⓓ Ⓔ	25 Ⓐ Ⓑ Ⓒ Ⓓ Ⓔ	35 Ⓐ Ⓑ Ⓒ Ⓓ Ⓔ
6 Ⓐ Ⓑ Ⓒ Ⓓ Ⓔ	16 Ⓐ Ⓑ Ⓒ Ⓓ Ⓔ	26 Ⓐ Ⓑ Ⓒ Ⓓ Ⓔ	36 Ⓐ Ⓑ Ⓒ Ⓓ Ⓔ
7 Ⓐ Ⓑ Ⓒ Ⓓ Ⓔ	17 Ⓐ Ⓑ Ⓒ Ⓓ Ⓔ	27 Ⓐ Ⓑ Ⓒ Ⓓ Ⓔ	37 Ⓐ Ⓑ Ⓒ Ⓓ Ⓔ
8 Ⓐ Ⓑ Ⓒ Ⓓ Ⓔ	18 Ⓐ Ⓑ Ⓒ Ⓓ Ⓔ	28 Ⓐ Ⓑ Ⓒ Ⓓ Ⓔ	38 Ⓐ Ⓑ Ⓒ Ⓓ Ⓔ
9 Ⓐ Ⓑ Ⓒ Ⓓ Ⓔ	19 Ⓐ Ⓑ Ⓒ Ⓓ Ⓔ	29 Ⓐ Ⓑ Ⓒ Ⓓ Ⓔ	39 Ⓐ Ⓑ Ⓒ Ⓓ Ⓔ
10 Ⓐ Ⓑ Ⓒ Ⓓ Ⓔ	20 Ⓐ Ⓑ Ⓒ Ⓓ Ⓔ	30 Ⓐ Ⓑ Ⓒ Ⓓ Ⓔ	40 Ⓐ Ⓑ Ⓒ Ⓓ Ⓔ

SECTION 10

1 Ⓐ Ⓑ Ⓒ Ⓓ Ⓔ	11 Ⓐ Ⓑ Ⓒ Ⓓ Ⓔ	21 Ⓐ Ⓑ Ⓒ Ⓓ Ⓔ	31 Ⓐ Ⓑ Ⓒ Ⓓ Ⓔ
2 Ⓐ Ⓑ Ⓒ Ⓓ Ⓔ	12 Ⓐ Ⓑ Ⓒ Ⓓ Ⓔ	22 Ⓐ Ⓑ Ⓒ Ⓓ Ⓔ	32 Ⓐ Ⓑ Ⓒ Ⓓ Ⓔ
3 Ⓐ Ⓑ Ⓒ Ⓓ Ⓔ	13 Ⓐ Ⓑ Ⓒ Ⓓ Ⓔ	23 Ⓐ Ⓑ Ⓒ Ⓓ Ⓔ	33 Ⓐ Ⓑ Ⓒ Ⓓ Ⓔ
4 Ⓐ Ⓑ Ⓒ Ⓓ Ⓔ	14 Ⓐ Ⓑ Ⓒ Ⓓ Ⓔ	24 Ⓐ Ⓑ Ⓒ Ⓓ Ⓔ	34 Ⓐ Ⓑ Ⓒ Ⓓ Ⓔ
5 Ⓐ Ⓑ Ⓒ Ⓓ Ⓔ	15 Ⓐ Ⓑ Ⓒ Ⓓ Ⓔ	25 Ⓐ Ⓑ Ⓒ Ⓓ Ⓔ	35 Ⓐ Ⓑ Ⓒ Ⓓ Ⓔ
6 Ⓐ Ⓑ Ⓒ Ⓓ Ⓔ	16 Ⓐ Ⓑ Ⓒ Ⓓ Ⓔ	26 Ⓐ Ⓑ Ⓒ Ⓓ Ⓔ	36 Ⓐ Ⓑ Ⓒ Ⓓ Ⓔ
7 Ⓐ Ⓑ Ⓒ Ⓓ Ⓔ	17 Ⓐ Ⓑ Ⓒ Ⓓ Ⓔ	27 Ⓐ Ⓑ Ⓒ Ⓓ Ⓔ	37 Ⓐ Ⓑ Ⓒ Ⓓ Ⓔ
8 Ⓐ Ⓑ Ⓒ Ⓓ Ⓔ	18 Ⓐ Ⓑ Ⓒ Ⓓ Ⓔ	28 Ⓐ Ⓑ Ⓒ Ⓓ Ⓔ	38 Ⓐ Ⓑ Ⓒ Ⓓ Ⓔ
9 Ⓐ Ⓑ Ⓒ Ⓓ Ⓔ	19 Ⓐ Ⓑ Ⓒ Ⓓ Ⓔ	29 Ⓐ Ⓑ Ⓒ Ⓓ Ⓔ	39 Ⓐ Ⓑ Ⓒ Ⓓ Ⓔ
10 Ⓐ Ⓑ Ⓒ Ⓓ Ⓔ	20 Ⓐ Ⓑ Ⓒ Ⓓ Ⓔ	30 Ⓐ Ⓑ Ⓒ Ⓓ Ⓔ	40 Ⓐ Ⓑ Ⓒ Ⓓ Ⓔ

PLEASE DO NOT WRITE IN THIS AREA

SERIAL #

Diagnostic Test Form

Use a No. 2 pencil only. Be sure each mark is dark and completely fills the intended oval. Completely erase any errors or stray marks.

1 Your Name:
(Print)
Last First M.I.

Signature: Date / /

Home Address:
Number and Street City State Zip Code

E-Mail: (Print) School: Class:

2 YOUR NAME
Last Name (First 4 Letters) | FIRST INIT | MID INIT

– ’ A B C D E F G H I J K L M N O P Q R S T U V W X Y Z

3 PHONE NUMBER

0 1 2 3 4 5 6 7 8 9

4 DATE OF BIRTH

MONTH	DAY		YEAR	
JAN				
FEB				
MAR	0	0		0
APR	1	1		1
MAY	2	2		2
JUN	3	3		3
JUL		4		4
AUG		5	5	5
SEP		6	6	6
OCT		7	7	7
NOV		8	8	8
DEC		9	9	9

5 SEX
MALE
FEMALE

IMPORTANT: Fill in items 6 and 7 exactly as shown on the preceding page.

6 TEST FORM
(Copy from back of test book)

7 TEST CODE

0 1 2 3 4 5 6 7 8 9

8 OTHER

1 A B C D E
2 A B C D E
3 A B C D E

OpScan *i*NSIGHT™ forms by Pearson NCS EM-253760-3:654321 Printed in U.S.A.

PLEASE DO NOT WRITE IN THIS AREA

SERIAL #

THIS PAGE INTENTIONALLY LEFT BLANK

The Princeton Review Diagnostic Test Form

ESSAY

SECTION

1

Begin your essay on this page. If you need more space, continue on the next page. Do not write outside of the essay box.

Continue on the opposite side if necessary.

PLEASE DO NOT WRITE IN THIS AREA

SERIAL #

Continuation of ESSAY Section 1 from previous page. Write below only if you need more space.

Start with number 1 for each new section. If a section has fewer questions than answer spaces, leave the extra answer spaces blank. Be sure to erase any errors or stray marks completely.

SECTION 2

1 Ⓐ Ⓑ Ⓒ Ⓓ Ⓔ	11 Ⓐ Ⓑ Ⓒ Ⓓ Ⓔ	21 Ⓐ Ⓑ Ⓒ Ⓓ Ⓔ	31 Ⓐ Ⓑ Ⓒ Ⓓ Ⓔ
2 Ⓐ Ⓑ Ⓒ Ⓓ Ⓔ	12 Ⓐ Ⓑ Ⓒ Ⓓ Ⓔ	22 Ⓐ Ⓑ Ⓒ Ⓓ Ⓔ	32 Ⓐ Ⓑ Ⓒ Ⓓ Ⓔ
3 Ⓐ Ⓑ Ⓒ Ⓓ Ⓔ	13 Ⓐ Ⓑ Ⓒ Ⓓ Ⓔ	23 Ⓐ Ⓑ Ⓒ Ⓓ Ⓔ	33 Ⓐ Ⓑ Ⓒ Ⓓ Ⓔ
4 Ⓐ Ⓑ Ⓒ Ⓓ Ⓔ	14 Ⓐ Ⓑ Ⓒ Ⓓ Ⓔ	24 Ⓐ Ⓑ Ⓒ Ⓓ Ⓔ	34 Ⓐ Ⓑ Ⓒ Ⓓ Ⓔ
5 Ⓐ Ⓑ Ⓒ Ⓓ Ⓔ	15 Ⓐ Ⓑ Ⓒ Ⓓ Ⓔ	25 Ⓐ Ⓑ Ⓒ Ⓓ Ⓔ	35 Ⓐ Ⓑ Ⓒ Ⓓ Ⓔ
6 Ⓐ Ⓑ Ⓒ Ⓓ Ⓔ	16 Ⓐ Ⓑ Ⓒ Ⓓ Ⓔ	26 Ⓐ Ⓑ Ⓒ Ⓓ Ⓔ	36 Ⓐ Ⓑ Ⓒ Ⓓ Ⓔ
7 Ⓐ Ⓑ Ⓒ Ⓓ Ⓔ	17 Ⓐ Ⓑ Ⓒ Ⓓ Ⓔ	27 Ⓐ Ⓑ Ⓒ Ⓓ Ⓔ	37 Ⓐ Ⓑ Ⓒ Ⓓ Ⓔ
8 Ⓐ Ⓑ Ⓒ Ⓓ Ⓔ	18 Ⓐ Ⓑ Ⓒ Ⓓ Ⓔ	28 Ⓐ Ⓑ Ⓒ Ⓓ Ⓔ	38 Ⓐ Ⓑ Ⓒ Ⓓ Ⓔ
9 Ⓐ Ⓑ Ⓒ Ⓓ Ⓔ	19 Ⓐ Ⓑ Ⓒ Ⓓ Ⓔ	29 Ⓐ Ⓑ Ⓒ Ⓓ Ⓔ	39 Ⓐ Ⓑ Ⓒ Ⓓ Ⓔ
10 Ⓐ Ⓑ Ⓒ Ⓓ Ⓔ	20 Ⓐ Ⓑ Ⓒ Ⓓ Ⓔ	30 Ⓐ Ⓑ Ⓒ Ⓓ Ⓔ	40 Ⓐ Ⓑ Ⓒ Ⓓ Ⓔ

SECTION 3

1 Ⓐ Ⓑ Ⓒ Ⓓ Ⓔ	11 Ⓐ Ⓑ Ⓒ Ⓓ Ⓔ	21 Ⓐ Ⓑ Ⓒ Ⓓ Ⓔ	31 Ⓐ Ⓑ Ⓒ Ⓓ Ⓔ
2 Ⓐ Ⓑ Ⓒ Ⓓ Ⓔ	12 Ⓐ Ⓑ Ⓒ Ⓓ Ⓔ	22 Ⓐ Ⓑ Ⓒ Ⓓ Ⓔ	32 Ⓐ Ⓑ Ⓒ Ⓓ Ⓔ
3 Ⓐ Ⓑ Ⓒ Ⓓ Ⓔ	13 Ⓐ Ⓑ Ⓒ Ⓓ Ⓔ	23 Ⓐ Ⓑ Ⓒ Ⓓ Ⓔ	33 Ⓐ Ⓑ Ⓒ Ⓓ Ⓔ
4 Ⓐ Ⓑ Ⓒ Ⓓ Ⓔ	14 Ⓐ Ⓑ Ⓒ Ⓓ Ⓔ	24 Ⓐ Ⓑ Ⓒ Ⓓ Ⓔ	34 Ⓐ Ⓑ Ⓒ Ⓓ Ⓔ
5 Ⓐ Ⓑ Ⓒ Ⓓ Ⓔ	15 Ⓐ Ⓑ Ⓒ Ⓓ Ⓔ	25 Ⓐ Ⓑ Ⓒ Ⓓ Ⓔ	35 Ⓐ Ⓑ Ⓒ Ⓓ Ⓔ
6 Ⓐ Ⓑ Ⓒ Ⓓ Ⓔ	16 Ⓐ Ⓑ Ⓒ Ⓓ Ⓔ	26 Ⓐ Ⓑ Ⓒ Ⓓ Ⓔ	36 Ⓐ Ⓑ Ⓒ Ⓓ Ⓔ
7 Ⓐ Ⓑ Ⓒ Ⓓ Ⓔ	17 Ⓐ Ⓑ Ⓒ Ⓓ Ⓔ	27 Ⓐ Ⓑ Ⓒ Ⓓ Ⓔ	37 Ⓐ Ⓑ Ⓒ Ⓓ Ⓔ
8 Ⓐ Ⓑ Ⓒ Ⓓ Ⓔ	18 Ⓐ Ⓑ Ⓒ Ⓓ Ⓔ	28 Ⓐ Ⓑ Ⓒ Ⓓ Ⓔ	38 Ⓐ Ⓑ Ⓒ Ⓓ Ⓔ
9 Ⓐ Ⓑ Ⓒ Ⓓ Ⓔ	19 Ⓐ Ⓑ Ⓒ Ⓓ Ⓔ	29 Ⓐ Ⓑ Ⓒ Ⓓ Ⓔ	39 Ⓐ Ⓑ Ⓒ Ⓓ Ⓔ
10 Ⓐ Ⓑ Ⓒ Ⓓ Ⓔ	20 Ⓐ Ⓑ Ⓒ Ⓓ Ⓔ	30 Ⓐ Ⓑ Ⓒ Ⓓ Ⓔ	40 Ⓐ Ⓑ Ⓒ Ⓓ Ⓔ

CAUTION Use the answer spaces in the grids below for Section 2 or Section 3 only if you are told to do so in your test book.

Student-Produced Responses

ONLY ANSWERS ENTERED IN THE OVALS IN EACH GRID WILL BE SCORED. YOU WILL NOT RECEIVE CREDIT FOR ANYTHING WRITTEN IN THE BOXES ABOVE THE OVALS.

9

	/	/	
.	.	.	.
	0	0	0
1	1	1	1
2	2	2	2
3	3	3	3
4	4	4	4
5	5	5	5
6	6	6	6
7	7	7	7
8	8	8	8
9	9	9	9

10

	/	/	
.	.	.	.
	0	0	0
1	1	1	1
2	2	2	2
3	3	3	3
4	4	4	4
5	5	5	5
6	6	6	6
7	7	7	7
8	8	8	8
9	9	9	9

11

	/	/	
.	.	.	.
	0	0	0
1	1	1	1
2	2	2	2
3	3	3	3
4	4	4	4
5	5	5	5
6	6	6	6
7	7	7	7
8	8	8	8
9	9	9	9

12

	/	/	
.	.	.	.
	0	0	0
1	1	1	1
2	2	2	2
3	3	3	3
4	4	4	4
5	5	5	5
6	6	6	6
7	7	7	7
8	8	8	8
9	9	9	9

13

	/	/	
.	.	.	.
	0	0	0
1	1	1	1
2	2	2	2
3	3	3	3
4	4	4	4
5	5	5	5
6	6	6	6
7	7	7	7
8	8	8	8
9	9	9	9

14

	/	/	
.	.	.	.
	0	0	0
1	1	1	1
2	2	2	2
3	3	3	3
4	4	4	4
5	5	5	5
6	6	6	6
7	7	7	7
8	8	8	8
9	9	9	9

15

	/	/	
.	.	.	.
	0	0	0
1	1	1	1
2	2	2	2
3	3	3	3
4	4	4	4
5	5	5	5
6	6	6	6
7	7	7	7
8	8	8	8
9	9	9	9

16

	/	/	
.	.	.	.
	0	0	0
1	1	1	1
2	2	2	2
3	3	3	3
4	4	4	4
5	5	5	5
6	6	6	6
7	7	7	7
8	8	8	8
9	9	9	9

17

	/	/	
.	.	.	.
	0	0	0
1	1	1	1
2	2	2	2
3	3	3	3
4	4	4	4
5	5	5	5
6	6	6	6
7	7	7	7
8	8	8	8
9	9	9	9

18

	/	/	
.	.	.	.
	0	0	0
1	1	1	1
2	2	2	2
3	3	3	3
4	4	4	4
5	5	5	5
6	6	6	6
7	7	7	7
8	8	8	8
9	9	9	9

Start with number 1 for each new section. If a section has fewer questions than answer spaces, leave the extra answer spaces blank. Be sure to erase any errors or stray marks completely.

SECTION 4

1 Ⓐ Ⓑ Ⓒ Ⓓ Ⓔ	11 Ⓐ Ⓑ Ⓒ Ⓓ Ⓔ	21 Ⓐ Ⓑ Ⓒ Ⓓ Ⓔ	31 Ⓐ Ⓑ Ⓒ Ⓓ Ⓔ
2 Ⓐ Ⓑ Ⓒ Ⓓ Ⓔ	12 Ⓐ Ⓑ Ⓒ Ⓓ Ⓔ	22 Ⓐ Ⓑ Ⓒ Ⓓ Ⓔ	32 Ⓐ Ⓑ Ⓒ Ⓓ Ⓔ
3 Ⓐ Ⓑ Ⓒ Ⓓ Ⓔ	13 Ⓐ Ⓑ Ⓒ Ⓓ Ⓔ	23 Ⓐ Ⓑ Ⓒ Ⓓ Ⓔ	33 Ⓐ Ⓑ Ⓒ Ⓓ Ⓔ
4 Ⓐ Ⓑ Ⓒ Ⓓ Ⓔ	14 Ⓐ Ⓑ Ⓒ Ⓓ Ⓔ	24 Ⓐ Ⓑ Ⓒ Ⓓ Ⓔ	34 Ⓐ Ⓑ Ⓒ Ⓓ Ⓔ
5 Ⓐ Ⓑ Ⓒ Ⓓ Ⓔ	15 Ⓐ Ⓑ Ⓒ Ⓓ Ⓔ	25 Ⓐ Ⓑ Ⓒ Ⓓ Ⓔ	35 Ⓐ Ⓑ Ⓒ Ⓓ Ⓔ
6 Ⓐ Ⓑ Ⓒ Ⓓ Ⓔ	16 Ⓐ Ⓑ Ⓒ Ⓓ Ⓔ	26 Ⓐ Ⓑ Ⓒ Ⓓ Ⓔ	36 Ⓐ Ⓑ Ⓒ Ⓓ Ⓔ
7 Ⓐ Ⓑ Ⓒ Ⓓ Ⓔ	17 Ⓐ Ⓑ Ⓒ Ⓓ Ⓔ	27 Ⓐ Ⓑ Ⓒ Ⓓ Ⓔ	37 Ⓐ Ⓑ Ⓒ Ⓓ Ⓔ
8 Ⓐ Ⓑ Ⓒ Ⓓ Ⓔ	18 Ⓐ Ⓑ Ⓒ Ⓓ Ⓔ	28 Ⓐ Ⓑ Ⓒ Ⓓ Ⓔ	38 Ⓐ Ⓑ Ⓒ Ⓓ Ⓔ
9 Ⓐ Ⓑ Ⓒ Ⓓ Ⓔ	19 Ⓐ Ⓑ Ⓒ Ⓓ Ⓔ	29 Ⓐ Ⓑ Ⓒ Ⓓ Ⓔ	39 Ⓐ Ⓑ Ⓒ Ⓓ Ⓔ
10 Ⓐ Ⓑ Ⓒ Ⓓ Ⓔ	20 Ⓐ Ⓑ Ⓒ Ⓓ Ⓔ	30 Ⓐ Ⓑ Ⓒ Ⓓ Ⓔ	40 Ⓐ Ⓑ Ⓒ Ⓓ Ⓔ

SECTION 5

1 Ⓐ Ⓑ Ⓒ Ⓓ Ⓔ	11 Ⓐ Ⓑ Ⓒ Ⓓ Ⓔ	21 Ⓐ Ⓑ Ⓒ Ⓓ Ⓔ	31 Ⓐ Ⓑ Ⓒ Ⓓ Ⓔ
2 Ⓐ Ⓑ Ⓒ Ⓓ Ⓔ	12 Ⓐ Ⓑ Ⓒ Ⓓ Ⓔ	22 Ⓐ Ⓑ Ⓒ Ⓓ Ⓔ	32 Ⓐ Ⓑ Ⓒ Ⓓ Ⓔ
3 Ⓐ Ⓑ Ⓒ Ⓓ Ⓔ	13 Ⓐ Ⓑ Ⓒ Ⓓ Ⓔ	23 Ⓐ Ⓑ Ⓒ Ⓓ Ⓔ	33 Ⓐ Ⓑ Ⓒ Ⓓ Ⓔ
4 Ⓐ Ⓑ Ⓒ Ⓓ Ⓔ	14 Ⓐ Ⓑ Ⓒ Ⓓ Ⓔ	24 Ⓐ Ⓑ Ⓒ Ⓓ Ⓔ	34 Ⓐ Ⓑ Ⓒ Ⓓ Ⓔ
5 Ⓐ Ⓑ Ⓒ Ⓓ Ⓔ	15 Ⓐ Ⓑ Ⓒ Ⓓ Ⓔ	25 Ⓐ Ⓑ Ⓒ Ⓓ Ⓔ	35 Ⓐ Ⓑ Ⓒ Ⓓ Ⓔ
6 Ⓐ Ⓑ Ⓒ Ⓓ Ⓔ	16 Ⓐ Ⓑ Ⓒ Ⓓ Ⓔ	26 Ⓐ Ⓑ Ⓒ Ⓓ Ⓔ	36 Ⓐ Ⓑ Ⓒ Ⓓ Ⓔ
7 Ⓐ Ⓑ Ⓒ Ⓓ Ⓔ	17 Ⓐ Ⓑ Ⓒ Ⓓ Ⓔ	27 Ⓐ Ⓑ Ⓒ Ⓓ Ⓔ	37 Ⓐ Ⓑ Ⓒ Ⓓ Ⓔ
8 Ⓐ Ⓑ Ⓒ Ⓓ Ⓔ	18 Ⓐ Ⓑ Ⓒ Ⓓ Ⓔ	28 Ⓐ Ⓑ Ⓒ Ⓓ Ⓔ	38 Ⓐ Ⓑ Ⓒ Ⓓ Ⓔ
9 Ⓐ Ⓑ Ⓒ Ⓓ Ⓔ	19 Ⓐ Ⓑ Ⓒ Ⓓ Ⓔ	29 Ⓐ Ⓑ Ⓒ Ⓓ Ⓔ	39 Ⓐ Ⓑ Ⓒ Ⓓ Ⓔ
10 Ⓐ Ⓑ Ⓒ Ⓓ Ⓔ	20 Ⓐ Ⓑ Ⓒ Ⓓ Ⓔ	30 Ⓐ Ⓑ Ⓒ Ⓓ Ⓔ	40 Ⓐ Ⓑ Ⓒ Ⓓ Ⓔ

CAUTION Use the answer spaces in the grids below for Section 4 or Section 5 only if you are told to do so in your test book.

Student-Produced Responses ONLY ANSWERS ENTERED IN THE OVALS IN EACH GRID WILL BE SCORED. YOU WILL NOT RECEIVE CREDIT FOR ANYTHING WRITTEN IN THE BOXES ABOVE THE OVALS.

Grids 9, 10, 11, 12, 13, 14, 15, 16, 17, 18 (each grid identical):

	/	/	
.	.	.	.
	0	0	0
1	1	1	1
2	2	2	2
3	3	3	3
4	4	4	4
5	5	5	5
6	6	6	6
7	7	7	7
8	8	8	8
9	9	9	9

PLEASE DO NOT WRITE IN THIS AREA

SERIAL #

Start with number 1 for each new section. If a section has fewer questions than answer spaces, leave the extra answer spaces blank. Be sure to erase any errors or stray marks completely.

SECTION 6

1 Ⓐ Ⓑ Ⓒ Ⓓ Ⓔ	11 Ⓐ Ⓑ Ⓒ Ⓓ Ⓔ	21 Ⓐ Ⓑ Ⓒ Ⓓ Ⓔ	31 Ⓐ Ⓑ Ⓒ Ⓓ Ⓔ
2 Ⓐ Ⓑ Ⓒ Ⓓ Ⓔ	12 Ⓐ Ⓑ Ⓒ Ⓓ Ⓔ	22 Ⓐ Ⓑ Ⓒ Ⓓ Ⓔ	32 Ⓐ Ⓑ Ⓒ Ⓓ Ⓔ
3 Ⓐ Ⓑ Ⓒ Ⓓ Ⓔ	13 Ⓐ Ⓑ Ⓒ Ⓓ Ⓔ	23 Ⓐ Ⓑ Ⓒ Ⓓ Ⓔ	33 Ⓐ Ⓑ Ⓒ Ⓓ Ⓔ
4 Ⓐ Ⓑ Ⓒ Ⓓ Ⓔ	14 Ⓐ Ⓑ Ⓒ Ⓓ Ⓔ	24 Ⓐ Ⓑ Ⓒ Ⓓ Ⓔ	34 Ⓐ Ⓑ Ⓒ Ⓓ Ⓔ
5 Ⓐ Ⓑ Ⓒ Ⓓ Ⓔ	15 Ⓐ Ⓑ Ⓒ Ⓓ Ⓔ	25 Ⓐ Ⓑ Ⓒ Ⓓ Ⓔ	35 Ⓐ Ⓑ Ⓒ Ⓓ Ⓔ
6 Ⓐ Ⓑ Ⓒ Ⓓ Ⓔ	16 Ⓐ Ⓑ Ⓒ Ⓓ Ⓔ	26 Ⓐ Ⓑ Ⓒ Ⓓ Ⓔ	36 Ⓐ Ⓑ Ⓒ Ⓓ Ⓔ
7 Ⓐ Ⓑ Ⓒ Ⓓ Ⓔ	17 Ⓐ Ⓑ Ⓒ Ⓓ Ⓔ	27 Ⓐ Ⓑ Ⓒ Ⓓ Ⓔ	37 Ⓐ Ⓑ Ⓒ Ⓓ Ⓔ
8 Ⓐ Ⓑ Ⓒ Ⓓ Ⓔ	18 Ⓐ Ⓑ Ⓒ Ⓓ Ⓔ	28 Ⓐ Ⓑ Ⓒ Ⓓ Ⓔ	38 Ⓐ Ⓑ Ⓒ Ⓓ Ⓔ
9 Ⓐ Ⓑ Ⓒ Ⓓ Ⓔ	19 Ⓐ Ⓑ Ⓒ Ⓓ Ⓔ	29 Ⓐ Ⓑ Ⓒ Ⓓ Ⓔ	39 Ⓐ Ⓑ Ⓒ Ⓓ Ⓔ
10 Ⓐ Ⓑ Ⓒ Ⓓ Ⓔ	20 Ⓐ Ⓑ Ⓒ Ⓓ Ⓔ	30 Ⓐ Ⓑ Ⓒ Ⓓ Ⓔ	40 Ⓐ Ⓑ Ⓒ Ⓓ Ⓔ

SECTION 7

1 Ⓐ Ⓑ Ⓒ Ⓓ Ⓔ	11 Ⓐ Ⓑ Ⓒ Ⓓ Ⓔ	21 Ⓐ Ⓑ Ⓒ Ⓓ Ⓔ	31 Ⓐ Ⓑ Ⓒ Ⓓ Ⓔ
2 Ⓐ Ⓑ Ⓒ Ⓓ Ⓔ	12 Ⓐ Ⓑ Ⓒ Ⓓ Ⓔ	22 Ⓐ Ⓑ Ⓒ Ⓓ Ⓔ	32 Ⓐ Ⓑ Ⓒ Ⓓ Ⓔ
3 Ⓐ Ⓑ Ⓒ Ⓓ Ⓔ	13 Ⓐ Ⓑ Ⓒ Ⓓ Ⓔ	23 Ⓐ Ⓑ Ⓒ Ⓓ Ⓔ	33 Ⓐ Ⓑ Ⓒ Ⓓ Ⓔ
4 Ⓐ Ⓑ Ⓒ Ⓓ Ⓔ	14 Ⓐ Ⓑ Ⓒ Ⓓ Ⓔ	24 Ⓐ Ⓑ Ⓒ Ⓓ Ⓔ	34 Ⓐ Ⓑ Ⓒ Ⓓ Ⓔ
5 Ⓐ Ⓑ Ⓒ Ⓓ Ⓔ	15 Ⓐ Ⓑ Ⓒ Ⓓ Ⓔ	25 Ⓐ Ⓑ Ⓒ Ⓓ Ⓔ	35 Ⓐ Ⓑ Ⓒ Ⓓ Ⓔ
6 Ⓐ Ⓑ Ⓒ Ⓓ Ⓔ	16 Ⓐ Ⓑ Ⓒ Ⓓ Ⓔ	26 Ⓐ Ⓑ Ⓒ Ⓓ Ⓔ	36 Ⓐ Ⓑ Ⓒ Ⓓ Ⓔ
7 Ⓐ Ⓑ Ⓒ Ⓓ Ⓔ	17 Ⓐ Ⓑ Ⓒ Ⓓ Ⓔ	27 Ⓐ Ⓑ Ⓒ Ⓓ Ⓔ	37 Ⓐ Ⓑ Ⓒ Ⓓ Ⓔ
8 Ⓐ Ⓑ Ⓒ Ⓓ Ⓔ	18 Ⓐ Ⓑ Ⓒ Ⓓ Ⓔ	28 Ⓐ Ⓑ Ⓒ Ⓓ Ⓔ	38 Ⓐ Ⓑ Ⓒ Ⓓ Ⓔ
9 Ⓐ Ⓑ Ⓒ Ⓓ Ⓔ	19 Ⓐ Ⓑ Ⓒ Ⓓ Ⓔ	29 Ⓐ Ⓑ Ⓒ Ⓓ Ⓔ	39 Ⓐ Ⓑ Ⓒ Ⓓ Ⓔ
10 Ⓐ Ⓑ Ⓒ Ⓓ Ⓔ	20 Ⓐ Ⓑ Ⓒ Ⓓ Ⓔ	30 Ⓐ Ⓑ Ⓒ Ⓓ Ⓔ	40 Ⓐ Ⓑ Ⓒ Ⓓ Ⓔ

CAUTION Use the answer spaces in the grids below for Section 6 or Section 7 only if you are told to do so in your test book.

Student-Produced Responses

ONLY ANSWERS ENTERED IN THE OVALS IN EACH GRID WILL BE SCORED. YOU WILL NOT RECEIVE CREDIT FOR ANYTHING WRITTEN IN THE BOXES ABOVE THE OVALS.

Grids 9, 10, 11, 12, 13, 14, 15, 16, 17, 18 (each grid identical):

	/	/	
.	.	.	.
	0	0	0
1	1	1	1
2	2	2	2
3	3	3	3
4	4	4	4
5	5	5	5
6	6	6	6
7	7	7	7
8	8	8	8
9	9	9	9

Start with number 1 for each new section. If a section has fewer questions than answer spaces, leave the extra answer spaces blank. Be sure to erase any errors or stray marks completely.

SECTION 8

1 Ⓐ Ⓑ Ⓒ Ⓓ Ⓔ	11 Ⓐ Ⓑ Ⓒ Ⓓ Ⓔ	21 Ⓐ Ⓑ Ⓒ Ⓓ Ⓔ	31 Ⓐ Ⓑ Ⓒ Ⓓ Ⓔ
2 Ⓐ Ⓑ Ⓒ Ⓓ Ⓔ	12 Ⓐ Ⓑ Ⓒ Ⓓ Ⓔ	22 Ⓐ Ⓑ Ⓒ Ⓓ Ⓔ	32 Ⓐ Ⓑ Ⓒ Ⓓ Ⓔ
3 Ⓐ Ⓑ Ⓒ Ⓓ Ⓔ	13 Ⓐ Ⓑ Ⓒ Ⓓ Ⓔ	23 Ⓐ Ⓑ Ⓒ Ⓓ Ⓔ	33 Ⓐ Ⓑ Ⓒ Ⓓ Ⓔ
4 Ⓐ Ⓑ Ⓒ Ⓓ Ⓔ	14 Ⓐ Ⓑ Ⓒ Ⓓ Ⓔ	24 Ⓐ Ⓑ Ⓒ Ⓓ Ⓔ	34 Ⓐ Ⓑ Ⓒ Ⓓ Ⓔ
5 Ⓐ Ⓑ Ⓒ Ⓓ Ⓔ	15 Ⓐ Ⓑ Ⓒ Ⓓ Ⓔ	25 Ⓐ Ⓑ Ⓒ Ⓓ Ⓔ	35 Ⓐ Ⓑ Ⓒ Ⓓ Ⓔ
6 Ⓐ Ⓑ Ⓒ Ⓓ Ⓔ	16 Ⓐ Ⓑ Ⓒ Ⓓ Ⓔ	26 Ⓐ Ⓑ Ⓒ Ⓓ Ⓔ	36 Ⓐ Ⓑ Ⓒ Ⓓ Ⓔ
7 Ⓐ Ⓑ Ⓒ Ⓓ Ⓔ	17 Ⓐ Ⓑ Ⓒ Ⓓ Ⓔ	27 Ⓐ Ⓑ Ⓒ Ⓓ Ⓔ	37 Ⓐ Ⓑ Ⓒ Ⓓ Ⓔ
8 Ⓐ Ⓑ Ⓒ Ⓓ Ⓔ	18 Ⓐ Ⓑ Ⓒ Ⓓ Ⓔ	28 Ⓐ Ⓑ Ⓒ Ⓓ Ⓔ	38 Ⓐ Ⓑ Ⓒ Ⓓ Ⓔ
9 Ⓐ Ⓑ Ⓒ Ⓓ Ⓔ	19 Ⓐ Ⓑ Ⓒ Ⓓ Ⓔ	29 Ⓐ Ⓑ Ⓒ Ⓓ Ⓔ	39 Ⓐ Ⓑ Ⓒ Ⓓ Ⓔ
10 Ⓐ Ⓑ Ⓒ Ⓓ Ⓔ	20 Ⓐ Ⓑ Ⓒ Ⓓ Ⓔ	30 Ⓐ Ⓑ Ⓒ Ⓓ Ⓔ	40 Ⓐ Ⓑ Ⓒ Ⓓ Ⓔ

SECTION 9

1 Ⓐ Ⓑ Ⓒ Ⓓ Ⓔ	11 Ⓐ Ⓑ Ⓒ Ⓓ Ⓔ	21 Ⓐ Ⓑ Ⓒ Ⓓ Ⓔ	31 Ⓐ Ⓑ Ⓒ Ⓓ Ⓔ
2 Ⓐ Ⓑ Ⓒ Ⓓ Ⓔ	12 Ⓐ Ⓑ Ⓒ Ⓓ Ⓔ	22 Ⓐ Ⓑ Ⓒ Ⓓ Ⓔ	32 Ⓐ Ⓑ Ⓒ Ⓓ Ⓔ
3 Ⓐ Ⓑ Ⓒ Ⓓ Ⓔ	13 Ⓐ Ⓑ Ⓒ Ⓓ Ⓔ	23 Ⓐ Ⓑ Ⓒ Ⓓ Ⓔ	33 Ⓐ Ⓑ Ⓒ Ⓓ Ⓔ
4 Ⓐ Ⓑ Ⓒ Ⓓ Ⓔ	14 Ⓐ Ⓑ Ⓒ Ⓓ Ⓔ	24 Ⓐ Ⓑ Ⓒ Ⓓ Ⓔ	34 Ⓐ Ⓑ Ⓒ Ⓓ Ⓔ
5 Ⓐ Ⓑ Ⓒ Ⓓ Ⓔ	15 Ⓐ Ⓑ Ⓒ Ⓓ Ⓔ	25 Ⓐ Ⓑ Ⓒ Ⓓ Ⓔ	35 Ⓐ Ⓑ Ⓒ Ⓓ Ⓔ
6 Ⓐ Ⓑ Ⓒ Ⓓ Ⓔ	16 Ⓐ Ⓑ Ⓒ Ⓓ Ⓔ	26 Ⓐ Ⓑ Ⓒ Ⓓ Ⓔ	36 Ⓐ Ⓑ Ⓒ Ⓓ Ⓔ
7 Ⓐ Ⓑ Ⓒ Ⓓ Ⓔ	17 Ⓐ Ⓑ Ⓒ Ⓓ Ⓔ	27 Ⓐ Ⓑ Ⓒ Ⓓ Ⓔ	37 Ⓐ Ⓑ Ⓒ Ⓓ Ⓔ
8 Ⓐ Ⓑ Ⓒ Ⓓ Ⓔ	18 Ⓐ Ⓑ Ⓒ Ⓓ Ⓔ	28 Ⓐ Ⓑ Ⓒ Ⓓ Ⓔ	38 Ⓐ Ⓑ Ⓒ Ⓓ Ⓔ
9 Ⓐ Ⓑ Ⓒ Ⓓ Ⓔ	19 Ⓐ Ⓑ Ⓒ Ⓓ Ⓔ	29 Ⓐ Ⓑ Ⓒ Ⓓ Ⓔ	39 Ⓐ Ⓑ Ⓒ Ⓓ Ⓔ
10 Ⓐ Ⓑ Ⓒ Ⓓ Ⓔ	20 Ⓐ Ⓑ Ⓒ Ⓓ Ⓔ	30 Ⓐ Ⓑ Ⓒ Ⓓ Ⓔ	40 Ⓐ Ⓑ Ⓒ Ⓓ Ⓔ

SECTION 10

1 Ⓐ Ⓑ Ⓒ Ⓓ Ⓔ	11 Ⓐ Ⓑ Ⓒ Ⓓ Ⓔ	21 Ⓐ Ⓑ Ⓒ Ⓓ Ⓔ	31 Ⓐ Ⓑ Ⓒ Ⓓ Ⓔ
2 Ⓐ Ⓑ Ⓒ Ⓓ Ⓔ	12 Ⓐ Ⓑ Ⓒ Ⓓ Ⓔ	22 Ⓐ Ⓑ Ⓒ Ⓓ Ⓔ	32 Ⓐ Ⓑ Ⓒ Ⓓ Ⓔ
3 Ⓐ Ⓑ Ⓒ Ⓓ Ⓔ	13 Ⓐ Ⓑ Ⓒ Ⓓ Ⓔ	23 Ⓐ Ⓑ Ⓒ Ⓓ Ⓔ	33 Ⓐ Ⓑ Ⓒ Ⓓ Ⓔ
4 Ⓐ Ⓑ Ⓒ Ⓓ Ⓔ	14 Ⓐ Ⓑ Ⓒ Ⓓ Ⓔ	24 Ⓐ Ⓑ Ⓒ Ⓓ Ⓔ	34 Ⓐ Ⓑ Ⓒ Ⓓ Ⓔ
5 Ⓐ Ⓑ Ⓒ Ⓓ Ⓔ	15 Ⓐ Ⓑ Ⓒ Ⓓ Ⓔ	25 Ⓐ Ⓑ Ⓒ Ⓓ Ⓔ	35 Ⓐ Ⓑ Ⓒ Ⓓ Ⓔ
6 Ⓐ Ⓑ Ⓒ Ⓓ Ⓔ	16 Ⓐ Ⓑ Ⓒ Ⓓ Ⓔ	26 Ⓐ Ⓑ Ⓒ Ⓓ Ⓔ	36 Ⓐ Ⓑ Ⓒ Ⓓ Ⓔ
7 Ⓐ Ⓑ Ⓒ Ⓓ Ⓔ	17 Ⓐ Ⓑ Ⓒ Ⓓ Ⓔ	27 Ⓐ Ⓑ Ⓒ Ⓓ Ⓔ	37 Ⓐ Ⓑ Ⓒ Ⓓ Ⓔ
8 Ⓐ Ⓑ Ⓒ Ⓓ Ⓔ	18 Ⓐ Ⓑ Ⓒ Ⓓ Ⓔ	28 Ⓐ Ⓑ Ⓒ Ⓓ Ⓔ	38 Ⓐ Ⓑ Ⓒ Ⓓ Ⓔ
9 Ⓐ Ⓑ Ⓒ Ⓓ Ⓔ	19 Ⓐ Ⓑ Ⓒ Ⓓ Ⓔ	29 Ⓐ Ⓑ Ⓒ Ⓓ Ⓔ	39 Ⓐ Ⓑ Ⓒ Ⓓ Ⓔ
10 Ⓐ Ⓑ Ⓒ Ⓓ Ⓔ	20 Ⓐ Ⓑ Ⓒ Ⓓ Ⓔ	30 Ⓐ Ⓑ Ⓒ Ⓓ Ⓔ	40 Ⓐ Ⓑ Ⓒ Ⓓ Ⓔ

PLEASE DO NOT WRITE IN THIS AREA

SERIAL #

Diagnostic Test Form

Use a No. 2 pencil only. Be sure each mark is dark and completely fills the intended oval. Completely erase any errors or stray marks.

1 Your Name:
(Print)
Last First M.I.

Signature: Date / /

Home Address:
Number and Street City State Zip Code

E-Mail: School: Class:
(Print)

2 YOUR NAME
Last Name (First 4 Letters) | FIRST INIT | MID INIT

				FIRST INIT	MID INIT
	–	–	–		
	'	'	'		
	◯	◯	◯		
A	A	A	A	A	A
B	B	B	B	B	B
C	C	C	C	C	C
D	D	D	D	D	D
E	E	E	E	E	E
F	F	F	F	F	F
G	G	G	G	G	G
H	H	H	H	H	H
I	I	I	I	I	I
J	J	J	J	J	J
K	K	K	K	K	K
L	L	L	L	L	L
M	M	M	M	M	M
N	N	N	N	N	N
O	O	O	O	O	O
P	P	P	P	P	P
Q	Q	Q	Q	Q	Q
R	R	R	R	R	R
S	S	S	S	S	S
T	T	T	T	T	T
U	U	U	U	U	U
V	V	V	V	V	V
W	W	W	W	W	W
X	X	X	X	X	X
Y	Y	Y	Y	Y	Y
Z	Z	Z	Z	Z	Z

3 PHONE NUMBER

			–			
0	0	0	0	0	0	0
1	1	1	1	1	1	1
2	2	2	2	2	2	2
3	3	3	3	3	3	3
4	4	4	4	4	4	4
5	5	5	5	5	5	5
6	6	6	6	6	6	6
7	7	7	7	7	7	7
8	8	8	8	8	8	8
9	9	9	9	9	9	9

IMPORTANT: Fill in items 6 and 7 exactly as shown on the preceding page.

6 TEST FORM
(Copy from back of test book)

7 TEST CODE

0	0	0	0
1	1	1	1
2	2	2	2
3	3	3	3
4	4	4	4
5	5	5	5
6	6	6	6
7	7	7	7
8	8	8	8
9	9	9	9

4 DATE OF BIRTH

MONTH	DAY		YEAR	
◯ JAN				
◯ FEB				
◯ MAR	0	0		0
◯ APR	1	1		1
◯ MAY	2	2		2
◯ JUN	3	3		3
◯ JUL		4		4
◯ AUG		5	5	5
◯ SEP		6	6	6
◯ OCT		7	7	7
◯ NOV		8	8	8
◯ DEC		9	9	9

8 OTHER
1 A B C D E
2 A B C D E
3 A B C D E

5 SEX
◯ MALE
◯ FEMALE

OpScan *i*NSIGHT™ forms by Pearson NCS EM-253760-3:654321 Printed in U.S.A.

PLEASE DO NOT WRITE IN THIS AREA

SERIAL #

THIS PAGE INTENTIONALLY LEFT BLANK

The Princeton Review Diagnostic Test Form

ESSAY

SECTION

1

Begin your essay on this page. If you need more space, continue on the next page. Do not write outside of the essay box.

Continue on the opposite side if necessary.

PLEASE DO NOT WRITE IN THIS AREA

SERIAL #

Continuation of ESSAY Section 1 from previous page. Write below only if you need more space.

Start with number 1 for each new section. If a section has fewer questions than answer spaces, leave the extra answer spaces blank. Be sure to erase any errors or stray marks completely.

SECTION 2

1 Ⓐ Ⓑ Ⓒ Ⓓ Ⓔ	11 Ⓐ Ⓑ Ⓒ Ⓓ Ⓔ	21 Ⓐ Ⓑ Ⓒ Ⓓ Ⓔ	31 Ⓐ Ⓑ Ⓒ Ⓓ Ⓔ
2 Ⓐ Ⓑ Ⓒ Ⓓ Ⓔ	12 Ⓐ Ⓑ Ⓒ Ⓓ Ⓔ	22 Ⓐ Ⓑ Ⓒ Ⓓ Ⓔ	32 Ⓐ Ⓑ Ⓒ Ⓓ Ⓔ
3 Ⓐ Ⓑ Ⓒ Ⓓ Ⓔ	13 Ⓐ Ⓑ Ⓒ Ⓓ Ⓔ	23 Ⓐ Ⓑ Ⓒ Ⓓ Ⓔ	33 Ⓐ Ⓑ Ⓒ Ⓓ Ⓔ
4 Ⓐ Ⓑ Ⓒ Ⓓ Ⓔ	14 Ⓐ Ⓑ Ⓒ Ⓓ Ⓔ	24 Ⓐ Ⓑ Ⓒ Ⓓ Ⓔ	34 Ⓐ Ⓑ Ⓒ Ⓓ Ⓔ
5 Ⓐ Ⓑ Ⓒ Ⓓ Ⓔ	15 Ⓐ Ⓑ Ⓒ Ⓓ Ⓔ	25 Ⓐ Ⓑ Ⓒ Ⓓ Ⓔ	35 Ⓐ Ⓑ Ⓒ Ⓓ Ⓔ
6 Ⓐ Ⓑ Ⓒ Ⓓ Ⓔ	16 Ⓐ Ⓑ Ⓒ Ⓓ Ⓔ	26 Ⓐ Ⓑ Ⓒ Ⓓ Ⓔ	36 Ⓐ Ⓑ Ⓒ Ⓓ Ⓔ
7 Ⓐ Ⓑ Ⓒ Ⓓ Ⓔ	17 Ⓐ Ⓑ Ⓒ Ⓓ Ⓔ	27 Ⓐ Ⓑ Ⓒ Ⓓ Ⓔ	37 Ⓐ Ⓑ Ⓒ Ⓓ Ⓔ
8 Ⓐ Ⓑ Ⓒ Ⓓ Ⓔ	18 Ⓐ Ⓑ Ⓒ Ⓓ Ⓔ	28 Ⓐ Ⓑ Ⓒ Ⓓ Ⓔ	38 Ⓐ Ⓑ Ⓒ Ⓓ Ⓔ
9 Ⓐ Ⓑ Ⓒ Ⓓ Ⓔ	19 Ⓐ Ⓑ Ⓒ Ⓓ Ⓔ	29 Ⓐ Ⓑ Ⓒ Ⓓ Ⓔ	39 Ⓐ Ⓑ Ⓒ Ⓓ Ⓔ
10 Ⓐ Ⓑ Ⓒ Ⓓ Ⓔ	20 Ⓐ Ⓑ Ⓒ Ⓓ Ⓔ	30 Ⓐ Ⓑ Ⓒ Ⓓ Ⓔ	40 Ⓐ Ⓑ Ⓒ Ⓓ Ⓔ

SECTION 3

1 Ⓐ Ⓑ Ⓒ Ⓓ Ⓔ	11 Ⓐ Ⓑ Ⓒ Ⓓ Ⓔ	21 Ⓐ Ⓑ Ⓒ Ⓓ Ⓔ	31 Ⓐ Ⓑ Ⓒ Ⓓ Ⓔ
2 Ⓐ Ⓑ Ⓒ Ⓓ Ⓔ	12 Ⓐ Ⓑ Ⓒ Ⓓ Ⓔ	22 Ⓐ Ⓑ Ⓒ Ⓓ Ⓔ	32 Ⓐ Ⓑ Ⓒ Ⓓ Ⓔ
3 Ⓐ Ⓑ Ⓒ Ⓓ Ⓔ	13 Ⓐ Ⓑ Ⓒ Ⓓ Ⓔ	23 Ⓐ Ⓑ Ⓒ Ⓓ Ⓔ	33 Ⓐ Ⓑ Ⓒ Ⓓ Ⓔ
4 Ⓐ Ⓑ Ⓒ Ⓓ Ⓔ	14 Ⓐ Ⓑ Ⓒ Ⓓ Ⓔ	24 Ⓐ Ⓑ Ⓒ Ⓓ Ⓔ	34 Ⓐ Ⓑ Ⓒ Ⓓ Ⓔ
5 Ⓐ Ⓑ Ⓒ Ⓓ Ⓔ	15 Ⓐ Ⓑ Ⓒ Ⓓ Ⓔ	25 Ⓐ Ⓑ Ⓒ Ⓓ Ⓔ	35 Ⓐ Ⓑ Ⓒ Ⓓ Ⓔ
6 Ⓐ Ⓑ Ⓒ Ⓓ Ⓔ	16 Ⓐ Ⓑ Ⓒ Ⓓ Ⓔ	26 Ⓐ Ⓑ Ⓒ Ⓓ Ⓔ	36 Ⓐ Ⓑ Ⓒ Ⓓ Ⓔ
7 Ⓐ Ⓑ Ⓒ Ⓓ Ⓔ	17 Ⓐ Ⓑ Ⓒ Ⓓ Ⓔ	27 Ⓐ Ⓑ Ⓒ Ⓓ Ⓔ	37 Ⓐ Ⓑ Ⓒ Ⓓ Ⓔ
8 Ⓐ Ⓑ Ⓒ Ⓓ Ⓔ	18 Ⓐ Ⓑ Ⓒ Ⓓ Ⓔ	28 Ⓐ Ⓑ Ⓒ Ⓓ Ⓔ	38 Ⓐ Ⓑ Ⓒ Ⓓ Ⓔ
9 Ⓐ Ⓑ Ⓒ Ⓓ Ⓔ	19 Ⓐ Ⓑ Ⓒ Ⓓ Ⓔ	29 Ⓐ Ⓑ Ⓒ Ⓓ Ⓔ	39 Ⓐ Ⓑ Ⓒ Ⓓ Ⓔ
10 Ⓐ Ⓑ Ⓒ Ⓓ Ⓔ	20 Ⓐ Ⓑ Ⓒ Ⓓ Ⓔ	30 Ⓐ Ⓑ Ⓒ Ⓓ Ⓔ	40 Ⓐ Ⓑ Ⓒ Ⓓ Ⓔ

CAUTION Use the answer spaces in the grids below for Section 2 or Section 3 only if you are told to do so in your test book.

Student-Produced Responses

ONLY ANSWERS ENTERED IN THE OVALS IN EACH GRID WILL BE SCORED. YOU WILL NOT RECEIVE CREDIT FOR ANYTHING WRITTEN IN THE BOXES ABOVE THE OVALS.

9

	/	/	
.	.	.	.
	0	0	0
1	1	1	1
2	2	2	2
3	3	3	3
4	4	4	4
5	5	5	5
6	6	6	6
7	7	7	7
8	8	8	8
9	9	9	9

10

	/	/	
.	.	.	.
	0	0	0
1	1	1	1
2	2	2	2
3	3	3	3
4	4	4	4
5	5	5	5
6	6	6	6
7	7	7	7
8	8	8	8
9	9	9	9

11

	/	/	
.	.	.	.
	0	0	0
1	1	1	1
2	2	2	2
3	3	3	3
4	4	4	4
5	5	5	5
6	6	6	6
7	7	7	7
8	8	8	8
9	9	9	9

12

	/	/	
.	.	.	.
	0	0	0
1	1	1	1
2	2	2	2
3	3	3	3
4	4	4	4
5	5	5	5
6	6	6	6
7	7	7	7
8	8	8	8
9	9	9	9

13

	/	/	
.	.	.	.
	0	0	0
1	1	1	1
2	2	2	2
3	3	3	3
4	4	4	4
5	5	5	5
6	6	6	6
7	7	7	7
8	8	8	8
9	9	9	9

14

	/	/	
.	.	.	.
	0	0	0
1	1	1	1
2	2	2	2
3	3	3	3
4	4	4	4
5	5	5	5
6	6	6	6
7	7	7	7
8	8	8	8
9	9	9	9

15

	/	/	
.	.	.	.
	0	0	0
1	1	1	1
2	2	2	2
3	3	3	3
4	4	4	4
5	5	5	5
6	6	6	6
7	7	7	7
8	8	8	8
9	9	9	9

16

	/	/	
.	.	.	.
	0	0	0
1	1	1	1
2	2	2	2
3	3	3	3
4	4	4	4
5	5	5	5
6	6	6	6
7	7	7	7
8	8	8	8
9	9	9	9

17

	/	/	
.	.	.	.
	0	0	0
1	1	1	1
2	2	2	2
3	3	3	3
4	4	4	4
5	5	5	5
6	6	6	6
7	7	7	7
8	8	8	8
9	9	9	9

18

	/	/	
.	.	.	.
	0	0	0
1	1	1	1
2	2	2	2
3	3	3	3
4	4	4	4
5	5	5	5
6	6	6	6
7	7	7	7
8	8	8	8
9	9	9	9

Start with number 1 for each new section. If a section has fewer questions than answer spaces, leave the extra answer spaces blank. Be sure to erase any errors or stray marks completely.

SECTION 4

1 Ⓐ Ⓑ Ⓒ Ⓓ Ⓔ	11 Ⓐ Ⓑ Ⓒ Ⓓ Ⓔ	21 Ⓐ Ⓑ Ⓒ Ⓓ Ⓔ	31 Ⓐ Ⓑ Ⓒ Ⓓ Ⓔ
2 Ⓐ Ⓑ Ⓒ Ⓓ Ⓔ	12 Ⓐ Ⓑ Ⓒ Ⓓ Ⓔ	22 Ⓐ Ⓑ Ⓒ Ⓓ Ⓔ	32 Ⓐ Ⓑ Ⓒ Ⓓ Ⓔ
3 Ⓐ Ⓑ Ⓒ Ⓓ Ⓔ	13 Ⓐ Ⓑ Ⓒ Ⓓ Ⓔ	23 Ⓐ Ⓑ Ⓒ Ⓓ Ⓔ	33 Ⓐ Ⓑ Ⓒ Ⓓ Ⓔ
4 Ⓐ Ⓑ Ⓒ Ⓓ Ⓔ	14 Ⓐ Ⓑ Ⓒ Ⓓ Ⓔ	24 Ⓐ Ⓑ Ⓒ Ⓓ Ⓔ	34 Ⓐ Ⓑ Ⓒ Ⓓ Ⓔ
5 Ⓐ Ⓑ Ⓒ Ⓓ Ⓔ	15 Ⓐ Ⓑ Ⓒ Ⓓ Ⓔ	25 Ⓐ Ⓑ Ⓒ Ⓓ Ⓔ	35 Ⓐ Ⓑ Ⓒ Ⓓ Ⓔ
6 Ⓐ Ⓑ Ⓒ Ⓓ Ⓔ	16 Ⓐ Ⓑ Ⓒ Ⓓ Ⓔ	26 Ⓐ Ⓑ Ⓒ Ⓓ Ⓔ	36 Ⓐ Ⓑ Ⓒ Ⓓ Ⓔ
7 Ⓐ Ⓑ Ⓒ Ⓓ Ⓔ	17 Ⓐ Ⓑ Ⓒ Ⓓ Ⓔ	27 Ⓐ Ⓑ Ⓒ Ⓓ Ⓔ	37 Ⓐ Ⓑ Ⓒ Ⓓ Ⓔ
8 Ⓐ Ⓑ Ⓒ Ⓓ Ⓔ	18 Ⓐ Ⓑ Ⓒ Ⓓ Ⓔ	28 Ⓐ Ⓑ Ⓒ Ⓓ Ⓔ	38 Ⓐ Ⓑ Ⓒ Ⓓ Ⓔ
9 Ⓐ Ⓑ Ⓒ Ⓓ Ⓔ	19 Ⓐ Ⓑ Ⓒ Ⓓ Ⓔ	29 Ⓐ Ⓑ Ⓒ Ⓓ Ⓔ	39 Ⓐ Ⓑ Ⓒ Ⓓ Ⓔ
10 Ⓐ Ⓑ Ⓒ Ⓓ Ⓔ	20 Ⓐ Ⓑ Ⓒ Ⓓ Ⓔ	30 Ⓐ Ⓑ Ⓒ Ⓓ Ⓔ	40 Ⓐ Ⓑ Ⓒ Ⓓ Ⓔ

SECTION 5

1 Ⓐ Ⓑ Ⓒ Ⓓ Ⓔ	11 Ⓐ Ⓑ Ⓒ Ⓓ Ⓔ	21 Ⓐ Ⓑ Ⓒ Ⓓ Ⓔ	31 Ⓐ Ⓑ Ⓒ Ⓓ Ⓔ
2 Ⓐ Ⓑ Ⓒ Ⓓ Ⓔ	12 Ⓐ Ⓑ Ⓒ Ⓓ Ⓔ	22 Ⓐ Ⓑ Ⓒ Ⓓ Ⓔ	32 Ⓐ Ⓑ Ⓒ Ⓓ Ⓔ
3 Ⓐ Ⓑ Ⓒ Ⓓ Ⓔ	13 Ⓐ Ⓑ Ⓒ Ⓓ Ⓔ	23 Ⓐ Ⓑ Ⓒ Ⓓ Ⓔ	33 Ⓐ Ⓑ Ⓒ Ⓓ Ⓔ
4 Ⓐ Ⓑ Ⓒ Ⓓ Ⓔ	14 Ⓐ Ⓑ Ⓒ Ⓓ Ⓔ	24 Ⓐ Ⓑ Ⓒ Ⓓ Ⓔ	34 Ⓐ Ⓑ Ⓒ Ⓓ Ⓔ
5 Ⓐ Ⓑ Ⓒ Ⓓ Ⓔ	15 Ⓐ Ⓑ Ⓒ Ⓓ Ⓔ	25 Ⓐ Ⓑ Ⓒ Ⓓ Ⓔ	35 Ⓐ Ⓑ Ⓒ Ⓓ Ⓔ
6 Ⓐ Ⓑ Ⓒ Ⓓ Ⓔ	16 Ⓐ Ⓑ Ⓒ Ⓓ Ⓔ	26 Ⓐ Ⓑ Ⓒ Ⓓ Ⓔ	36 Ⓐ Ⓑ Ⓒ Ⓓ Ⓔ
7 Ⓐ Ⓑ Ⓒ Ⓓ Ⓔ	17 Ⓐ Ⓑ Ⓒ Ⓓ Ⓔ	27 Ⓐ Ⓑ Ⓒ Ⓓ Ⓔ	37 Ⓐ Ⓑ Ⓒ Ⓓ Ⓔ
8 Ⓐ Ⓑ Ⓒ Ⓓ Ⓔ	18 Ⓐ Ⓑ Ⓒ Ⓓ Ⓔ	28 Ⓐ Ⓑ Ⓒ Ⓓ Ⓔ	38 Ⓐ Ⓑ Ⓒ Ⓓ Ⓔ
9 Ⓐ Ⓑ Ⓒ Ⓓ Ⓔ	19 Ⓐ Ⓑ Ⓒ Ⓓ Ⓔ	29 Ⓐ Ⓑ Ⓒ Ⓓ Ⓔ	39 Ⓐ Ⓑ Ⓒ Ⓓ Ⓔ
10 Ⓐ Ⓑ Ⓒ Ⓓ Ⓔ	20 Ⓐ Ⓑ Ⓒ Ⓓ Ⓔ	30 Ⓐ Ⓑ Ⓒ Ⓓ Ⓔ	40 Ⓐ Ⓑ Ⓒ Ⓓ Ⓔ

CAUTION Use the answer spaces in the grids below for Section 4 or Section 5 only if you are told to do so in your test book.

Student-Produced Responses ONLY ANSWERS ENTERED IN THE OVALS IN EACH GRID WILL BE SCORED. YOU WILL NOT RECEIVE CREDIT FOR ANYTHING WRITTEN IN THE BOXES ABOVE THE OVALS.

Grid	Column 1	Column 2	Column 3	Column 4
9	. 1 2 3 4 5 6 7 8 9	/ . 0 1 2 3 4 5 6 7 8 9	/ . 0 1 2 3 4 5 6 7 8 9	. 0 1 2 3 4 5 6 7 8 9
10	. 1 2 3 4 5 6 7 8 9	/ . 0 1 2 3 4 5 6 7 8 9	/ . 0 1 2 3 4 5 6 7 8 9	. 0 1 2 3 4 5 6 7 8 9
11	. 1 2 3 4 5 6 7 8 9	/ . 0 1 2 3 4 5 6 7 8 9	/ . 0 1 2 3 4 5 6 7 8 9	. 0 1 2 3 4 5 6 7 8 9
12	. 1 2 3 4 5 6 7 8 9	/ . 0 1 2 3 4 5 6 7 8 9	/ . 0 1 2 3 4 5 6 7 8 9	. 0 1 2 3 4 5 6 7 8 9
13	. 1 2 3 4 5 6 7 8 9	/ . 0 1 2 3 4 5 6 7 8 9	/ . 0 1 2 3 4 5 6 7 8 9	. 0 1 2 3 4 5 6 7 8 9
14	. 1 2 3 4 5 6 7 8 9	/ . 0 1 2 3 4 5 6 7 8 9	/ . 0 1 2 3 4 5 6 7 8 9	. 0 1 2 3 4 5 6 7 8 9
15	. 1 2 3 4 5 6 7 8 9	/ . 0 1 2 3 4 5 6 7 8 9	/ . 0 1 2 3 4 5 6 7 8 9	. 0 1 2 3 4 5 6 7 8 9
16	. 1 2 3 4 5 6 7 8 9	/ . 0 1 2 3 4 5 6 7 8 9	/ . 0 1 2 3 4 5 6 7 8 9	. 0 1 2 3 4 5 6 7 8 9
17	. 1 2 3 4 5 6 7 8 9	/ . 0 1 2 3 4 5 6 7 8 9	/ . 0 1 2 3 4 5 6 7 8 9	. 0 1 2 3 4 5 6 7 8 9
18	. 1 2 3 4 5 6 7 8 9	/ . 0 1 2 3 4 5 6 7 8 9	/ . 0 1 2 3 4 5 6 7 8 9	. 0 1 2 3 4 5 6 7 8 9

Start with number 1 for each new section. If a section has fewer questions than answer spaces, leave the extra answer spaces blank. Be sure to erase any errors or stray marks completely.

SECTION 6

1 Ⓐ Ⓑ Ⓒ Ⓓ Ⓔ	11 Ⓐ Ⓑ Ⓒ Ⓓ Ⓔ	21 Ⓐ Ⓑ Ⓒ Ⓓ Ⓔ	31 Ⓐ Ⓑ Ⓒ Ⓓ Ⓔ
2 Ⓐ Ⓑ Ⓒ Ⓓ Ⓔ	12 Ⓐ Ⓑ Ⓒ Ⓓ Ⓔ	22 Ⓐ Ⓑ Ⓒ Ⓓ Ⓔ	32 Ⓐ Ⓑ Ⓒ Ⓓ Ⓔ
3 Ⓐ Ⓑ Ⓒ Ⓓ Ⓔ	13 Ⓐ Ⓑ Ⓒ Ⓓ Ⓔ	23 Ⓐ Ⓑ Ⓒ Ⓓ Ⓔ	33 Ⓐ Ⓑ Ⓒ Ⓓ Ⓔ
4 Ⓐ Ⓑ Ⓒ Ⓓ Ⓔ	14 Ⓐ Ⓑ Ⓒ Ⓓ Ⓔ	24 Ⓐ Ⓑ Ⓒ Ⓓ Ⓔ	34 Ⓐ Ⓑ Ⓒ Ⓓ Ⓔ
5 Ⓐ Ⓑ Ⓒ Ⓓ Ⓔ	15 Ⓐ Ⓑ Ⓒ Ⓓ Ⓔ	25 Ⓐ Ⓑ Ⓒ Ⓓ Ⓔ	35 Ⓐ Ⓑ Ⓒ Ⓓ Ⓔ
6 Ⓐ Ⓑ Ⓒ Ⓓ Ⓔ	16 Ⓐ Ⓑ Ⓒ Ⓓ Ⓔ	26 Ⓐ Ⓑ Ⓒ Ⓓ Ⓔ	36 Ⓐ Ⓑ Ⓒ Ⓓ Ⓔ
7 Ⓐ Ⓑ Ⓒ Ⓓ Ⓔ	17 Ⓐ Ⓑ Ⓒ Ⓓ Ⓔ	27 Ⓐ Ⓑ Ⓒ Ⓓ Ⓔ	37 Ⓐ Ⓑ Ⓒ Ⓓ Ⓔ
8 Ⓐ Ⓑ Ⓒ Ⓓ Ⓔ	18 Ⓐ Ⓑ Ⓒ Ⓓ Ⓔ	28 Ⓐ Ⓑ Ⓒ Ⓓ Ⓔ	38 Ⓐ Ⓑ Ⓒ Ⓓ Ⓔ
9 Ⓐ Ⓑ Ⓒ Ⓓ Ⓔ	19 Ⓐ Ⓑ Ⓒ Ⓓ Ⓔ	29 Ⓐ Ⓑ Ⓒ Ⓓ Ⓔ	39 Ⓐ Ⓑ Ⓒ Ⓓ Ⓔ
10 Ⓐ Ⓑ Ⓒ Ⓓ Ⓔ	20 Ⓐ Ⓑ Ⓒ Ⓓ Ⓔ	30 Ⓐ Ⓑ Ⓒ Ⓓ Ⓔ	40 Ⓐ Ⓑ Ⓒ Ⓓ Ⓔ

SECTION 7

1 Ⓐ Ⓑ Ⓒ Ⓓ Ⓔ	11 Ⓐ Ⓑ Ⓒ Ⓓ Ⓔ	21 Ⓐ Ⓑ Ⓒ Ⓓ Ⓔ	31 Ⓐ Ⓑ Ⓒ Ⓓ Ⓔ
2 Ⓐ Ⓑ Ⓒ Ⓓ Ⓔ	12 Ⓐ Ⓑ Ⓒ Ⓓ Ⓔ	22 Ⓐ Ⓑ Ⓒ Ⓓ Ⓔ	32 Ⓐ Ⓑ Ⓒ Ⓓ Ⓔ
3 Ⓐ Ⓑ Ⓒ Ⓓ Ⓔ	13 Ⓐ Ⓑ Ⓒ Ⓓ Ⓔ	23 Ⓐ Ⓑ Ⓒ Ⓓ Ⓔ	33 Ⓐ Ⓑ Ⓒ Ⓓ Ⓔ
4 Ⓐ Ⓑ Ⓒ Ⓓ Ⓔ	14 Ⓐ Ⓑ Ⓒ Ⓓ Ⓔ	24 Ⓐ Ⓑ Ⓒ Ⓓ Ⓔ	34 Ⓐ Ⓑ Ⓒ Ⓓ Ⓔ
5 Ⓐ Ⓑ Ⓒ Ⓓ Ⓔ	15 Ⓐ Ⓑ Ⓒ Ⓓ Ⓔ	25 Ⓐ Ⓑ Ⓒ Ⓓ Ⓔ	35 Ⓐ Ⓑ Ⓒ Ⓓ Ⓔ
6 Ⓐ Ⓑ Ⓒ Ⓓ Ⓔ	16 Ⓐ Ⓑ Ⓒ Ⓓ Ⓔ	26 Ⓐ Ⓑ Ⓒ Ⓓ Ⓔ	36 Ⓐ Ⓑ Ⓒ Ⓓ Ⓔ
7 Ⓐ Ⓑ Ⓒ Ⓓ Ⓔ	17 Ⓐ Ⓑ Ⓒ Ⓓ Ⓔ	27 Ⓐ Ⓑ Ⓒ Ⓓ Ⓔ	37 Ⓐ Ⓑ Ⓒ Ⓓ Ⓔ
8 Ⓐ Ⓑ Ⓒ Ⓓ Ⓔ	18 Ⓐ Ⓑ Ⓒ Ⓓ Ⓔ	28 Ⓐ Ⓑ Ⓒ Ⓓ Ⓔ	38 Ⓐ Ⓑ Ⓒ Ⓓ Ⓔ
9 Ⓐ Ⓑ Ⓒ Ⓓ Ⓔ	19 Ⓐ Ⓑ Ⓒ Ⓓ Ⓔ	29 Ⓐ Ⓑ Ⓒ Ⓓ Ⓔ	39 Ⓐ Ⓑ Ⓒ Ⓓ Ⓔ
10 Ⓐ Ⓑ Ⓒ Ⓓ Ⓔ	20 Ⓐ Ⓑ Ⓒ Ⓓ Ⓔ	30 Ⓐ Ⓑ Ⓒ Ⓓ Ⓔ	40 Ⓐ Ⓑ Ⓒ Ⓓ Ⓔ

CAUTION Use the answer spaces in the grids below for Section 6 or Section 7 only if you are told to do so in your test book.

Student-Produced Responses

ONLY ANSWERS ENTERED IN THE OVALS IN EACH GRID WILL BE SCORED. YOU WILL NOT RECEIVE CREDIT FOR ANYTHING WRITTEN IN THE BOXES ABOVE THE OVALS.

Grids 9, 10, 11, 12, 13, 14, 15, 16, 17, 18 — each grid has four columns:

	/	/	
.	.	.	.
	0	0	0
1	1	1	1
2	2	2	2
3	3	3	3
4	4	4	4
5	5	5	5
6	6	6	6
7	7	7	7
8	8	8	8
9	9	9	9

Start with number 1 for each new section. If a section has fewer questions than answer spaces, leave the extra answer spaces blank. Be sure to erase any errors or stray marks completely.

SECTION 8

1 Ⓐ Ⓑ Ⓒ Ⓓ Ⓔ	11 Ⓐ Ⓑ Ⓒ Ⓓ Ⓔ	21 Ⓐ Ⓑ Ⓒ Ⓓ Ⓔ	31 Ⓐ Ⓑ Ⓒ Ⓓ Ⓔ
2 Ⓐ Ⓑ Ⓒ Ⓓ Ⓔ	12 Ⓐ Ⓑ Ⓒ Ⓓ Ⓔ	22 Ⓐ Ⓑ Ⓒ Ⓓ Ⓔ	32 Ⓐ Ⓑ Ⓒ Ⓓ Ⓔ
3 Ⓐ Ⓑ Ⓒ Ⓓ Ⓔ	13 Ⓐ Ⓑ Ⓒ Ⓓ Ⓔ	23 Ⓐ Ⓑ Ⓒ Ⓓ Ⓔ	33 Ⓐ Ⓑ Ⓒ Ⓓ Ⓔ
4 Ⓐ Ⓑ Ⓒ Ⓓ Ⓔ	14 Ⓐ Ⓑ Ⓒ Ⓓ Ⓔ	24 Ⓐ Ⓑ Ⓒ Ⓓ Ⓔ	34 Ⓐ Ⓑ Ⓒ Ⓓ Ⓔ
5 Ⓐ Ⓑ Ⓒ Ⓓ Ⓔ	15 Ⓐ Ⓑ Ⓒ Ⓓ Ⓔ	25 Ⓐ Ⓑ Ⓒ Ⓓ Ⓔ	35 Ⓐ Ⓑ Ⓒ Ⓓ Ⓔ
6 Ⓐ Ⓑ Ⓒ Ⓓ Ⓔ	16 Ⓐ Ⓑ Ⓒ Ⓓ Ⓔ	26 Ⓐ Ⓑ Ⓒ Ⓓ Ⓔ	36 Ⓐ Ⓑ Ⓒ Ⓓ Ⓔ
7 Ⓐ Ⓑ Ⓒ Ⓓ Ⓔ	17 Ⓐ Ⓑ Ⓒ Ⓓ Ⓔ	27 Ⓐ Ⓑ Ⓒ Ⓓ Ⓔ	37 Ⓐ Ⓑ Ⓒ Ⓓ Ⓔ
8 Ⓐ Ⓑ Ⓒ Ⓓ Ⓔ	18 Ⓐ Ⓑ Ⓒ Ⓓ Ⓔ	28 Ⓐ Ⓑ Ⓒ Ⓓ Ⓔ	38 Ⓐ Ⓑ Ⓒ Ⓓ Ⓔ
9 Ⓐ Ⓑ Ⓒ Ⓓ Ⓔ	19 Ⓐ Ⓑ Ⓒ Ⓓ Ⓔ	29 Ⓐ Ⓑ Ⓒ Ⓓ Ⓔ	39 Ⓐ Ⓑ Ⓒ Ⓓ Ⓔ
10 Ⓐ Ⓑ Ⓒ Ⓓ Ⓔ	20 Ⓐ Ⓑ Ⓒ Ⓓ Ⓔ	30 Ⓐ Ⓑ Ⓒ Ⓓ Ⓔ	40 Ⓐ Ⓑ Ⓒ Ⓓ Ⓔ

SECTION 9

1 Ⓐ Ⓑ Ⓒ Ⓓ Ⓔ	11 Ⓐ Ⓑ Ⓒ Ⓓ Ⓔ	21 Ⓐ Ⓑ Ⓒ Ⓓ Ⓔ	31 Ⓐ Ⓑ Ⓒ Ⓓ Ⓔ
2 Ⓐ Ⓑ Ⓒ Ⓓ Ⓔ	12 Ⓐ Ⓑ Ⓒ Ⓓ Ⓔ	22 Ⓐ Ⓑ Ⓒ Ⓓ Ⓔ	32 Ⓐ Ⓑ Ⓒ Ⓓ Ⓔ
3 Ⓐ Ⓑ Ⓒ Ⓓ Ⓔ	13 Ⓐ Ⓑ Ⓒ Ⓓ Ⓔ	23 Ⓐ Ⓑ Ⓒ Ⓓ Ⓔ	33 Ⓐ Ⓑ Ⓒ Ⓓ Ⓔ
4 Ⓐ Ⓑ Ⓒ Ⓓ Ⓔ	14 Ⓐ Ⓑ Ⓒ Ⓓ Ⓔ	24 Ⓐ Ⓑ Ⓒ Ⓓ Ⓔ	34 Ⓐ Ⓑ Ⓒ Ⓓ Ⓔ
5 Ⓐ Ⓑ Ⓒ Ⓓ Ⓔ	15 Ⓐ Ⓑ Ⓒ Ⓓ Ⓔ	25 Ⓐ Ⓑ Ⓒ Ⓓ Ⓔ	35 Ⓐ Ⓑ Ⓒ Ⓓ Ⓔ
6 Ⓐ Ⓑ Ⓒ Ⓓ Ⓔ	16 Ⓐ Ⓑ Ⓒ Ⓓ Ⓔ	26 Ⓐ Ⓑ Ⓒ Ⓓ Ⓔ	36 Ⓐ Ⓑ Ⓒ Ⓓ Ⓔ
7 Ⓐ Ⓑ Ⓒ Ⓓ Ⓔ	17 Ⓐ Ⓑ Ⓒ Ⓓ Ⓔ	27 Ⓐ Ⓑ Ⓒ Ⓓ Ⓔ	37 Ⓐ Ⓑ Ⓒ Ⓓ Ⓔ
8 Ⓐ Ⓑ Ⓒ Ⓓ Ⓔ	18 Ⓐ Ⓑ Ⓒ Ⓓ Ⓔ	28 Ⓐ Ⓑ Ⓒ Ⓓ Ⓔ	38 Ⓐ Ⓑ Ⓒ Ⓓ Ⓔ
9 Ⓐ Ⓑ Ⓒ Ⓓ Ⓔ	19 Ⓐ Ⓑ Ⓒ Ⓓ Ⓔ	29 Ⓐ Ⓑ Ⓒ Ⓓ Ⓔ	39 Ⓐ Ⓑ Ⓒ Ⓓ Ⓔ
10 Ⓐ Ⓑ Ⓒ Ⓓ Ⓔ	20 Ⓐ Ⓑ Ⓒ Ⓓ Ⓔ	30 Ⓐ Ⓑ Ⓒ Ⓓ Ⓔ	40 Ⓐ Ⓑ Ⓒ Ⓓ Ⓔ

SECTION 10

1 Ⓐ Ⓑ Ⓒ Ⓓ Ⓔ	11 Ⓐ Ⓑ Ⓒ Ⓓ Ⓔ	21 Ⓐ Ⓑ Ⓒ Ⓓ Ⓔ	31 Ⓐ Ⓑ Ⓒ Ⓓ Ⓔ
2 Ⓐ Ⓑ Ⓒ Ⓓ Ⓔ	12 Ⓐ Ⓑ Ⓒ Ⓓ Ⓔ	22 Ⓐ Ⓑ Ⓒ Ⓓ Ⓔ	32 Ⓐ Ⓑ Ⓒ Ⓓ Ⓔ
3 Ⓐ Ⓑ Ⓒ Ⓓ Ⓔ	13 Ⓐ Ⓑ Ⓒ Ⓓ Ⓔ	23 Ⓐ Ⓑ Ⓒ Ⓓ Ⓔ	33 Ⓐ Ⓑ Ⓒ Ⓓ Ⓔ
4 Ⓐ Ⓑ Ⓒ Ⓓ Ⓔ	14 Ⓐ Ⓑ Ⓒ Ⓓ Ⓔ	24 Ⓐ Ⓑ Ⓒ Ⓓ Ⓔ	34 Ⓐ Ⓑ Ⓒ Ⓓ Ⓔ
5 Ⓐ Ⓑ Ⓒ Ⓓ Ⓔ	15 Ⓐ Ⓑ Ⓒ Ⓓ Ⓔ	25 Ⓐ Ⓑ Ⓒ Ⓓ Ⓔ	35 Ⓐ Ⓑ Ⓒ Ⓓ Ⓔ
6 Ⓐ Ⓑ Ⓒ Ⓓ Ⓔ	16 Ⓐ Ⓑ Ⓒ Ⓓ Ⓔ	26 Ⓐ Ⓑ Ⓒ Ⓓ Ⓔ	36 Ⓐ Ⓑ Ⓒ Ⓓ Ⓔ
7 Ⓐ Ⓑ Ⓒ Ⓓ Ⓔ	17 Ⓐ Ⓑ Ⓒ Ⓓ Ⓔ	27 Ⓐ Ⓑ Ⓒ Ⓓ Ⓔ	37 Ⓐ Ⓑ Ⓒ Ⓓ Ⓔ
8 Ⓐ Ⓑ Ⓒ Ⓓ Ⓔ	18 Ⓐ Ⓑ Ⓒ Ⓓ Ⓔ	28 Ⓐ Ⓑ Ⓒ Ⓓ Ⓔ	38 Ⓐ Ⓑ Ⓒ Ⓓ Ⓔ
9 Ⓐ Ⓑ Ⓒ Ⓓ Ⓔ	19 Ⓐ Ⓑ Ⓒ Ⓓ Ⓔ	29 Ⓐ Ⓑ Ⓒ Ⓓ Ⓔ	39 Ⓐ Ⓑ Ⓒ Ⓓ Ⓔ
10 Ⓐ Ⓑ Ⓒ Ⓓ Ⓔ	20 Ⓐ Ⓑ Ⓒ Ⓓ Ⓔ	30 Ⓐ Ⓑ Ⓒ Ⓓ Ⓔ	40 Ⓐ Ⓑ Ⓒ Ⓓ Ⓔ

PLEASE DO NOT WRITE IN THIS AREA

SERIAL #

NOTES

The Princeton Review
SAT® Vocab Challenge
for iPhone™ and iPod touch®
$4.99
Brought to you by the experts at The Princeton Review and Modality, Inc.
◀ From the home screen you can easily see your mastered words add up!
SAT Vocab Challenge
127
Start
Stats
Word Index
335
Beneficial
credulous
groundless
abundant
Swipe & flick ▶ through hundreds of words in just minutes
The Princeton Review SAT
▲ Available now in the Apple® App Store
250 need-to-know SAT vocab terms
4 fast-paced games to test your knowledge and build your skills
$4.99 A small price to pay for true vocab mastery
SAT mark is owned by the College Board. iPhone, iPod and Apple marks are owned by Apple, Inc. The Princeton Review is not affiliated with Princeton University.
www.PrincetonReview.com
STUDY ANYWHERE
www.modality.com